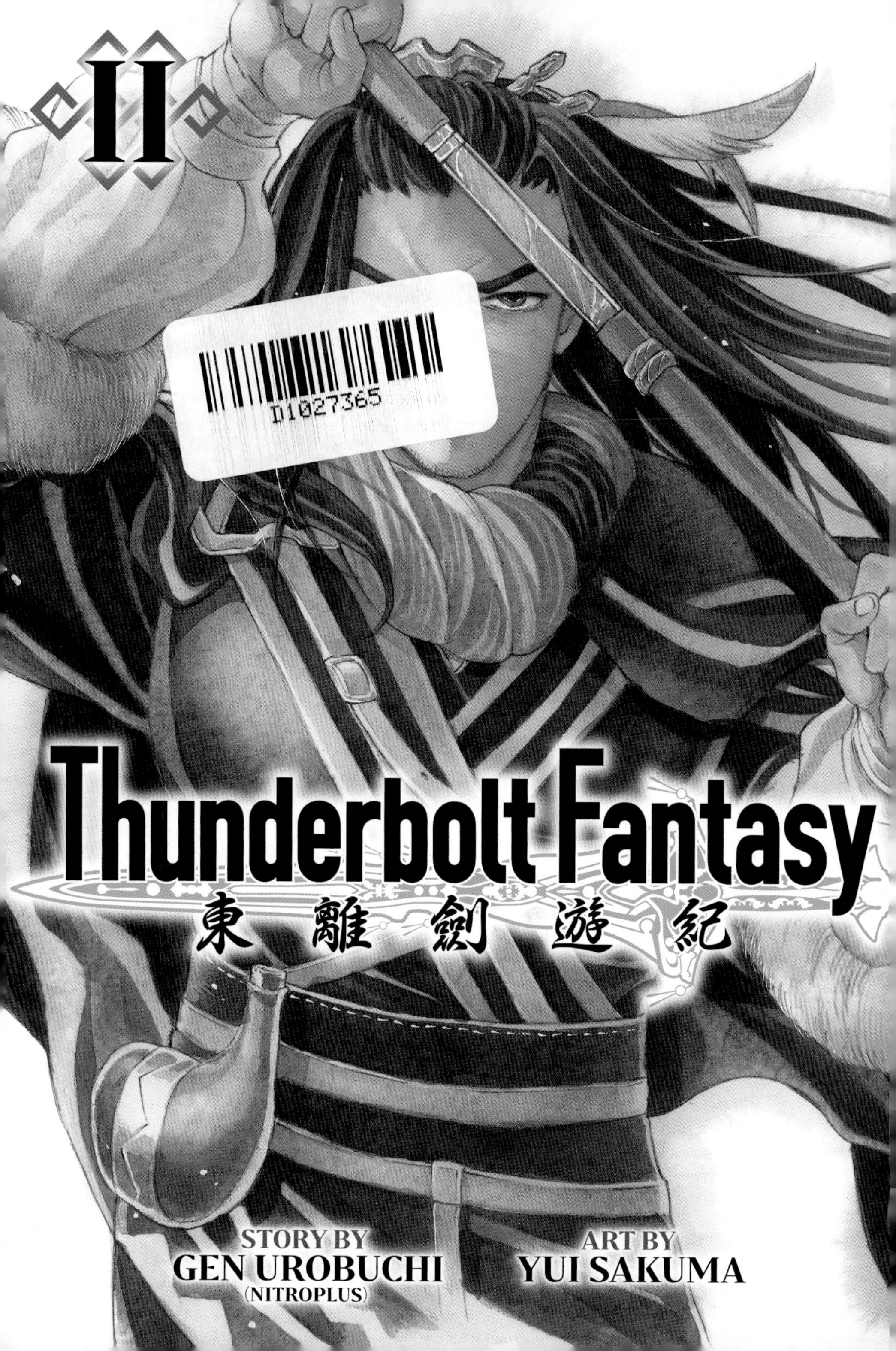
II
Thunderbolt Fantasy
東離劍遊紀
STORY BY
GEN UROBUCHI
(NITROPLUS)
ART BY
YUI SAKUMA

TABLE OF CONTENTS

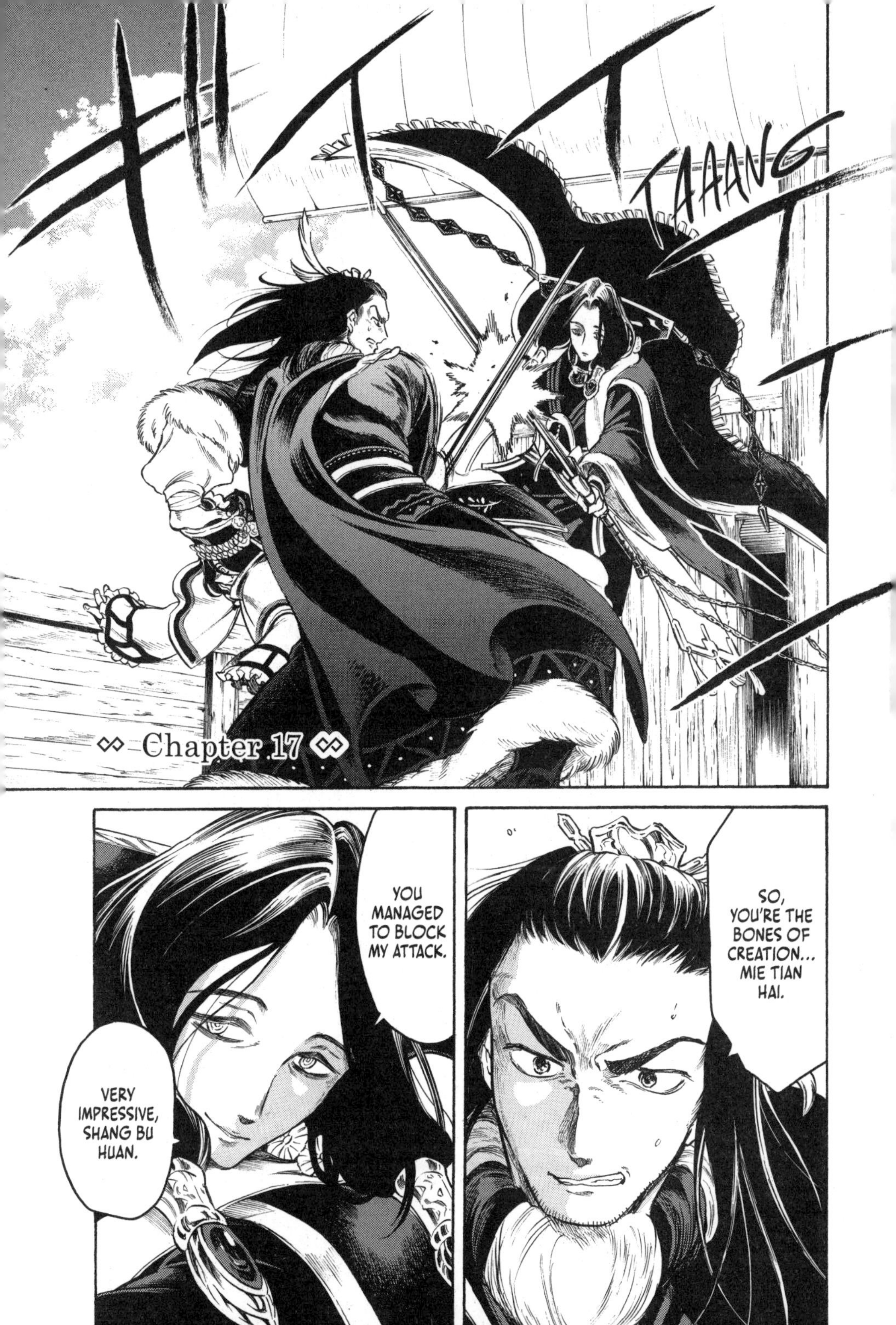
TAAANG
Chapter 17
SO, YOU'RE THE BONES OF CREATION... MIE TIAN HAI.
YOU MANAGED TO BLOCK MY ATTACK.
VERY IMPRESSIVE, SHANG BU HUAN.

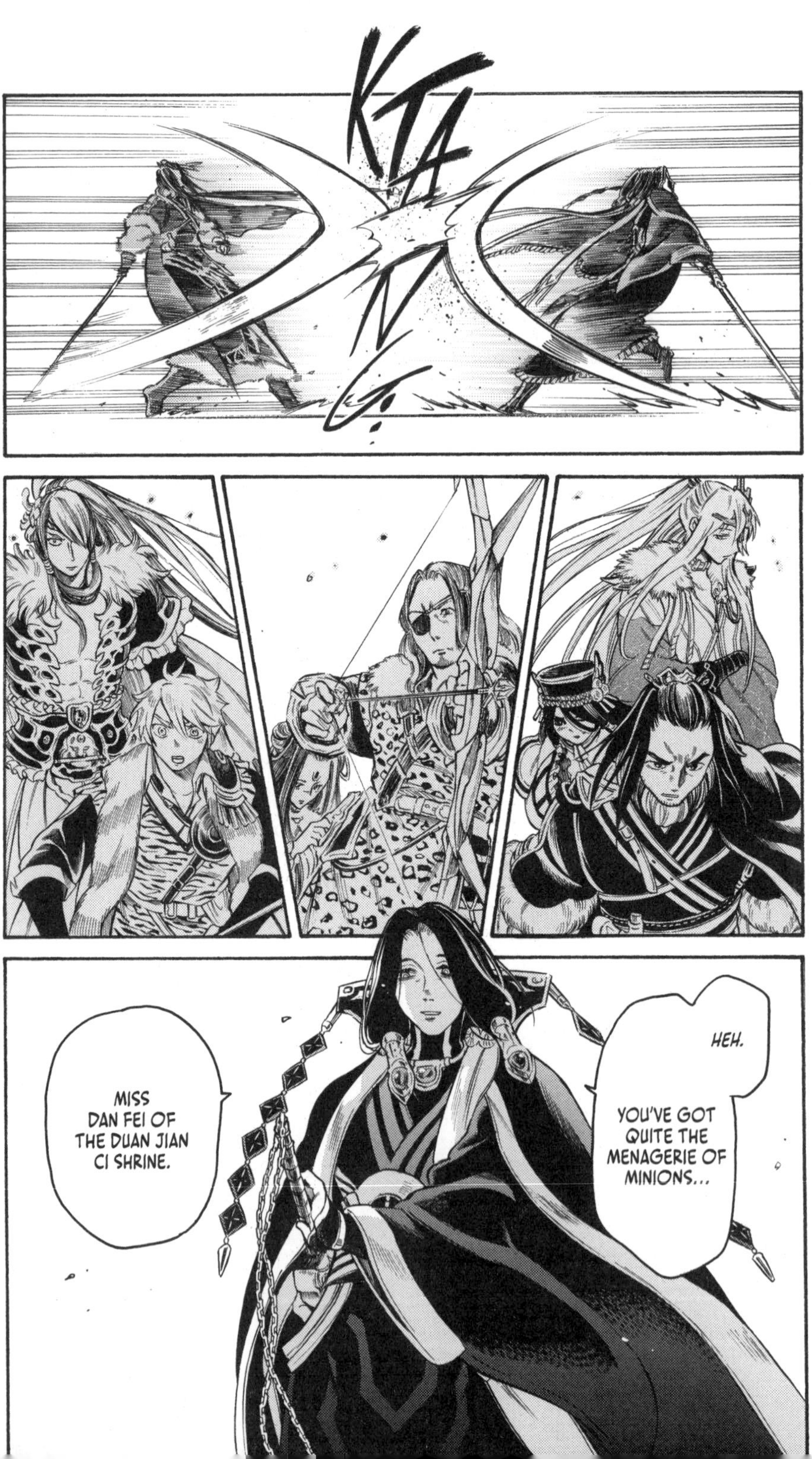
KTANG
HEH.
YOU'VE GOT QUITE THE MENAGERIE OF MINIONS...
MISS DAN FEI OF THE DUAN JIAN CI SHRINE.

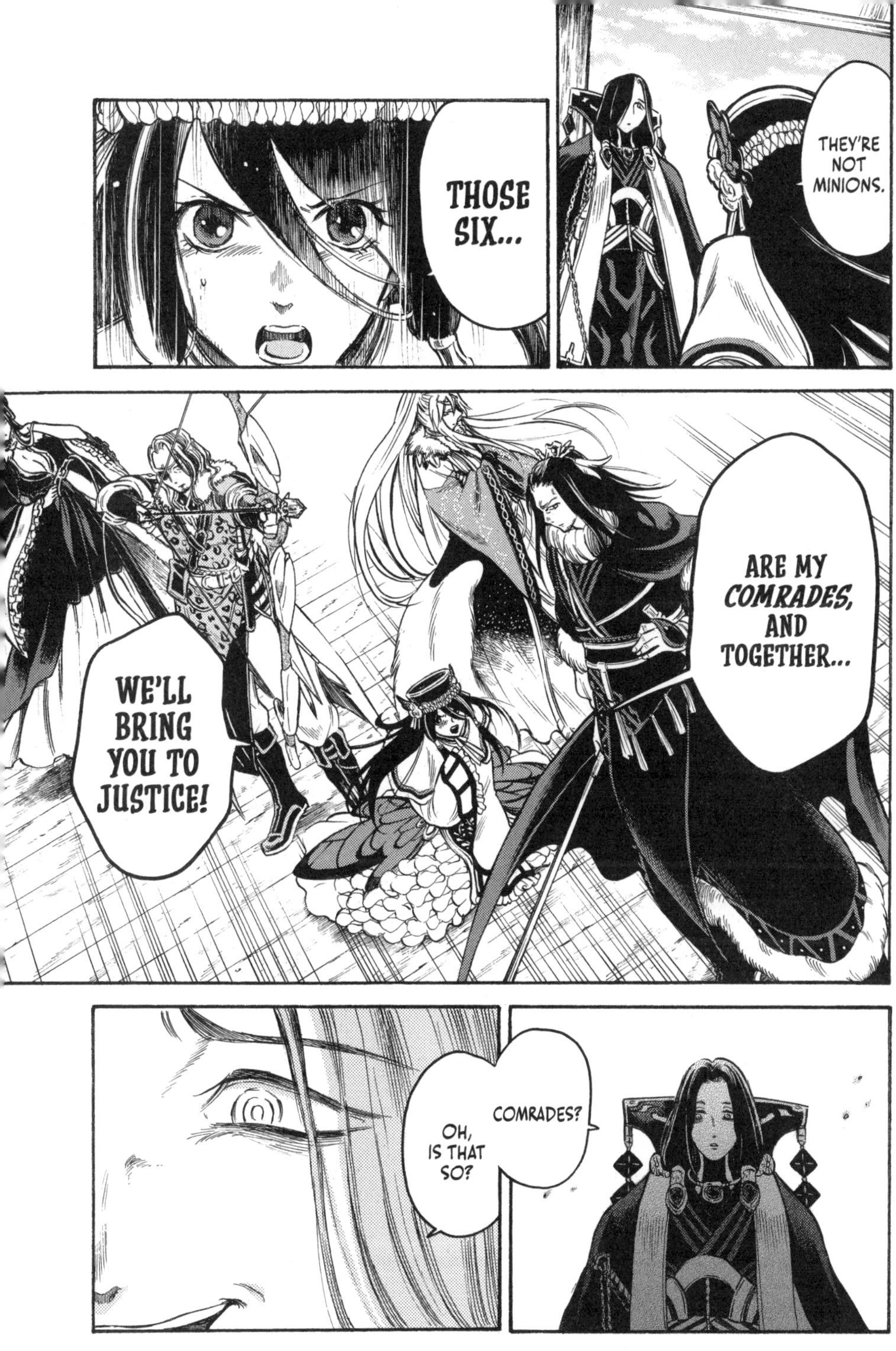
THEY'RE NOT MINIONS.
THOSE SIX...
ARE MY *COMRADES,* AND TOGETHER...
WE'LL BRING YOU TO JUSTICE!
COMRADES?
OH, IS THAT SO?

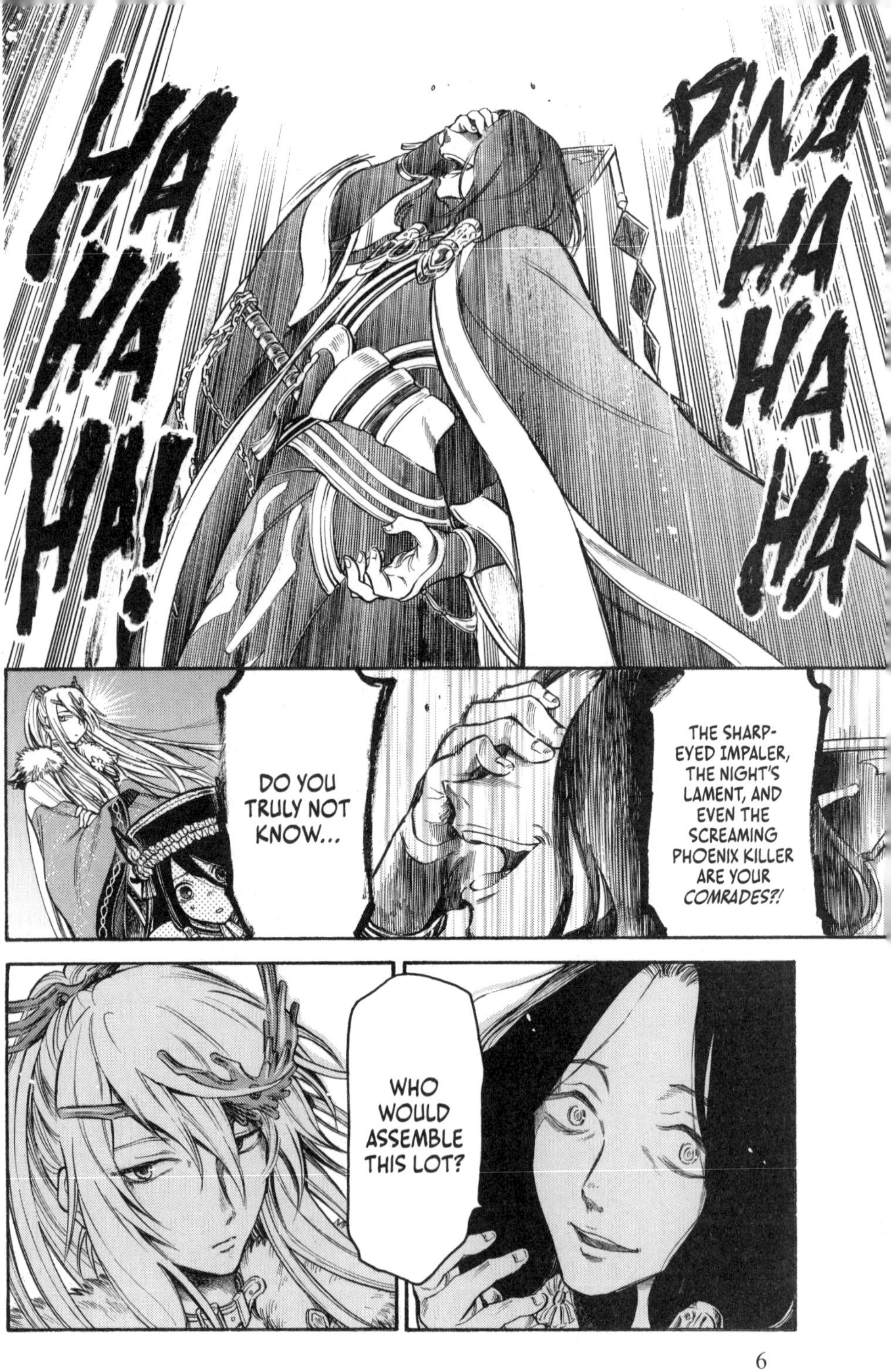
PWAHAHAHAHA
HAHAHAHA!
THE SHARP-EYED IMPALER, THE NIGHT'S LAMENT, AND EVEN THE SCREAMING PHOENIX KILLER ARE YOUR *COMRADES*?!
DO YOU TRULY NOT KNOW...
WHO WOULD ASSEMBLE THIS LOT?

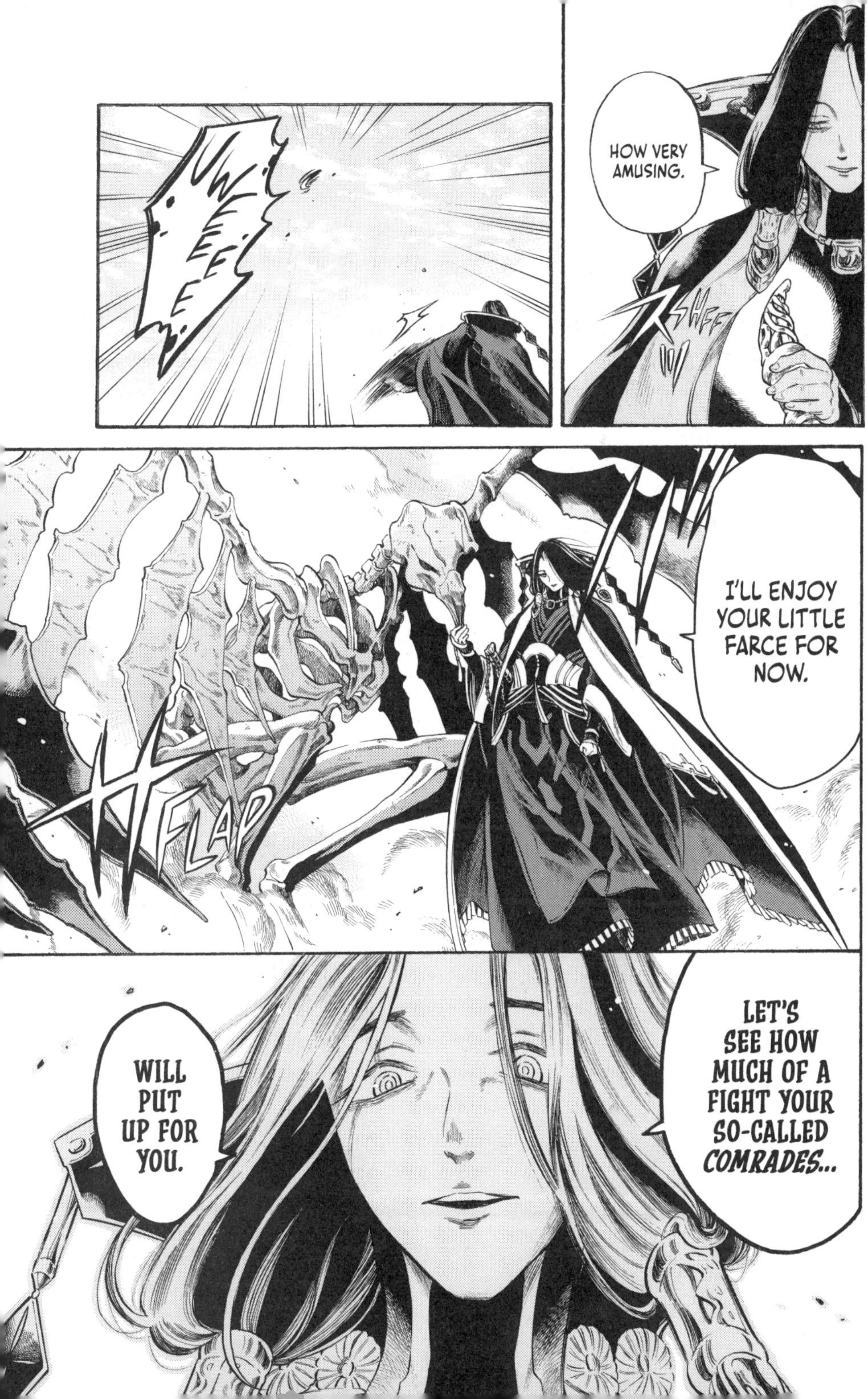
HOW VERY AMUSING.
I'LL ENJOY YOUR LITTLE FARCE FOR NOW.
FLAP
LET'S SEE HOW MUCH OF A FIGHT YOUR SO-CALLED *COMRADES*...
WILL PUT UP FOR YOU.

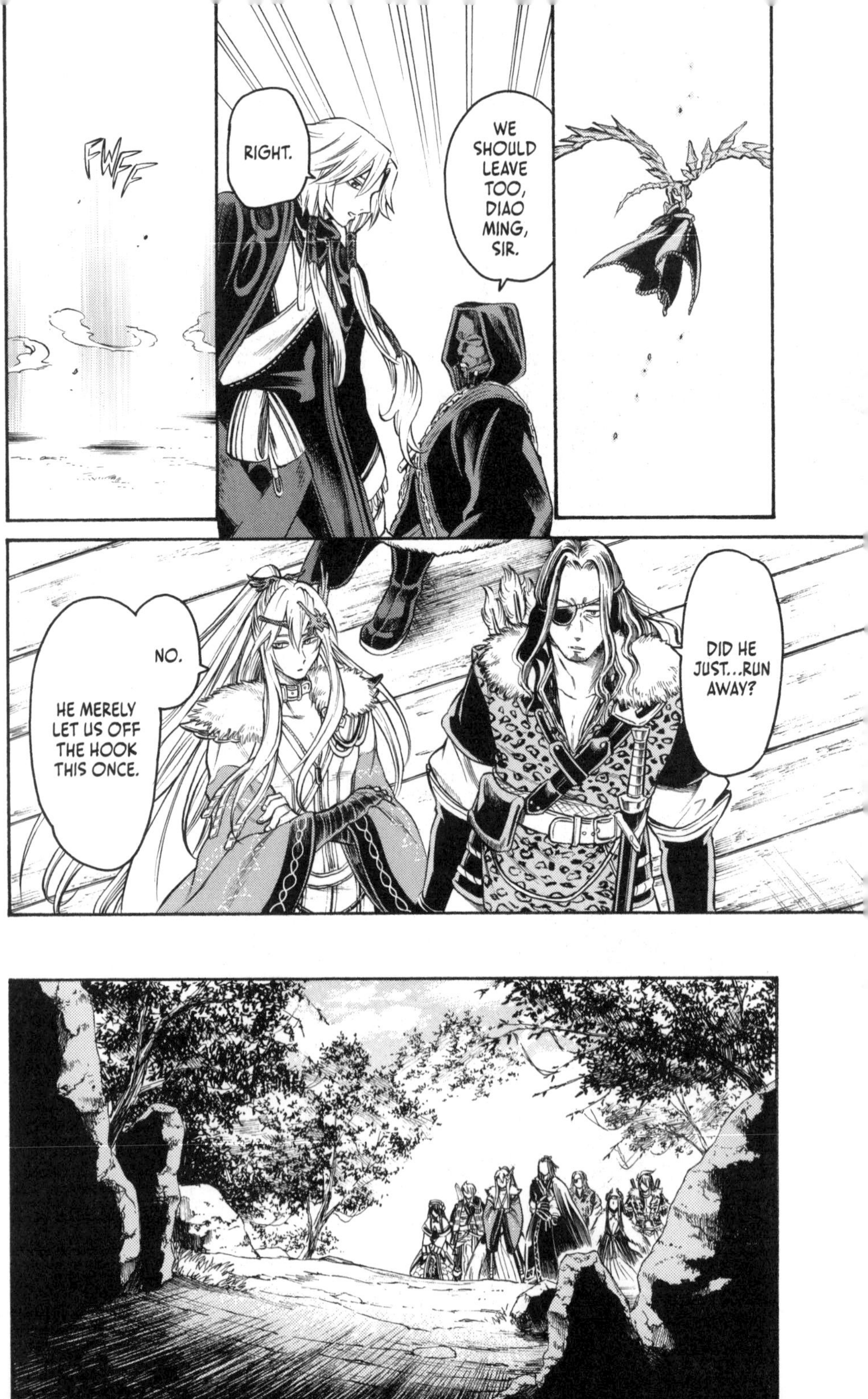
WE SHOULD LEAVE TOO, DIAO MING, SIR.
RIGHT.
FWFF
DID HE JUST...RUN AWAY?
NO.
HE MERELY LET US OFF THE HOOK THIS ONCE.

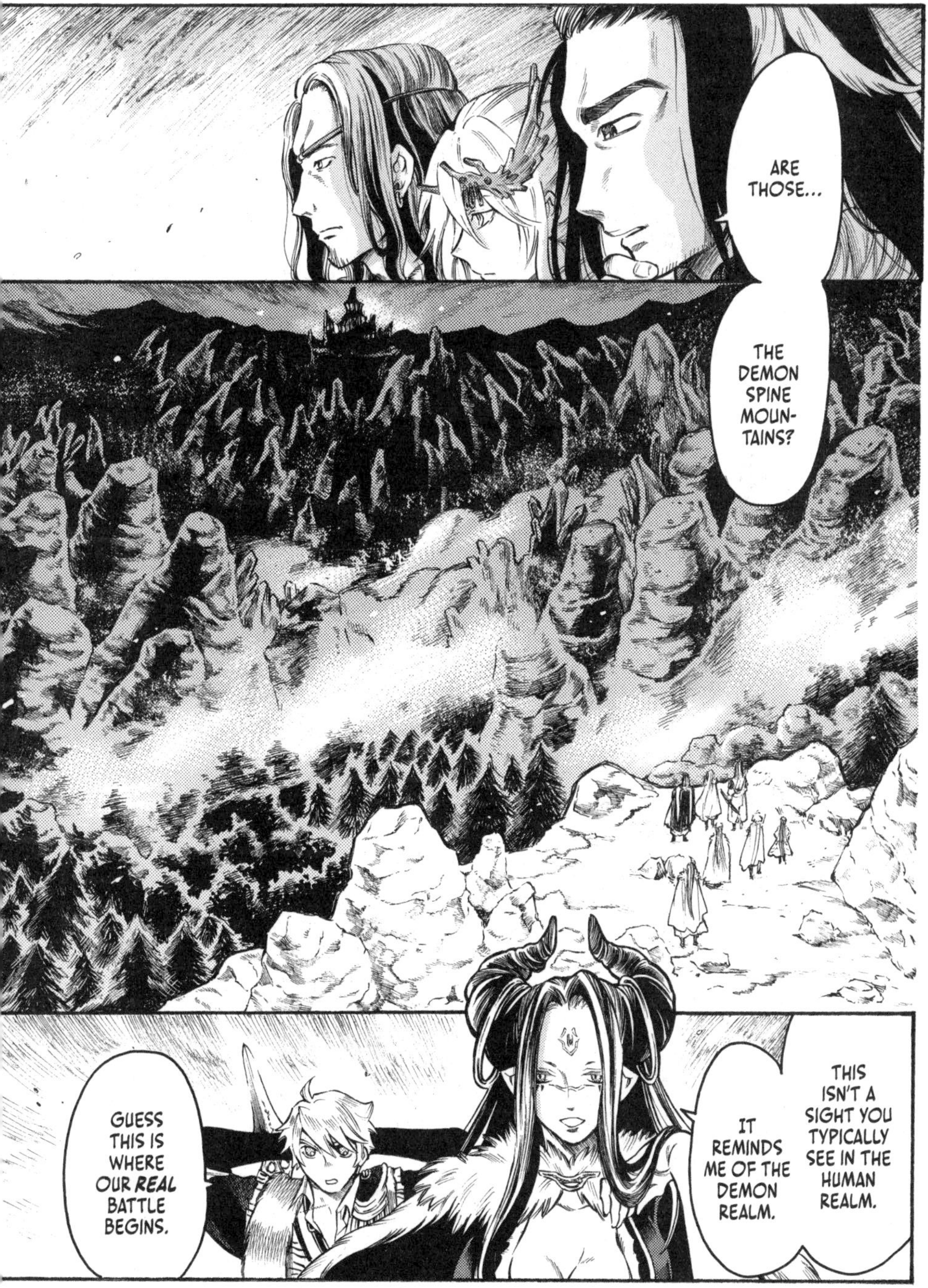
ARE THOSE...
THE DEMON SPINE MOUNTAINS?
THIS ISN'T A SIGHT YOU TYPICALLY SEE IN THE HUMAN REALM.
IT REMINDS ME OF THE DEMON REALM.
GUESS THIS IS WHERE OUR *REAL* BATTLE BEGINS.

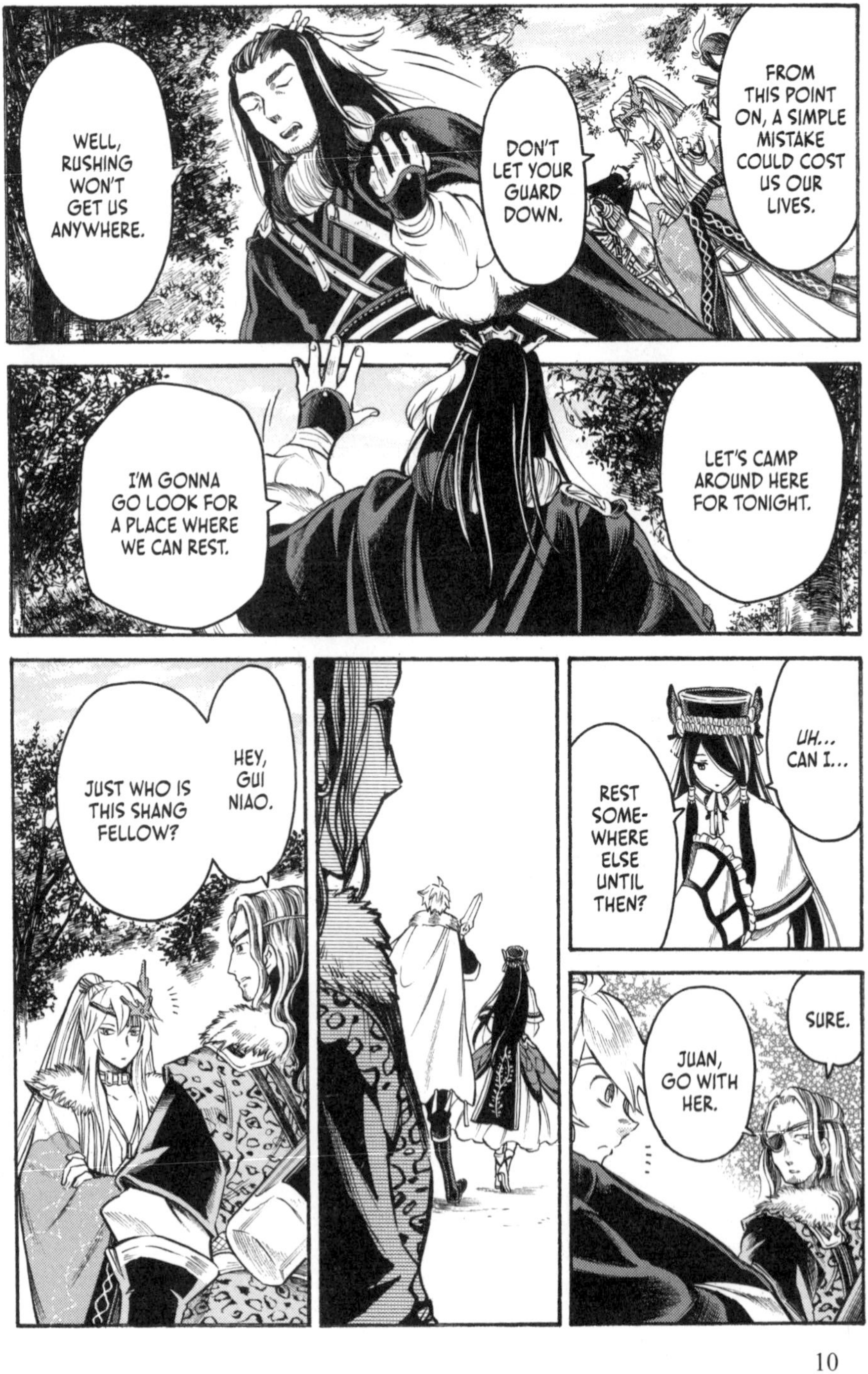
FROM THIS POINT ON, A SIMPLE MISTAKE COULD COST US OUR LIVES.
DON'T LET YOUR GUARD DOWN.
WELL, RUSHING WON'T GET US ANYWHERE.
LET'S CAMP AROUND HERE FOR TONIGHT.
I'M GONNA GO LOOK FOR A PLACE WHERE WE CAN REST.
UH... CAN I...
REST SOME-WHERE ELSE UNTIL THEN?
SURE.
JUAN, GO WITH HER.
...
HEY, GUI NIAO.
JUST WHO IS THIS SHANG FELLOW?

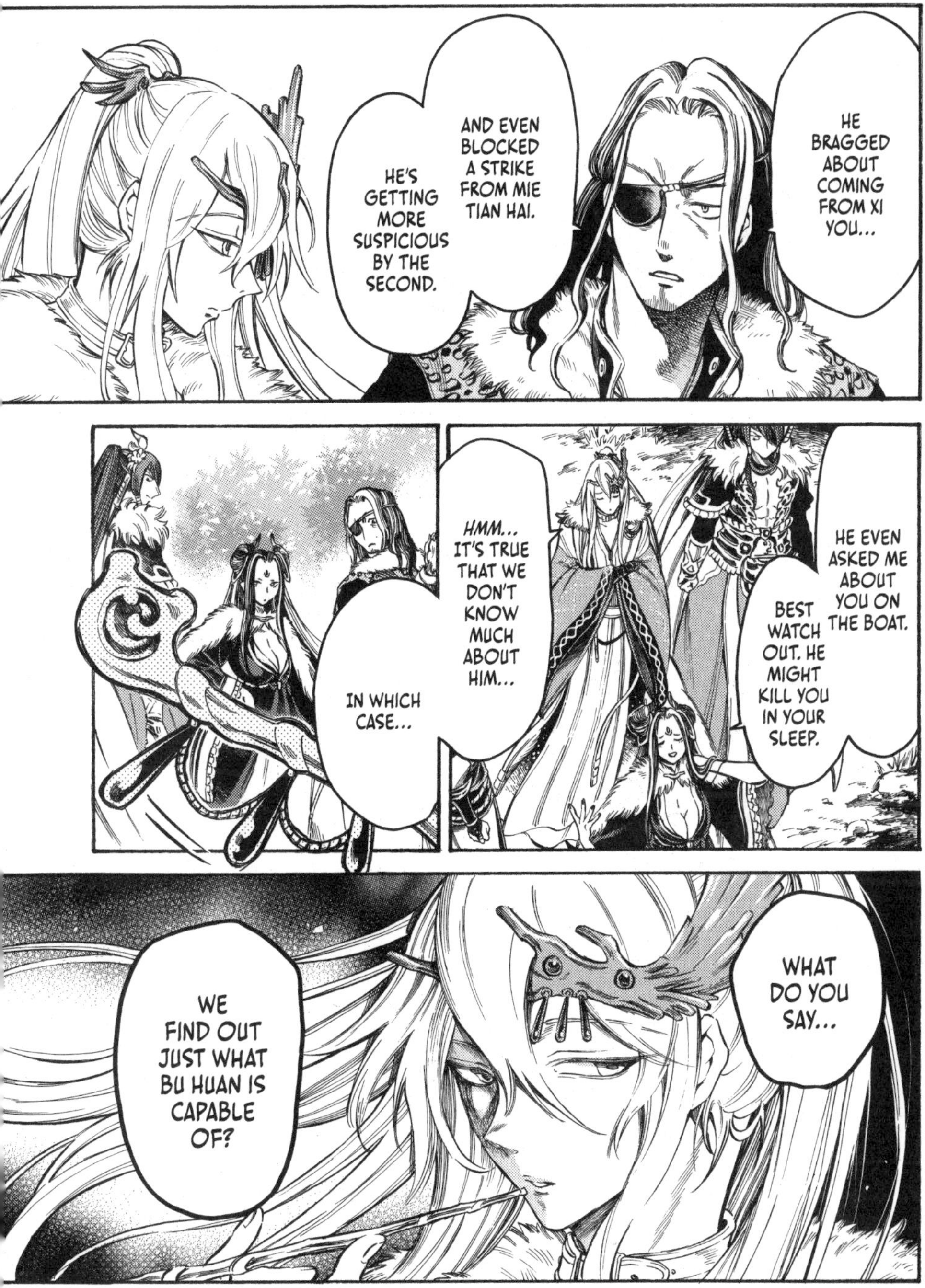
HE BRAGGED ABOUT COMING FROM XI YOU...
AND EVEN BLOCKED A STRIKE FROM MIE TIAN HAI.
HE'S GETTING MORE SUSPICIOUS BY THE SECOND.
HE EVEN ASKED ME ABOUT YOU ON THE BOAT.
BEST WATCH OUT. HE MIGHT KILL YOU IN YOUR SLEEP.
HMM... IT'S TRUE THAT WE DON'T KNOW MUCH ABOUT HIM...
IN WHICH CASE...
WHAT DO YOU SAY...
WE FIND OUT JUST WHAT BU HUAN IS CAPABLE OF?

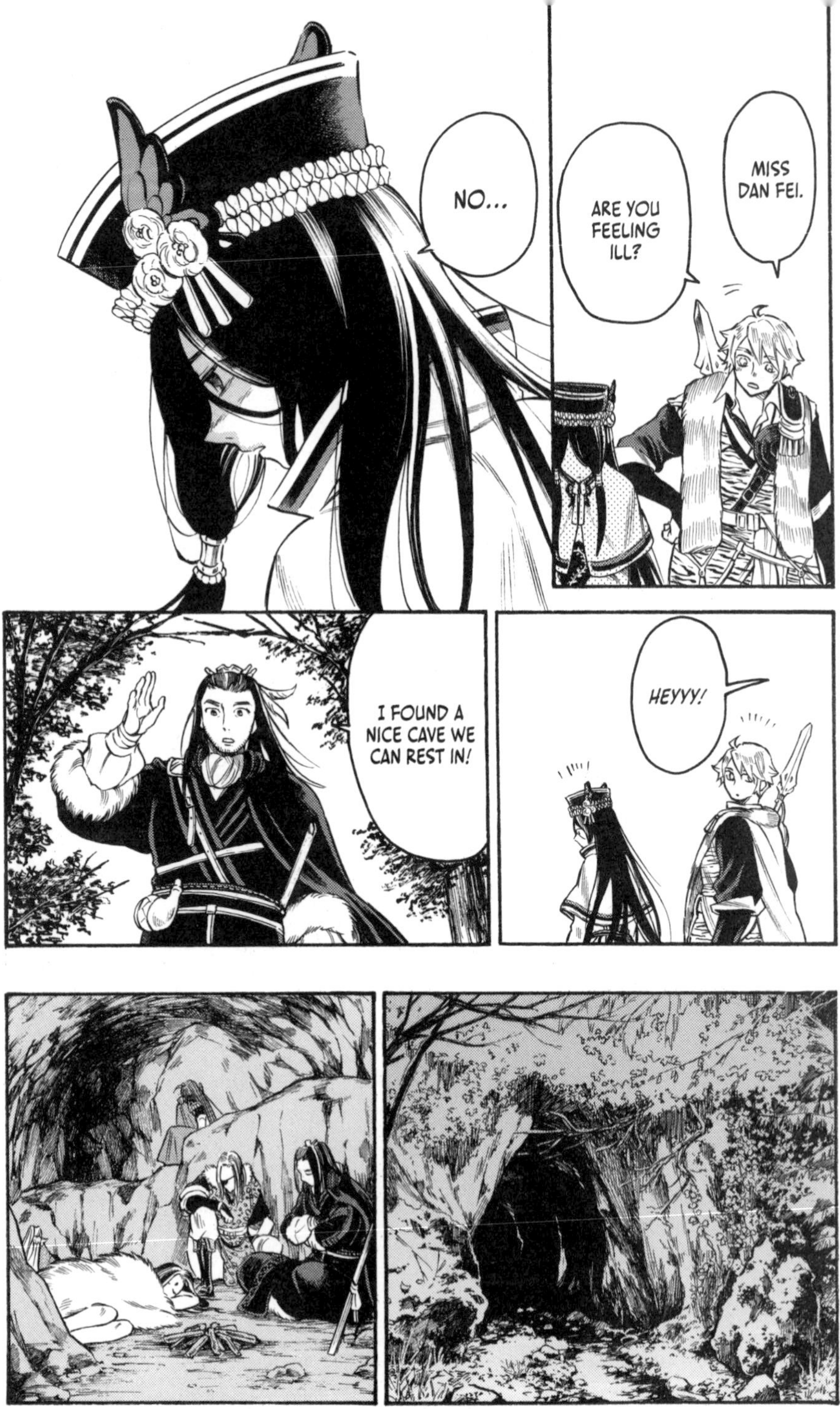
MISS DAN FEI.
ARE YOU FEELING ILL?
NO...
HEYYY!
I FOUND A NICE CAVE WE CAN REST IN!

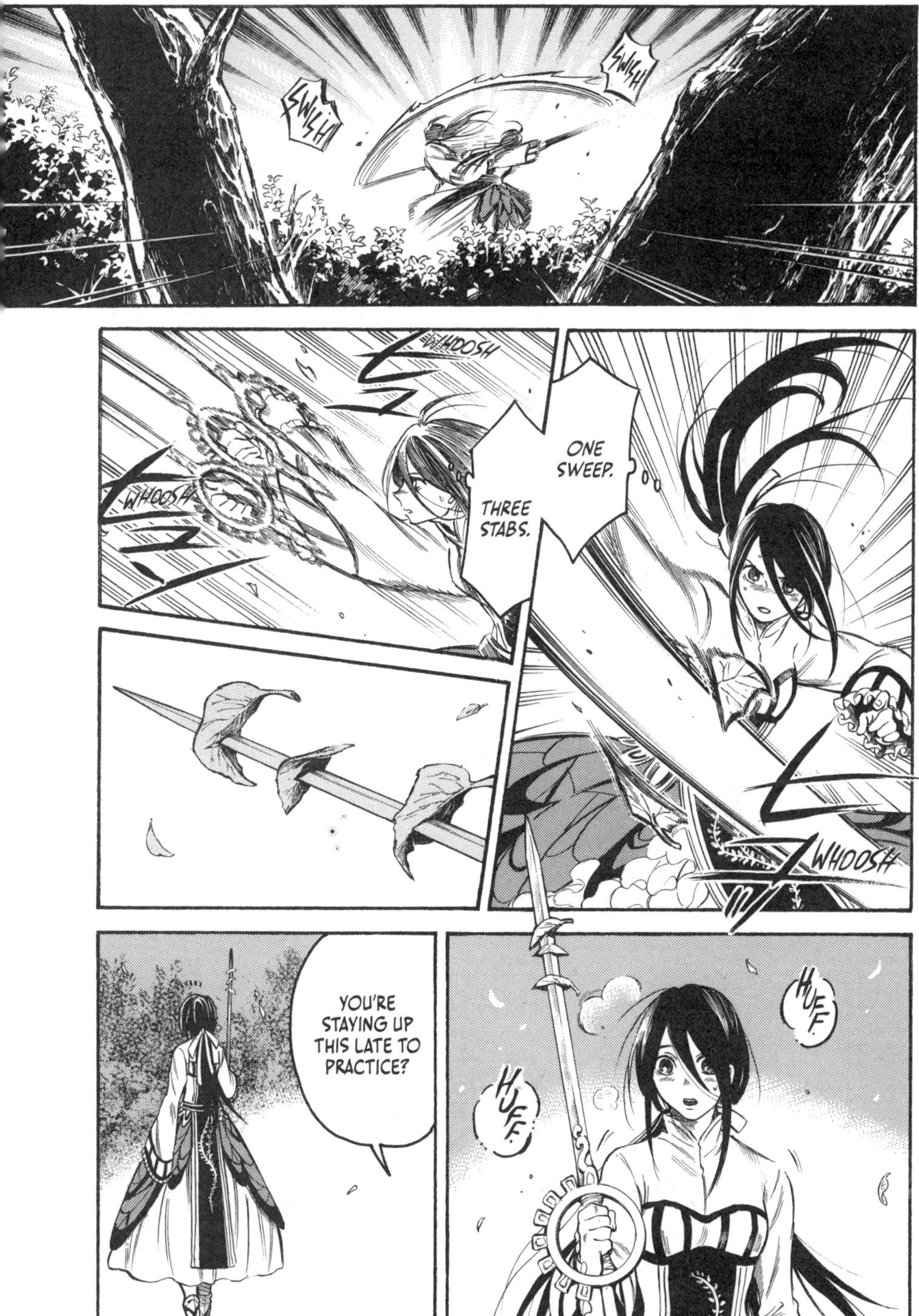
SWISH
SWISH
ONE SWEEP.
THREE STABS.
WHOOSH
WHOOSH
WHOOSH
HUFF
HUFF
YOU'RE STAYING UP THIS LATE TO PRACTICE?

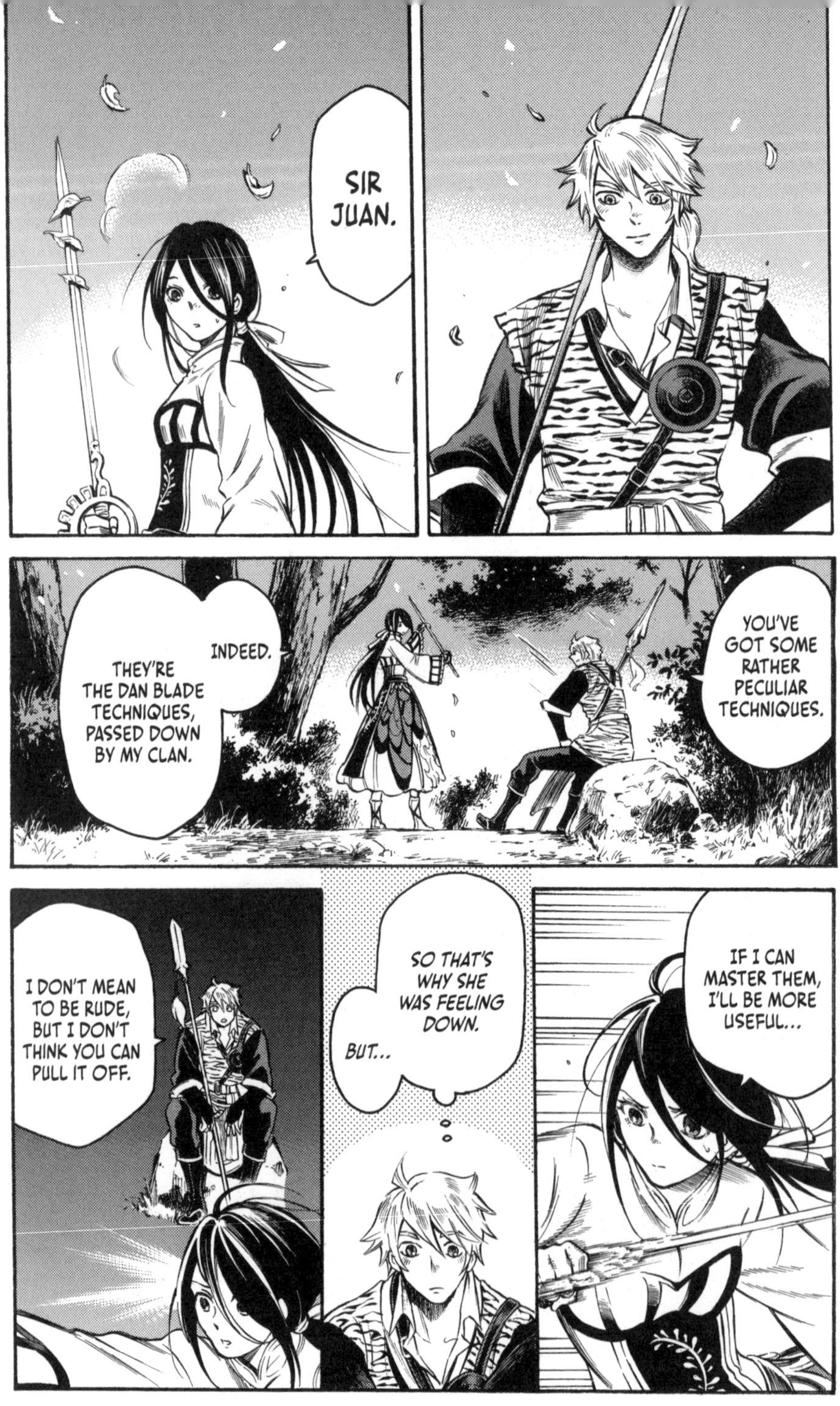
SIR JUAN.
YOU'VE GOT SOME RATHER PECULIAR TECHNIQUES.
INDEED.
THEY'RE THE DAN BLADE TECHNIQUES, PASSED DOWN BY MY CLAN.
IF I CAN MASTER THEM, I'LL BE MORE USEFUL...
SO THAT'S WHY SHE WAS FEELING DOWN.
BUT...
I DON'T MEAN TO BE RUDE, BUT I DON'T THINK YOU CAN PULL IT OFF.

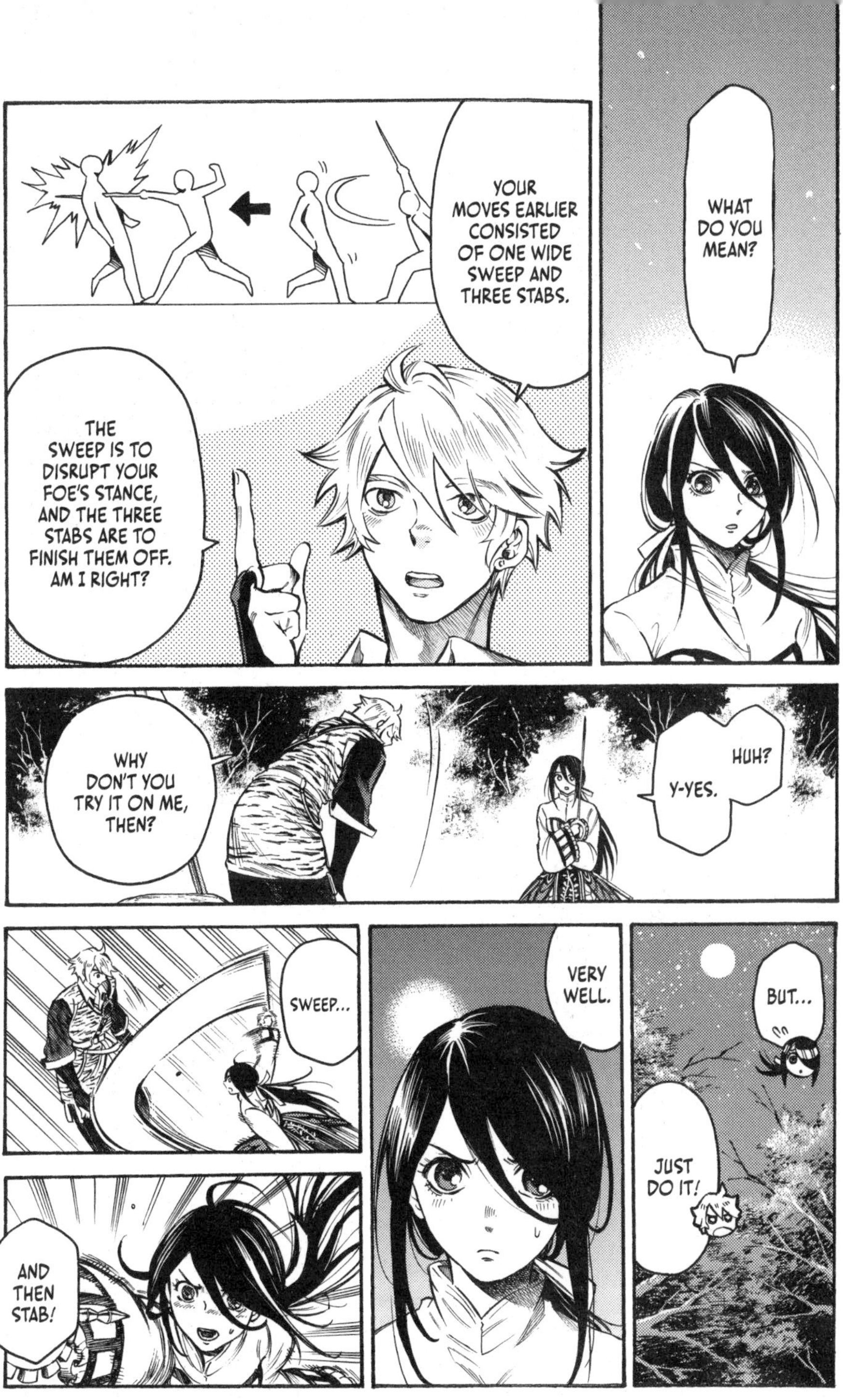
WHAT DO YOU MEAN?
YOUR MOVES EARLIER CONSISTED OF ONE WIDE SWEEP AND THREE STABS.
THE SWEEP IS TO DISRUPT YOUR FOE'S STANCE, AND THE THREE STABS ARE TO FINISH THEM OFF. AM I RIGHT?
HUH?
Y-YES.
WHY DON'T YOU TRY IT ON ME, THEN?
BUT...
JUST DO IT!
VERY WELL.
SWEEP...
AND THEN STAB!

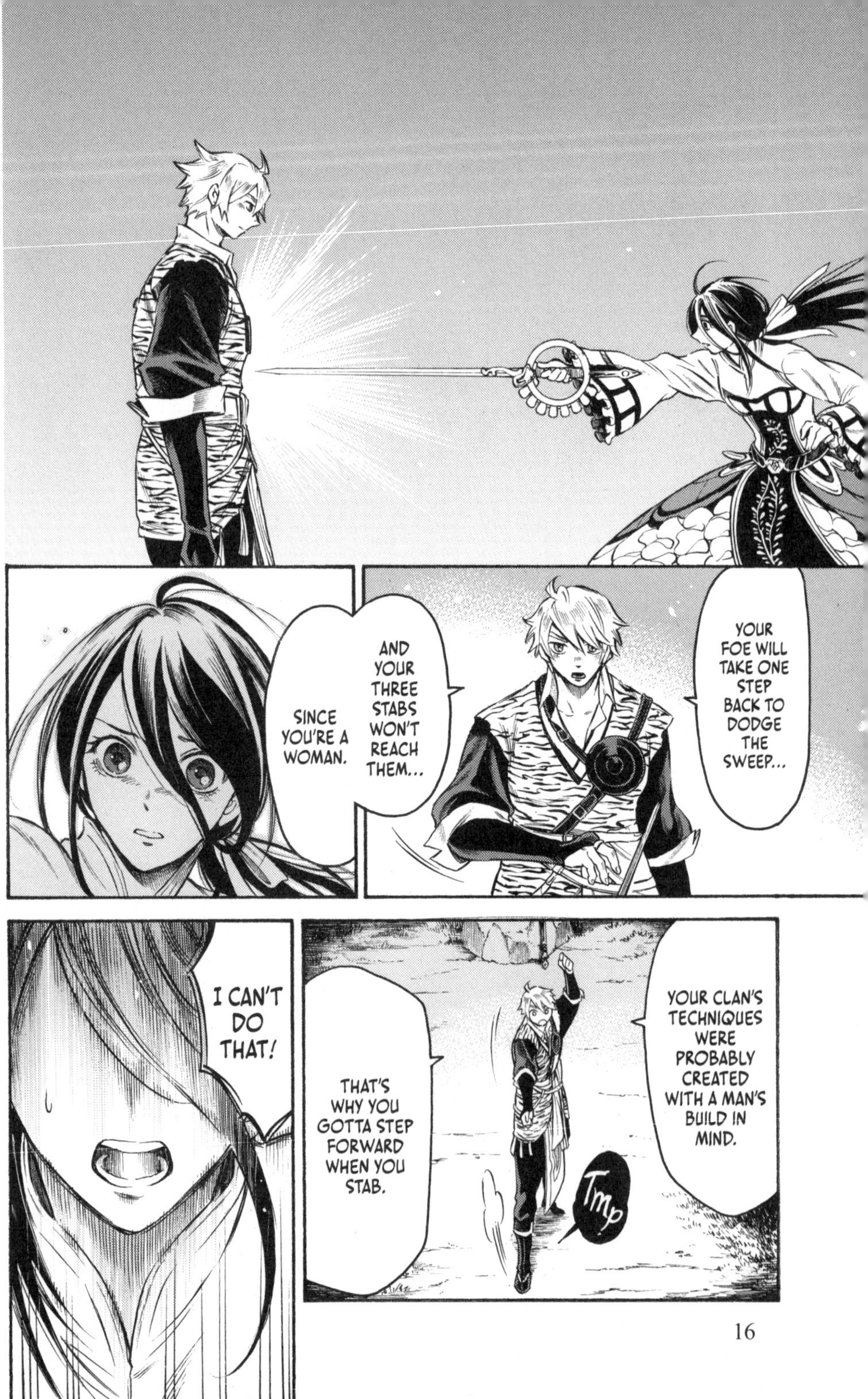

YOUR FOE WILL TAKE ONE STEP BACK TO DODGE THE SWEEP...
AND YOUR THREE STABS WON'T REACH THEM...
SINCE YOU'RE A WOMAN.
YOUR CLAN'S TECHNIQUES WERE PROBABLY CREATED WITH A MAN'S BUILD IN MIND.
THAT'S WHY YOU GOTTA STEP FORWARD WHEN YOU STAB.
Tmp
I CAN'T DO THAT!

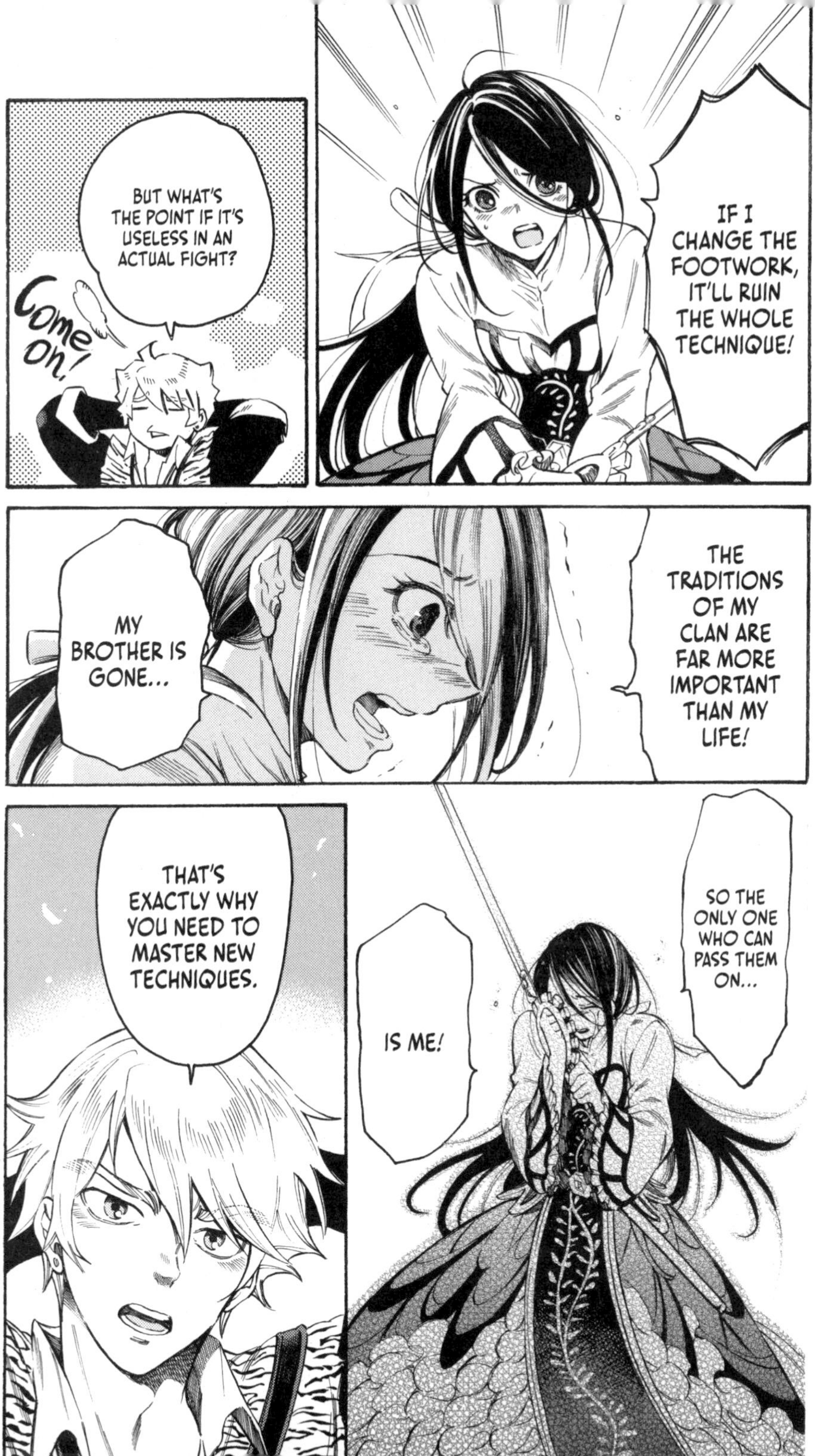
IF I CHANGE THE FOOTWORK, IT'LL RUIN THE WHOLE TECHNIQUE!
BUT WHAT'S THE POINT IF IT'S USELESS IN AN ACTUAL FIGHT?
Come on!
THE TRADITIONS OF MY CLAN ARE FAR MORE IMPORTANT THAN MY LIFE!
MY BROTHER IS GONE...
SO THE ONLY ONE WHO CAN PASS THEM ON...
IS ME!
THAT'S EXACTLY WHY YOU NEED TO MASTER NEW TECHNIQUES.

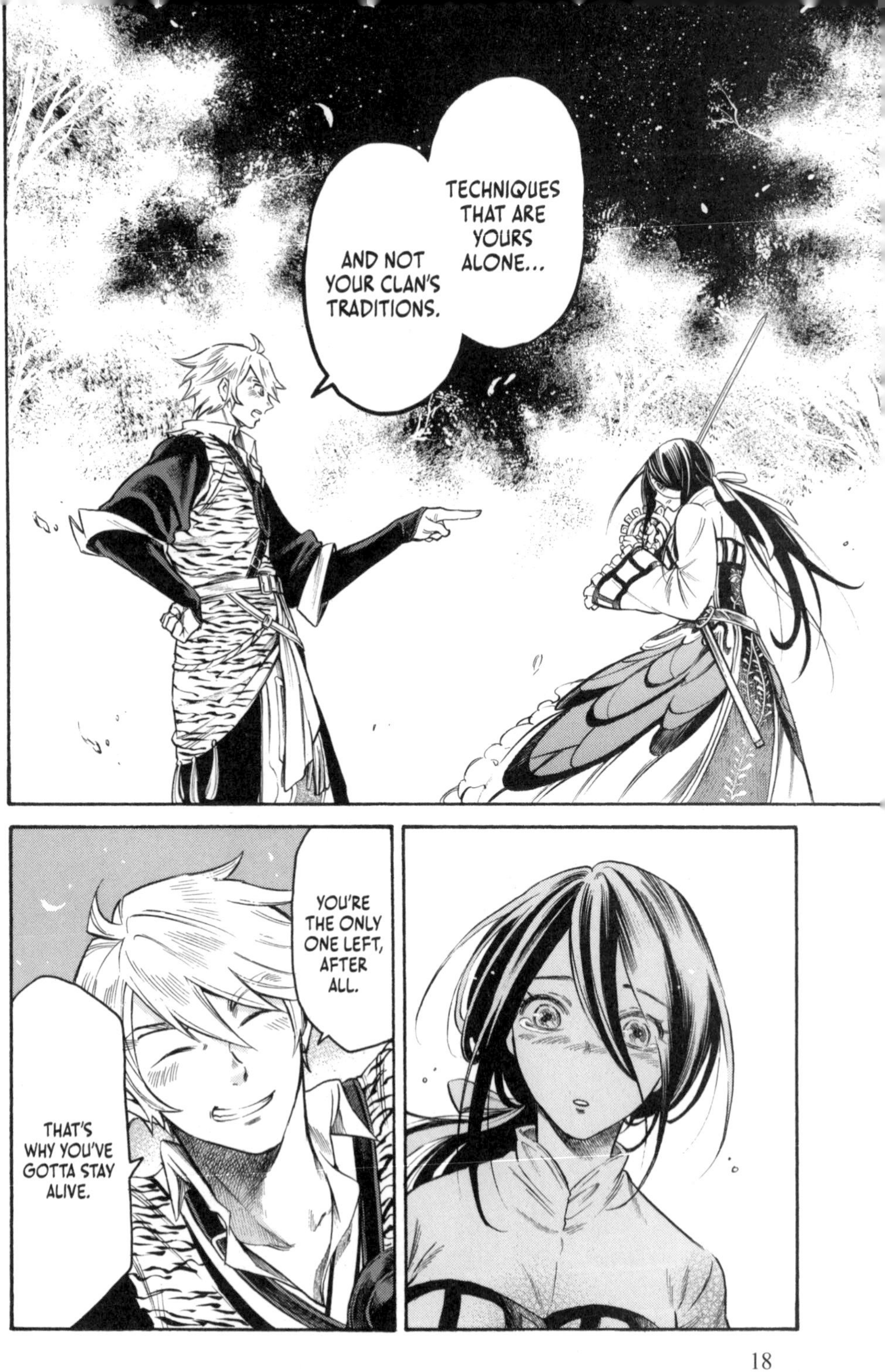
TECHNIQUES THAT ARE YOURS ALONE...
AND NOT YOUR CLAN'S TRADITIONS.
YOU'RE THE ONLY ONE LEFT, AFTER ALL.
THAT'S WHY YOU'VE GOTTA STAY ALIVE.

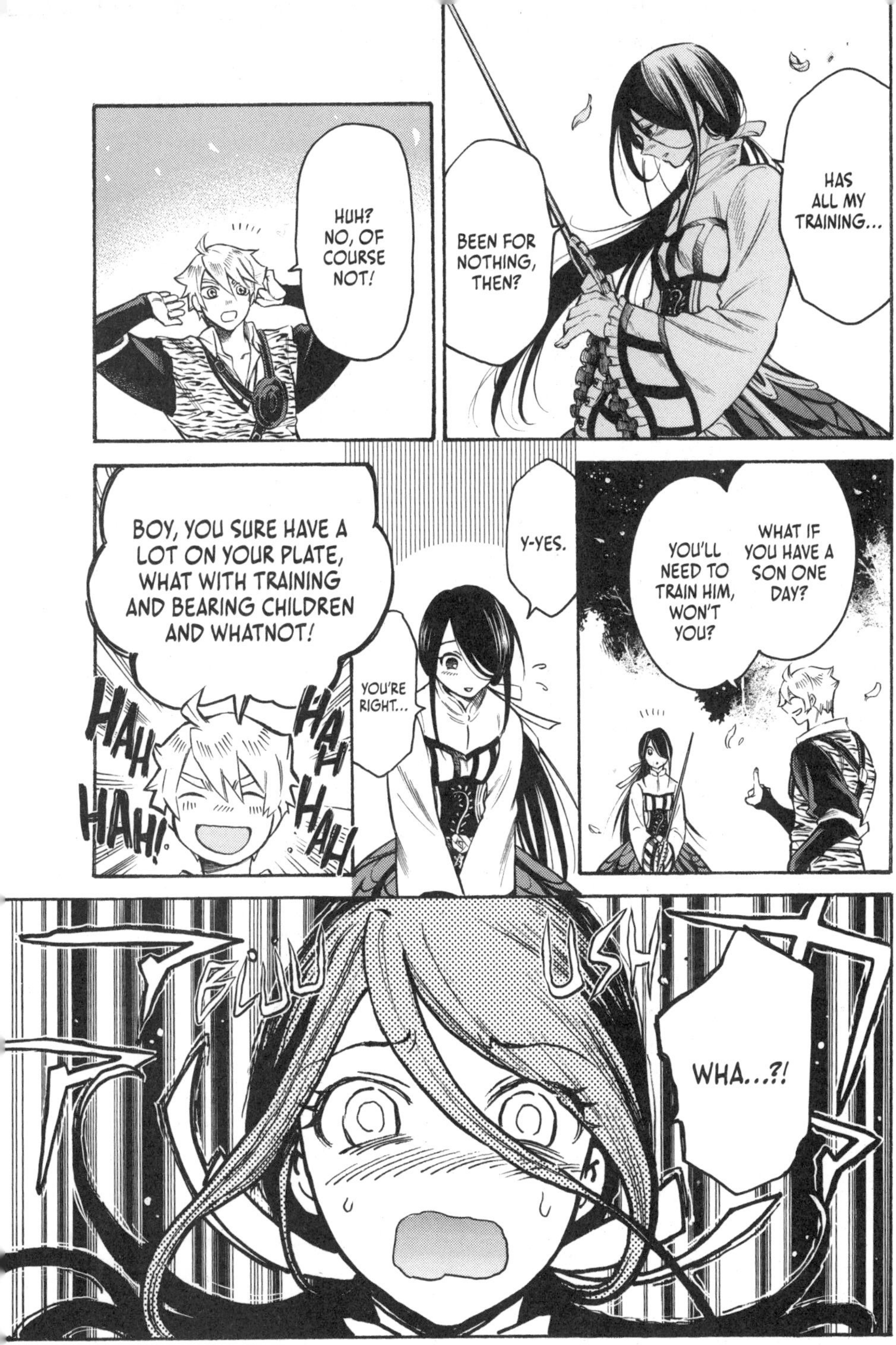
HAS ALL MY TRAINING...
BEEN FOR NOTHING, THEN?
HUH? NO, OF COURSE NOT!
WHAT IF YOU HAVE A SON ONE DAY?
YOU'LL NEED TO TRAIN HIM, WON'T YOU?
Y-YES.
YOU'RE RIGHT...
BOY, YOU SURE HAVE A LOT ON YOUR PLATE, WHAT WITH TRAINING AND BEARING CHILDREN AND WHATNOT!
HAH HAH HAH HAH
HAH HAH HAH!
BLUUUSH
WHA...?!

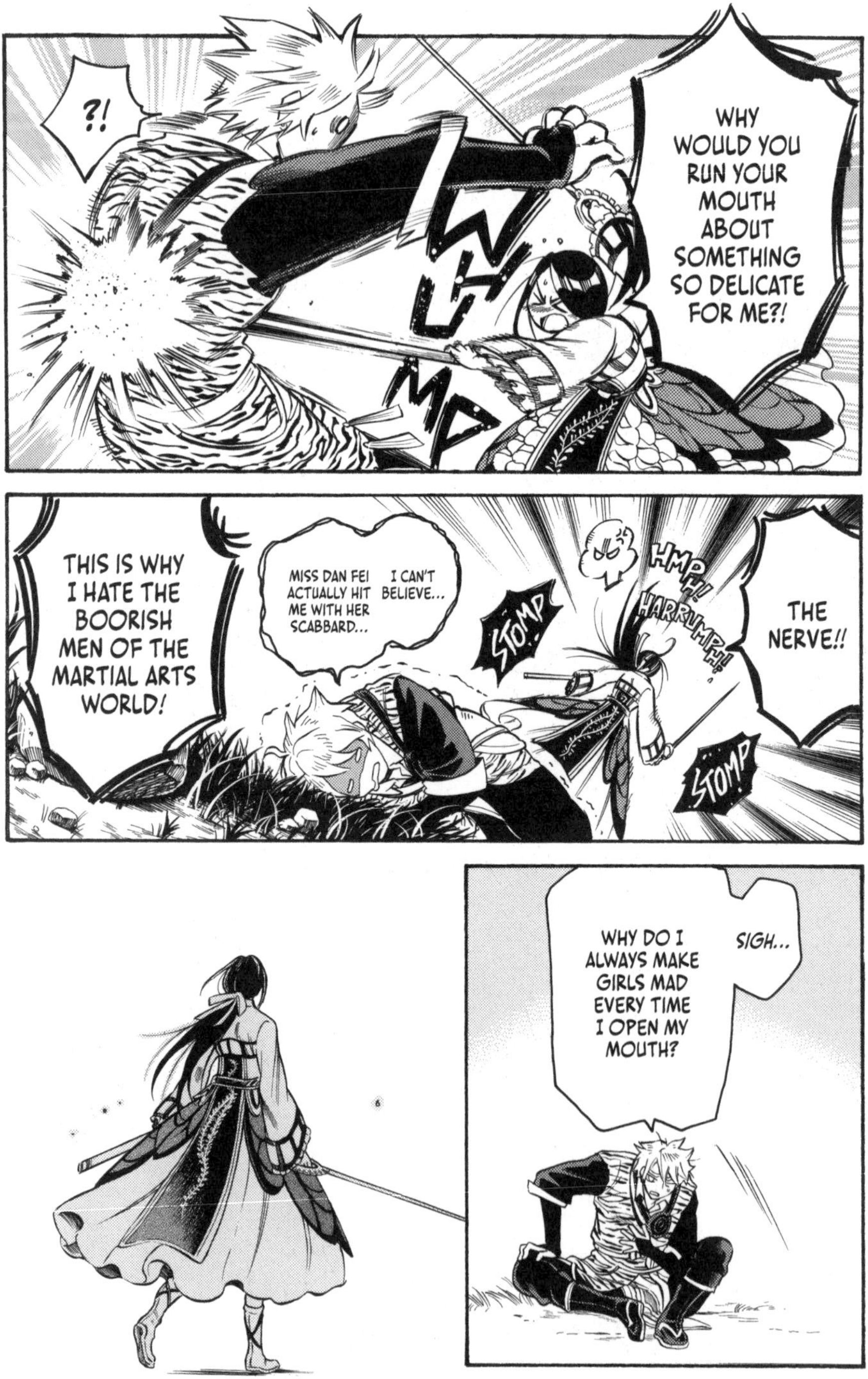
WHY WOULD YOU RUN YOUR MOUTH ABOUT SOMETHING SO DELICATE FOR ME?!
WHUMP
?!
THE NERVE!!
HMPH! HARRUMPH!
STOMP
STOMP
I CAN'T BELIEVE...
MISS DAN FEI ACTUALLY HIT ME WITH HER SCABBARD...
THIS IS WHY I HATE THE BOORISH MEN OF THE MARTIAL ARTS WORLD!
SIGH...
WHY DO I ALWAYS MAKE GIRLS MAD EVERY TIME I OPEN MY MOUTH?

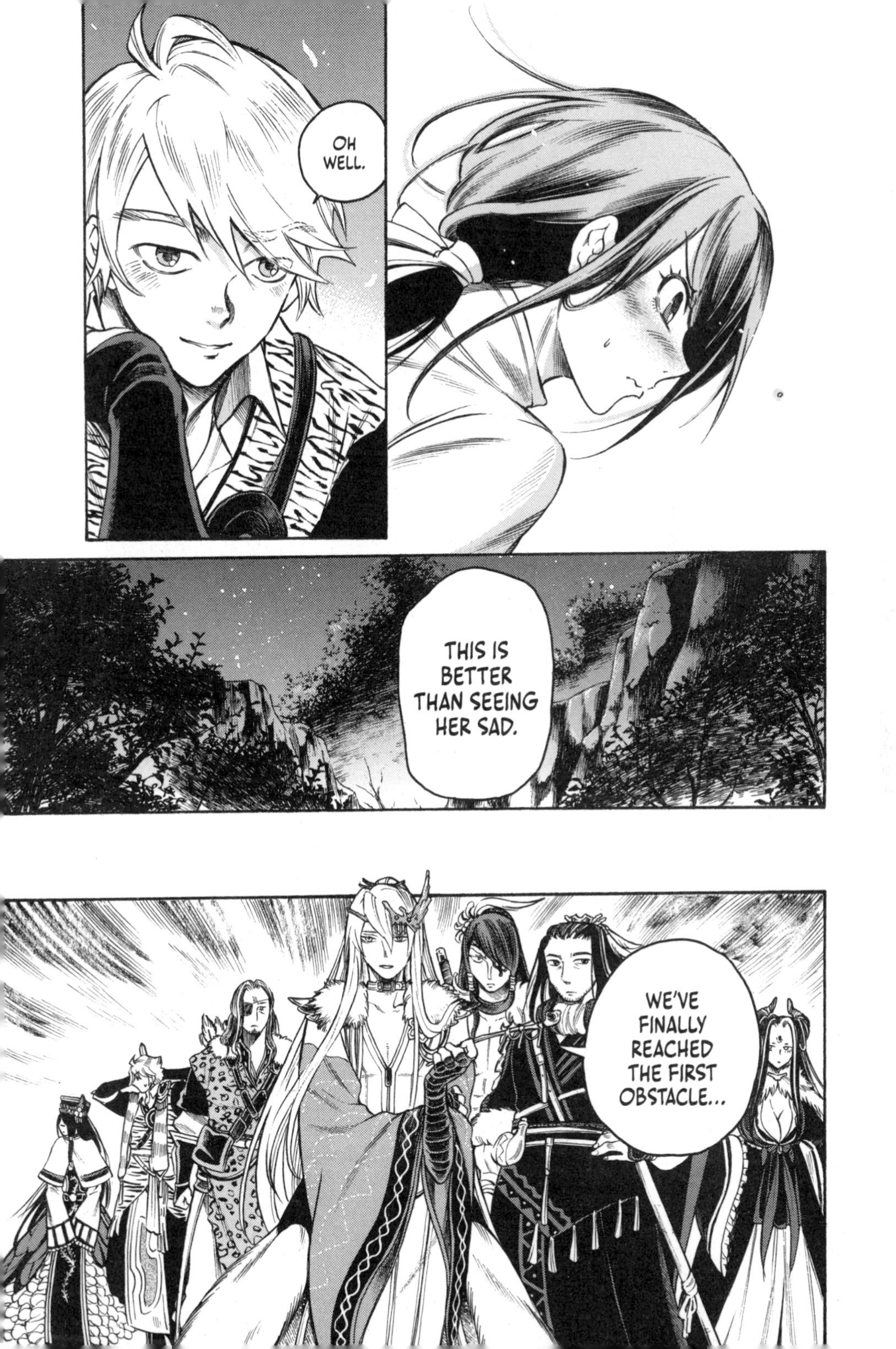
OH WELL.
THIS IS BETTER THAN SEEING HER SAD.
WE'VE FINALLY REACHED THE FIRST OBSTACLE...

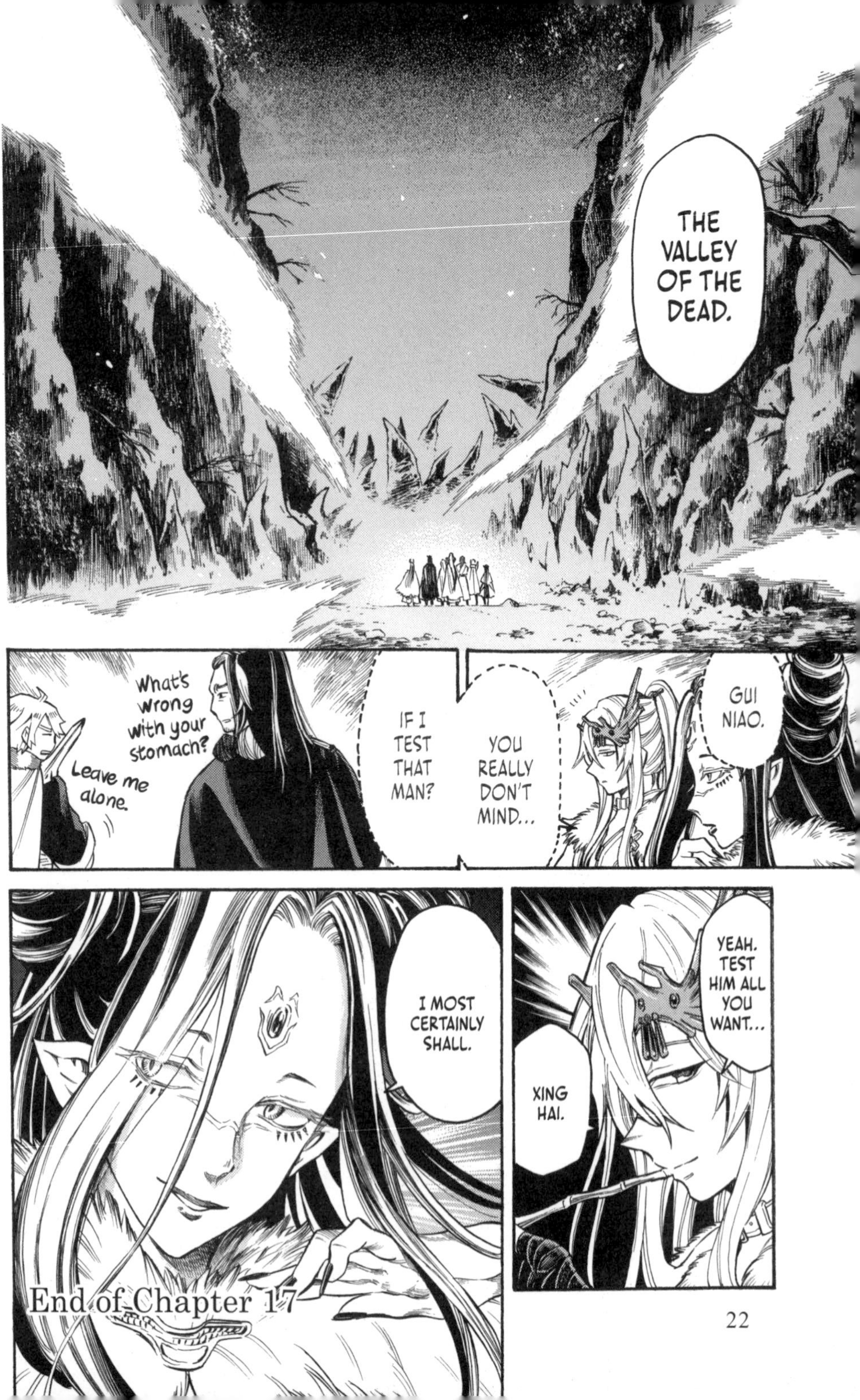
THE VALLEY OF THE DEAD.
GUI NIAO.
YOU REALLY DON'T MIND...
IF I TEST THAT MAN?
What's wrong with your stomach?
Leave me alone.
YEAH. TEST HIM ALL YOU WANT...
XING HAI.
I MOST CERTAINLY SHALL.
End of Chapter 17

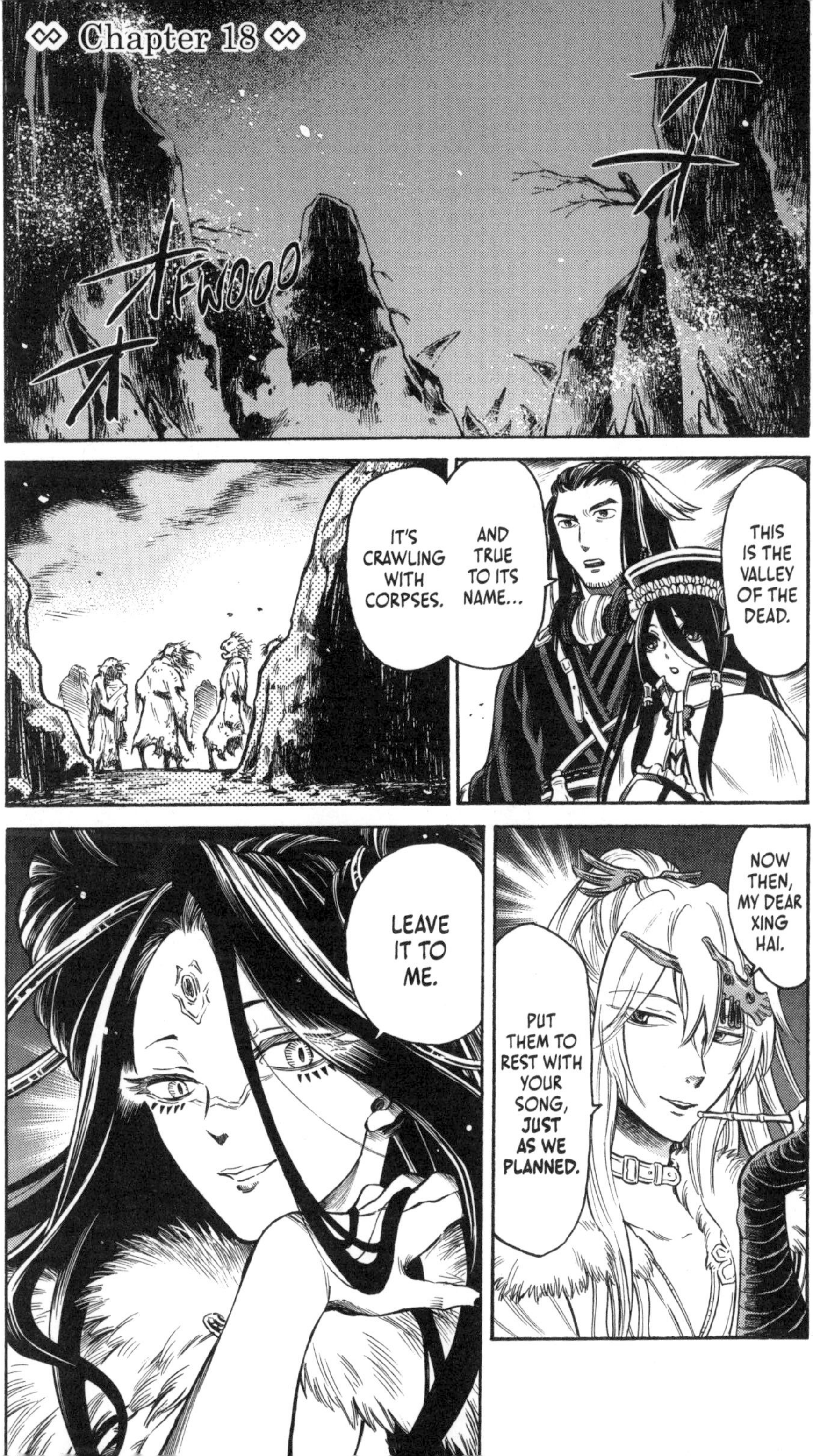
Chapter 18
FWOOO
THIS IS THE VALLEY OF THE DEAD.
AND TRUE TO ITS NAME...
IT'S CRAWLING WITH CORPSES.
NOW THEN, MY DEAR XING HAI.
PUT THEM TO REST WITH YOUR SONG, JUST AS WE PLANNED.
LEAVE IT TO ME.

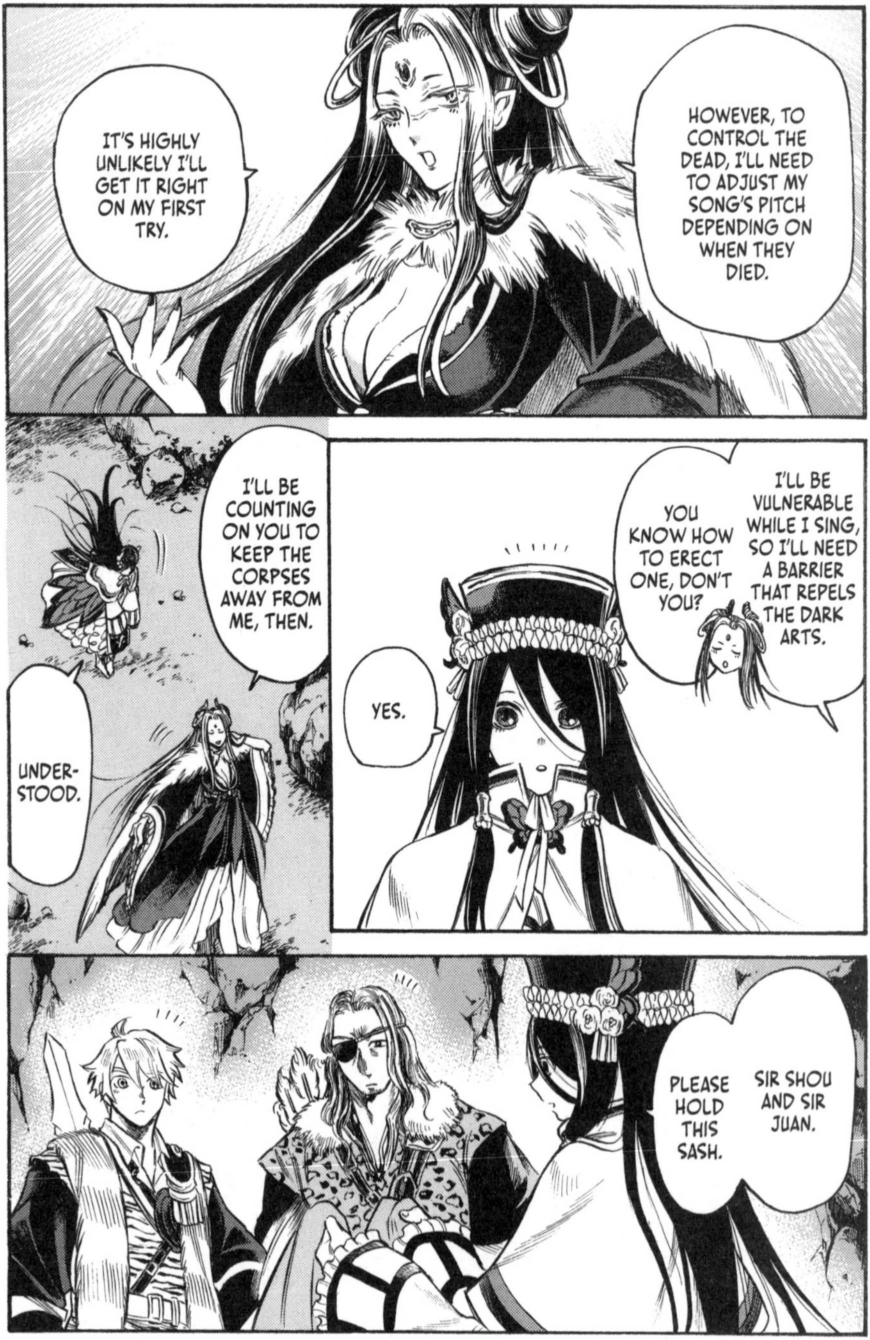
HOWEVER, TO CONTROL THE DEAD, I'LL NEED TO ADJUST MY SONG'S PITCH DEPENDING ON WHEN THEY DIED.
IT'S HIGHLY UNLIKELY I'LL GET IT RIGHT ON MY FIRST TRY.
I'LL BE VULNERABLE WHILE I SING, SO I'LL NEED A BARRIER THAT REPELS THE DARK ARTS.
YOU KNOW HOW TO ERECT ONE, DON'T YOU?
YES.
I'LL BE COUNTING ON YOU TO KEEP THE CORPSES AWAY FROM ME, THEN.
UNDER-STOOD.
SIR SHOU AND SIR JUAN.
PLEASE HOLD THIS SASH.

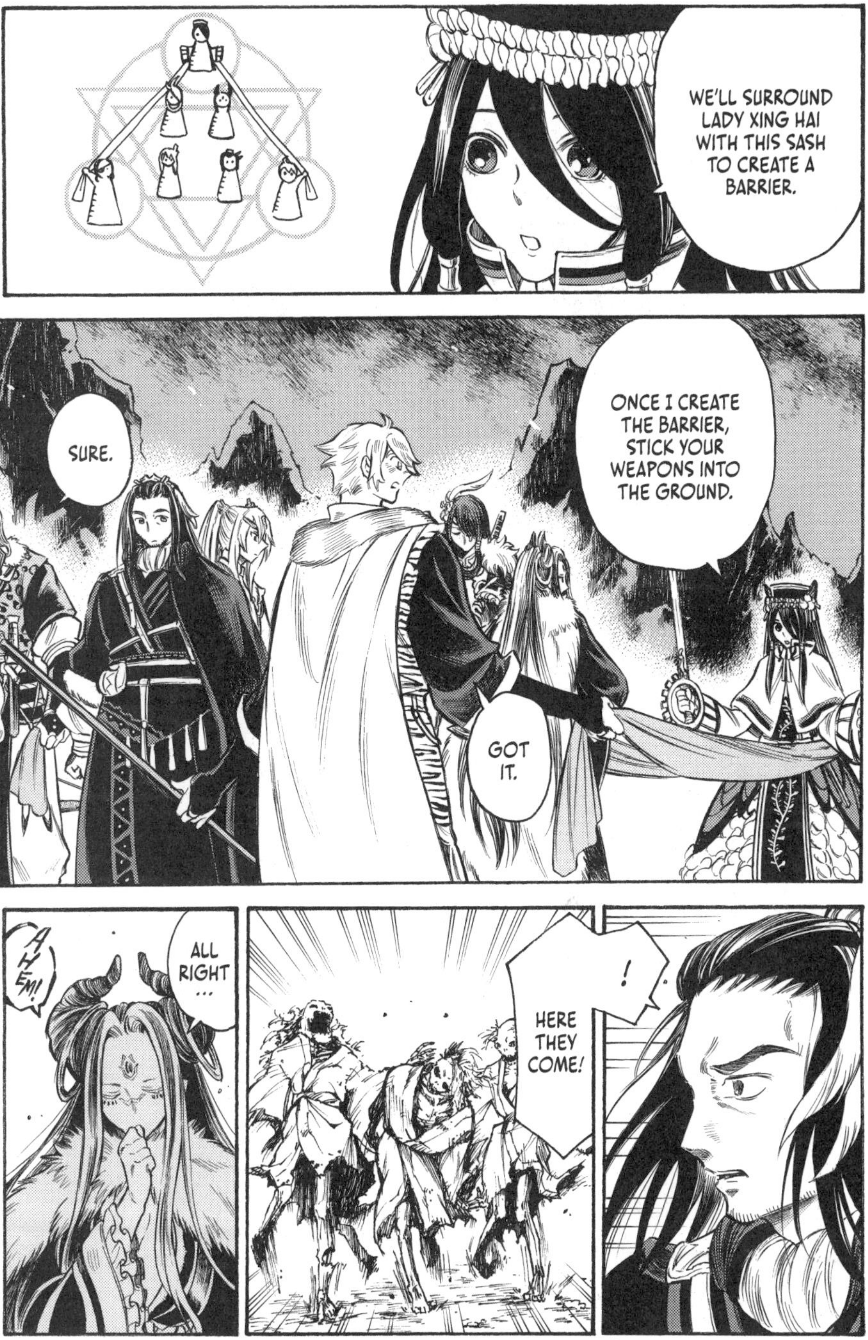
WE'LL SURROUND LADY XING HAI WITH THIS SASH TO CREATE A BARRIER.
ONCE I CREATE THE BARRIER, STICK YOUR WEAPONS INTO THE GROUND.
GOT IT.
SURE.
!
HERE THEY COME!
ALL RIGHT ...
AHEM!

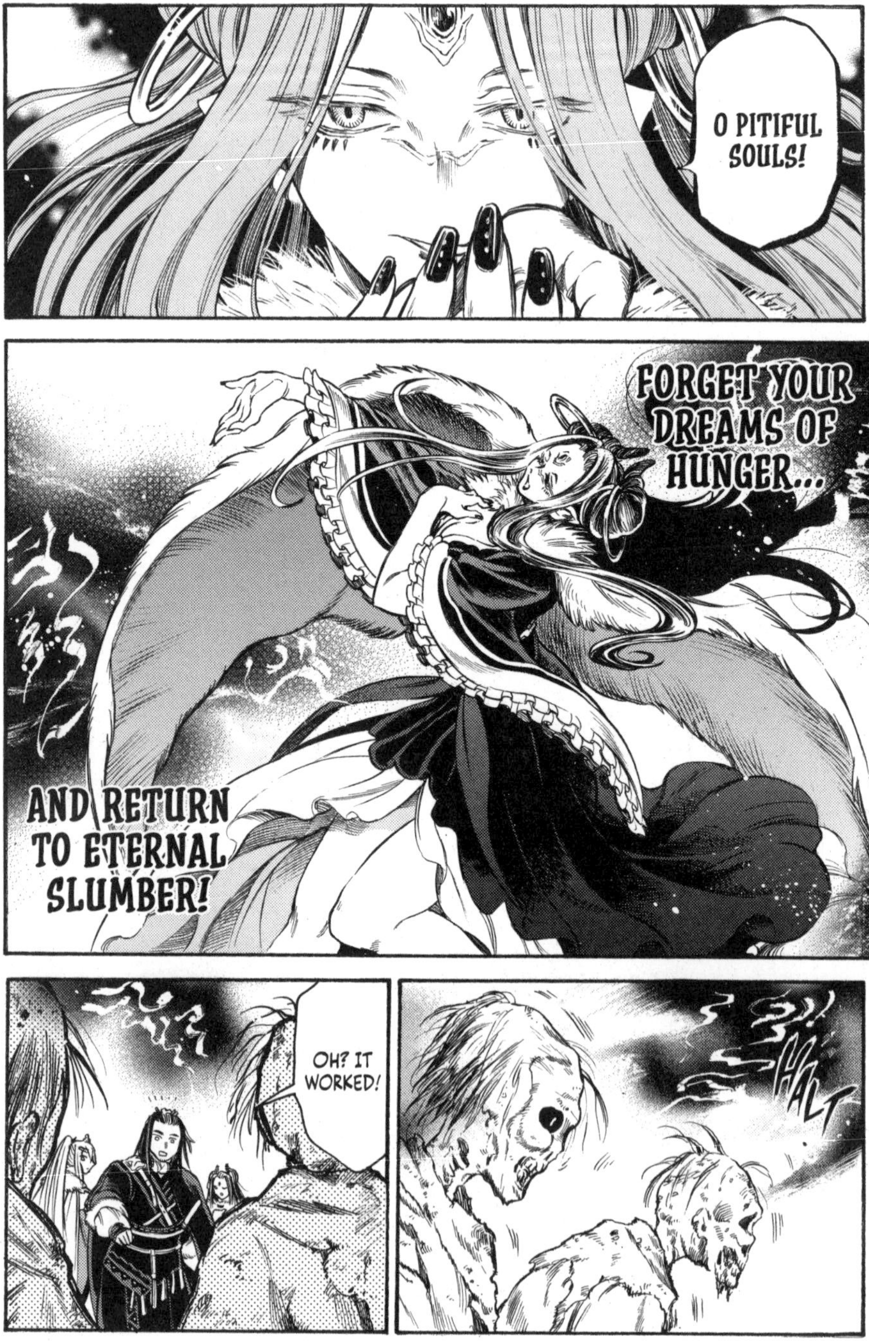
O PITIFUL SOULS!
FORGET YOUR DREAMS OF HUNGER...
AND RETURN TO ETERNAL SLUMBER!
HALT
OH? IT WORKED!

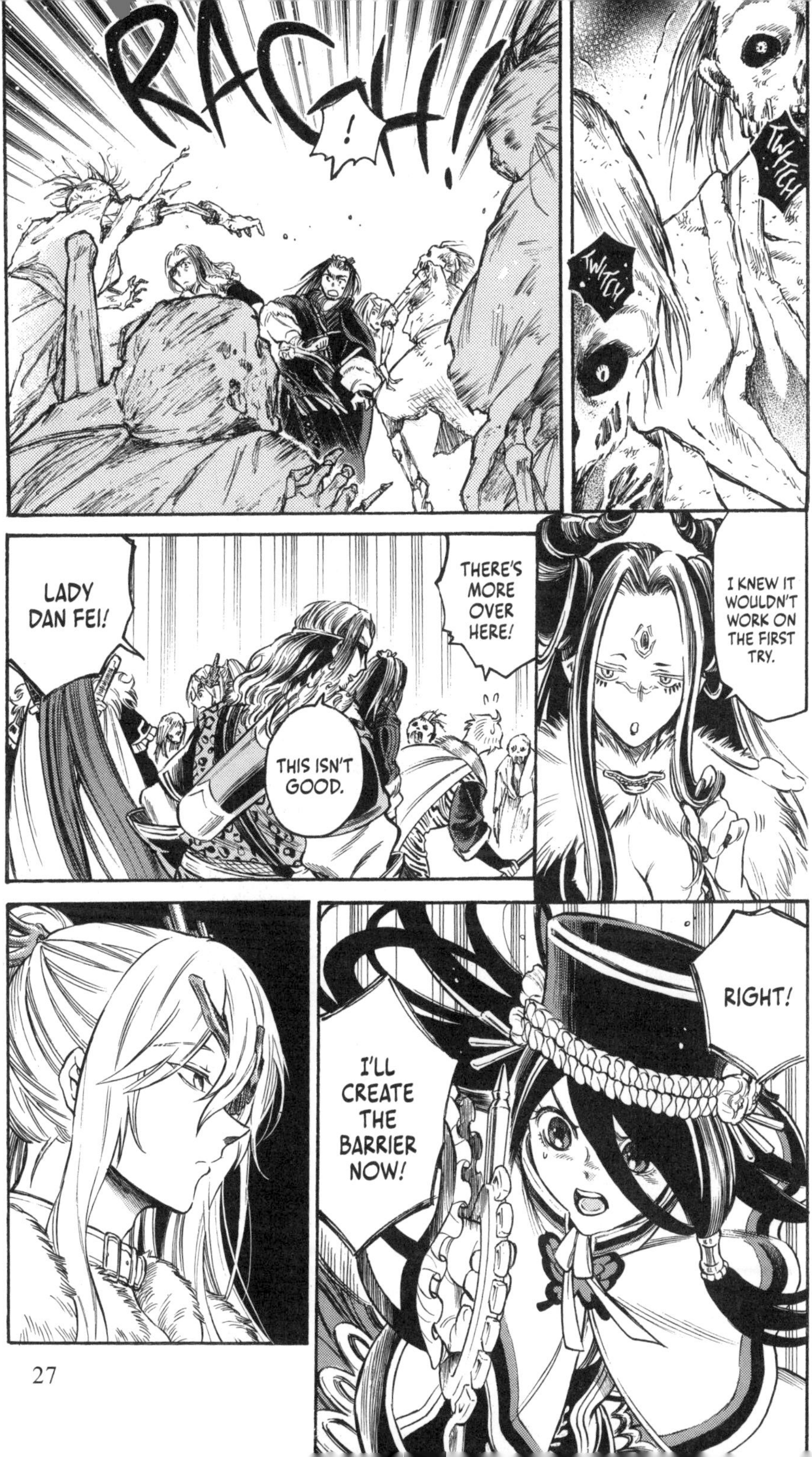
TWITCH
TWITCH
RACH!!
!
I KNEW IT WOULDN'T WORK ON THE FIRST TRY.
THERE'S MORE OVER HERE!
LADY DAN FEI!
THIS ISN'T GOOD.
RIGHT!
I'LL CREATE THE BARRIER NOW!

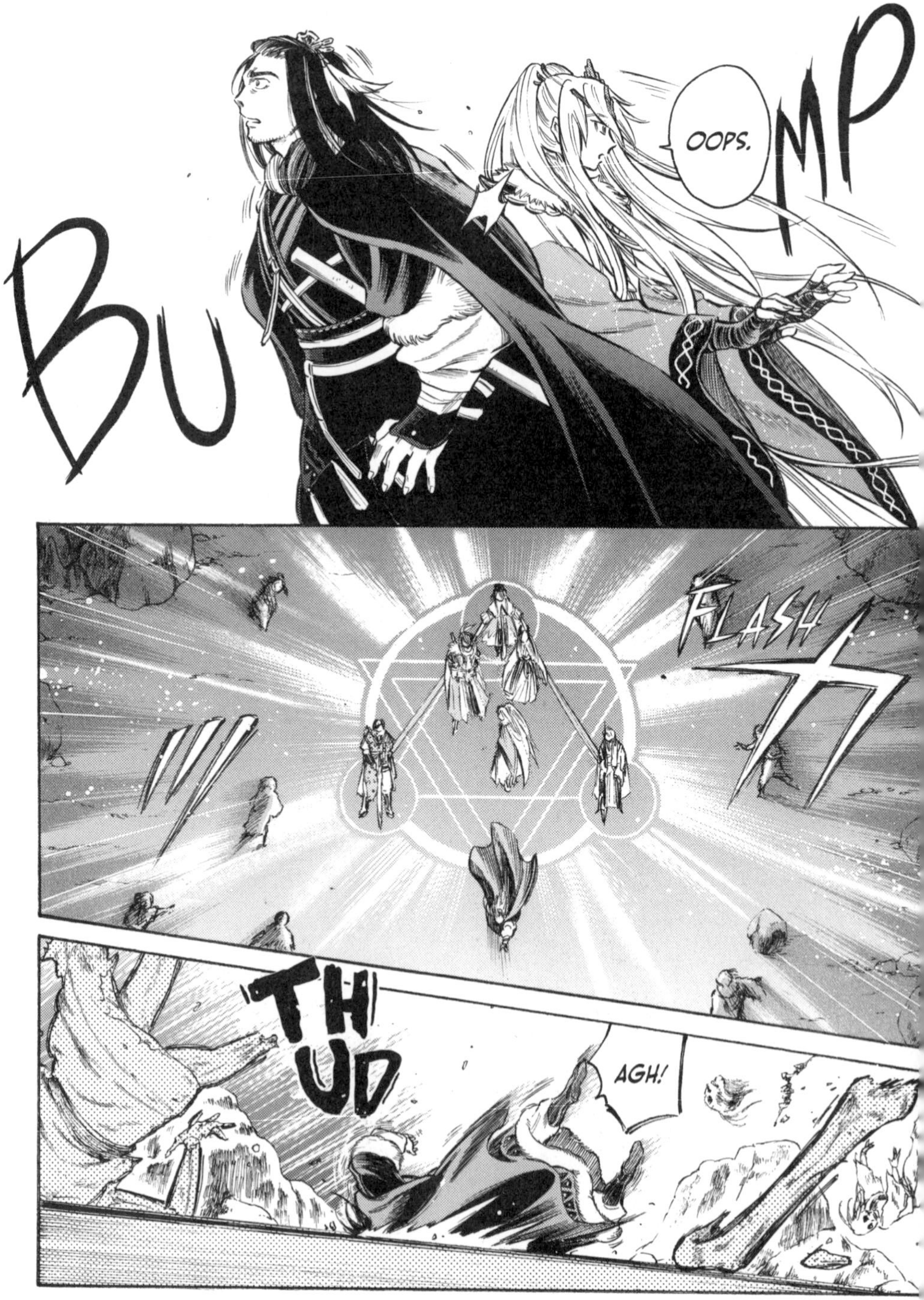
OOPS.
BUMP
FLASH
AGH!
THUD

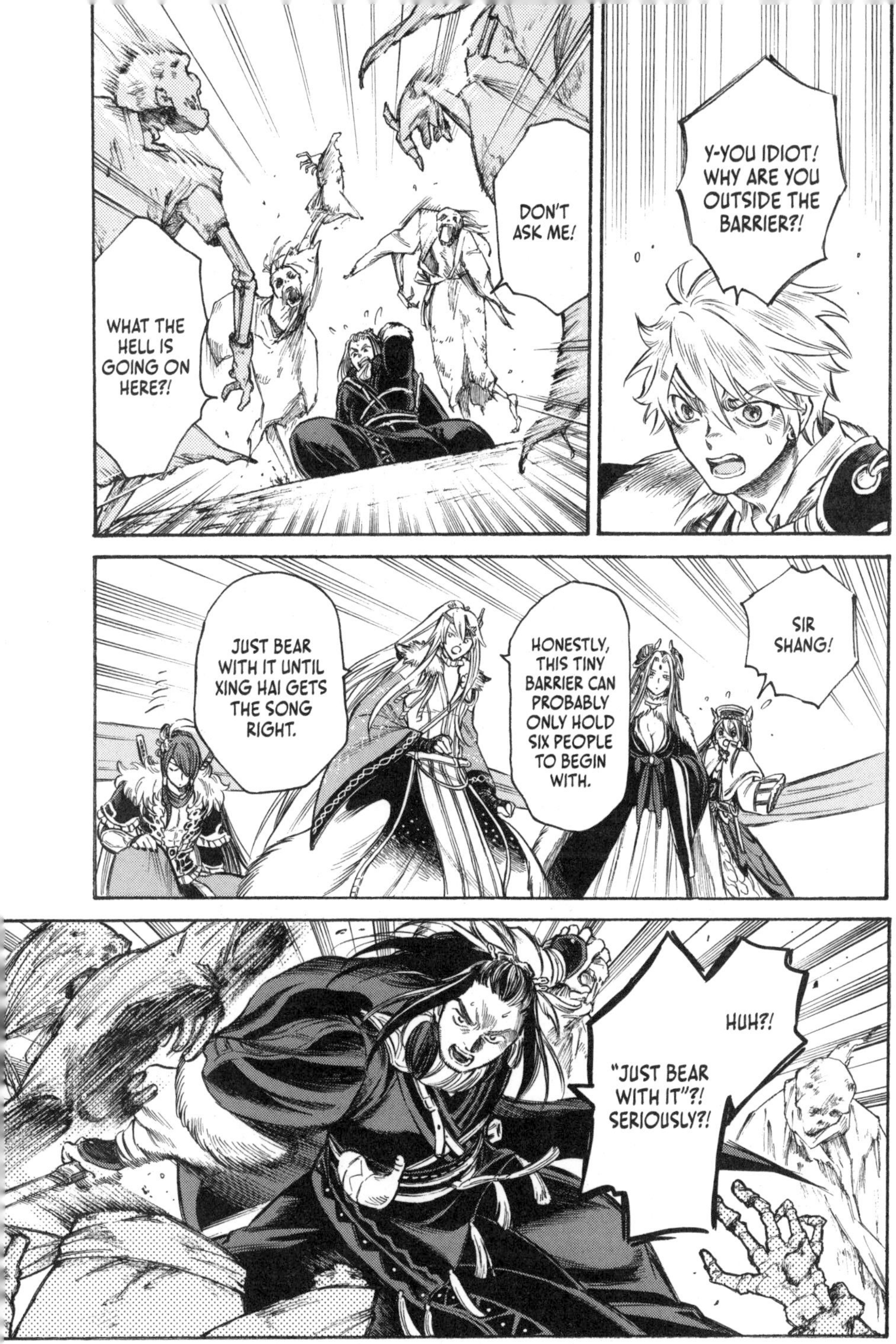
Y-YOU IDIOT! WHY ARE YOU OUTSIDE THE BARRIER?!
DON'T ASK ME!
WHAT THE HELL IS GOING ON HERE?!
SIR SHANG!
HONESTLY, THIS TINY BARRIER CAN PROBABLY ONLY HOLD SIX PEOPLE TO BEGIN WITH.
JUST BEAR WITH IT UNTIL XING HAI GETS THE SONG RIGHT.
HUH?!
"JUST BEAR WITH IT"?! SERIOUSLY?!

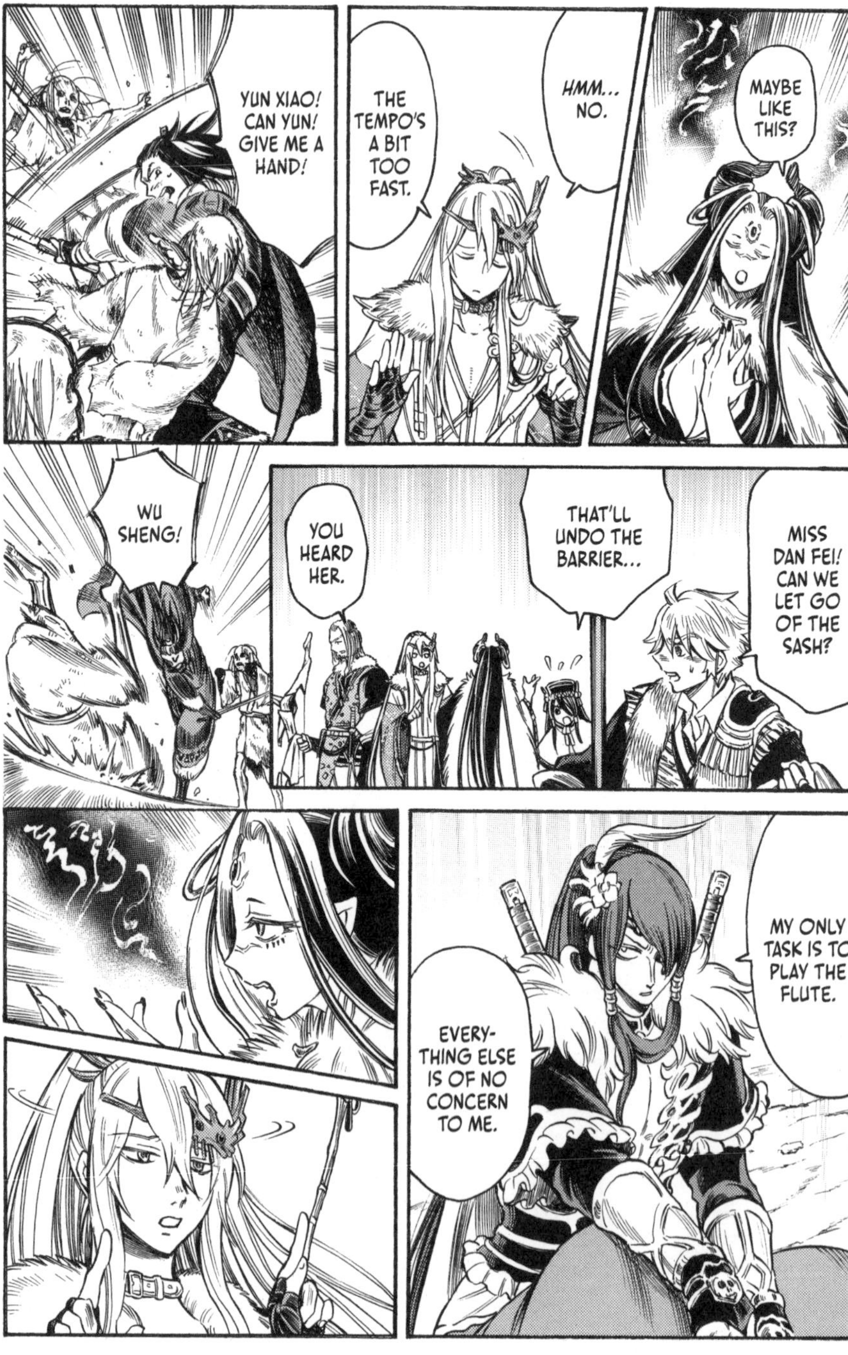
MAYBE LIKE THIS?
HMM... NO.
THE TEMPO'S A BIT TOO FAST.
YUN XIAO! CAN YUN! GIVE ME A HAND!
MISS DAN FEI! CAN WE LET GO OF THE SASH?
THAT'LL UNDO THE BARRIER...
YOU HEARD HER.
WU SHENG!
MY ONLY TASK IS TO PLAY THE FLUTE.
EVERY-THING ELSE IS OF NO CONCERN TO ME.

WE'RE BUSY RIGHT NOW.

BE QUIET.

GUI NIAO...

GRIK

GRIK

YOU BASTARDS...

GIVE ME A DAMN BREAK!

WHOMP!!

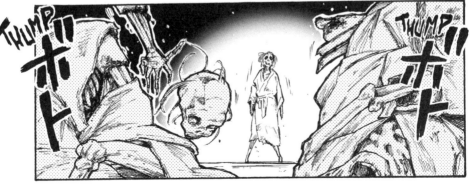

THUMP!!

THUMP!!

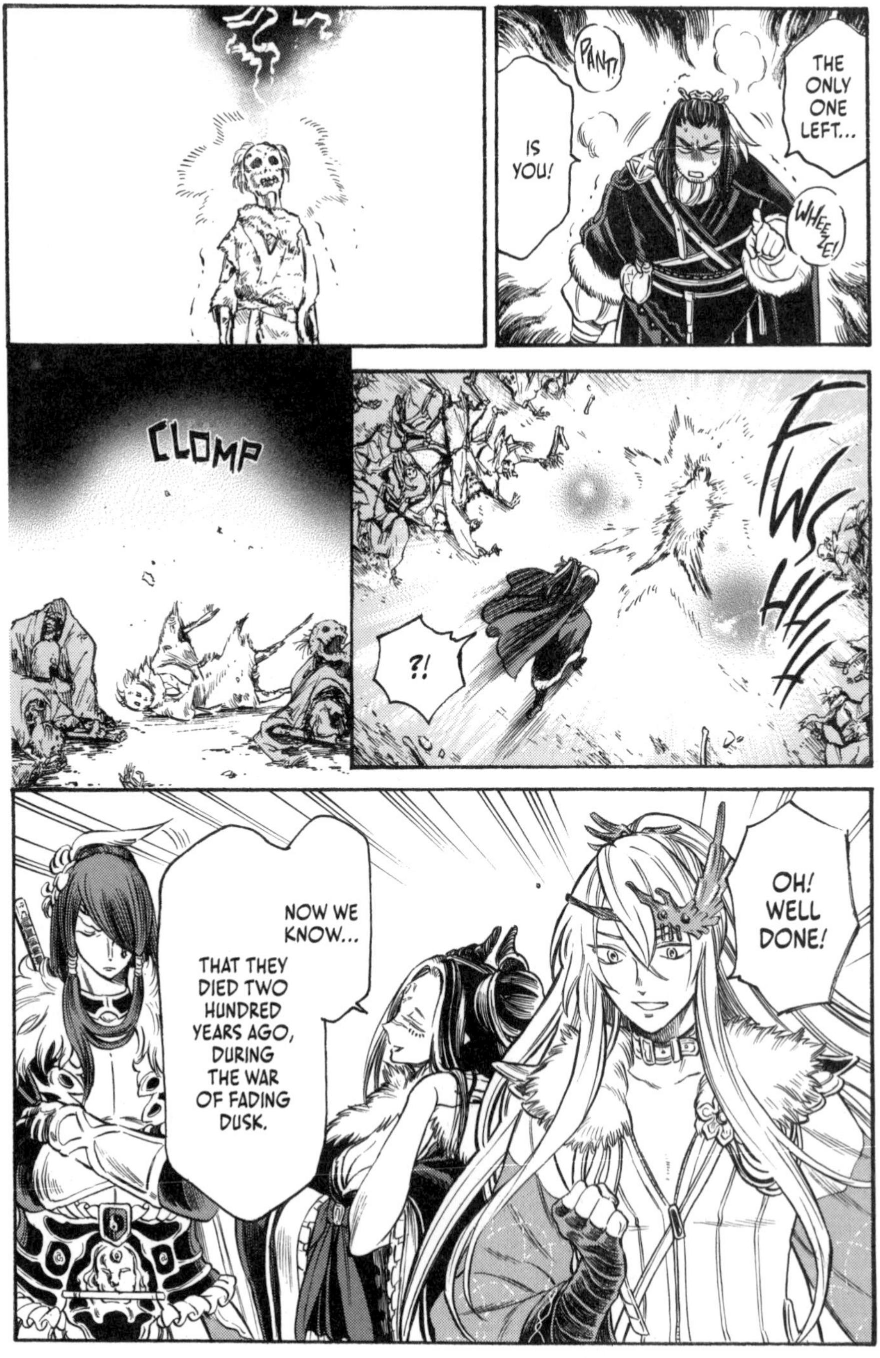
THE ONLY ONE LEFT...
PANT!
IS YOU!
WHEEZE!
FWSHHHH
?!
CLOMP
OH! WELL DONE!
NOW WE KNOW...
THAT THEY DIED TWO HUNDRED YEARS AGO, DURING THE WAR OF FADING DUSK.

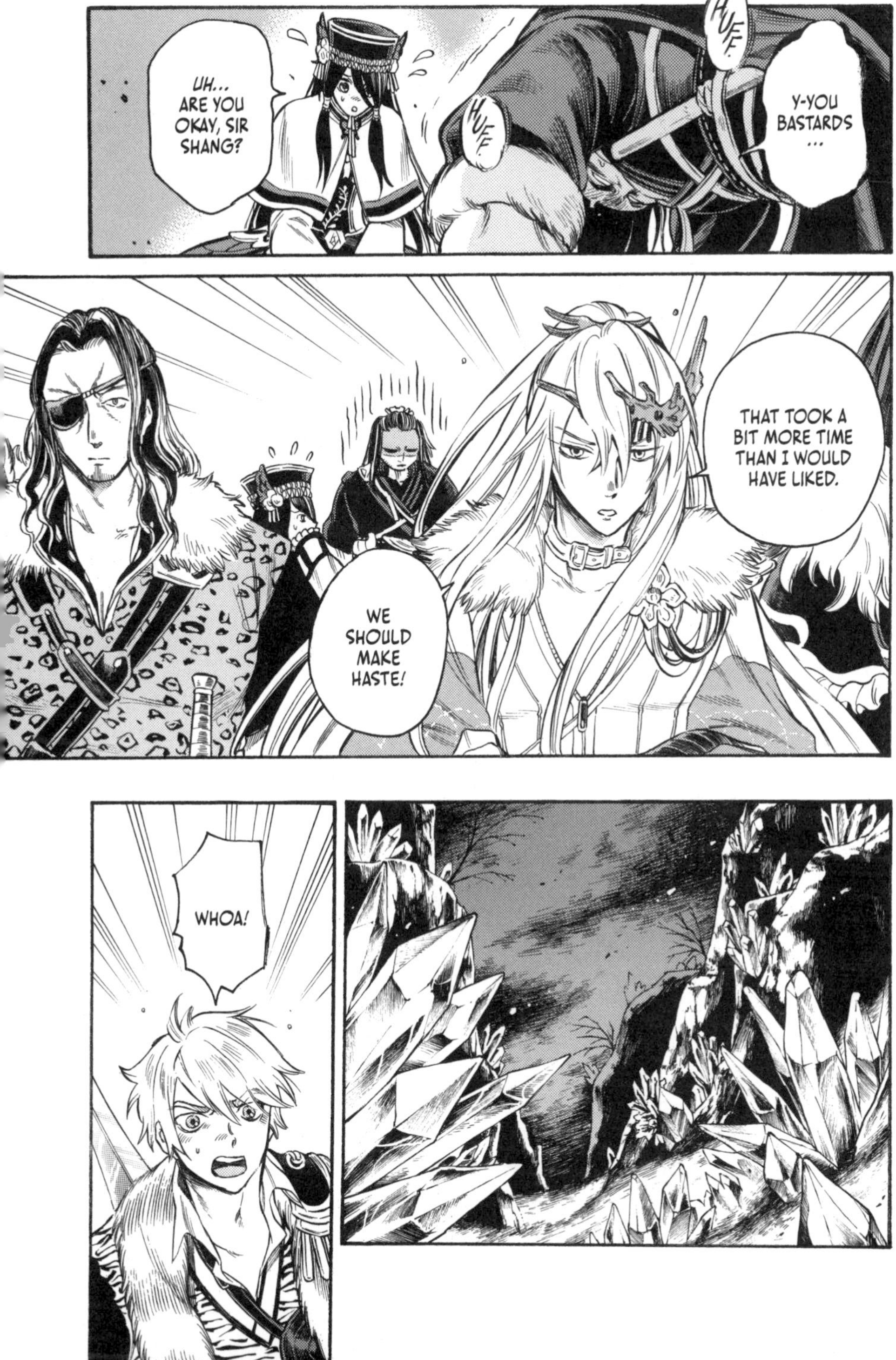
HUFF
Y-YOU BASTARDS ...
HUFF
UH... ARE YOU OKAY, SIR SHANG?
THAT TOOK A BIT MORE TIME THAN I WOULD HAVE LIKED.
WE SHOULD MAKE HASTE!
WHOA!

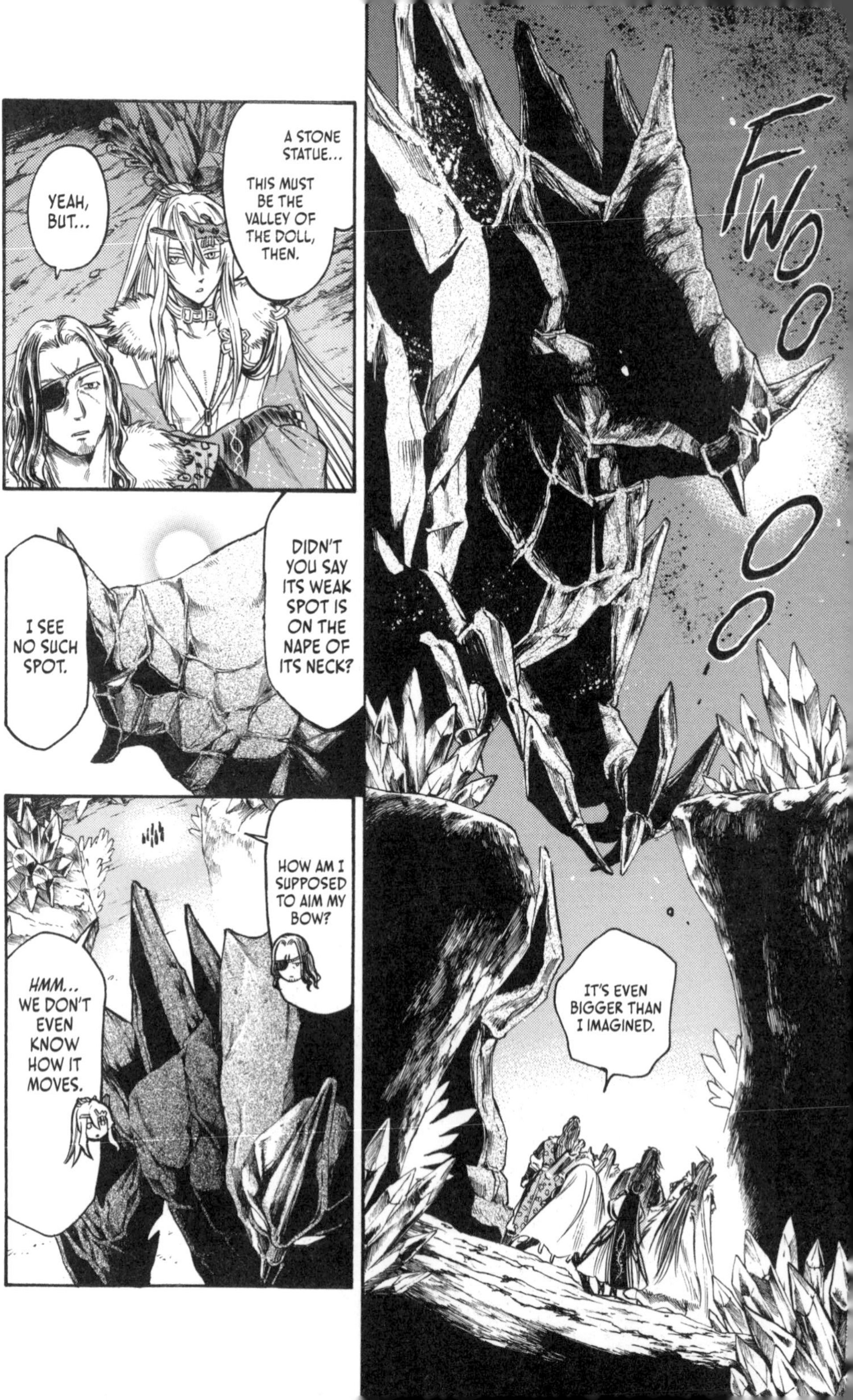
FWOOOOOOO
IT'S EVEN BIGGER THAN I IMAGINED.
A STONE STATUE...
THIS MUST BE THE VALLEY OF THE DOLL, THEN.
YEAH, BUT...
DIDN'T YOU SAY ITS WEAK SPOT IS ON THE NAPE OF ITS NECK?
I SEE NO SUCH SPOT.
HOW AM I SUPPOSED TO AIM MY BOW?
HMM... WE DON'T EVEN KNOW HOW IT MOVES.

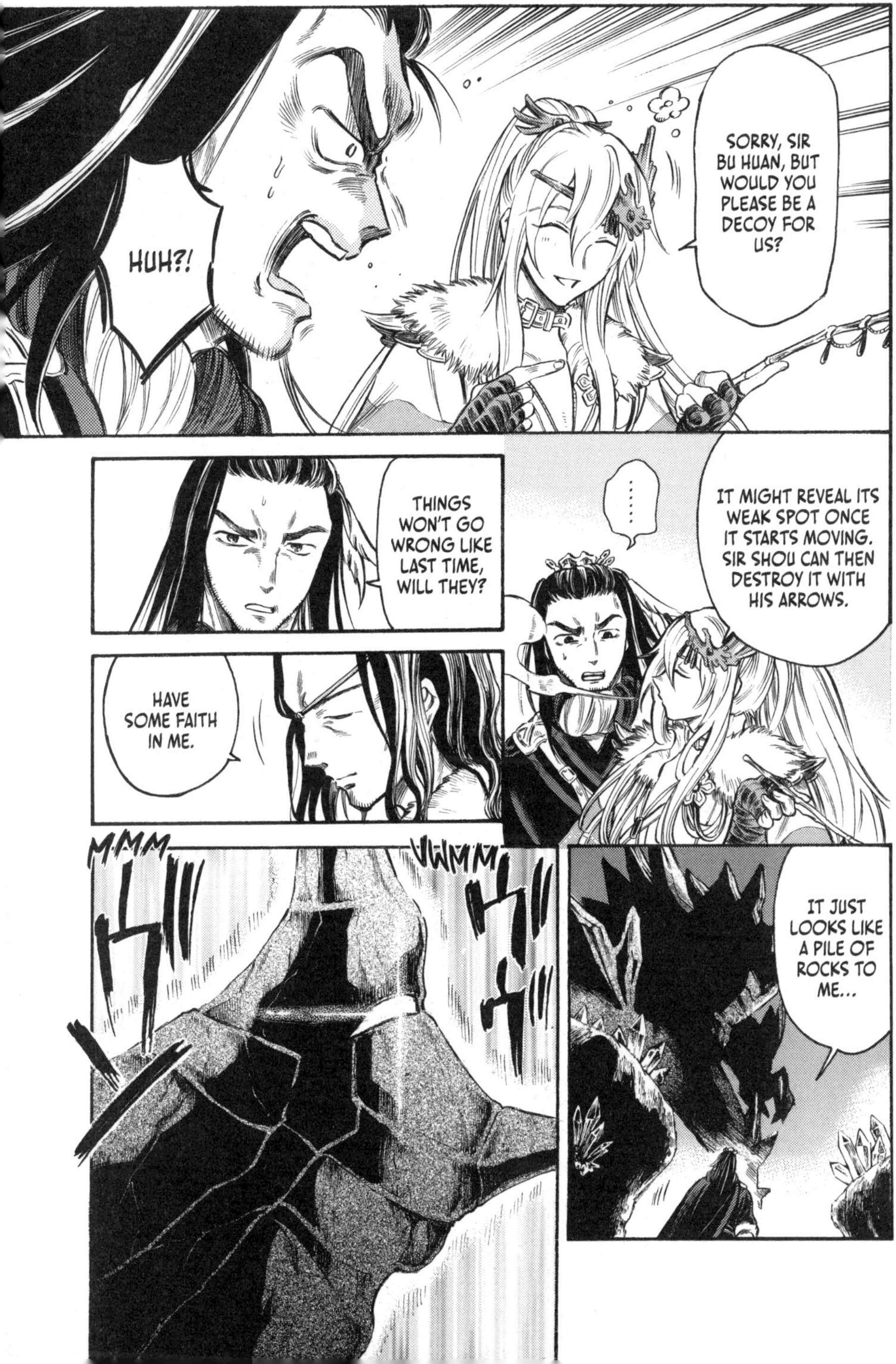
SORRY, SIR BU HUAN, BUT WOULD YOU PLEASE BE A DECOY FOR US?
HUH?!
IT MIGHT REVEAL ITS WEAK SPOT ONCE IT STARTS MOVING. SIR SHOU CAN THEN DESTROY IT WITH HIS ARROWS.
......
THINGS WON'T GO WRONG LIKE LAST TIME, WILL THEY?
HAVE SOME FAITH IN ME.
IT JUST LOOKS LIKE A PILE OF ROCKS TO ME...
VWMM
MMM

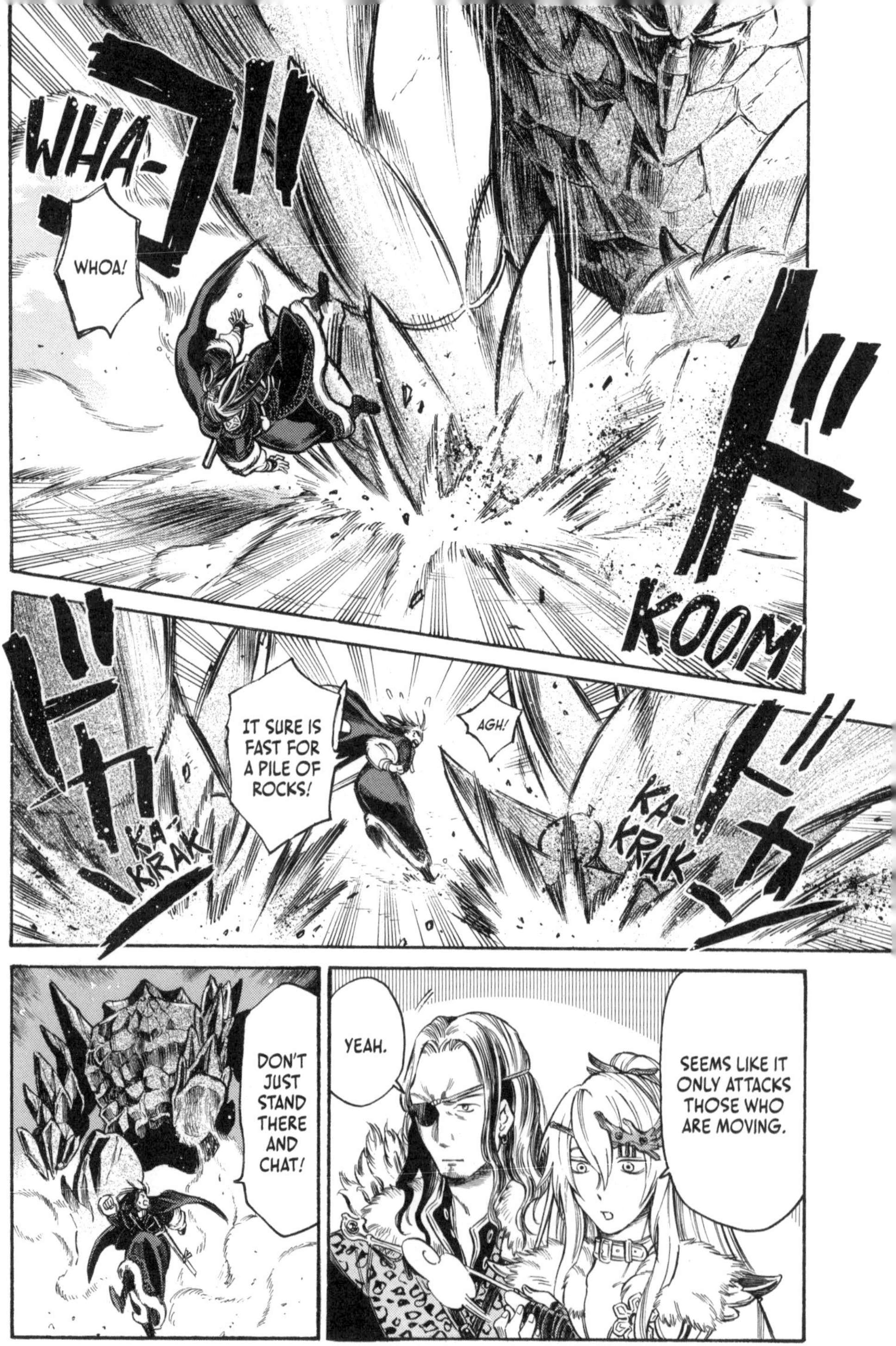
WHA-
WHOA!
KOOM
AGH!
IT SURE IS FAST FOR A PILE OF ROCKS!
KA-KRAK
KA-KRAK
SEEMS LIKE IT ONLY ATTACKS THOSE WHO ARE MOVING.
YEAH.
DON'T JUST STAND THERE AND CHAT!

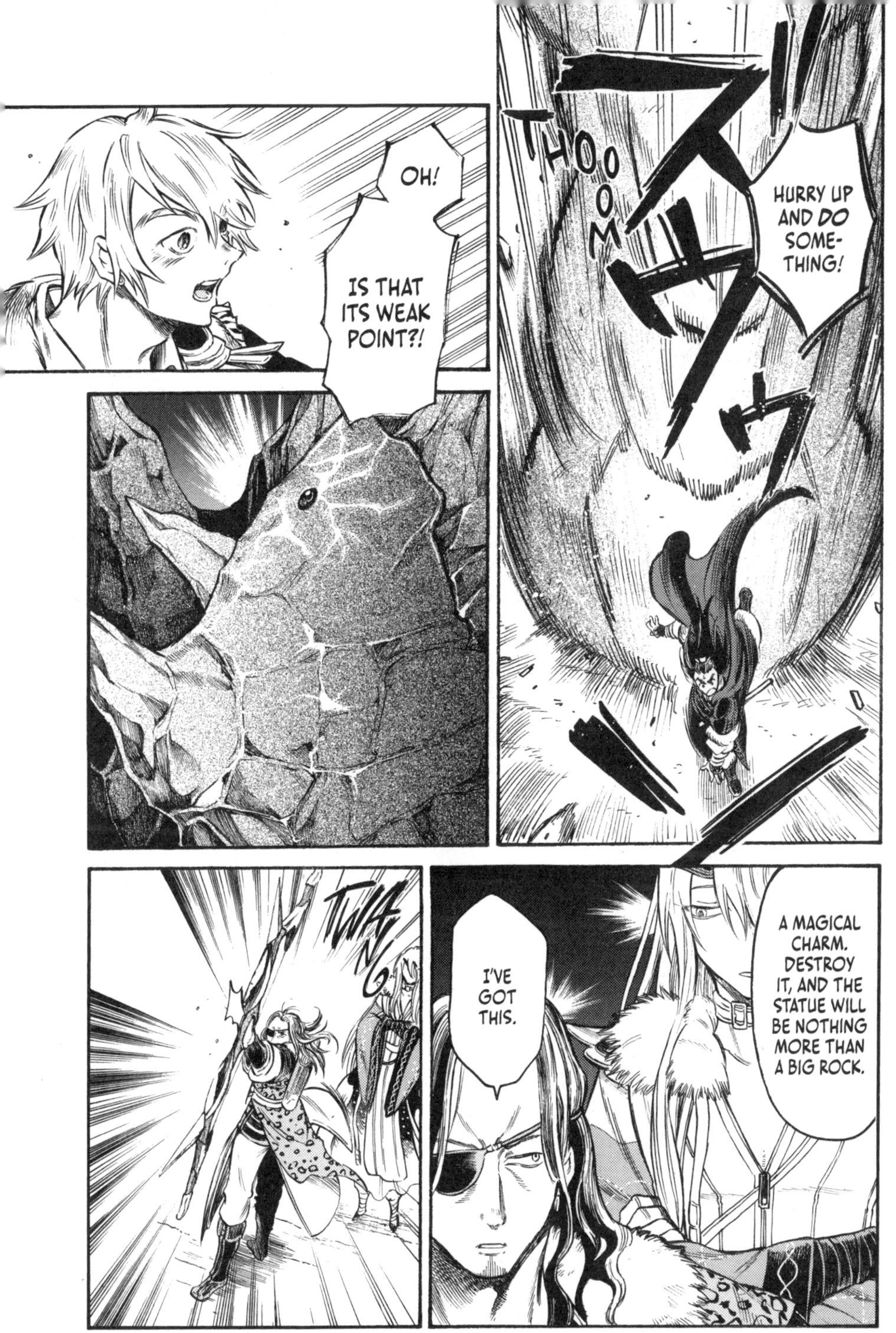
THOOOOM
HURRY UP AND DO SOME-THING!
OH!
IS THAT ITS WEAK POINT?!
A MAGICAL CHARM. DESTROY IT, AND THE STATUE WILL BE NOTHING MORE THAN A BIG ROCK.
I'VE GOT THIS.
TWANG

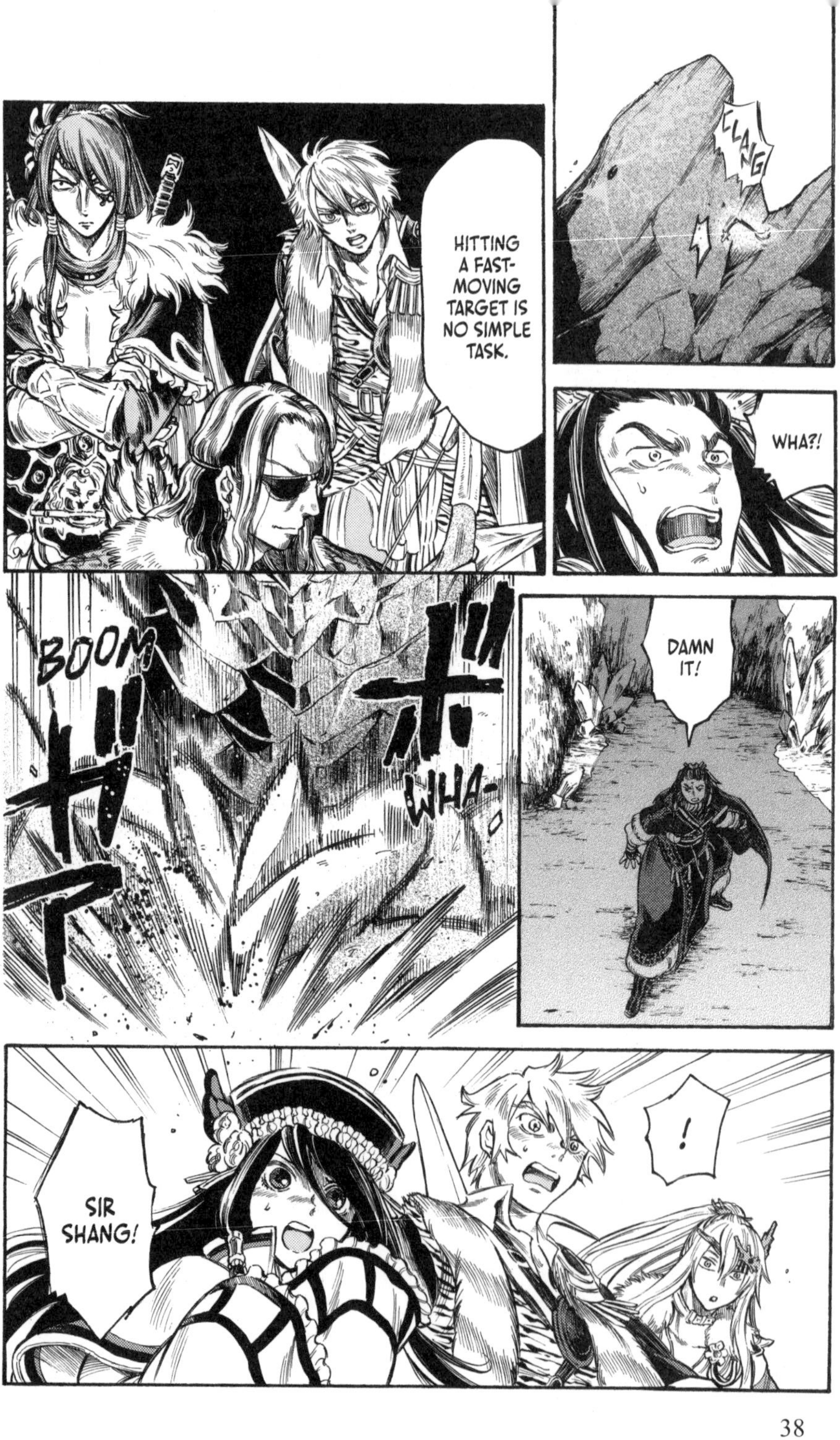
CLANG
WHA?!
HITTING A FAST-MOVING TARGET IS NO SIMPLE TASK.
DAMN IT!
BOOM
WHA-
!
SIR SHANG!

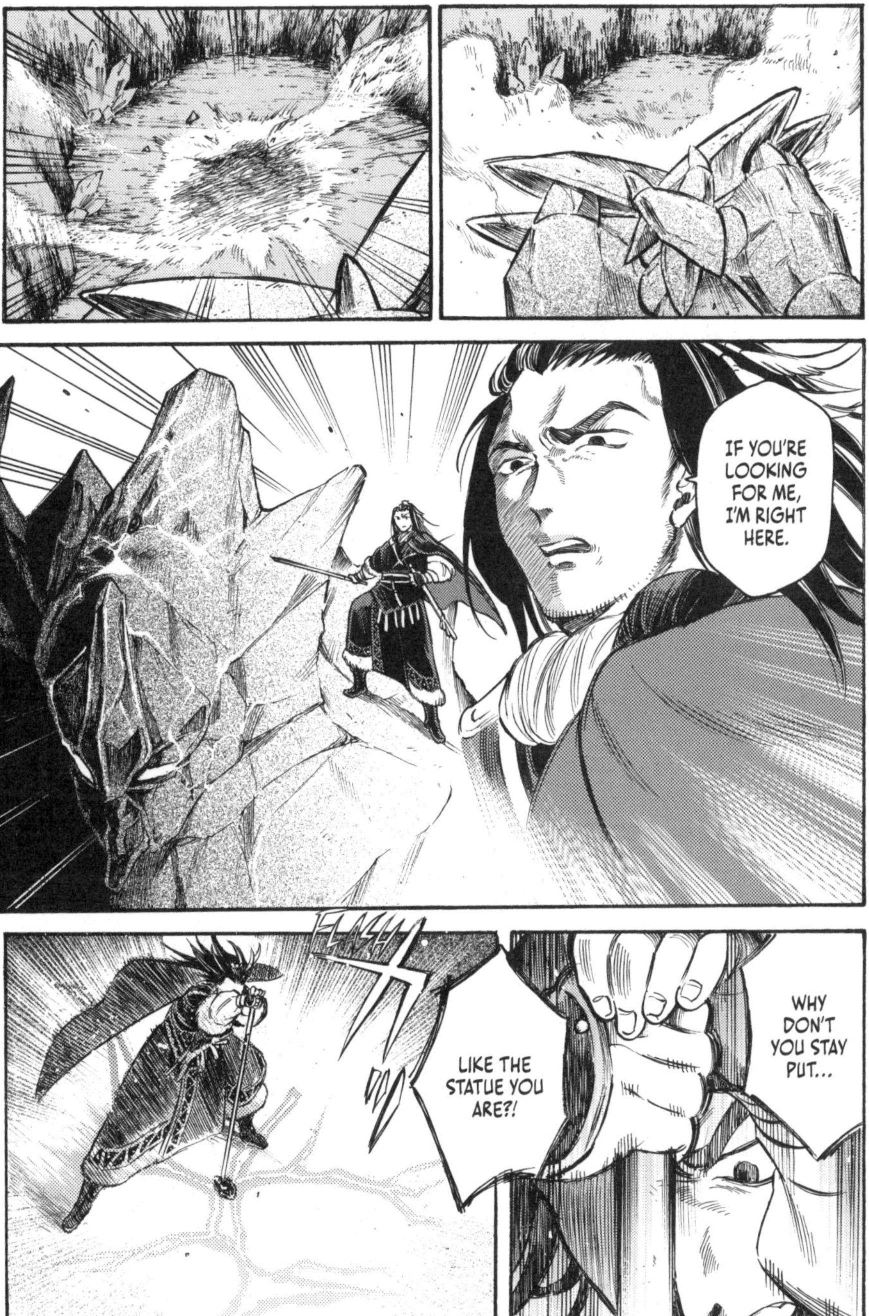
IF YOU'RE LOOKING FOR ME, I'M RIGHT HERE.
WHY DON'T YOU STAY PUT...
LIKE THE STATUE YOU ARE?!
FLASH

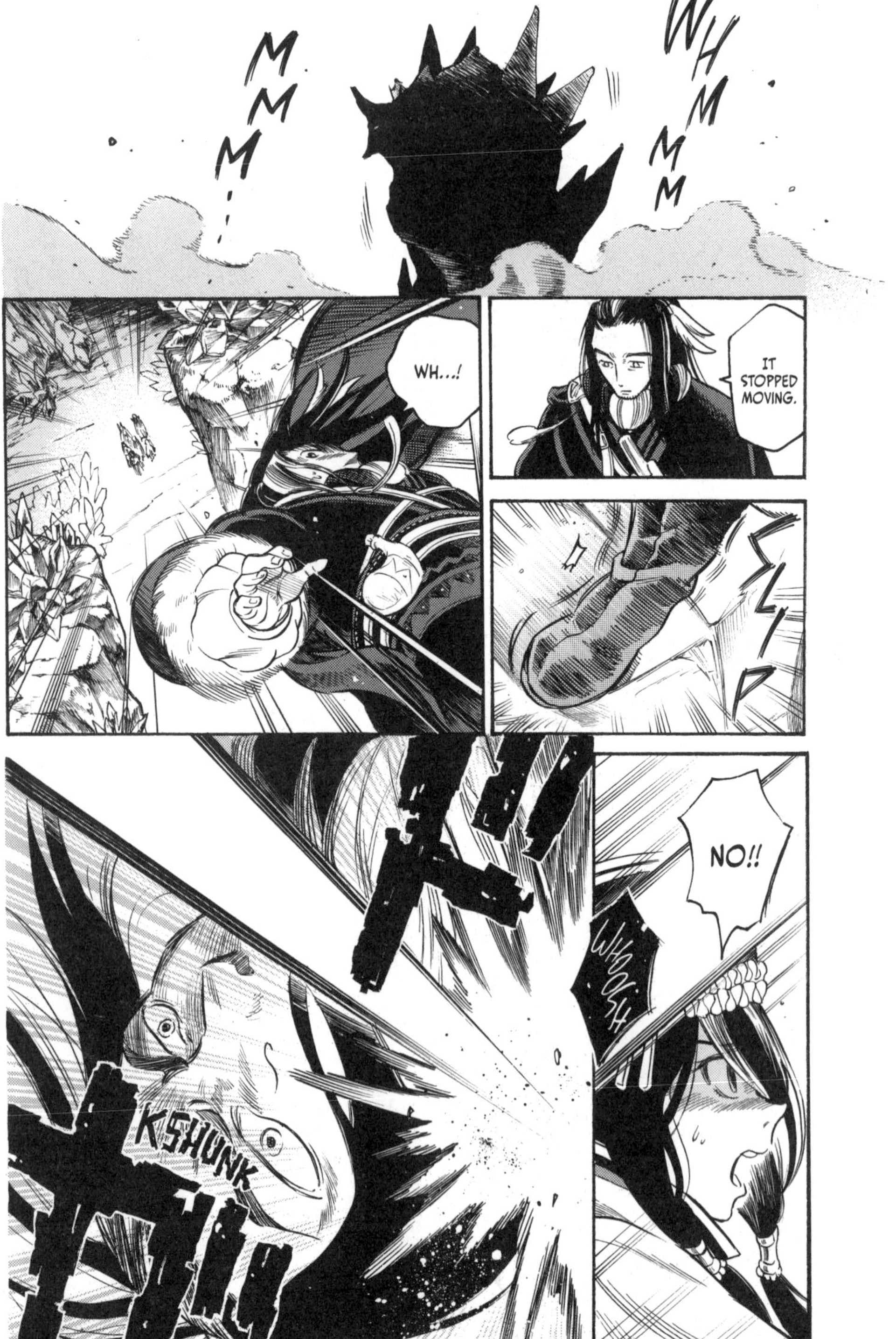
WHMMM
MMM...!
IT STOPPED MOVING.
SLIP
WH...!
NO!!
WHOOSH
KSHUNK

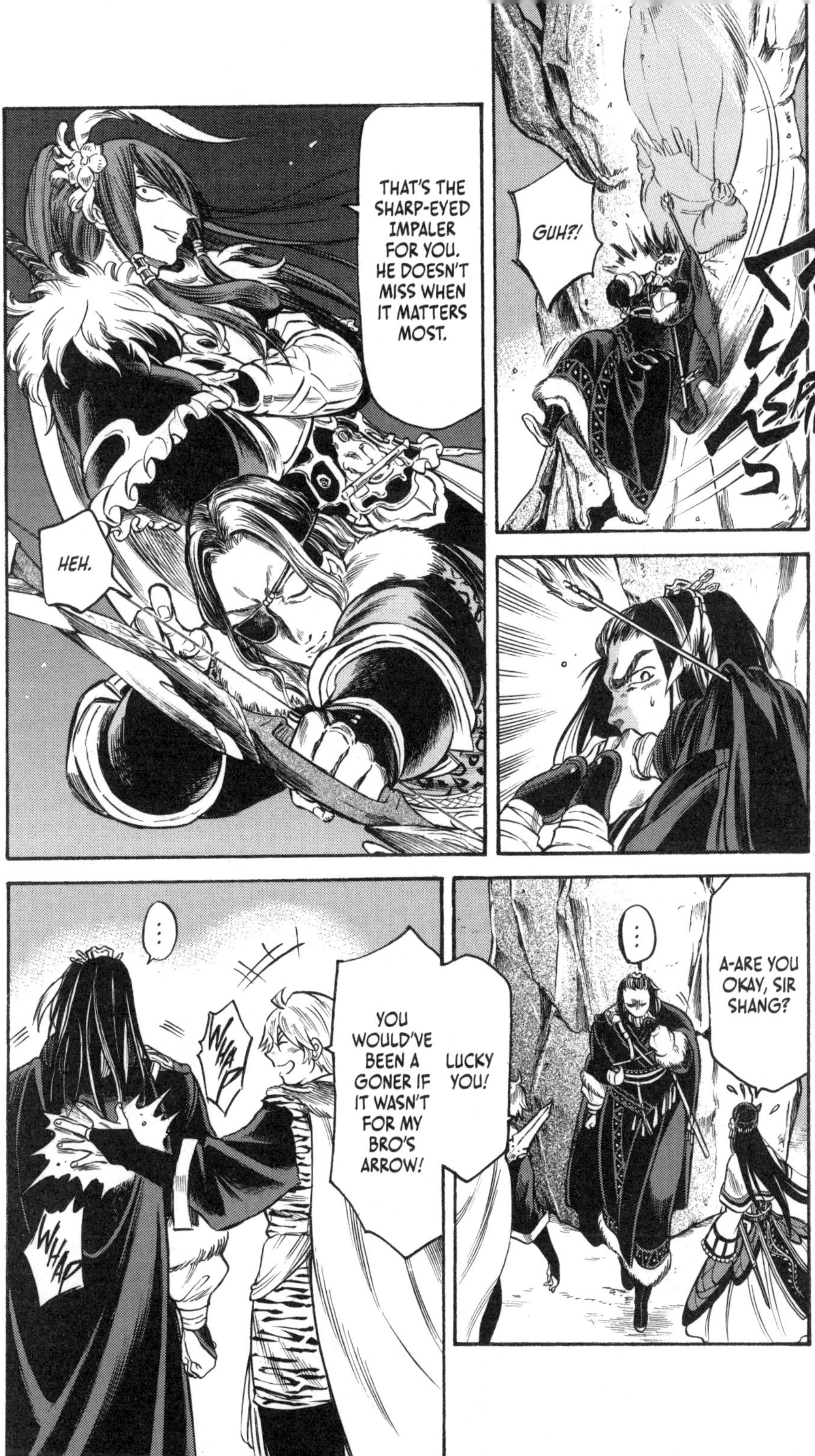
GUH?!
SPIN
THAT'S THE SHARP-EYED IMPALER FOR YOU. HE DOESN'T MISS WHEN IT MATTERS MOST.
HEH.
A-ARE YOU OKAY, SIR SHANG?
...
LUCKY YOU!
YOU WOULD'VE BEEN A GONER IF IT WASN'T FOR MY BRO'S ARROW!
WHAP
...
WHAP

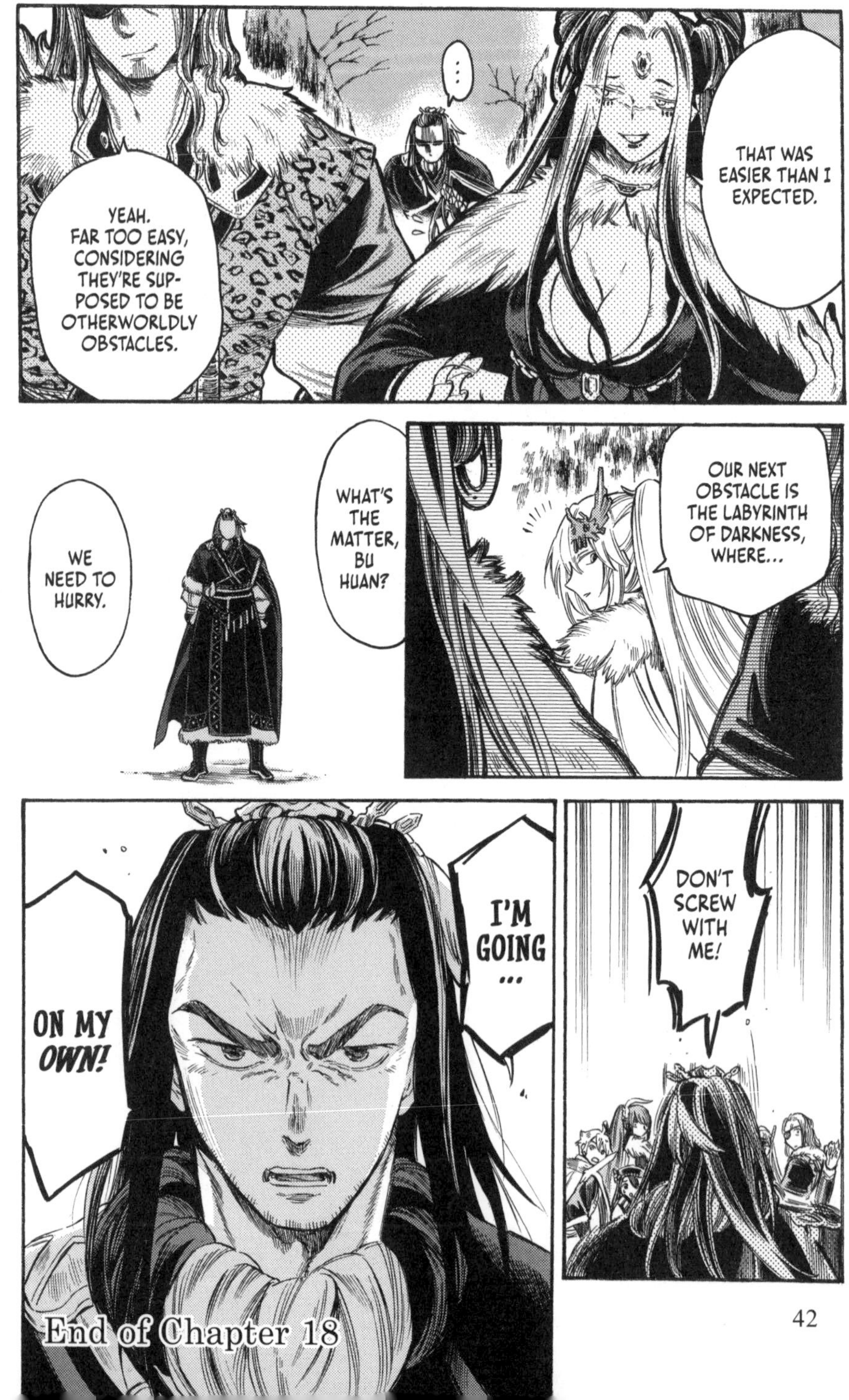

THAT WAS EASIER THAN I EXPECTED.
...
YEAH. FAR TOO EASY, CONSIDERING THEY'RE SUP-POSED TO BE OTHERWORLDLY OBSTACLES.
OUR NEXT OBSTACLE IS THE LABYRINTH OF DARKNESS, WHERE...
WHAT'S THE MATTER, BU HUAN?
WE NEED TO HURRY.
DON'T SCREW WITH ME!
I'M GOING...
ON MY OWN!

End of Chapter 18

Chapter 19

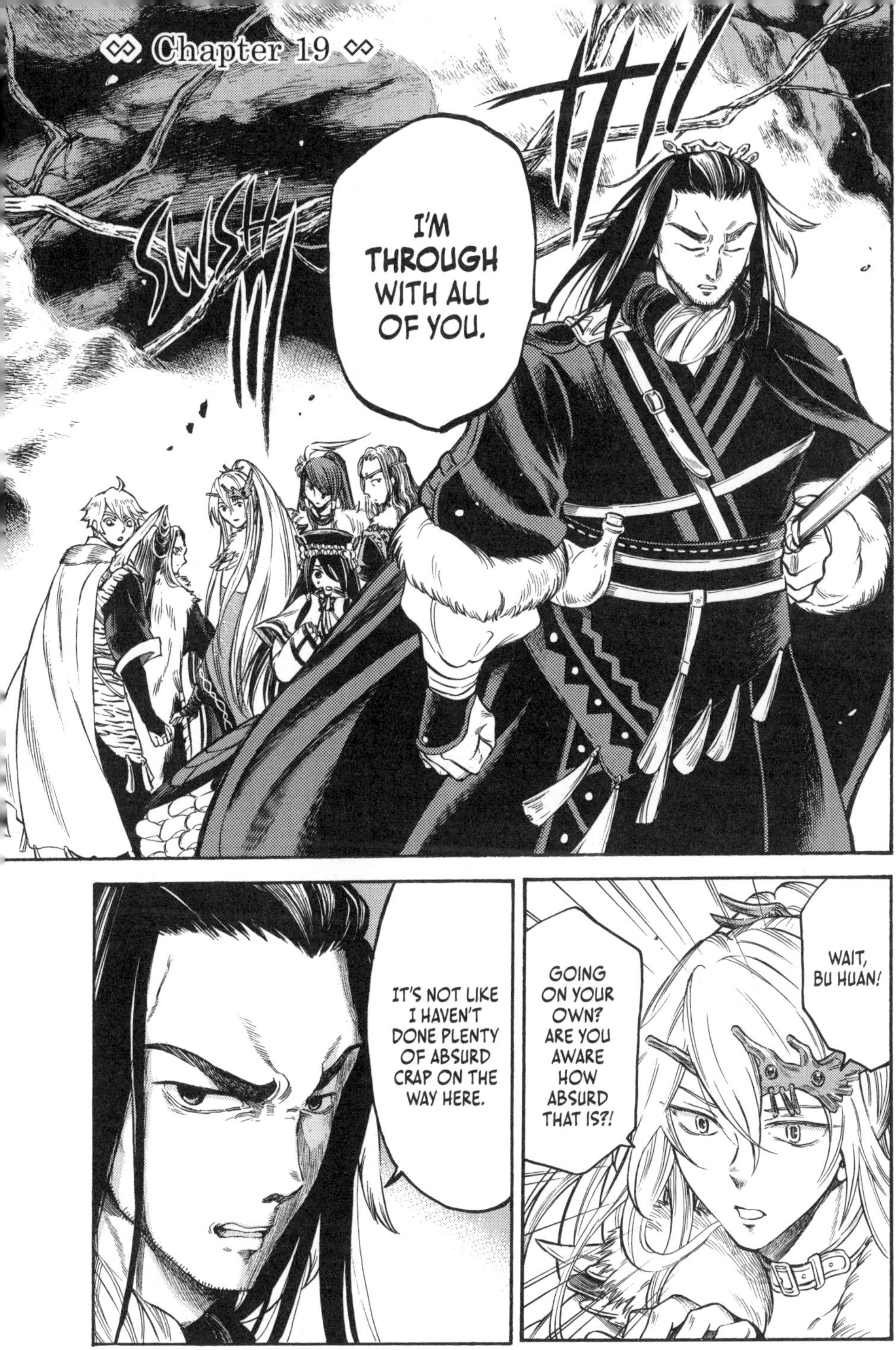
SWISH
I'M THROUGH WITH ALL OF YOU.
WAIT, BU HUAN!
GOING ON YOUR OWN? ARE YOU AWARE HOW ABSURD THAT IS?!
IT'S NOT LIKE I HAVEN'T DONE PLENTY OF ABSURD CRAP ON THE WAY HERE.

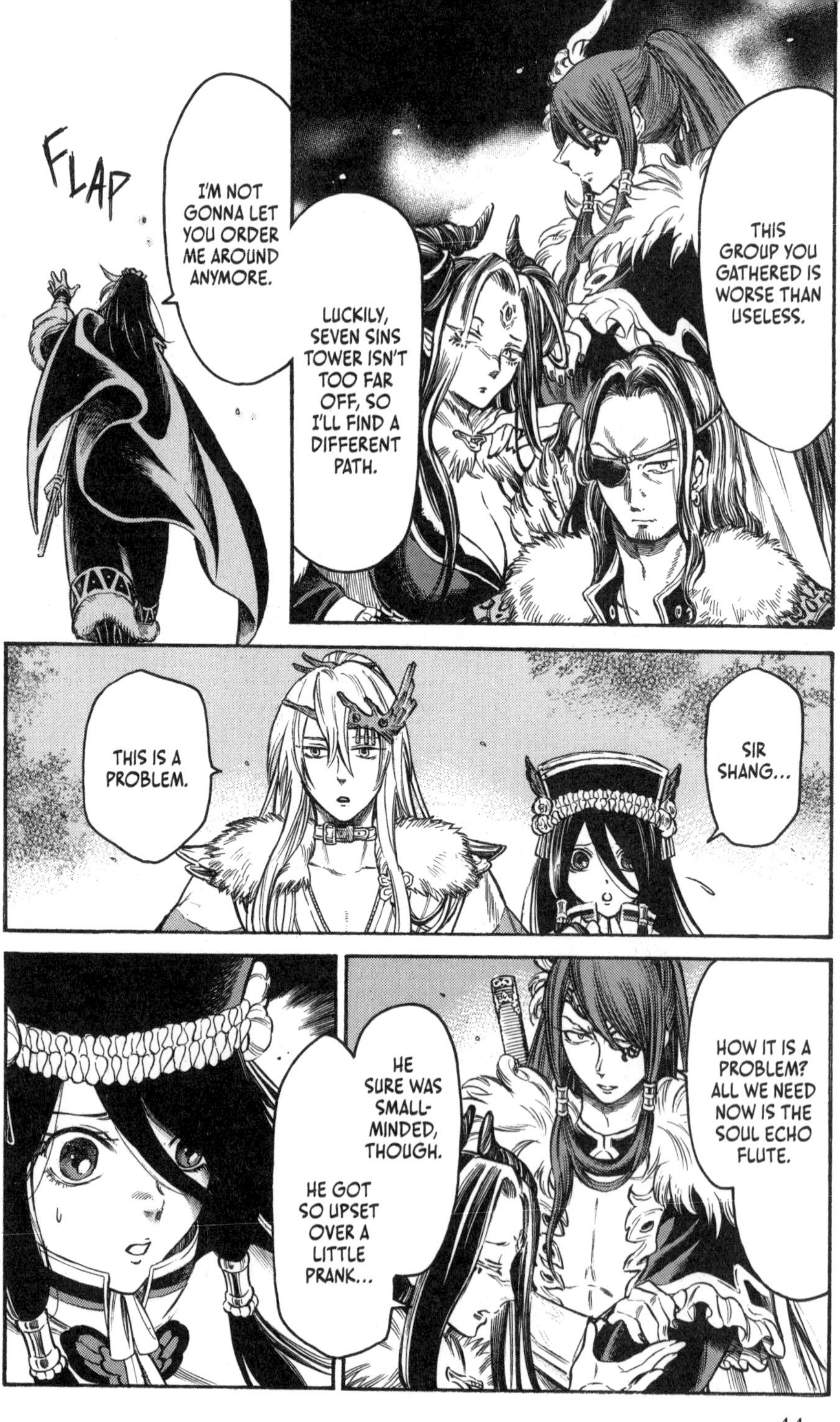
THIS GROUP YOU GATHERED IS WORSE THAN USELESS.
I'M NOT GONNA LET YOU ORDER ME AROUND ANYMORE.
LUCKILY, SEVEN SINS TOWER ISN'T TOO FAR OFF, SO I'LL FIND A DIFFERENT PATH.
FLAP
SIR SHANG...
THIS IS A PROBLEM.
HOW IT IS A PROBLEM? ALL WE NEED NOW IS THE SOUL ECHO FLUTE.
HE SURE WAS SMALL-MINDED, THOUGH.
HE GOT SO UPSET OVER A LITTLE PRANK...

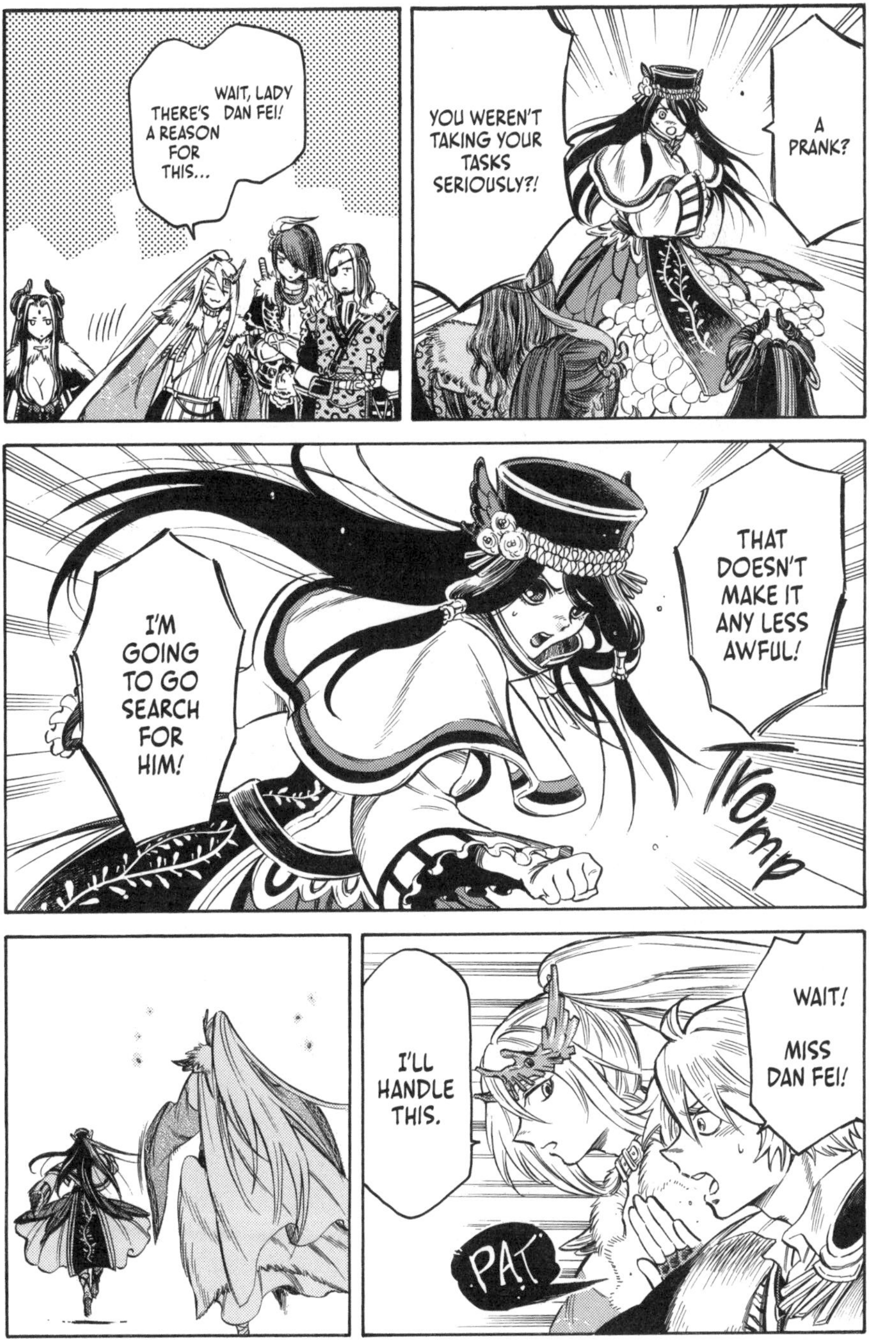

A PRANK?
YOU WEREN'T TAKING YOUR TASKS SERIOUSLY?!
WAIT, LADY DAN FEI! THERE'S A REASON FOR THIS...
THAT DOESN'T MAKE IT ANY LESS AWFUL!
I'M GOING TO GO SEARCH FOR HIM!
Tromp
WAIT! MISS DAN FEI!
I'LL HANDLE THIS.
PAT

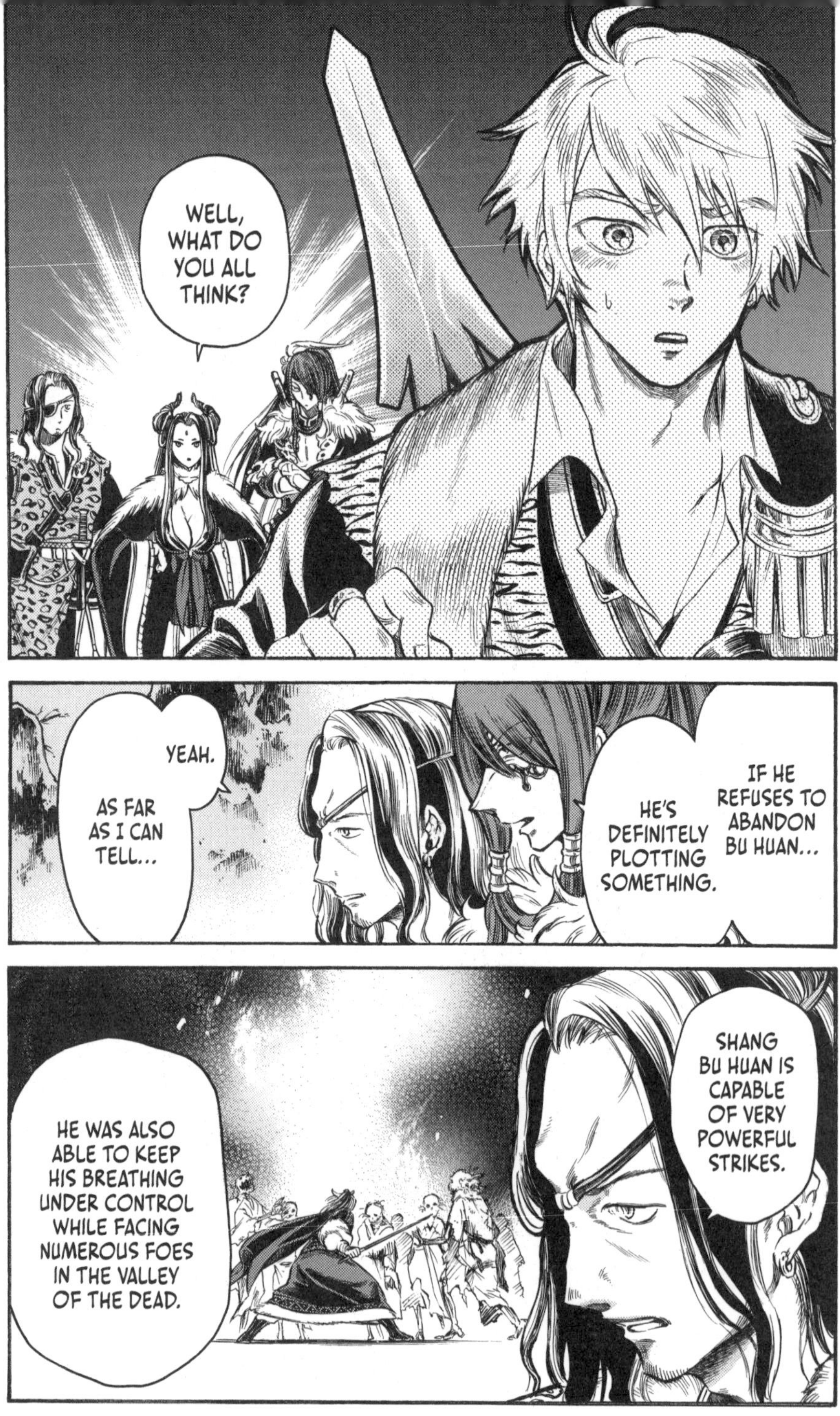
WELL, WHAT DO YOU ALL THINK?
IF HE REFUSES TO ABANDON BU HUAN...
HE'S DEFINITELY PLOTTING SOMETHING.
YEAH.
AS FAR AS I CAN TELL...
SHANG BU HUAN IS CAPABLE OF VERY POWERFUL STRIKES.
HE WAS ALSO ABLE TO KEEP HIS BREATHING UNDER CONTROL WHILE FACING NUMEROUS FOES IN THE VALLEY OF THE DEAD.

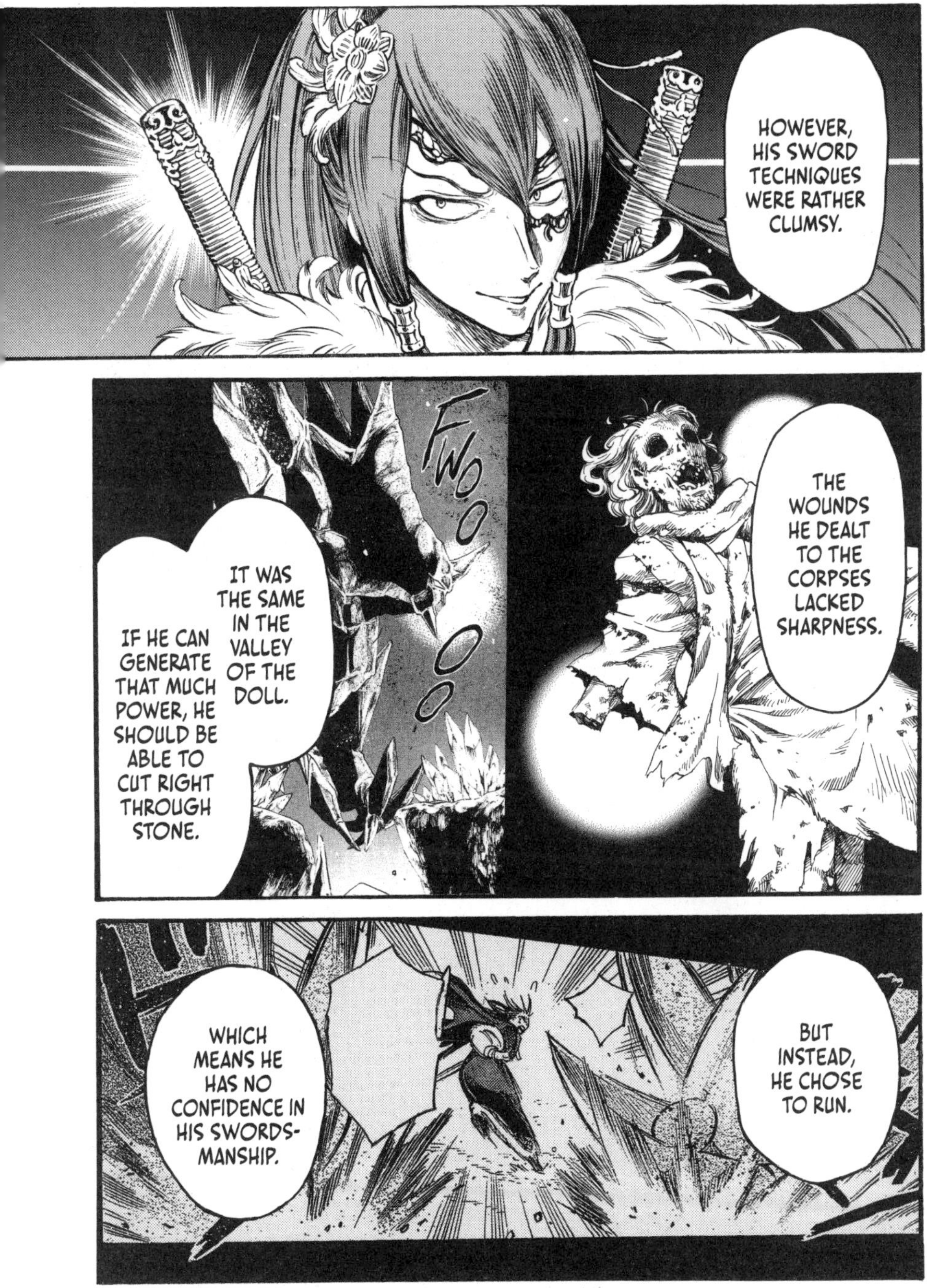
HOWEVER, HIS SWORD TECHNIQUES WERE RATHER CLUMSY.
THE WOUNDS HE DEALT TO THE CORPSES LACKED SHARPNESS.
FWOOOOO
IT WAS THE SAME IN THE VALLEY OF THE DOLL.
IF HE CAN GENERATE THAT MUCH POWER, HE SHOULD BE ABLE TO CUT RIGHT THROUGH STONE.
BUT INSTEAD, HE CHOSE TO RUN.
WHICH MEANS HE HAS NO CONFIDENCE IN HIS SWORDS-MANSHIP.

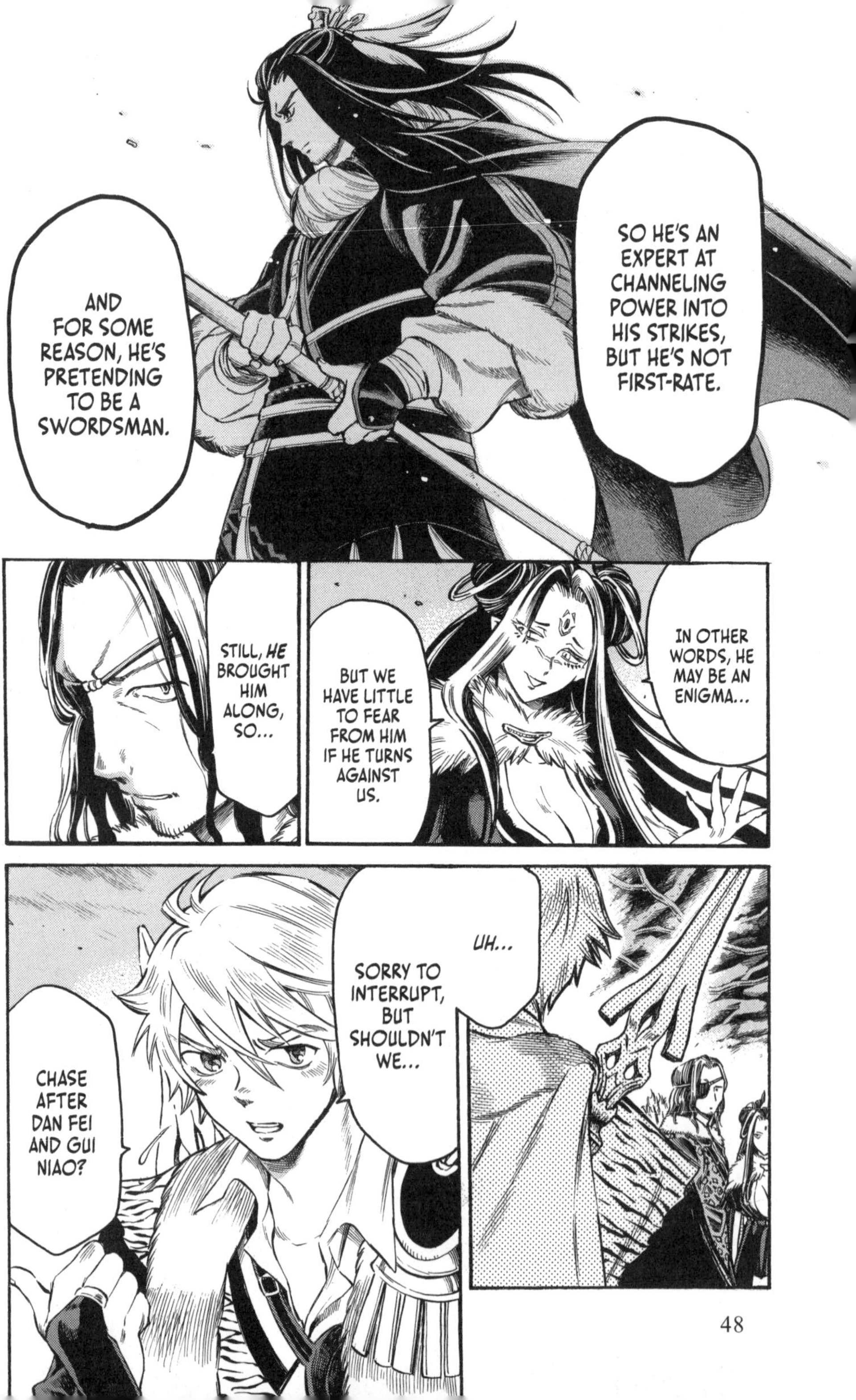
SO HE'S AN EXPERT AT CHANNELING POWER INTO HIS STRIKES, BUT HE'S NOT FIRST-RATE.
AND FOR SOME REASON, HE'S PRETENDING TO BE A SWORDSMAN.
IN OTHER WORDS, HE MAY BE AN ENIGMA...
BUT WE HAVE LITTLE TO FEAR FROM HIM IF HE TURNS AGAINST US.
STILL, *HE* BROUGHT HIM ALONG, SO...
UH...
SORRY TO INTERRUPT, BUT SHOULDN'T WE...
CHASE AFTER DAN FEI AND GUI NIAO?

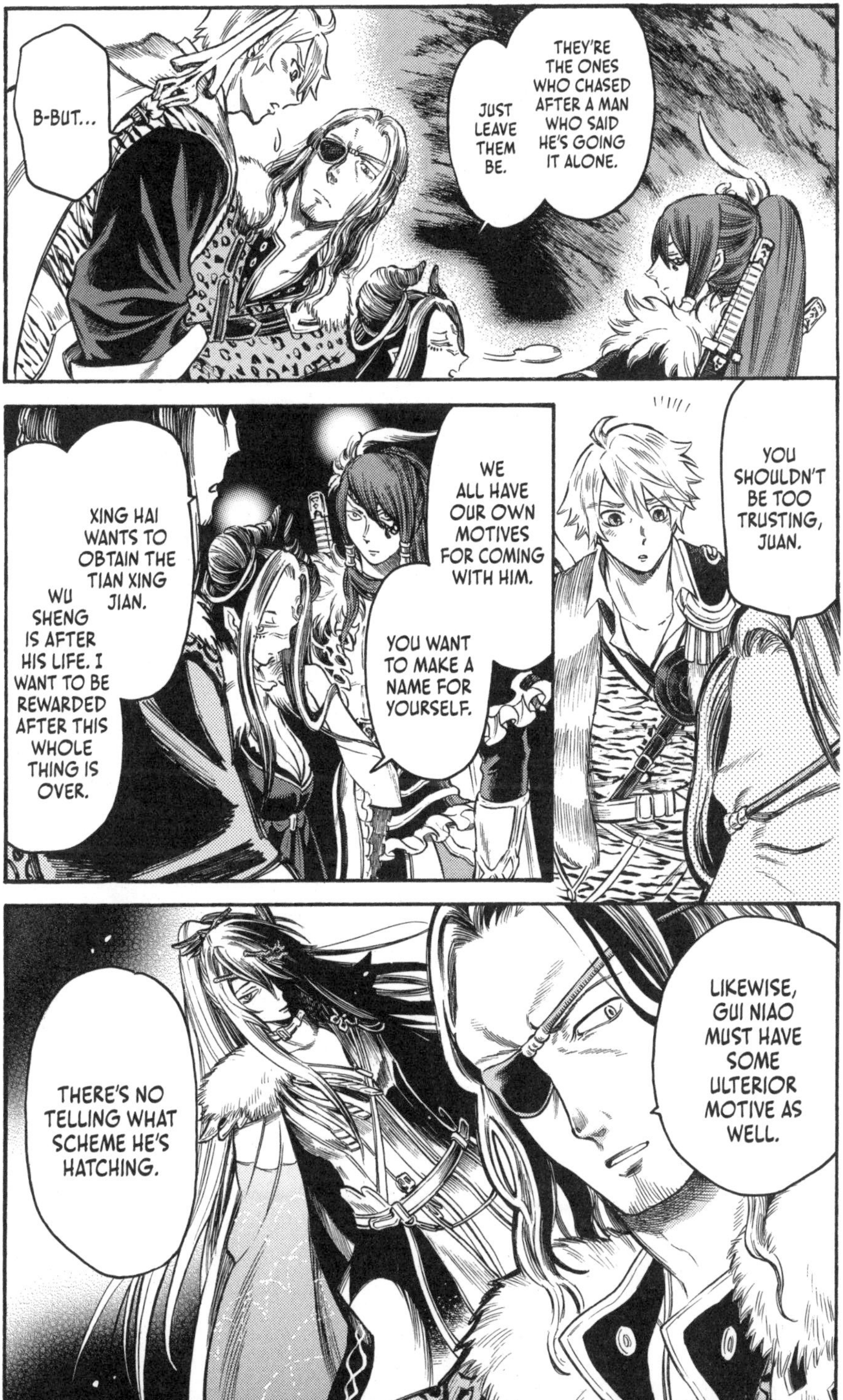

JUST LEAVE THEM BE. THEY'RE THE ONES WHO CHASED AFTER A MAN WHO SAID HE'S GOING IT ALONE.
B-BUT...
YOU SHOULDN'T BE TOO TRUSTING, JUAN.
WE ALL HAVE OUR OWN MOTIVES FOR COMING WITH HIM.
XING HAI WANTS TO OBTAIN THE TIAN XING JIAN. WU SHENG IS AFTER HIS LIFE. I WANT TO BE REWARDED AFTER THIS WHOLE THING IS OVER.
YOU WANT TO MAKE A NAME FOR YOURSELF.
LIKEWISE, GUI NIAO MUST HAVE SOME ULTERIOR MOTIVE AS WELL.
THERE'S NO TELLING WHAT SCHEME HE'S HATCHING.

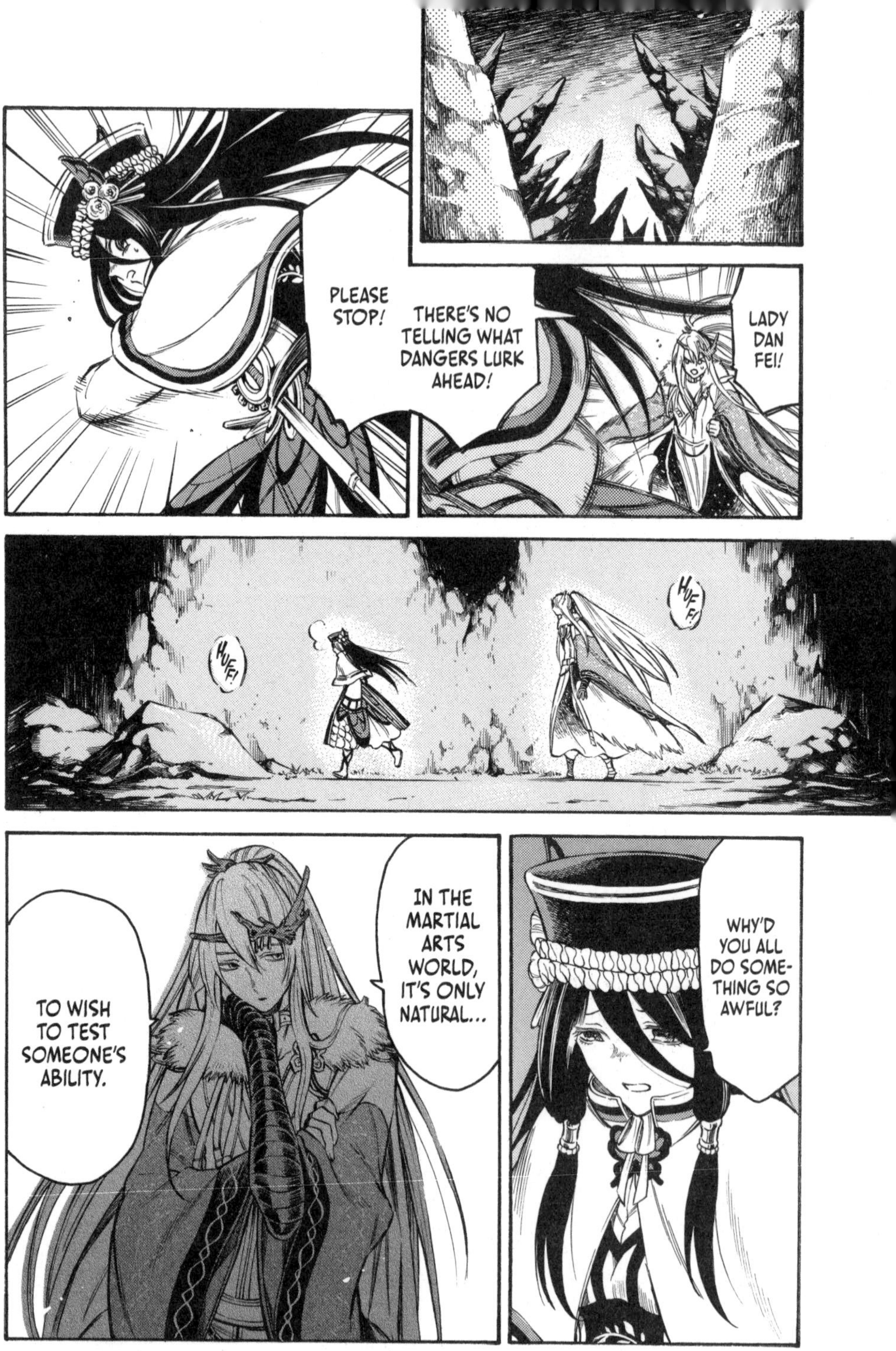
LADY DAN FEI!
THERE'S NO TELLING WHAT DANGERS LURK AHEAD!
PLEASE STOP!
HUFF!
HUFF!
WHY'D YOU ALL DO SOMETHING SO AWFUL?
IN THE MARTIAL ARTS WORLD, IT'S ONLY NATURAL...
TO WISH TO TEST SOMEONE'S ABILITY.

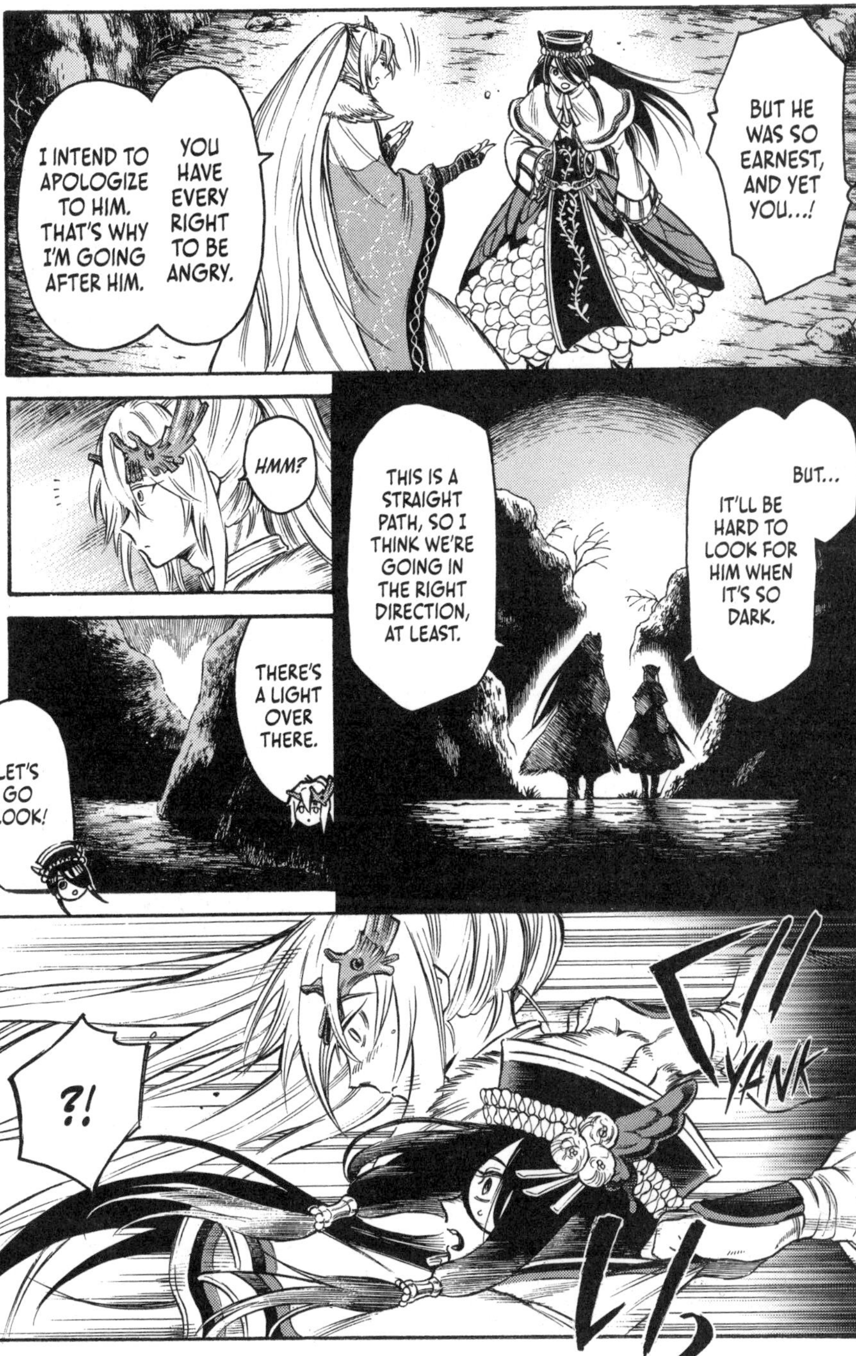
BUT HE WAS SO EARNEST, AND YET YOU...!
YOU HAVE EVERY RIGHT TO BE ANGRY.
I INTEND TO APOLOGIZE TO HIM. THAT'S WHY I'M GOING AFTER HIM.
BUT...
IT'LL BE HARD TO LOOK FOR HIM WHEN IT'S SO DARK.
THIS IS A STRAIGHT PATH, SO I THINK WE'RE GOING IN THE RIGHT DIRECTION, AT LEAST.
HMM?
THERE'S A LIGHT OVER THERE.
LET'S GO LOOK!
YANK
?!

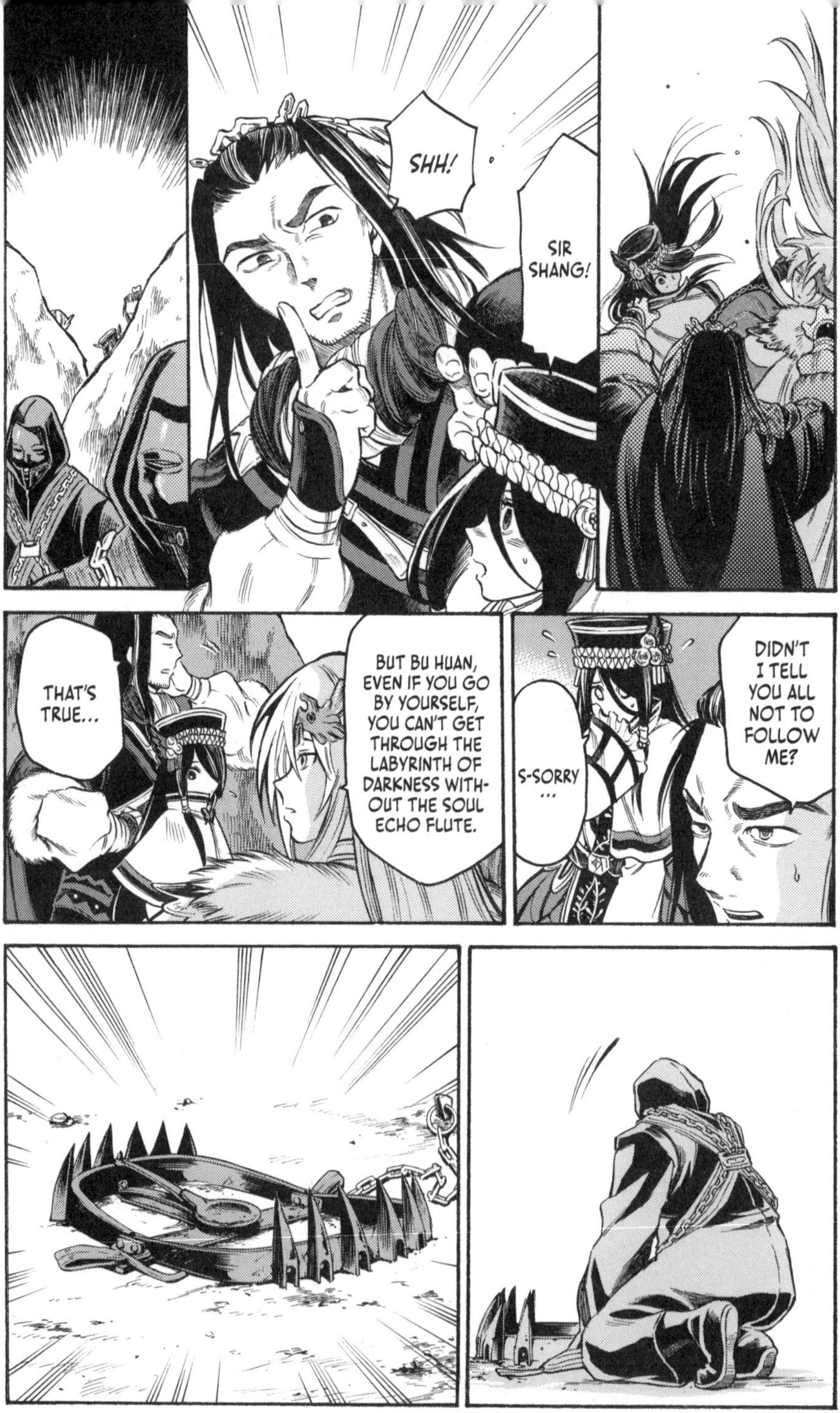
SIR SHANG!
SHH!
DIDN'T I TELL YOU ALL NOT TO FOLLOW ME?
S-SORRY...
BUT BU HUAN, EVEN IF YOU GO BY YOURSELF, YOU CAN'T GET THROUGH THE LABYRINTH OF DARKNESS WITHOUT THE SOUL ECHO FLUTE.
THAT'S TRUE...

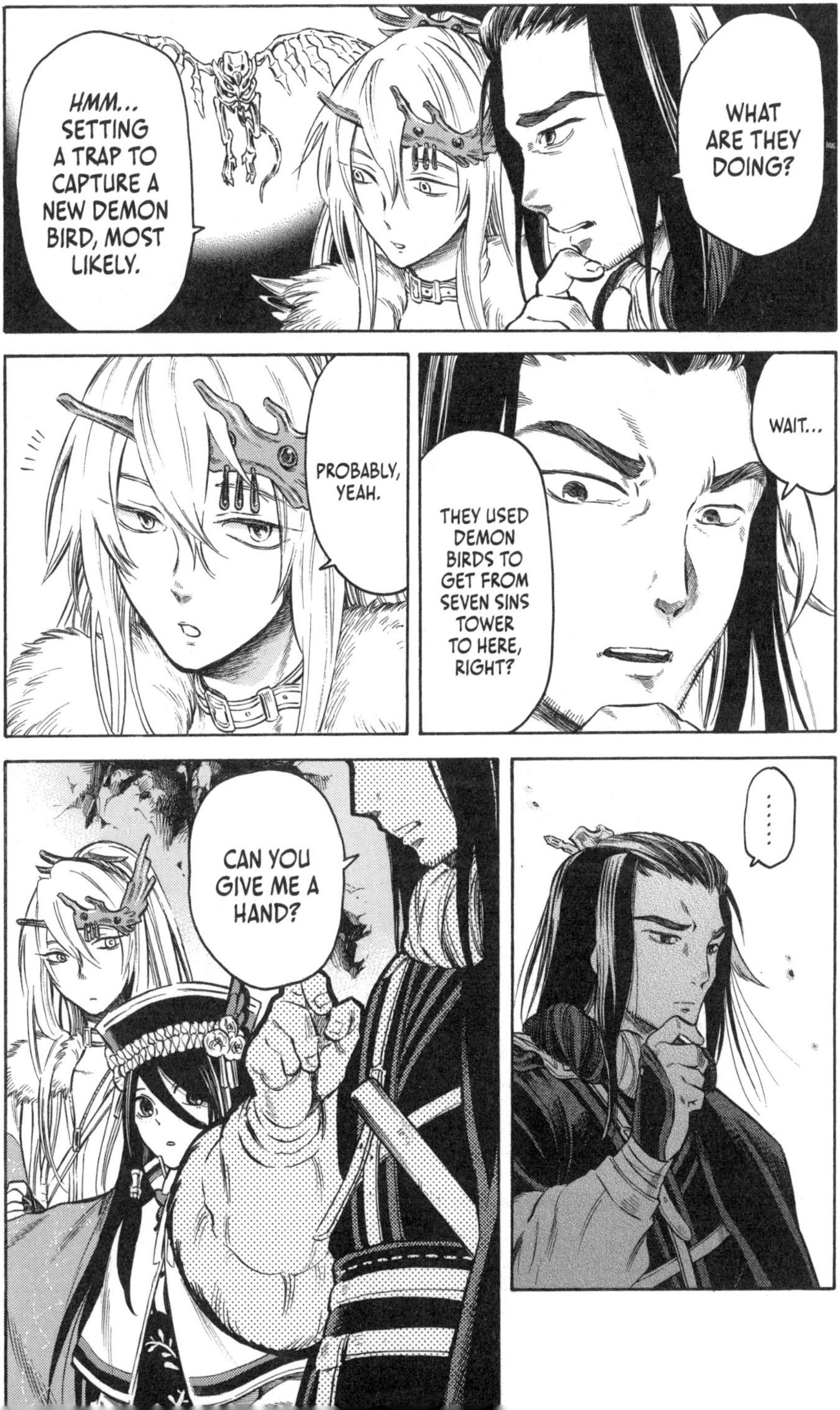
WHAT ARE THEY DOING?
HMM... SETTING A TRAP TO CAPTURE A NEW DEMON BIRD, MOST LIKELY.
WAIT...
THEY USED DEMON BIRDS TO GET FROM SEVEN SINS TOWER TO HERE, RIGHT?
PROBABLY, YEAH.
......
CAN YOU GIVE ME A HAND?

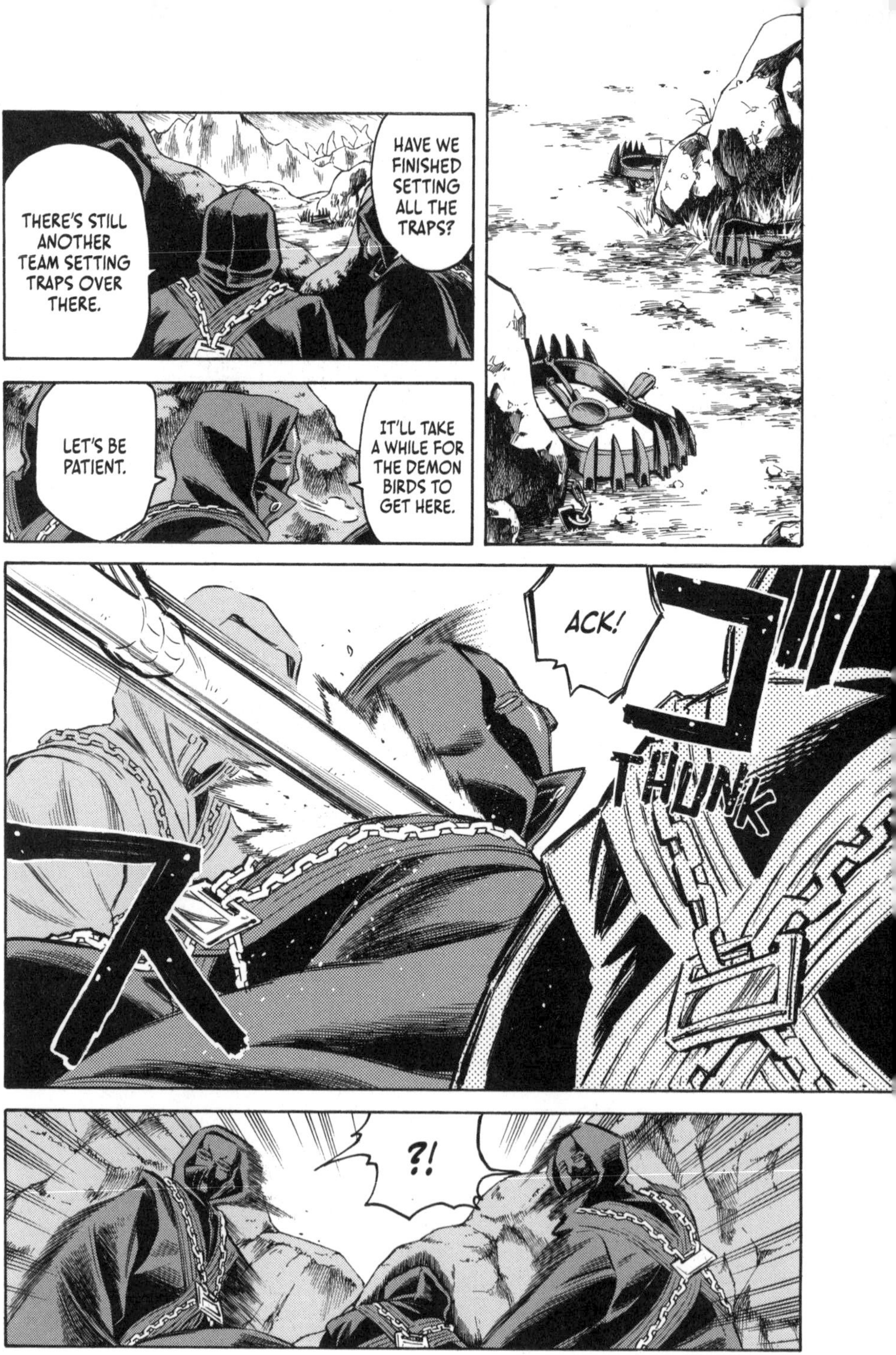
HAVE WE FINISHED SETTING ALL THE TRAPS?
THERE'S STILL ANOTHER TEAM SETTING TRAPS OVER THERE.
IT'LL TAKE A WHILE FOR THE DEMON BIRDS TO GET HERE.
LET'S BE PATIENT.
ACK!
THUNK
?!

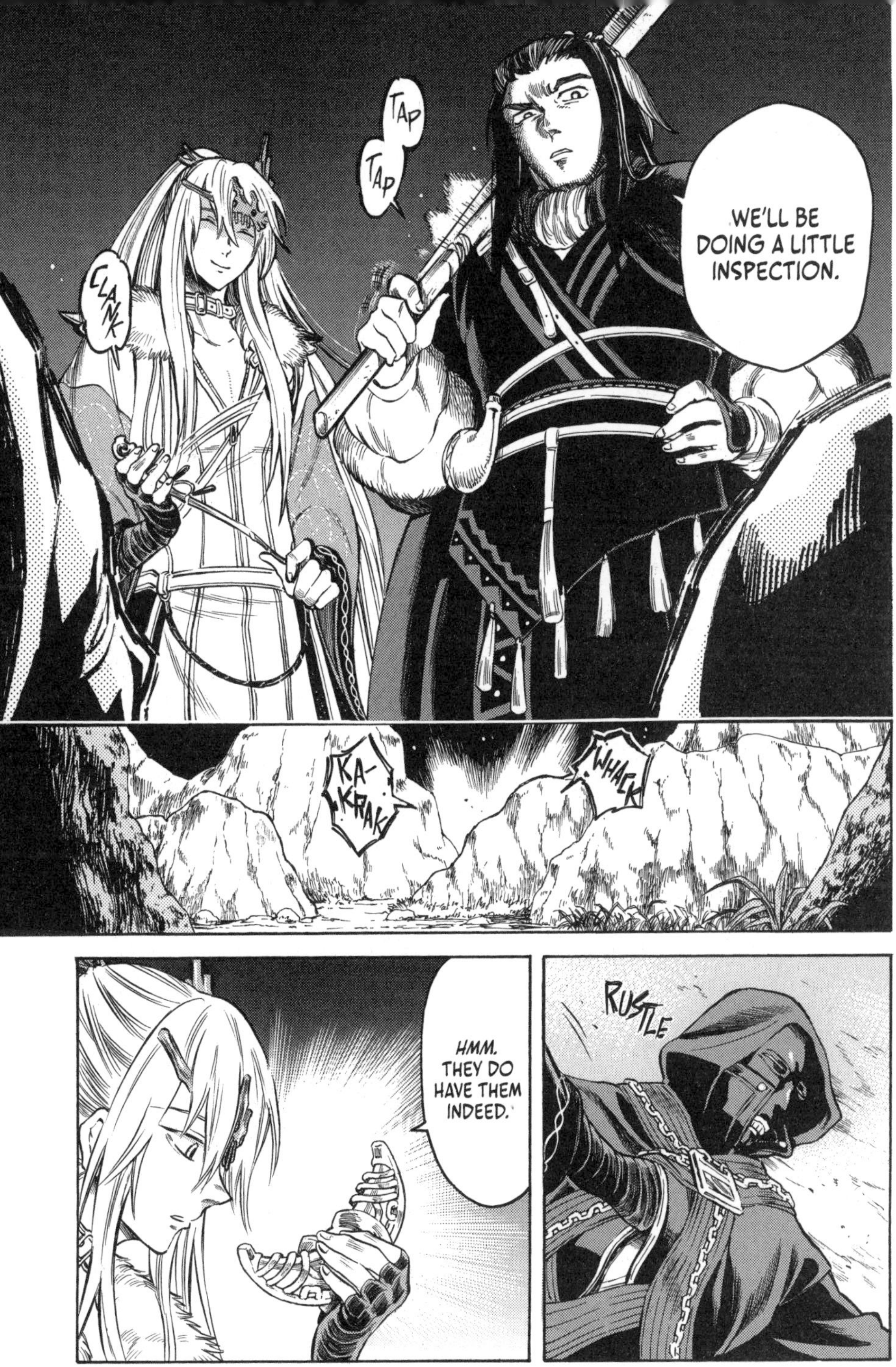
WE'LL BE DOING A LITTLE INSPECTION.
TAP TAP
CLANK
WHACK
KA-KRAK
RUSTLE
HMM. THEY DO HAVE THEM INDEED.

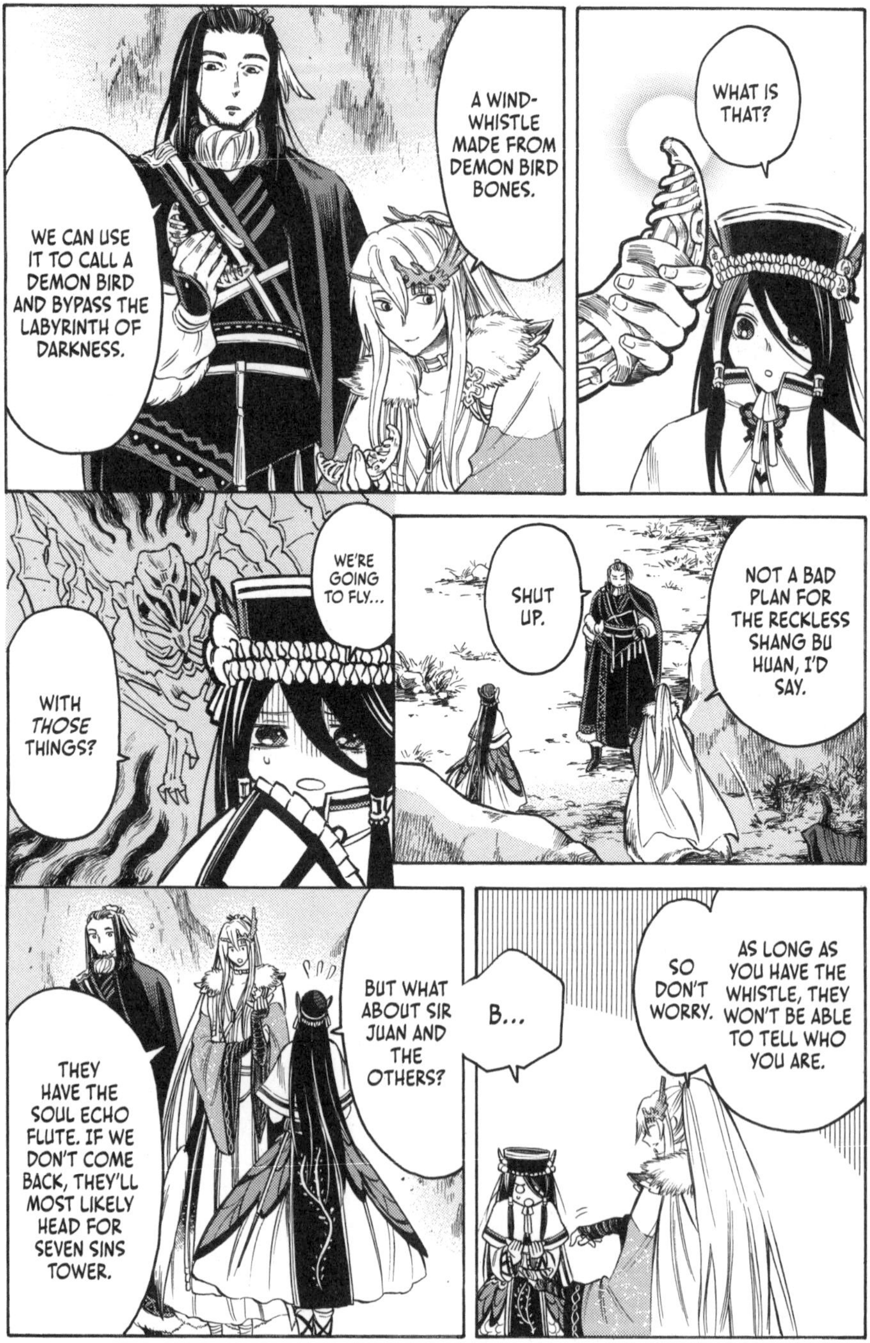
WHAT IS THAT?
A WIND-WHISTLE MADE FROM DEMON BIRD BONES.
WE CAN USE IT TO CALL A DEMON BIRD AND BYPASS THE LABYRINTH OF DARKNESS.
NOT A BAD PLAN FOR THE RECKLESS SHANG BU HUAN, I'D SAY.
SHUT UP.
WE'RE GOING TO FLY...
WITH *THOSE* THINGS?
AS LONG AS YOU HAVE THE WHISTLE, THEY WON'T BE ABLE TO TELL WHO YOU ARE.
SO DON'T WORRY.
B...
BUT WHAT ABOUT SIR JUAN AND THE OTHERS?
THEY HAVE THE SOUL ECHO FLUTE. IF WE DON'T COME BACK, THEY'LL MOST LIKELY HEAD FOR SEVEN SINS TOWER.

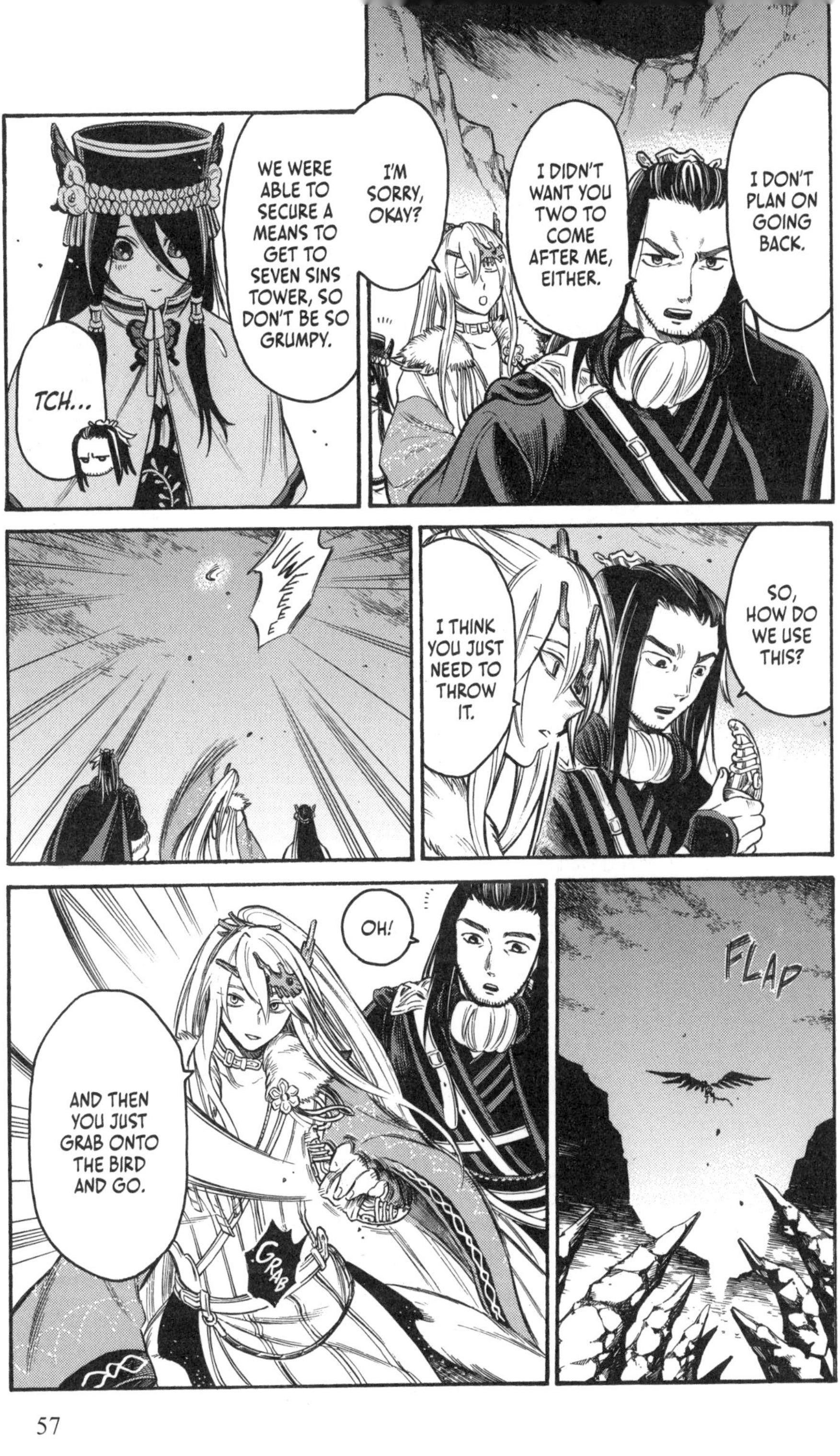
I DON'T PLAN ON GOING BACK.
I DIDN'T WANT YOU TWO TO COME AFTER ME, EITHER.
I'M SORRY, OKAY?
WE WERE ABLE TO SECURE A MEANS TO GET TO SEVEN SINS TOWER, SO DON'T BE SO GRUMPY.
TCH...
SO, HOW DO WE USE THIS?
I THINK YOU JUST NEED TO THROW IT.
UWEEEE
FLAP
OH!
AND THEN YOU JUST GRAB ONTO THE BIRD AND GO.
GRAB

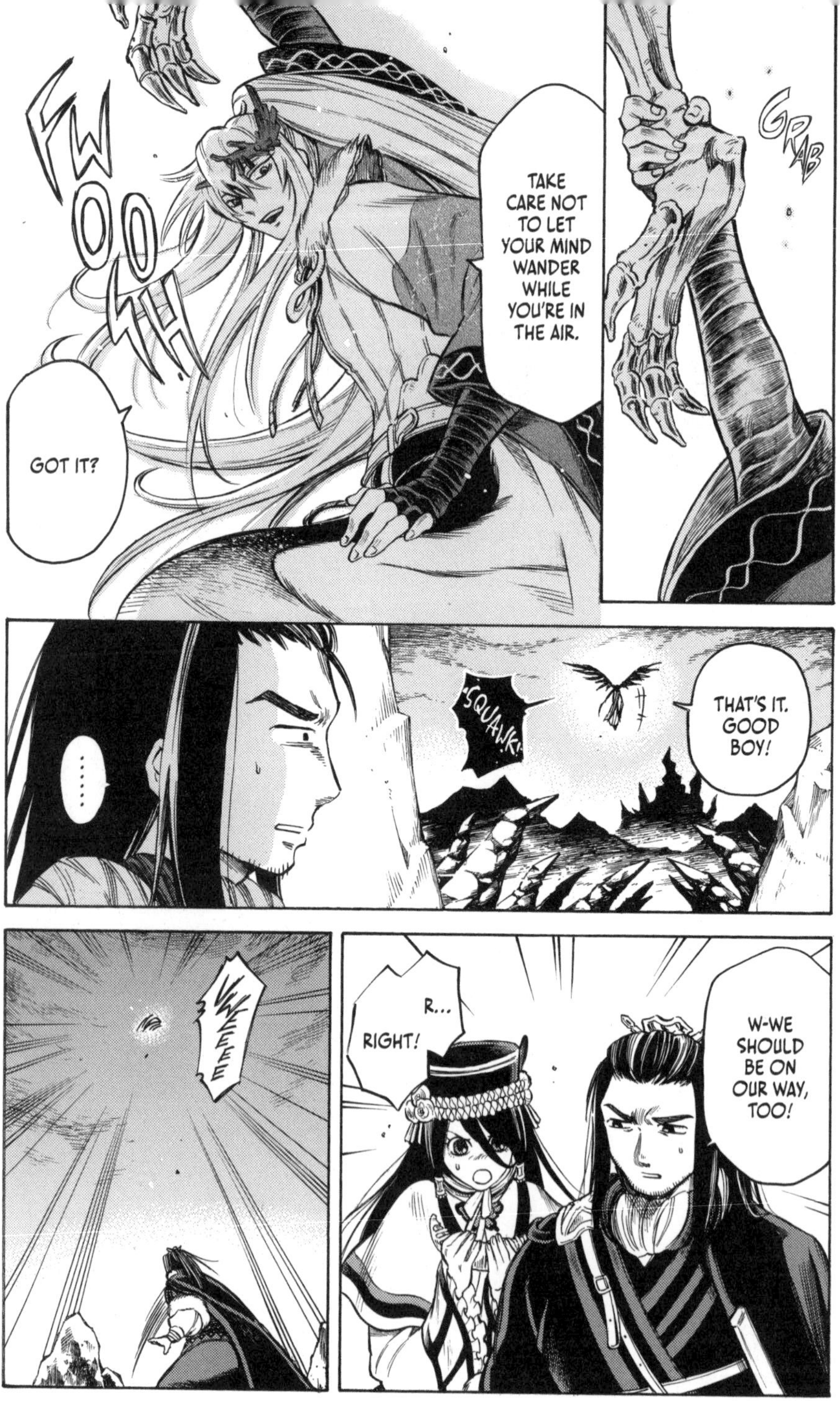
GRAB
TAKE CARE NOT TO LET YOUR MIND WANDER WHILE YOU'RE IN THE AIR.
FWOOSH!
GOT IT?
THAT'S IT. GOOD BOY!
SQUAWK!
......
W-WE SHOULD BE ON OUR WAY, TOO!
R... RIGHT!
VWEEEEE

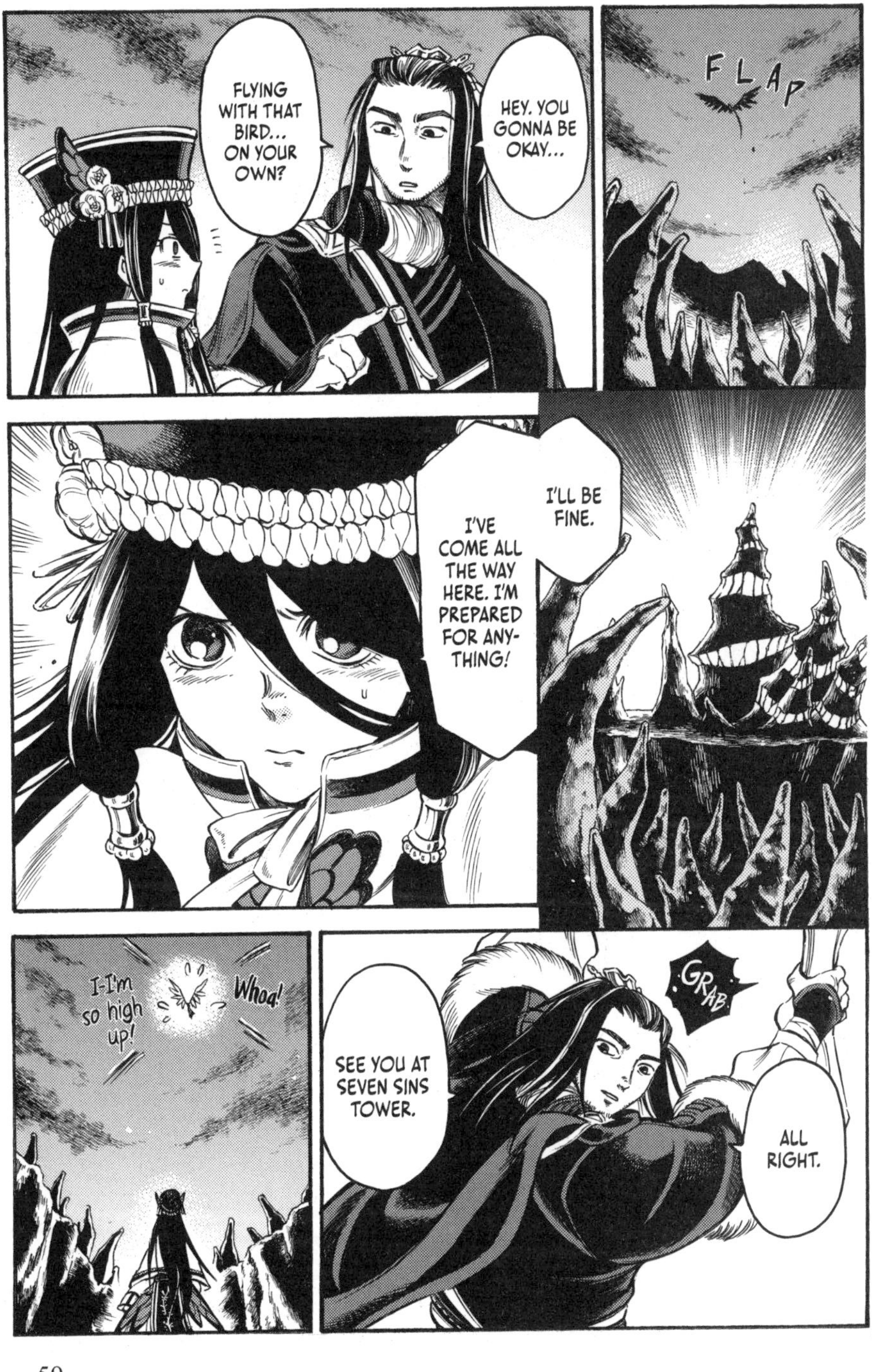
FLAP
HEY. YOU GONNA BE OKAY...
FLYING WITH THAT BIRD... ON YOUR OWN?
I'LL BE FINE.
I'VE COME ALL THE WAY HERE. I'M PREPARED FOR ANY-THING!
GRAB
SEE YOU AT SEVEN SINS TOWER.
ALL RIGHT.
Whoa!
I-I'm so high up!

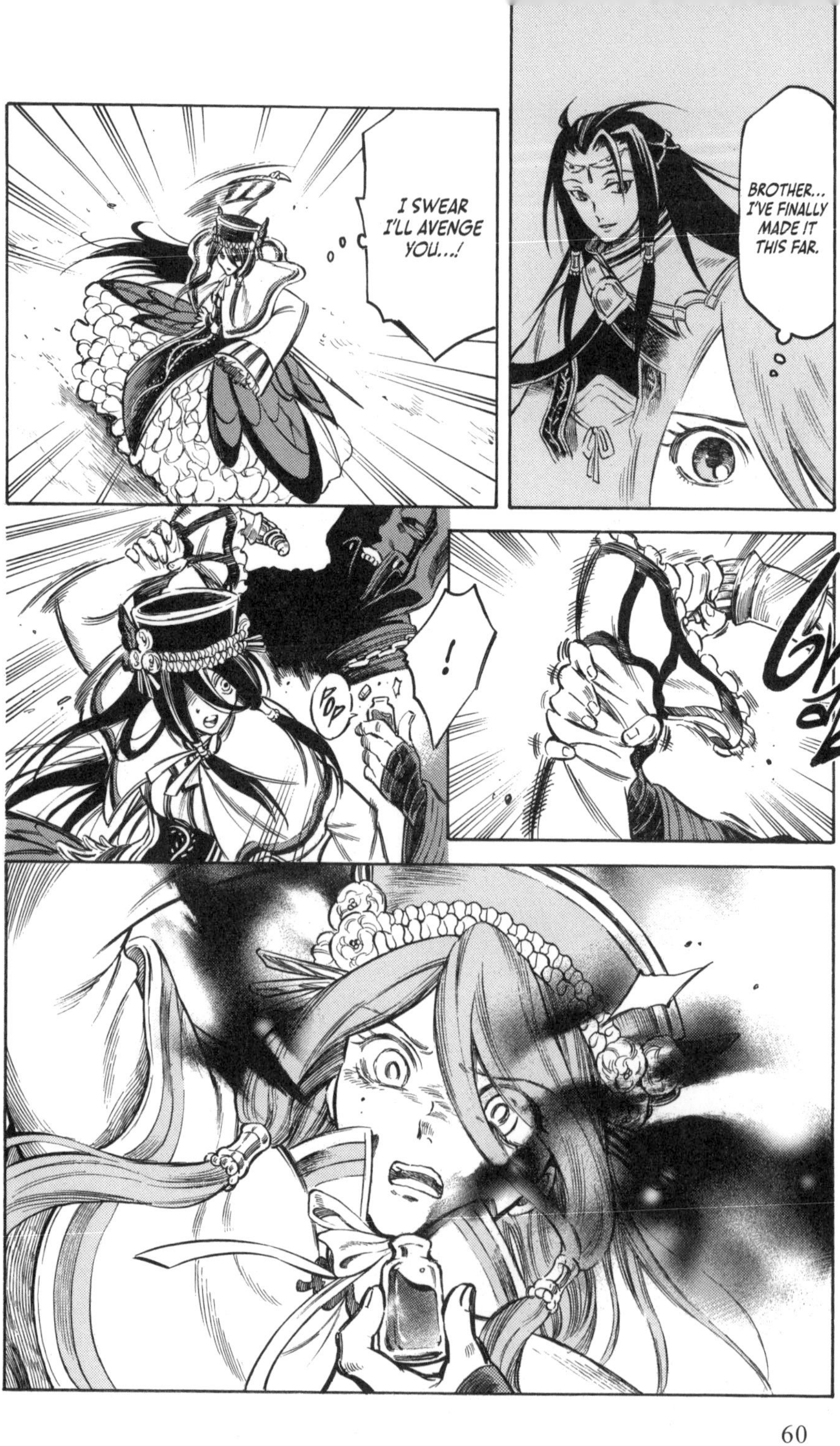
BROTHER... I'VE FINALLY MADE IT THIS FAR.
I SWEAR I'LL AVENGE YOU...!
GRAB
!
POP

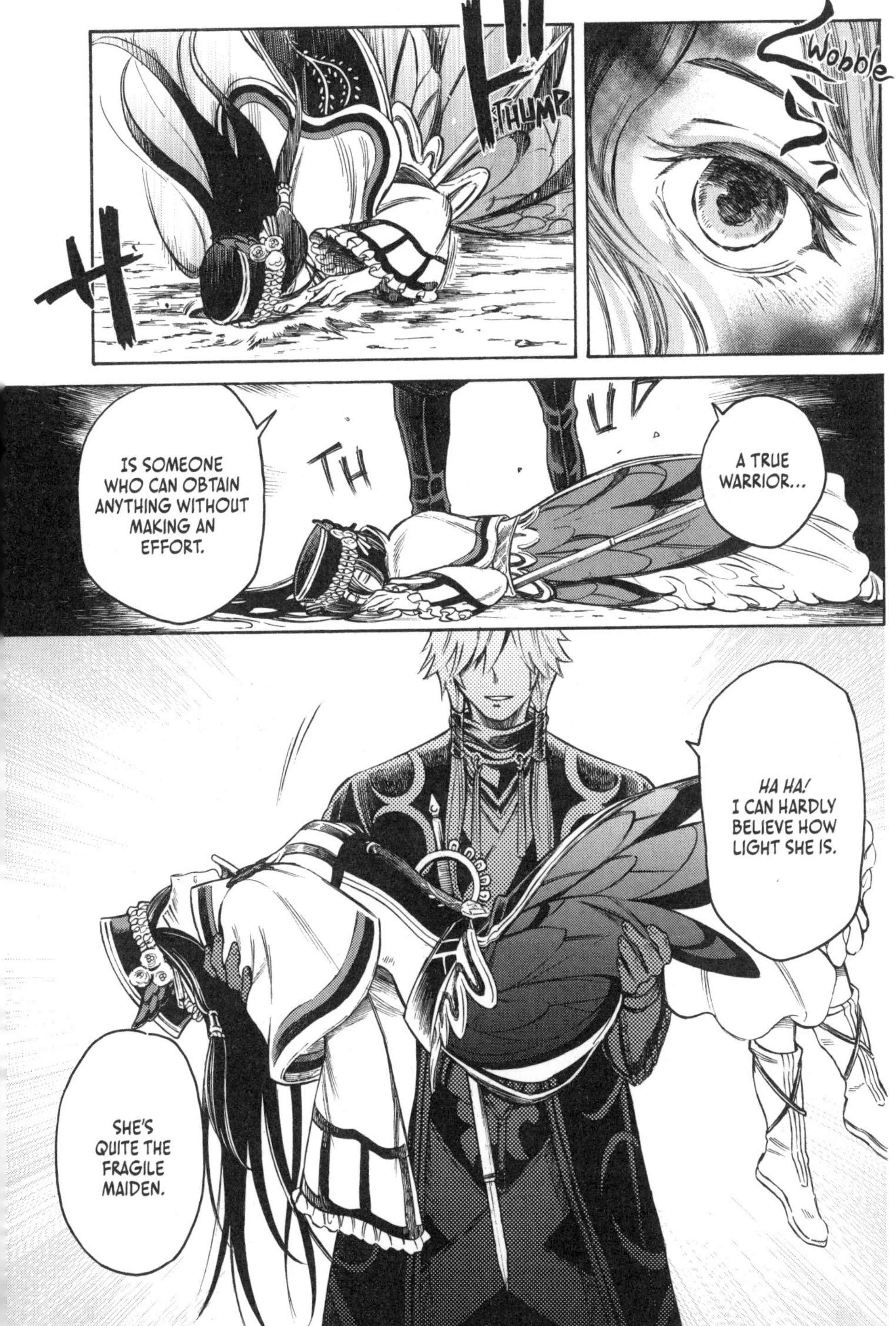
Wobble
THUMP
A TRUE WARRIOR...
IS SOMEONE WHO CAN OBTAIN ANYTHING WITHOUT MAKING AN EFFORT.
THUD
HA HA! I CAN HARDLY BELIEVE HOW LIGHT SHE IS.
SHE'S QUITE THE FRAGILE MAIDEN.

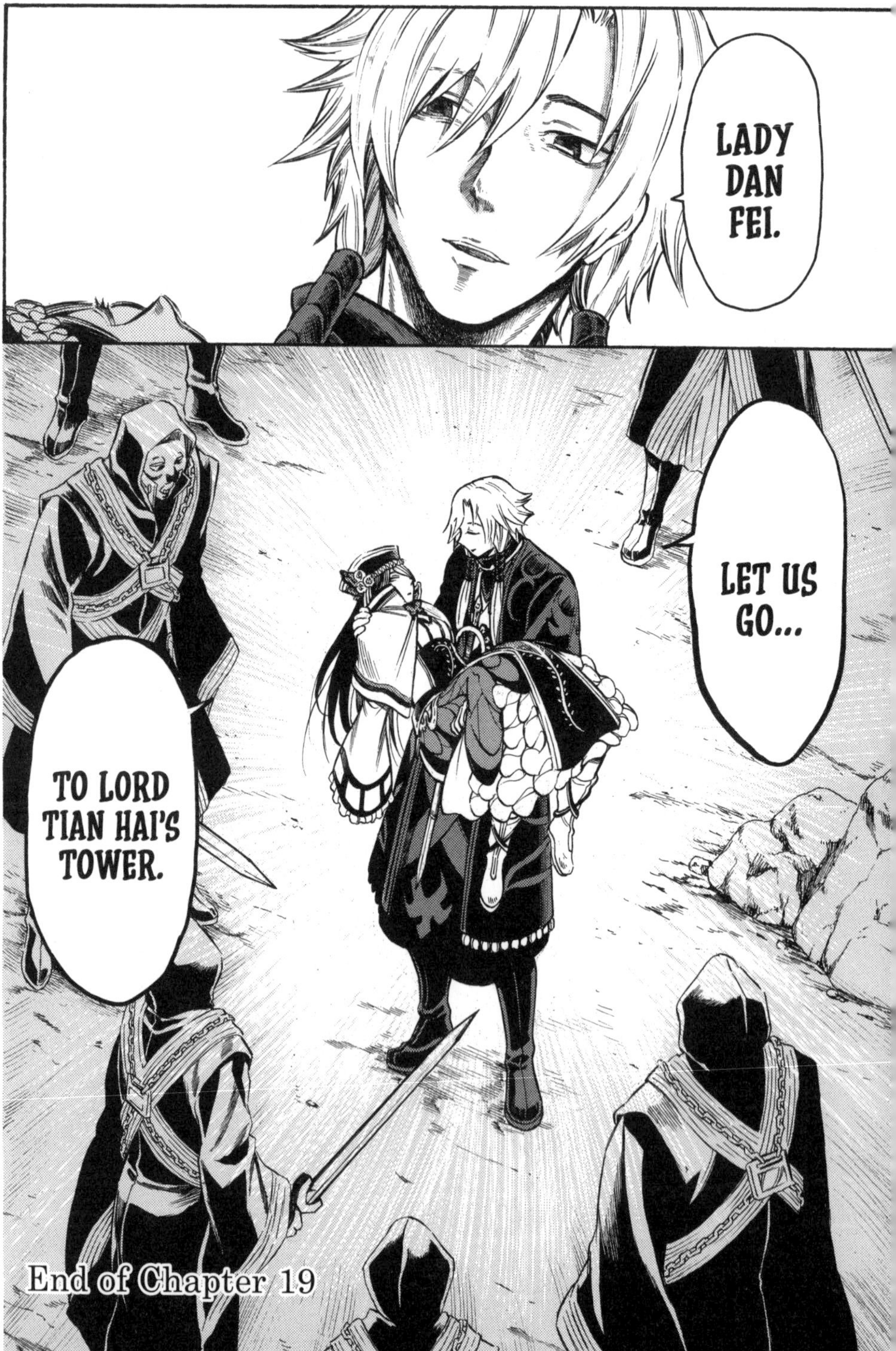
LADY DAN FEI.
LET US GO...
TO LORD TIAN HAI'S TOWER.
End of Chapter 19

◇ Chapter 20 ◇

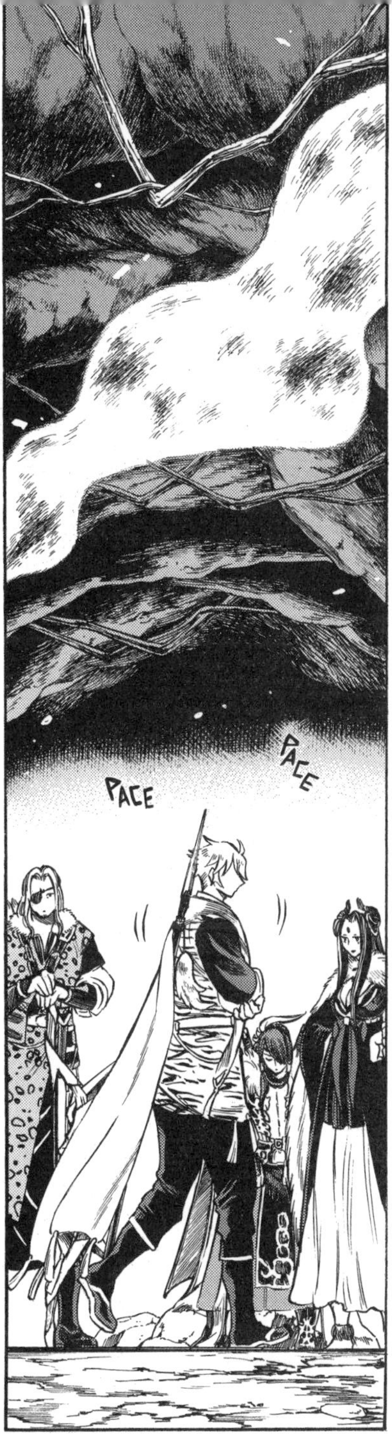
PACE
PACE

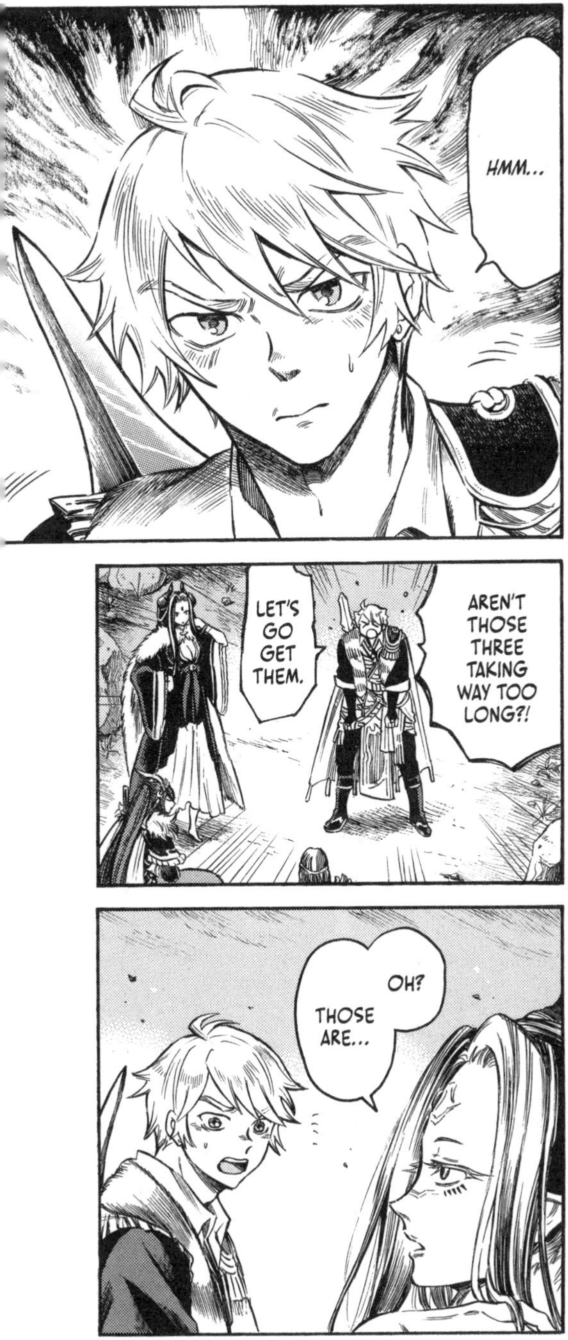
HMM...
AREN'T THOSE THREE TAKING WAY TOO LONG?!
LET'S GO GET THEM.
OH? THOSE ARE...

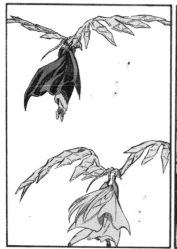

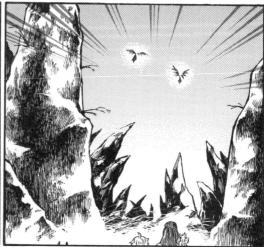

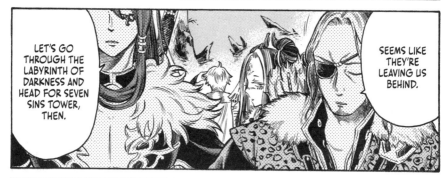

SEEMS LIKE THEY'RE LEAVING US BEHIND.
LET'S GO THROUGH THE LABYRINTH OF DARKNESS AND HEAD FOR SEVEN SINS TOWER, THEN.
MISS DAN FEI...
IS NOWHERE TO BE SEEN, THOUGH...

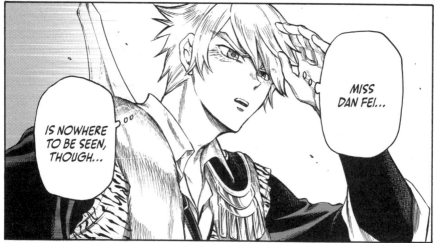

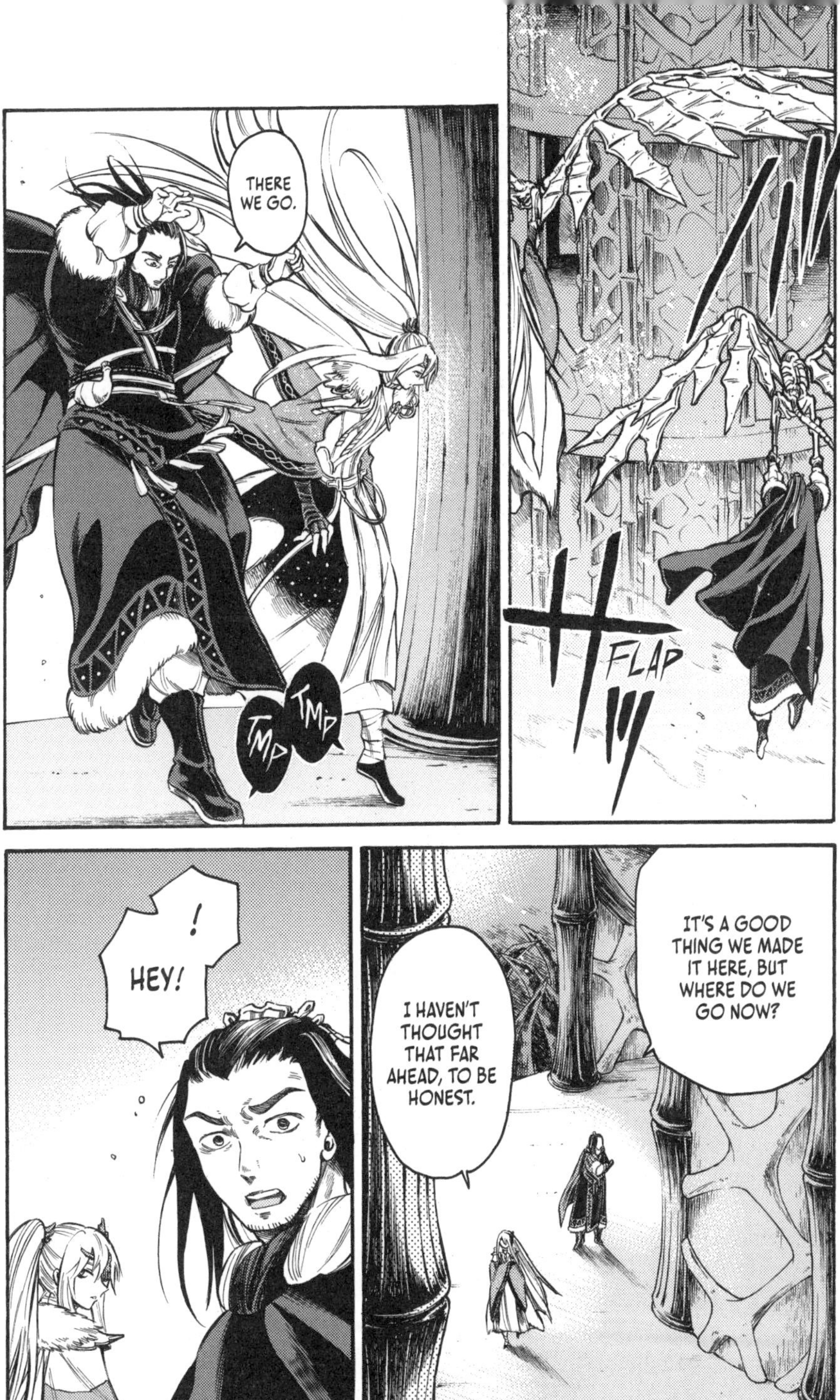
FLAP
THERE WE GO.
TMP TMP
IT'S A GOOD THING WE MADE IT HERE, BUT WHERE DO WE GO NOW?
I HAVEN'T THOUGHT THAT FAR AHEAD, TO BE HONEST.
!
HEY!

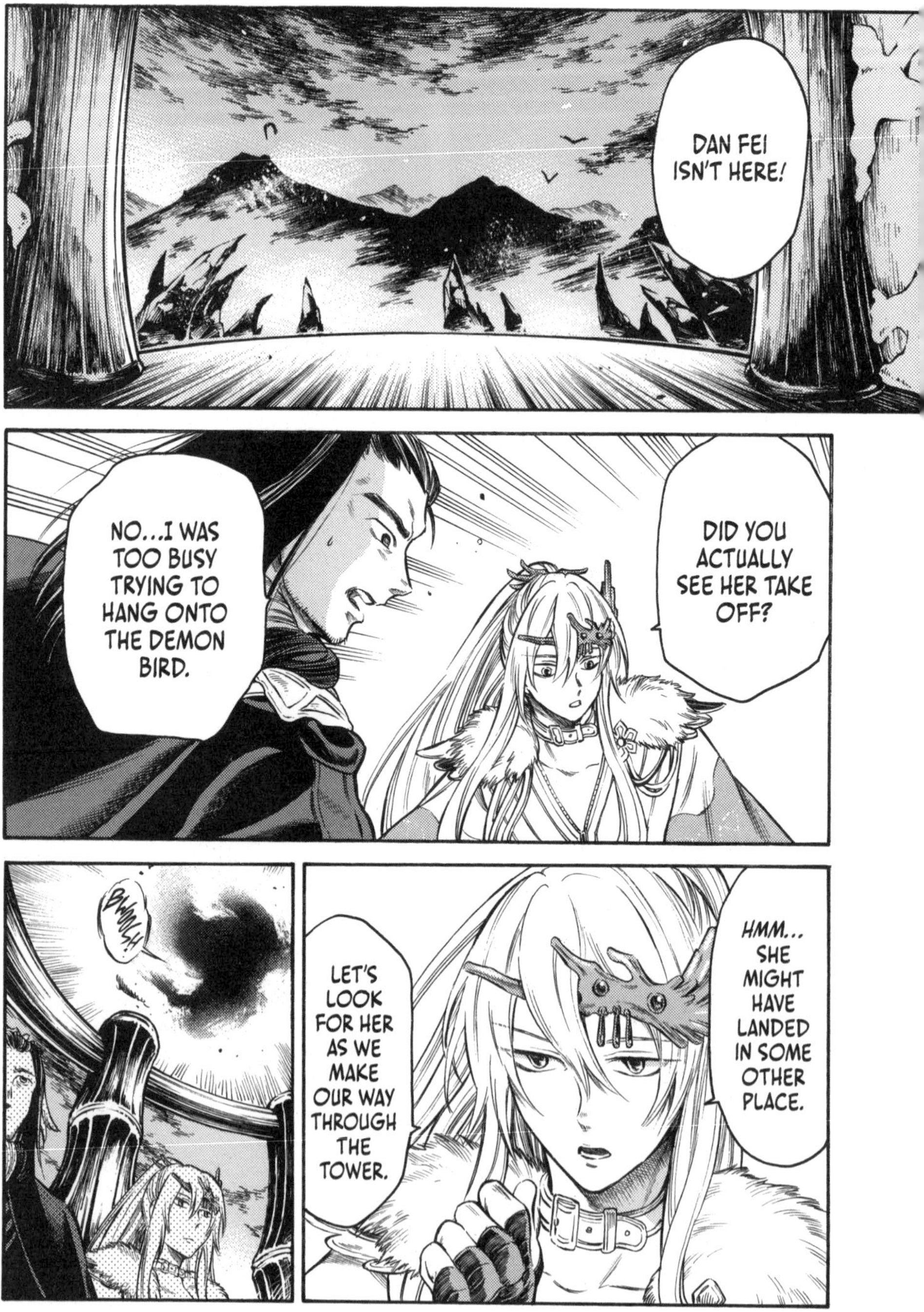
DAN FEI ISN'T HERE!
DID YOU ACTUALLY SEE HER TAKE OFF?
NO...I WAS TOO BUSY TRYING TO HANG ONTO THE DEMON BIRD.
HMM... SHE MIGHT HAVE LANDED IN SOME OTHER PLACE.
LET'S LOOK FOR HER AS WE MAKE OUR WAY THROUGH THE TOWER.
BWOOSH!

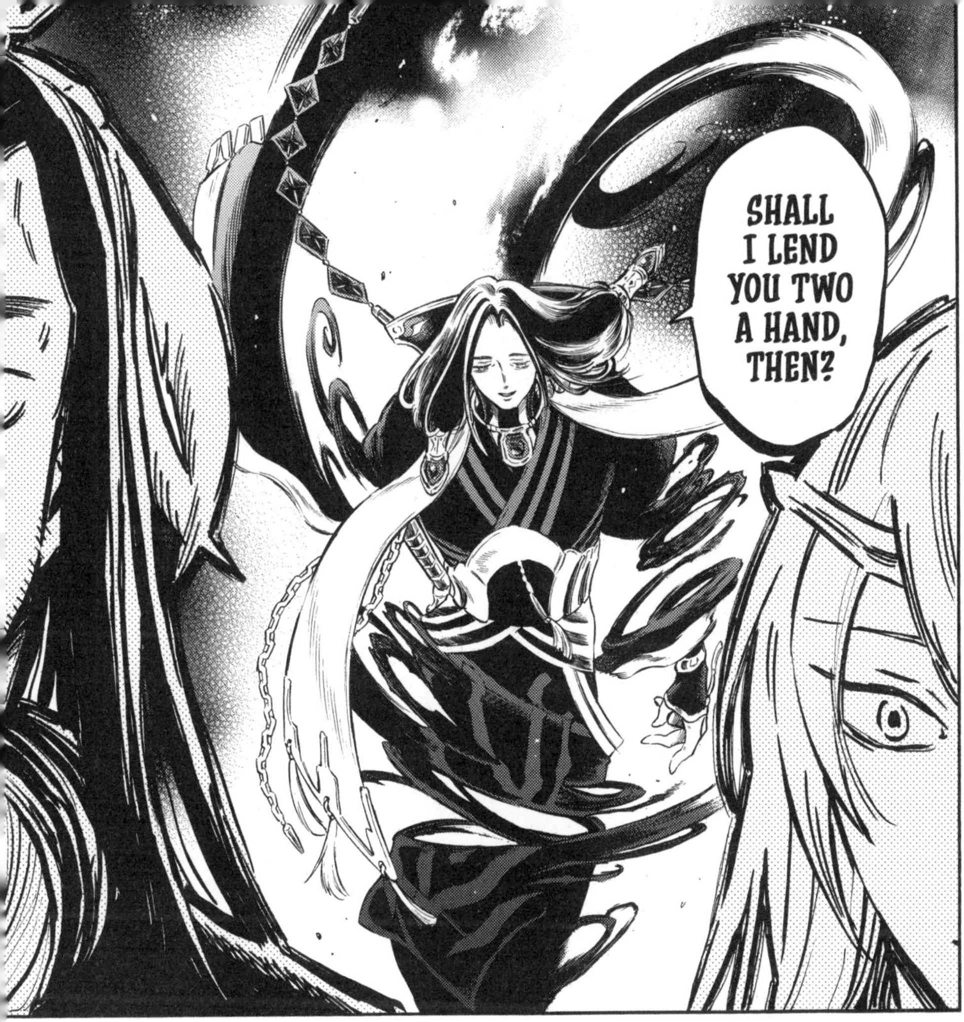
SHALL I LEND YOU TWO A HAND, THEN?

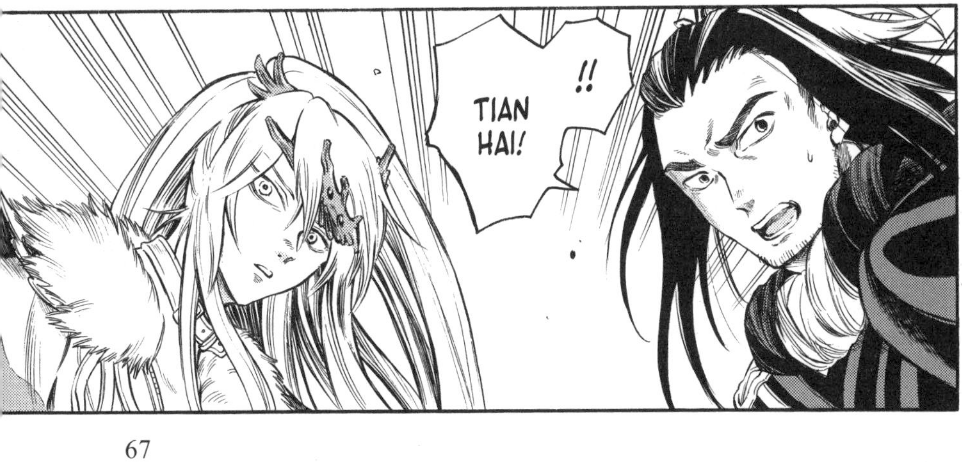
!!
TIAN HAI!

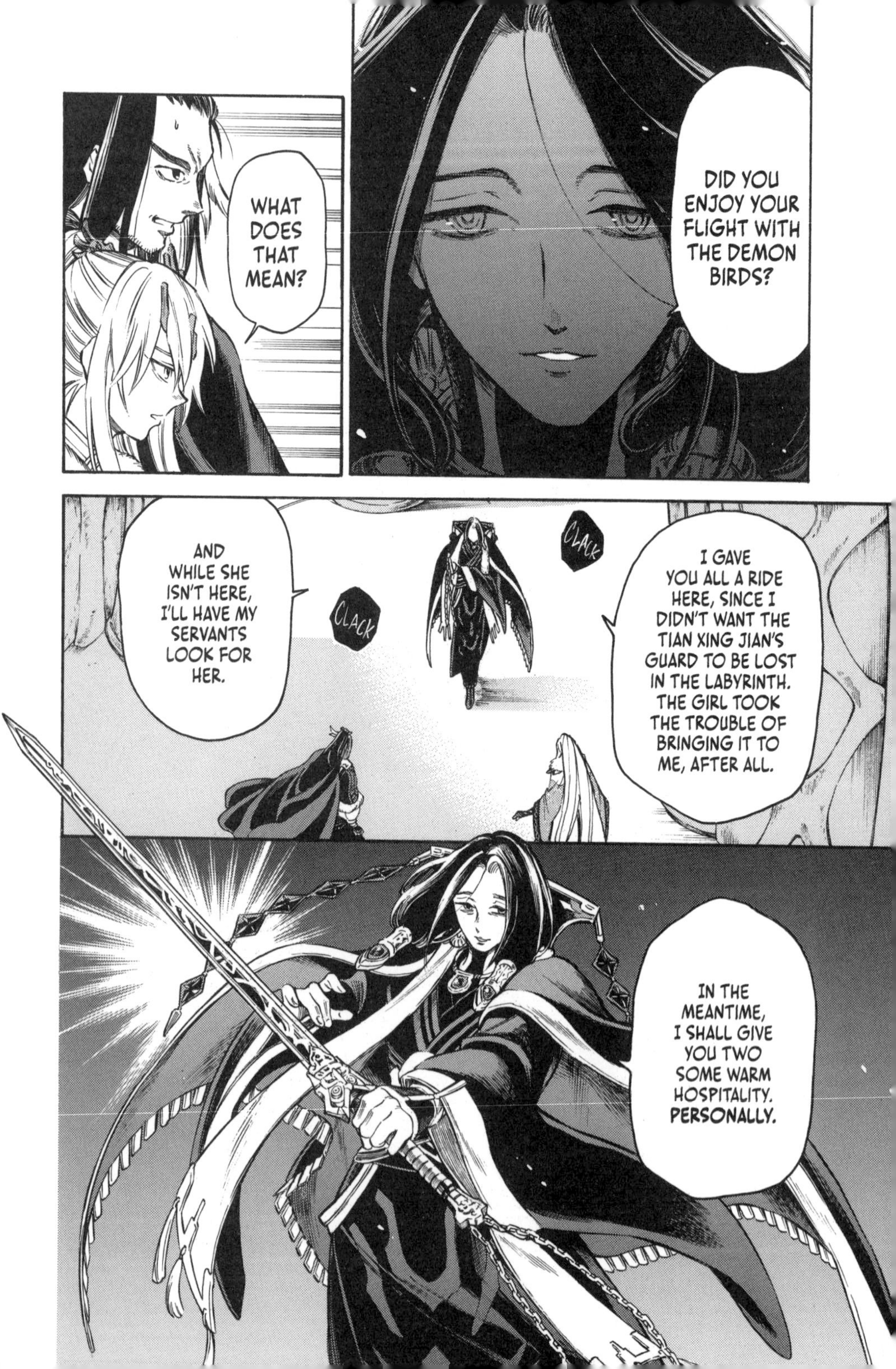
DID YOU ENJOY YOUR FLIGHT WITH THE DEMON BIRDS?
WHAT DOES THAT MEAN?
I GAVE YOU ALL A RIDE HERE, SINCE I DIDN'T WANT THE TIAN XING JIAN'S GUARD TO BE LOST IN THE LABYRINTH. THE GIRL TOOK THE TROUBLE OF BRINGING IT TO ME, AFTER ALL.
CLACK
CLACK
AND WHILE SHE ISN'T HERE, I'LL HAVE MY SERVANTS LOOK FOR HER.
IN THE MEANTIME, I SHALL GIVE YOU TWO SOME WARM HOSPITALITY. PERSONALLY.

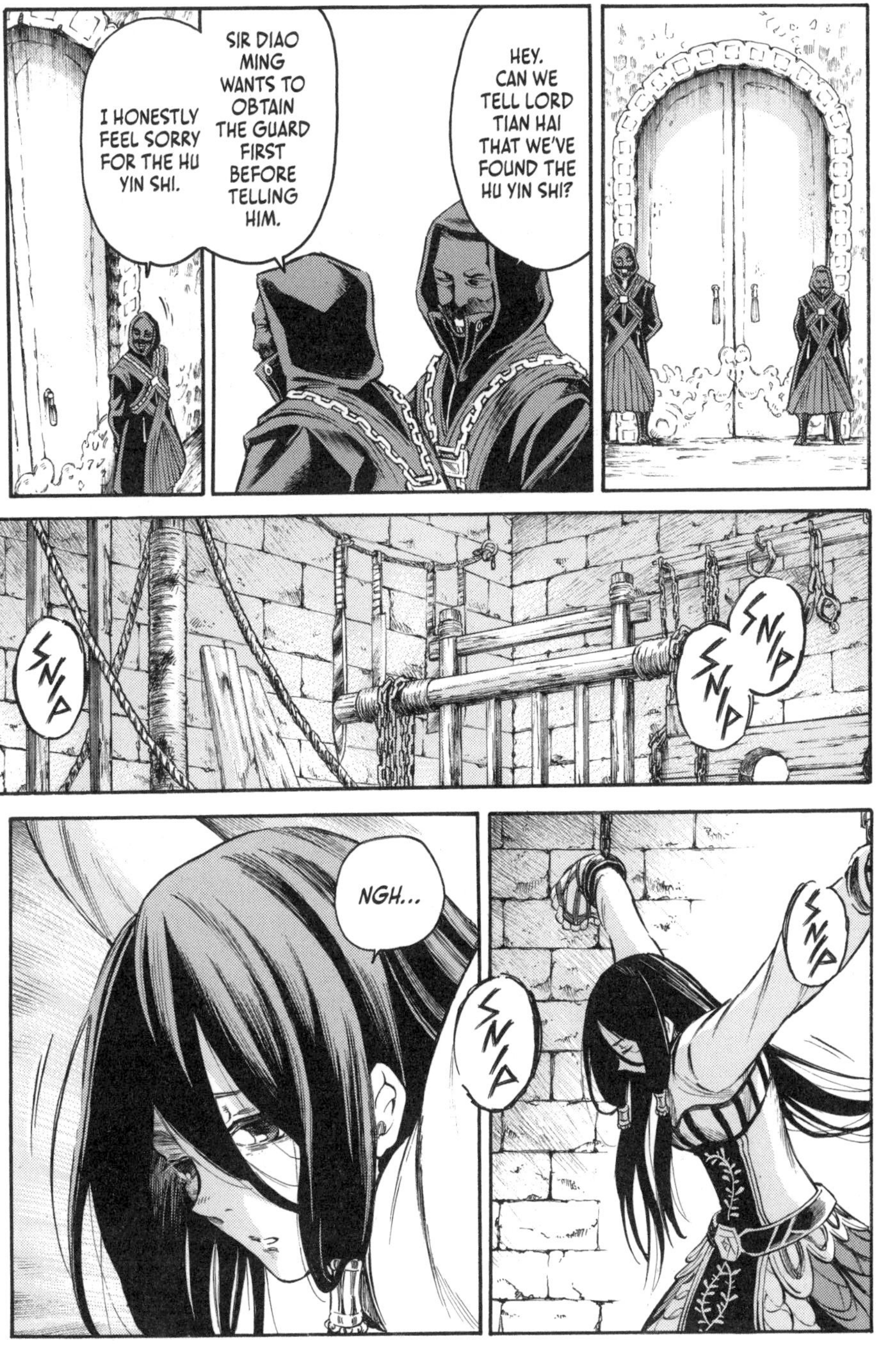
HEY. CAN WE TELL LORD TIAN HAI THAT WE'VE FOUND THE HU YIN SHI?
SIR DIAO MING WANTS TO OBTAIN THE GUARD FIRST BEFORE TELLING HIM.
I HONESTLY FEEL SORRY FOR THE HU YIN SHI.
SNIP
SNIP
SNIP
SNIP
SNIP
NGH...

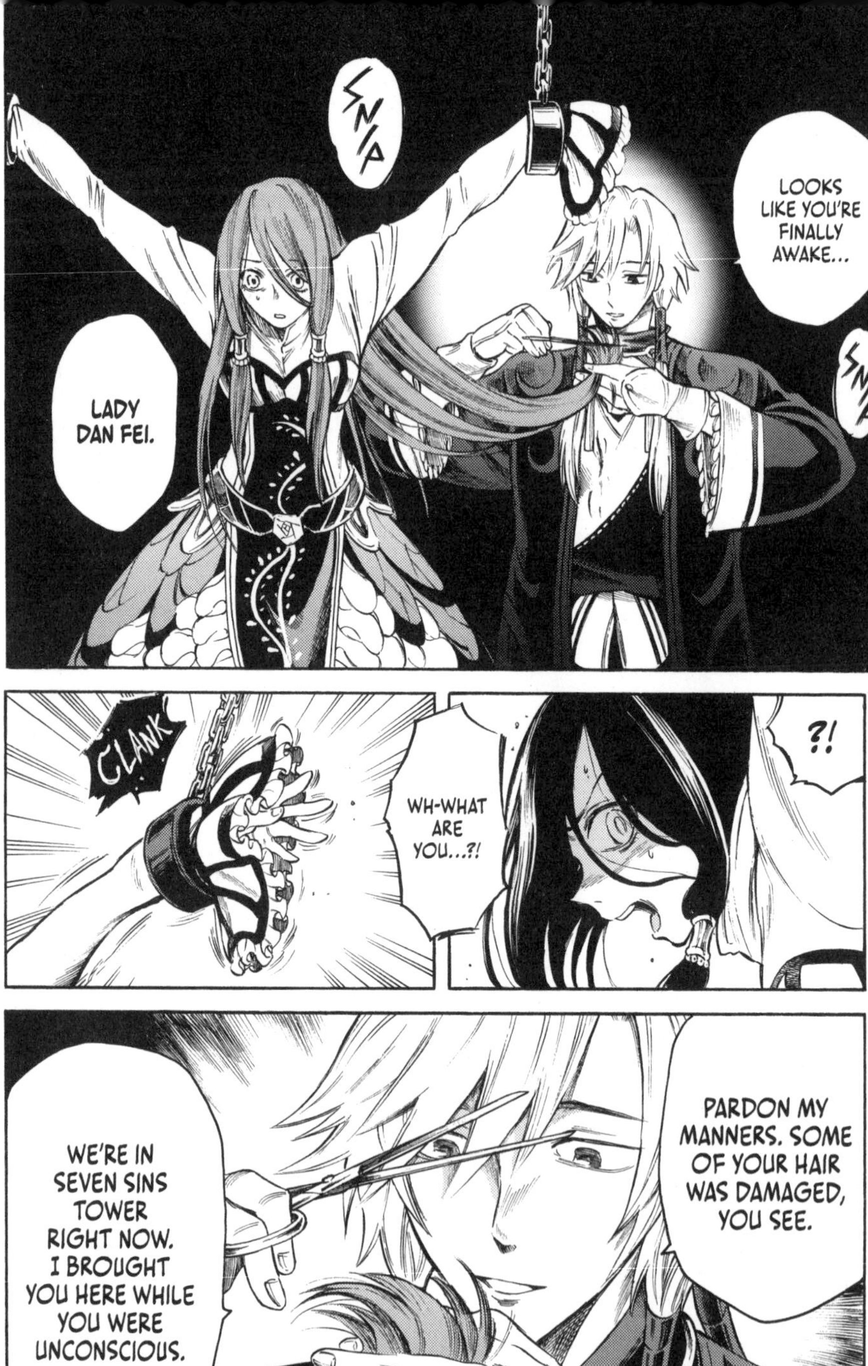
LOOKS LIKE YOU'RE FINALLY AWAKE...
SNIP
SNIP
LADY DAN FEI.
?!
WH-WHAT ARE YOU...?!
CLANK
PARDON MY MANNERS. SOME OF YOUR HAIR WAS DAMAGED, YOU SEE.
WE'RE IN SEVEN SINS TOWER RIGHT NOW. I BROUGHT YOU HERE WHILE YOU WERE UNCONSCIOUS.

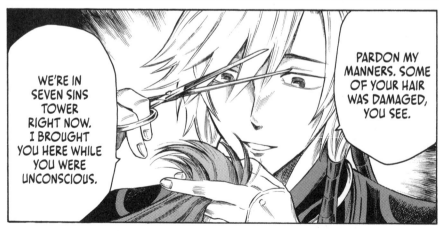

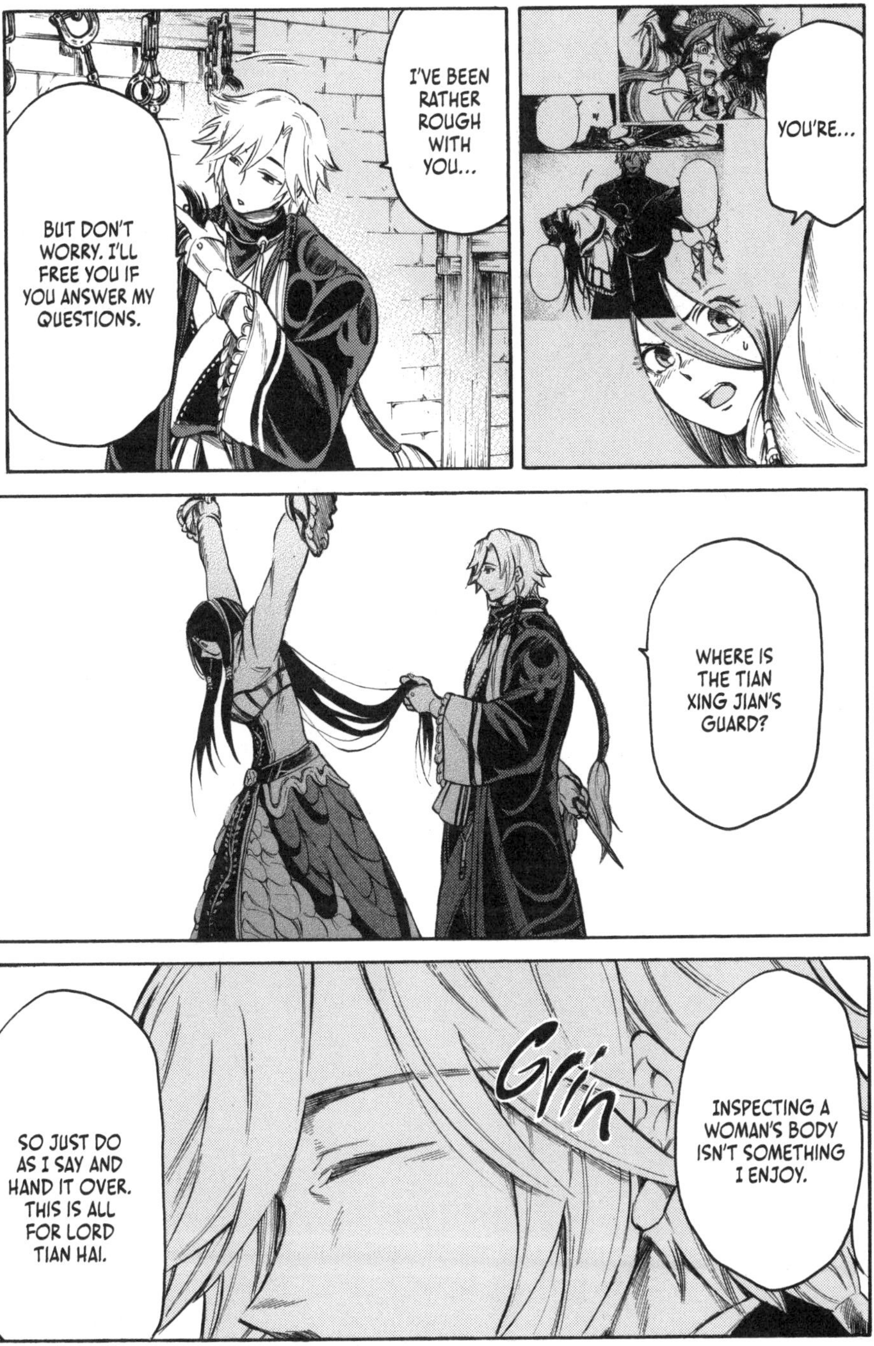
YOU'RE...
I'VE BEEN RATHER ROUGH WITH YOU...
BUT DON'T WORRY. I'LL FREE YOU IF YOU ANSWER MY QUESTIONS.
WHERE IS THE TIAN XING JIAN'S GUARD?
INSPECTING A WOMAN'S BODY ISN'T SOMETHING I ENJOY.
Grin
SO JUST DO AS I SAY AND HAND IT OVER. THIS IS ALL FOR LORD TIAN HAI.

I REFUSE TO TELL--

N-NO!

TIAN... HAI...

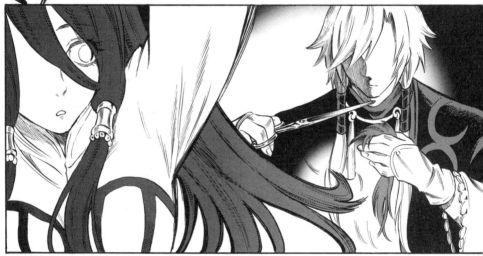

THAT'S...

LORD TIAN HAI TO YOU...

LADY DAN FEI.

FWSH

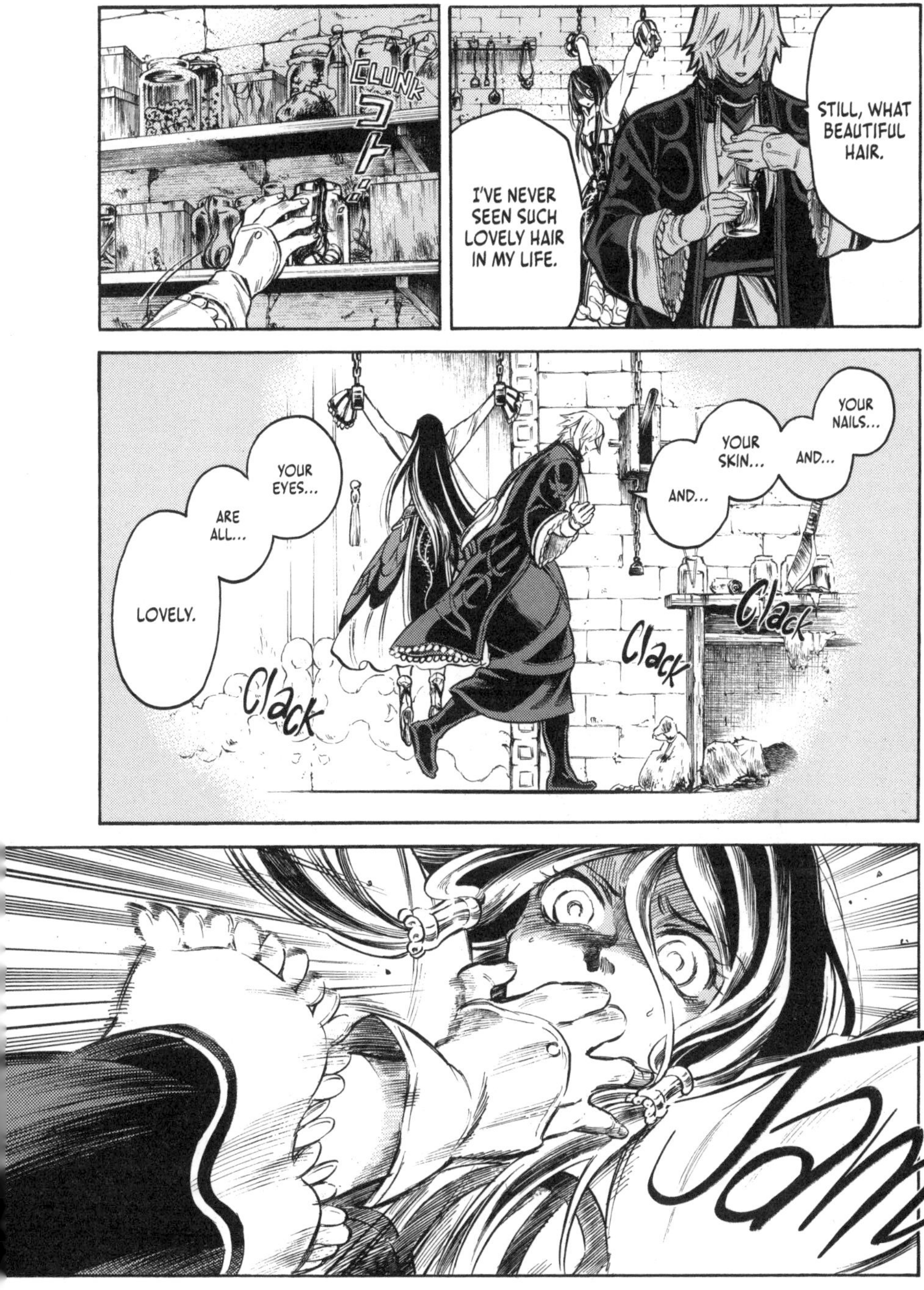
STILL, WHAT BEAUTIFUL HAIR.
I'VE NEVER SEEN SUCH LOVELY HAIR IN MY LIFE.
CLUNK
コト…
YOUR NAILS…
AND…
YOUR SKIN…
AND…
YOUR EYES…
ARE ALL…
LOVELY.
Clack
Clack
Clack
Tan

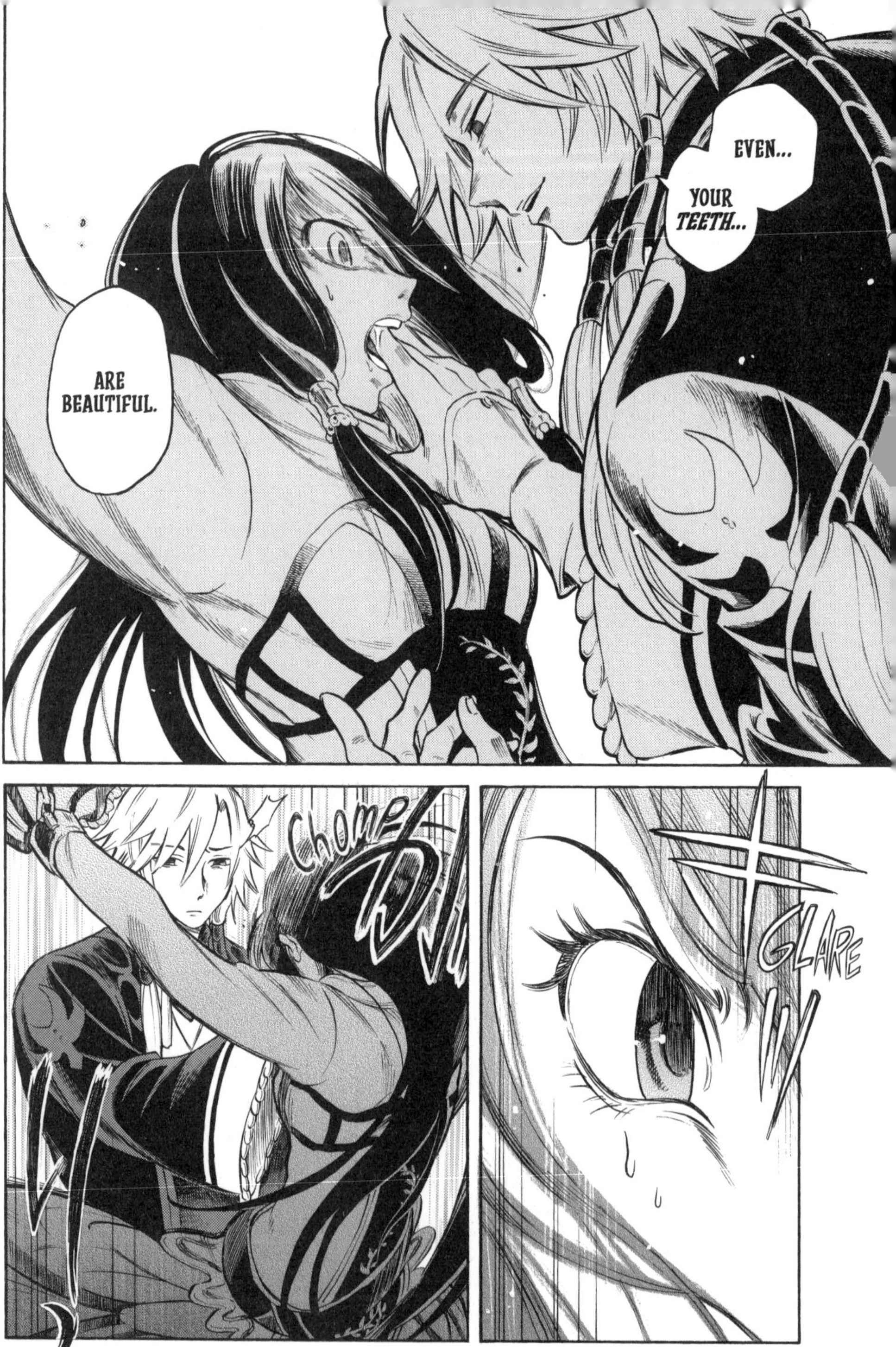
EVEN...
YOUR TEETH...
ARE BEAUTIFUL.
GLARE
Chomp

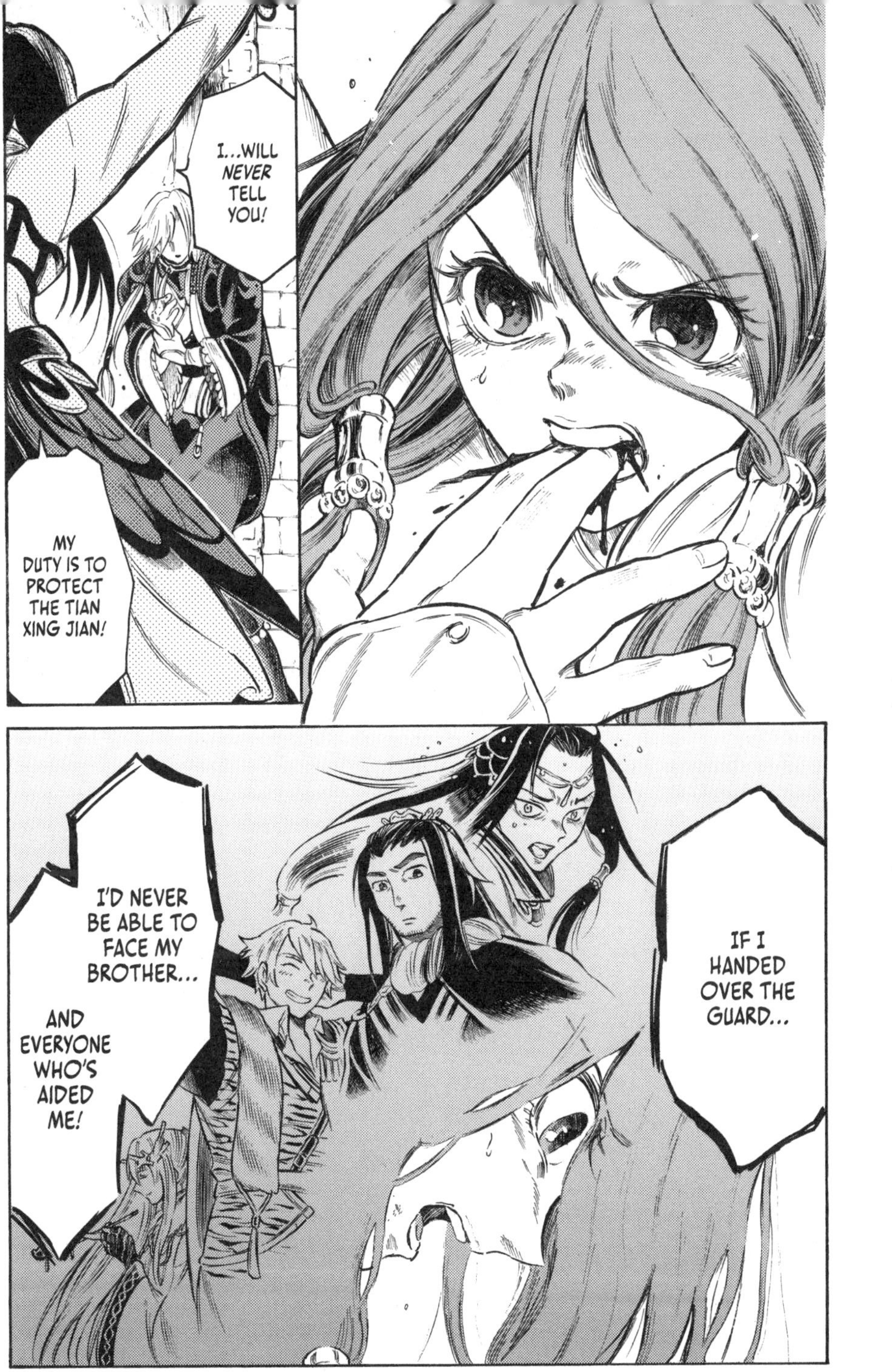
I...WILL NEVER TELL YOU!
MY DUTY IS TO PROTECT THE TIAN XING JIAN!
IF I HANDED OVER THE GUARD...
I'D NEVER BE ABLE TO FACE MY BROTHER...
AND EVERYONE WHO'S AIDED ME!

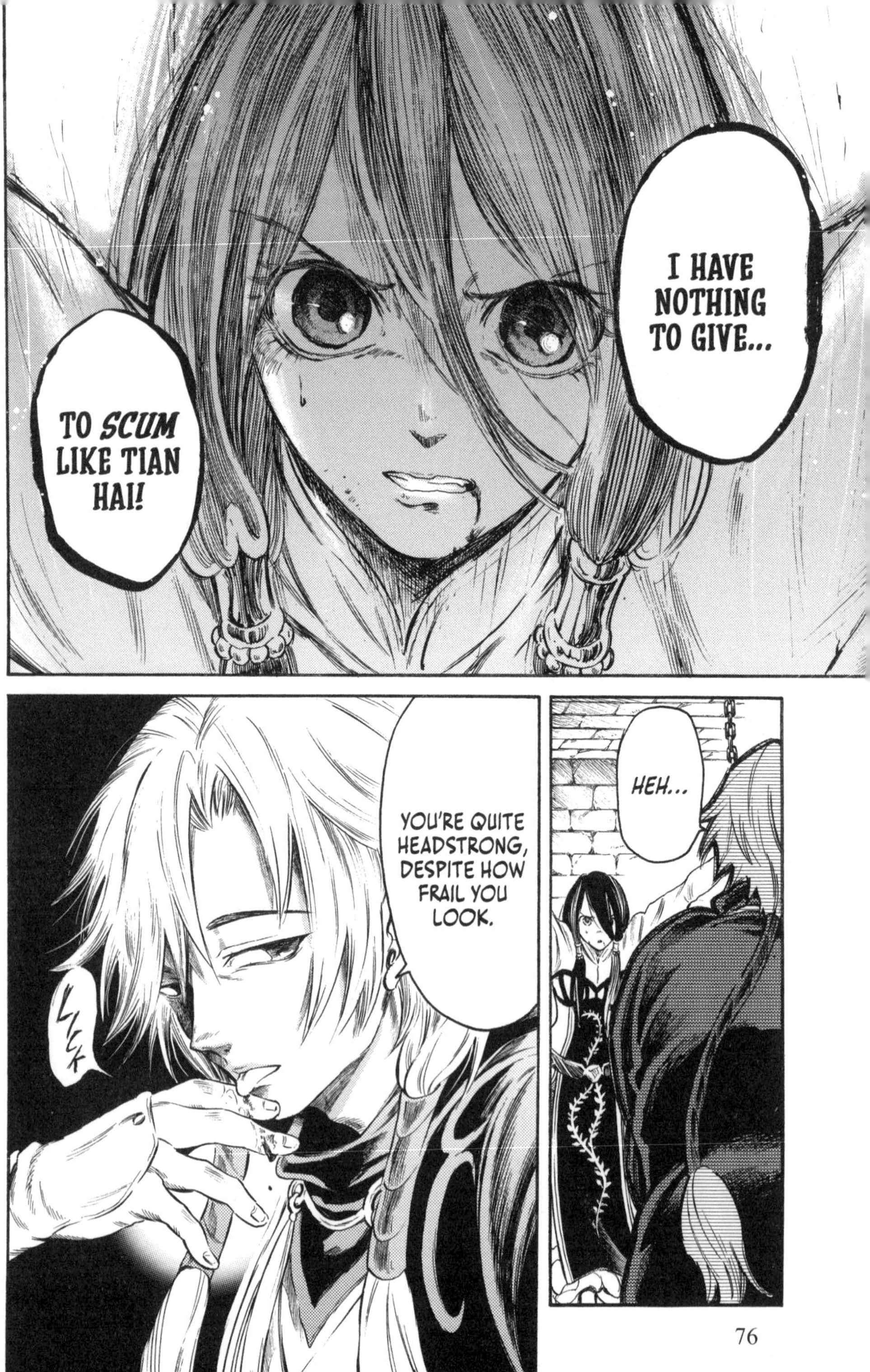
I HAVE NOTHING TO GIVE...
TO *SCUM* LIKE TIAN HAI!
HEH...
YOU'RE QUITE HEADSTRONG, DESPITE HOW FRAIL YOU LOOK.
LICK

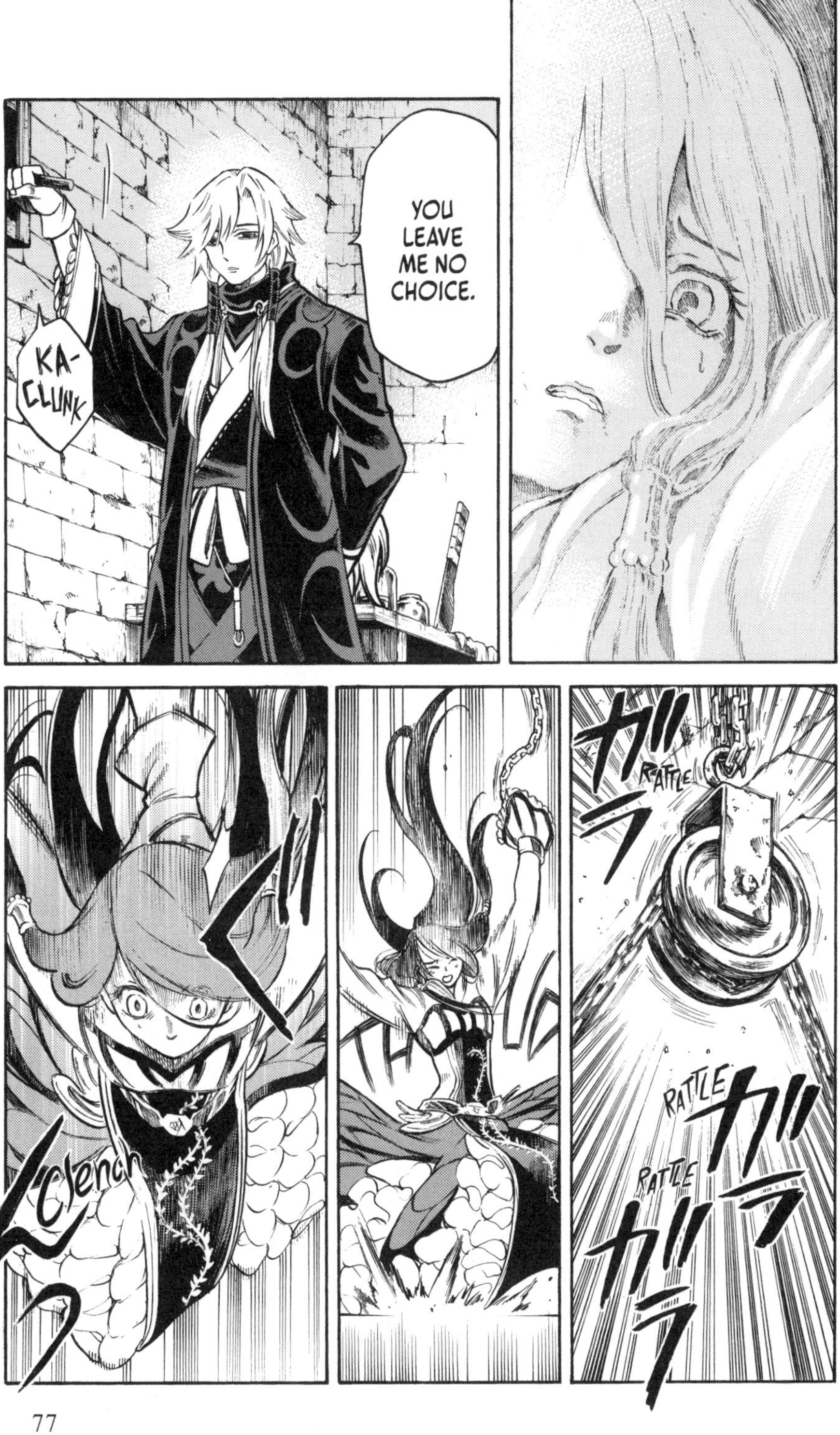
YOU LEAVE ME NO CHOICE.
KA-CLUNK
ガラ
RATTLE
ガラ
RATTLE
ガラ
RATTLE
clench

IF YOU WON'T GIVE IT TO ME...

I'LL JUST HAVE TO TORMENT YOU UNTIL YOU DO.

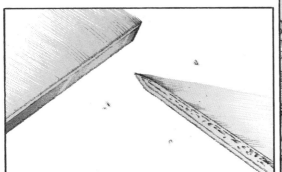

WHAT'S WRONG?

TIRED FROM YOUR LONG JOURNEY?

DAMMIT!

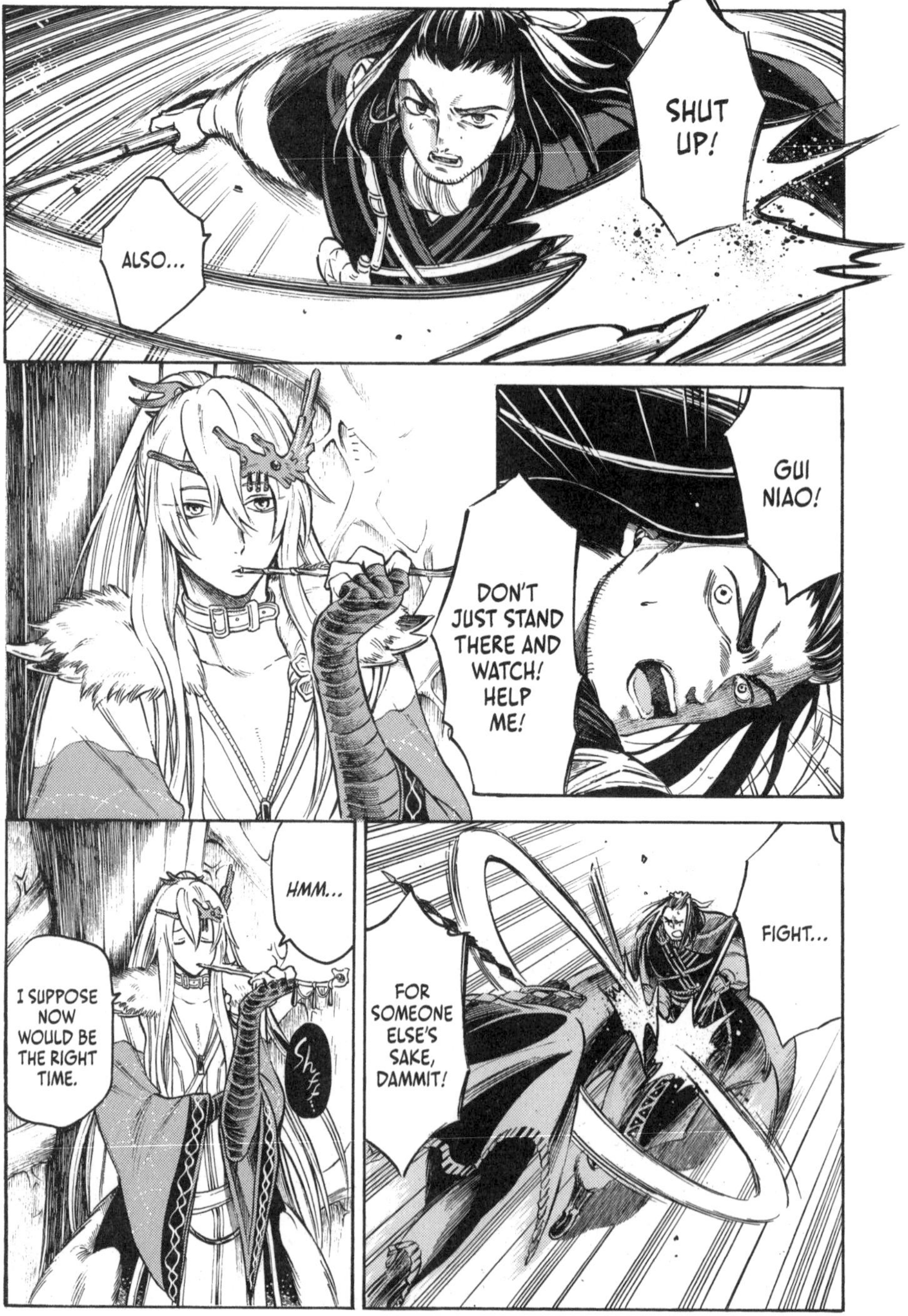
SHUT UP!
ALSO...
GUI NIAO!
DON'T JUST STAND THERE AND WATCH! HELP ME!
FIGHT...
FOR SOMEONE ELSE'S SAKE, DAMMIT!
HMM...
I SUPPOSE NOW WOULD BE THE RIGHT TIME.

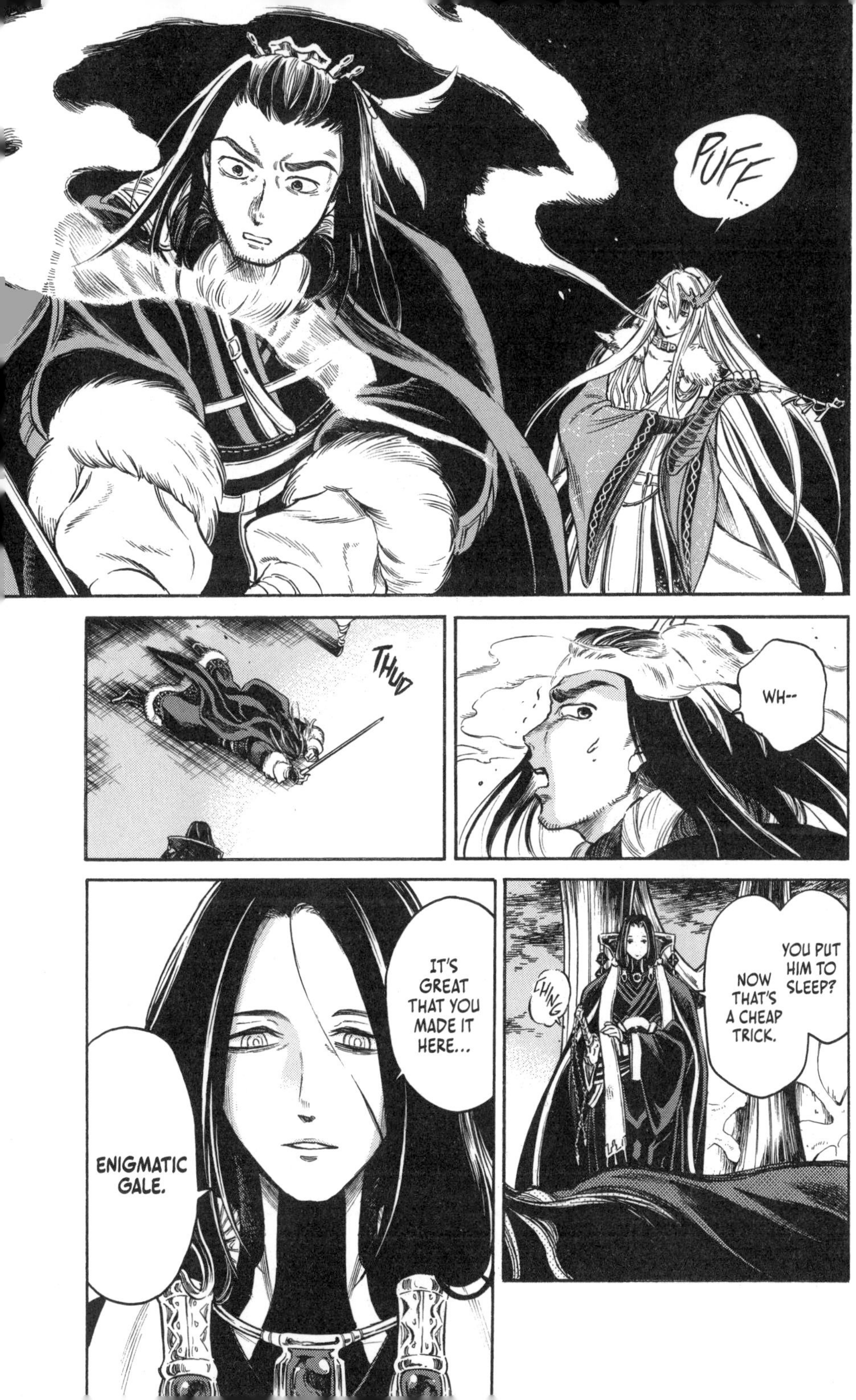
PUFF...
WH--
THUD
YOU PUT HIM TO SLEEP?
NOW THAT'S A CHEAP TRICK.
CHING
IT'S GREAT THAT YOU MADE IT HERE...
ENIGMATIC GALE.

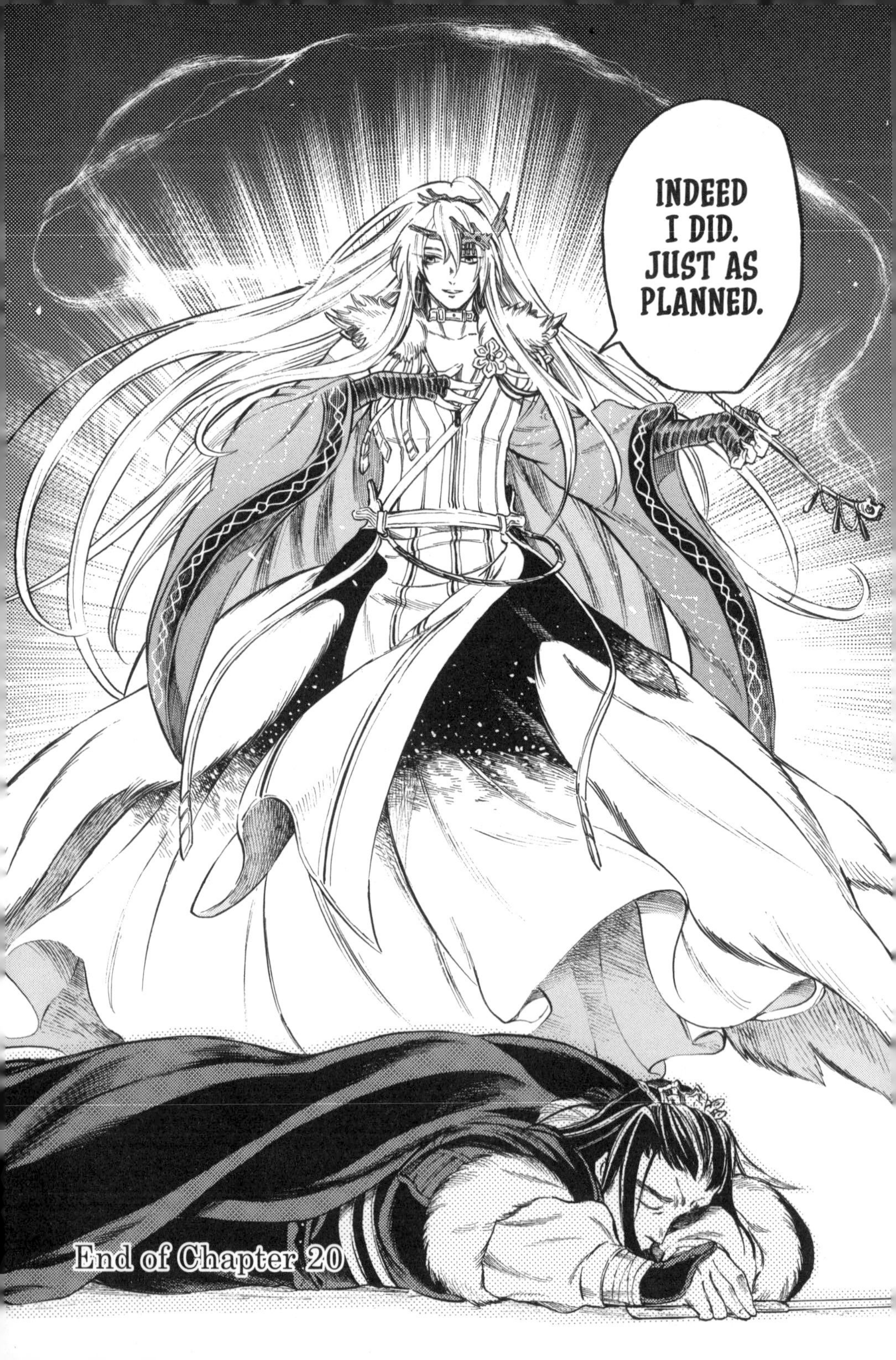
INDEED I DID. JUST AS PLANNED.
End of Chapter 20

Chapter 21

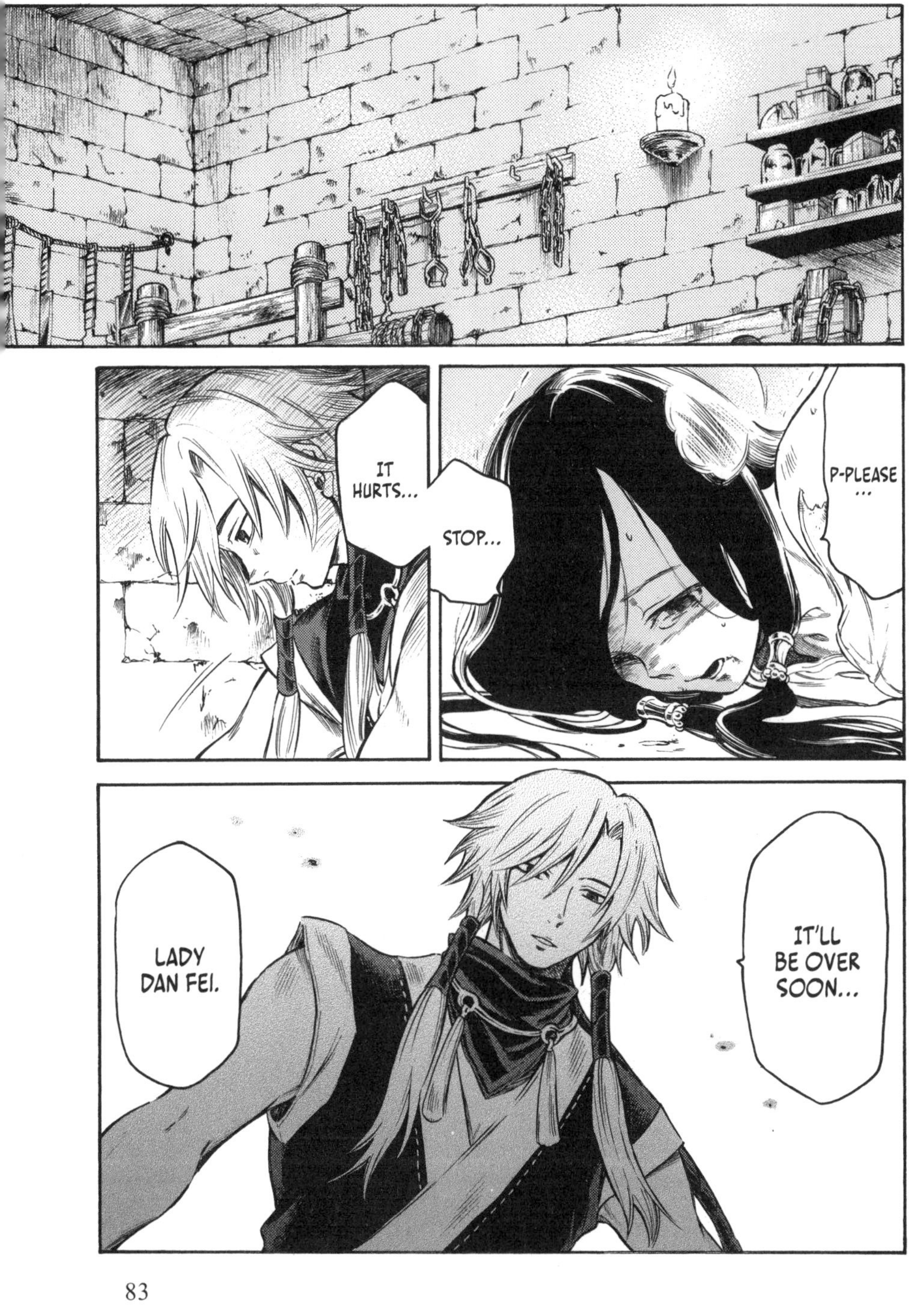
P-PLEASE...
STOP...
IT HURTS...
IT'LL BE OVER SOON...
LADY DAN FEI.

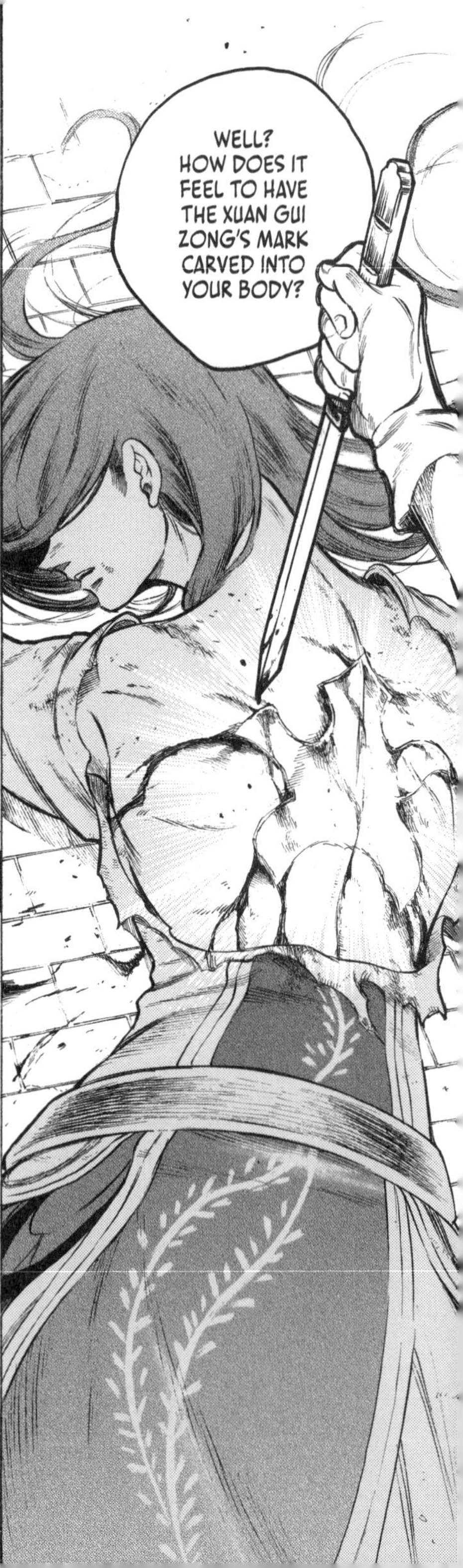
WELL? HOW DOES IT FEEL TO HAVE THE XUAN GUI ZONG'S MARK CARVED INTO YOUR BODY?

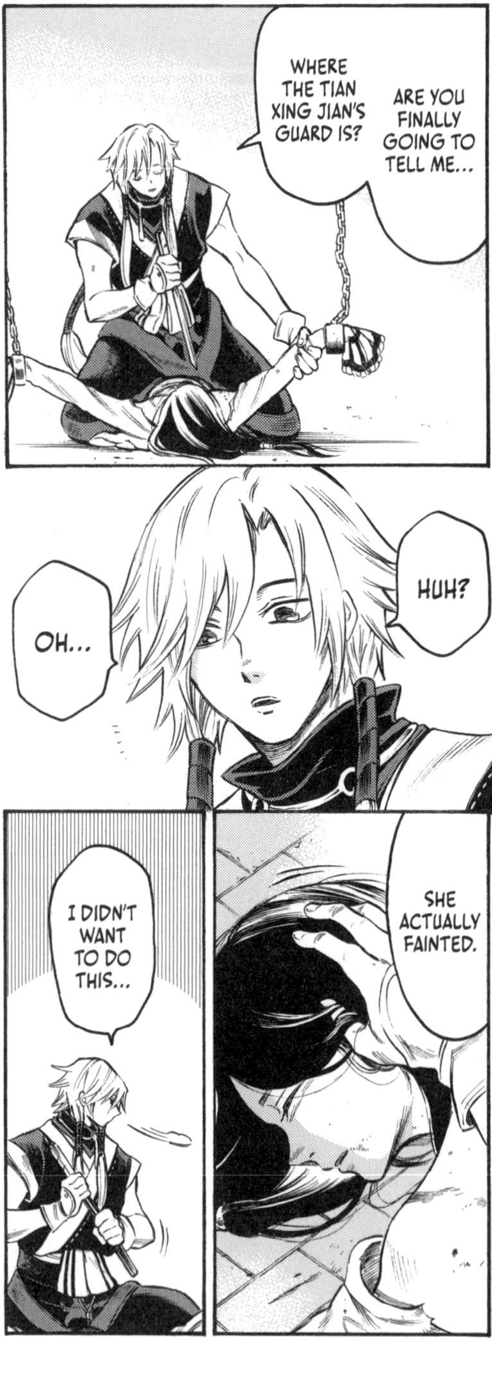
ARE YOU FINALLY GOING TO TELL ME...
WHERE THE TIAN XING JIAN'S GUARD IS?
HUH?
OH...
SHE ACTUALLY FAINTED.
I DIDN'T WANT TO DO THIS...

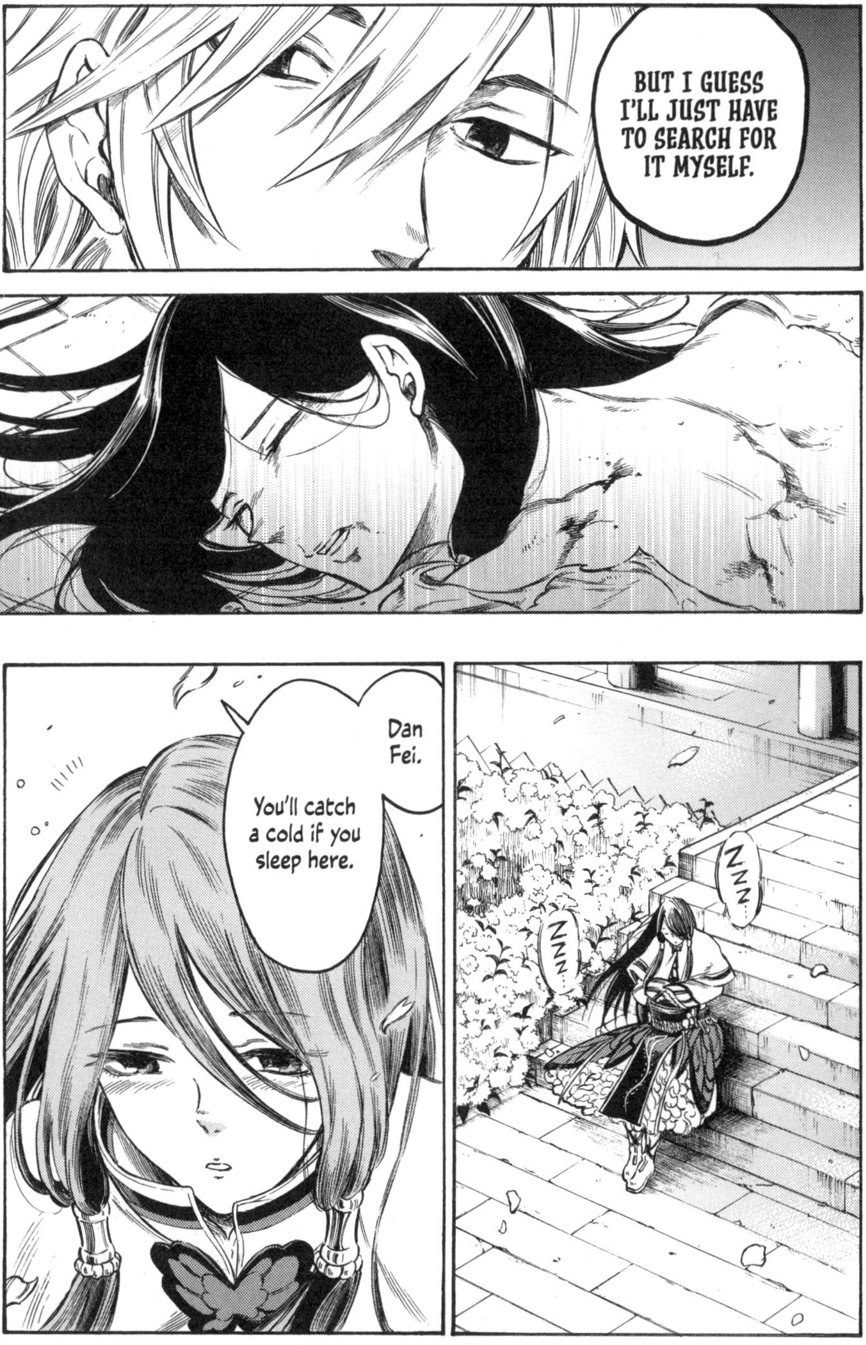
BUT I GUESS I'LL JUST HAVE TO SEARCH FOR IT MYSELF.
Nnn...
Nnn...
Dan Fei.
You'll catch a cold if you sleep here.

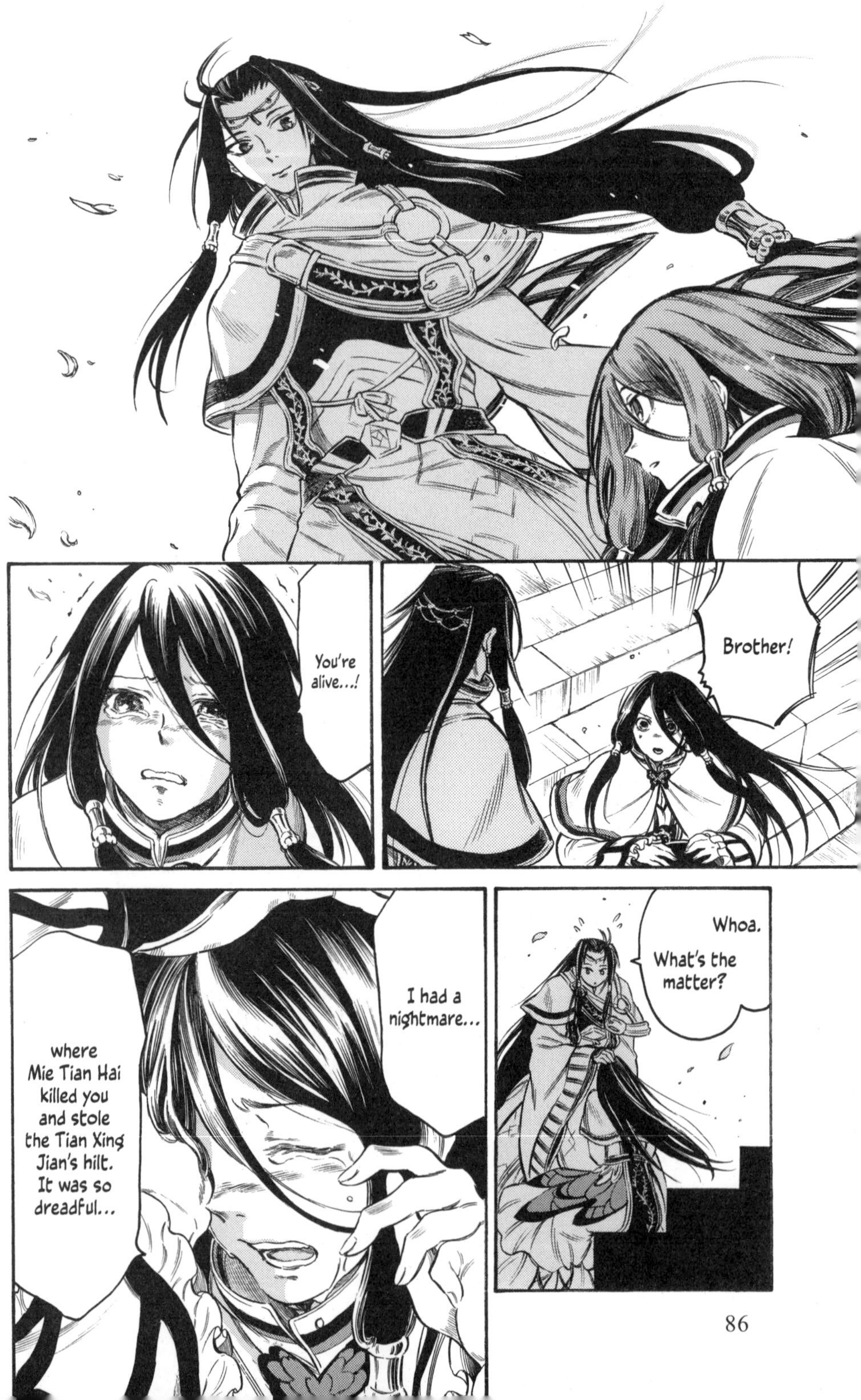
Brother!
You're alive...!
Whoa.
What's the matter?
I had a nightmare...
where Mie Tian Hai killed you and stole the Tian Xing Jian's hilt. It was so dreadful...

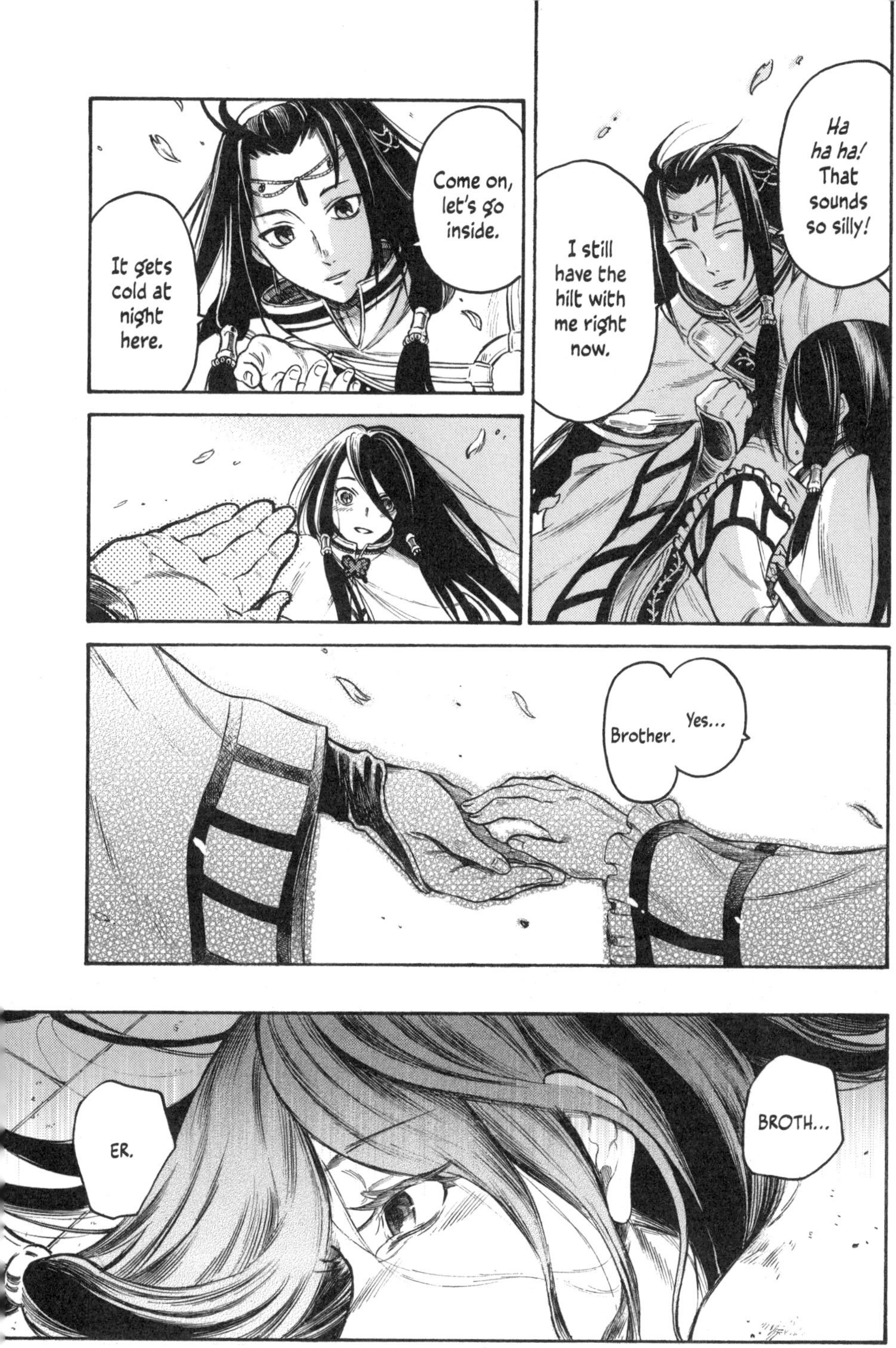
Ha ha ha! That sounds so silly!
I still have the hilt with me right now.
Come on, let's go inside.
It gets cold at night here.
Yes... Brother.
BROTH...
ER.

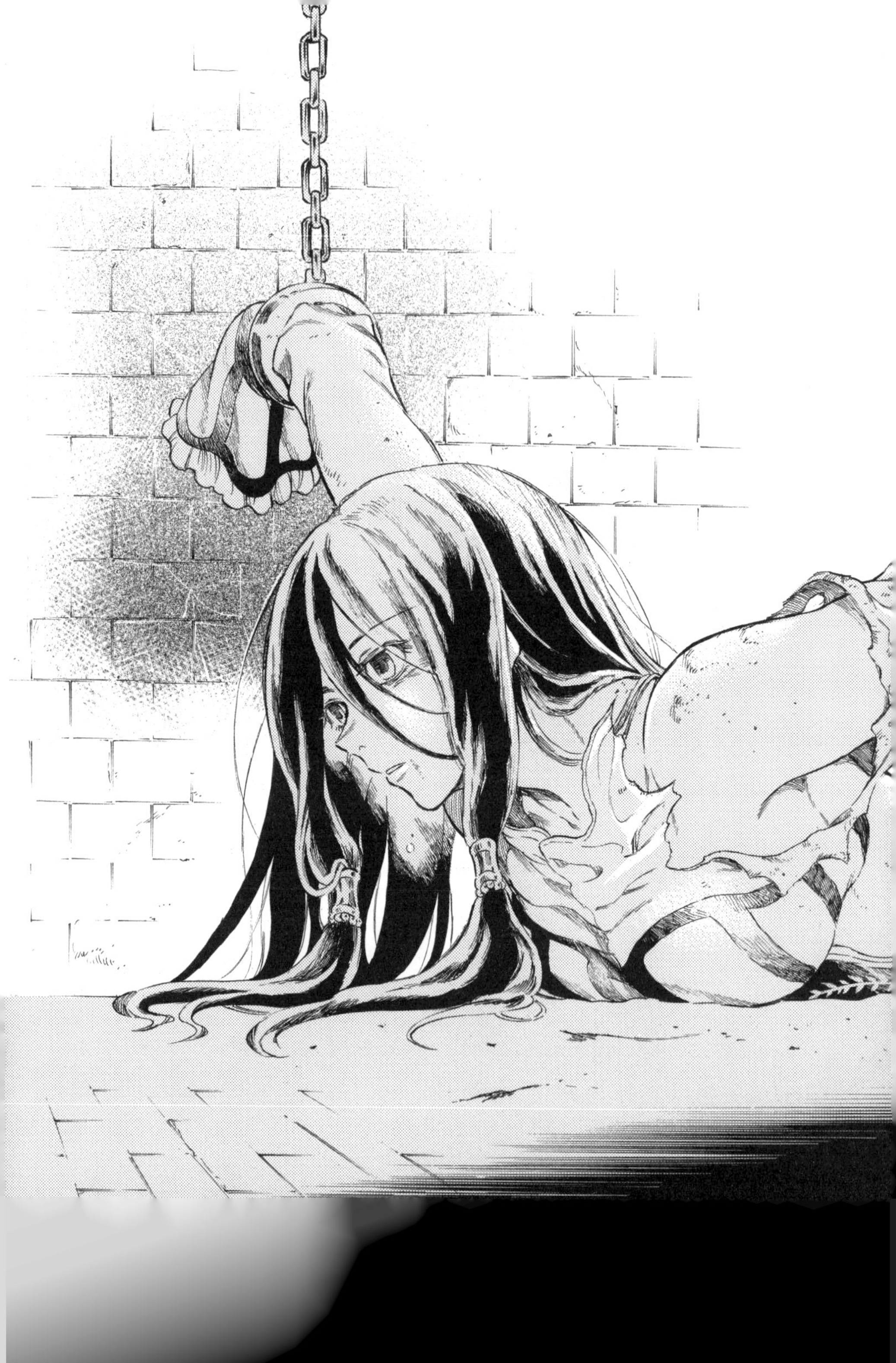

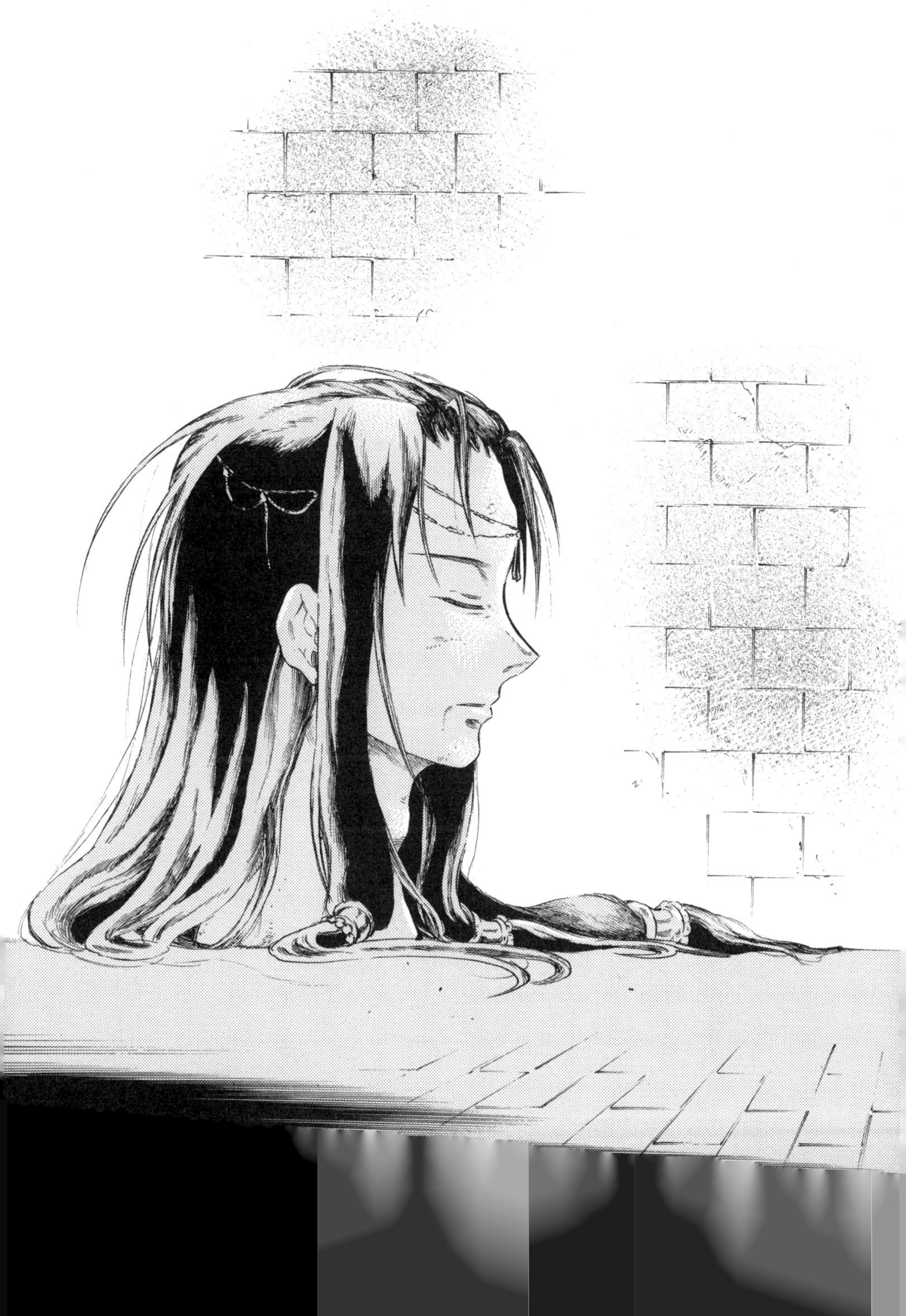

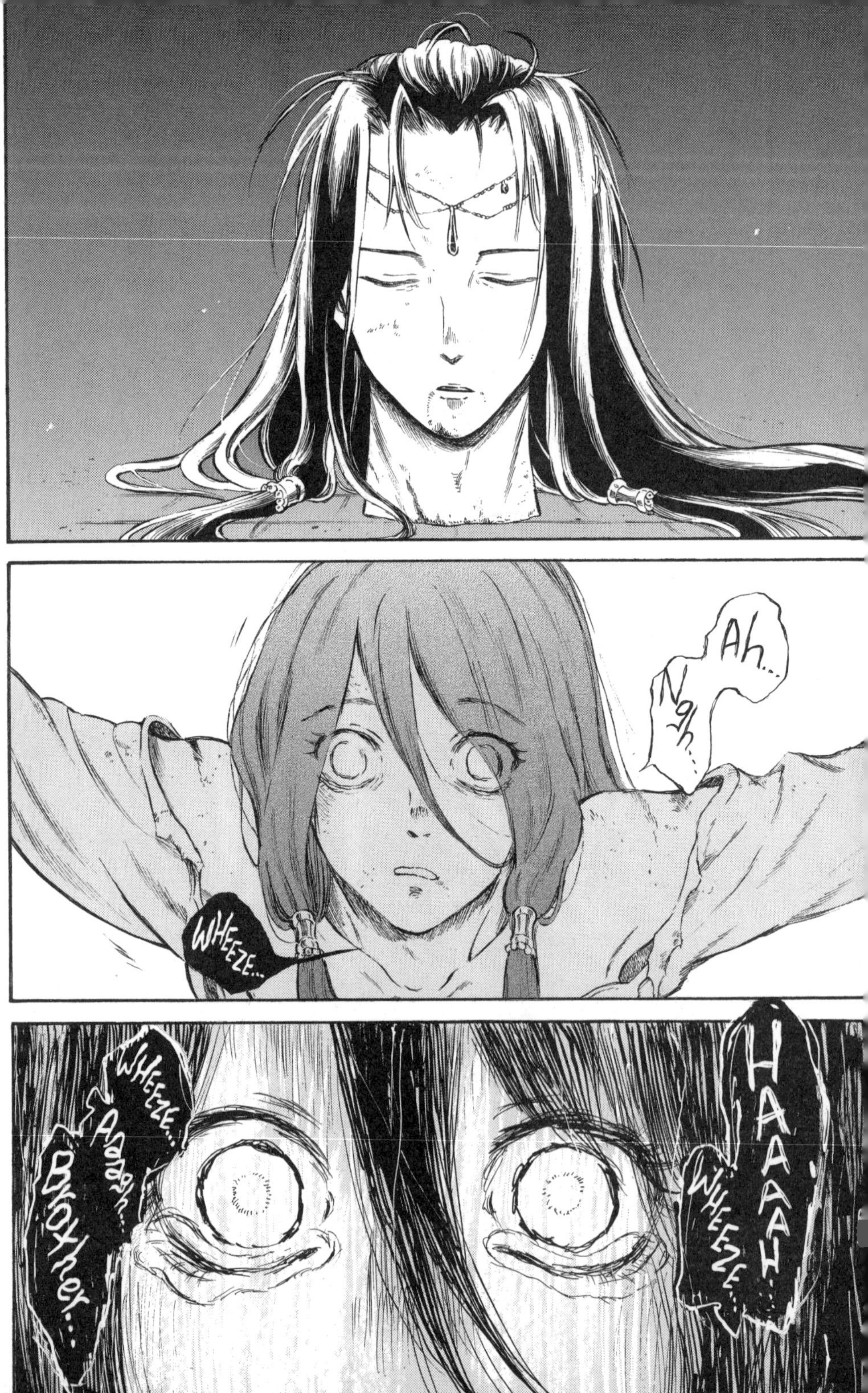
Ah... Ngh...
WHEEZE...
HAAAAH...
WHEEZE...
WHEEZE... Aaagh... Brother...

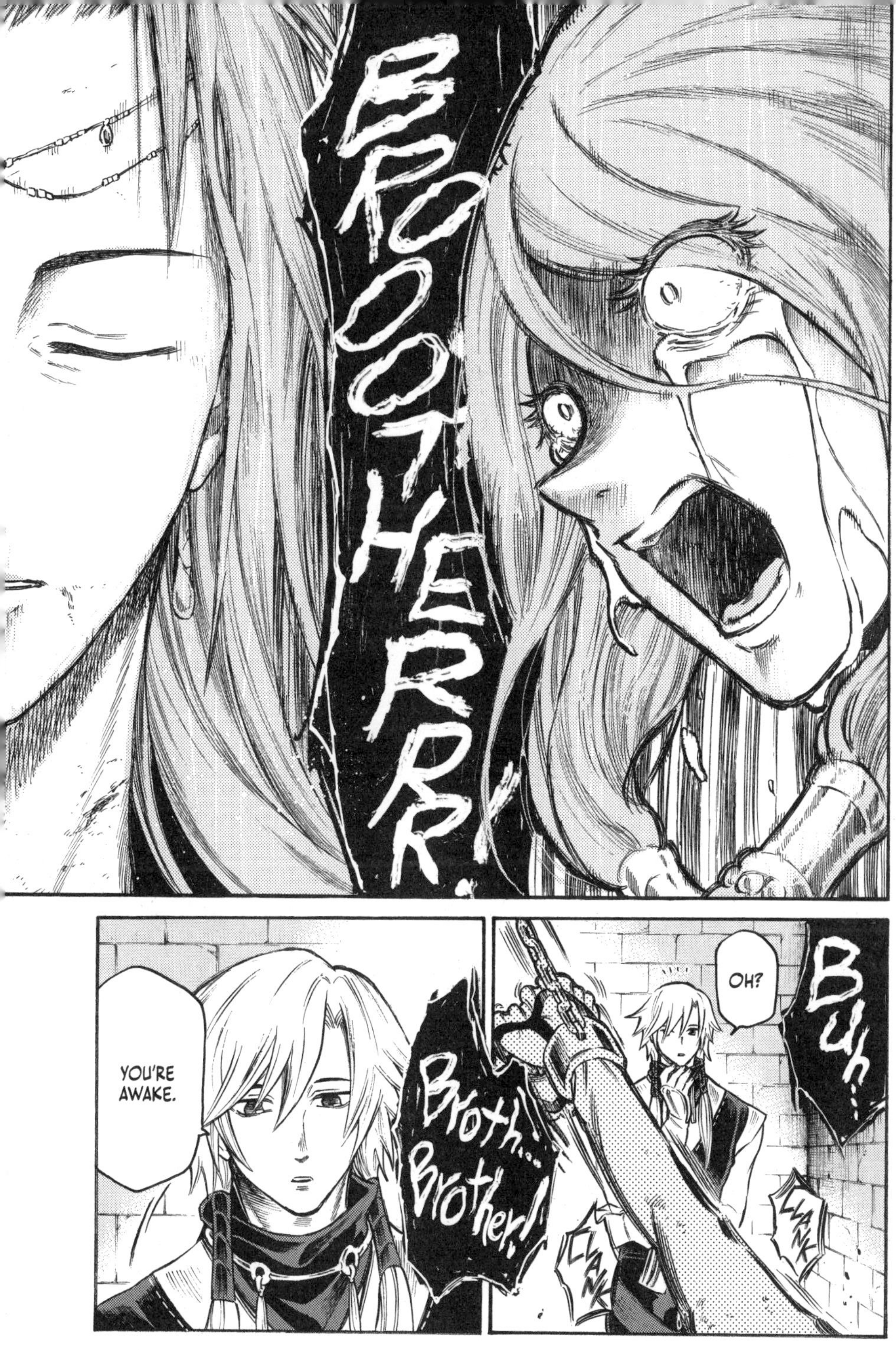
BROOOTHERRR!
OH?
Buh...
Broth... Brother!
CLANK
CLANK
YOU'RE AWAKE.

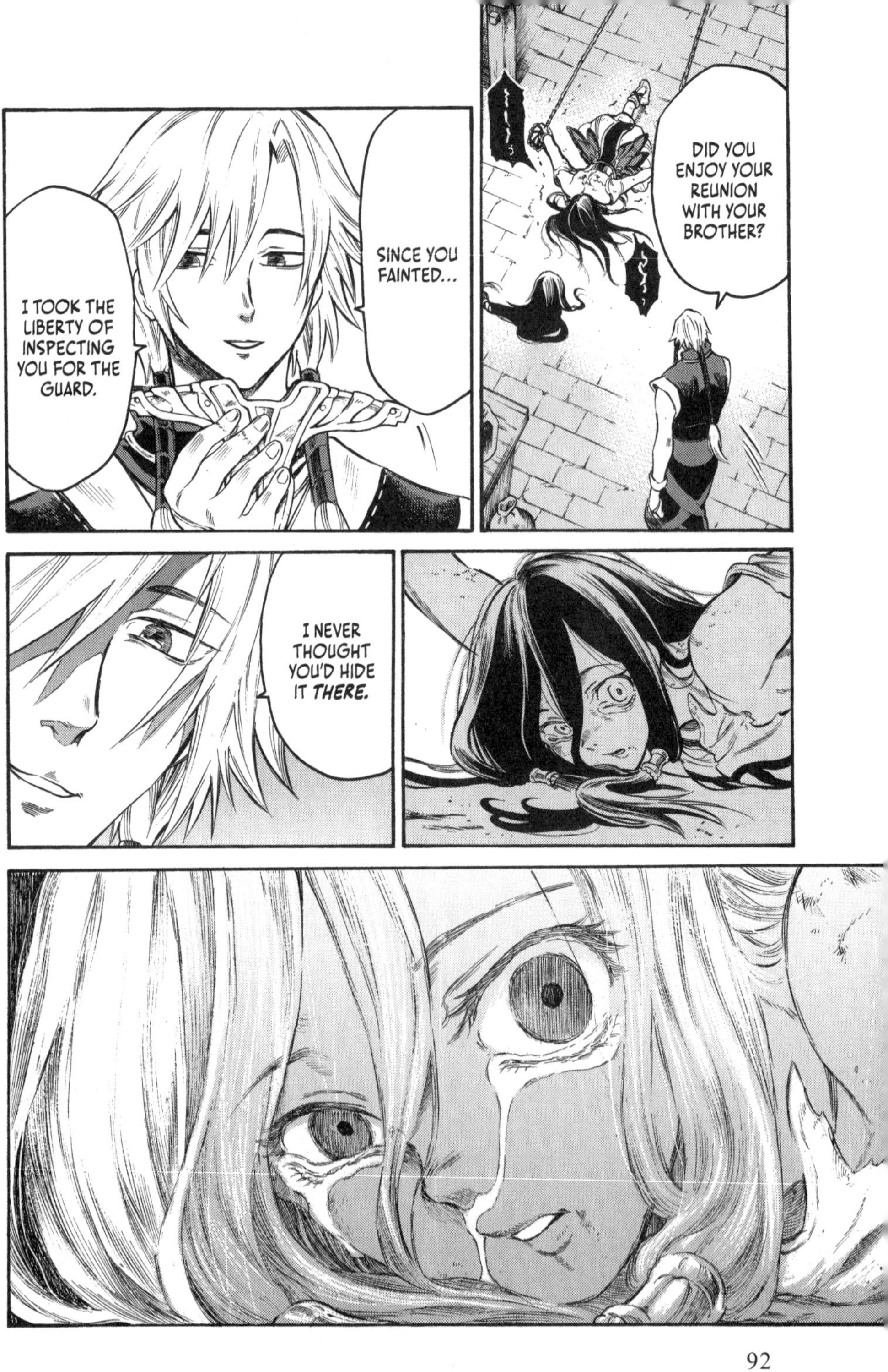
DID YOU ENJOY YOUR REUNION WITH YOUR BROTHER?
SINCE YOU FAINTED...
I TOOK THE LIBERTY OF INSPECTING YOU FOR THE GUARD.
I NEVER THOUGHT YOU'D HIDE IT *THERE.*

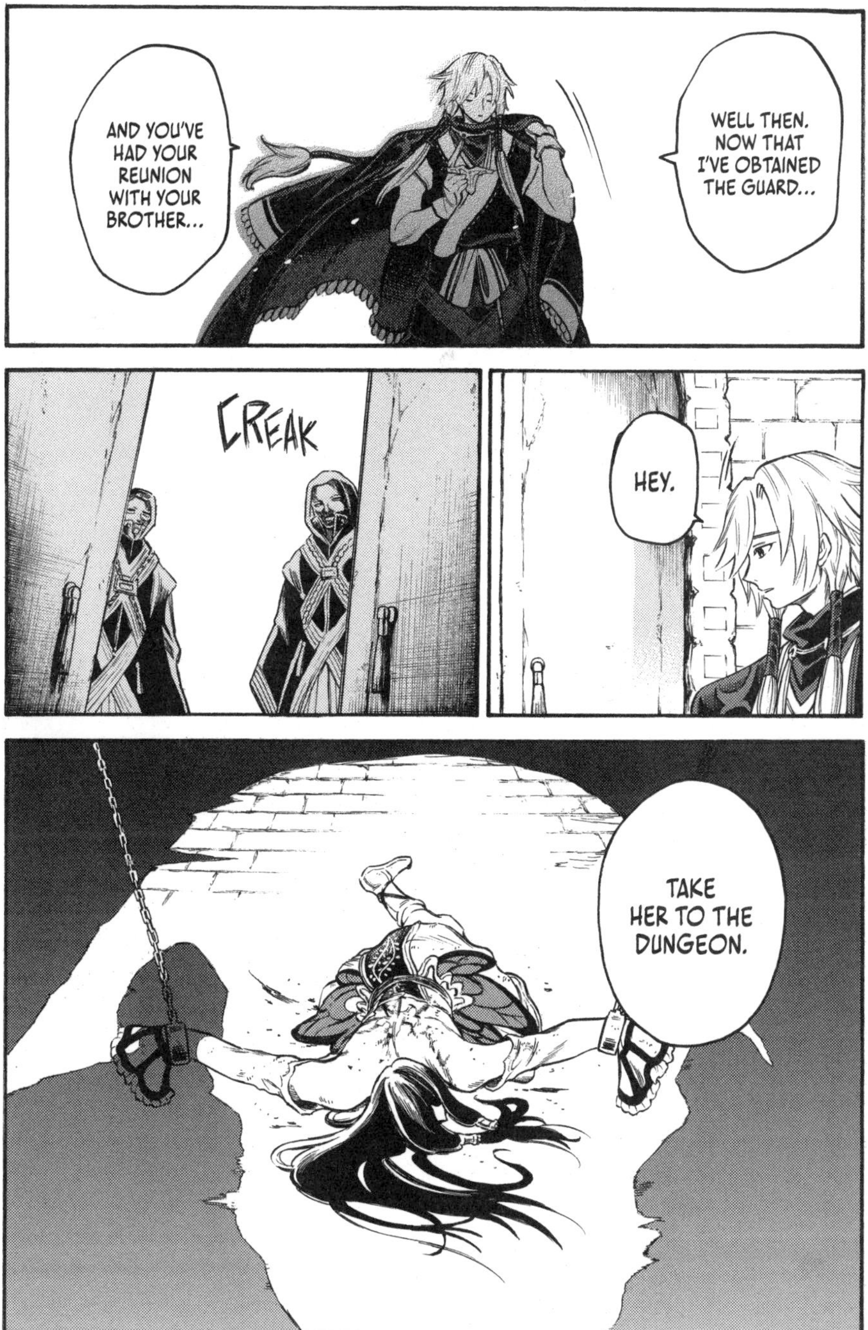
WELL THEN. NOW THAT I'VE OBTAINED THE GUARD...
AND YOU'VE HAD YOUR REUNION WITH YOUR BROTHER...
HEY.
CREAK
TAKE HER TO THE DUNGEON.

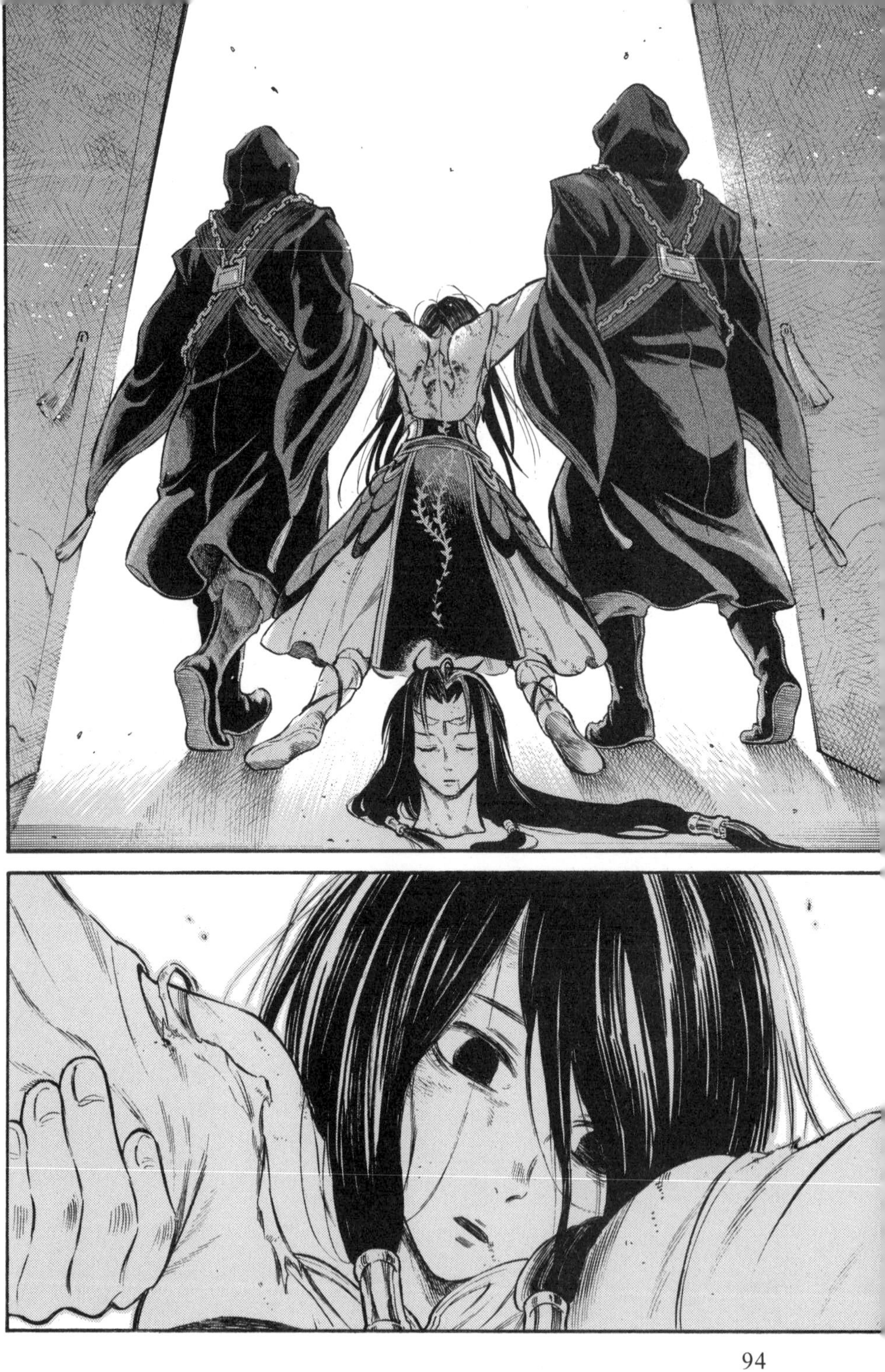

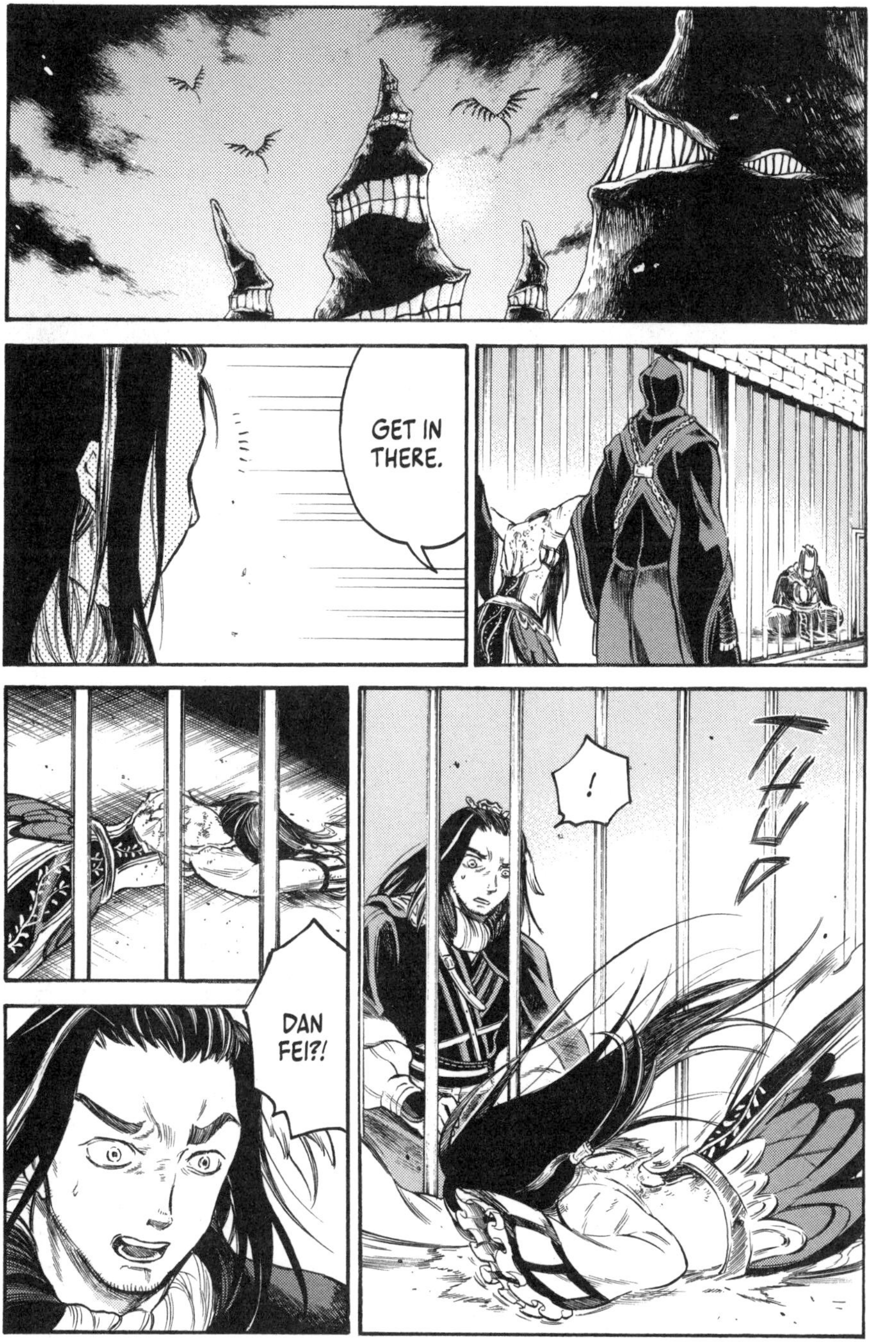
GET IN THERE.
!
THUD
DAN FEI?!

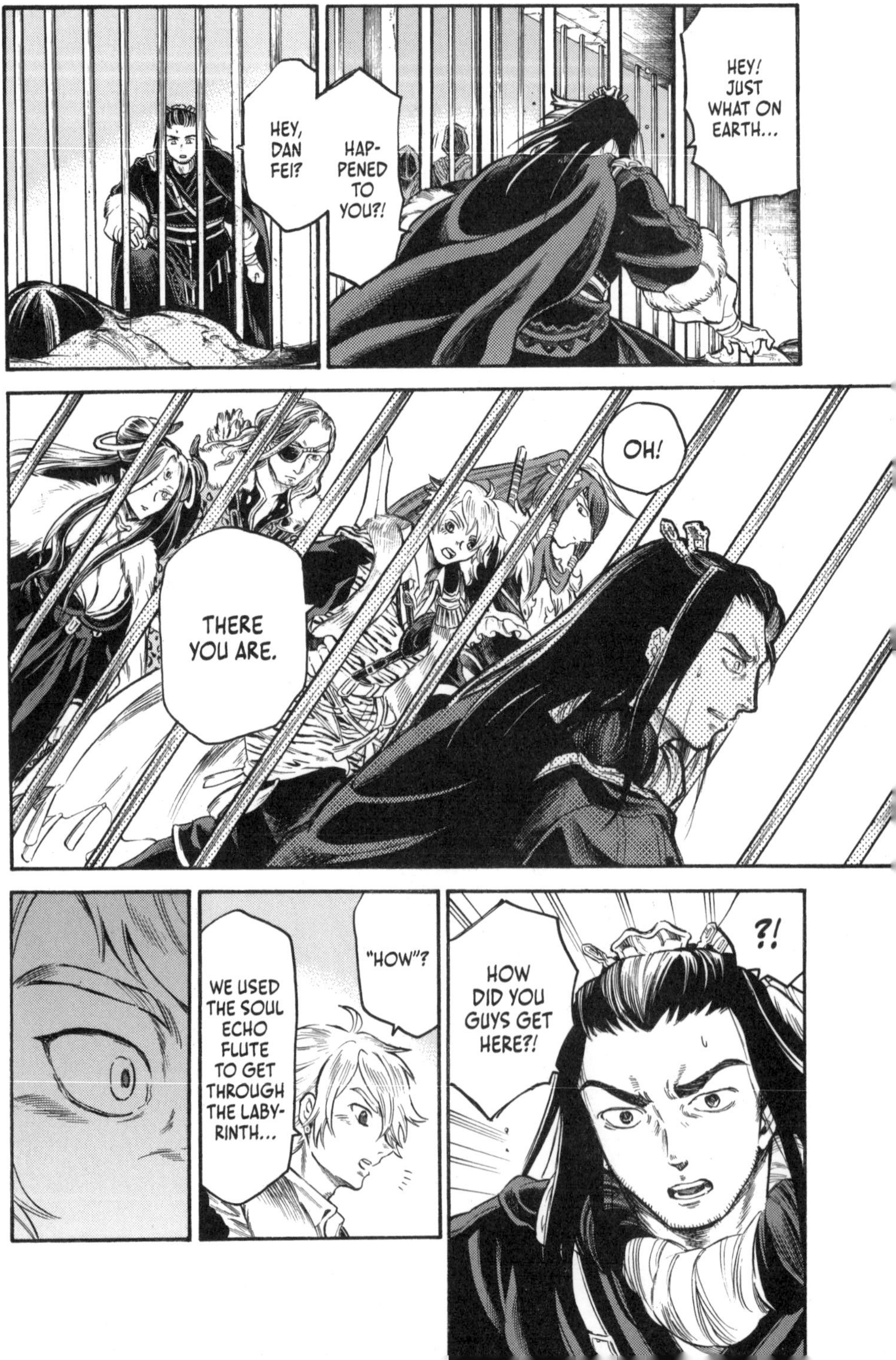
HEY! JUST WHAT ON EARTH...
HAP-PENED TO YOU?!
HEY, DAN FEI?
OH!
THERE YOU ARE.
?!
HOW DID YOU GUYS GET HERE?!
"HOW"?
WE USED THE SOUL ECHO FLUTE TO GET THROUGH THE LABY-RINTH...

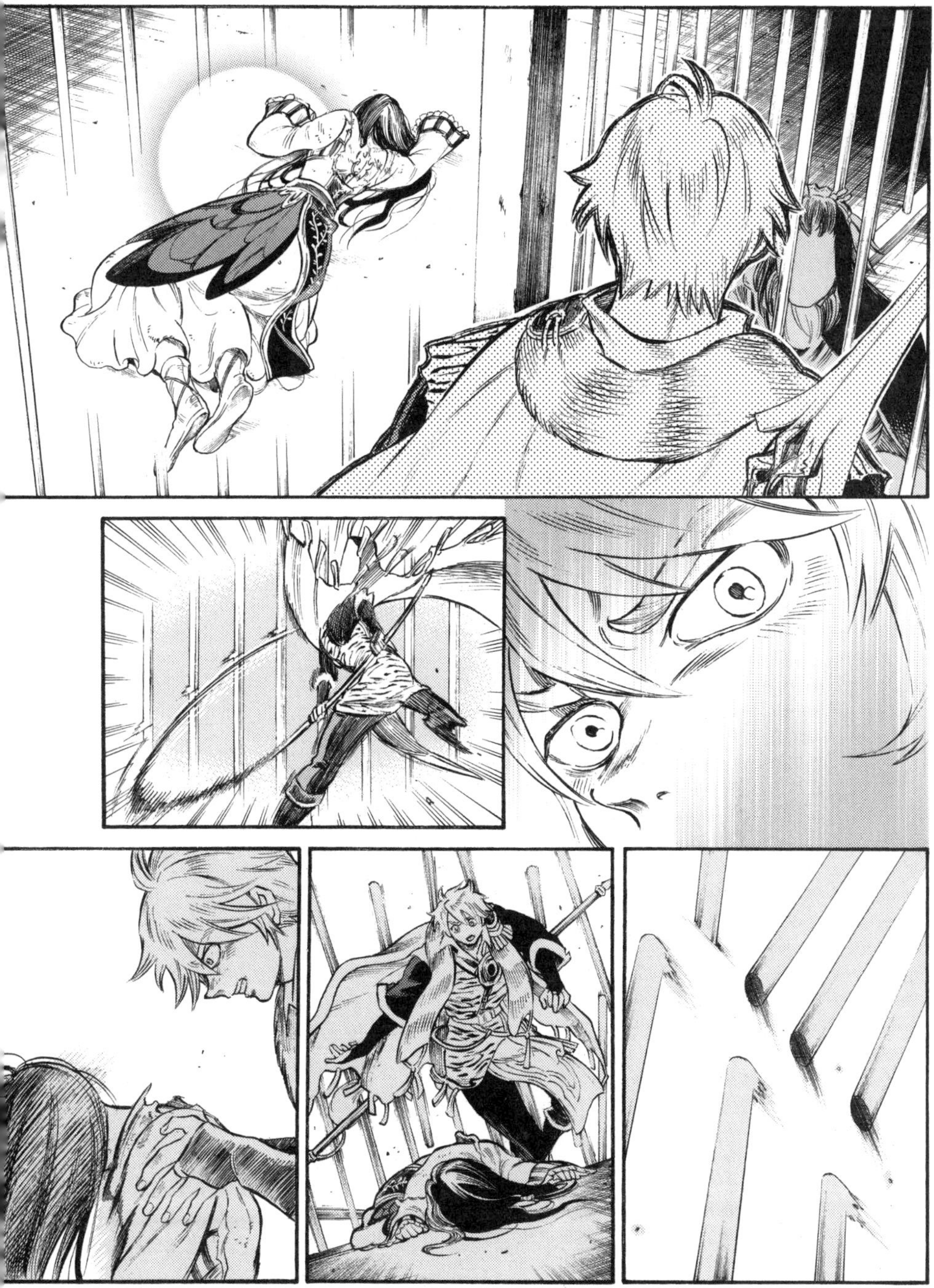

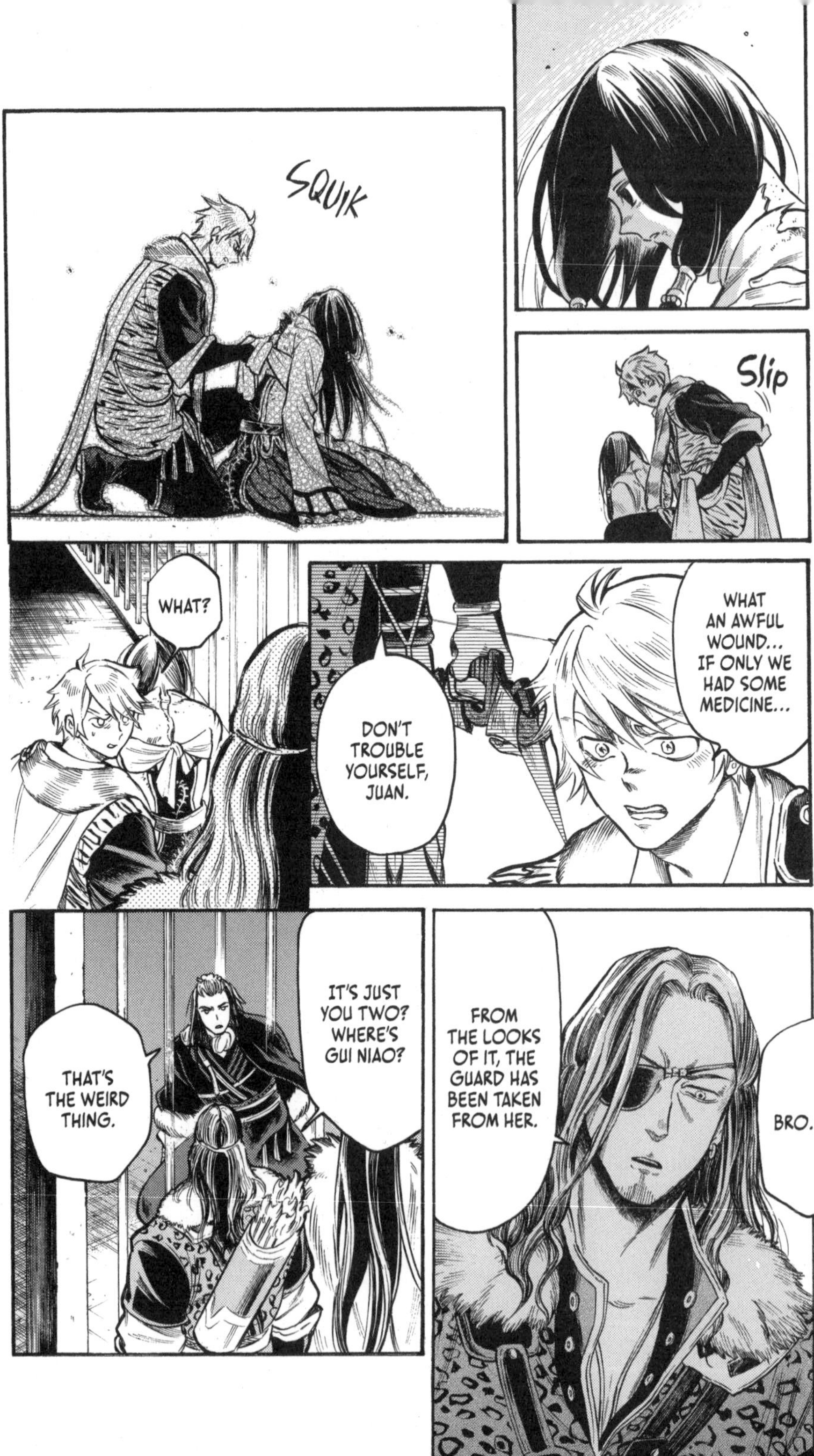
Slip
SQUIK
WHAT AN AWFUL WOUND... IF ONLY WE HAD SOME MEDICINE...
DON'T TROUBLE YOURSELF, JUAN.
WHAT?
BRO...?
FROM THE LOOKS OF IT, THE GUARD HAS BEEN TAKEN FROM HER.
IT'S JUST YOU TWO? WHERE'S GUI NIAO?
THAT'S THE WEIRD THING.

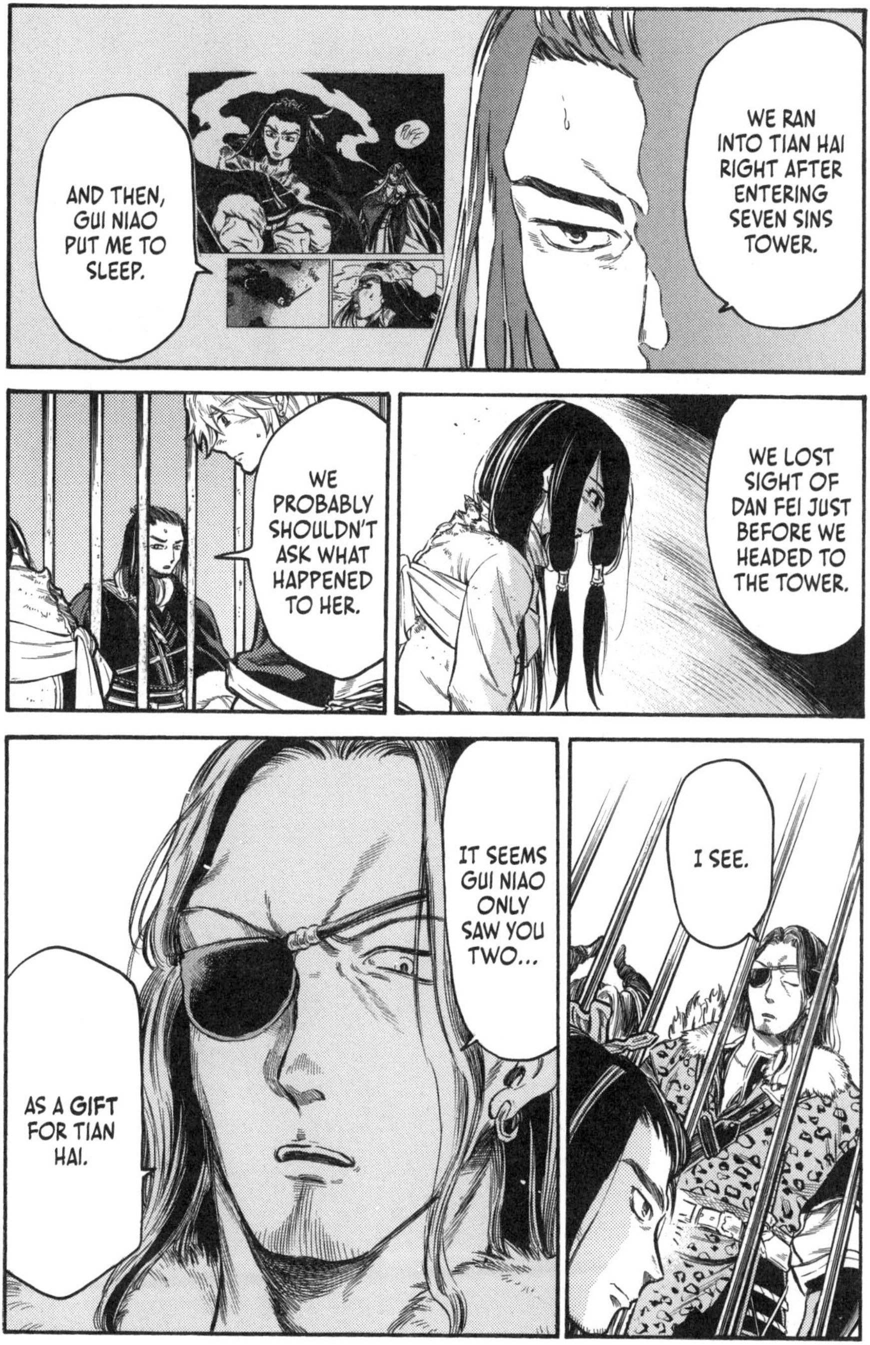
WE RAN INTO TIAN HAI RIGHT AFTER ENTERING SEVEN SINS TOWER.
AND THEN, GUI NIAO PUT ME TO SLEEP.
WE LOST SIGHT OF DAN FEI JUST BEFORE WE HEADED TO THE TOWER.
WE PROBABLY SHOULDN'T ASK WHAT HAPPENED TO HER.
I SEE.
IT SEEMS GUI NIAO ONLY SAW YOU TWO...
AS A GIFT FOR TIAN HAI.

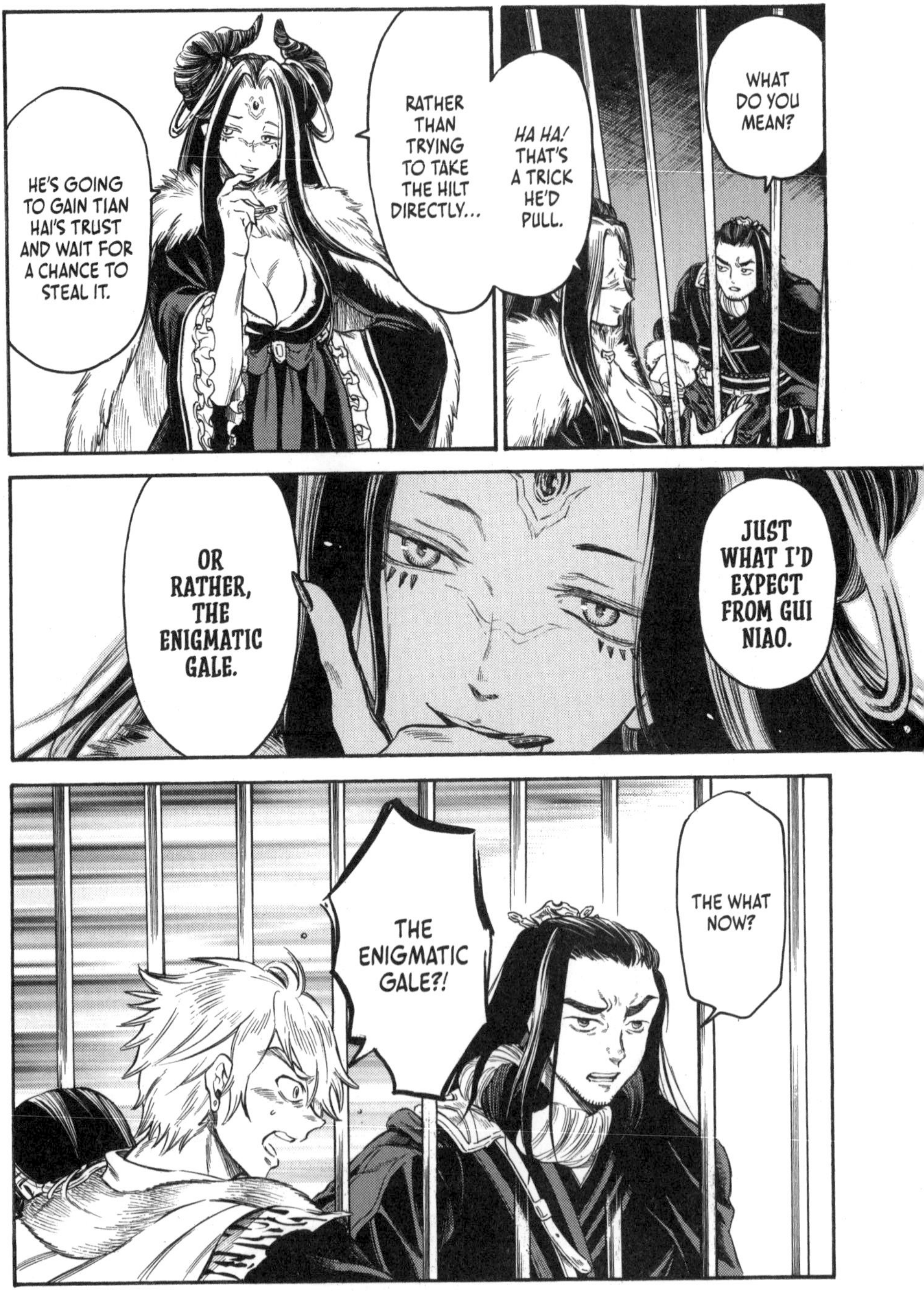
WHAT DO YOU MEAN?
HA HA! THAT'S A TRICK HE'D PULL.
RATHER THAN TRYING TO TAKE THE HILT DIRECTLY…
HE'S GOING TO GAIN TIAN HAI'S TRUST AND WAIT FOR A CHANCE TO STEAL IT.
JUST WHAT I'D EXPECT FROM GUI NIAO.
OR RATHER, THE ENIGMATIC GALE.
THE WHAT NOW?
THE ENIGMATIC GALE?!

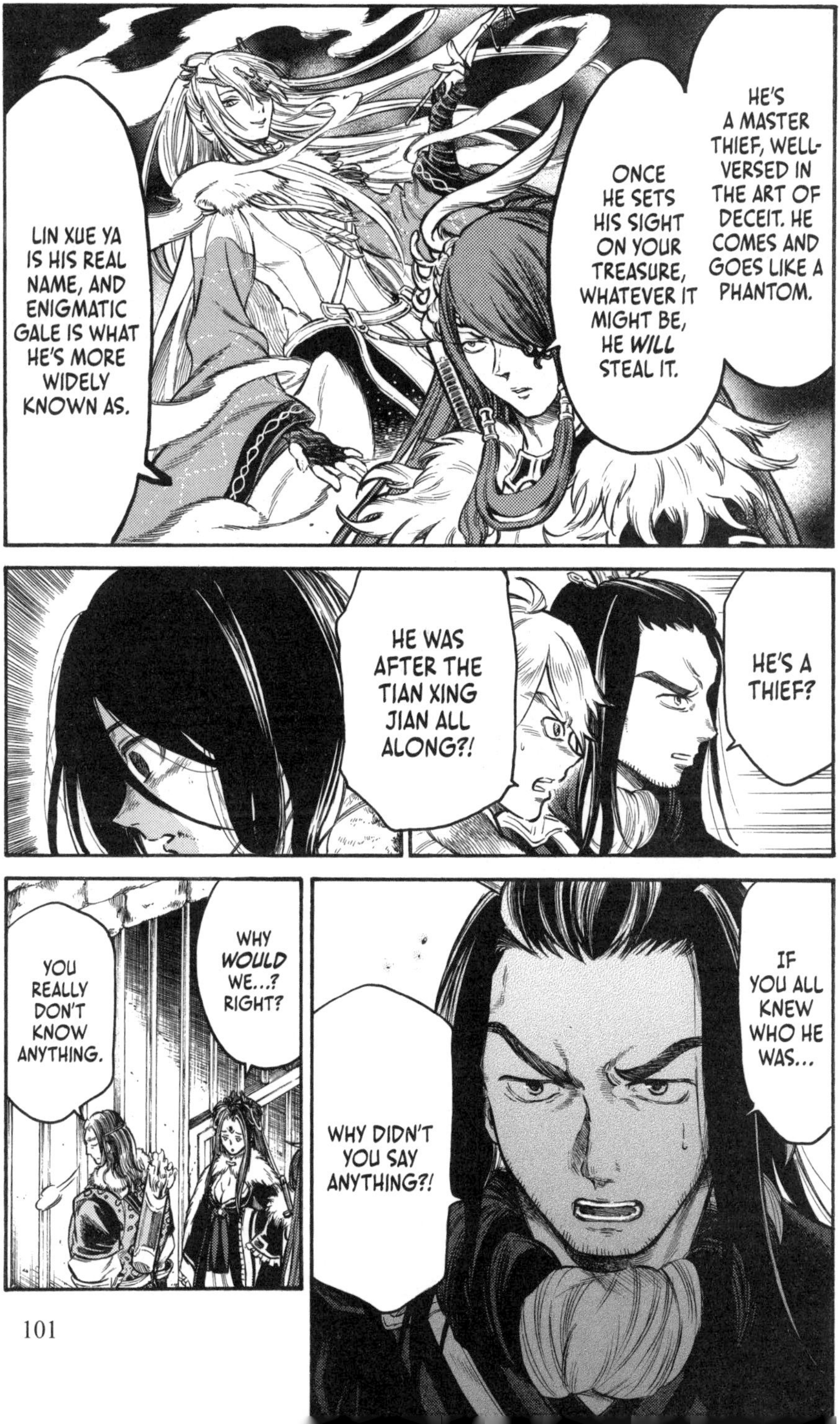
HE'S A MASTER THIEF, WELL-VERSED IN THE ART OF DECEIT. HE COMES AND GOES LIKE A PHANTOM.
ONCE HE SETS HIS SIGHT ON YOUR TREASURE, WHATEVER IT MIGHT BE, HE *WILL* STEAL IT.
LIN XUE YA IS HIS REAL NAME, AND ENIGMATIC GALE IS WHAT HE'S MORE WIDELY KNOWN AS.
HE'S A THIEF?
HE WAS AFTER THE TIAN XING JIAN ALL ALONG?!
IF YOU ALL KNEW WHO HE WAS...
WHY DIDN'T YOU SAY ANYTHING?!
WHY *WOULD* WE...? RIGHT?
YOU REALLY DON'T KNOW ANYTHING.

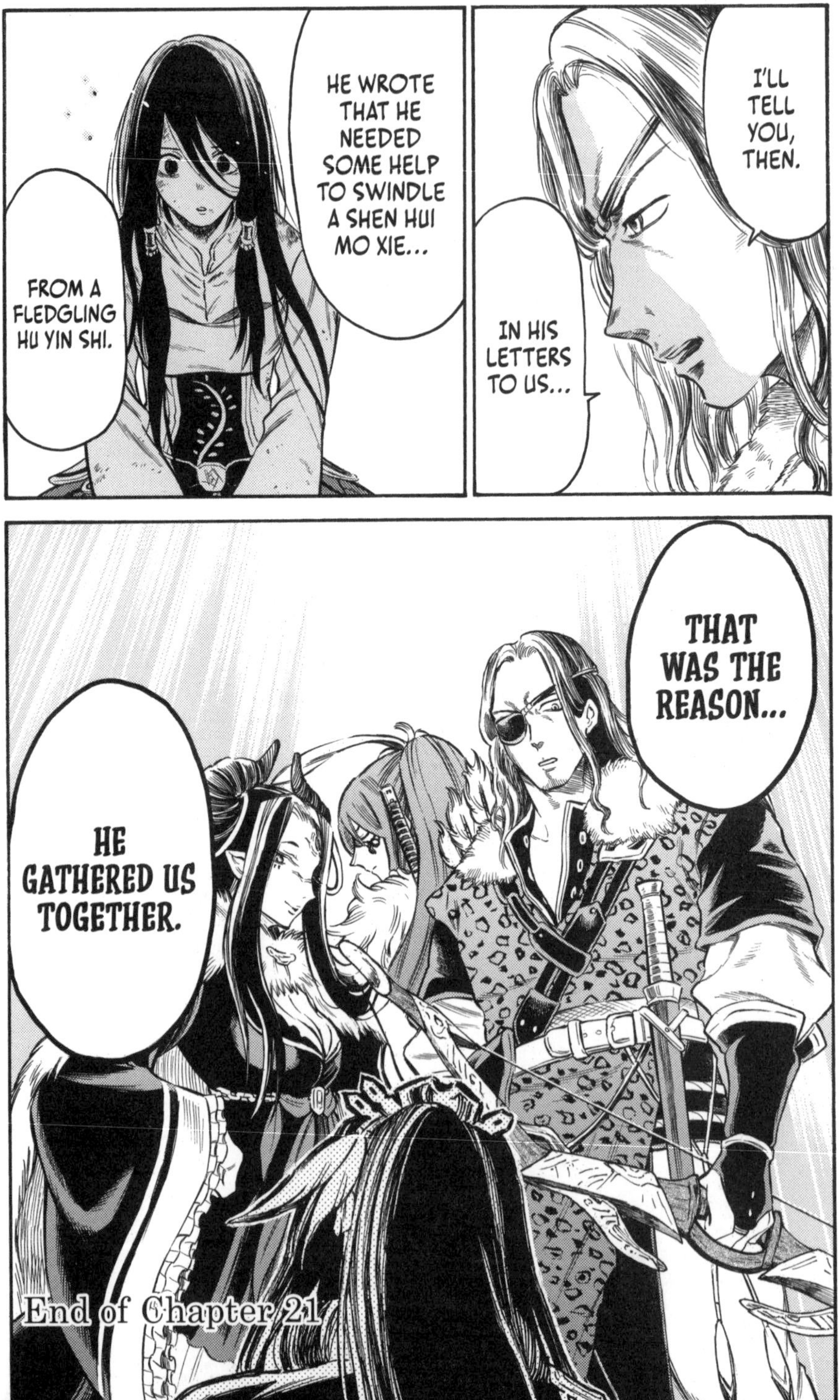
I'LL TELL YOU, THEN.
IN HIS LETTERS TO US...
HE WROTE THAT HE NEEDED SOME HELP TO SWINDLE A SHEN HUI MO XIE...
FROM A FLEDGLING HU YIN SHI.
THAT WAS THE REASON...
HE GATHERED US TOGETHER.
End of Chapter 21

∽ Chapter 22 ∽

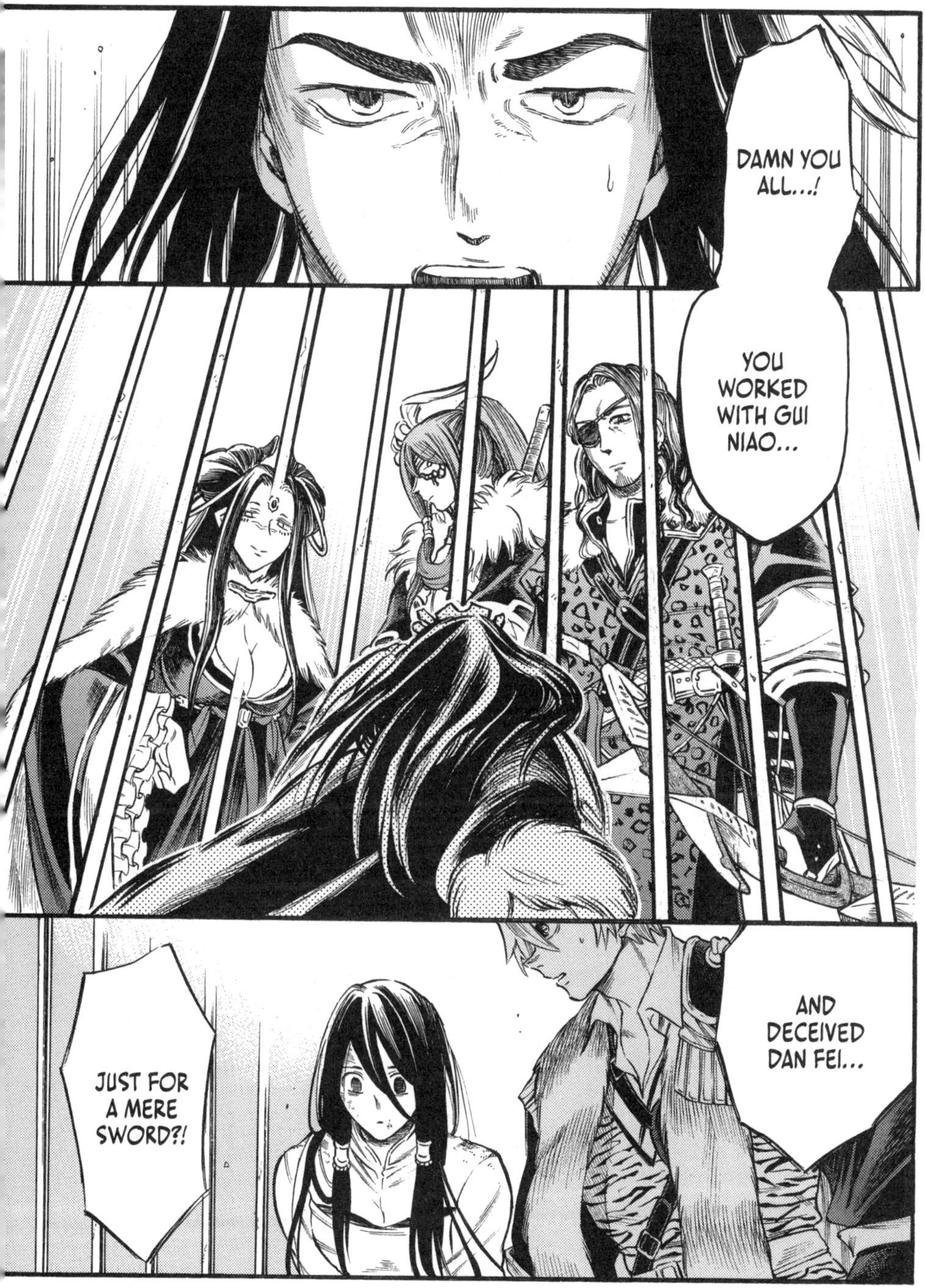
DAMN YOU ALL...!
YOU WORKED WITH GUI NIAO...
AND DECEIVED DAN FEI...
JUST FOR A MERE SWORD?!

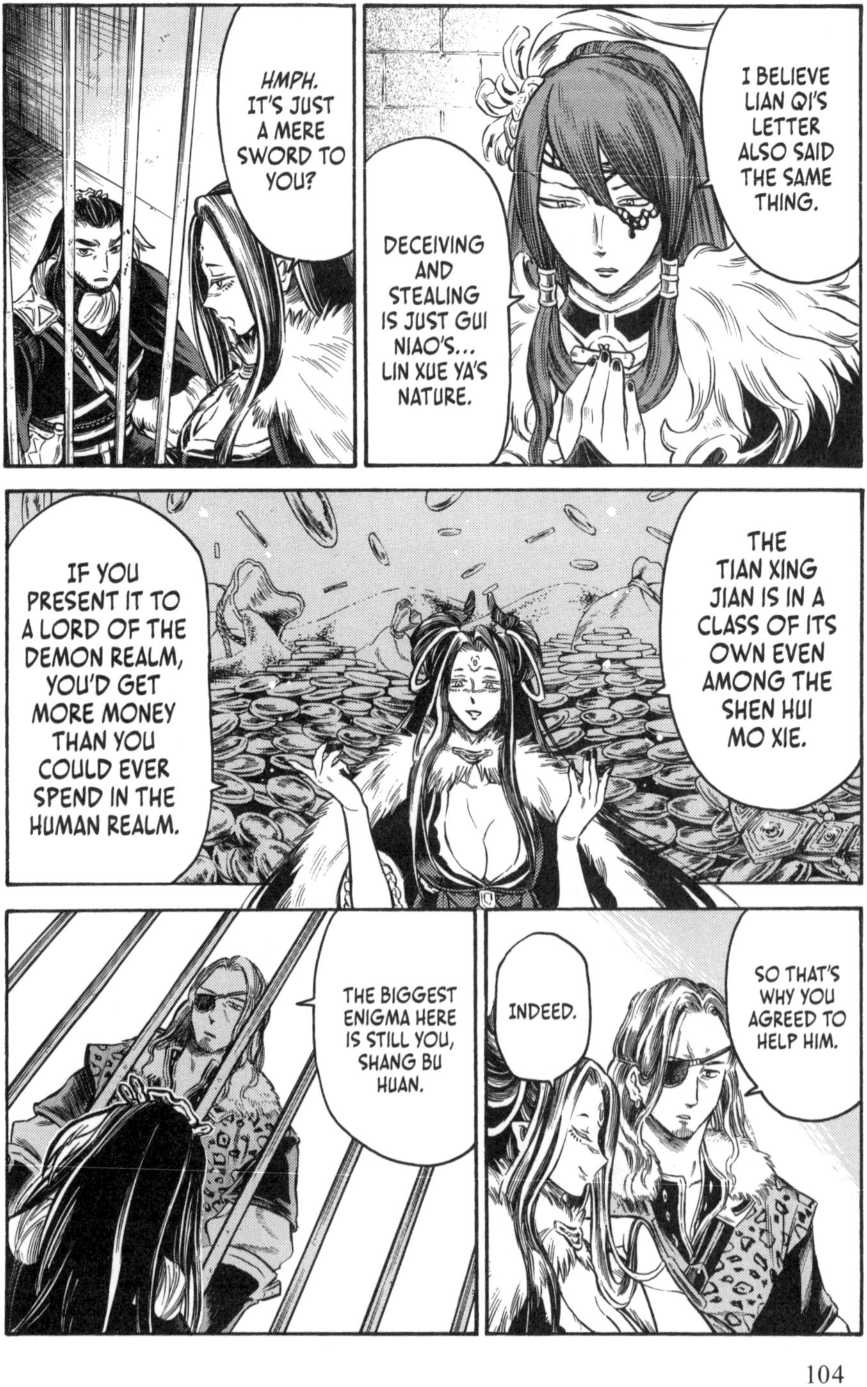
I BELIEVE LIAN QI'S LETTER ALSO SAID THE SAME THING.
DECEIVING AND STEALING IS JUST GUI NIAO'S... LIN XUE YA'S NATURE.
HMPH. IT'S JUST A MERE SWORD TO YOU?
THE TIAN XING JIAN IS IN A CLASS OF ITS OWN EVEN AMONG THE SHEN HUI MO XIE.
IF YOU PRESENT IT TO A LORD OF THE DEMON REALM, YOU'D GET MORE MONEY THAN YOU COULD EVER SPEND IN THE HUMAN REALM.
SO THAT'S WHY YOU AGREED TO HELP HIM.
INDEED.
THE BIGGEST ENIGMA HERE IS STILL YOU, SHANG BU HUAN.

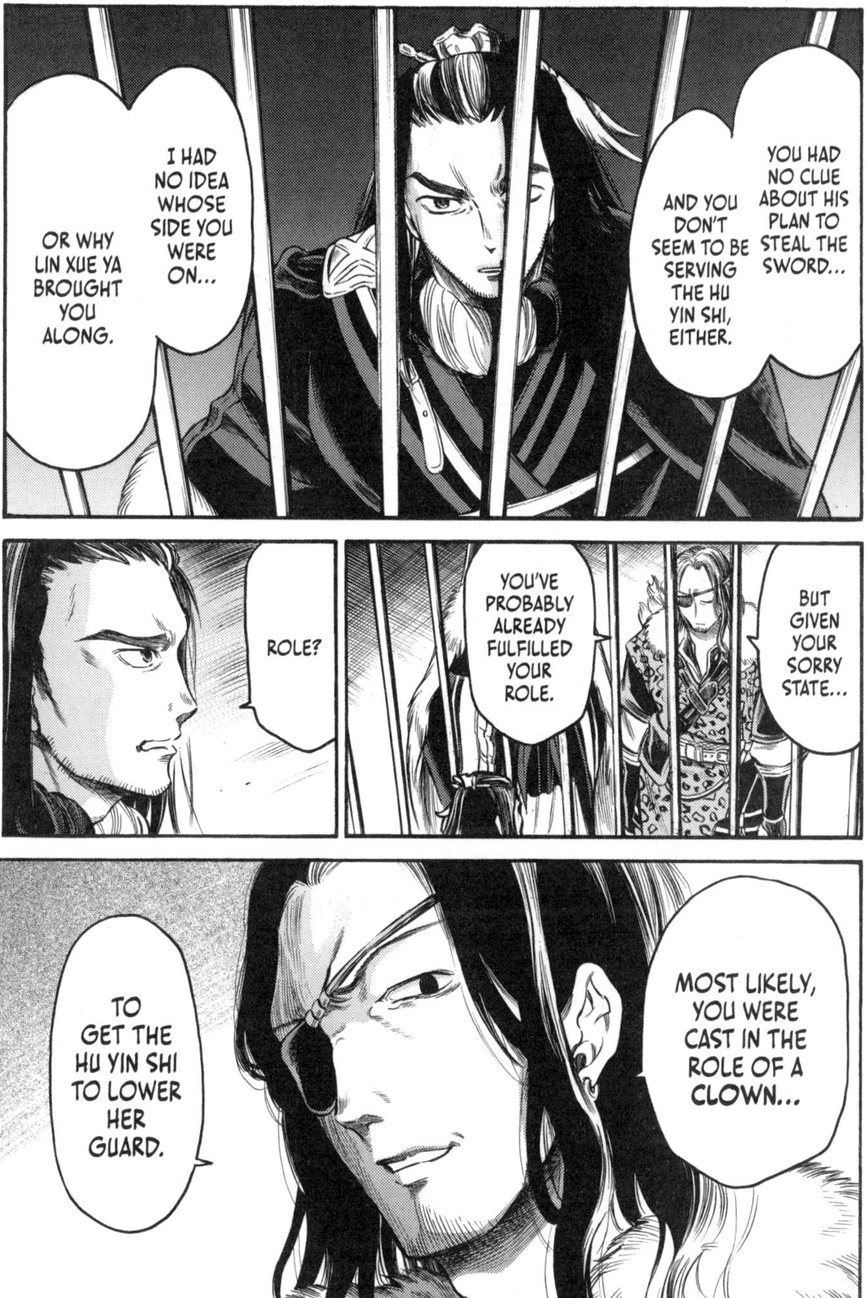
YOU HAD NO CLUE ABOUT HIS PLAN TO STEAL THE SWORD...
AND YOU DON'T SEEM TO BE SERVING THE HU YIN SHI, EITHER.
I HAD NO IDEA WHOSE SIDE YOU WERE ON...
OR WHY LIN XUE YA BROUGHT YOU ALONG.
BUT GIVEN YOUR SORRY STATE...
YOU'VE PROBABLY ALREADY FULFILLED YOUR ROLE.
ROLE?
MOST LIKELY, YOU WERE CAST IN THE ROLE OF A CLOWN...
TO GET THE HU YIN SHI TO LOWER HER GUARD.

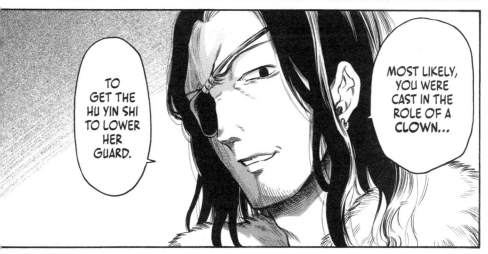

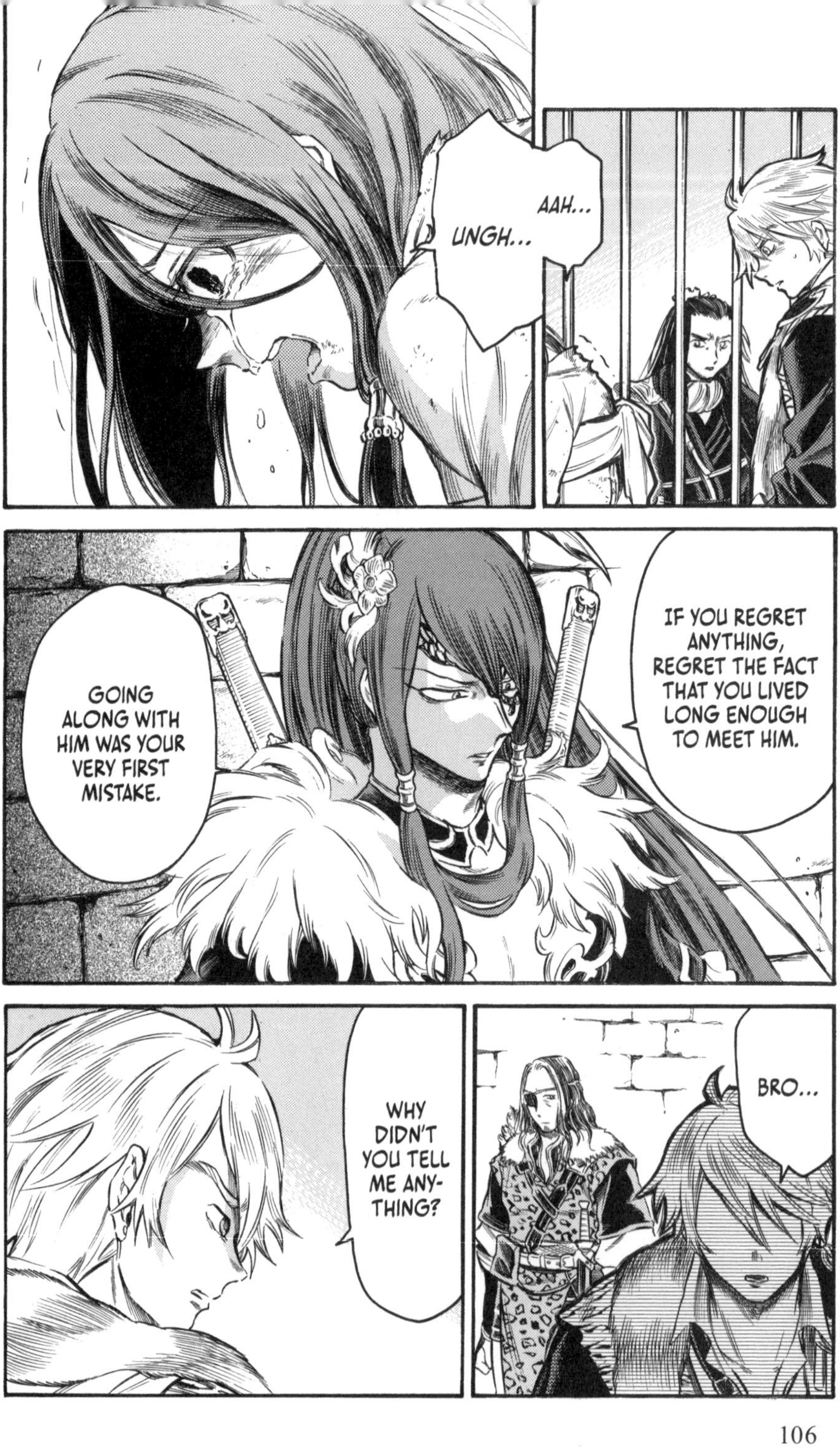
AAH... UNGH...
IF YOU REGRET ANYTHING, REGRET THE FACT THAT YOU LIVED LONG ENOUGH TO MEET HIM.
GOING ALONG WITH HIM WAS YOUR VERY FIRST MISTAKE.
BRO...
WHY DIDN'T YOU TELL ME ANY-THING?

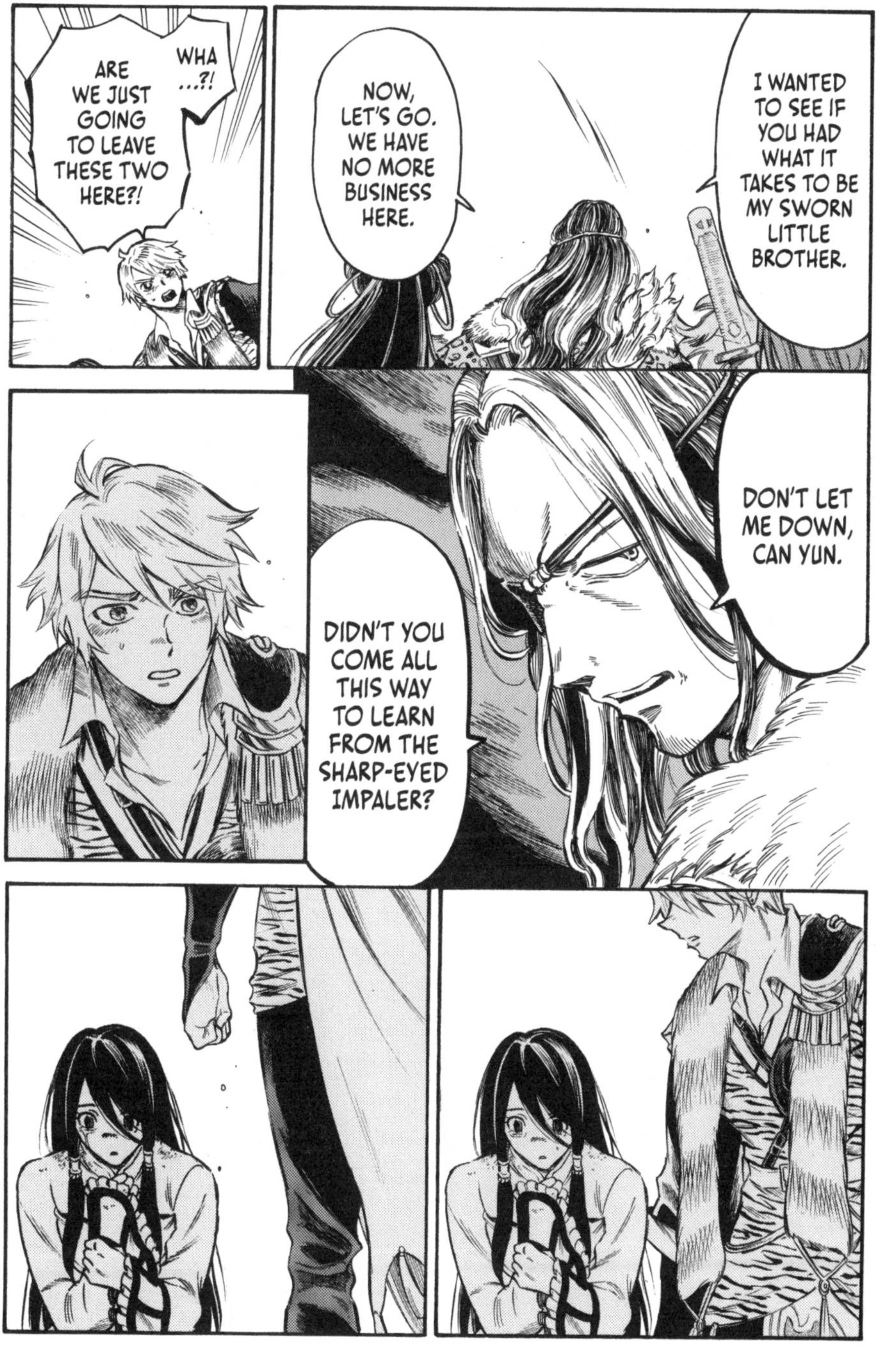
I WANTED TO SEE IF YOU HAD WHAT IT TAKES TO BE MY SWORN LITTLE BROTHER.
NOW, LET'S GO. WE HAVE NO MORE BUSINESS HERE.
WHA ...?!
ARE WE JUST GOING TO LEAVE THESE TWO HERE?!
DON'T LET ME DOWN, CAN YUN.
DIDN'T YOU COME ALL THIS WAY TO LEARN FROM THE SHARP-EYED IMPALER?

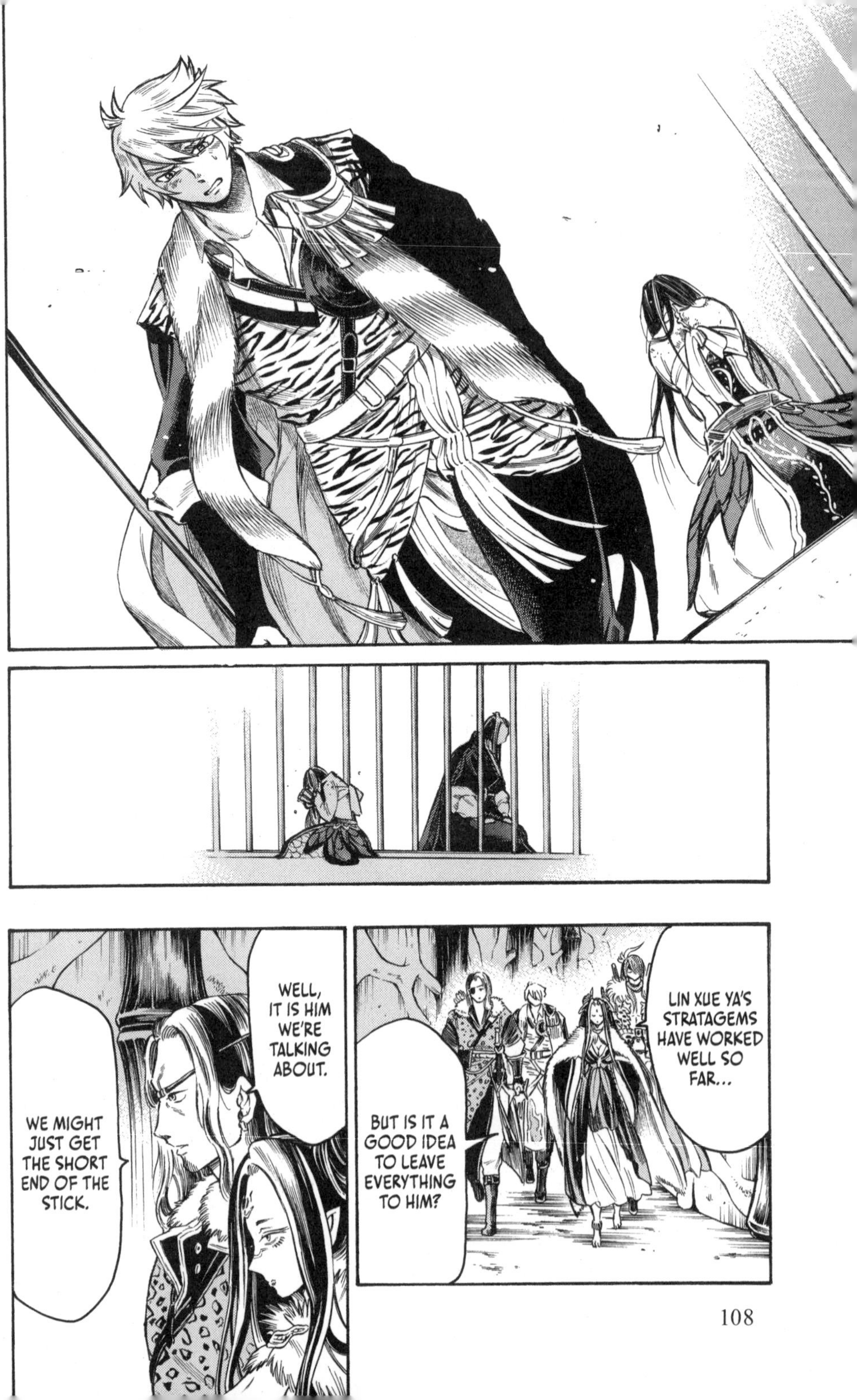
LIN XUE YA'S STRATAGEMS HAVE WORKED WELL SO FAR...
BUT IS IT A GOOD IDEA TO LEAVE EVERYTHING TO HIM?
WELL, IT IS HIM WE'RE TALKING ABOUT.
WE MIGHT JUST GET THE SHORT END OF THE STICK.

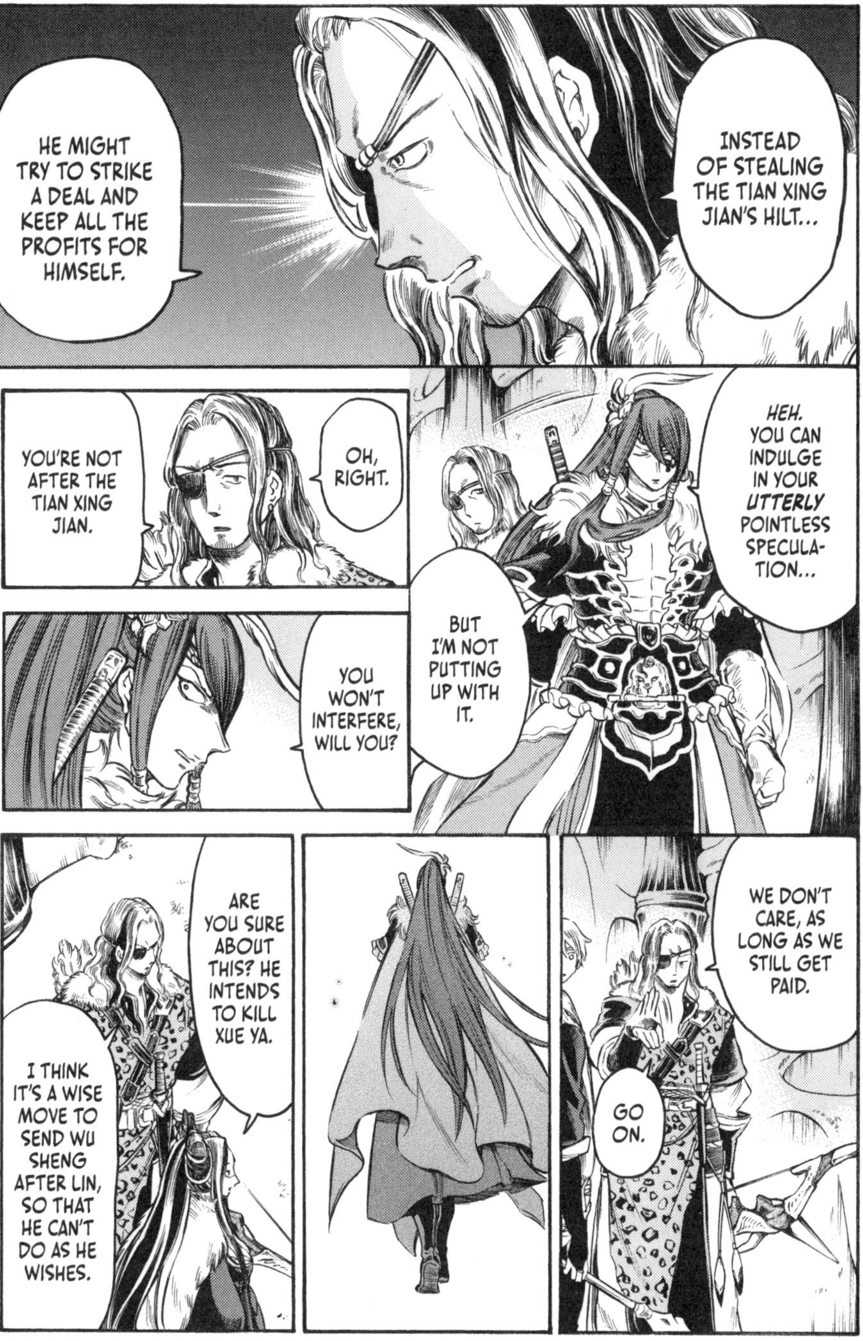
INSTEAD OF STEALING THE TIAN XING JIAN'S HILT...
HE MIGHT TRY TO STRIKE A DEAL AND KEEP ALL THE PROFITS FOR HIMSELF.
HEH. YOU CAN INDULGE IN YOUR ***UTTERLY*** POINTLESS SPECULA-TION...
BUT I'M NOT PUTTING UP WITH IT.
OH, RIGHT.
YOU'RE NOT AFTER THE TIAN XING JIAN.
YOU WON'T INTERFERE, WILL YOU?
WE DON'T CARE, AS LONG AS WE STILL GET PAID.
GO ON.
ARE YOU SURE ABOUT THIS? HE INTENDS TO KILL XUE YA.
I THINK IT'S A WISE MOVE TO SEND WU SHENG AFTER LIN, SO THAT HE CAN'T DO AS HE WISHES.

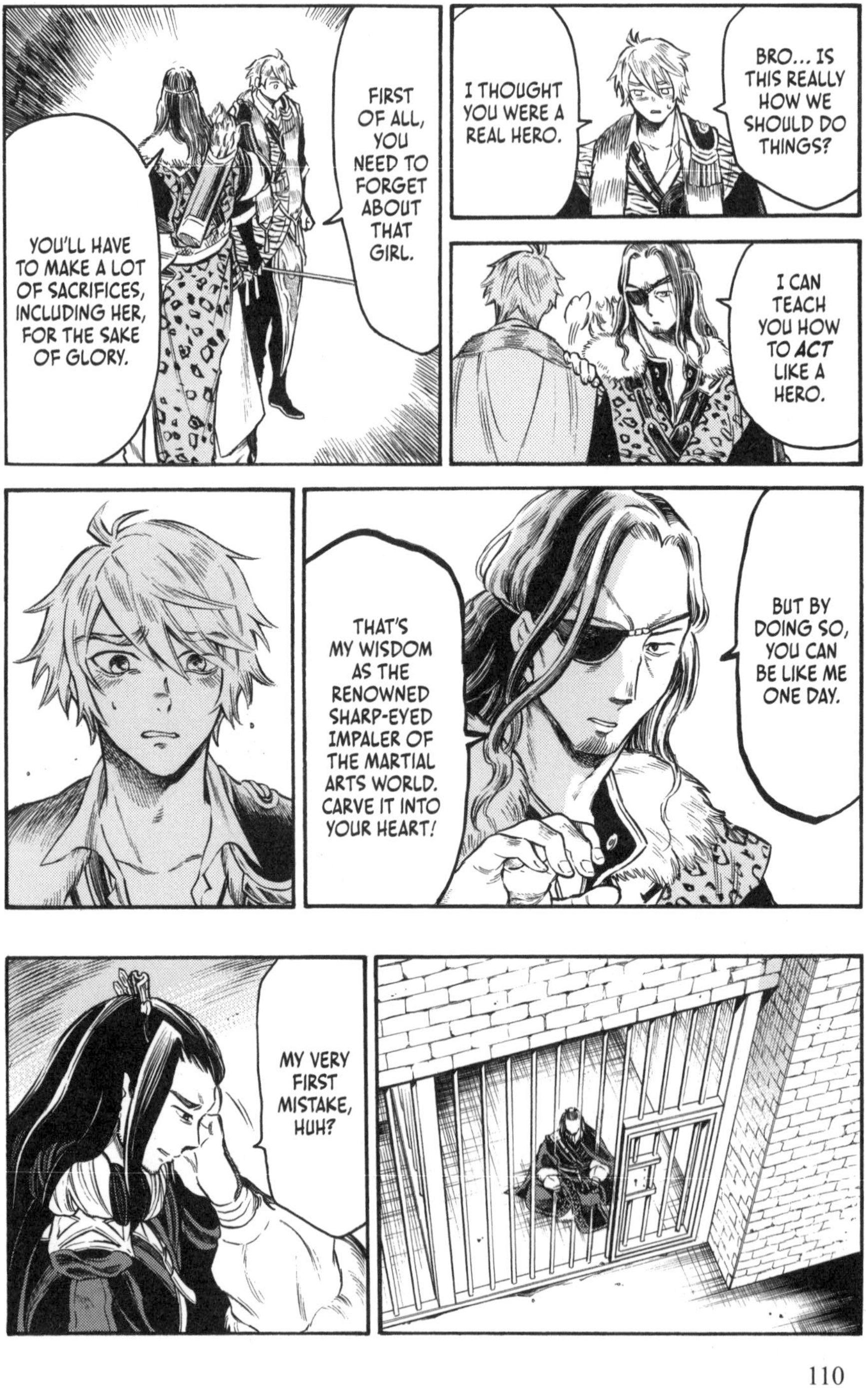
BRO... IS THIS REALLY HOW WE SHOULD DO THINGS?
I THOUGHT YOU WERE A REAL HERO.
I CAN TEACH YOU HOW TO ACT LIKE A HERO.
FIRST OF ALL, YOU NEED TO FORGET ABOUT THAT GIRL.
YOU'LL HAVE TO MAKE A LOT OF SACRIFICES, INCLUDING HER, FOR THE SAKE OF GLORY.
BUT BY DOING SO, YOU CAN BE LIKE ME ONE DAY.
THAT'S MY WISDOM AS THE RENOWNED SHARP-EYED IMPALER OF THE MARTIAL ARTS WORLD. CARVE IT INTO YOUR HEART!
MY VERY FIRST MISTAKE, HUH?

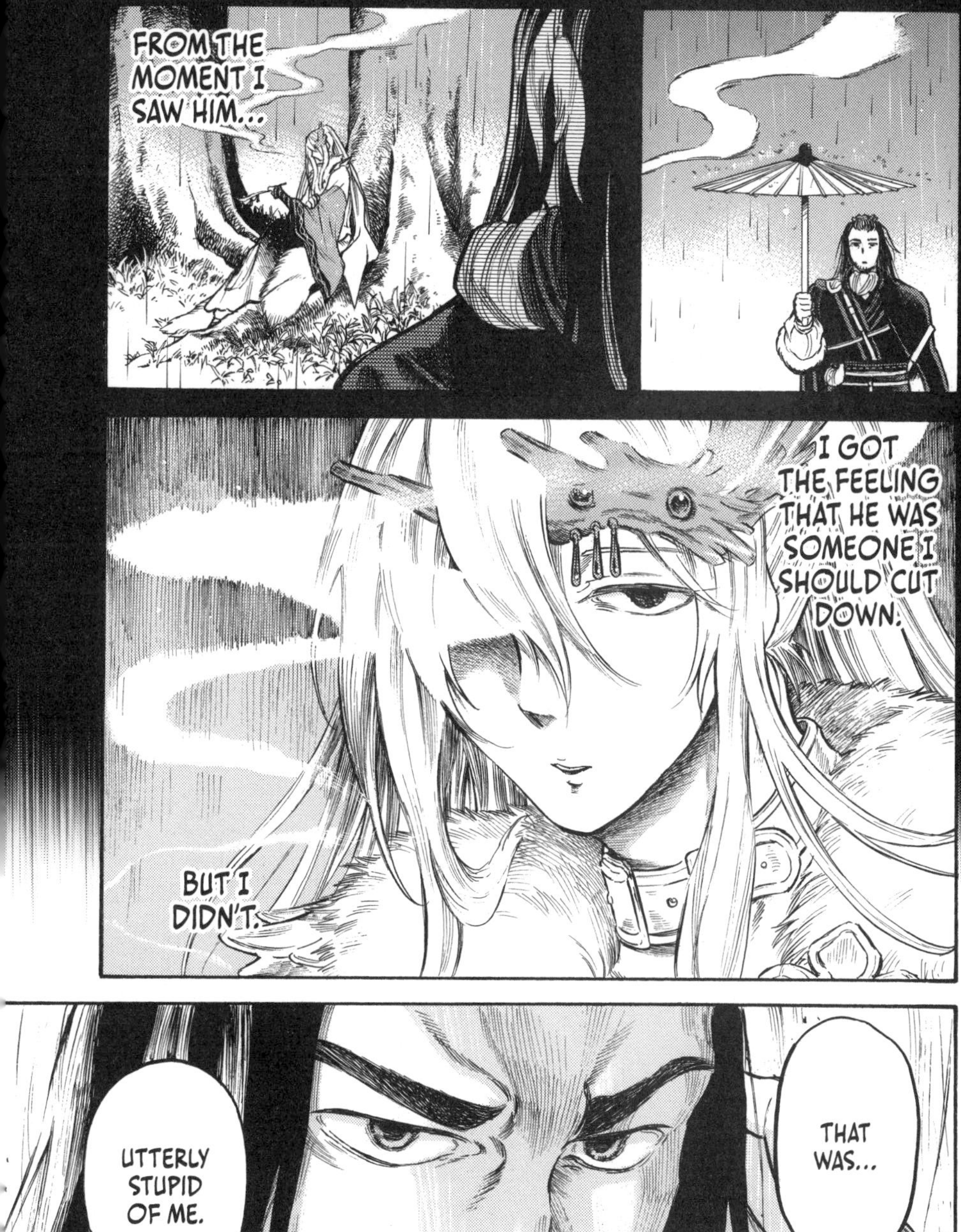
FROM THE MOMENT I SAW HIM...
I GOT THE FEELING THAT HE WAS SOMEONE I SHOULD CUT DOWN.
BUT I DIDN'T.
THAT WAS...
UTTERLY STUPID OF ME.

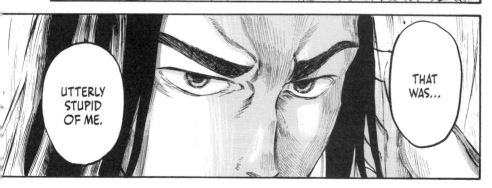

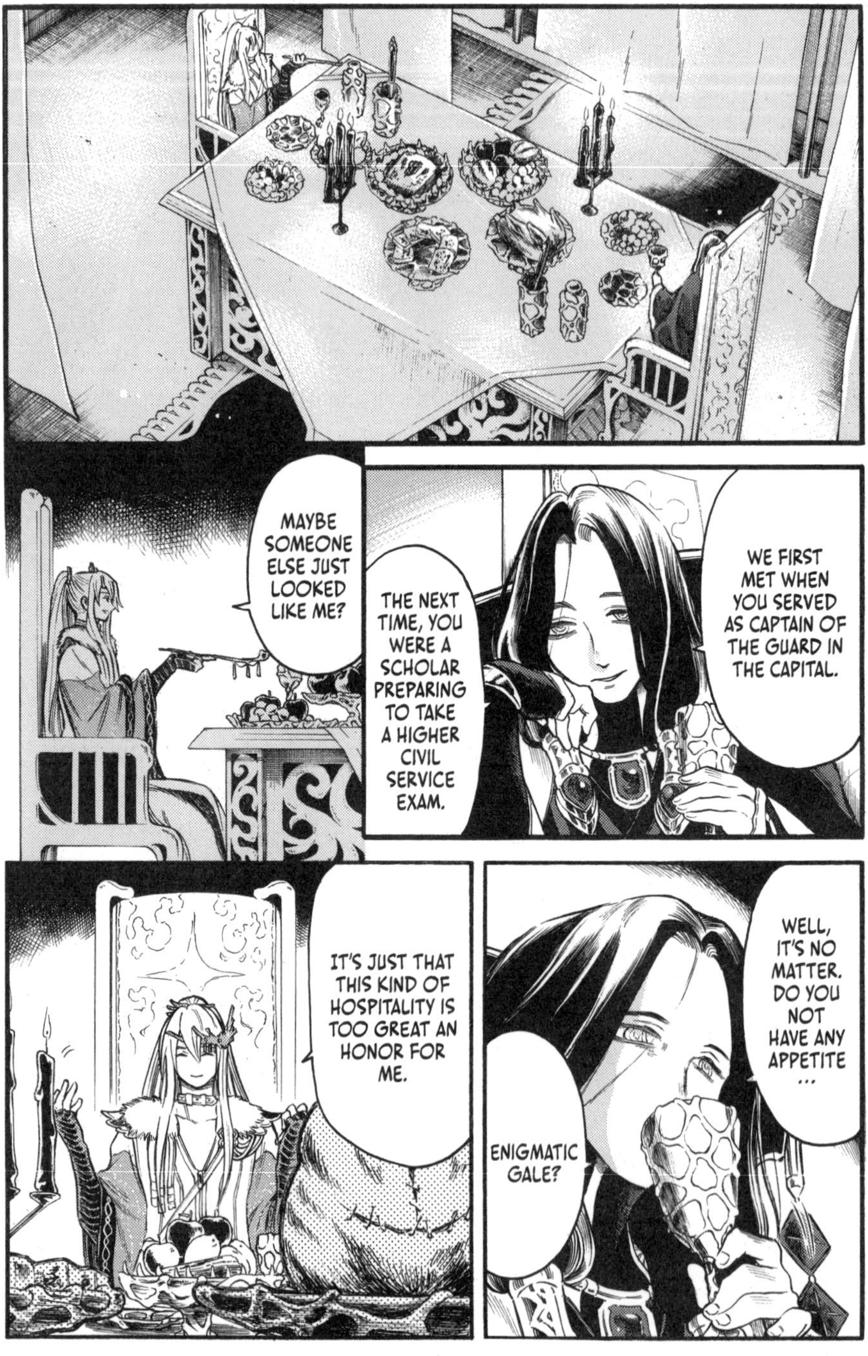
WE FIRST MET WHEN YOU SERVED AS CAPTAIN OF THE GUARD IN THE CAPITAL.
THE NEXT TIME, YOU WERE A SCHOLAR PREPARING TO TAKE A HIGHER CIVIL SERVICE EXAM.
MAYBE SOMEONE ELSE JUST LOOKED LIKE ME?
WELL, IT'S NO MATTER. DO YOU NOT HAVE ANY APPETITE...
ENIGMATIC GALE?
IT'S JUST THAT THIS KIND OF HOSPITALITY IS TOO GREAT AN HONOR FOR ME.

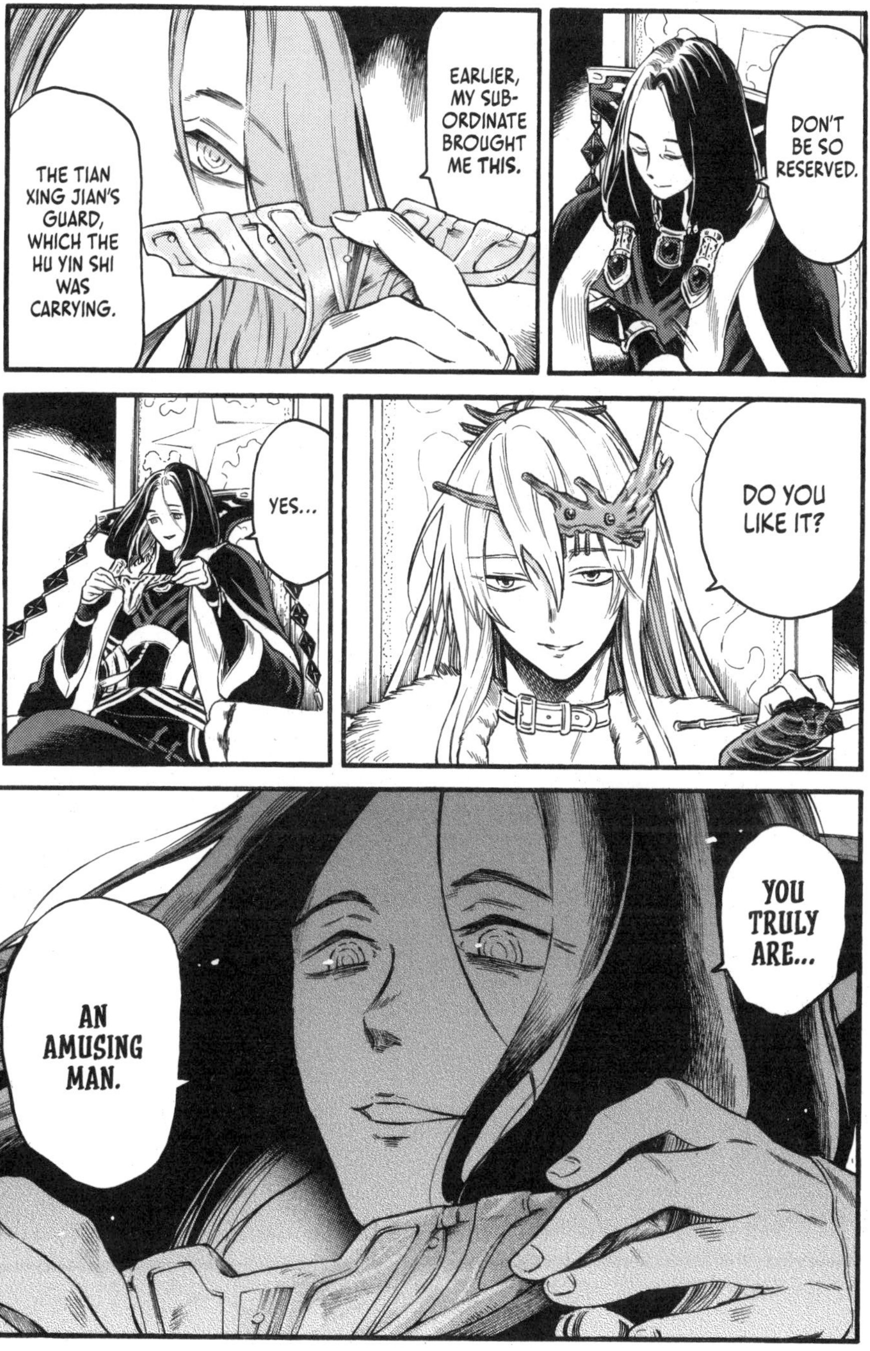
DON'T BE SO RESERVED.
EARLIER, MY SUB-ORDINATE BROUGHT ME THIS.
THE TIAN XING JIAN'S GUARD, WHICH THE HU YIN SHI WAS CARRYING.
DO YOU LIKE IT?
YES...
YOU TRULY ARE...
AN AMUSING MAN.

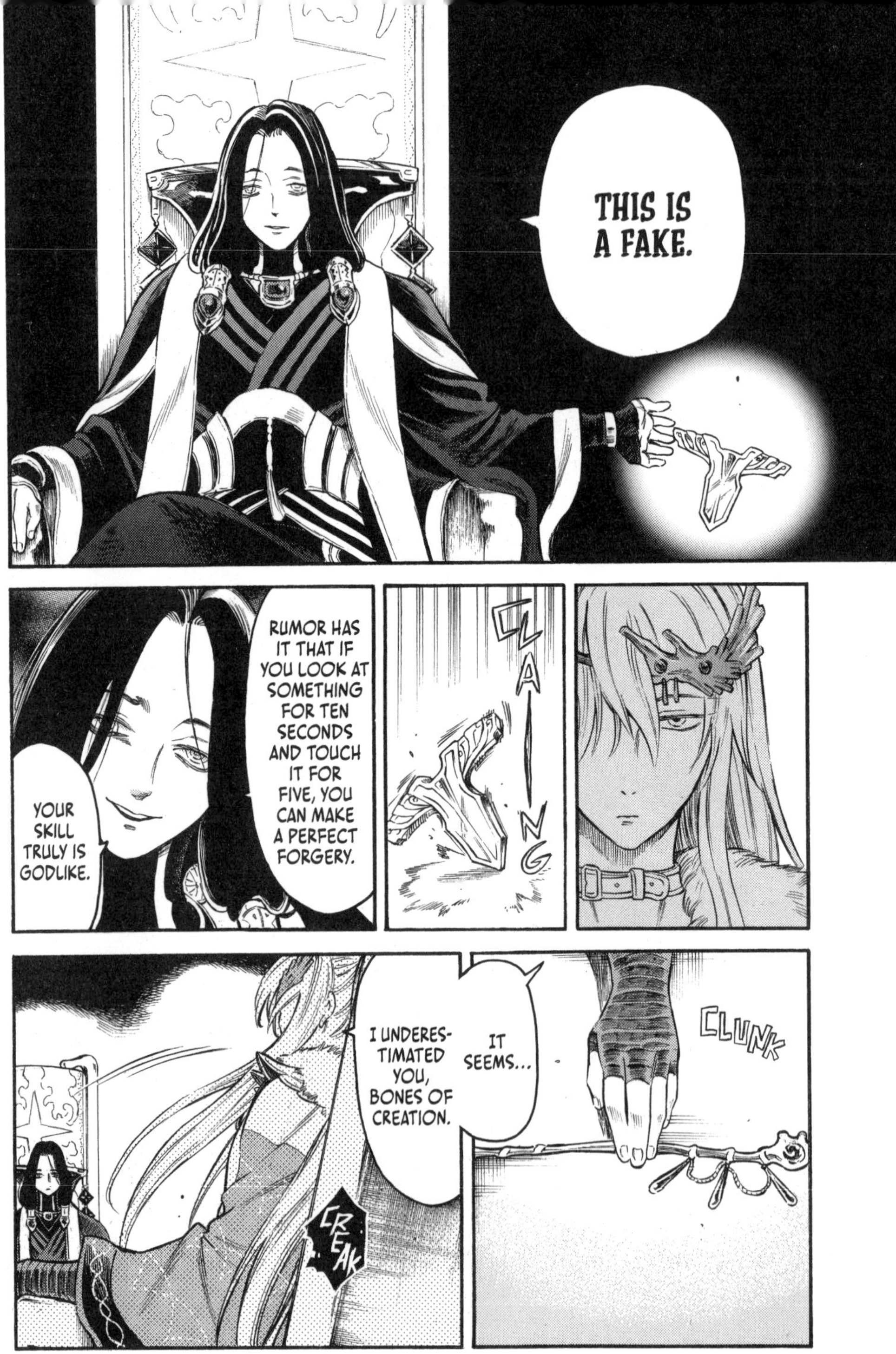
THIS IS A FAKE.
CLAING
RUMOR HAS IT THAT IF YOU LOOK AT SOMETHING FOR TEN SECONDS AND TOUCH IT FOR FIVE, YOU CAN MAKE A PERFECT FORGERY.
YOUR SKILL TRULY IS GODLIKE.
CLUNK
IT SEEMS...
I UNDERES-TIMATED YOU, BONES OF CREATION.
CREAK

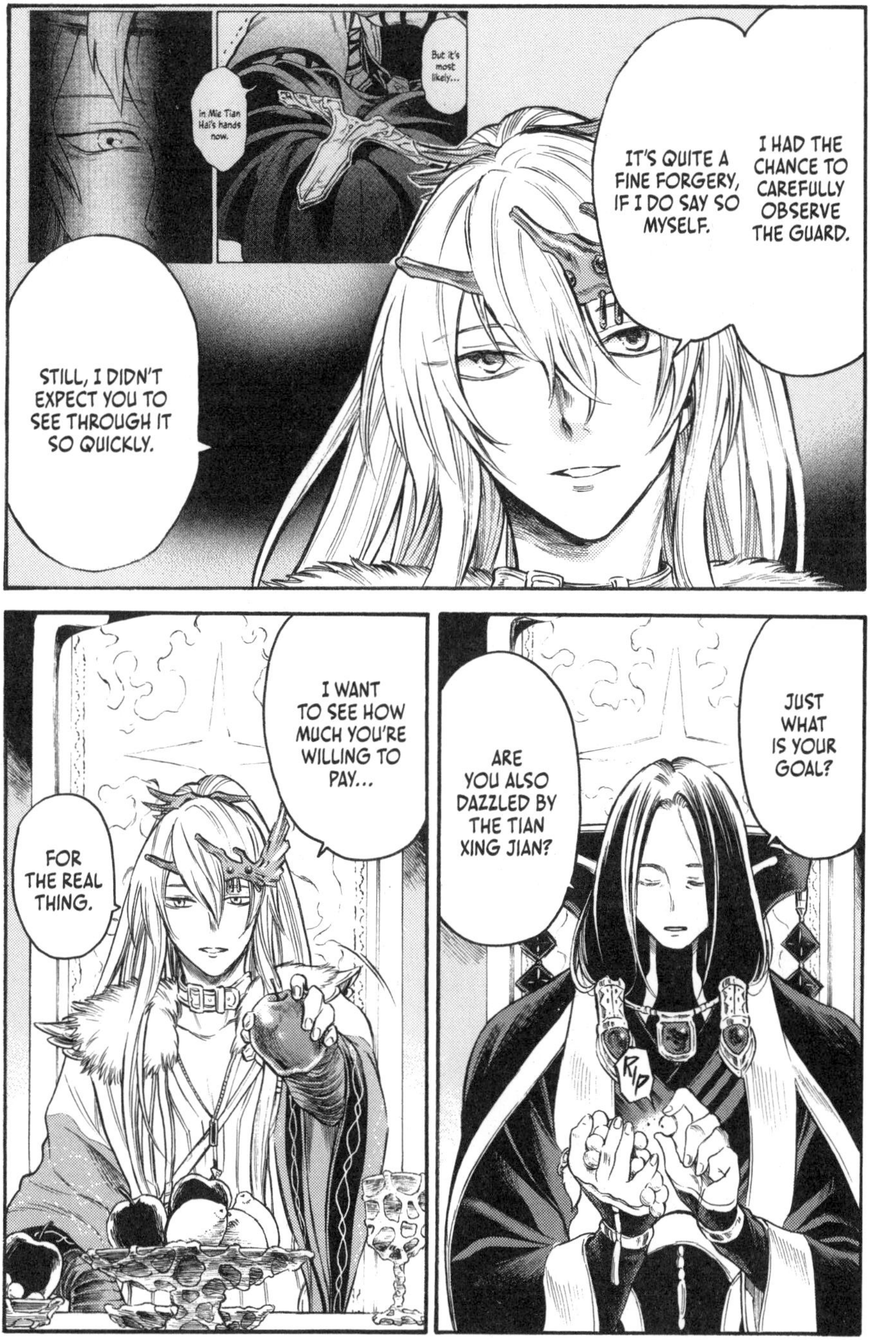
I HAD THE CHANCE TO CAREFULLY OBSERVE THE GUARD.
IT'S QUITE A FINE FORGERY, IF I DO SAY SO MYSELF.
But it's most likely...
in Mie Tian Hai's hands now.
STILL, I DIDN'T EXPECT YOU TO SEE THROUGH IT SO QUICKLY.
JUST WHAT IS YOUR GOAL?
ARE YOU ALSO DAZZLED BY THE TIAN XING JIAN?
RIP
I WANT TO SEE HOW MUCH YOU'RE WILLING TO PAY...
FOR THE REAL THING.

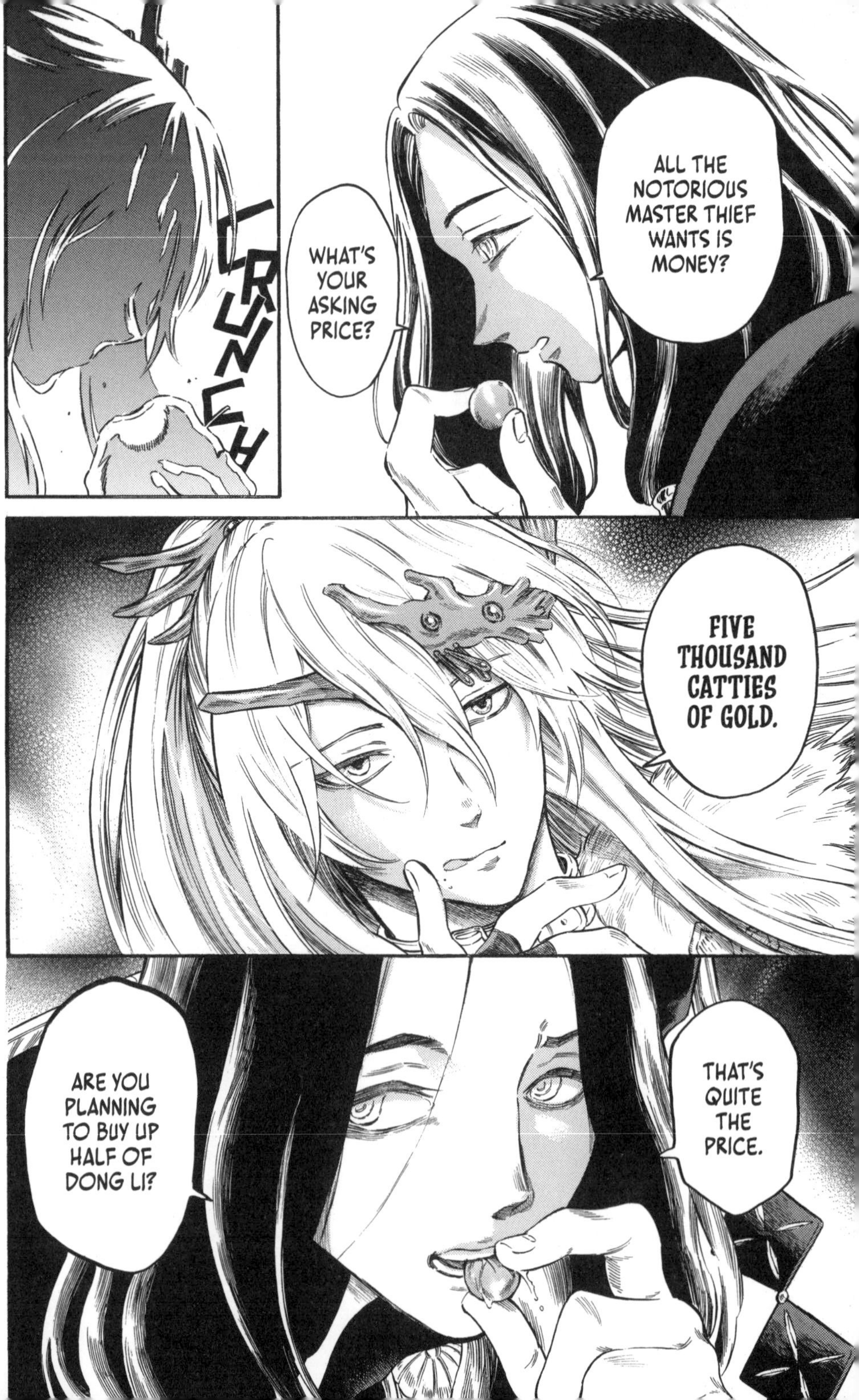
ALL THE NOTORIOUS MASTER THIEF WANTS IS MONEY?
WHAT'S YOUR ASKING PRICE?
CRUNCH
FIVE THOUSAND CATTIES OF GOLD.
THAT'S QUITE THE PRICE.
ARE YOU PLANNING TO BUY UP HALF OF DONG LI?

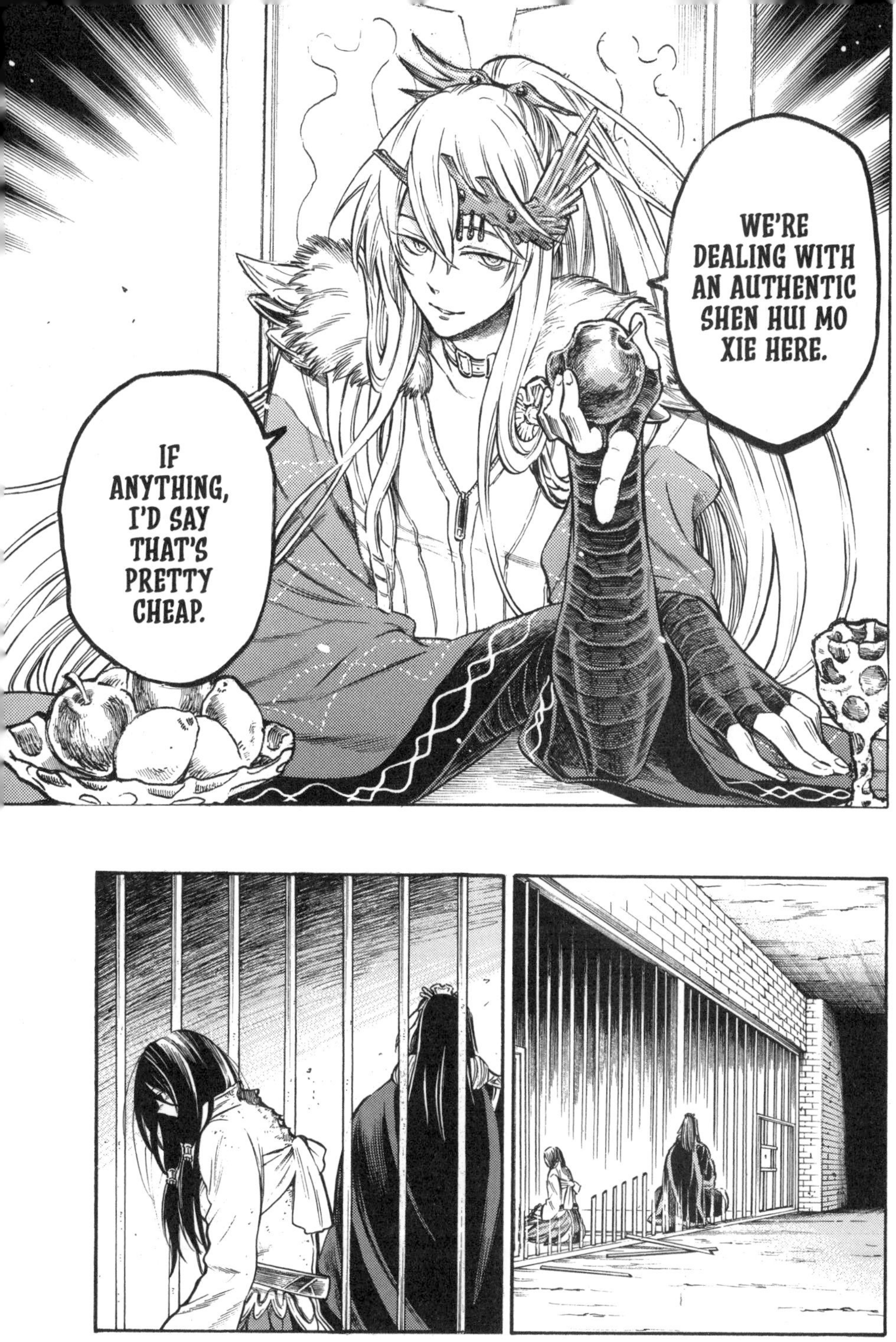
WE'RE DEALING WITH AN AUTHENTIC SHEN HUI MO XIE HERE.
IF ANYTHING, I'D SAY THAT'S PRETTY CHEAP.

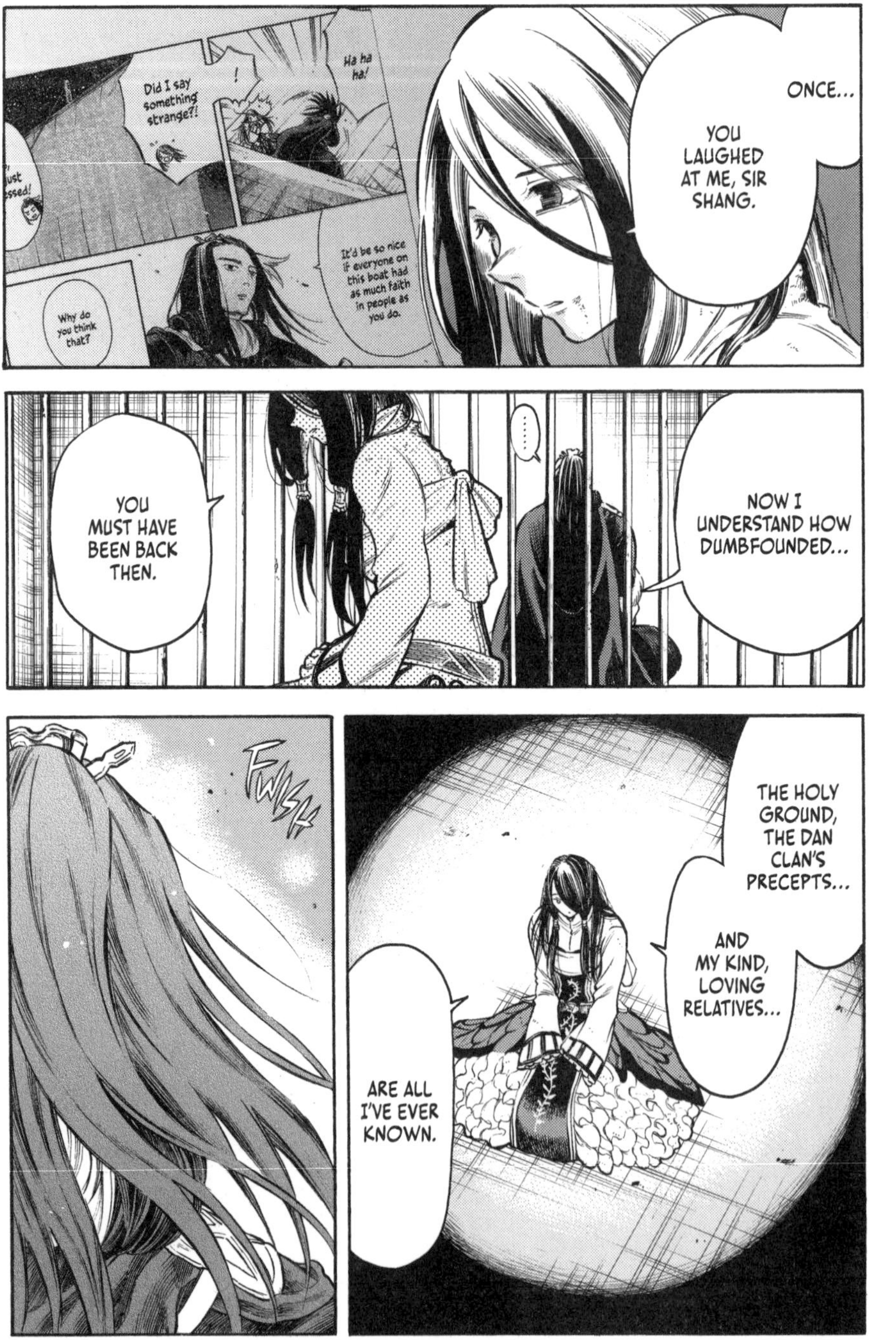
ONCE...
YOU LAUGHED AT ME, SIR SHANG.
Ha ha ha!
!
Did I say something strange?!
It'd be so nice if everyone on this boat had as much faith in people as you do.
Why do you think that?
NOW I UNDERSTAND HOW DUMBFOUNDED...
......
YOU MUST HAVE BEEN BACK THEN.
THE HOLY GROUND, THE DAN CLAN'S PRECEPTS...
AND MY KIND, LOVING RELATIVES...
ARE ALL I'VE EVER KNOWN.
FWISH

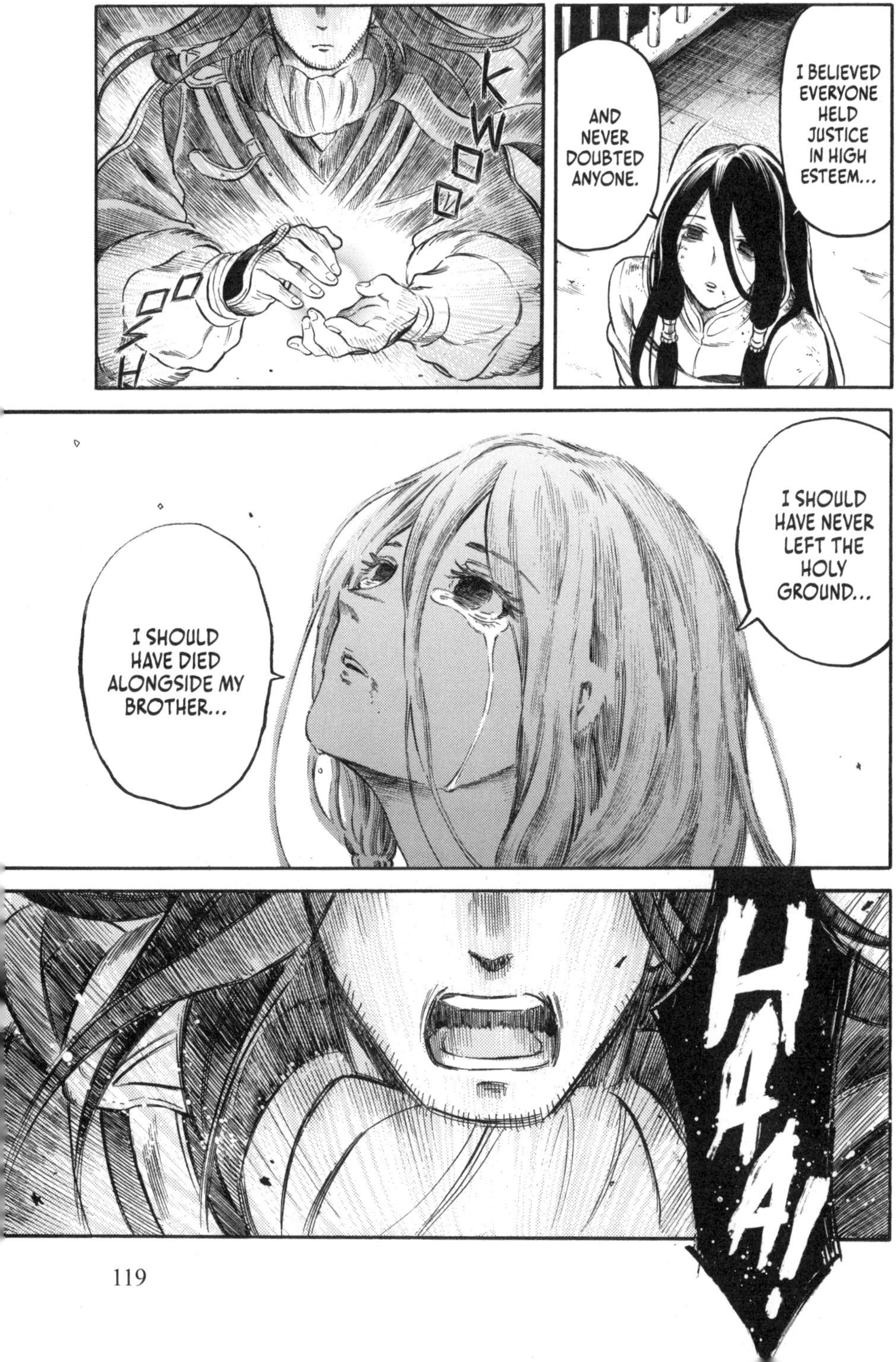
I BELIEVED EVERYONE HELD JUSTICE IN HIGH ESTEEM...
AND NEVER DOUBTED ANYONE.
KWOO
I SHOULD HAVE NEVER LEFT THE HOLY GROUND...
I SHOULD HAVE DIED ALONGSIDE MY BROTHER...
HAAI!

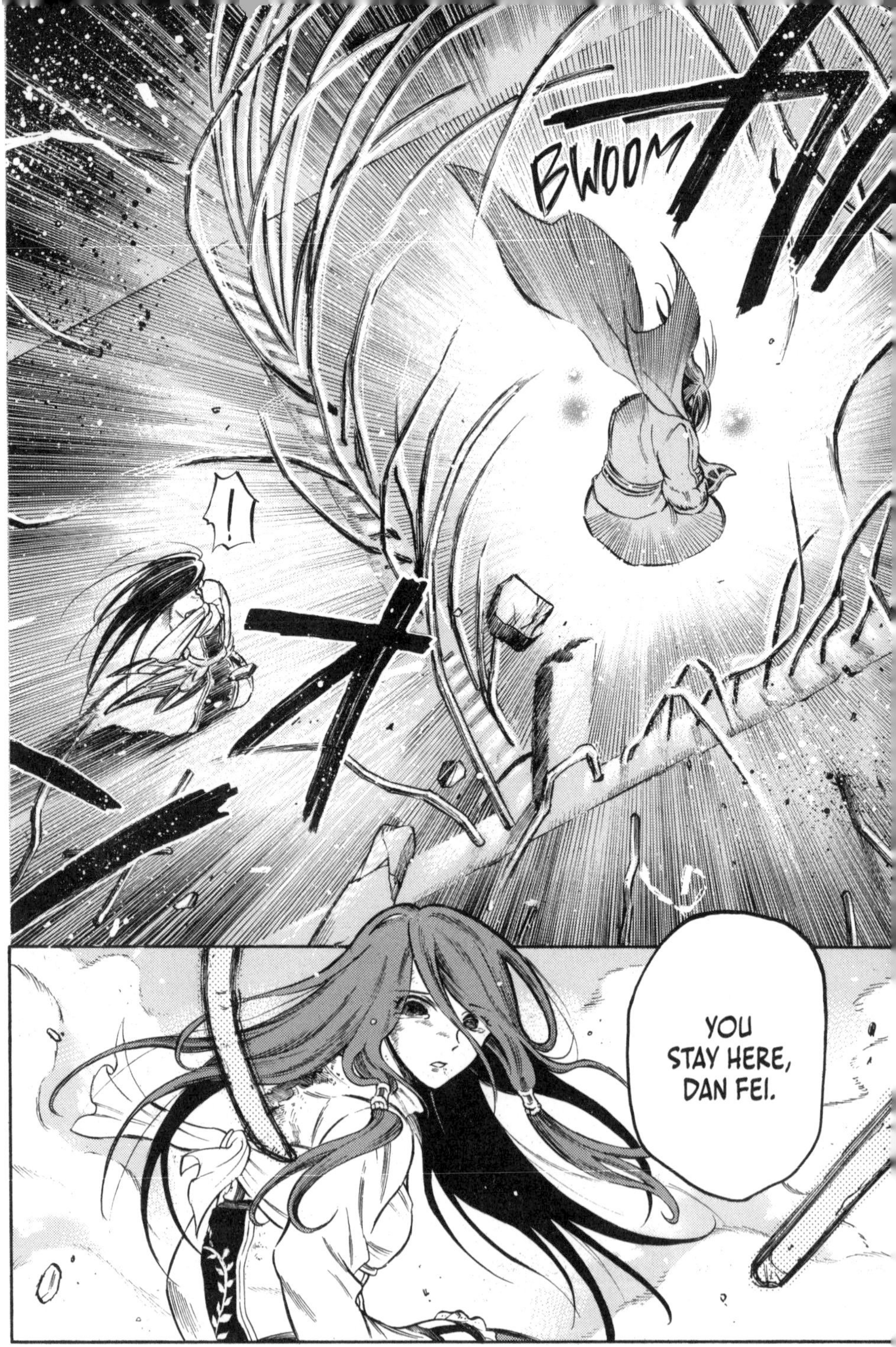
BWOOM
!
YOU STAY HERE, DAN FEI.

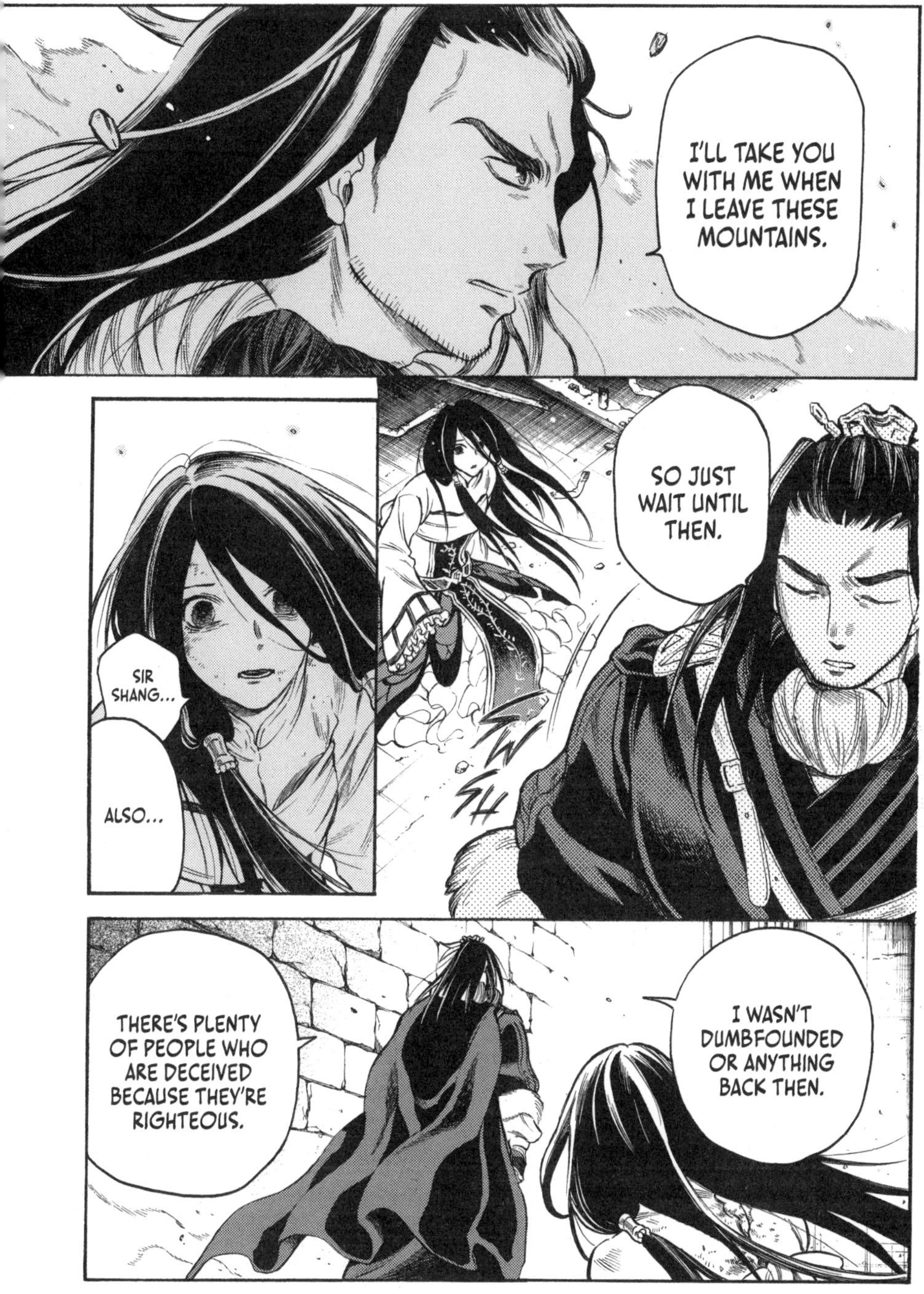
I'LL TAKE YOU WITH ME WHEN I LEAVE THESE MOUNTAINS.
SO JUST WAIT UNTIL THEN.
SIR SHANG...
ALSO...
I WASN'T DUMBFOUNDED OR ANYTHING BACK THEN.
THERE'S PLENTY OF PEOPLE WHO ARE DECEIVED BECAUSE THEY'RE RIGHTEOUS.

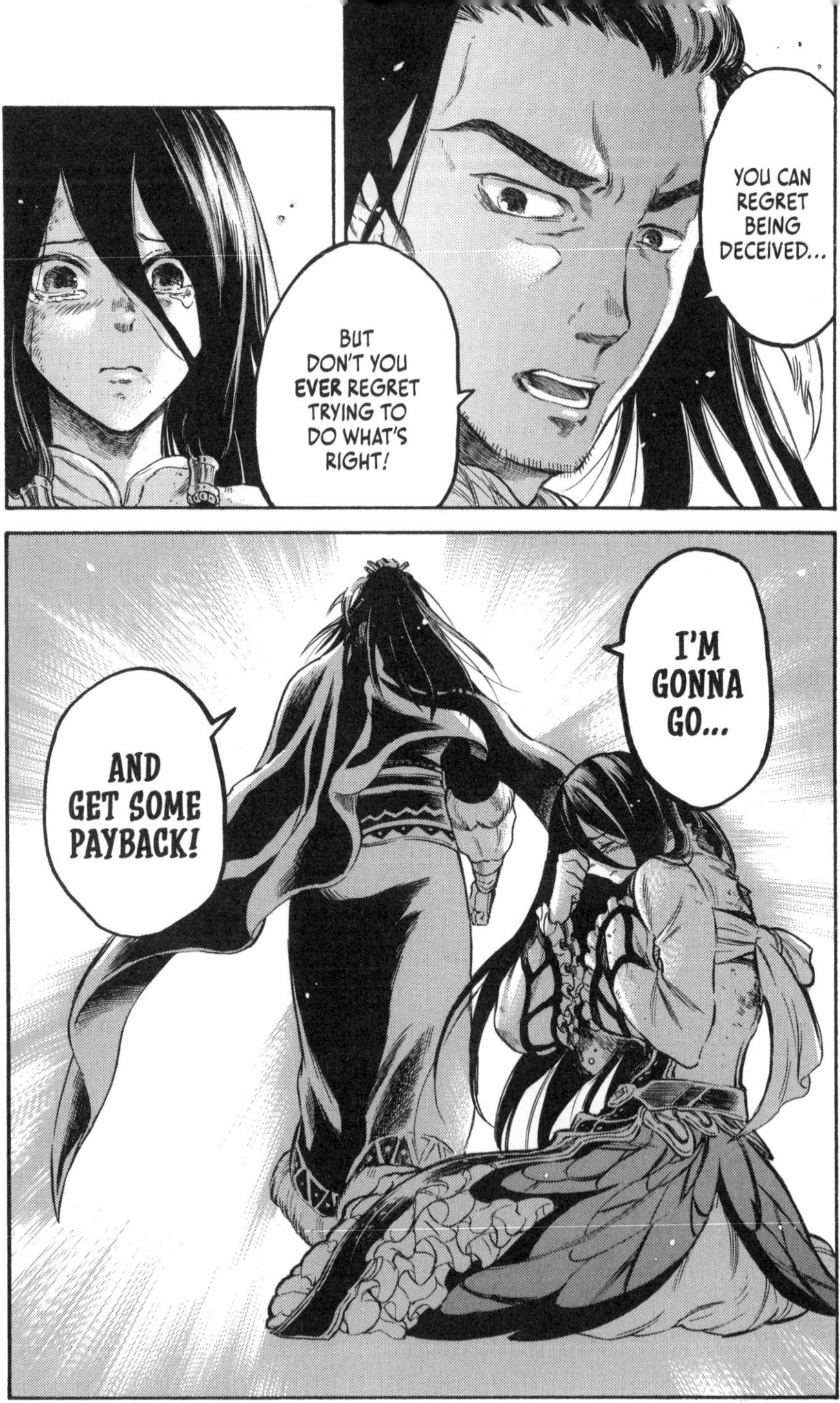
YOU CAN REGRET BEING DECEIVED...
BUT DON'T YOU EVER REGRET TRYING TO DO WHAT'S RIGHT!
I'M GONNA GO...
AND GET SOME PAYBACK!

End of Chapter 22

Character Designs

Here are a few character designs, drawn by Yui Sakuma before the serialization of the manga began!

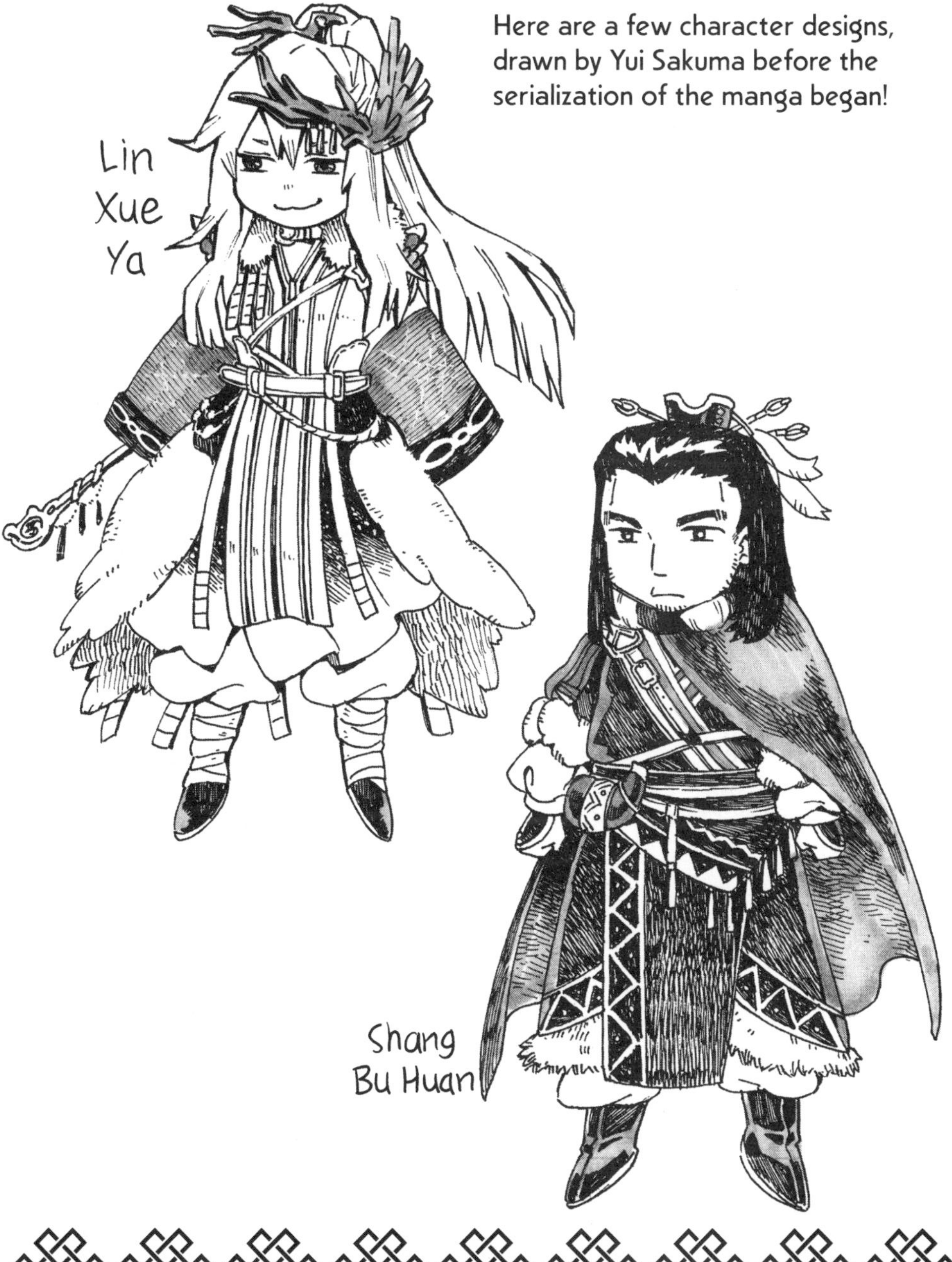
Lin Xue Ya
Shang Bu Huan

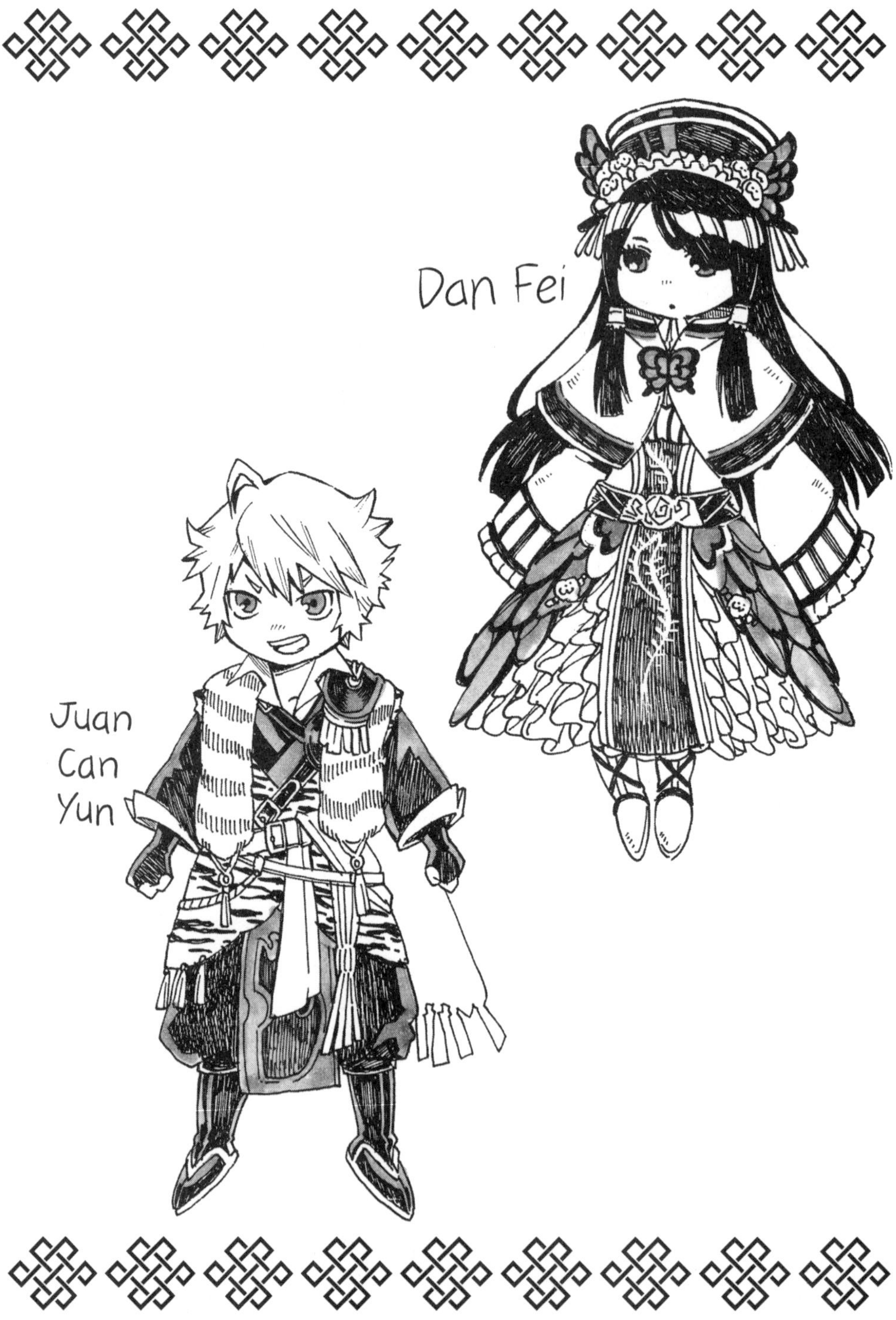
Dan Fei
Juan Can Yun

∽ Chapter 23 ∽

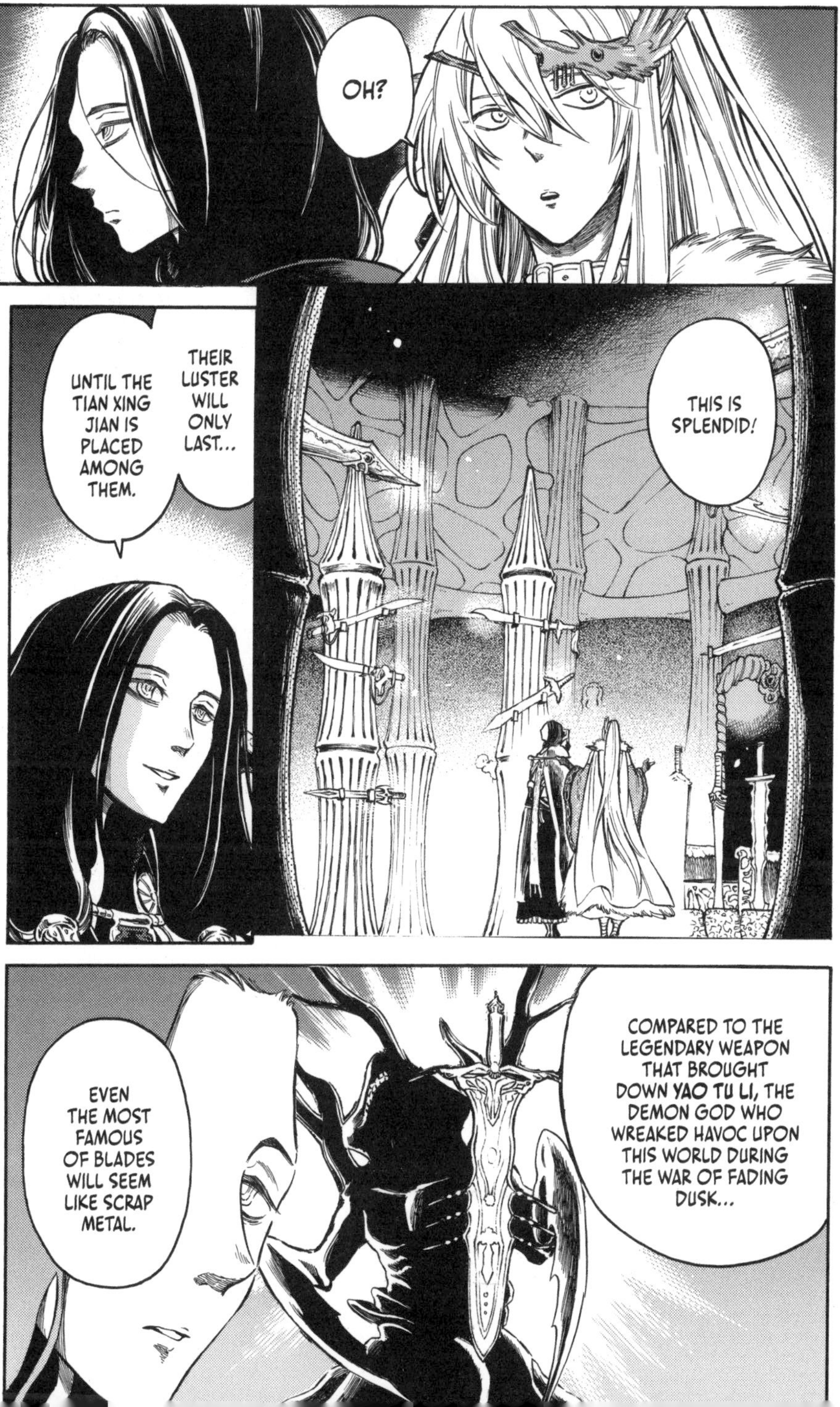
OH?
THIS IS SPLENDID!
THEIR LUSTER WILL ONLY LAST...
UNTIL THE TIAN XING JIAN IS PLACED AMONG THEM.
COMPARED TO THE LEGENDARY WEAPON THAT BROUGHT DOWN YAO TU LI, THE DEMON GOD WHO WREAKED HAVOC UPON THIS WORLD DURING THE WAR OF FADING DUSK...
EVEN THE MOST FAMOUS OF BLADES WILL SEEM LIKE SCRAP METAL.

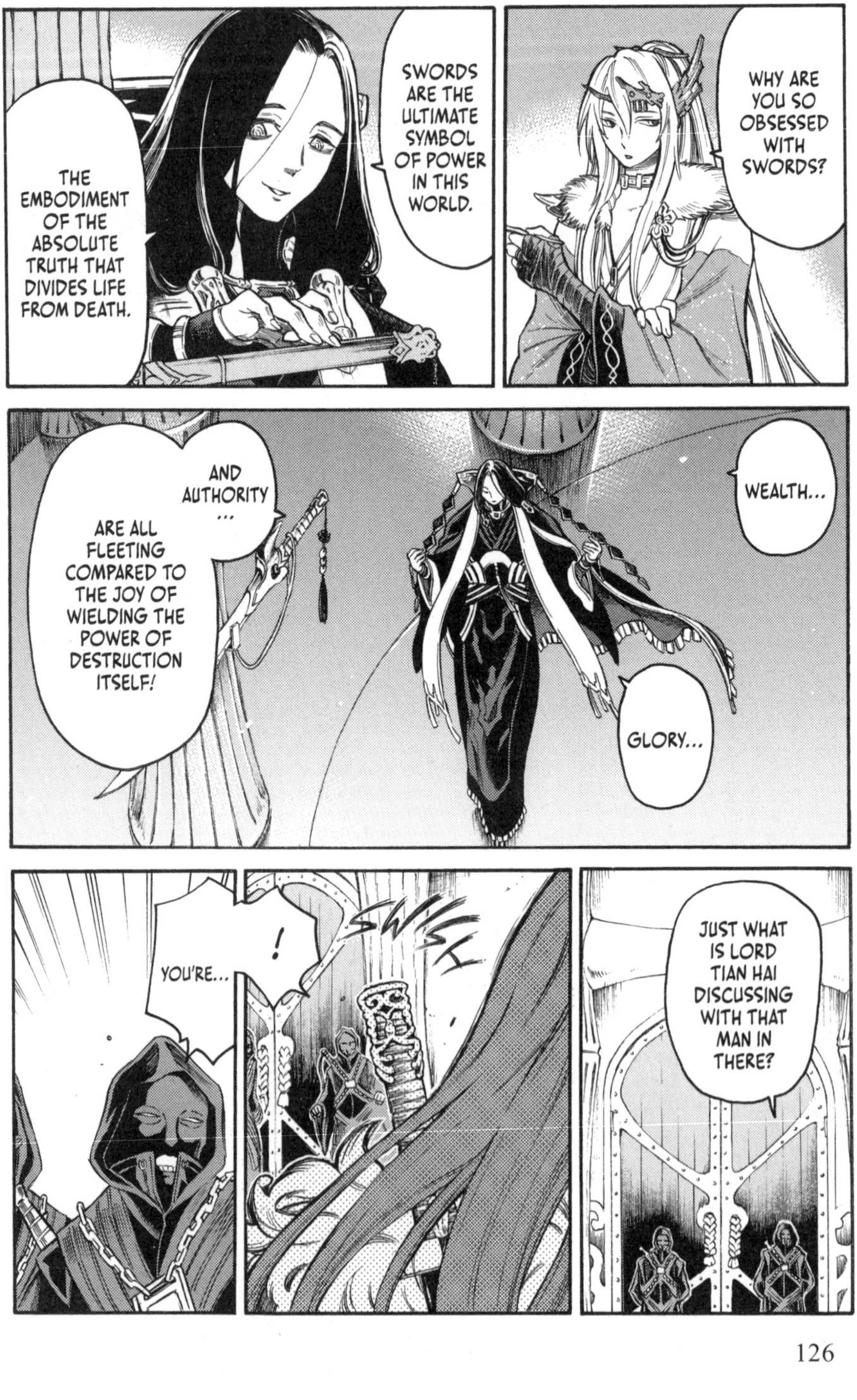
WHY ARE YOU SO OBSESSED WITH SWORDS?
SWORDS ARE THE ULTIMATE SYMBOL OF POWER IN THIS WORLD.
THE EMBODIMENT OF THE ABSOLUTE TRUTH THAT DIVIDES LIFE FROM DEATH.
WEALTH...
GLORY...
AND AUTHORITY...
ARE ALL FLEETING COMPARED TO THE JOY OF WIELDING THE POWER OF DESTRUCTION ITSELF!
JUST WHAT IS LORD TIAN HAI DISCUSSING WITH THAT MAN IN THERE?
SWISH
!
YOU'RE...

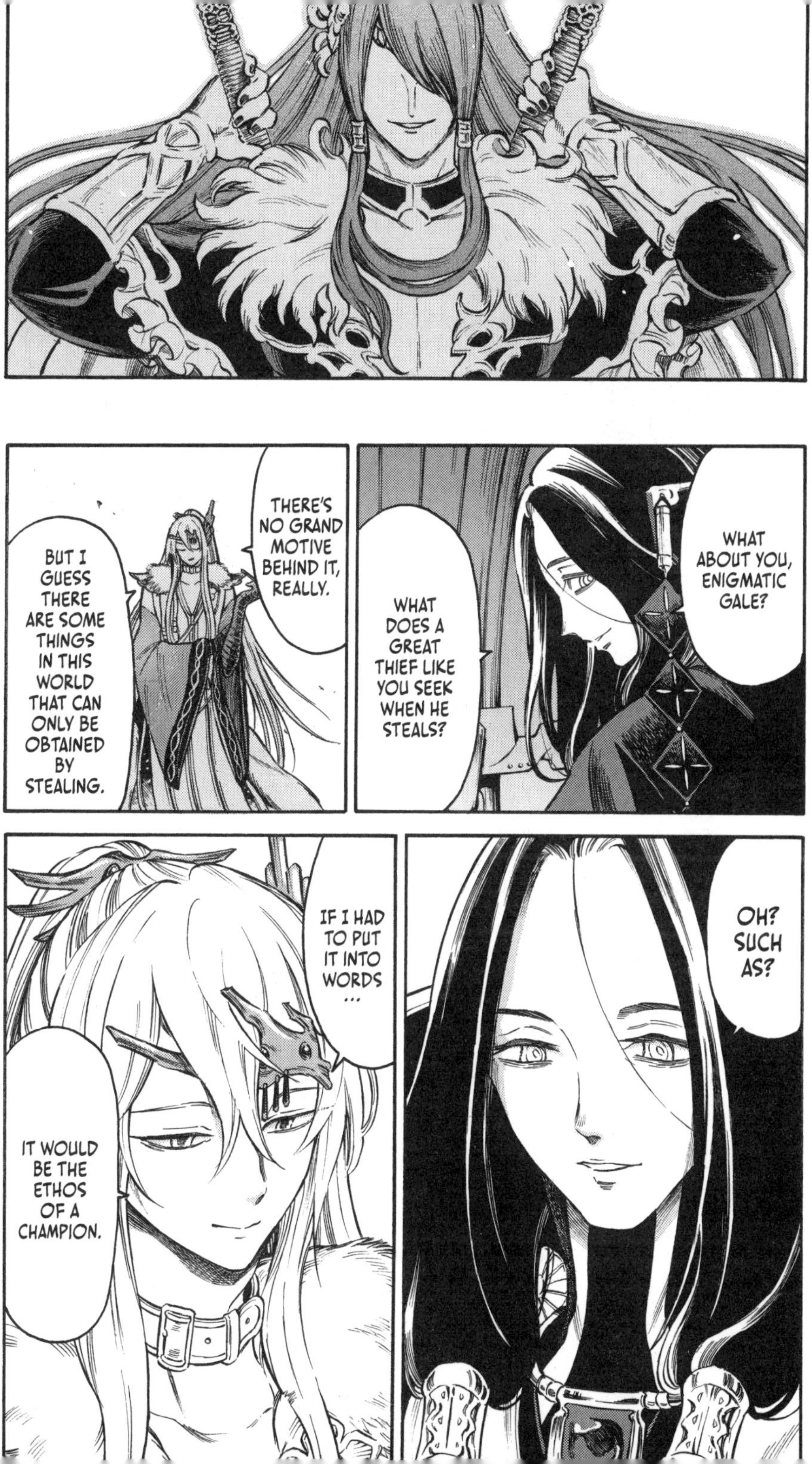
WHAT ABOUT YOU, ENIGMATIC GALE?
WHAT DOES A GREAT THIEF LIKE YOU SEEK WHEN HE STEALS?
THERE'S NO GRAND MOTIVE BEHIND IT, REALLY.
BUT I GUESS THERE ARE SOME THINGS IN THIS WORLD THAT CAN ONLY BE OBTAINED BY STEALING.
OH? SUCH AS?
IF I HAD TO PUT IT INTO WORDS ...
IT WOULD BE THE ETHOS OF A CHAMPION.

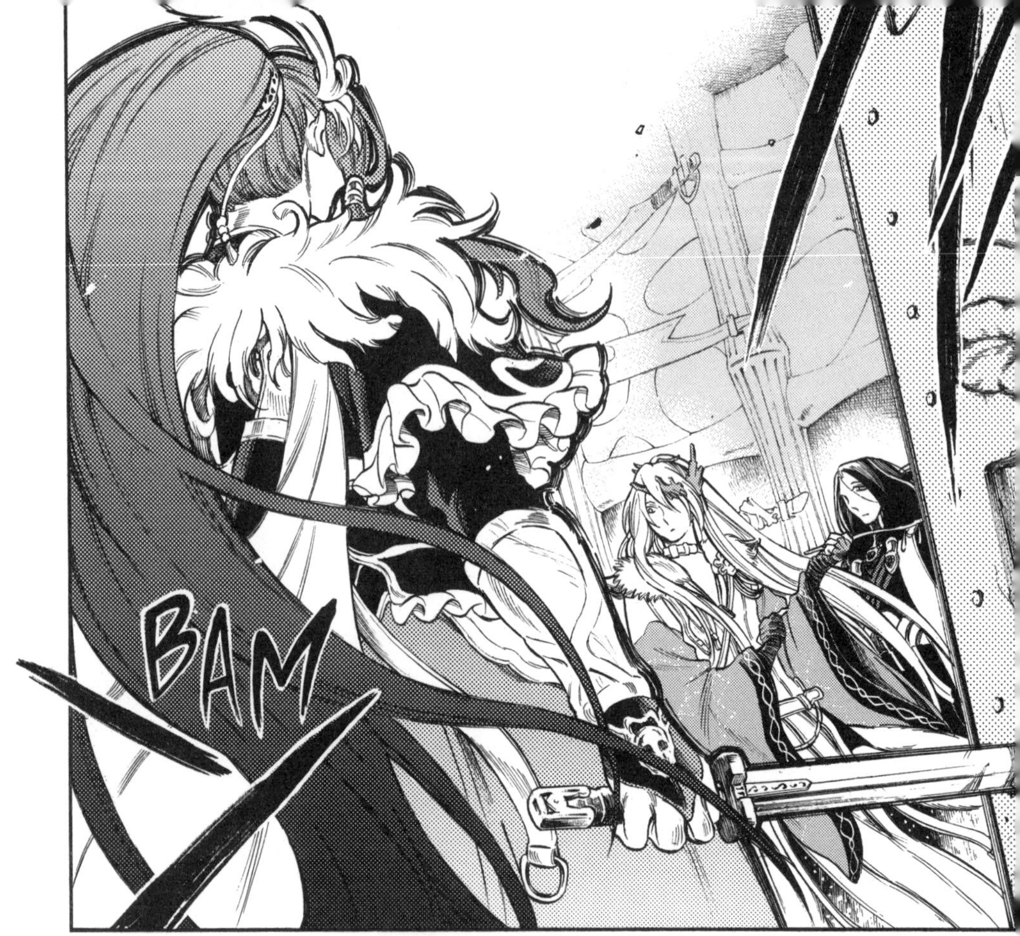
BAM
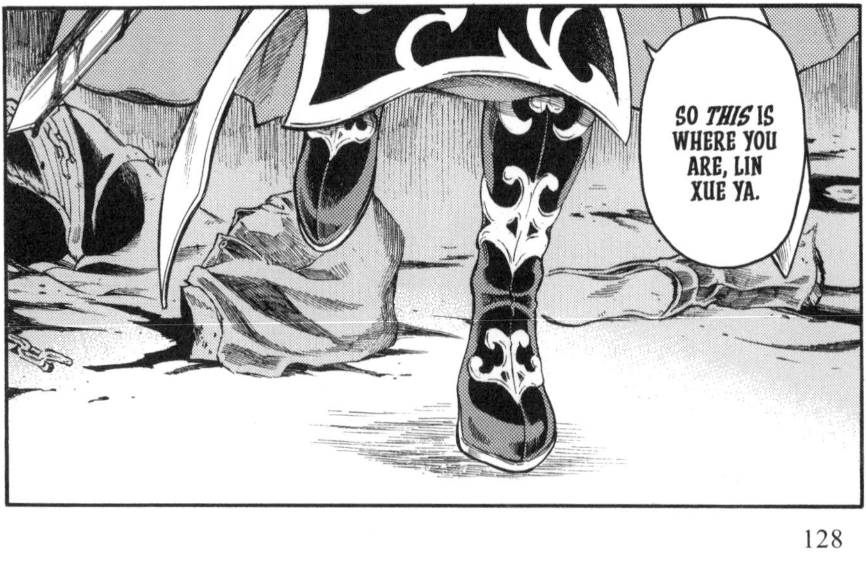
SO *THIS* IS WHERE YOU ARE, LIN XUE YA.

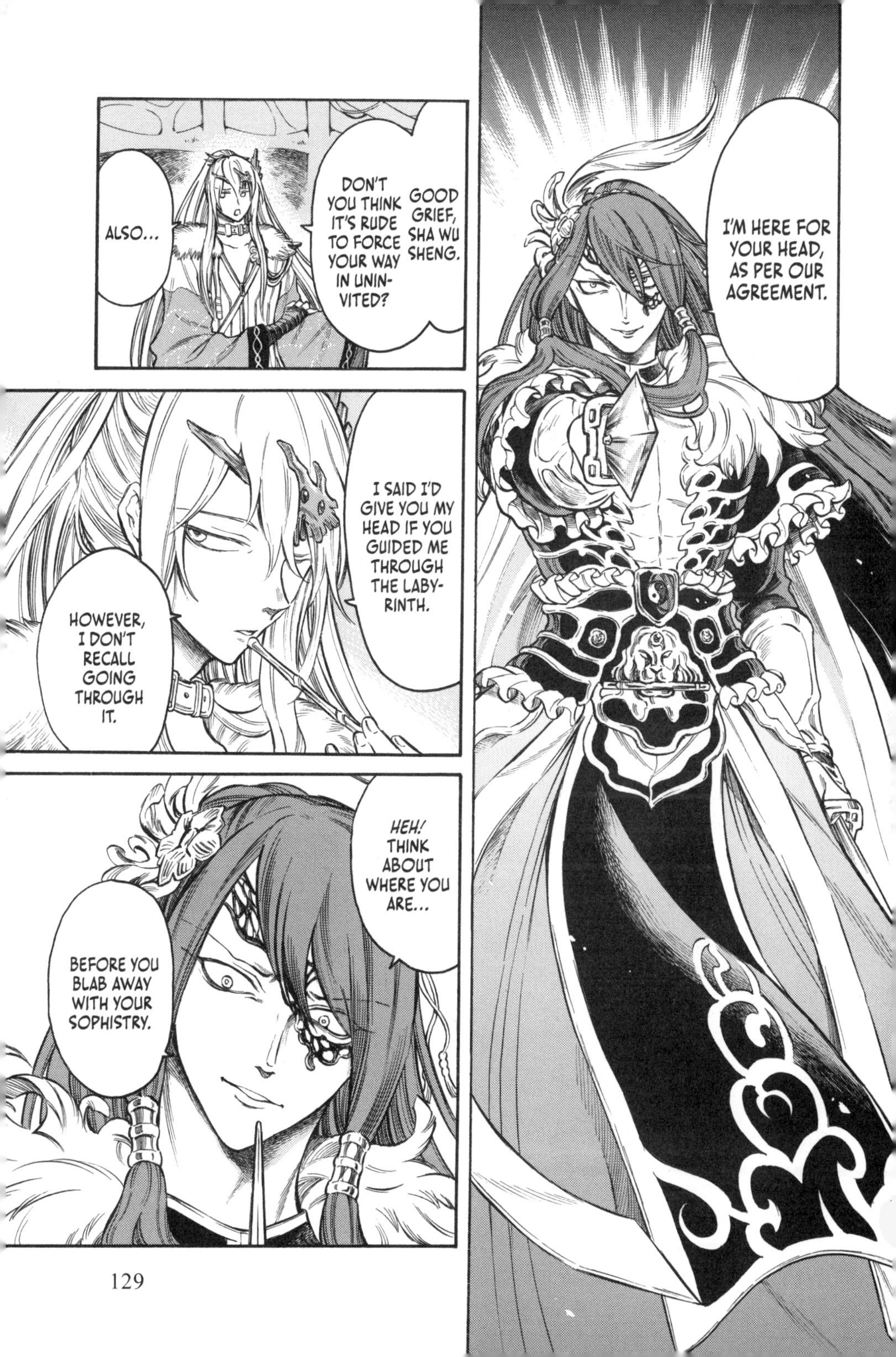

I'M HERE FOR YOUR HEAD, AS PER OUR AGREEMENT.
GOOD GRIEF, SHA WU SHENG.
DON'T YOU THINK IT'S RUDE TO FORCE YOUR WAY IN UNIN-VITED?
ALSO...
I SAID I'D GIVE YOU MY HEAD IF YOU GUIDED ME THROUGH THE LABY-RINTH.
HOWEVER, I DON'T RECALL GOING THROUGH IT.
HEH! THINK ABOUT WHERE YOU ARE...
BEFORE YOU BLAB AWAY WITH YOUR SOPHISTRY.

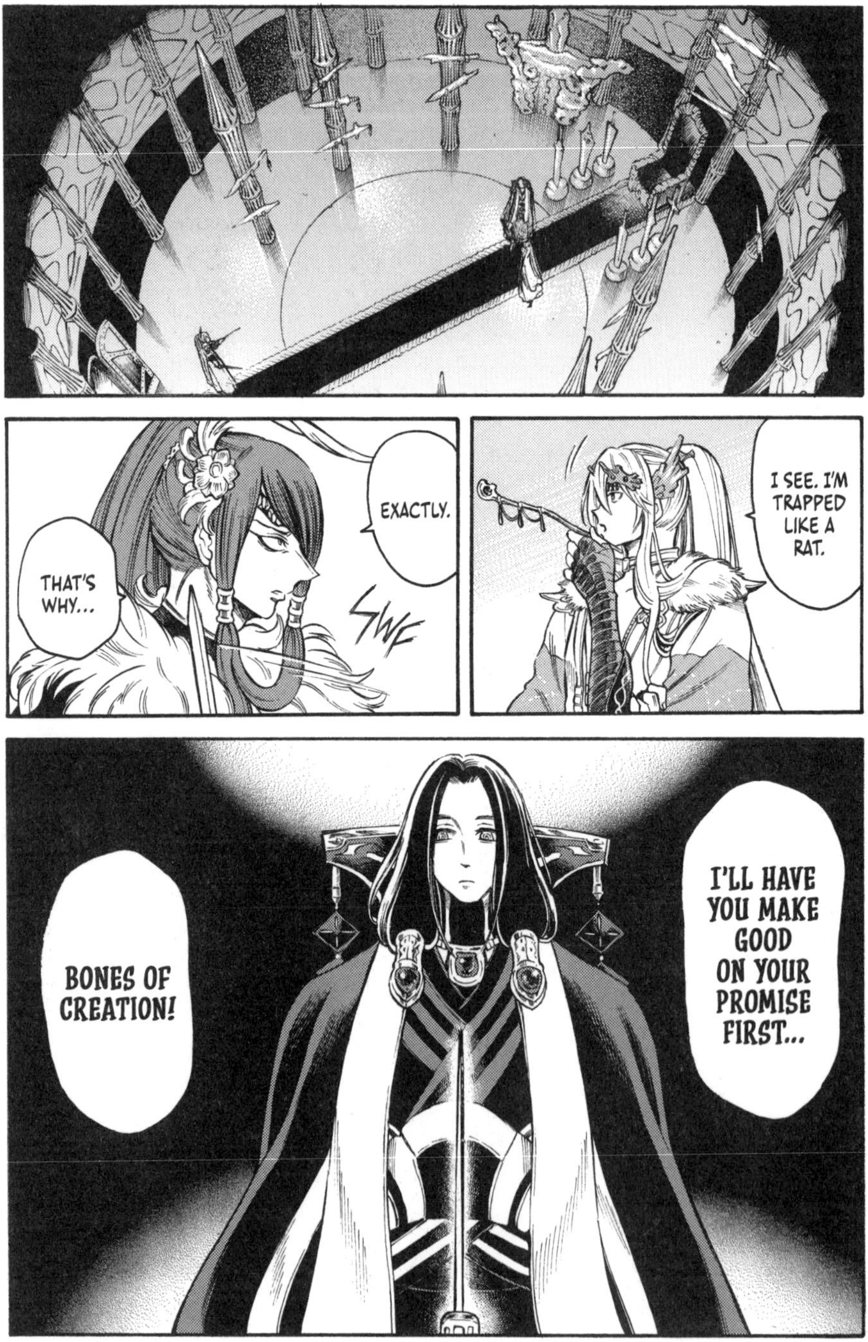
I SEE. I'M TRAPPED LIKE A RAT.
EXACTLY.
THAT'S WHY...
SWF
I'LL HAVE YOU MAKE GOOD ON YOUR PROMISE FIRST...
BONES OF CREATION!

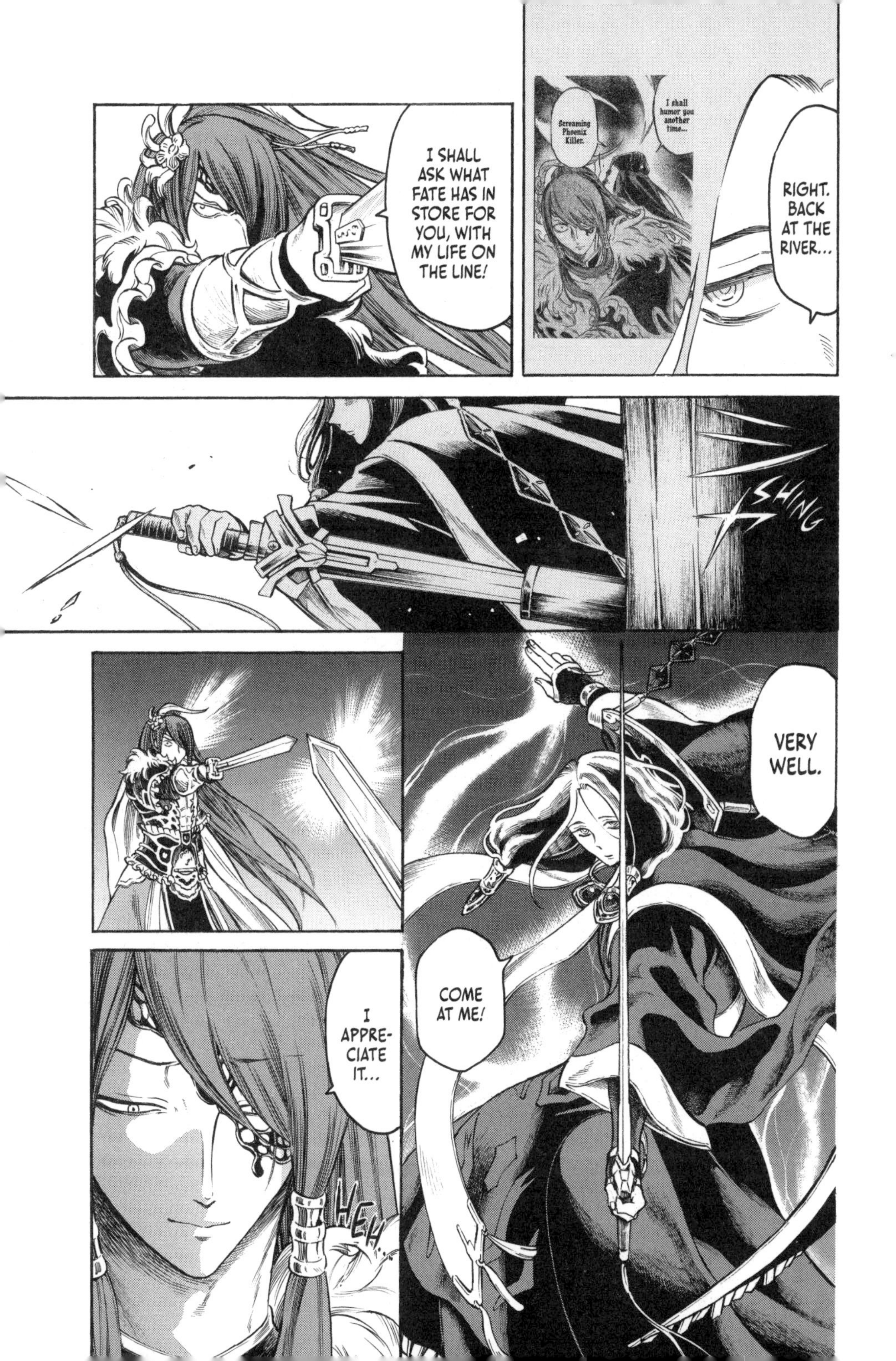
RIGHT. BACK AT THE RIVER...
I shall humor you another time...
Screaming Phoenix Killer.
I SHALL ASK WHAT FATE HAS IN STORE FOR YOU, WITH MY LIFE ON THE LINE!
SHING
VERY WELL.
COME AT ME!
I APPRE-CIATE IT...
HEH...

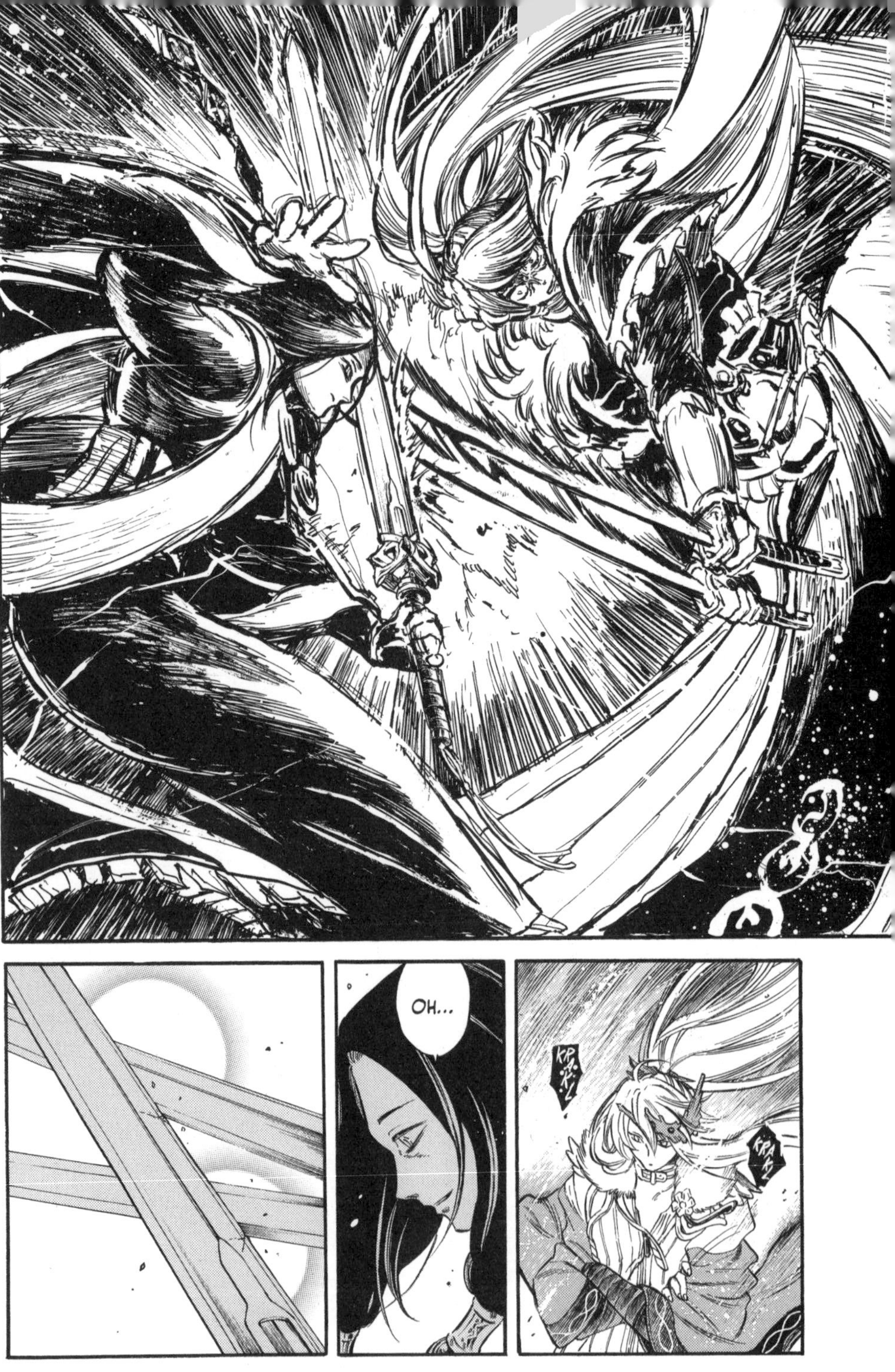
KRAKL
KRAKL
OH...

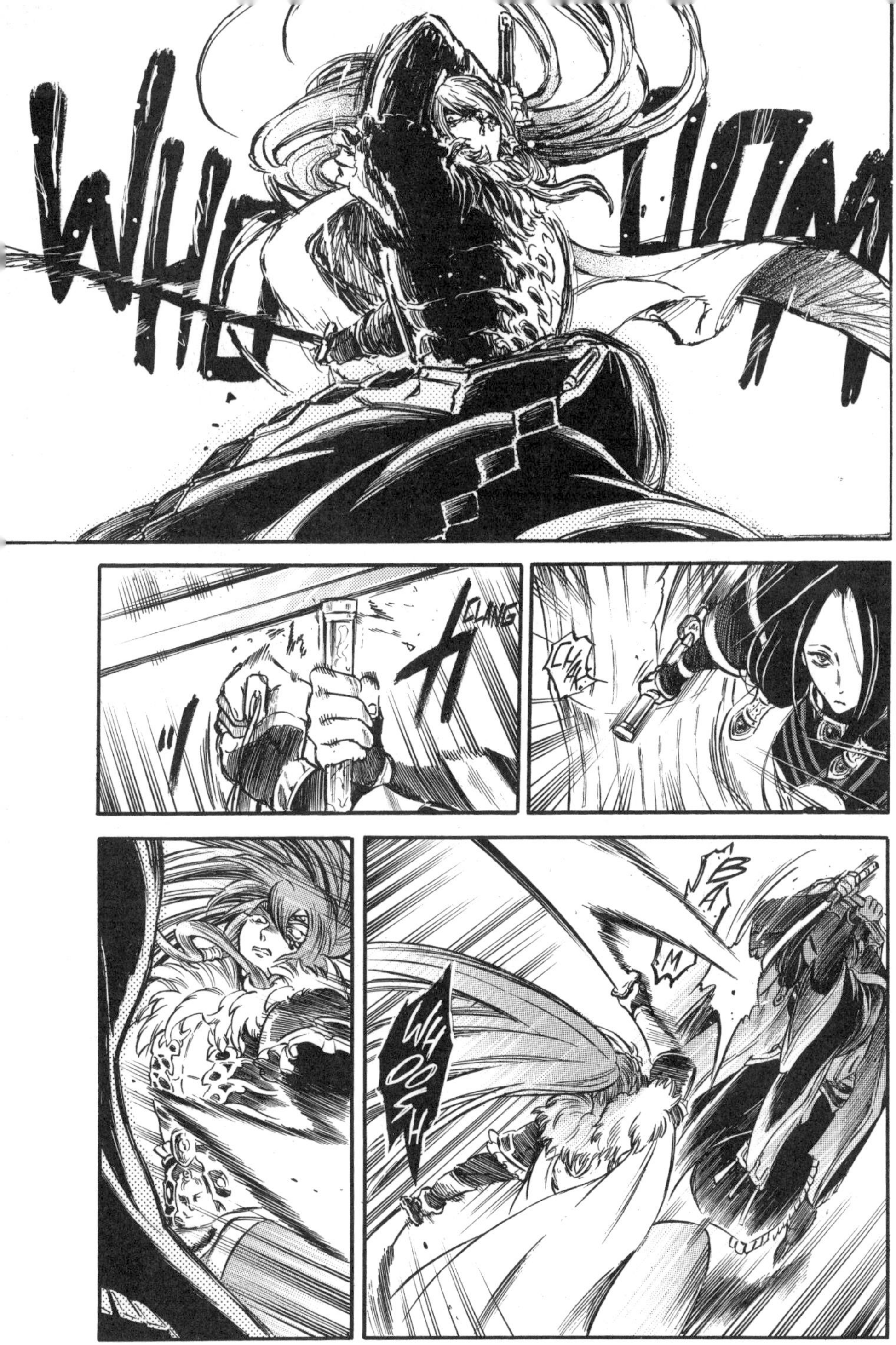
WHO
OOM
CHAK
CLANG
BAM
WHOOSH

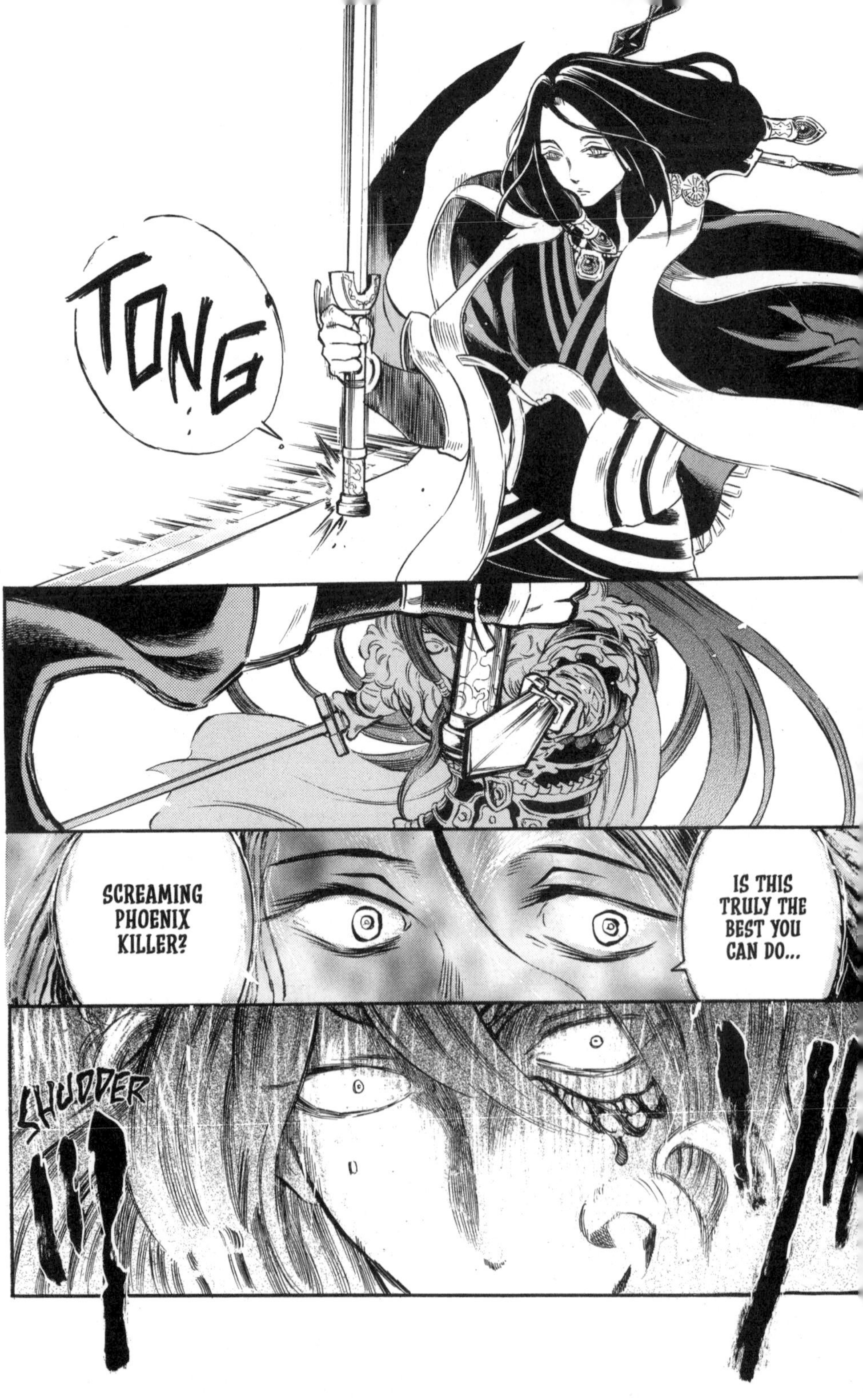
TONG
IS THIS TRULY THE BEST YOU CAN DO...
SCREAMING PHOENIX KILLER?
SHUDDER

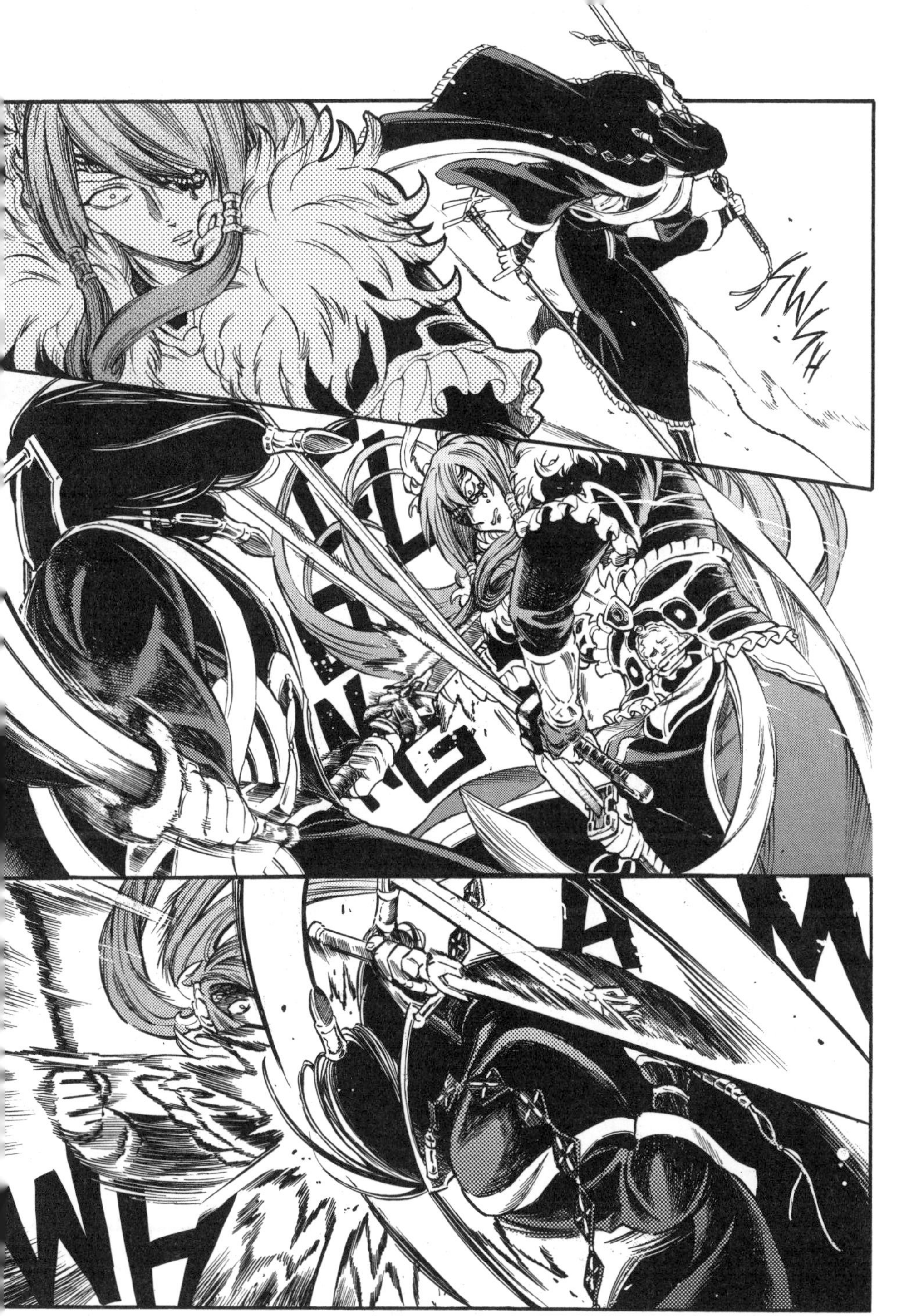
SWSH

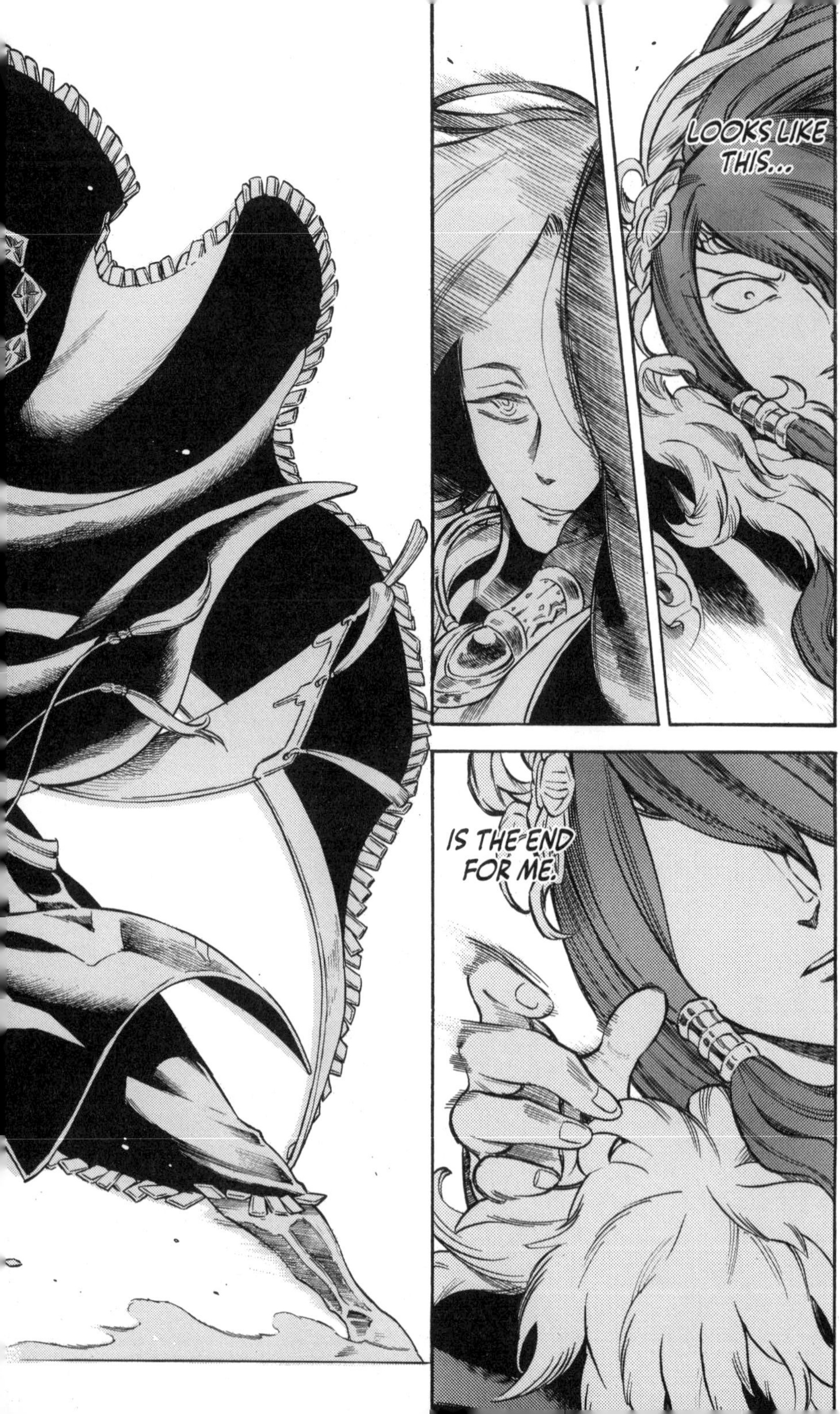
LOOKS LIKE THIS...
IS THE END FOR ME.

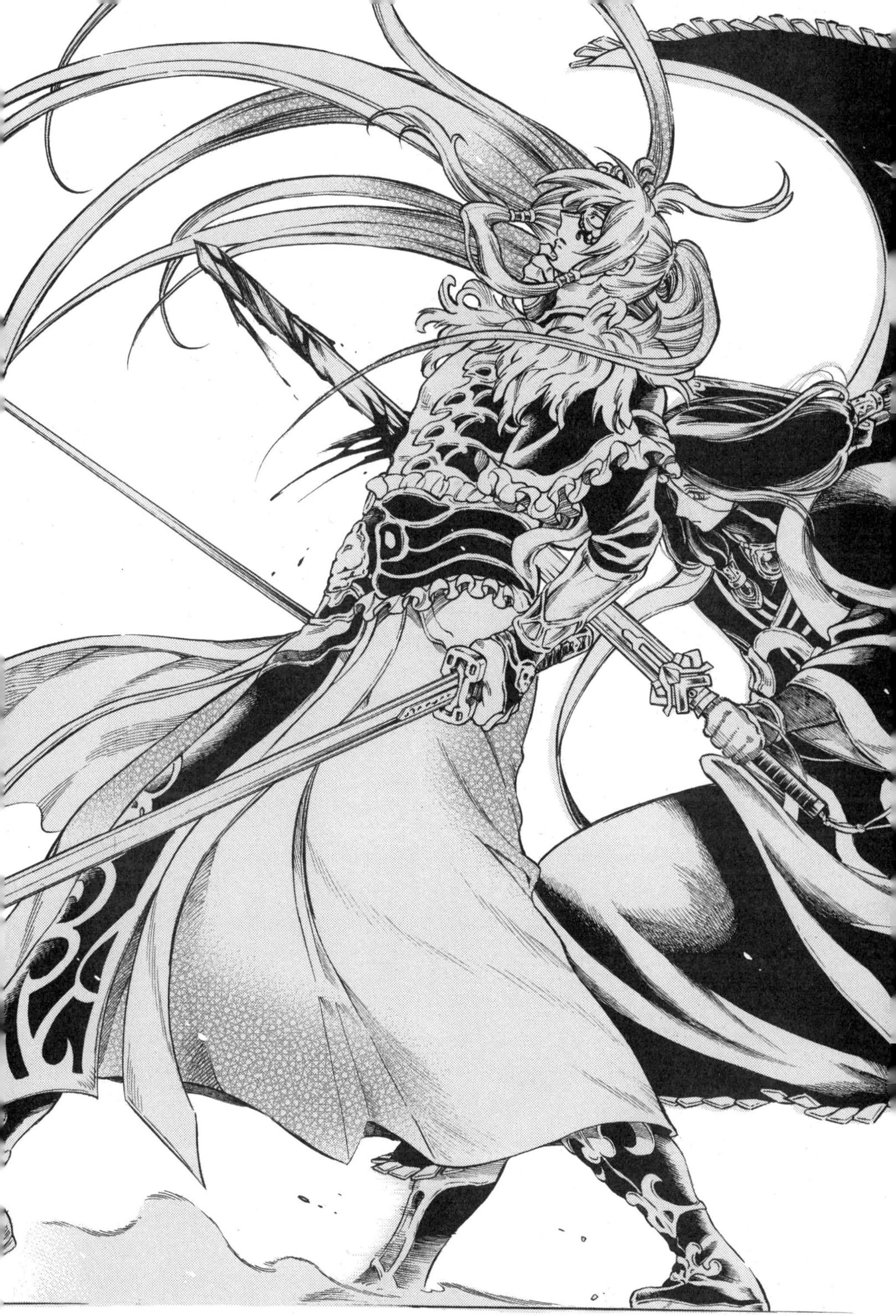

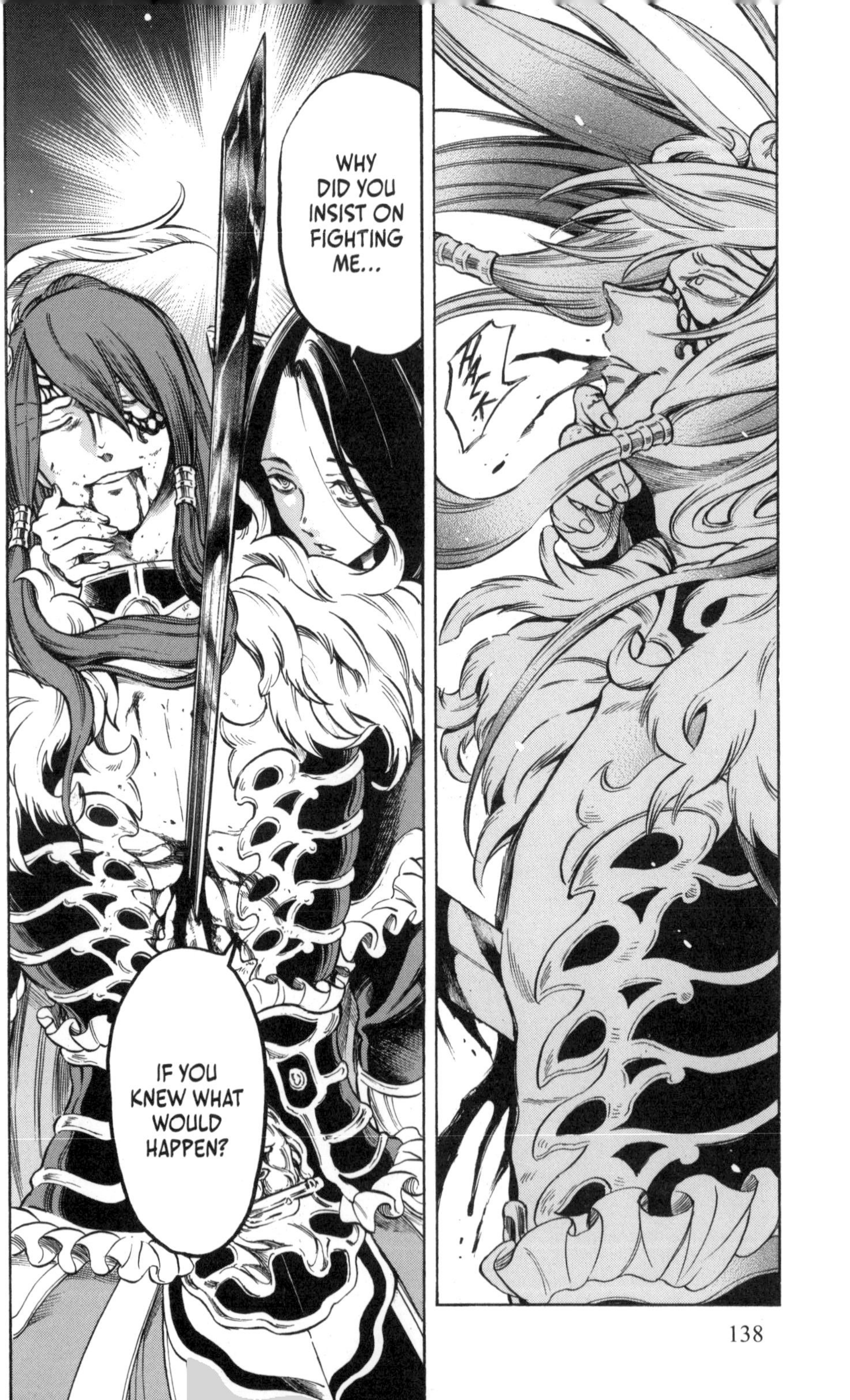
HACK
WHY DID YOU INSIST ON FIGHTING ME...
IF YOU KNEW WHAT WOULD HAPPEN?

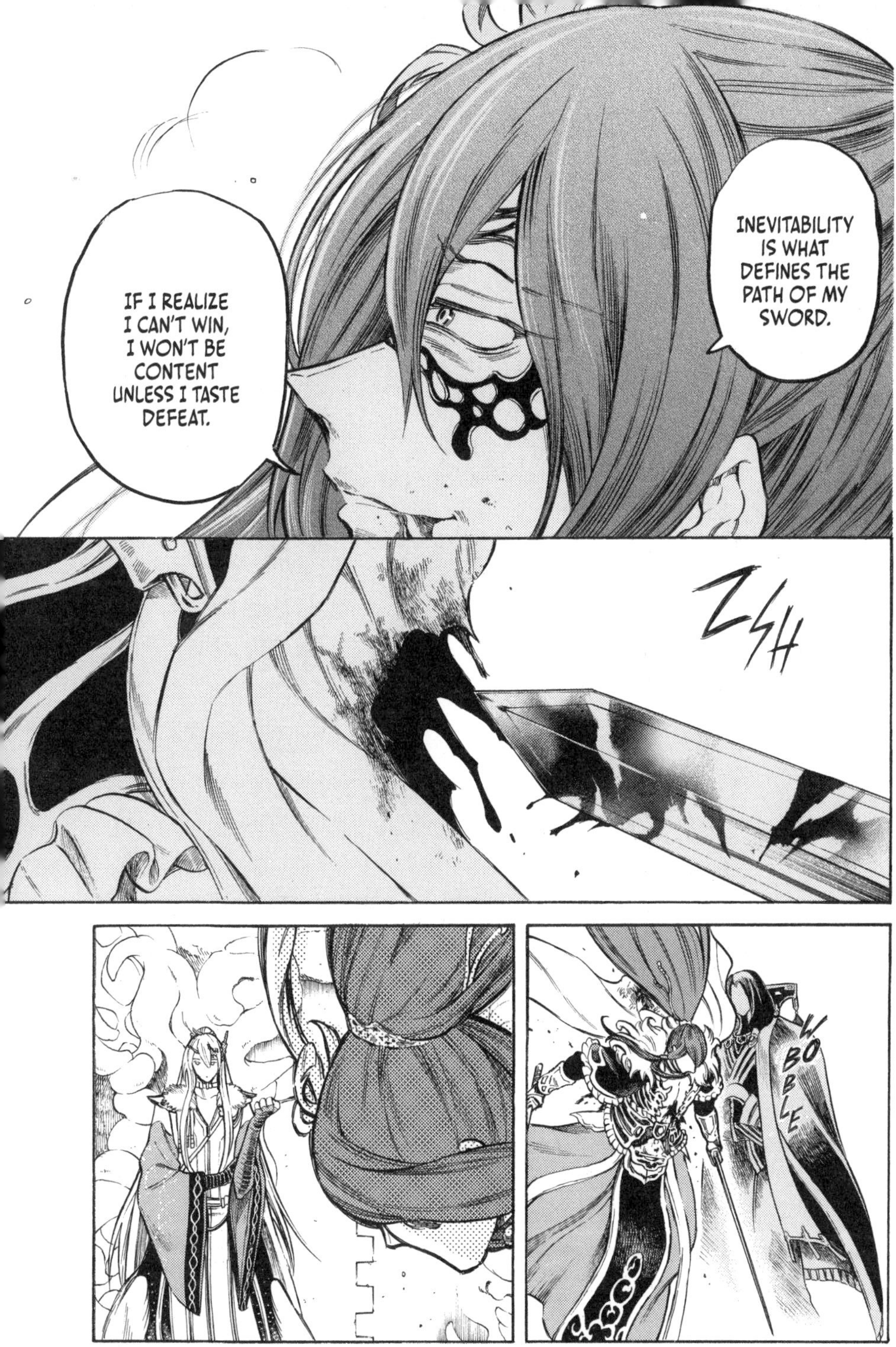
INEVITABILITY IS WHAT DEFINES THE PATH OF MY SWORD.
IF I REALIZE I CAN'T WIN, I WON'T BE CONTENT UNLESS I TASTE DEFEAT.
ZSH
WOBBLE

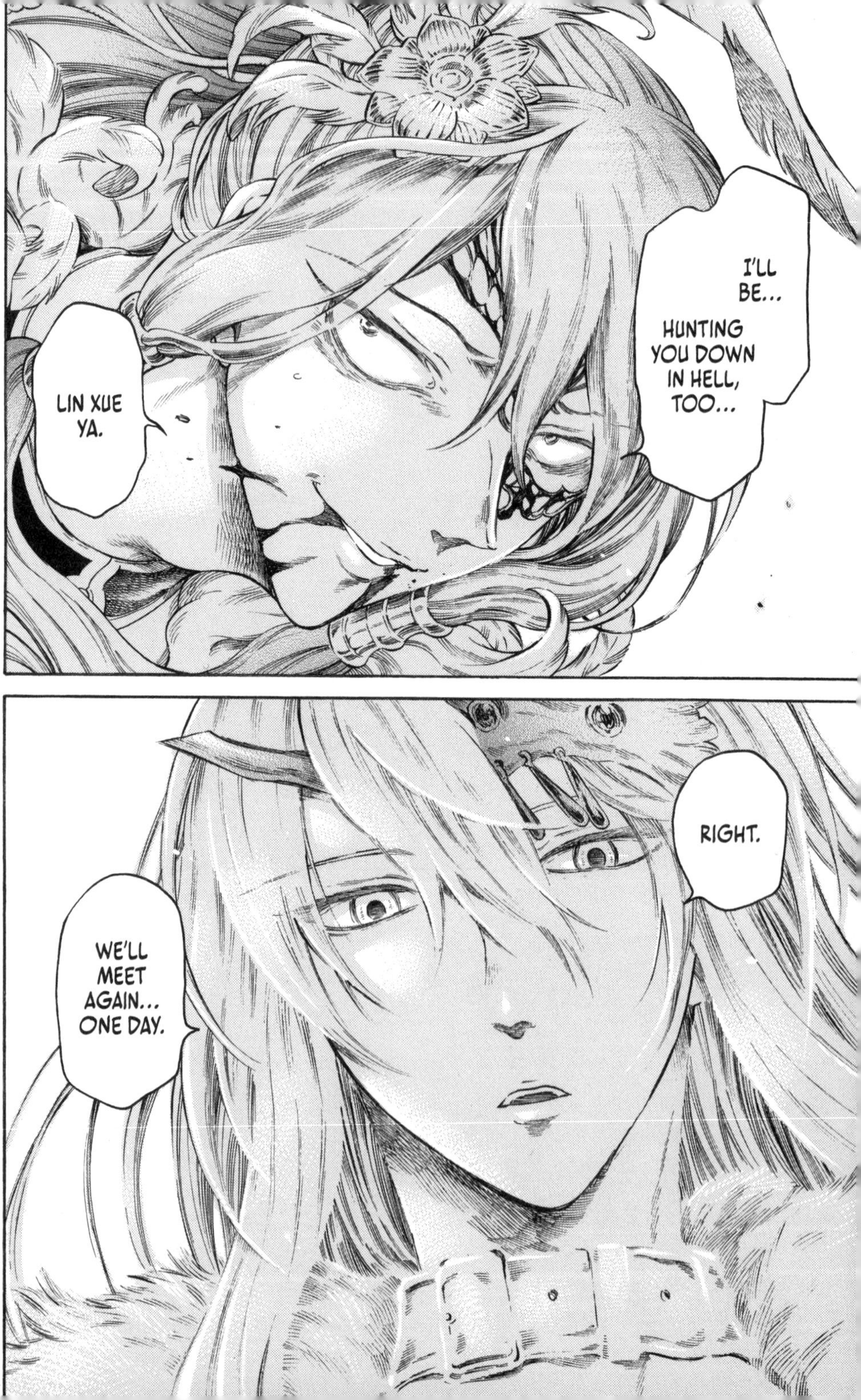
I'LL BE... HUNTING YOU DOWN IN HELL, TOO...
LIN XUE YA.
RIGHT.
WE'LL MEET AGAIN... ONE DAY.

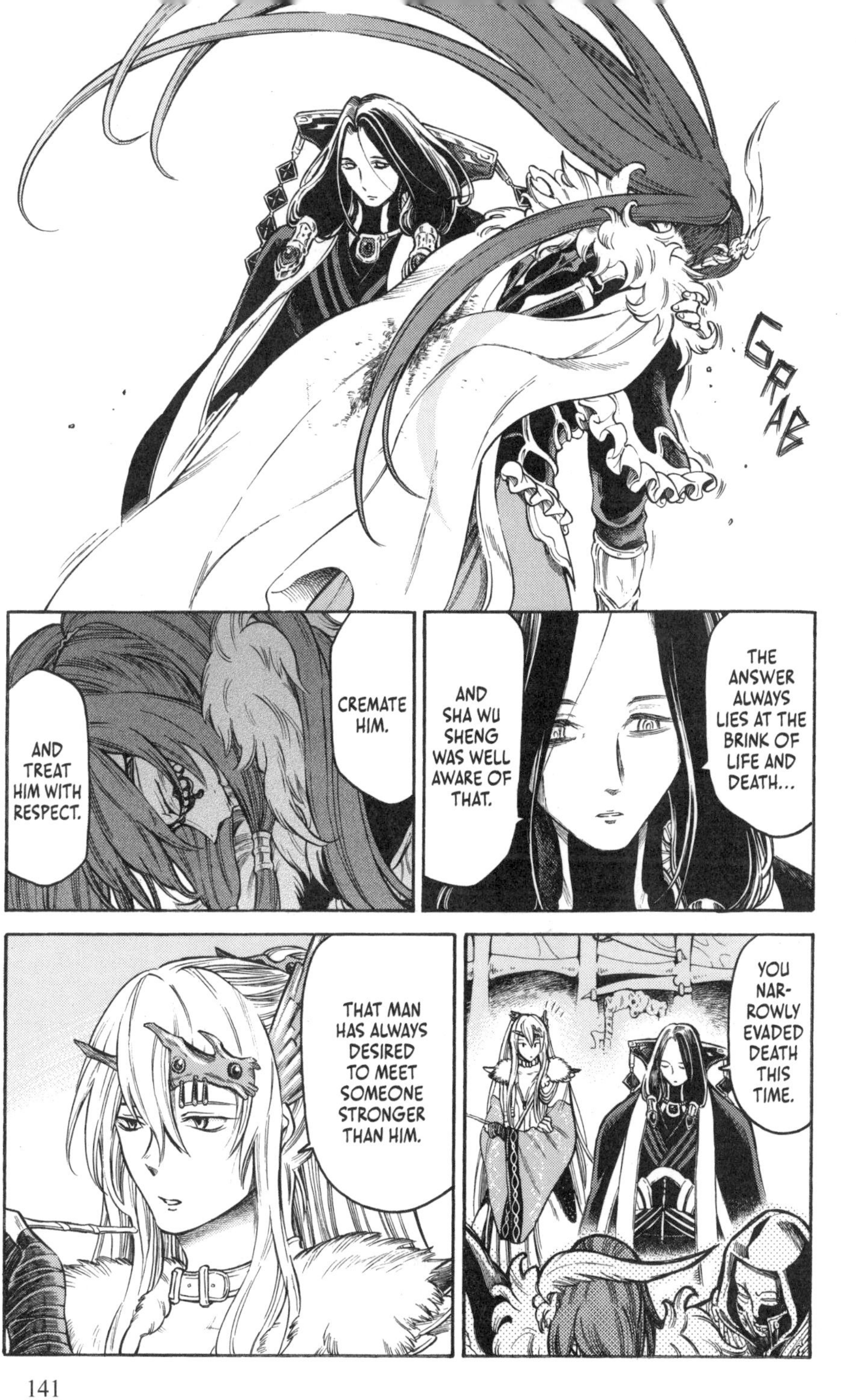
GRAB
THE ANSWER ALWAYS LIES AT THE BRINK OF LIFE AND DEATH…
AND SHA WU SHENG WAS WELL AWARE OF THAT.
CREMATE HIM.
AND TREAT HIM WITH RESPECT.
YOU NAR-ROWLY EVADED DEATH THIS TIME.
THAT MAN HAS ALWAYS DESIRED TO MEET SOMEONE STRONGER THAN HIM.

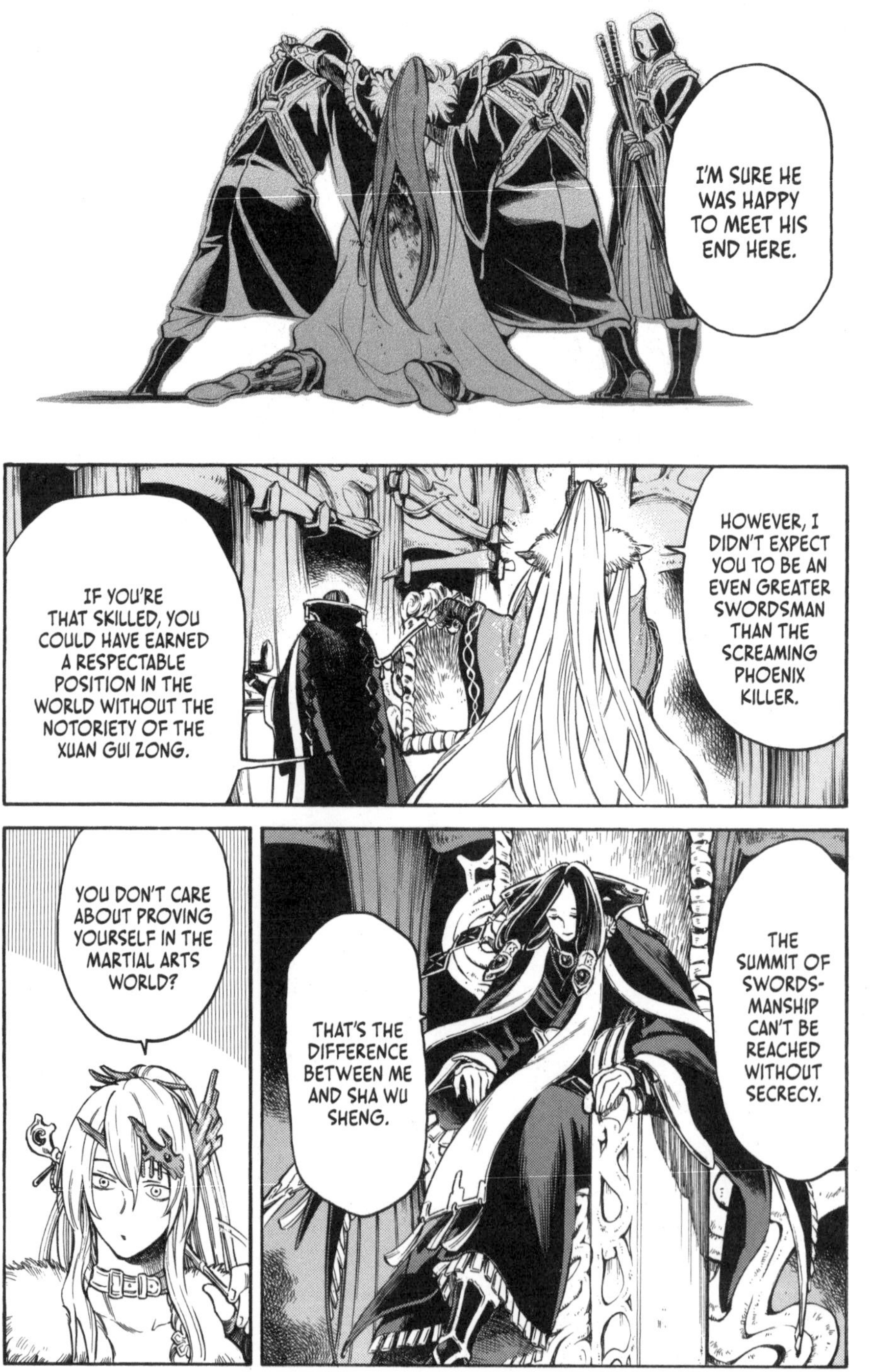
I'M SURE HE WAS HAPPY TO MEET HIS END HERE.
HOWEVER, I DIDN'T EXPECT YOU TO BE AN EVEN GREATER SWORDSMAN THAN THE SCREAMING PHOENIX KILLER.
IF YOU'RE THAT SKILLED, YOU COULD HAVE EARNED A RESPECTABLE POSITION IN THE WORLD WITHOUT THE NOTORIETY OF THE XUAN GUI ZONG.
THE SUMMIT OF SWORDS-MANSHIP CAN'T BE REACHED WITHOUT SECRECY.
THAT'S THE DIFFERENCE BETWEEN ME AND SHA WU SHENG.
YOU DON'T CARE ABOUT PROVING YOURSELF IN THE MARTIAL ARTS WORLD?

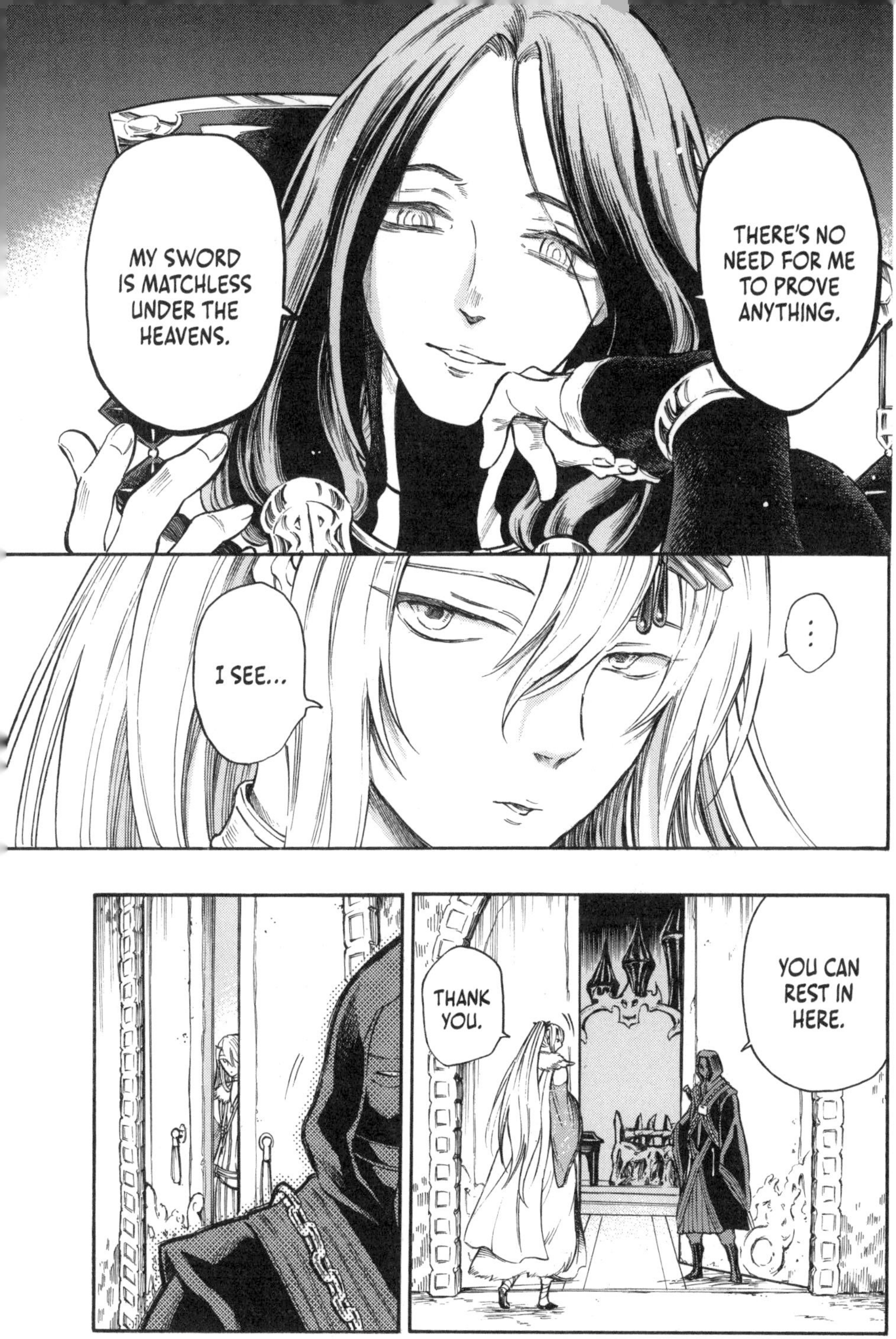
THERE'S NO NEED FOR ME TO PROVE ANYTHING.
MY SWORD IS MATCHLESS UNDER THE HEAVENS.
...
I SEE...
YOU CAN REST IN HERE.
THANK YOU.

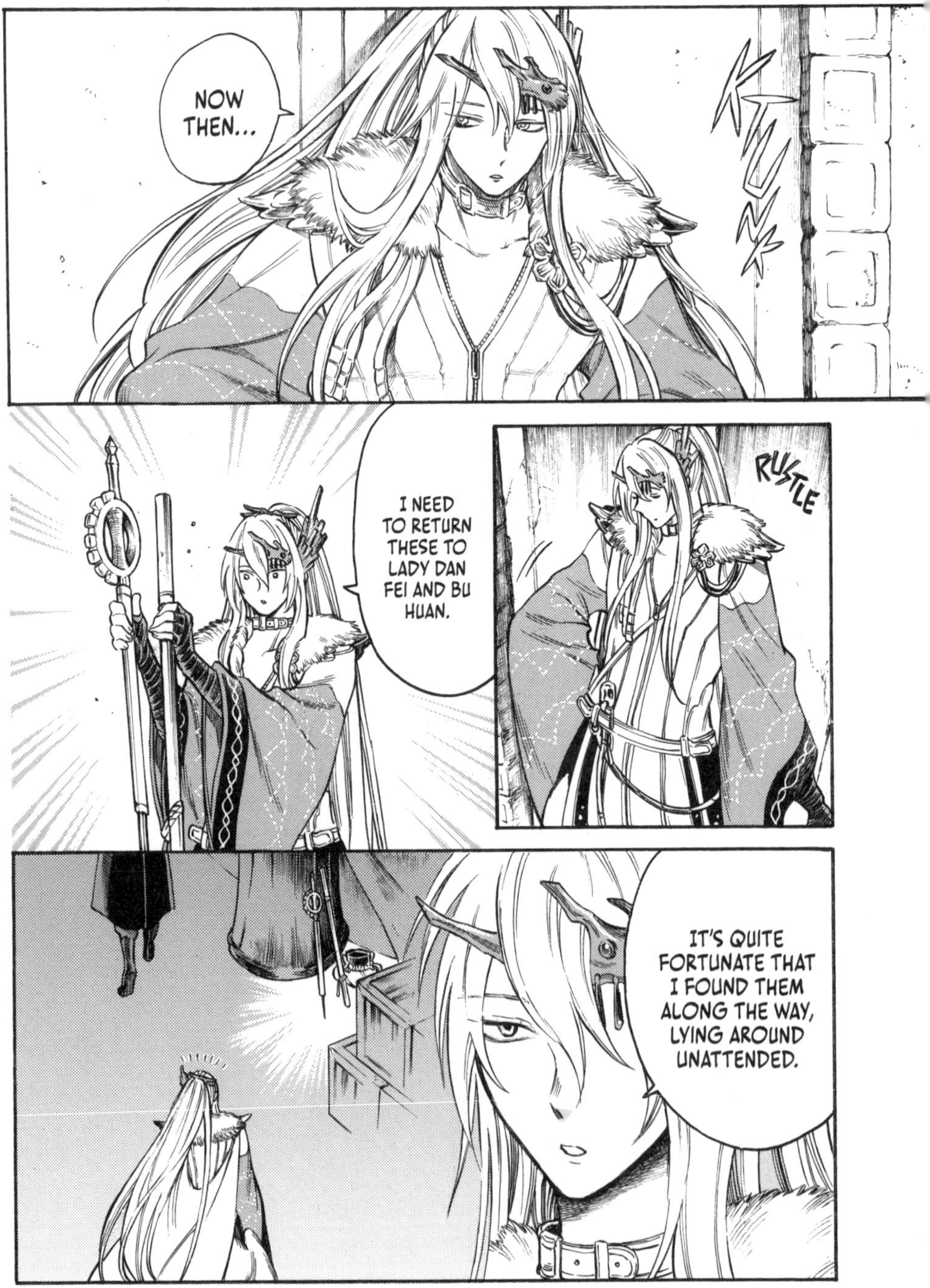
KTUNK
NOW THEN...
RUSTLE
I NEED TO RETURN THESE TO LADY DAN FEI AND BU HUAN.
IT'S QUITE FORTUNATE THAT I FOUND THEM ALONG THE WAY, LYING AROUND UNATTENDED.

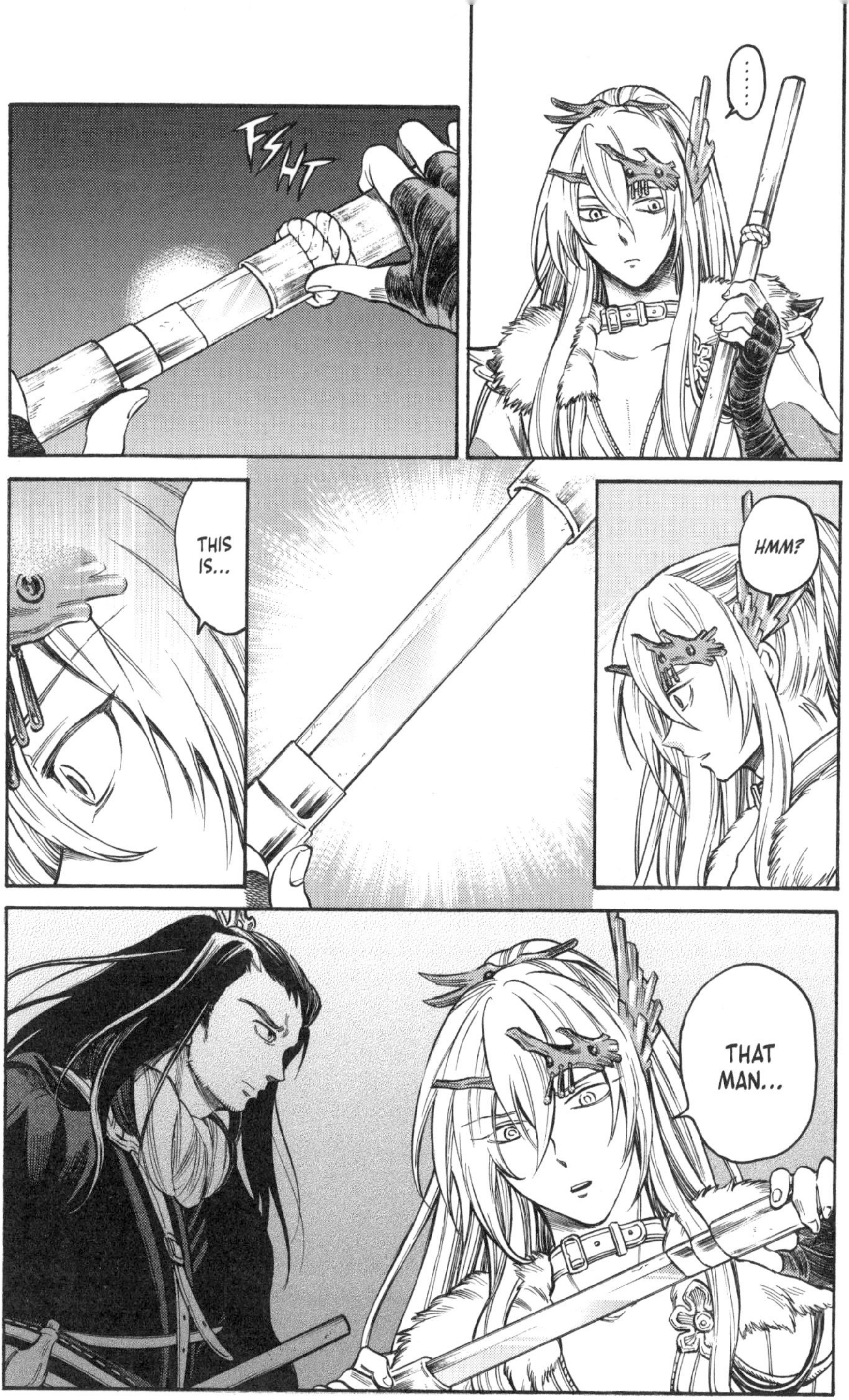
......
FSHT
HMM?
THIS IS...
THAT MAN...

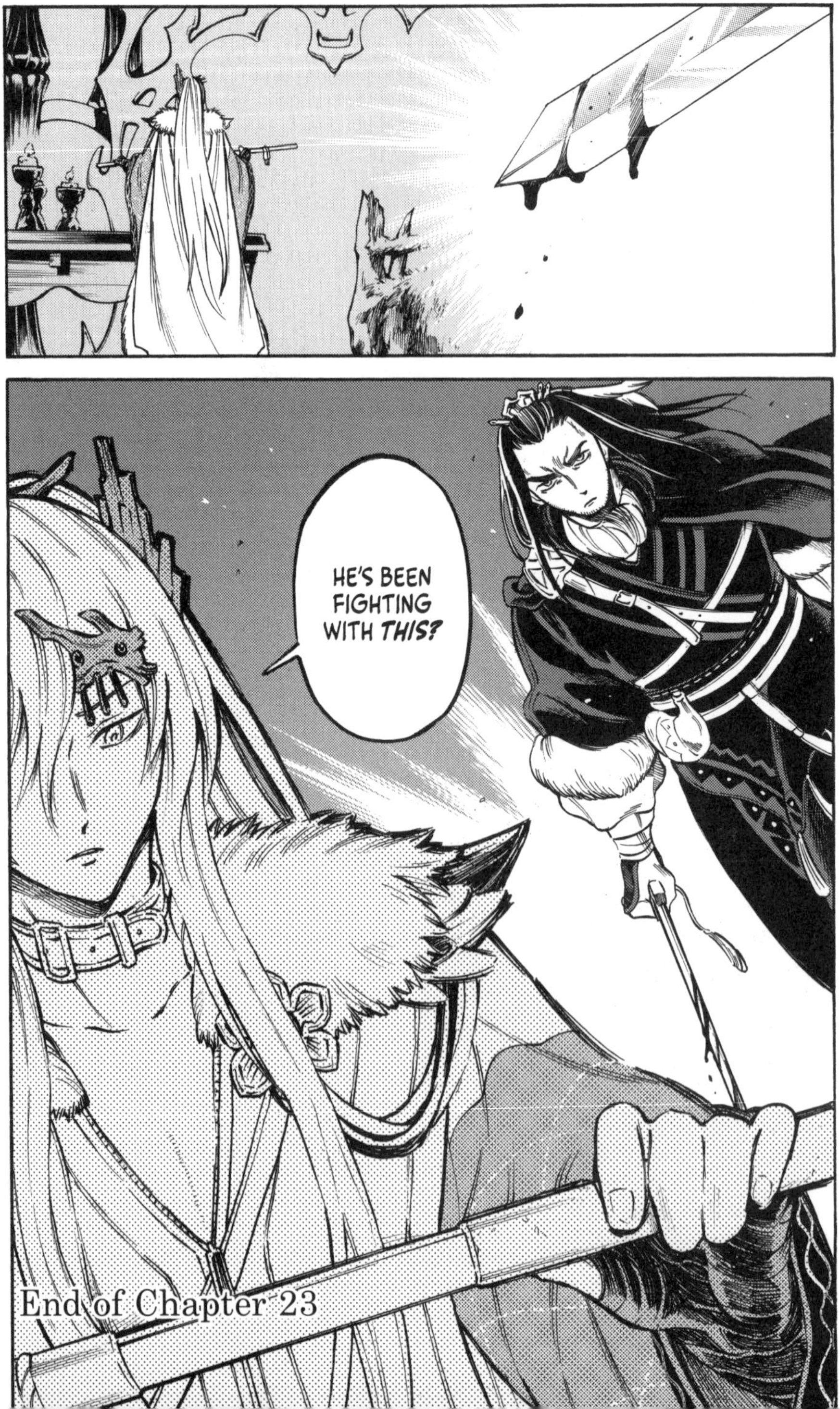
HE'S BEEN FIGHTING WITH THIS?
End of Chapter 23

Chapter 24

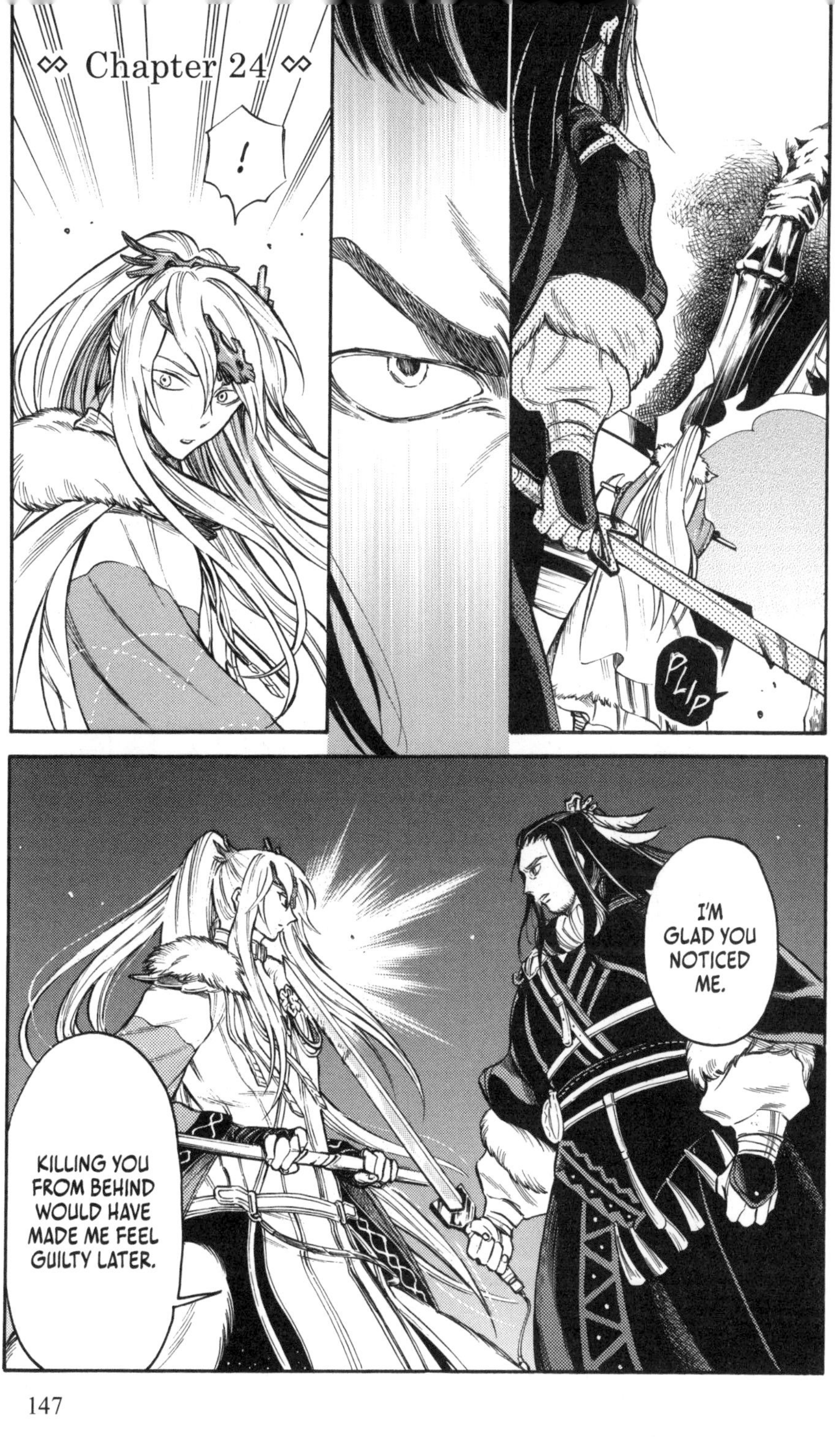
PLIP
!
I'M GLAD YOU NOTICED ME.
KILLING YOU FROM BEHIND WOULD HAVE MADE ME FEEL GUILTY LATER.

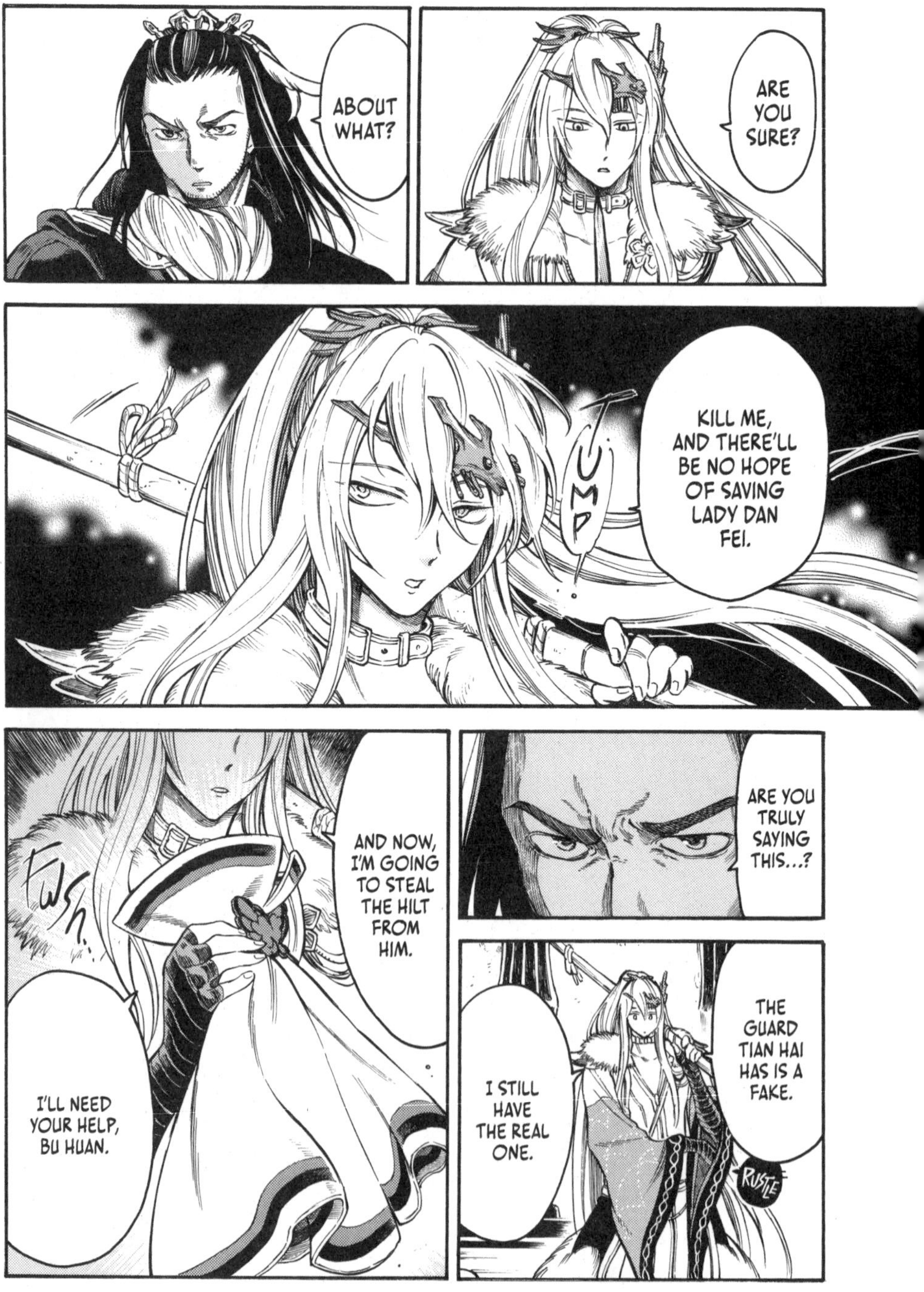
ARE YOU SURE?
ABOUT WHAT?
THUMP
KILL ME, AND THERE'LL BE NO HOPE OF SAVING LADY DAN FEI.
ARE YOU TRULY SAYING THIS...?
THE GUARD TIAN HAI HAS IS A FAKE.
I STILL HAVE THE REAL ONE.
RUSTLE
AND NOW, I'M GOING TO STEAL THE HILT FROM HIM.
FWSH
I'LL NEED YOUR HELP, BU HUAN.

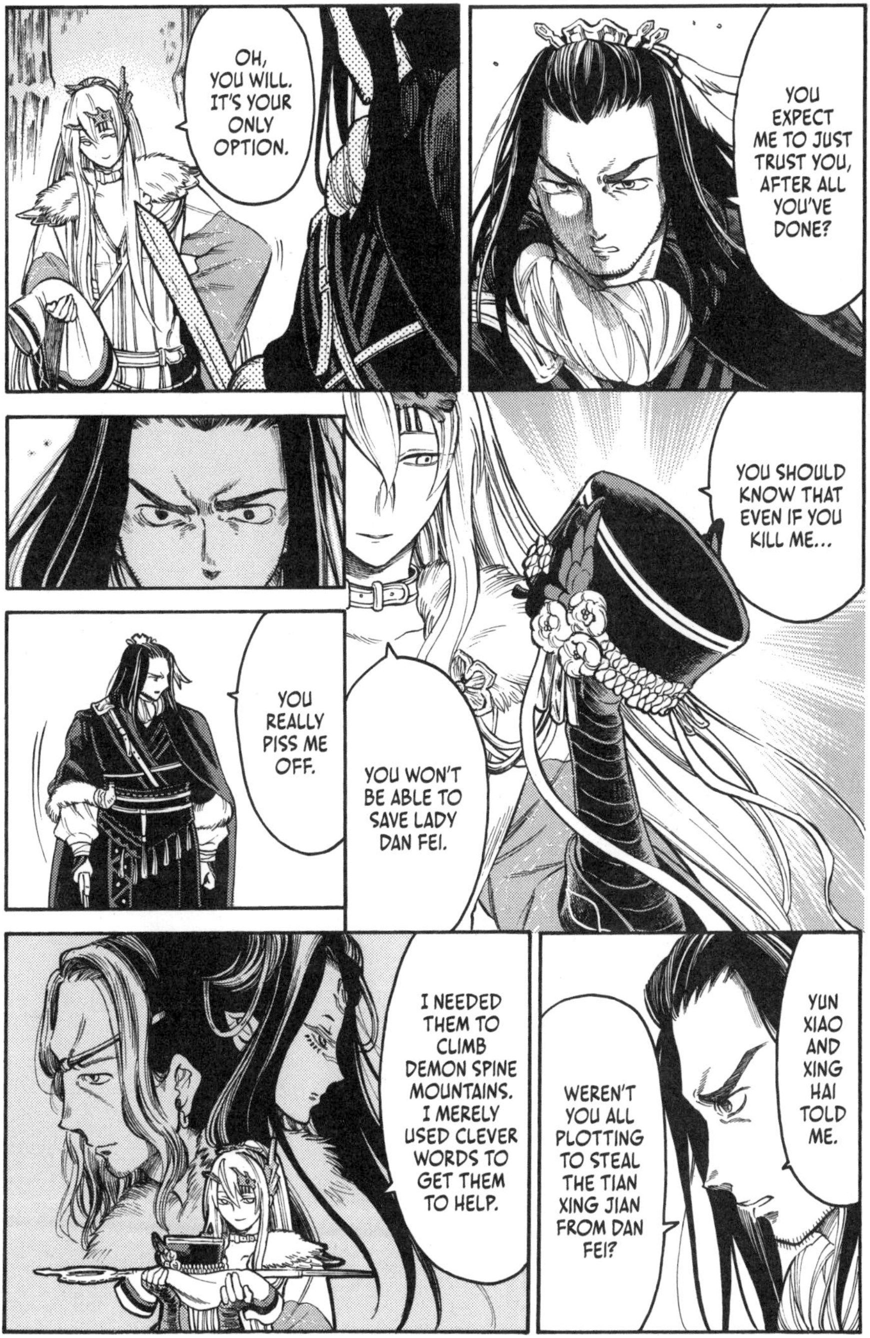
YOU EXPECT ME TO JUST TRUST YOU, AFTER ALL YOU'VE DONE?
OH, YOU WILL. IT'S YOUR ONLY OPTION.
YOU SHOULD KNOW THAT EVEN IF YOU KILL ME...
YOU WON'T BE ABLE TO SAVE LADY DAN FEI.
YOU REALLY PISS ME OFF.
YUN XIAO AND XING HAI TOLD ME.
WEREN'T YOU ALL PLOTTING TO STEAL THE TIAN XING JIAN FROM DAN FEI?
I NEEDED THEM TO CLIMB DEMON SPINE MOUNTAINS. I MERELY USED CLEVER WORDS TO GET THEM TO HELP.

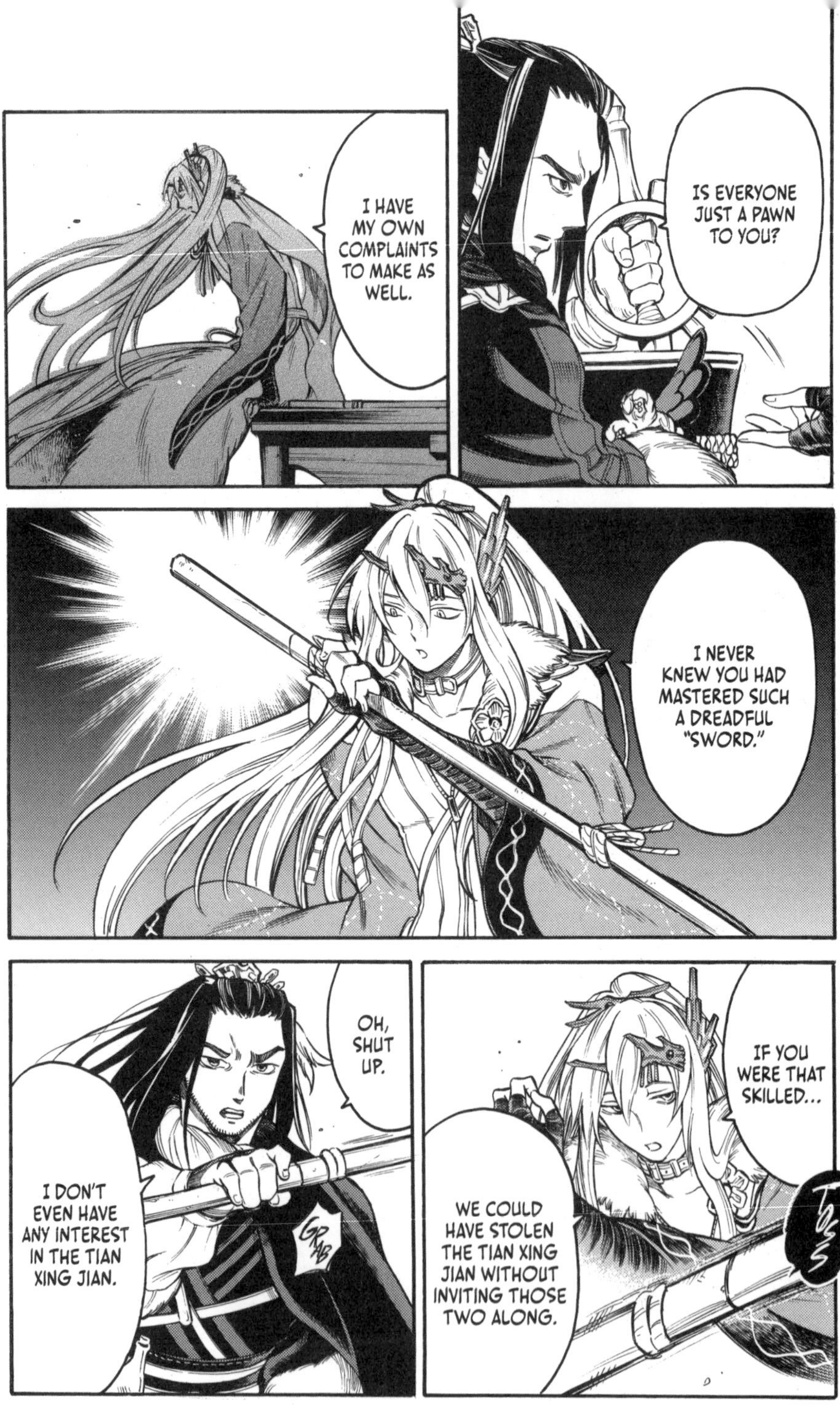
IS EVERYONE JUST A PAWN TO YOU?
I HAVE MY OWN COMPLAINTS TO MAKE AS WELL.
I NEVER KNEW YOU HAD MASTERED SUCH A DREADFUL "SWORD."
IF YOU WERE THAT SKILLED...
WE COULD HAVE STOLEN THE TIAN XING JIAN WITHOUT INVITING THOSE TWO ALONG.
TOSS
OH, SHUT UP.
I DON'T EVEN HAVE ANY INTEREST IN THE TIAN XING JIAN.
GRAB

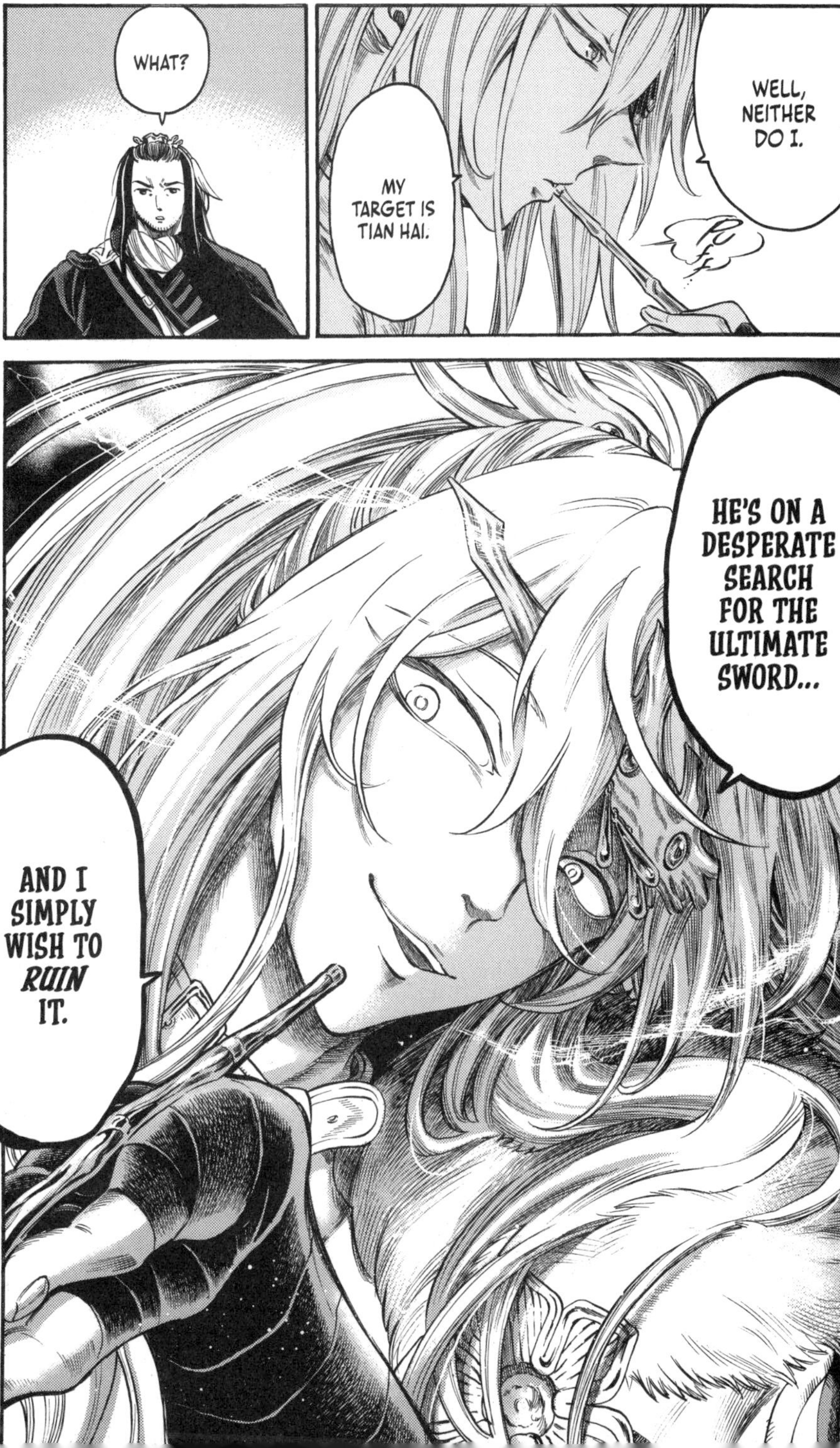
WELL, NEITHER DO I.
MY TARGET IS TIAN HAI.
WHAT?
HE'S ON A DESPERATE SEARCH FOR THE ULTIMATE SWORD...
AND I SIMPLY WISH TO *RUIN* IT.

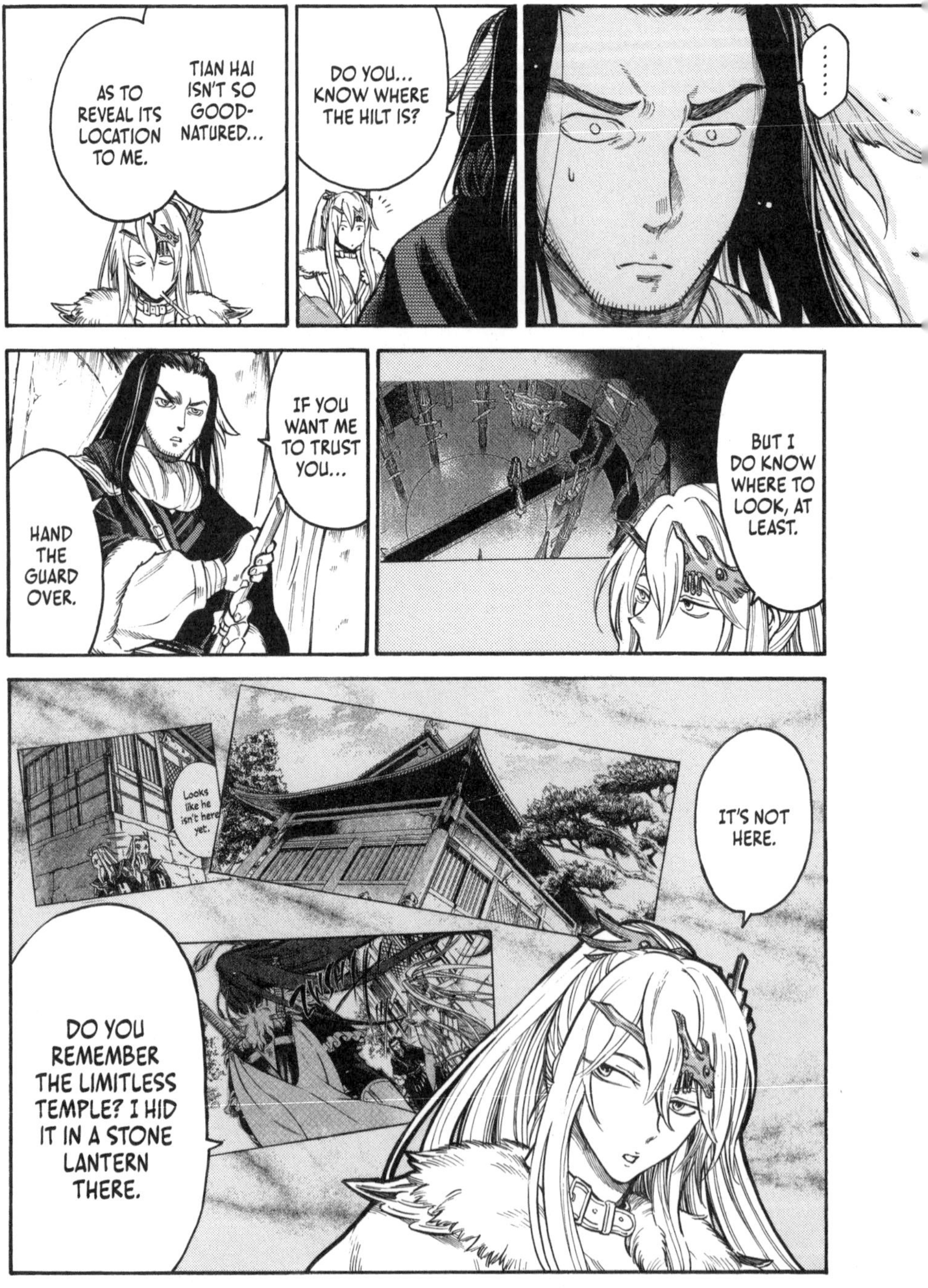
……
DO YOU… KNOW WHERE THE HILT IS?
TIAN HAI ISN'T SO GOOD-NATURED…
AS TO REVEAL ITS LOCATION TO ME.
BUT I DO KNOW WHERE TO LOOK, AT LEAST.
IF YOU WANT ME TO TRUST YOU…
HAND THE GUARD OVER.
IT'S NOT HERE.
Looks like he isn't here yet.
DO YOU REMEMBER THE LIMITLESS TEMPLE? I HID IT IN A STONE LANTERN THERE.

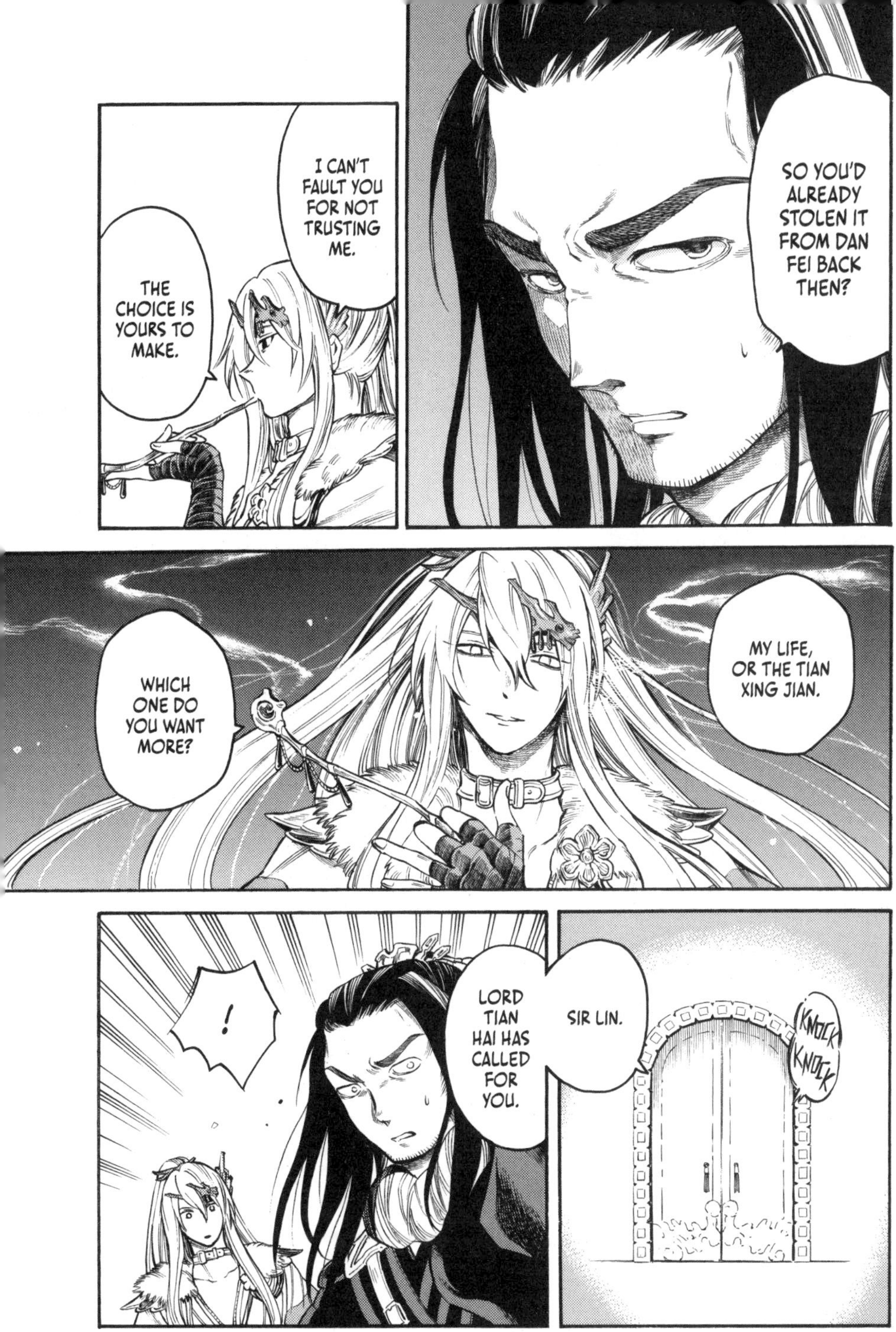
SO YOU'D ALREADY STOLEN IT FROM DAN FEI BACK THEN?
I CAN'T FAULT YOU FOR NOT TRUSTING ME.
THE CHOICE IS YOURS TO MAKE.
MY LIFE, OR THE TIAN XING JIAN.
WHICH ONE DO YOU WANT MORE?
KNOCK KNOCK
SIR LIN.
LORD TIAN HAI HAS CALLED FOR YOU.
!

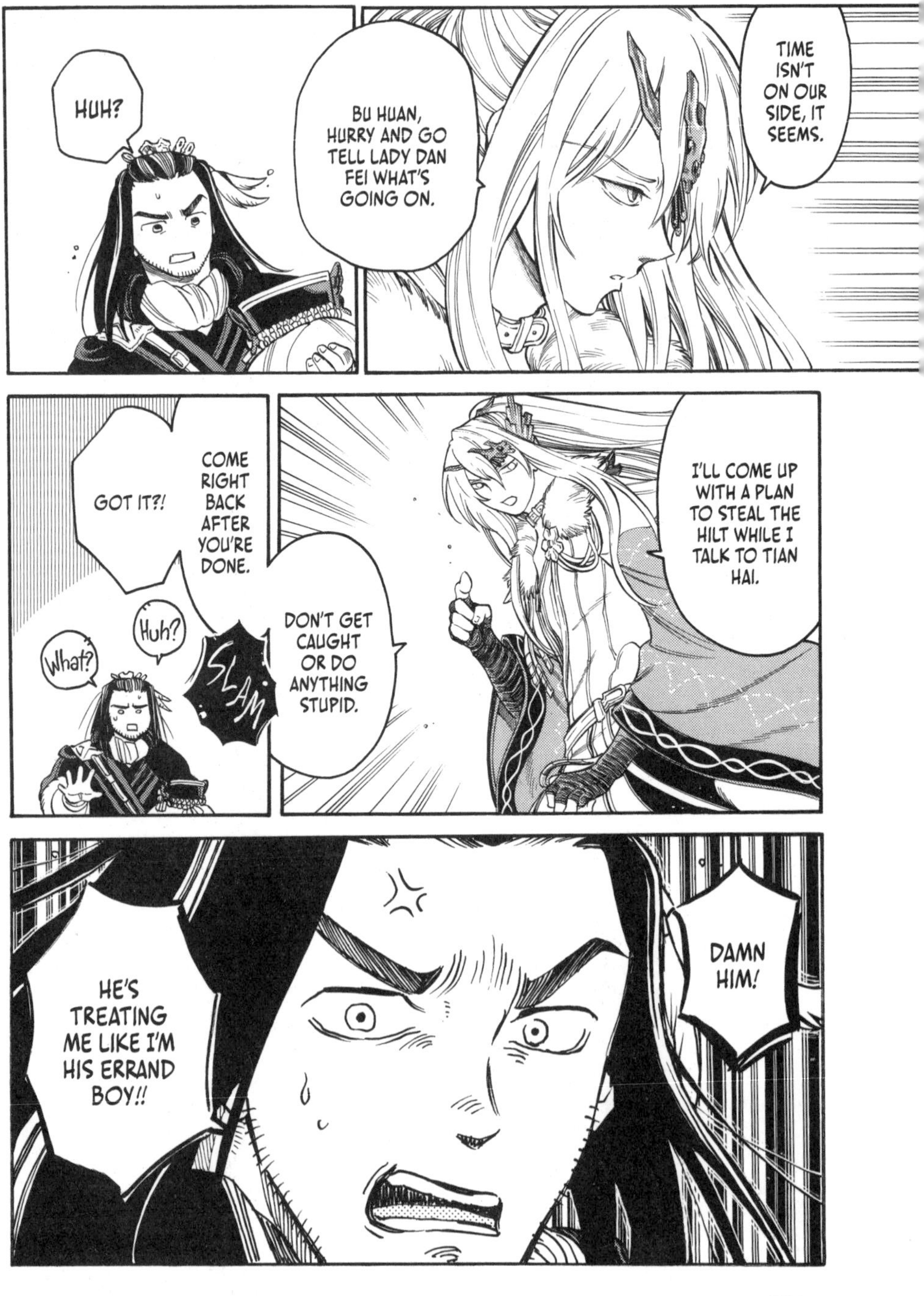
TIME ISN'T ON OUR SIDE, IT SEEMS.
BU HUAN, HURRY AND GO TELL LADY DAN FEI WHAT'S GOING ON.
HUH?
I'LL COME UP WITH A PLAN TO STEAL THE HILT WHILE I TALK TO TIAN HAI.
COME RIGHT BACK AFTER YOU'RE DONE.
GOT IT?!
DON'T GET CAUGHT OR DO ANYTHING STUPID.
SLAM
Huh?
What?
DAMN HIM!
HE'S TREATING ME LIKE I'M HIS ERRAND BOY!!

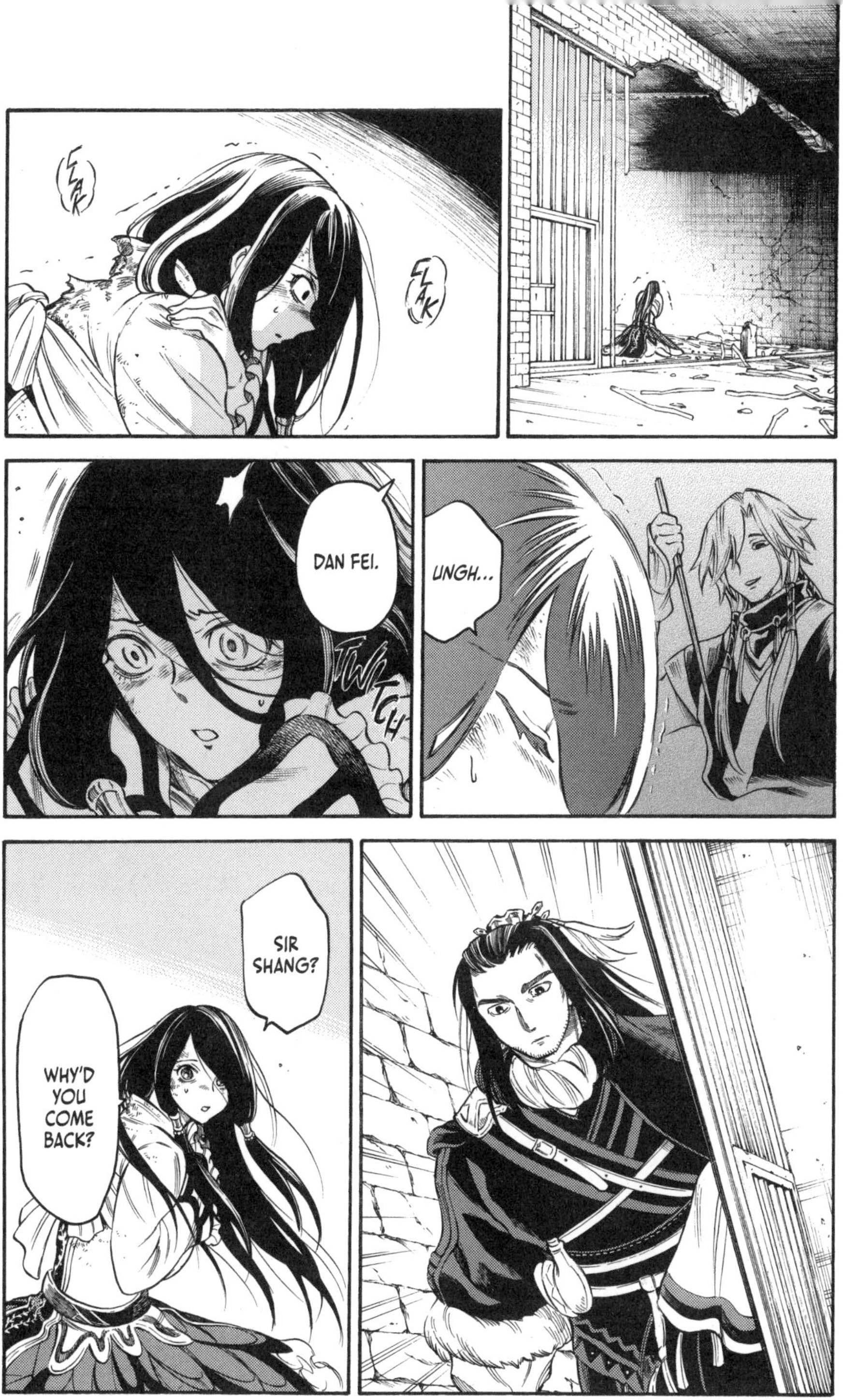
FLAK
FLAK
UNGH...
DAN FEI.
TWITCH
SIR SHANG?
WHY'D YOU COME BACK?

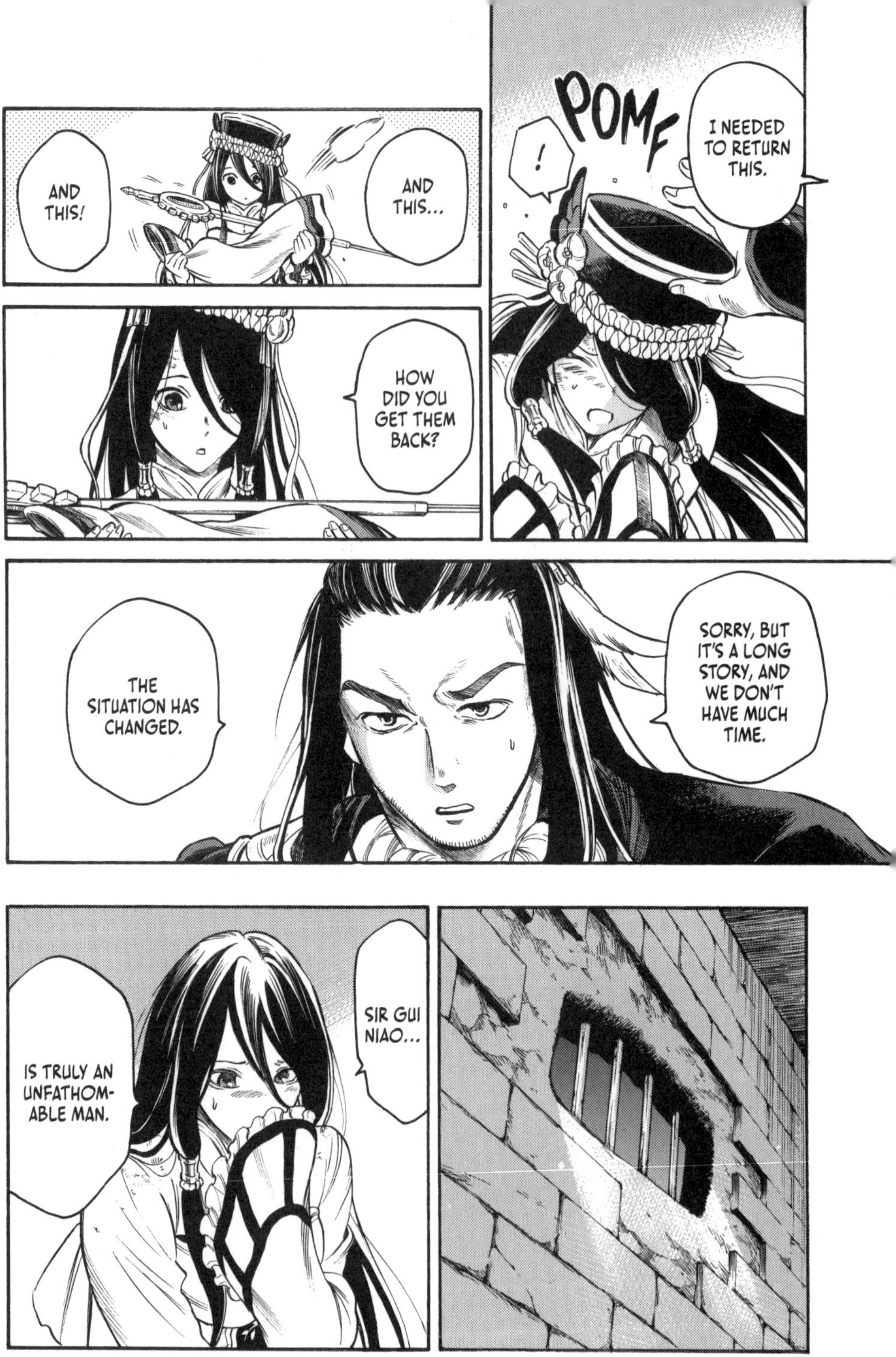
I NEEDED TO RETURN THIS.
POMF
!
AND THIS...
AND THIS!
HOW DID YOU GET THEM BACK?
SORRY, BUT IT'S A LONG STORY, AND WE DON'T HAVE MUCH TIME.
THE SITUATION HAS CHANGED.
SIR GUI NIAO...
IS TRULY AN UNFATHOM-ABLE MAN.

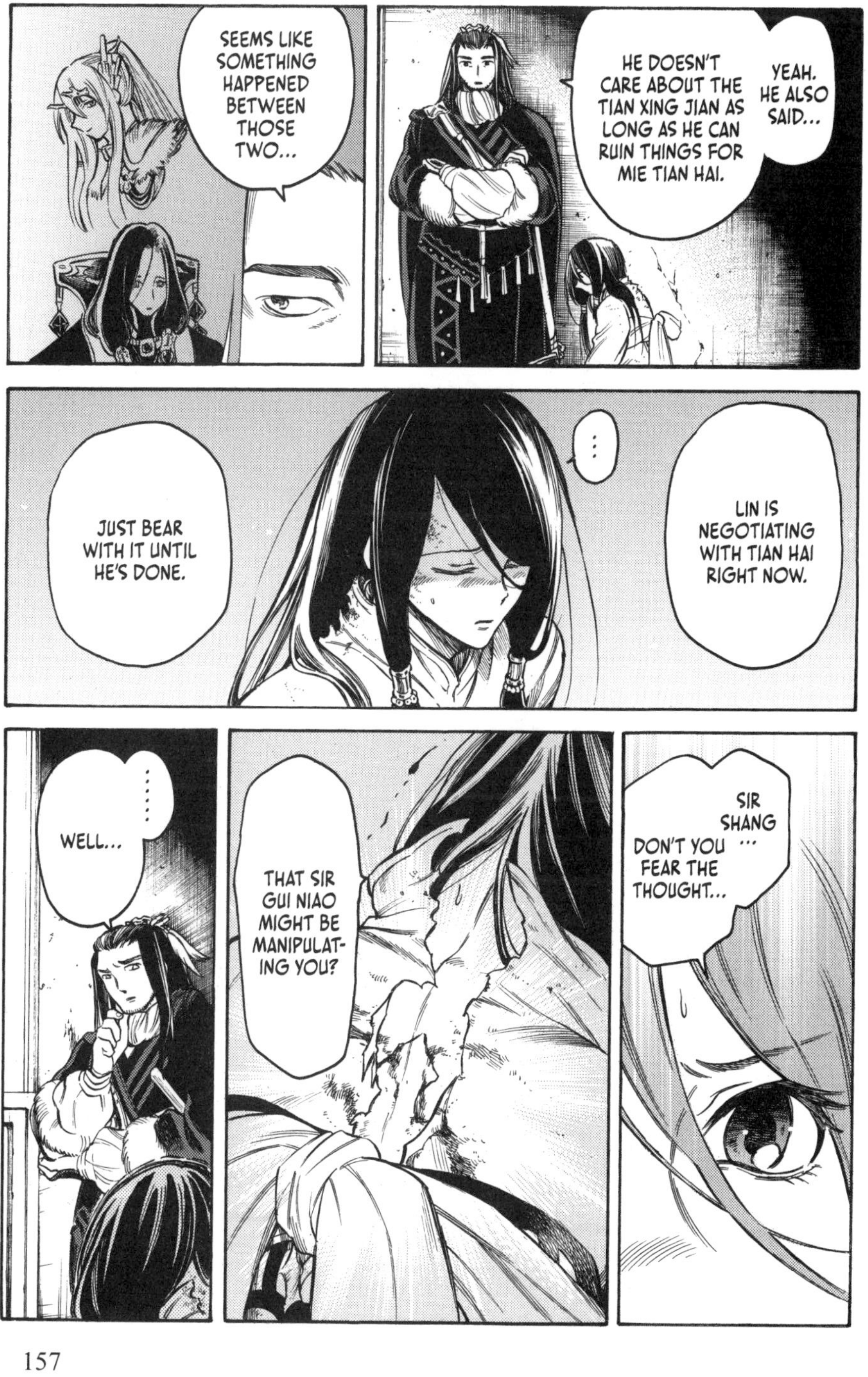
YEAH. HE ALSO SAID…
HE DOESN'T CARE ABOUT THE TIAN XING JIAN AS LONG AS HE CAN RUIN THINGS FOR MIE TIAN HAI.
SEEMS LIKE SOMETHING HAPPENED BETWEEN THOSE TWO…
LIN IS NEGOTIATING WITH TIAN HAI RIGHT NOW.
…
JUST BEAR WITH IT UNTIL HE'S DONE.
SIR SHANG …
DON'T YOU FEAR THE THOUGHT…
THAT SIR GUI NIAO MIGHT BE MANIPULATING YOU?
……
WELL…

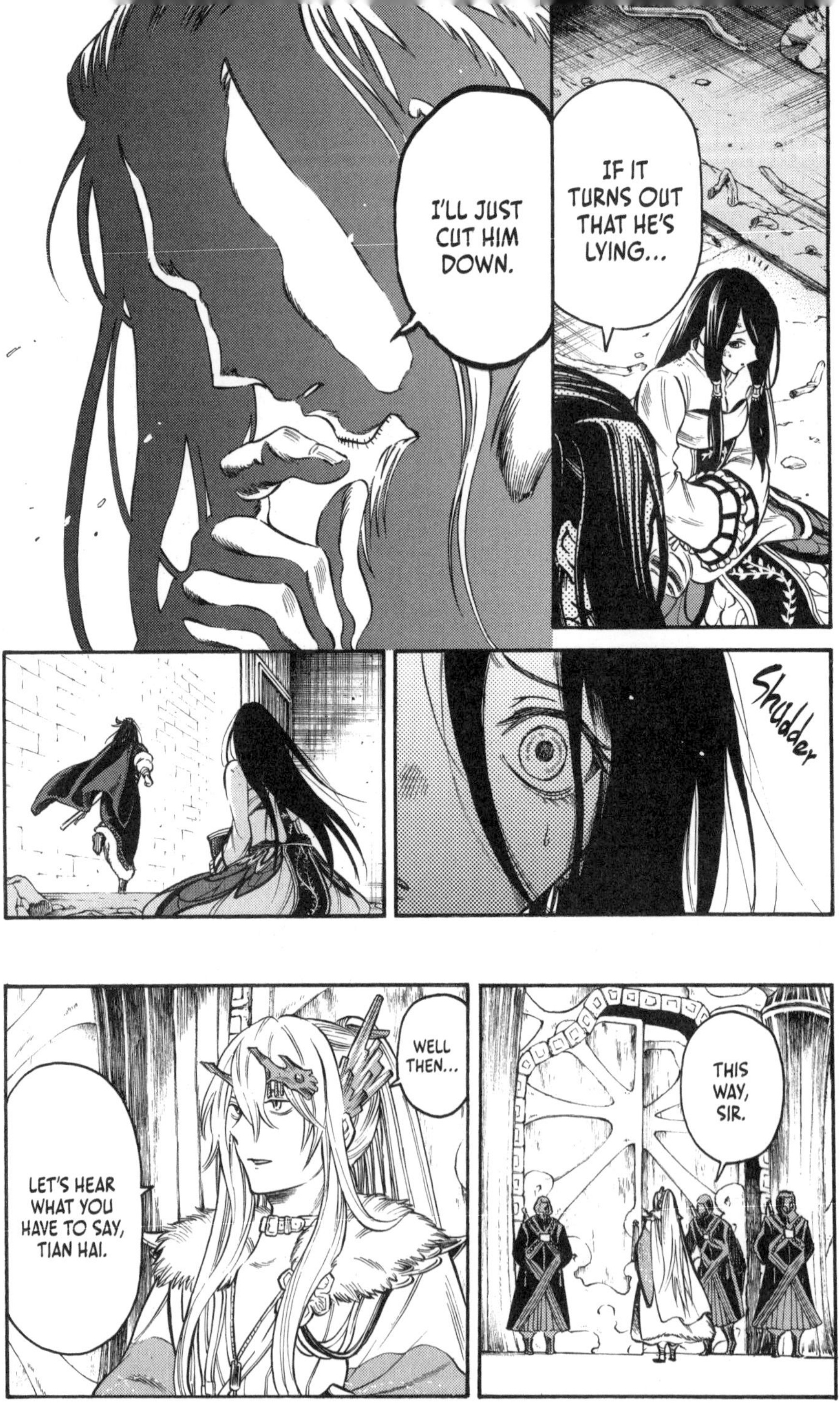
IF IT TURNS OUT THAT HE'S LYING...
I'LL JUST CUT HIM DOWN.
Shudder
THIS WAY, SIR.
WELL THEN...
LET'S HEAR WHAT YOU HAVE TO SAY, TIAN HAI.

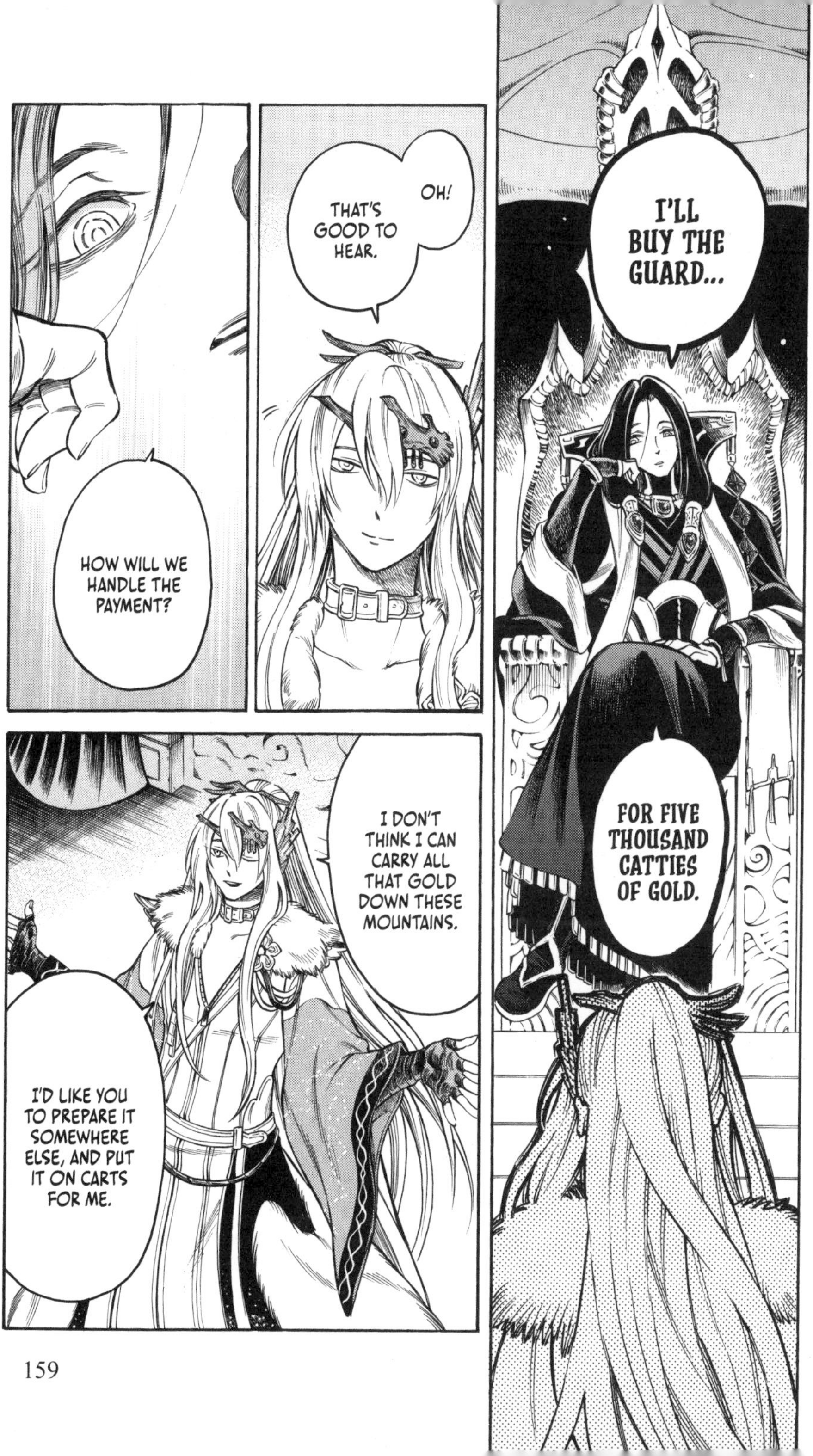
I'LL BUY THE GUARD...
FOR FIVE THOUSAND CATTIES OF GOLD.
OH!
THAT'S GOOD TO HEAR.
HOW WILL WE HANDLE THE PAYMENT?
I DON'T THINK I CAN CARRY ALL THAT GOLD DOWN THESE MOUNTAINS.
I'D LIKE YOU TO PREPARE IT SOMEWHERE ELSE, AND PUT IT ON CARTS FOR ME.

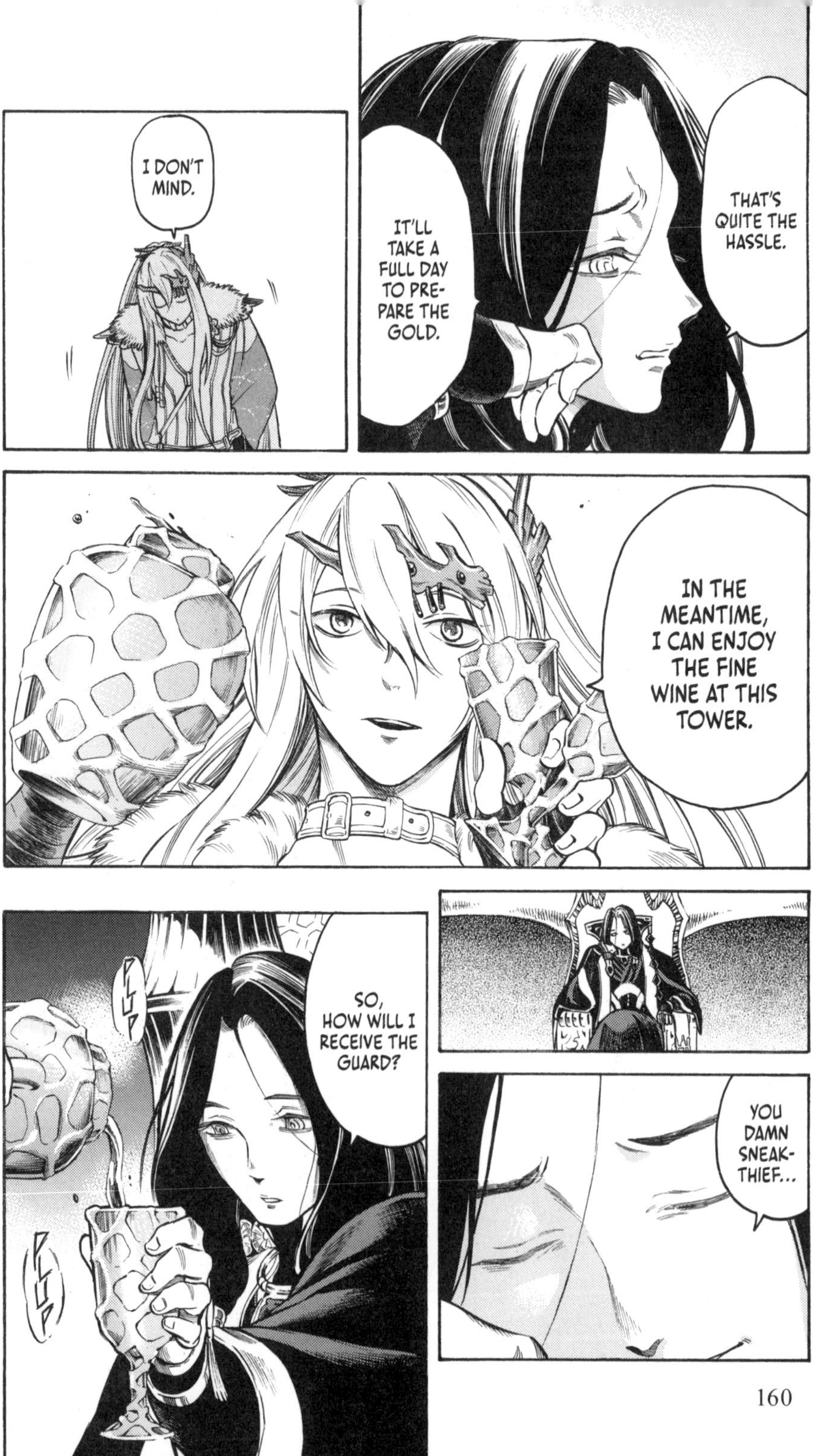
THAT'S QUITE THE HASSLE.
IT'LL TAKE A FULL DAY TO PRE-PARE THE GOLD.
I DON'T MIND.
IN THE MEANTIME, I CAN ENJOY THE FINE WINE AT THIS TOWER.
YOU DAMN SNEAK-THIEF...
SO, HOW WILL I RECEIVE THE GUARD?
PLUP
PLUP

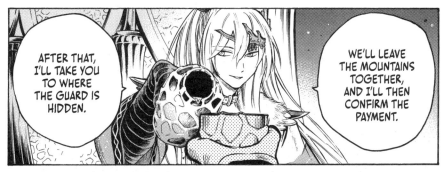

WE'LL LEAVE THE MOUNTAINS TOGETHER, AND I'LL THEN CONFIRM THE PAYMENT.
AFTER THAT, I'LL TAKE YOU TO WHERE THE GUARD IS HIDDEN.
HOW DO I KNOW YOU WON'T JUST TAKE THE GOLD AND RUN?
I MAY BE AN INFAMOUS THIEF...
BUT EVEN I CAN'T RUN AND HIDE WHILE CARRYING ALL THAT GOLD AROUND.
THAT IS TRUE.
I'LL SEE TO THE PREPARATIONS RIGHT AWAY.
THEN, LET US TOAST TO THE NEW MASTER...
OF THE TIAN XING JIAN.

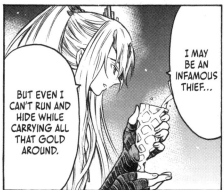

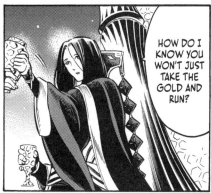

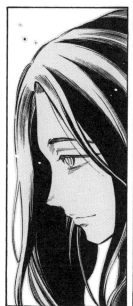

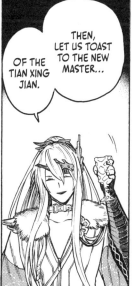

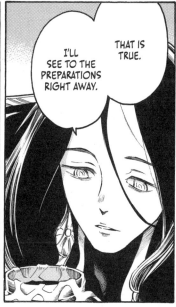

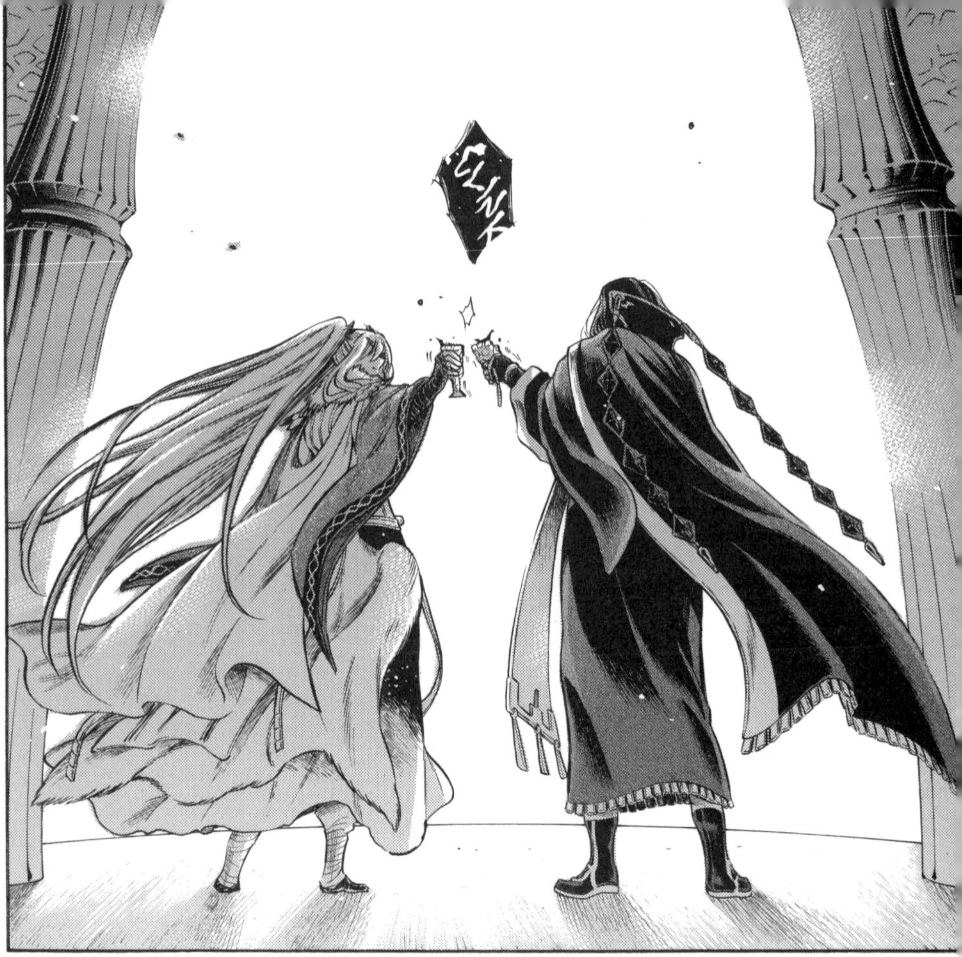
CLINK

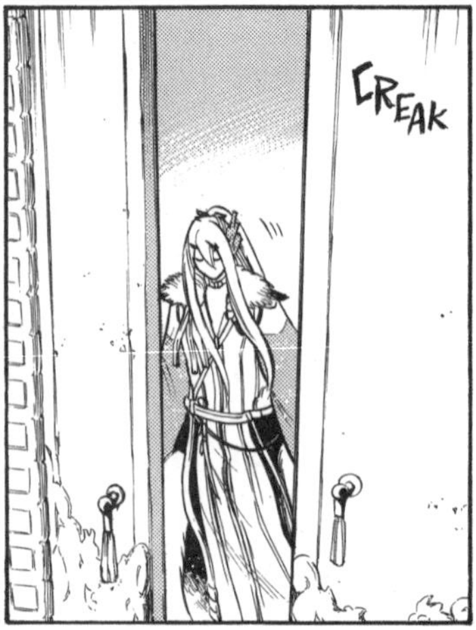
CREAK

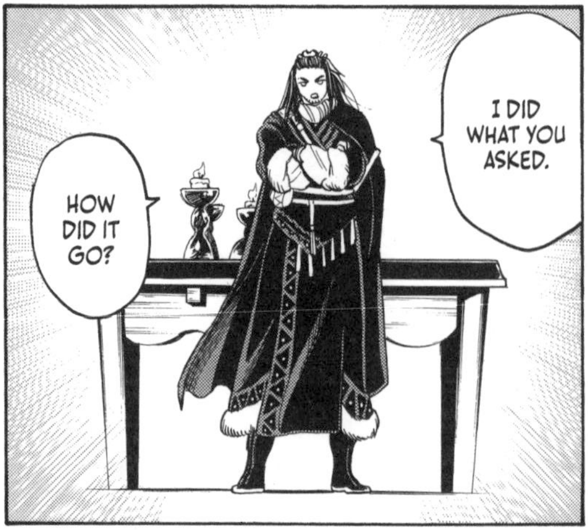
I DID WHAT YOU ASKED.
HOW DID IT GO?

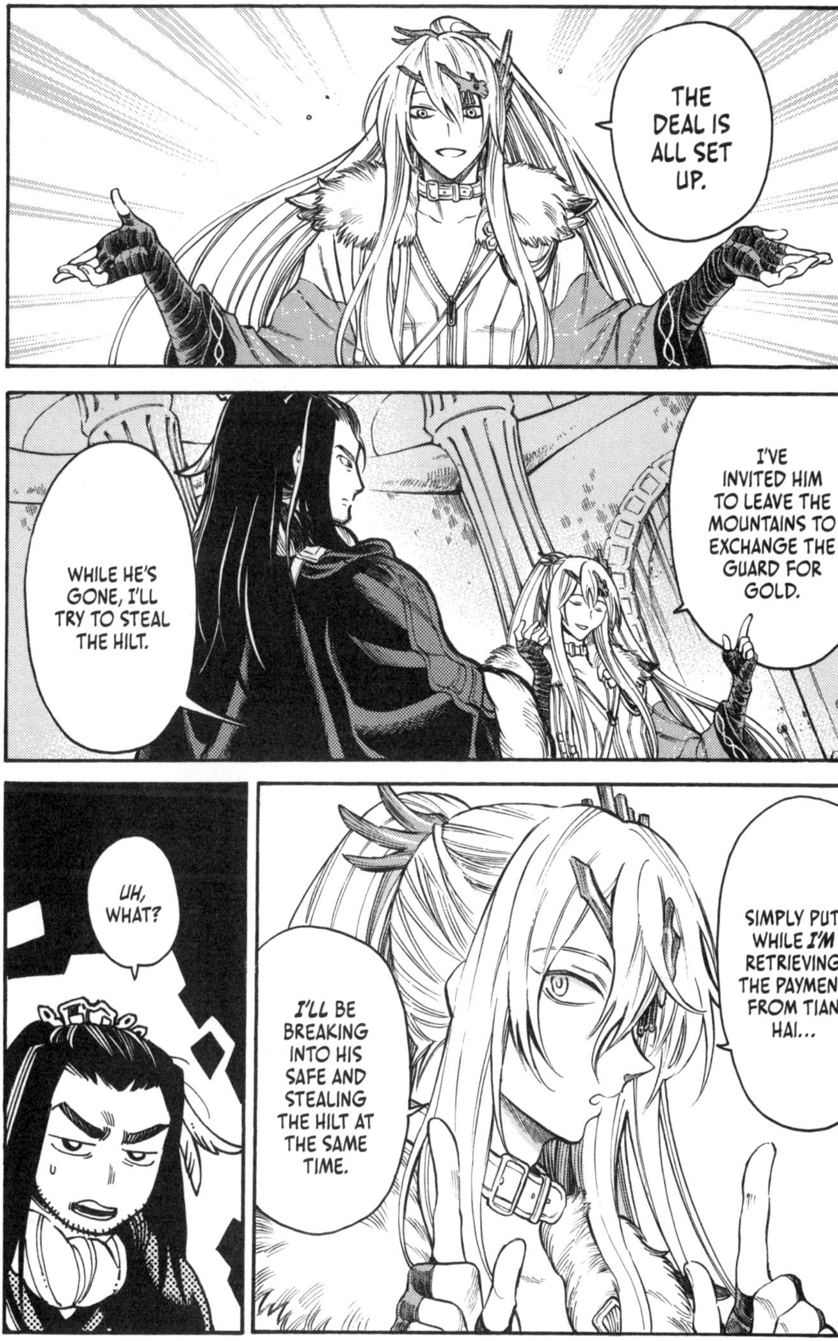
THE DEAL IS ALL SET UP.
I'VE INVITED HIM TO LEAVE THE MOUNTAINS TO EXCHANGE THE GUARD FOR GOLD.
WHILE HE'S GONE, I'LL TRY TO STEAL THE HILT.
SIMPLY PUT, WHILE *I'M* RETRIEVING THE PAYMENT FROM TIAN HAI...
I'LL BE BREAKING INTO HIS SAFE AND STEALING THE HILT AT THE SAME TIME.
UH, WHAT?

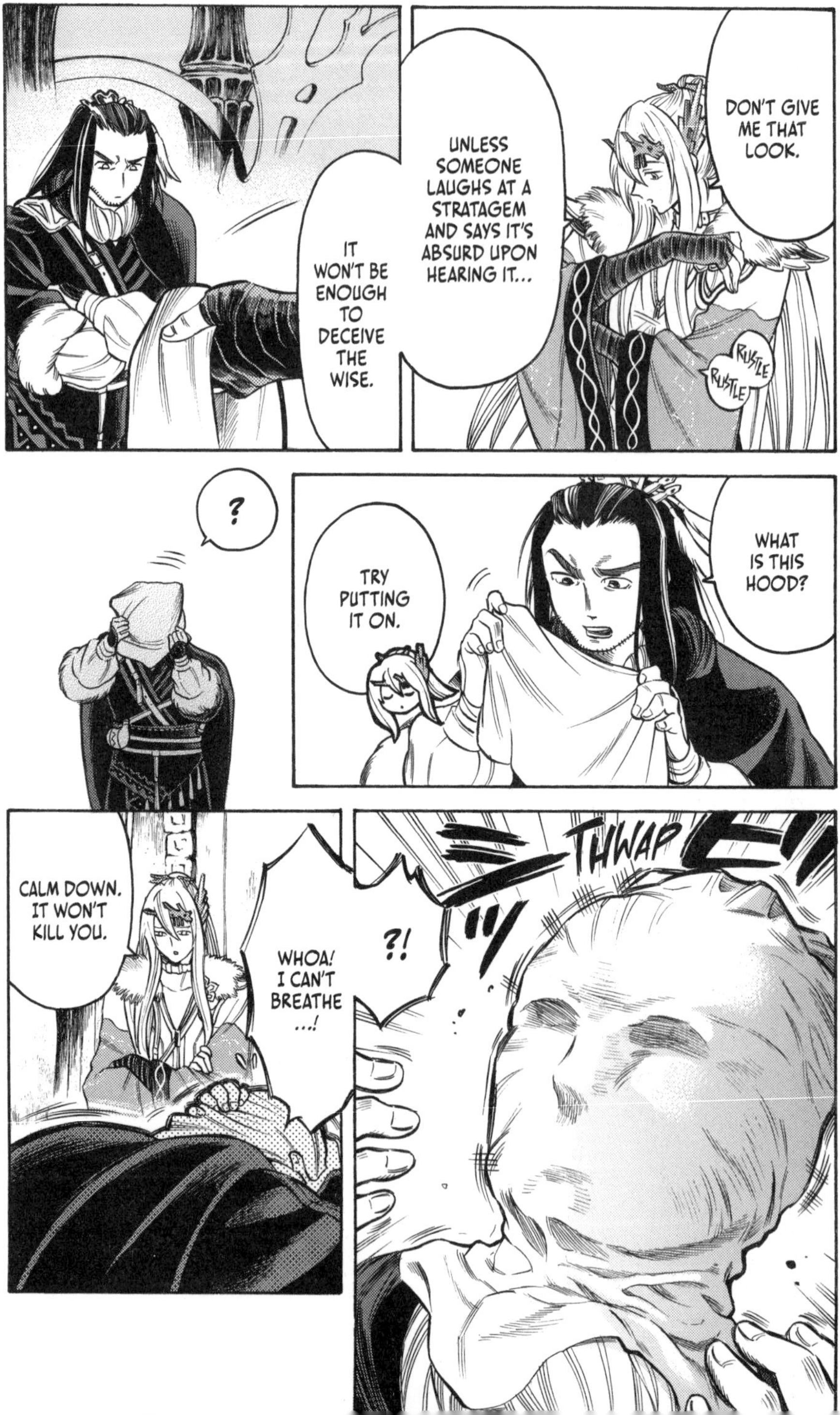
DON'T GIVE ME THAT LOOK.
RUSTLE RUSTLE
UNLESS SOMEONE LAUGHS AT A STRATAGEM AND SAYS IT'S ABSURD UPON HEARING IT...
IT WON'T BE ENOUGH TO DECEIVE THE WISE.
WHAT IS THIS HOOD?
TRY PUTTING IT ON.
?
THWAP
?!
WHOA! I CAN'T BREATHE...!
CALM DOWN. IT WON'T KILL YOU.

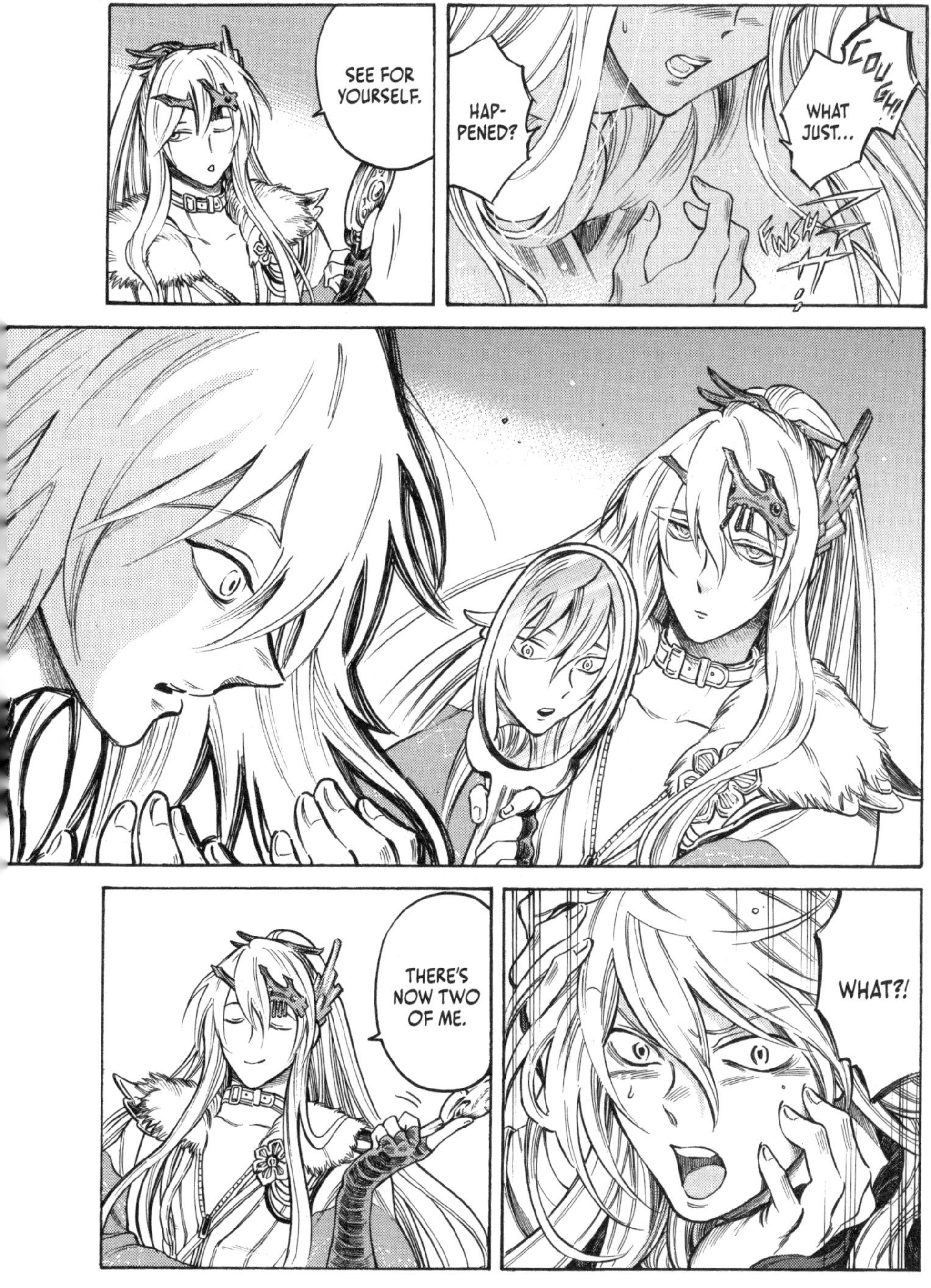
COUGH!!
WHAT JUST...
HAP-PENED?
FWSH
SEE FOR YOURSELF.
WHAT?!
THERE'S NOW TWO OF ME.

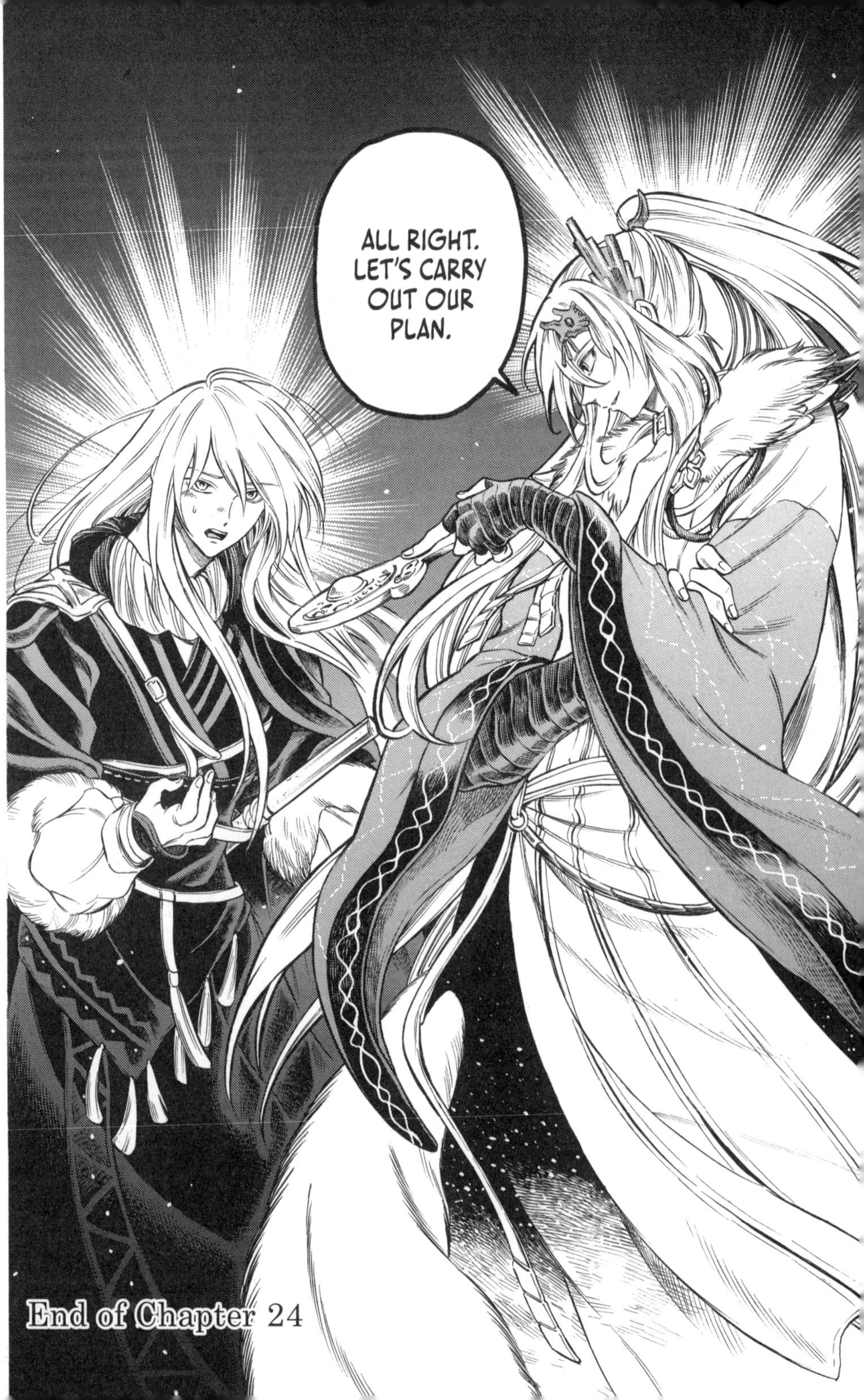
ALL RIGHT. LET'S CARRY OUT OUR PLAN.
End of Chapter 24

◇◇ Chapter 25 ◇◇

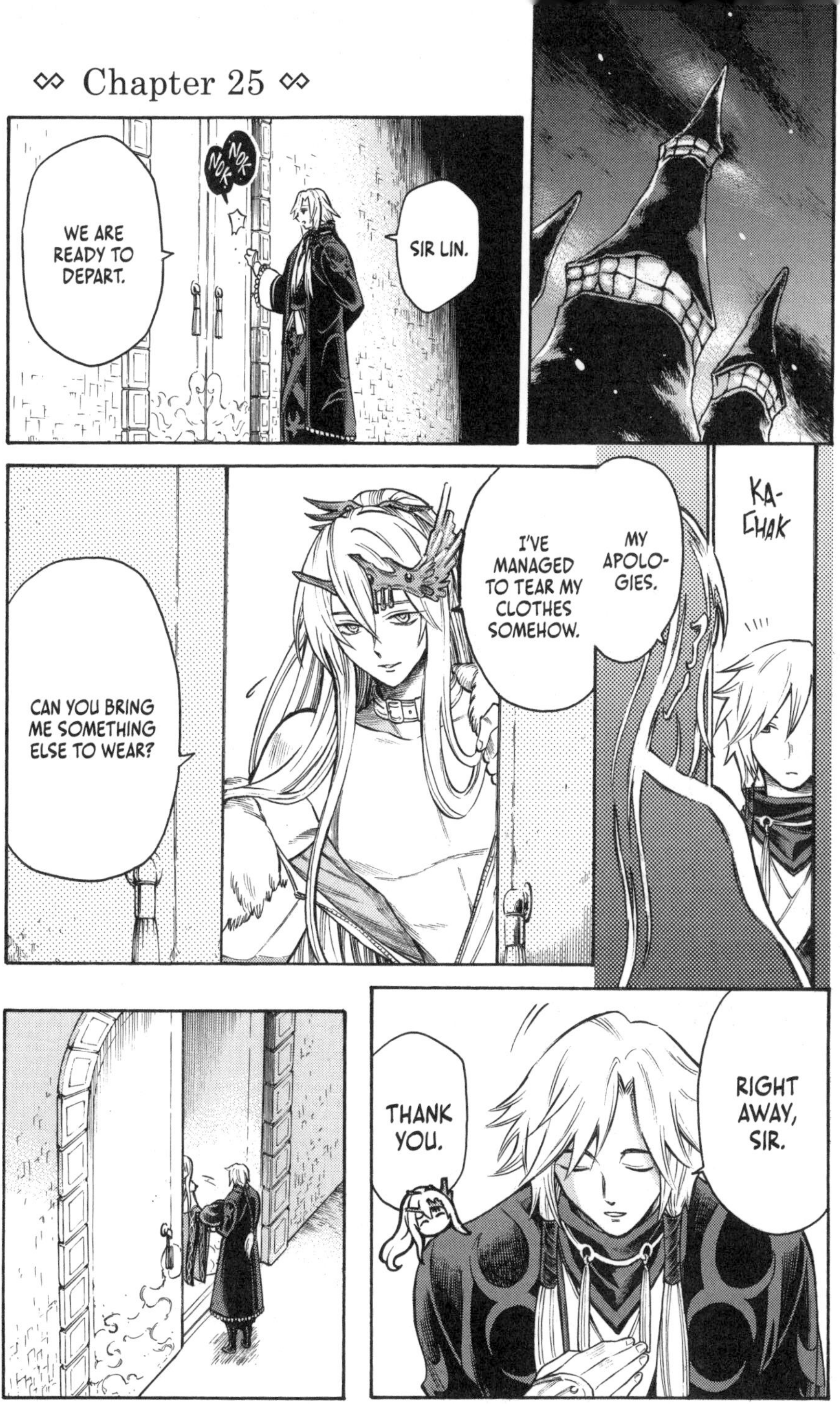
NOK NOK
SIR LIN.
WE ARE READY TO DEPART.
KA-CHAK
MY APOLOGIES.
I'VE MANAGED TO TEAR MY CLOTHES SOMEHOW.
CAN YOU BRING ME SOMETHING ELSE TO WEAR?
RIGHT AWAY, SIR.
THANK YOU.

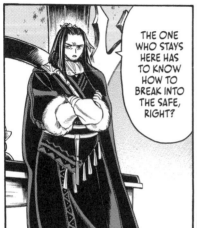

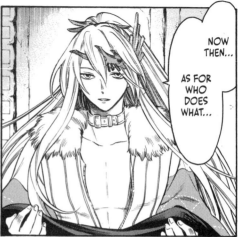

NOW THEN...
AS FOR WHO DOES WHAT...
THE ONE WHO STAYS HERE HAS TO KNOW HOW TO BREAK INTO THE SAFE, RIGHT?
WHICH MEANS I GET THE RAW DEAL AND HAVE TO LURE TIAN HAI AWAY.
I'M GLAD YOU'RE SO QUICK TO UNDER-STAND.
Shff
SO...
WHAT DO I DO AFTER I'VE RECEIVED THE GOLD?

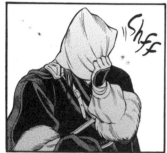

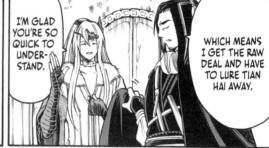

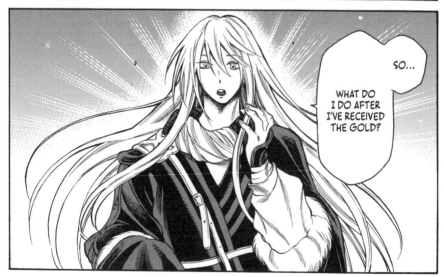

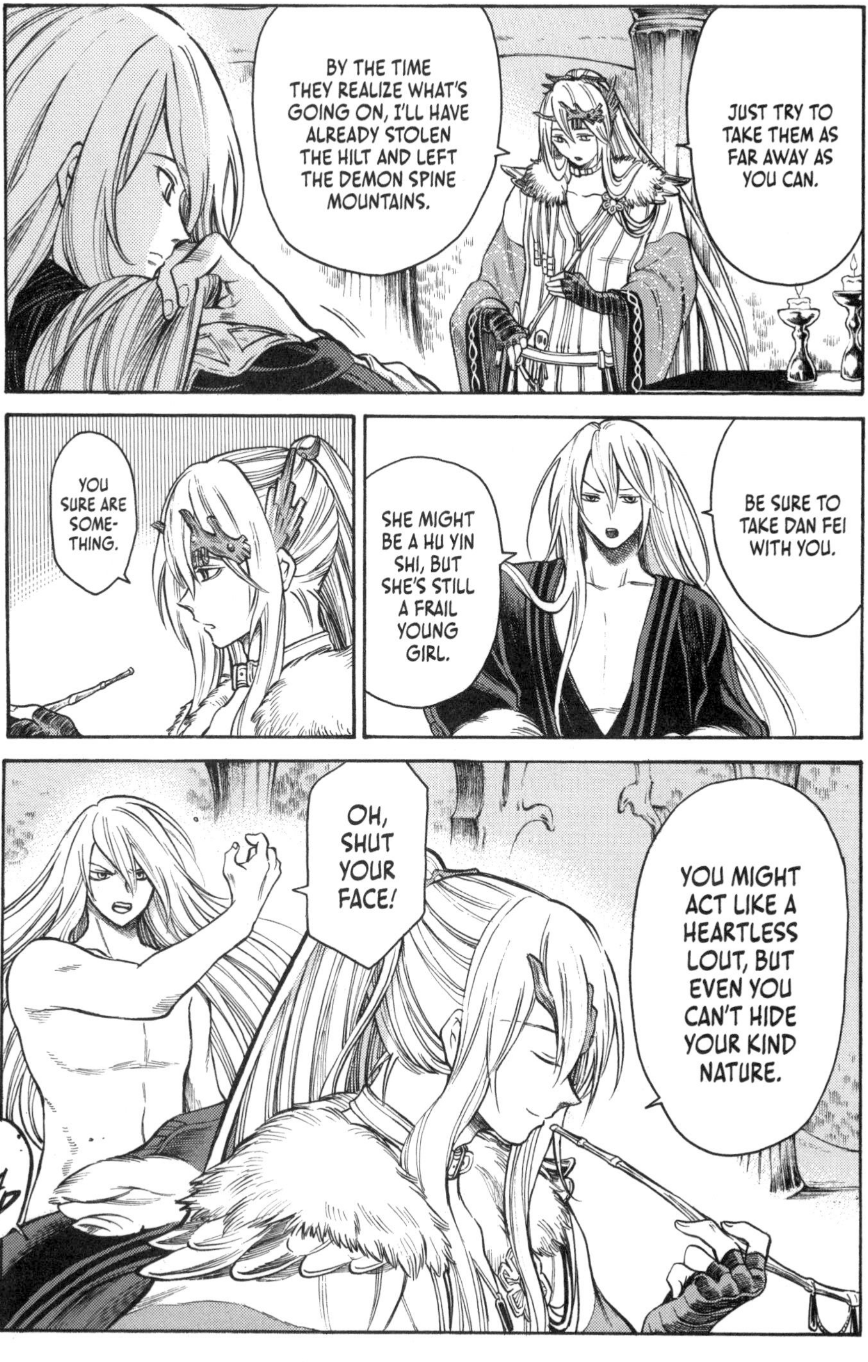
JUST TRY TO TAKE THEM AS FAR AWAY AS YOU CAN.
BY THE TIME THEY REALIZE WHAT'S GOING ON, I'LL HAVE ALREADY STOLEN THE HILT AND LEFT THE DEMON SPINE MOUNTAINS.
BE SURE TO TAKE DAN FEI WITH YOU.
SHE MIGHT BE A HU YIN SHI, BUT SHE'S STILL A FRAIL YOUNG GIRL.
YOU SURE ARE SOME-THING.
YOU MIGHT ACT LIKE A HEARTLESS LOUT, BUT EVEN YOU CAN'T HIDE YOUR KIND NATURE.
OH, SHUT YOUR FACE!
FLAP

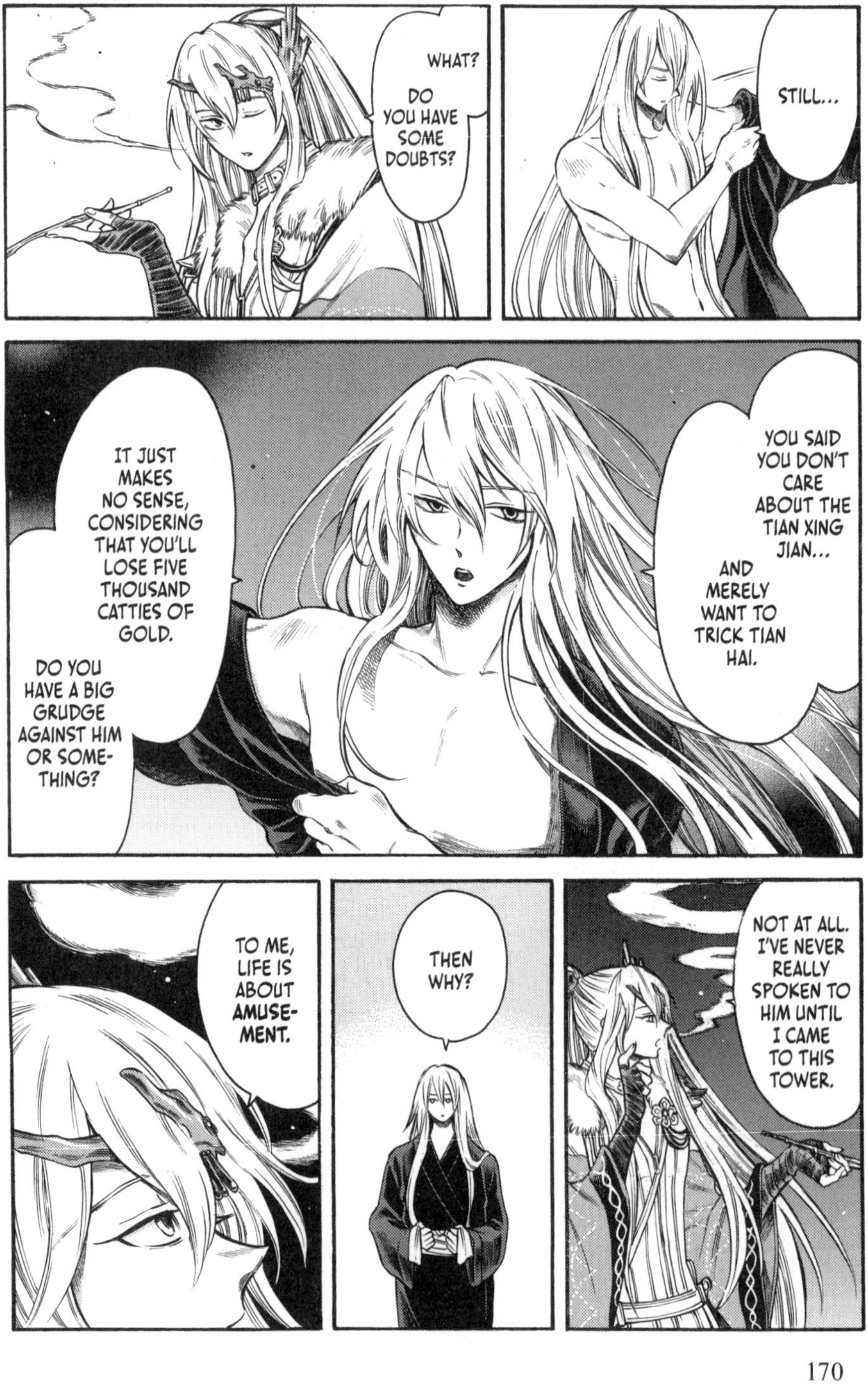
STILL...
WHAT?
DO YOU HAVE SOME DOUBTS?
YOU SAID YOU DON'T CARE ABOUT THE TIAN XING JIAN...
AND MERELY WANT TO TRICK TIAN HAI.
IT JUST MAKES NO SENSE, CONSIDERING THAT YOU'LL LOSE FIVE THOUSAND CATTIES OF GOLD.
DO YOU HAVE A BIG GRUDGE AGAINST HIM OR SOME-THING?
NOT AT ALL. I'VE NEVER REALLY SPOKEN TO HIM UNTIL I CAME TO THIS TOWER.
THEN WHY?
TO ME, LIFE IS ABOUT **AMUSE-MENT.**

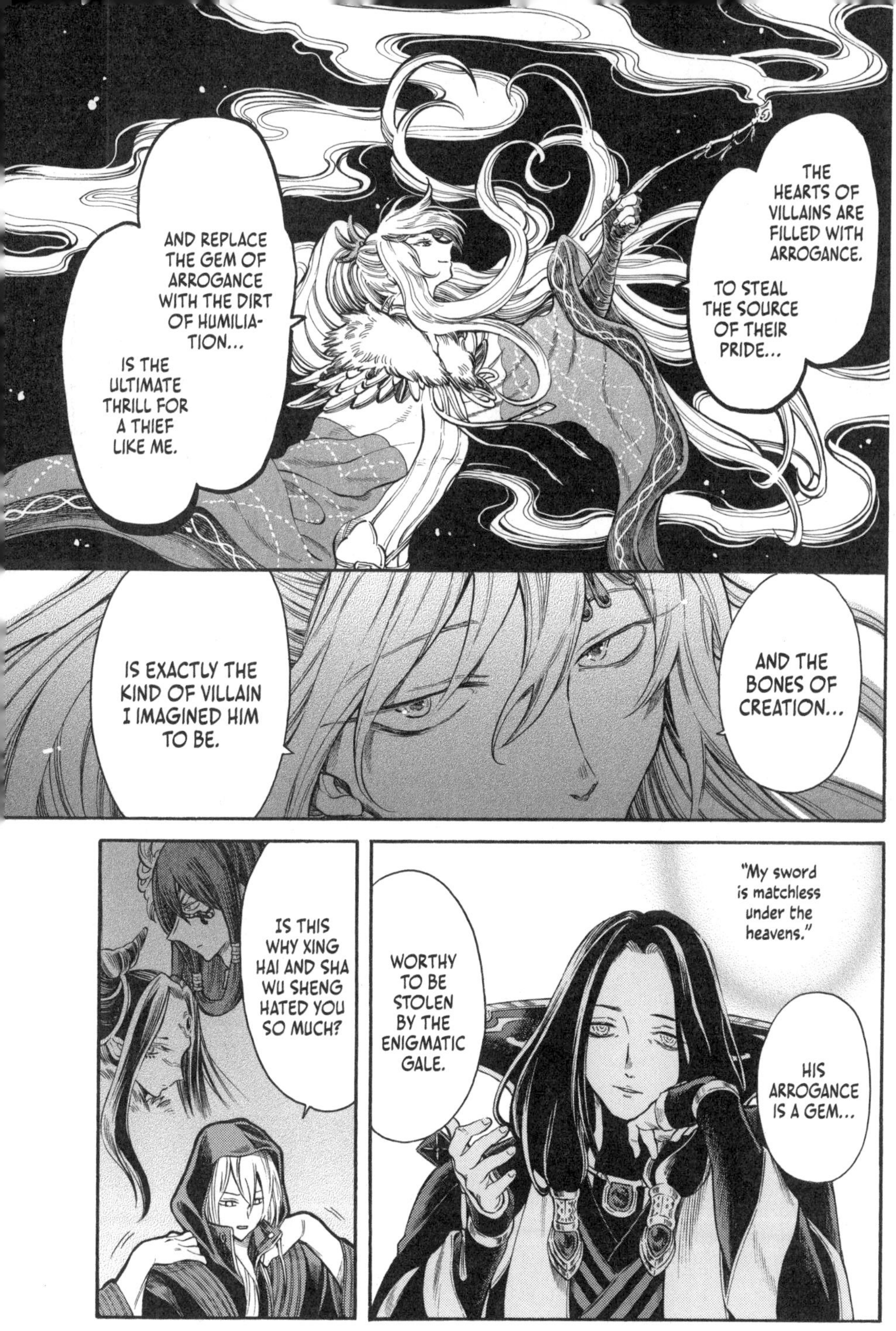
THE HEARTS OF VILLAINS ARE FILLED WITH ARROGANCE.
TO STEAL THE SOURCE OF THEIR PRIDE...
AND REPLACE THE GEM OF ARROGANCE WITH THE DIRT OF HUMILIATION...
IS THE ULTIMATE THRILL FOR A THIEF LIKE ME.
AND THE BONES OF CREATION...
IS EXACTLY THE KIND OF VILLAIN I IMAGINED HIM TO BE.
"My sword is matchless under the heavens."
HIS ARROGANCE IS A GEM...
WORTHY TO BE STOLEN BY THE ENIGMATIC GALE.
IS THIS WHY XING HAI AND SHA WU SHENG HATED YOU SO MUCH?

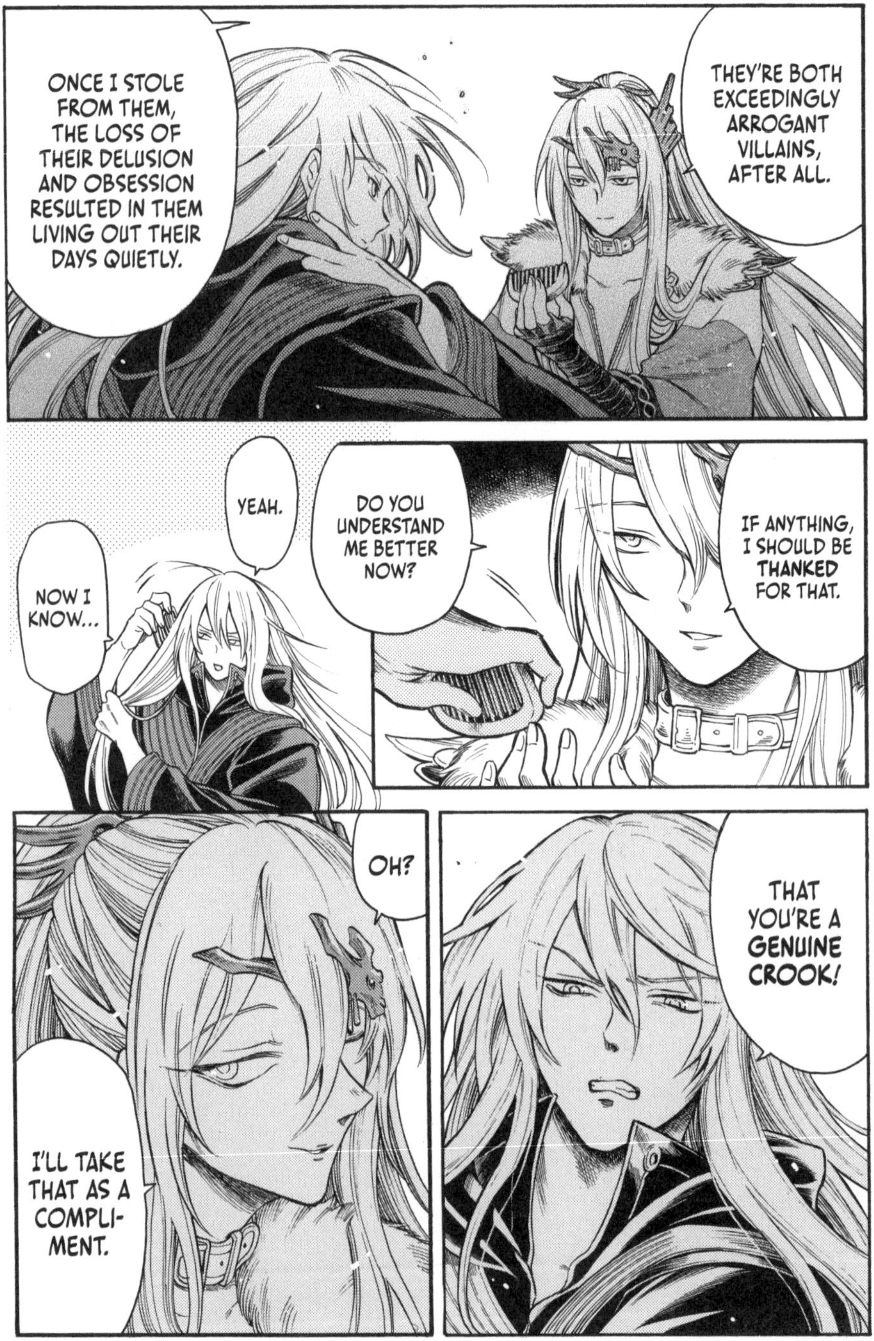
THEY'RE BOTH EXCEEDINGLY ARROGANT VILLAINS, AFTER ALL.
ONCE I STOLE FROM THEM, THE LOSS OF THEIR DELUSION AND OBSESSION RESULTED IN THEM LIVING OUT THEIR DAYS QUIETLY.
IF ANYTHING, I SHOULD BE THANKED FOR THAT.
DO YOU UNDERSTAND ME BETTER NOW?
YEAH.
NOW I KNOW...
THAT YOU'RE A GENUINE CROOK!
OH?
I'LL TAKE THAT AS A COMPLIMENT.

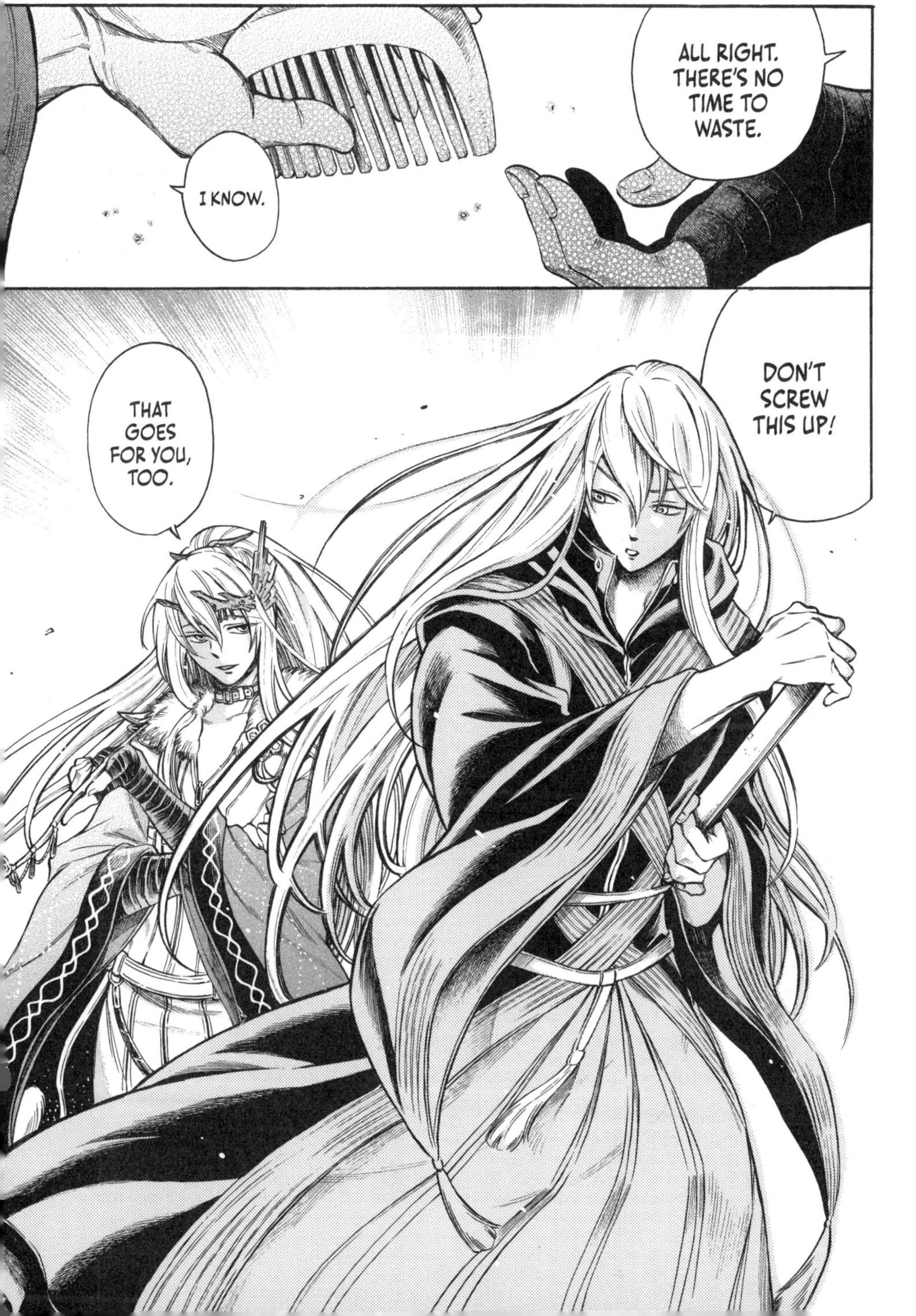
ALL RIGHT. THERE'S NO TIME TO WASTE.
I KNOW.
DON'T SCREW THIS UP!
THAT GOES FOR YOU, TOO.

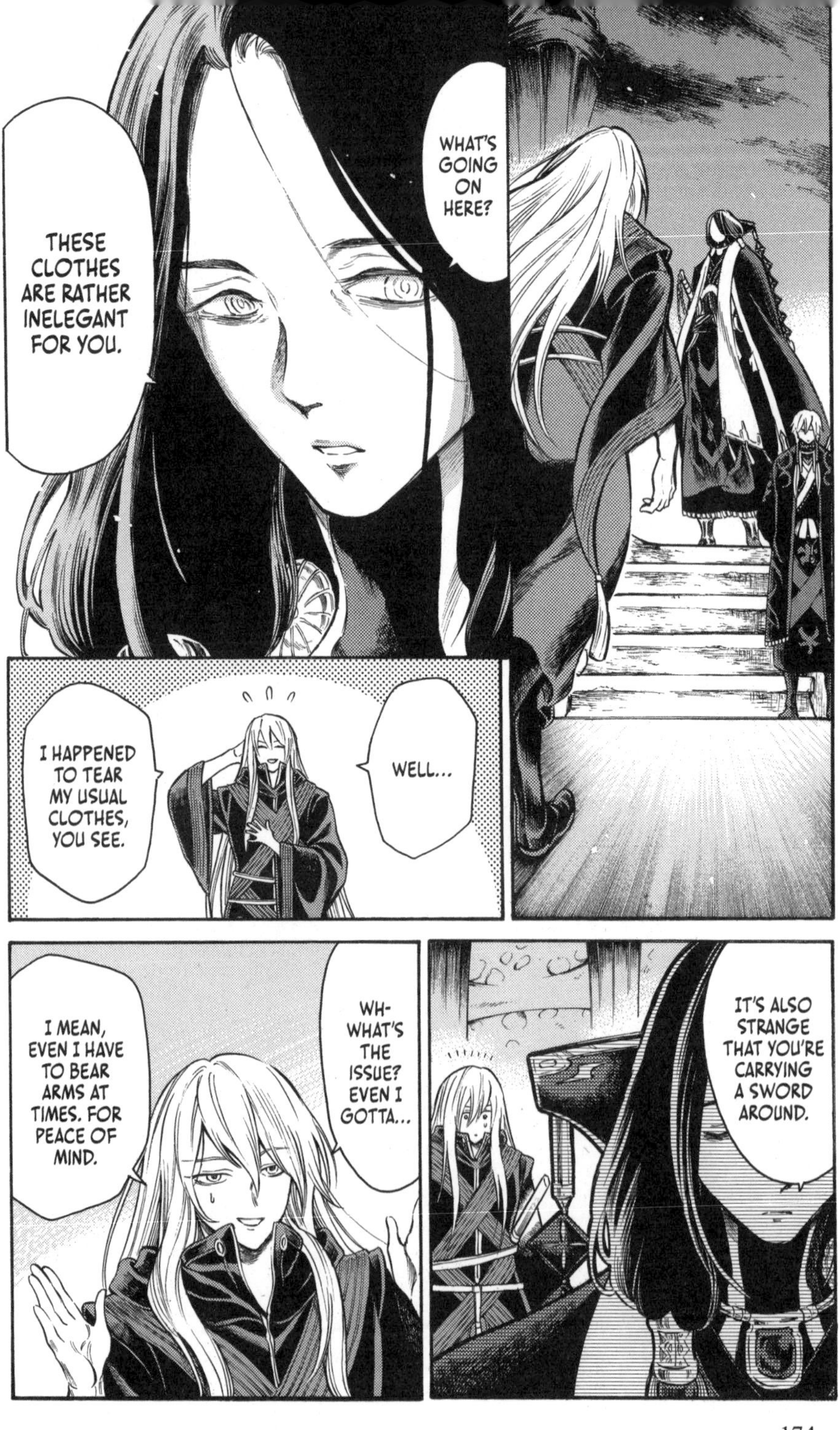
WHAT'S GOING ON HERE?
THESE CLOTHES ARE RATHER INELEGANT FOR YOU.
WELL...
I HAPPENED TO TEAR MY USUAL CLOTHES, YOU SEE.
IT'S ALSO STRANGE THAT YOU'RE CARRYING A SWORD AROUND.
WH-WHAT'S THE ISSUE? EVEN I GOTTA...
I MEAN, EVEN I HAVE TO BEAR ARMS AT TIMES. FOR PEACE OF MIND.

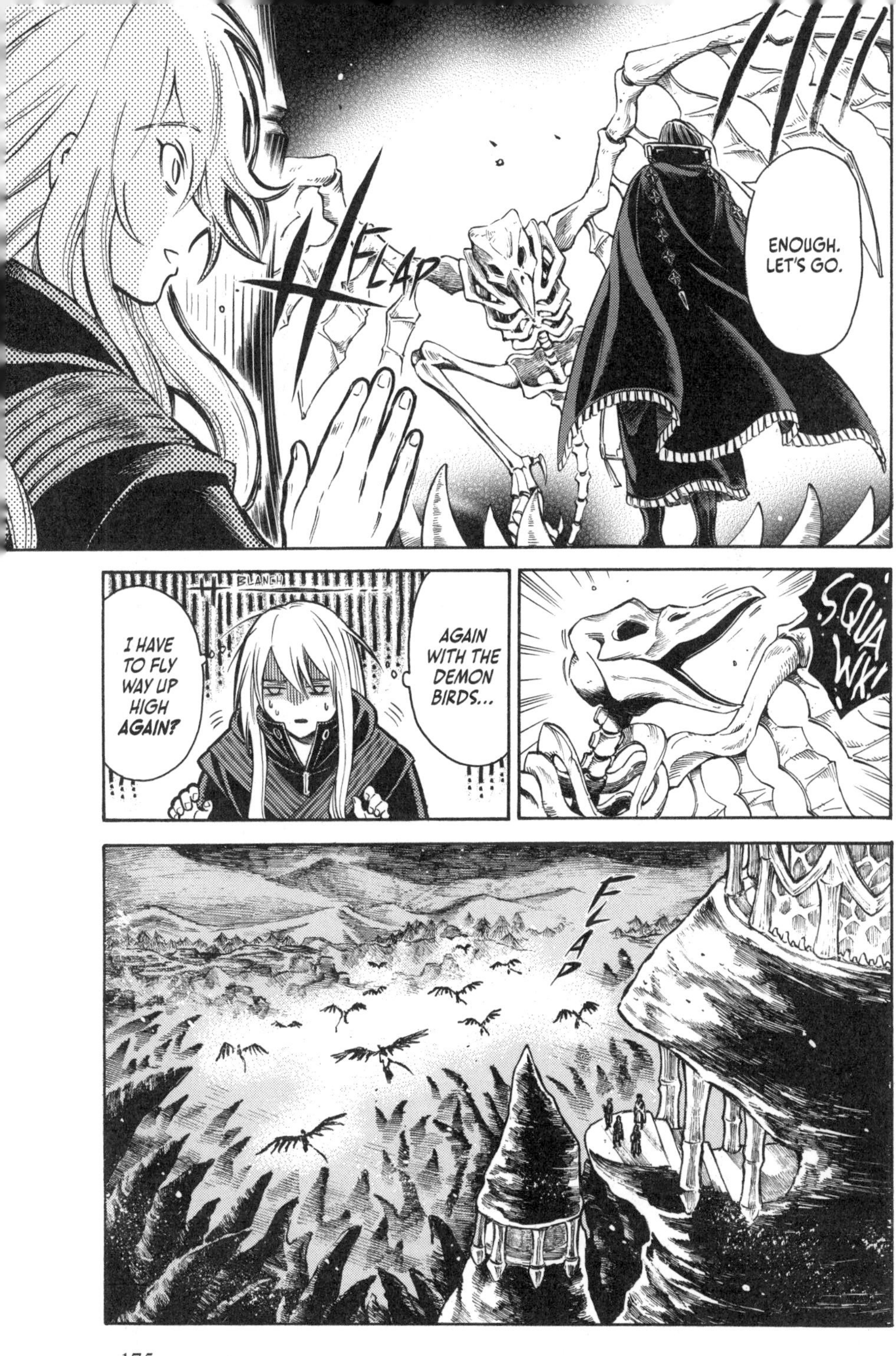
FLAP
ENOUGH. LET'S GO.
SQUAWK!
BLANCH
AGAIN WITH THE DEMON BIRDS...
I HAVE TO FLY WAY UP HIGH AGAIN?
FLAP

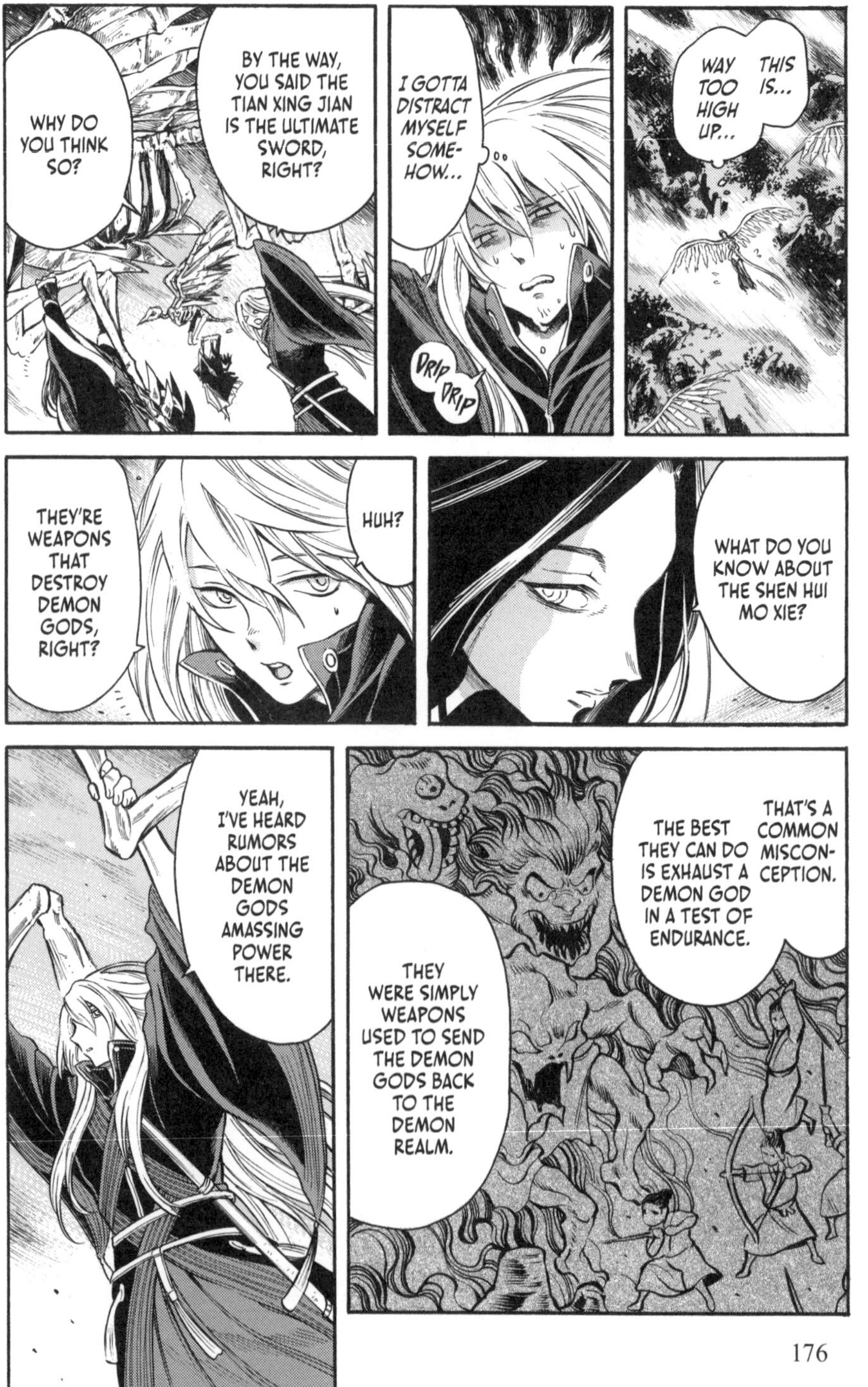
THIS IS...
WAY TOO HIGH UP...
I GOTTA DISTRACT MYSELF SOMEHOW...
DRIP DRIP
BY THE WAY, YOU SAID THE TIAN XING JIAN IS THE ULTIMATE SWORD, RIGHT?
WHY DO YOU THINK SO?
WHAT DO YOU KNOW ABOUT THE SHEN HUI MO XIE?
HUH?
THEY'RE WEAPONS THAT DESTROY DEMON GODS, RIGHT?
THAT'S A COMMON MISCONCEPTION.
THE BEST THEY CAN DO IS EXHAUST A DEMON GOD IN A TEST OF ENDURANCE.
THEY WERE SIMPLY WEAPONS USED TO SEND THE DEMON GODS BACK TO THE DEMON REALM.
YEAH, I'VE HEARD RUMORS ABOUT THE DEMON GODS AMASSING POWER THERE.

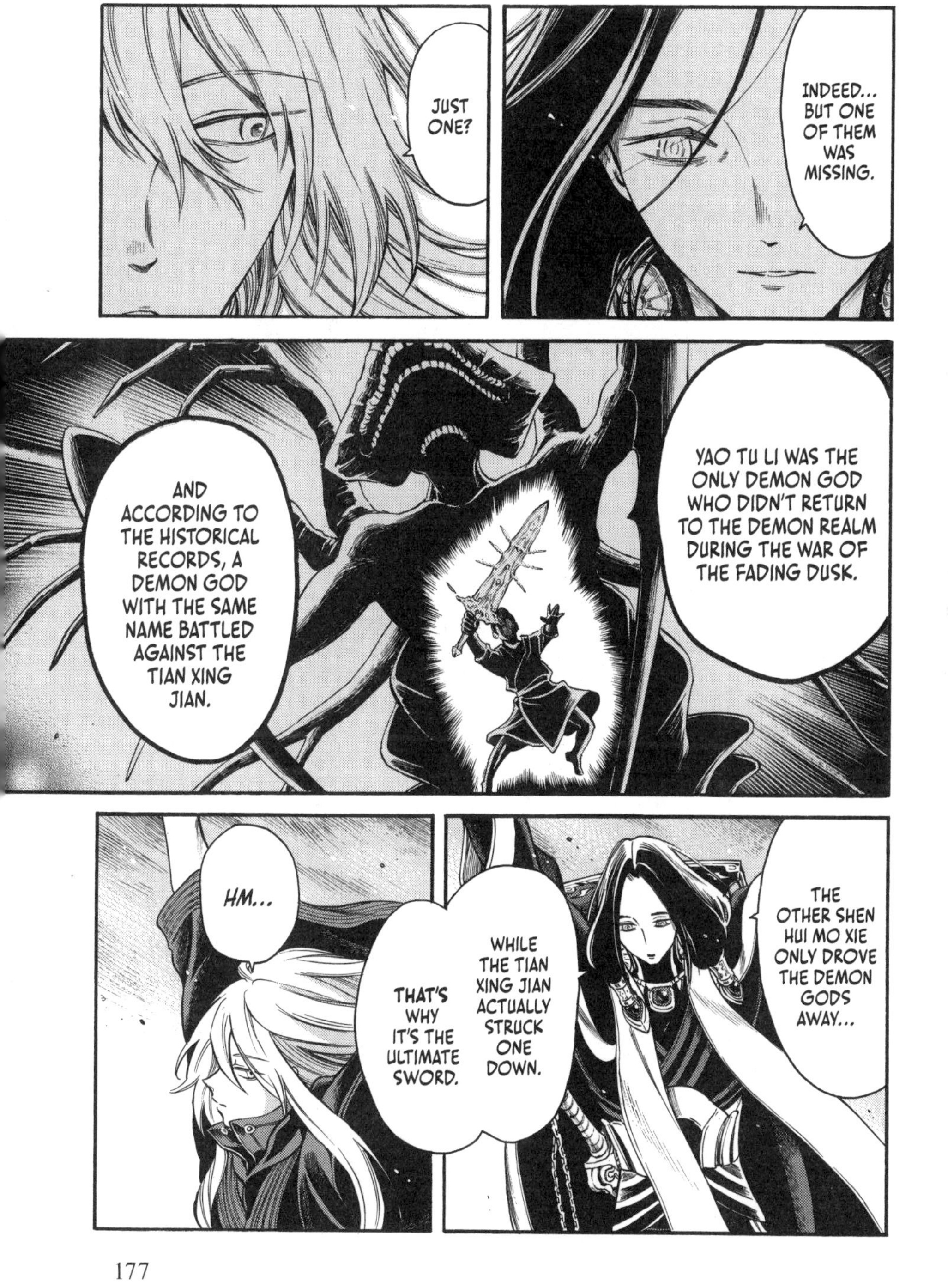
INDEED... BUT ONE OF THEM WAS MISSING.
JUST ONE?
YAO TU LI WAS THE ONLY DEMON GOD WHO DIDN'T RETURN TO THE DEMON REALM DURING THE WAR OF THE FADING DUSK.
AND ACCORDING TO THE HISTORICAL RECORDS, A DEMON GOD WITH THE SAME NAME BATTLED AGAINST THE TIAN XING JIAN.
THE OTHER SHEN HUI MO XIE ONLY DROVE THE DEMON GODS AWAY...
WHILE THE TIAN XING JIAN ACTUALLY STRUCK ONE DOWN.
THAT'S WHY IT'S THE ULTIMATE SWORD.
HM...

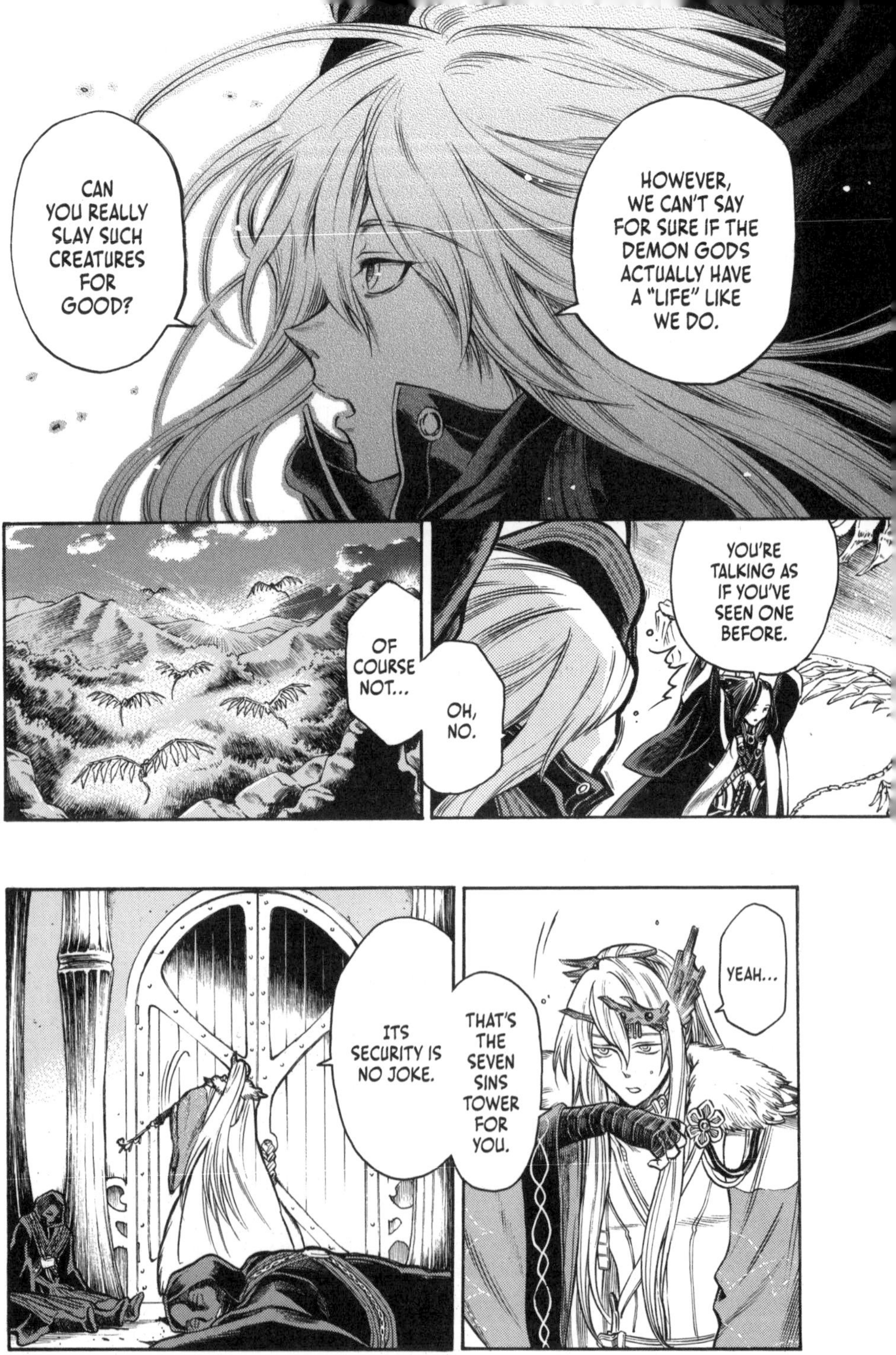
HOWEVER, WE CAN'T SAY FOR SURE IF THE DEMON GODS ACTUALLY HAVE A "LIFE" LIKE WE DO.
CAN YOU REALLY SLAY SUCH CREATURES FOR GOOD?
YOU'RE TALKING AS IF YOU'VE SEEN ONE BEFORE.
OH, NO.
OF COURSE NOT...
YEAH...
THAT'S THE SEVEN SINS TOWER FOR YOU.
ITS SECURITY IS NO JOKE.

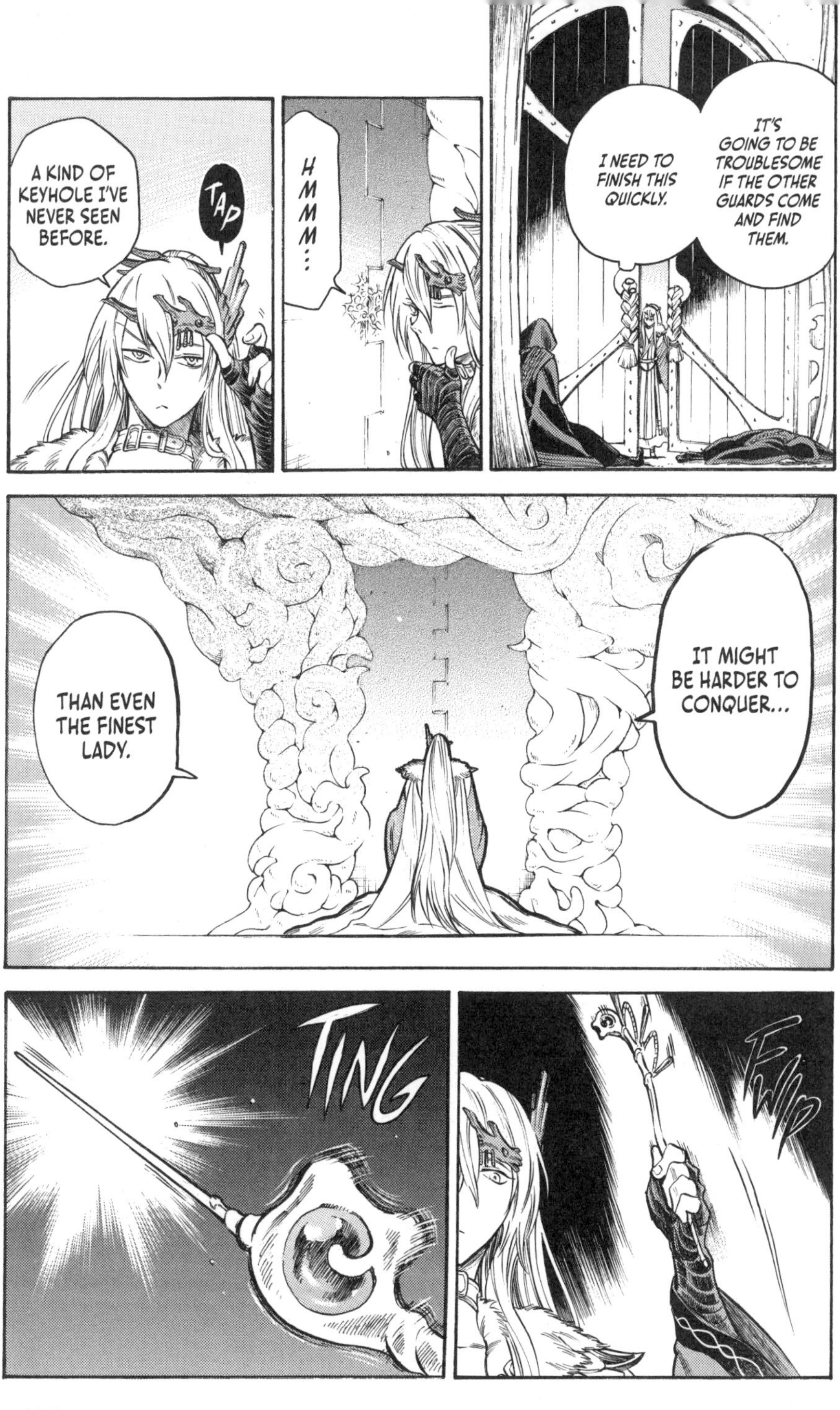
IT'S GOING TO BE TROUBLESOME IF THE OTHER GUARDS COME AND FIND THEM.
I NEED TO FINISH THIS QUICKLY.
HMMM...
TAP
A KIND OF KEYHOLE I'VE NEVER SEEN BEFORE.
IT MIGHT BE HARDER TO CONQUER...
THAN EVEN THE FINEST LADY.
FWIP
TING

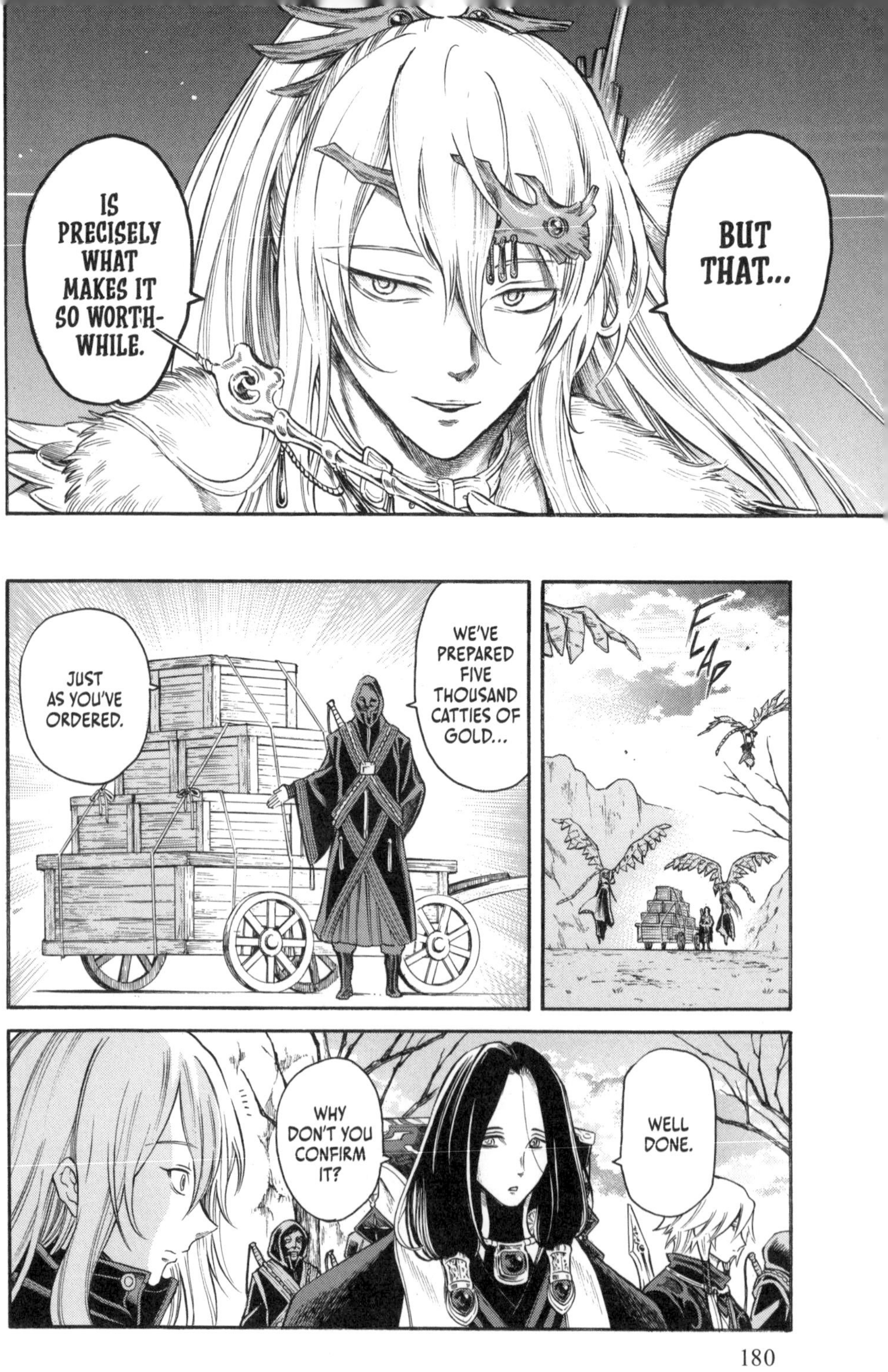
BUT THAT...
IS PRECISELY WHAT MAKES IT SO WORTH-WHILE.
FLAP
WE'VE PREPARED FIVE THOUSAND CATTIES OF GOLD...
JUST AS YOU'VE ORDERED.
WELL DONE.
WHY DON'T YOU CONFIRM IT?

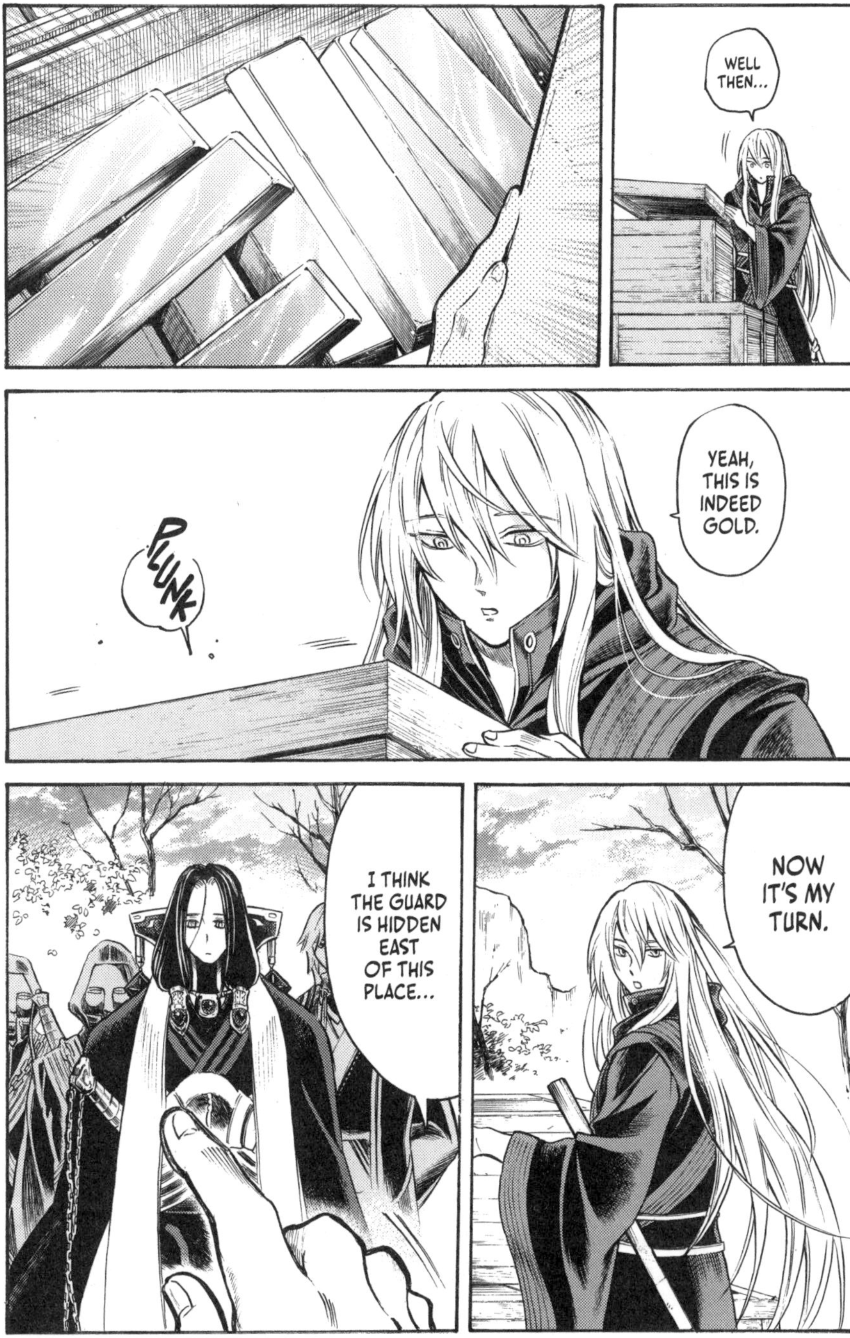
WELL THEN...
YEAH, THIS IS INDEED GOLD.
PLUNK
NOW IT'S MY TURN.
I THINK THE GUARD IS HIDDEN EAST OF THIS PLACE...

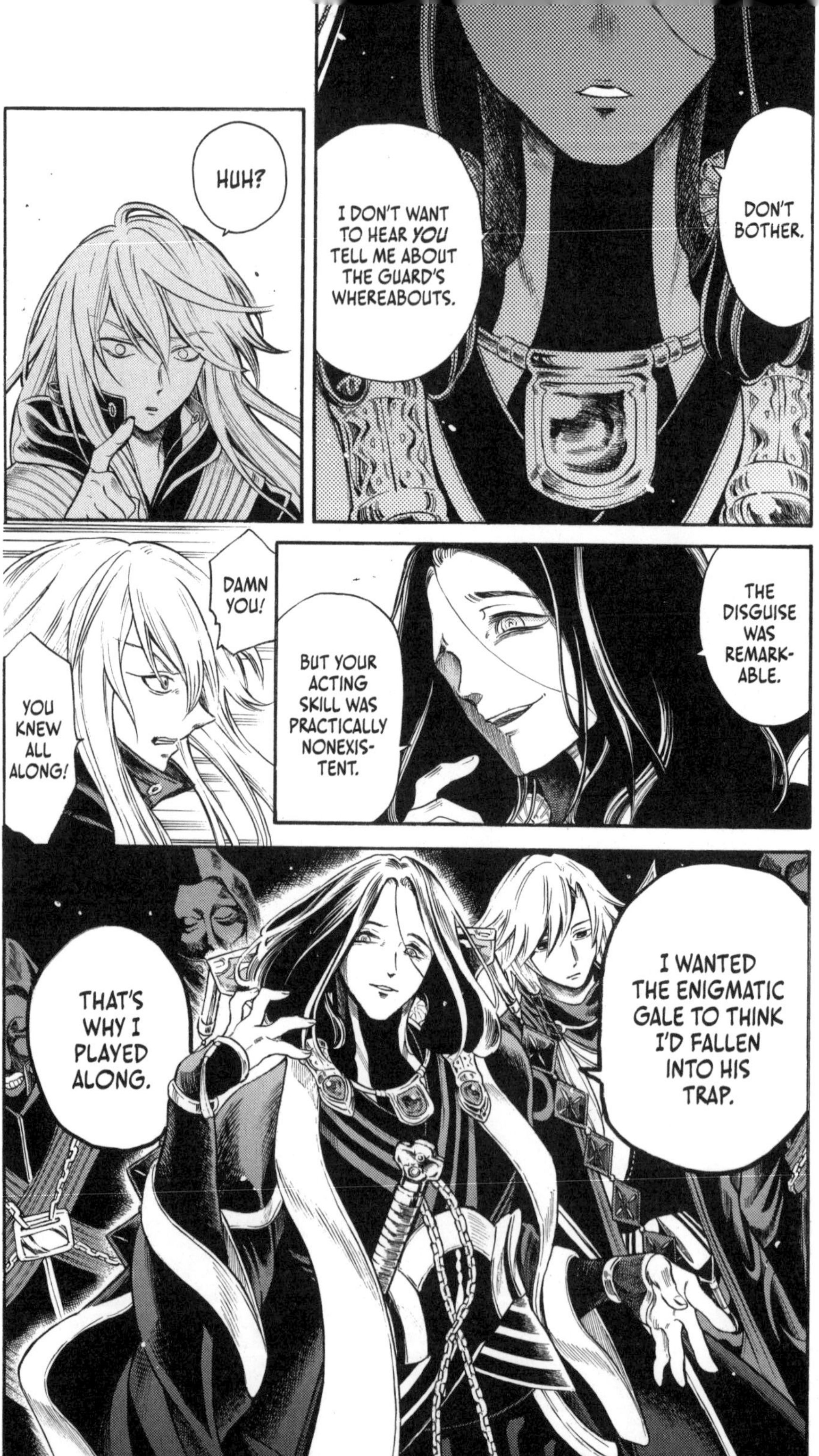
DON'T BOTHER.
I DON'T WANT TO HEAR *YOU* TELL ME ABOUT THE GUARD'S WHEREABOUTS.
HUH?
THE DISGUISE WAS REMARKABLE.
BUT YOUR ACTING SKILL WAS PRACTICALLY NONEXISTENT.
DAMN YOU!
YOU KNEW ALL ALONG!
I WANTED THE ENIGMATIC GALE TO THINK I'D FALLEN INTO HIS TRAP.
THAT'S WHY I PLAYED ALONG.

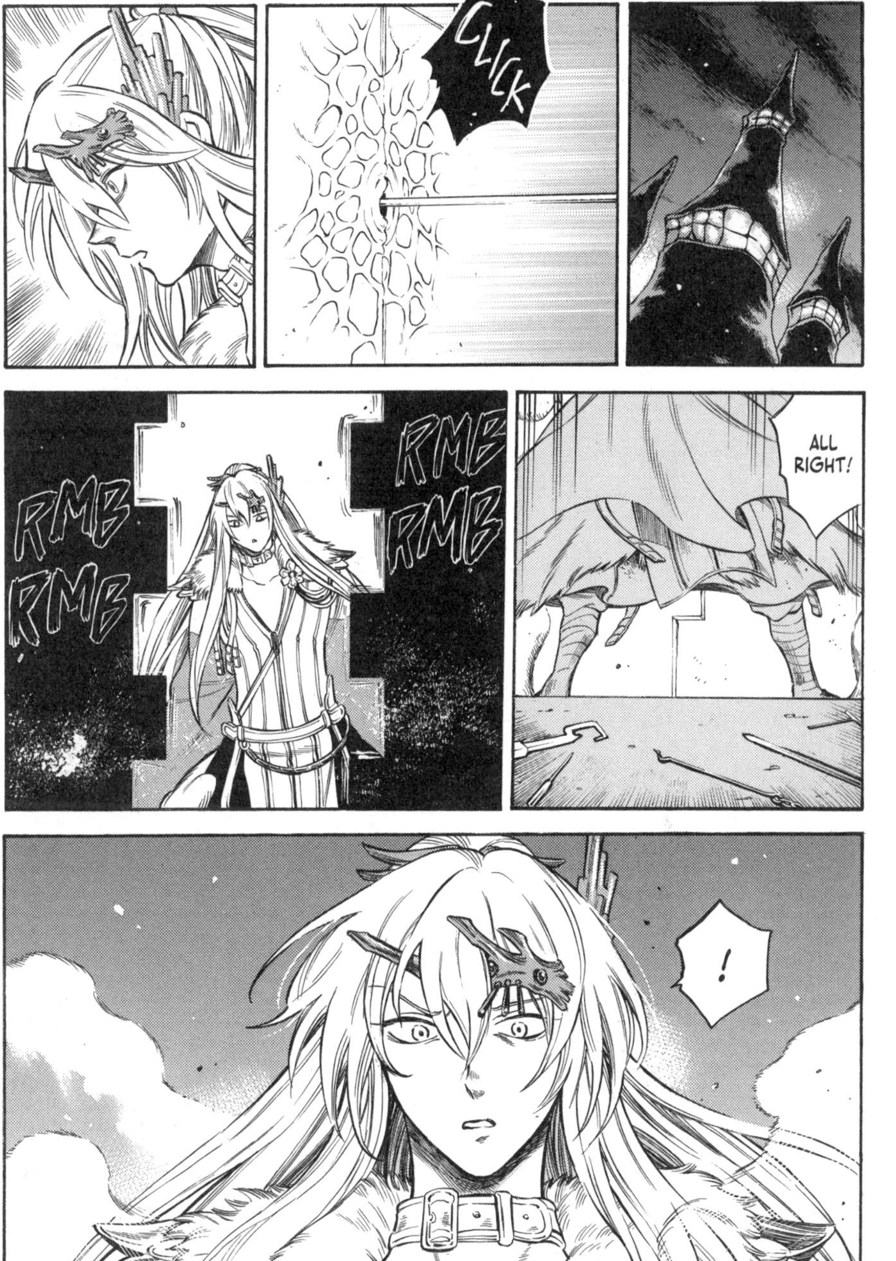
CLICK
ALL RIGHT!
RMB RMB
RMB RMB
!

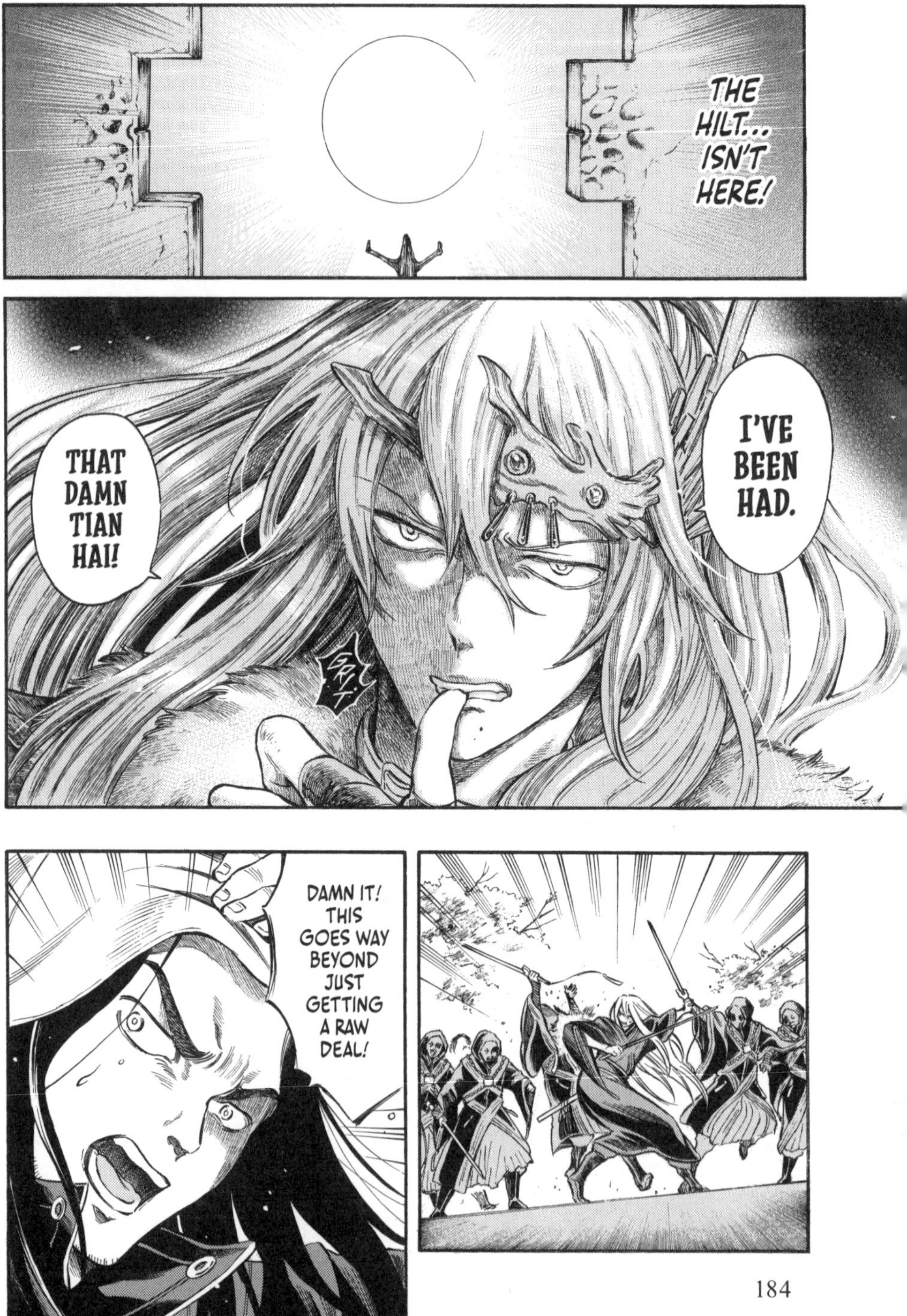
THE HILT... ISN'T HERE!
I'VE BEEN HAD.
THAT DAMN TIAN HAI!
GRIT
DAMN IT! THIS GOES WAY BEYOND JUST GETTING A RAW DEAL!

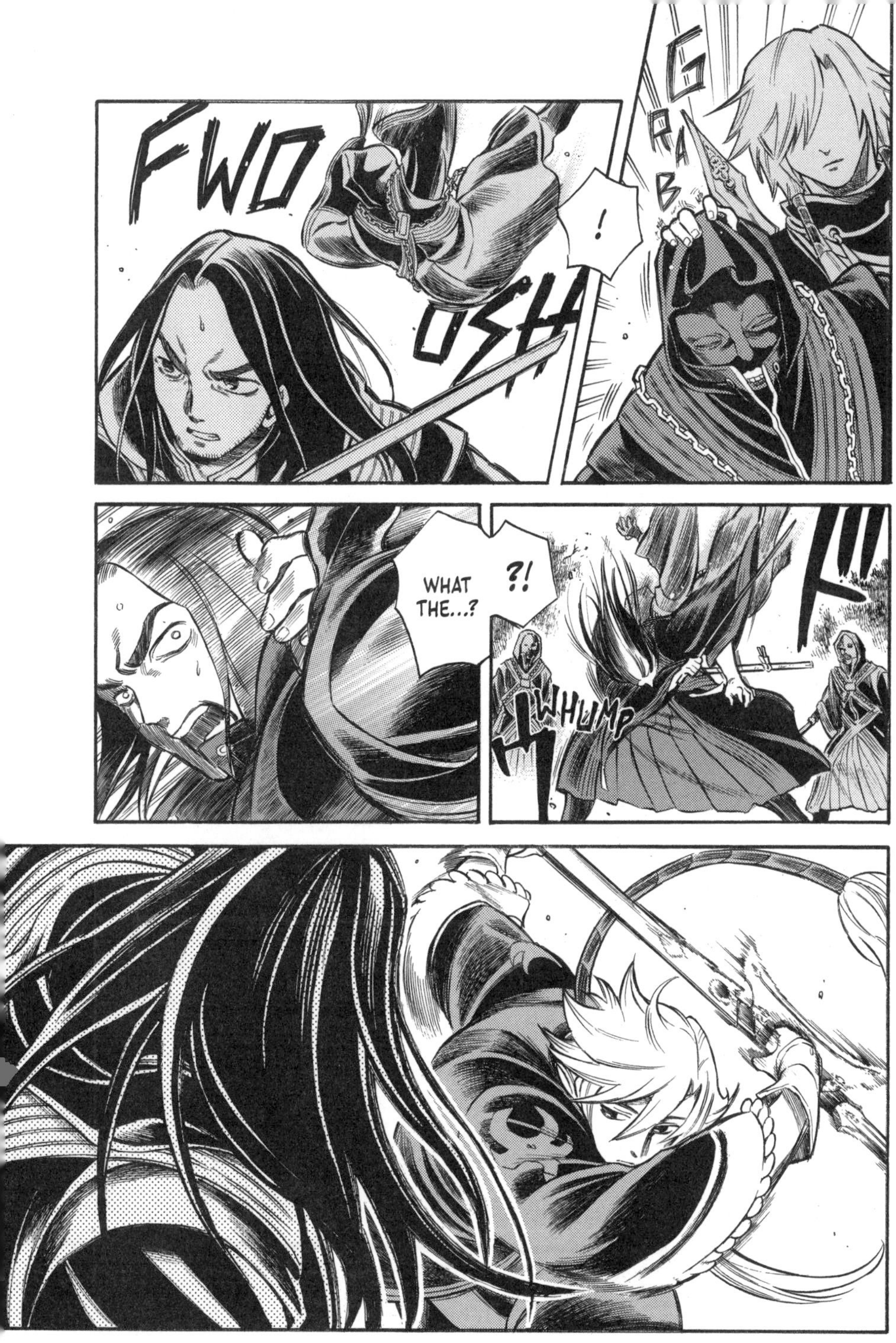
GRAB
!
FWOOSH
?!
WHAT THE...?
WHUMP

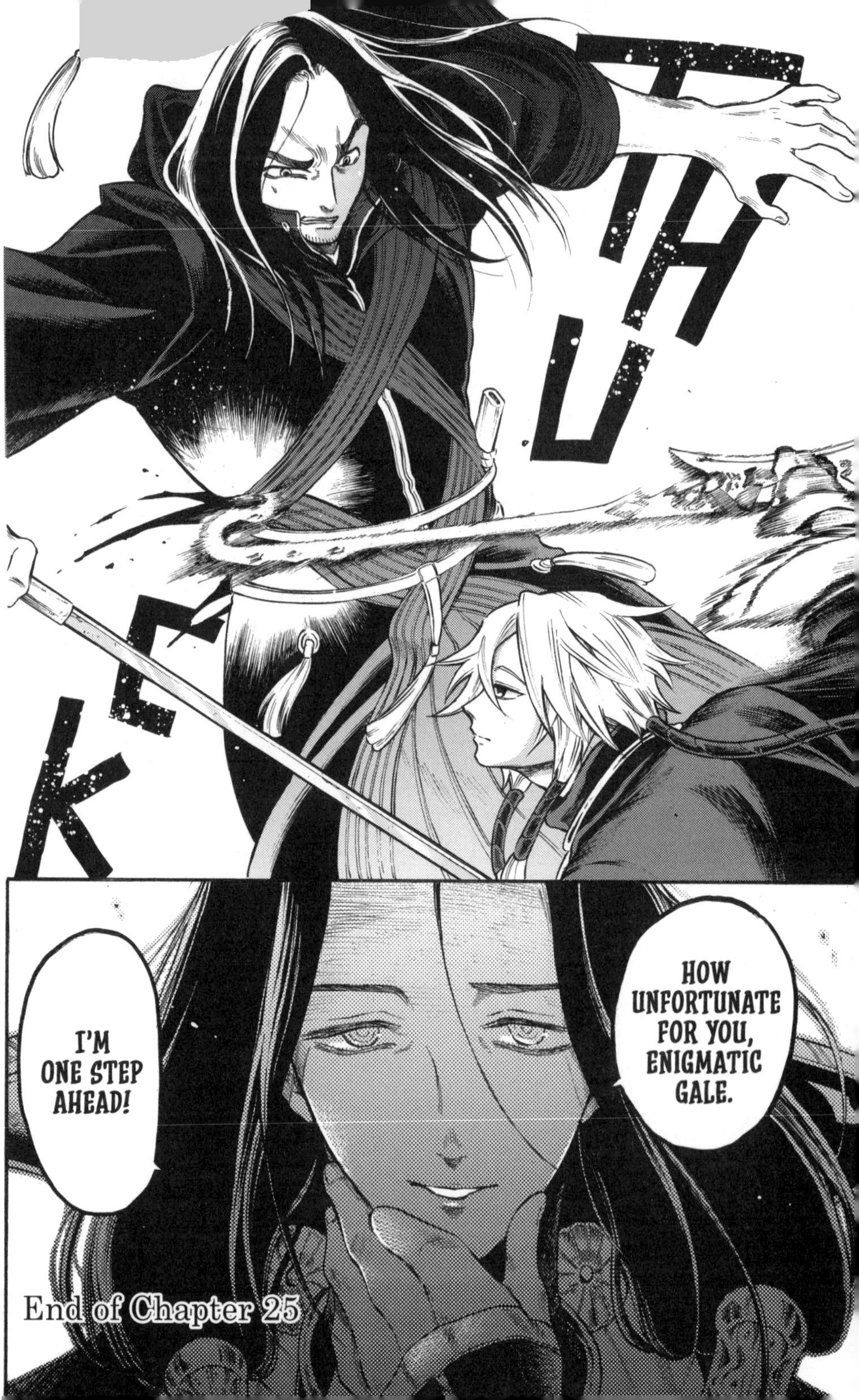
HOW UNFORTUNATE FOR YOU, ENIGMATIC GALE.
I'M ONE STEP AHEAD!

End of Chapter 25

∽ Chapter 26 ∽

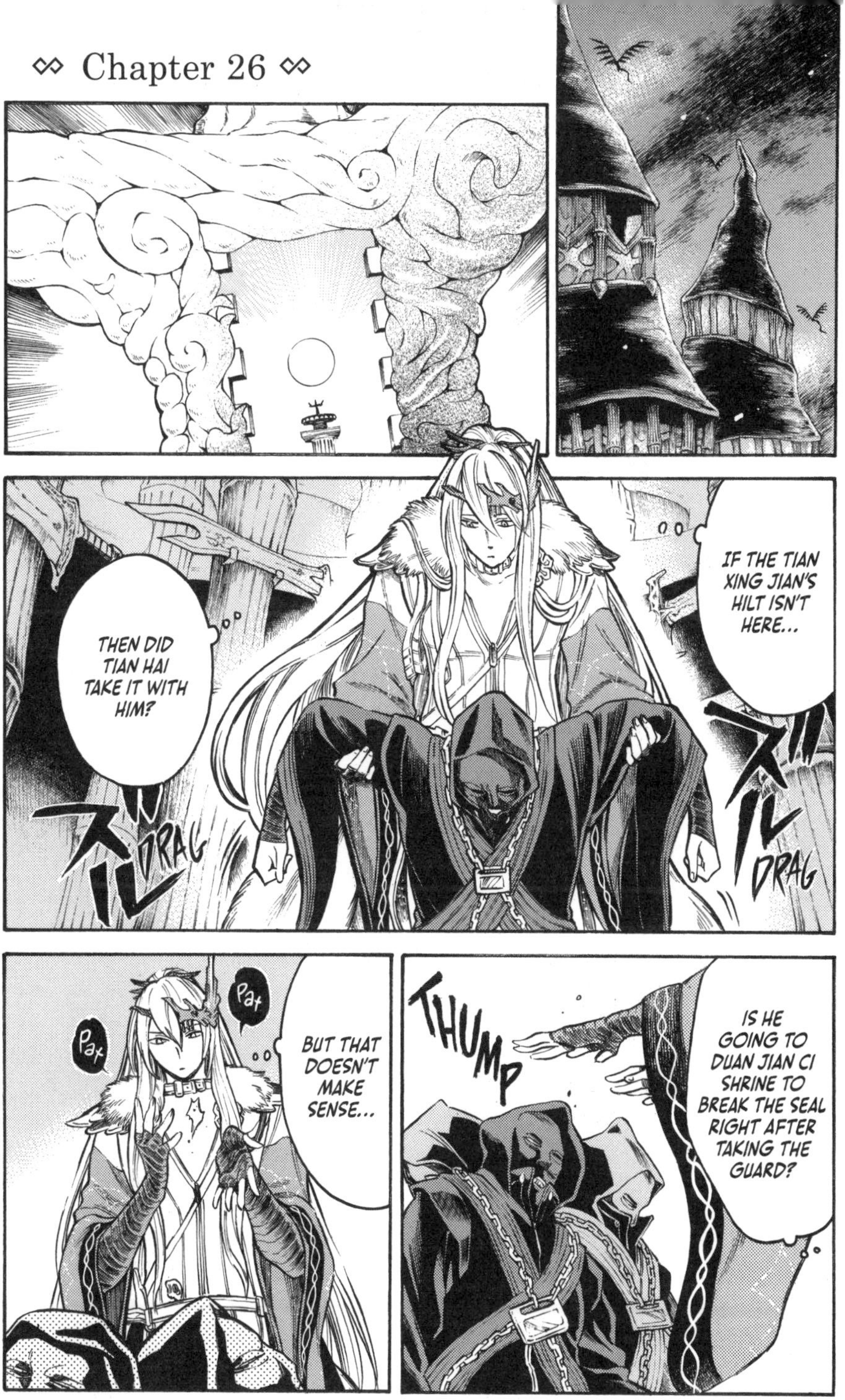
IF THE TIAN XING JIAN'S HILT ISN'T HERE...
THEN DID TIAN HAI TAKE IT WITH HIM?
DRAG
DRAG
IS HE GOING TO DUAN JIAN CI SHRINE TO BREAK THE SEAL RIGHT AFTER TAKING THE GUARD?
THUMP
BUT THAT DOESN'T MAKE SENSE...
Pat
Pat

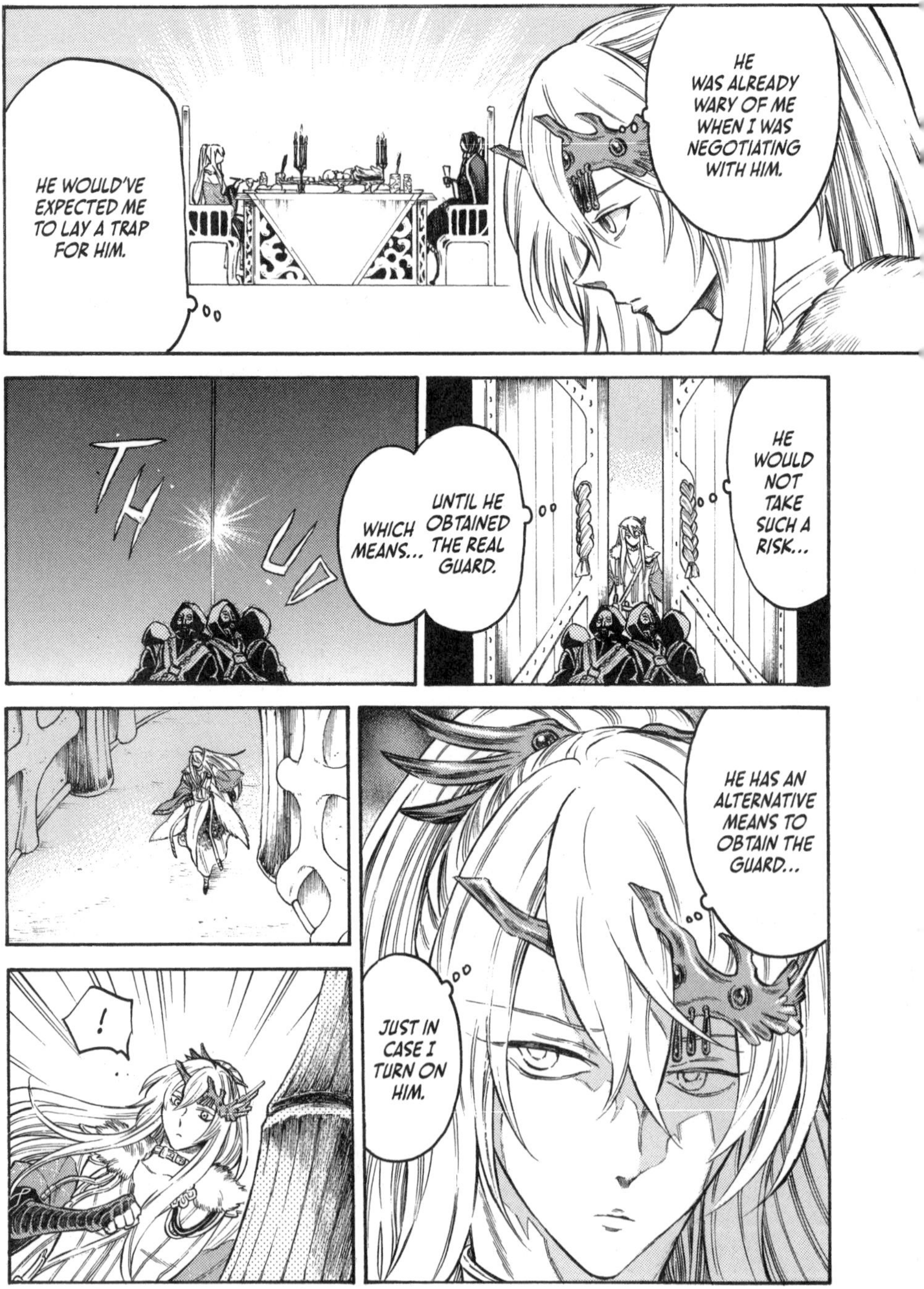
HE WAS ALREADY WARY OF ME WHEN I WAS NEGOTIATING WITH HIM.
HE WOULD'VE EXPECTED ME TO LAY A TRAP FOR HIM.
HE WOULD NOT TAKE SUCH A RISK...
UNTIL HE OBTAINED THE REAL GUARD.
WHICH MEANS...
THUD
HE HAS AN ALTERNATIVE MEANS TO OBTAIN THE GUARD...
JUST IN CASE I TURN ON HIM.
!

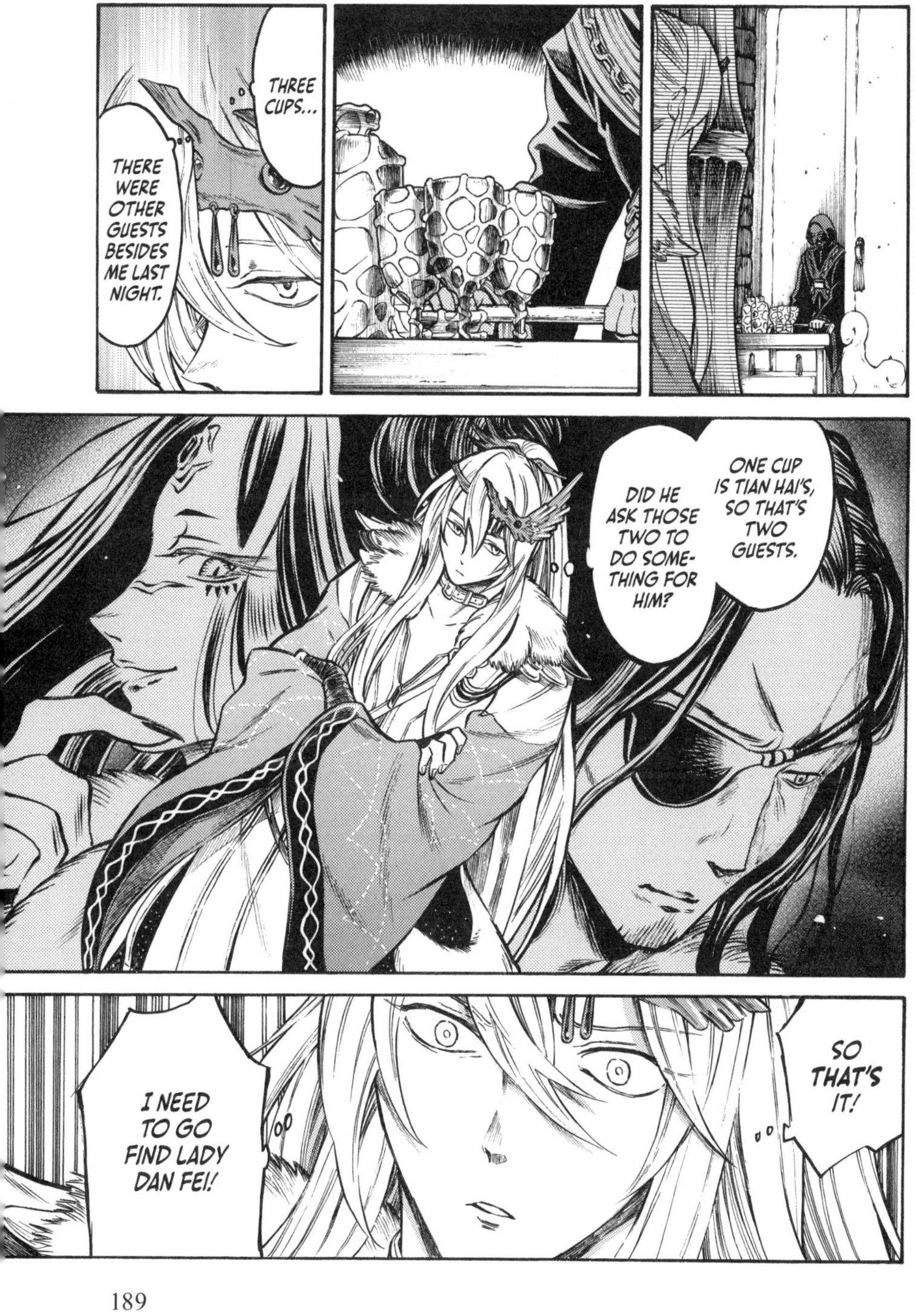
THREE CUPS...
THERE WERE OTHER GUESTS BESIDES ME LAST NIGHT.
ONE CUP IS TIAN HAI'S, SO THAT'S TWO GUESTS.
DID HE ASK THOSE TWO TO DO SOME-THING FOR HIM?
SO THAT'S IT!
I NEED TO GO FIND LADY DAN FEI!

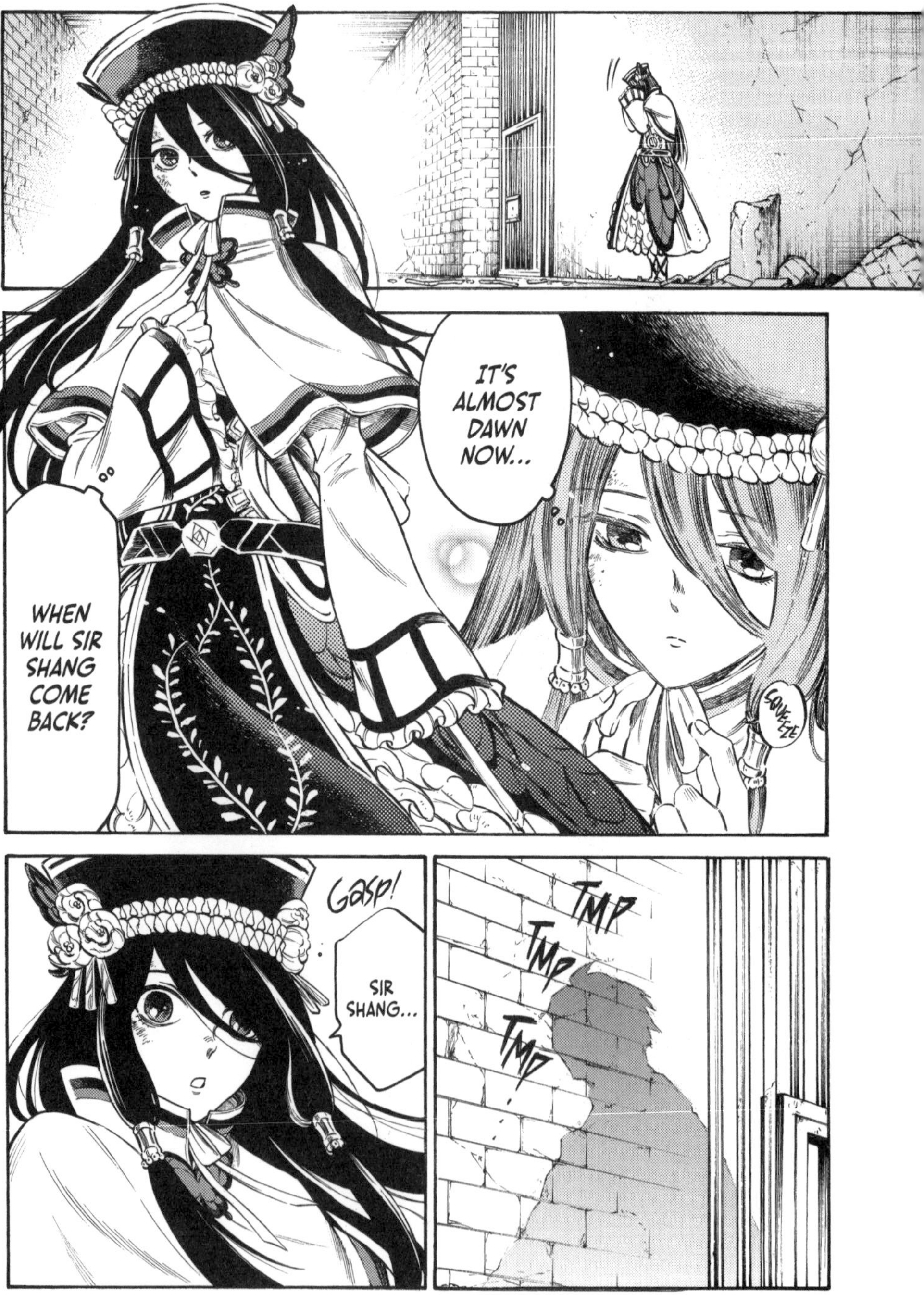
IT'S ALMOST DAWN NOW...
SQUEEZE
WHEN WILL SIR SHANG COME BACK?
TMP
TMP
TMP
Gasp!
SIR SHANG...

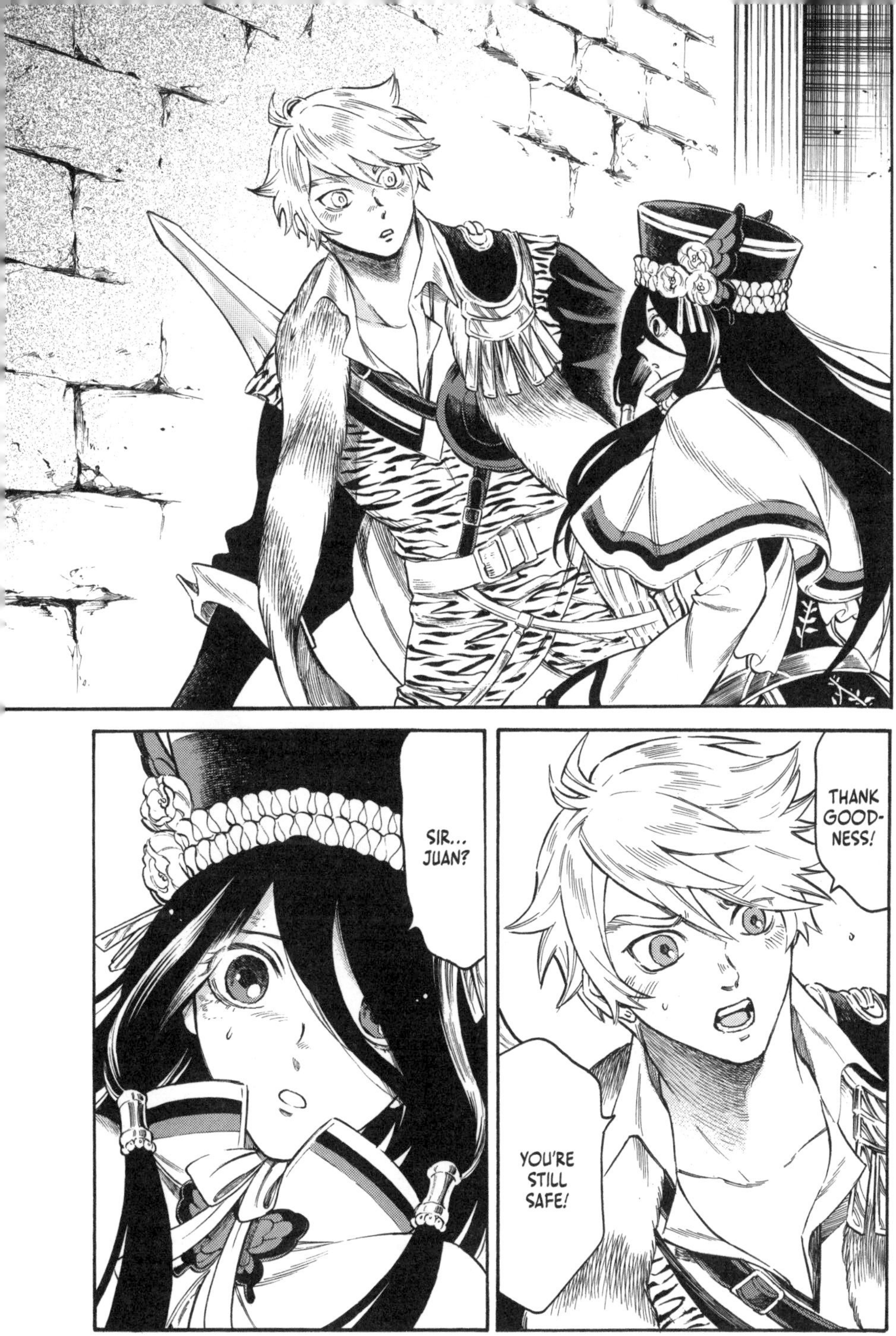
THANK GOOD-NESS!
YOU'RE STILL SAFE!
SIR... JUAN?

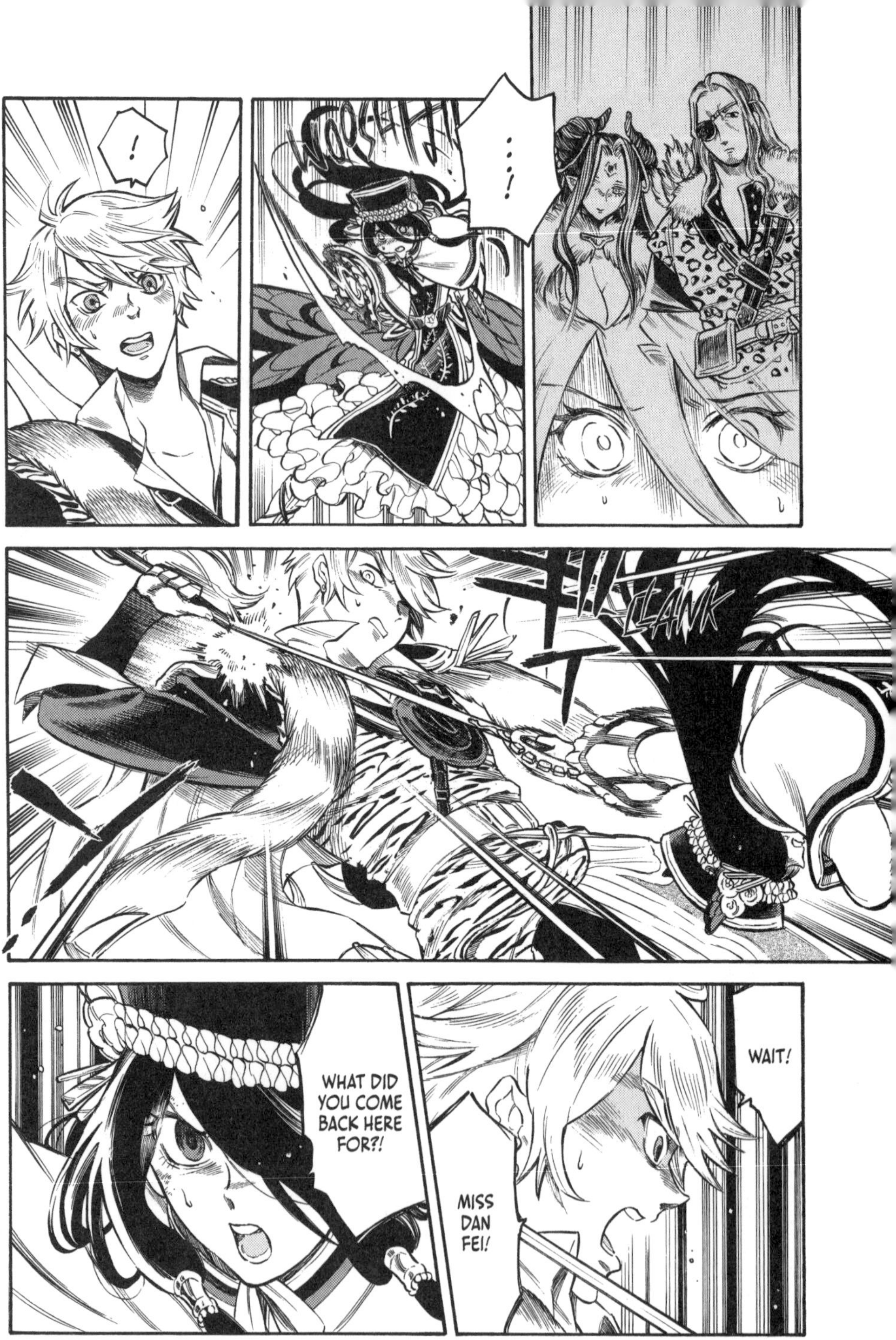
...!
WOOSH!!
!
CLANK
WAIT!
MISS DAN FEI!
WHAT DID YOU COME BACK HERE FOR?!

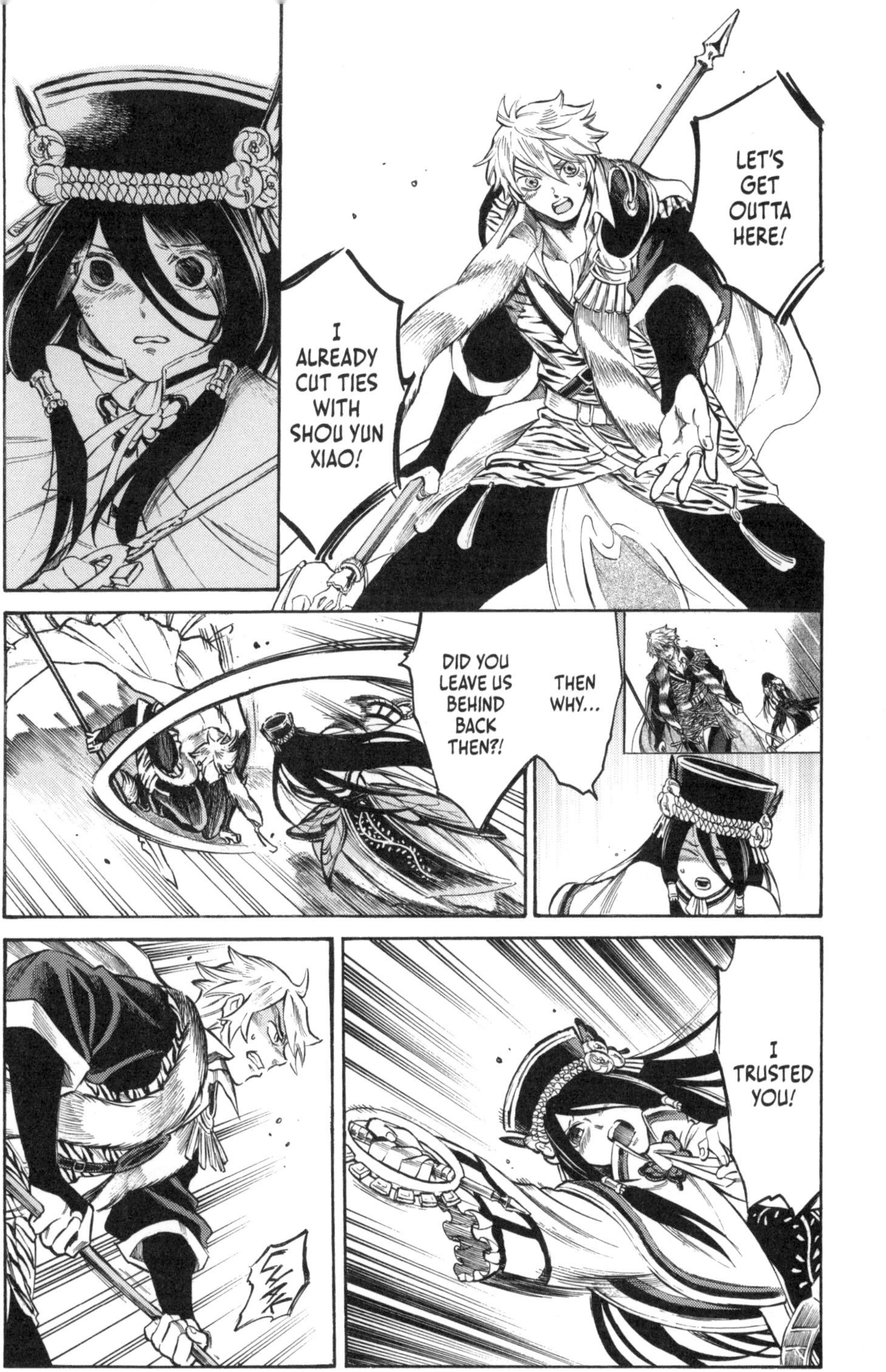
LET'S GET OUTTA HERE!
I ALREADY CUT TIES WITH SHOU YUN XIAO!
THEN WHY...
DID YOU LEAVE US BEHIND BACK THEN?!
I TRUSTED YOU!

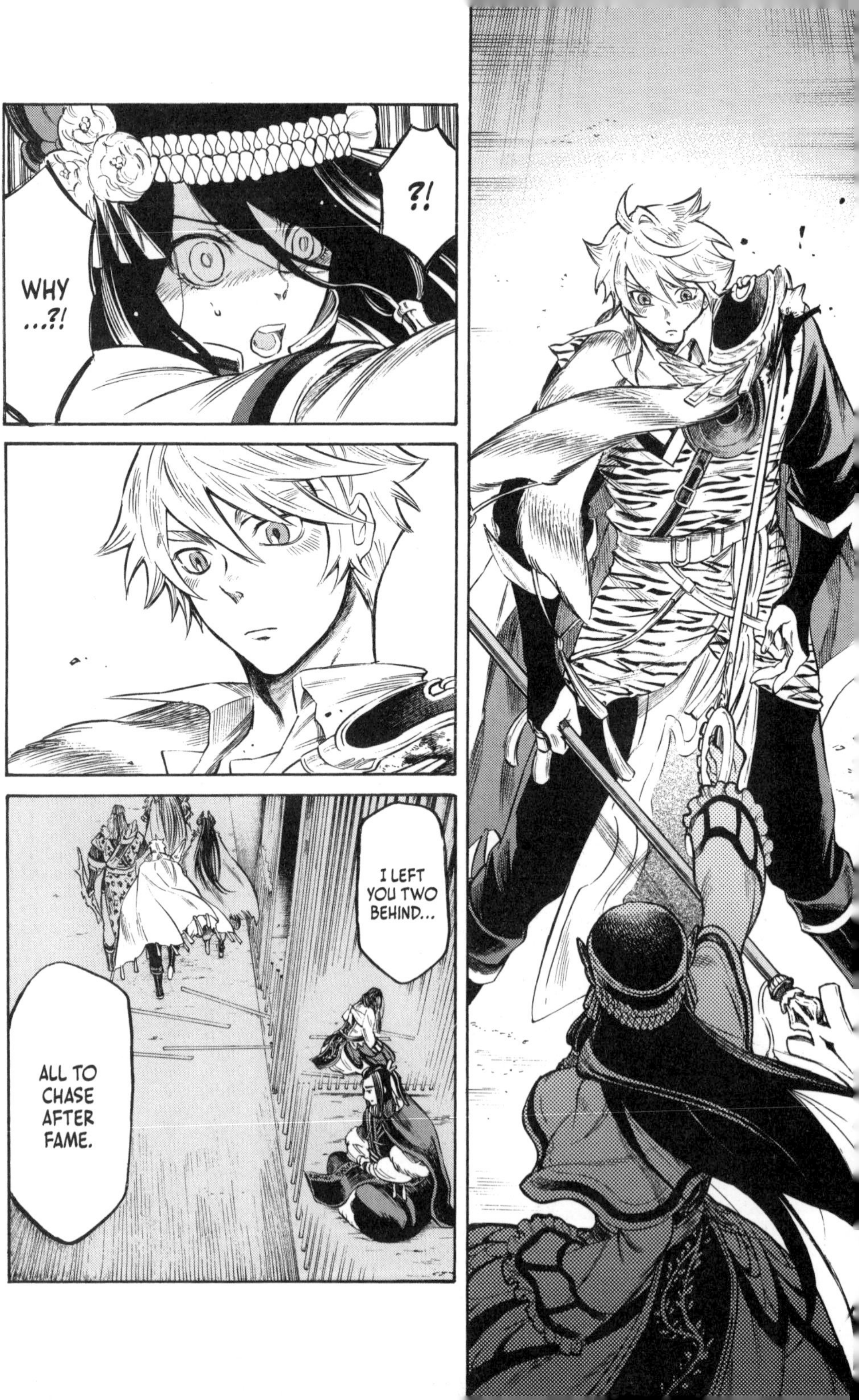
!
?!
WHY ...?!
I LEFT YOU TWO BEHIND...
ALL TO CHASE AFTER FAME.

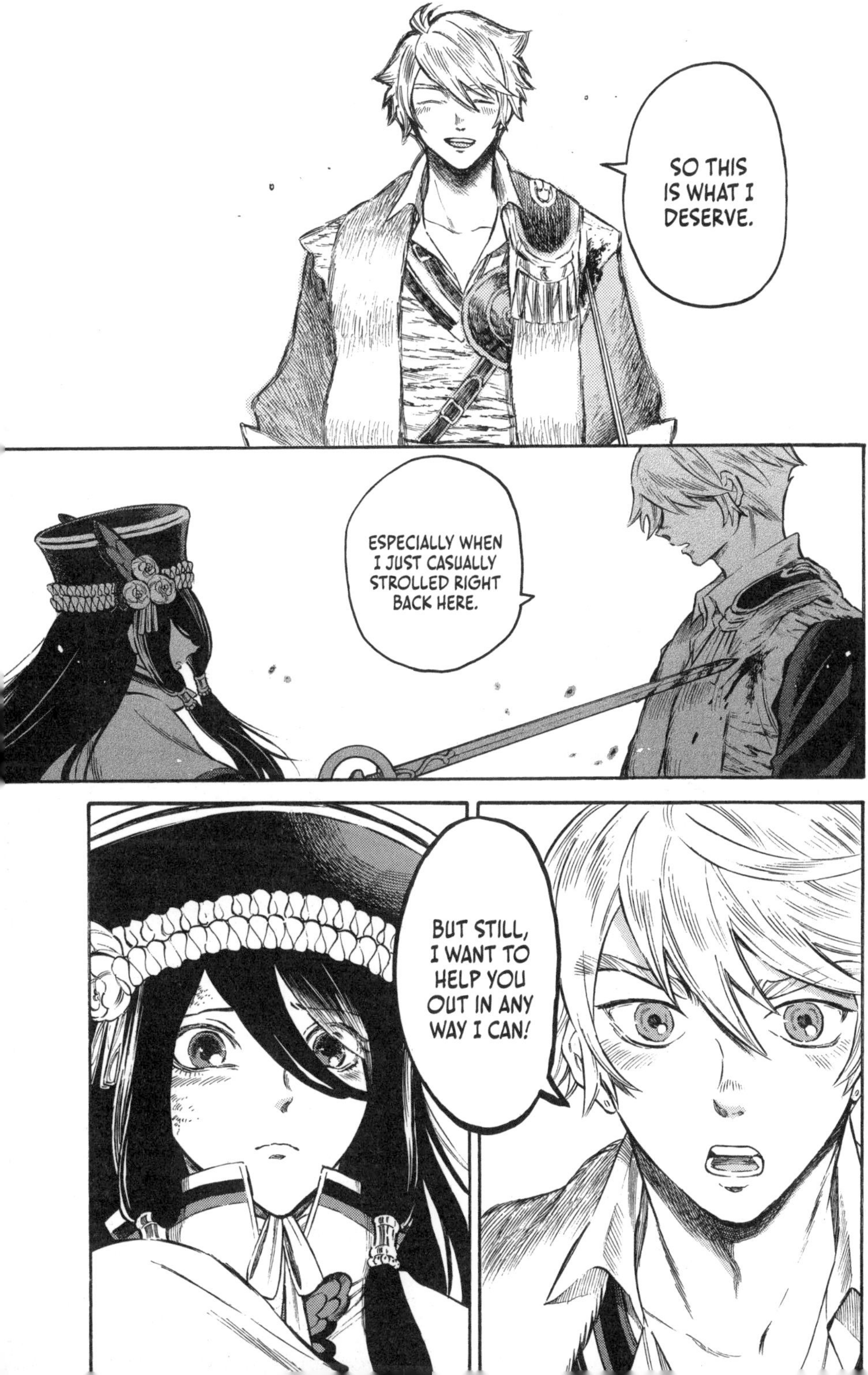
SO THIS IS WHAT I DESERVE.
ESPECIALLY WHEN I JUST CASUALLY STROLLED RIGHT BACK HERE.
BUT STILL, I WANT TO HELP YOU OUT IN ANY WAY I CAN!

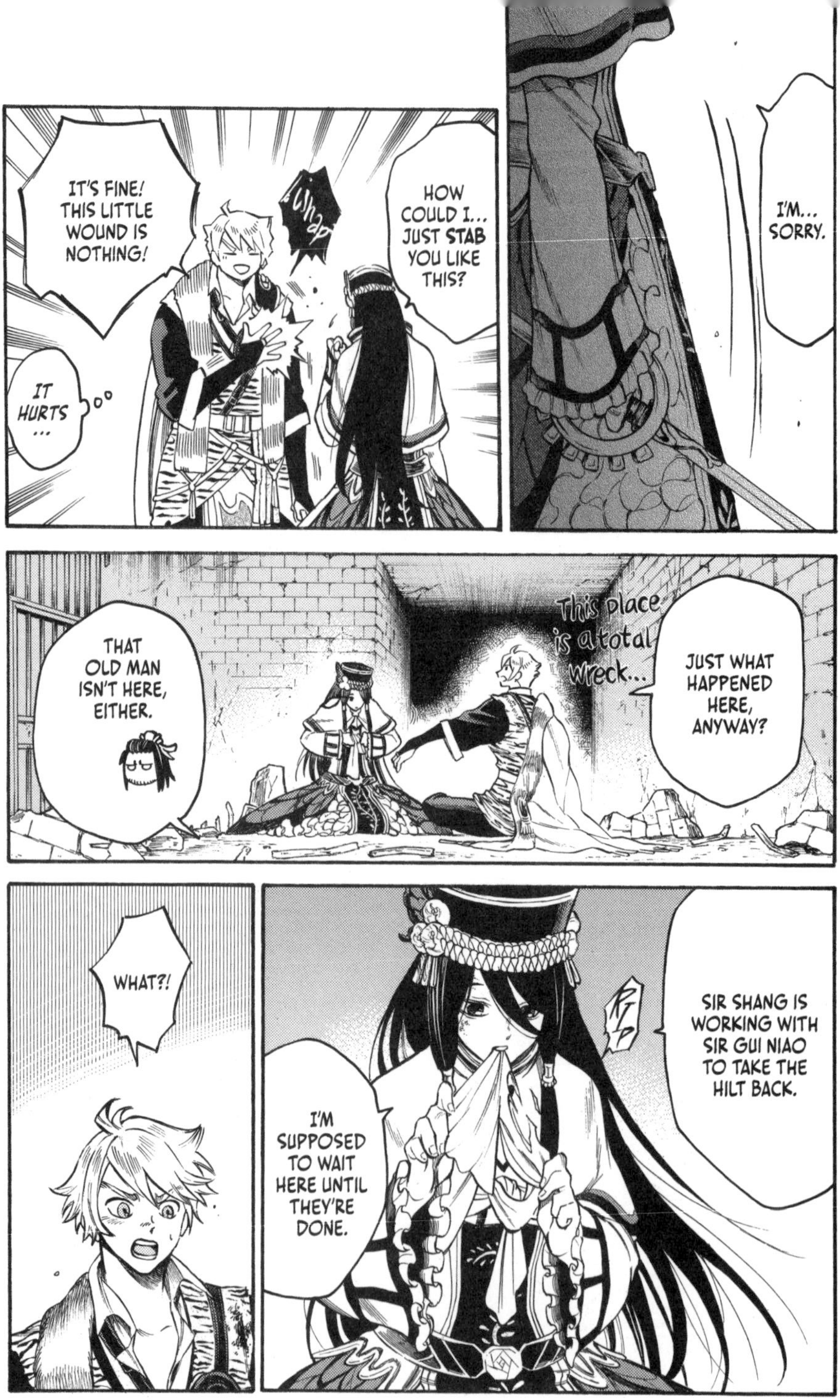
I'M... SORRY.
HOW COULD I... JUST STAB YOU LIKE THIS?
IT'S FINE! THIS LITTLE WOUND IS NOTHING!
IT HURTS...
This place is a total wreck...
JUST WHAT HAPPENED HERE, ANYWAY?
THAT OLD MAN ISN'T HERE, EITHER.
SIR SHANG IS WORKING WITH SIR GUI NIAO TO TAKE THE HILT BACK.
Rip
I'M SUPPOSED TO WAIT HERE UNTIL THEY'RE DONE.
WHAT?!

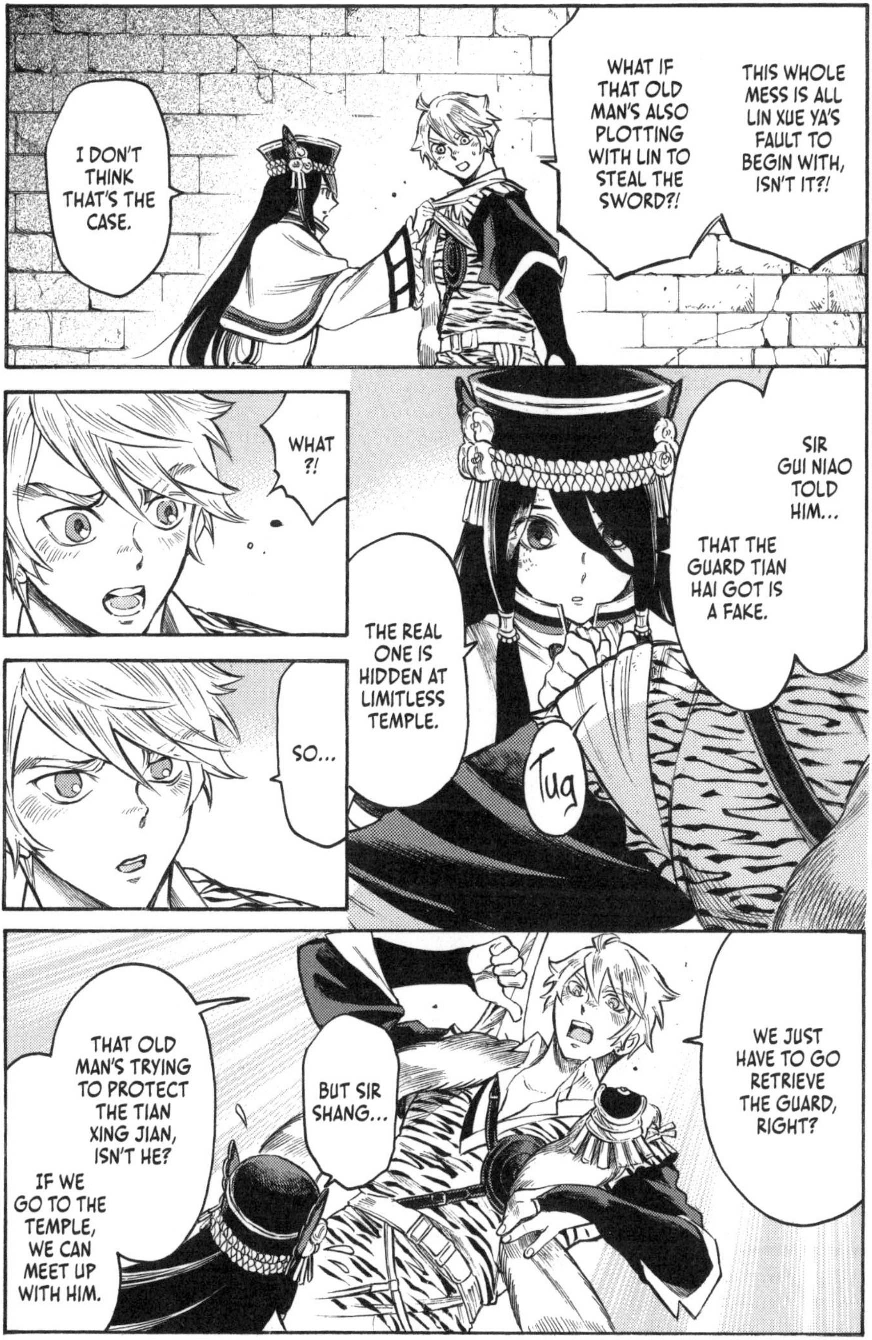
THIS WHOLE MESS IS ALL LIN XUE YA'S FAULT TO BEGIN WITH, ISN'T IT?!
WHAT IF THAT OLD MAN'S ALSO PLOTTING WITH LIN TO STEAL THE SWORD?!
I DON'T THINK THAT'S THE CASE.
SIR GUI NIAO TOLD HIM...
THAT THE GUARD TIAN HAI GOT IS A FAKE.
THE REAL ONE IS HIDDEN AT LIMITLESS TEMPLE.
Tug
WHAT ?!
SO...
WE JUST HAVE TO GO RETRIEVE THE GUARD, RIGHT?
BUT SIR SHANG...
THAT OLD MAN'S TRYING TO PROTECT THE TIAN XING JIAN, ISN'T HE?
IF WE GO TO THE TEMPLE, WE CAN MEET UP WITH HIM.

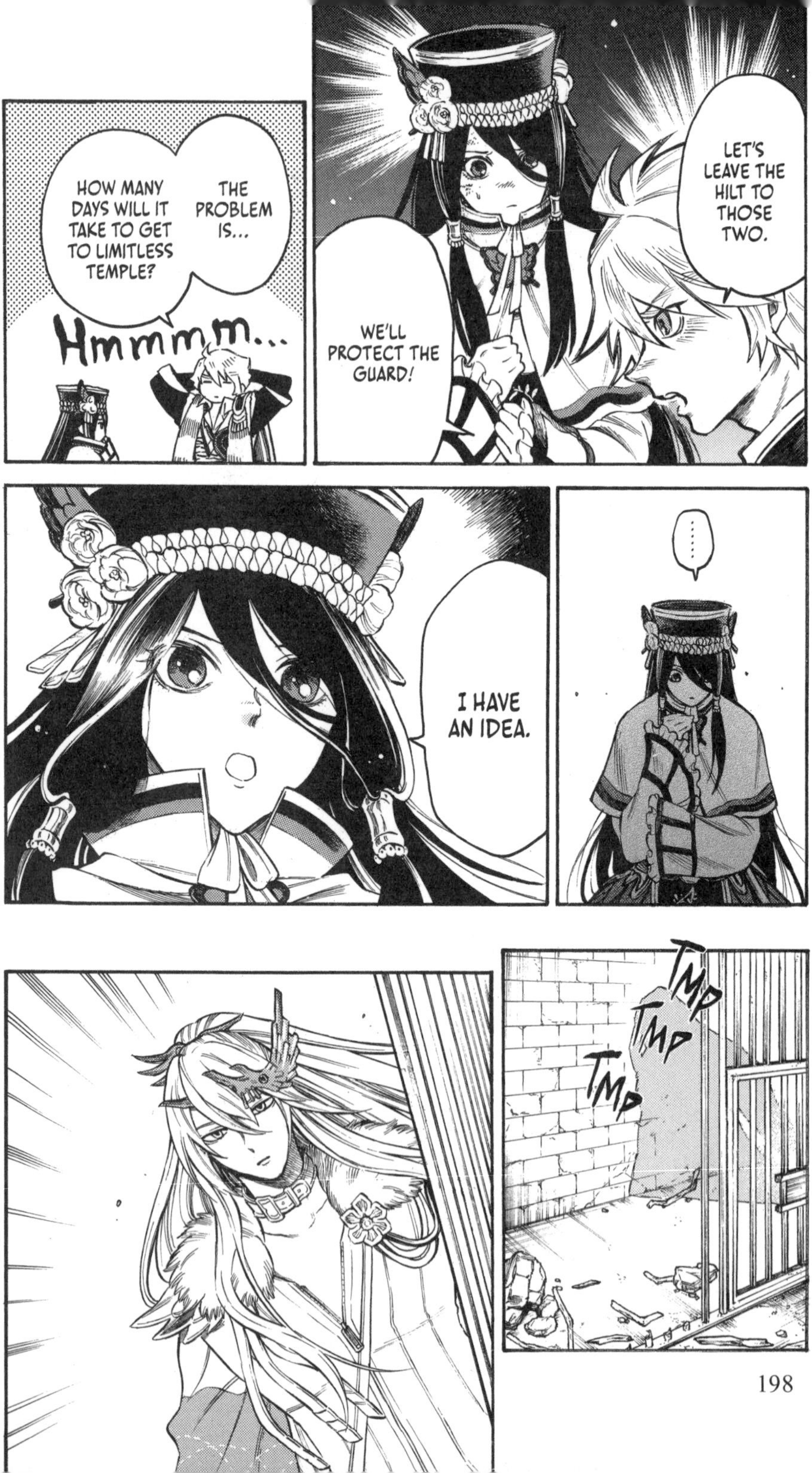
LET'S LEAVE THE HILT TO THOSE TWO.
WE'LL PROTECT THE GUARD!
THE PROBLEM IS...
HOW MANY DAYS WILL IT TAKE TO GET TO LIMITLESS TEMPLE?
Hmmmm...
......
I HAVE AN IDEA.
TMP TMP TMP

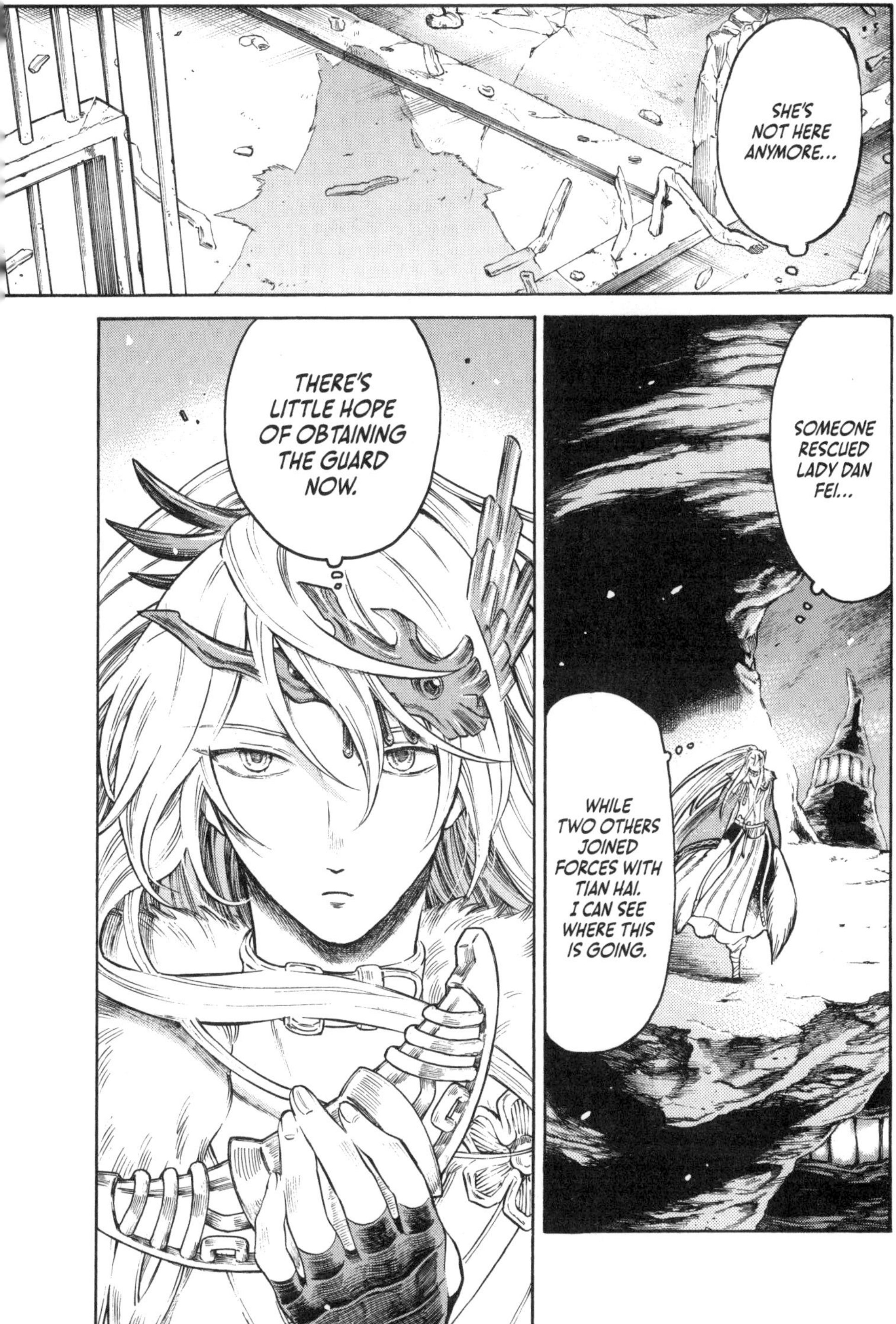
SHE'S NOT HERE ANYMORE...
SOMEONE RESCUED LADY DAN FEI...
WHILE TWO OTHERS JOINED FORCES WITH TIAN HAI. I CAN SEE WHERE THIS IS GOING.
THERE'S LITTLE HOPE OF OBTAINING THE GUARD NOW.

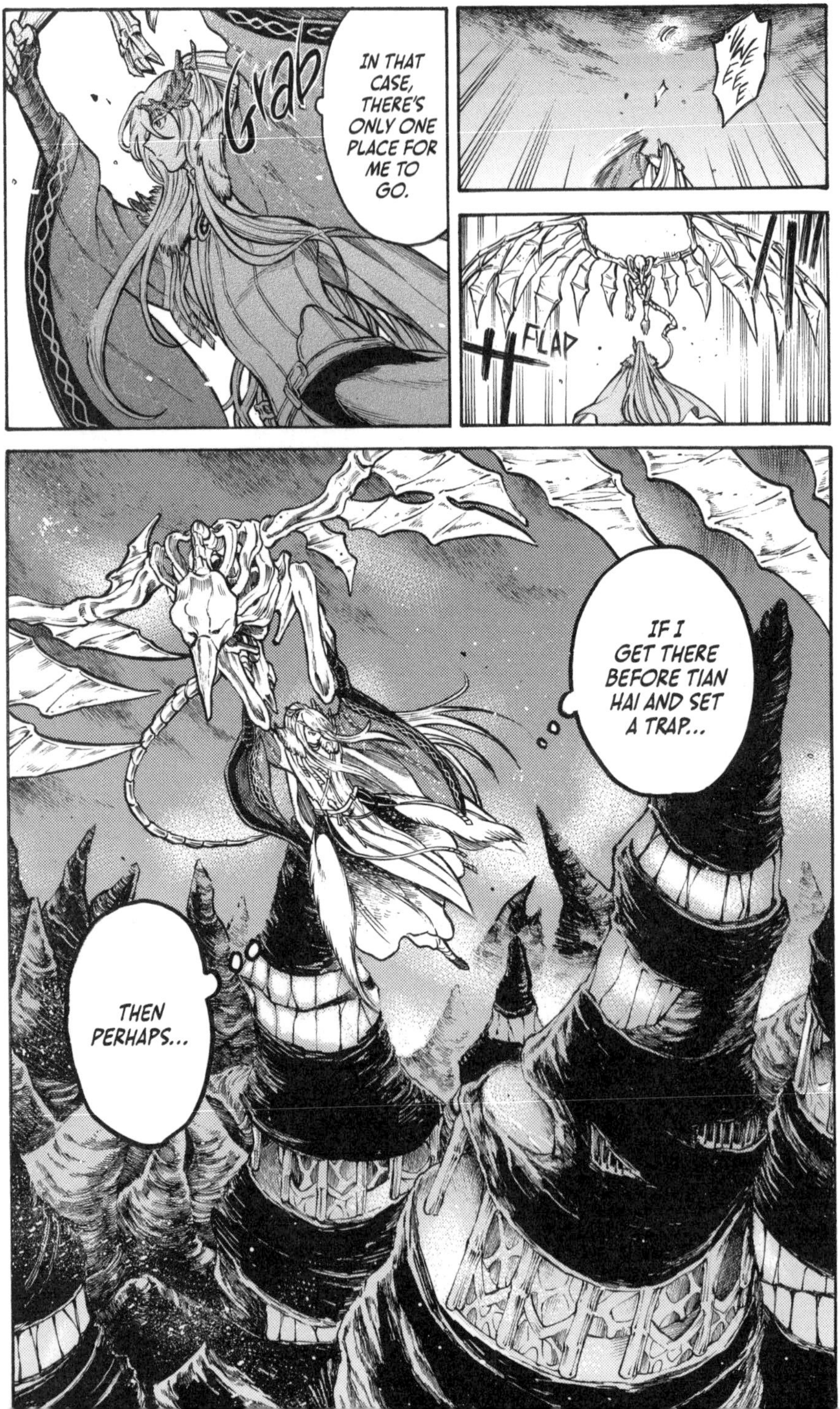
VWEEEE
FLAP
Grab
IN THAT CASE, THERE'S ONLY ONE PLACE FOR ME TO GO.
IF I GET THERE BEFORE TIAN HAI AND SET A TRAP...
THEN PERHAPS...

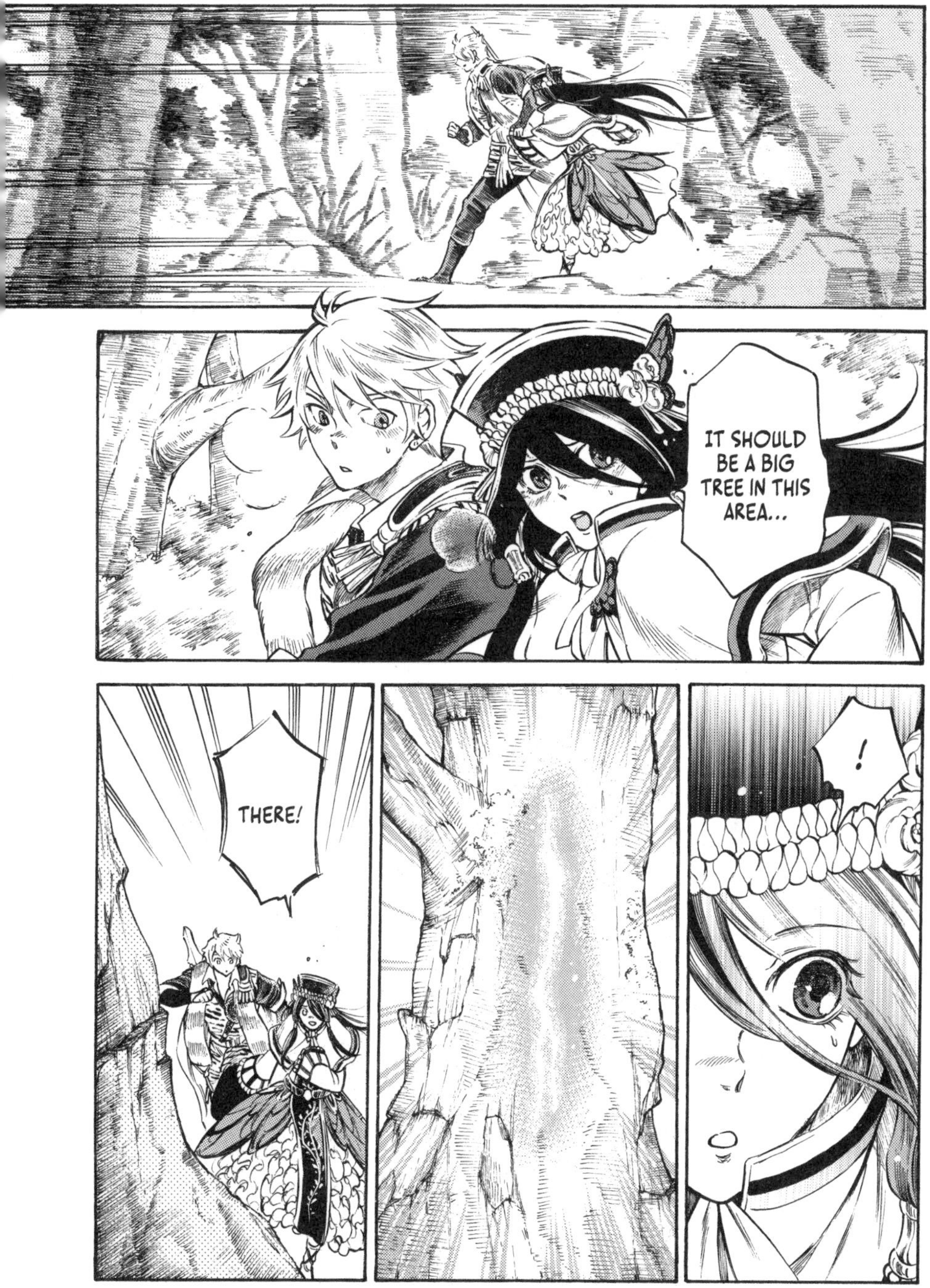
IT SHOULD BE A BIG TREE IN THIS AREA...
!
THERE!

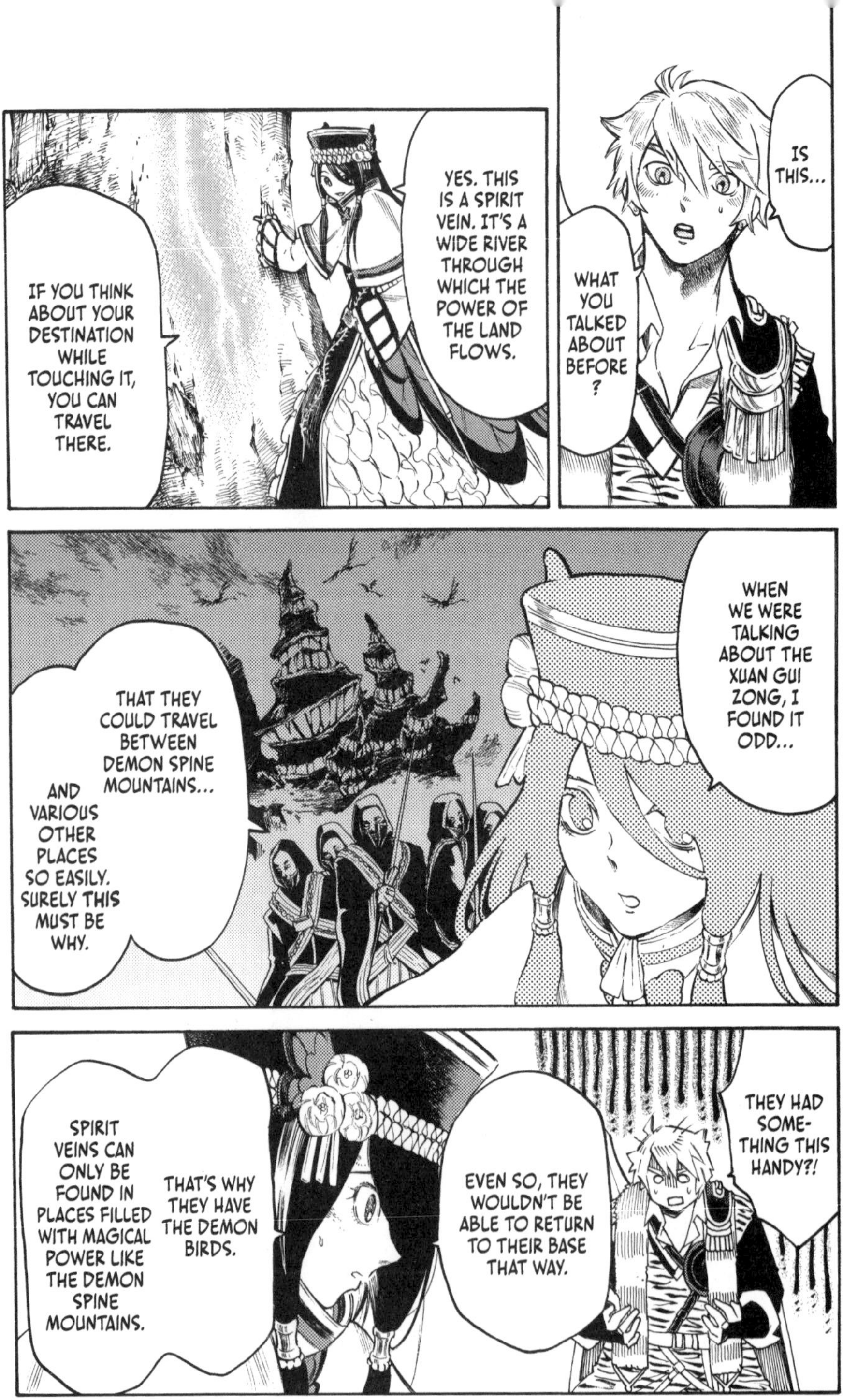
IS THIS...
WHAT YOU TALKED ABOUT BEFORE?
YES. THIS IS A SPIRIT VEIN. IT'S A WIDE RIVER THROUGH WHICH THE POWER OF THE LAND FLOWS.
IF YOU THINK ABOUT YOUR DESTINATION WHILE TOUCHING IT, YOU CAN TRAVEL THERE.
WHEN WE WERE TALKING ABOUT THE XUAN GUI ZONG, I FOUND IT ODD...
THAT THEY COULD TRAVEL BETWEEN DEMON SPINE MOUNTAINS...
AND VARIOUS OTHER PLACES SO EASILY. SURELY THIS MUST BE WHY.
THEY HAD SOME-THING THIS HANDY?!
EVEN SO, THEY WOULDN'T BE ABLE TO RETURN TO THEIR BASE THAT WAY.
THAT'S WHY THEY HAVE THE DEMON BIRDS.
SPIRIT VEINS CAN ONLY BE FOUND IN PLACES FILLED WITH MAGICAL POWER LIKE THE DEMON SPINE MOUNTAINS.

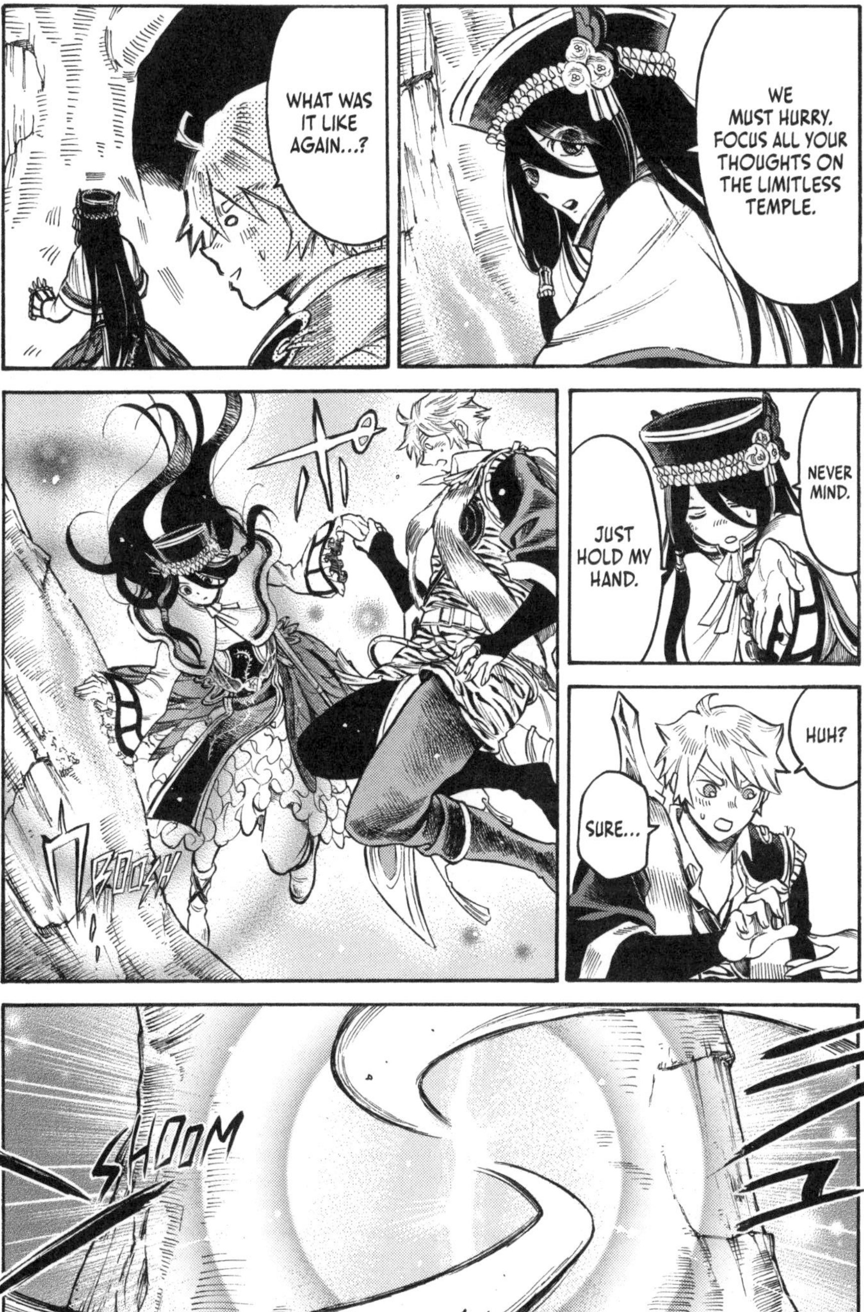
WE MUST HURRY. FOCUS ALL YOUR THOUGHTS ON THE LIMITLESS TEMPLE.
WHAT WAS IT LIKE AGAIN...?
NEVER MIND.
JUST HOLD MY HAND.
HUH?
SURE...
SHOOM

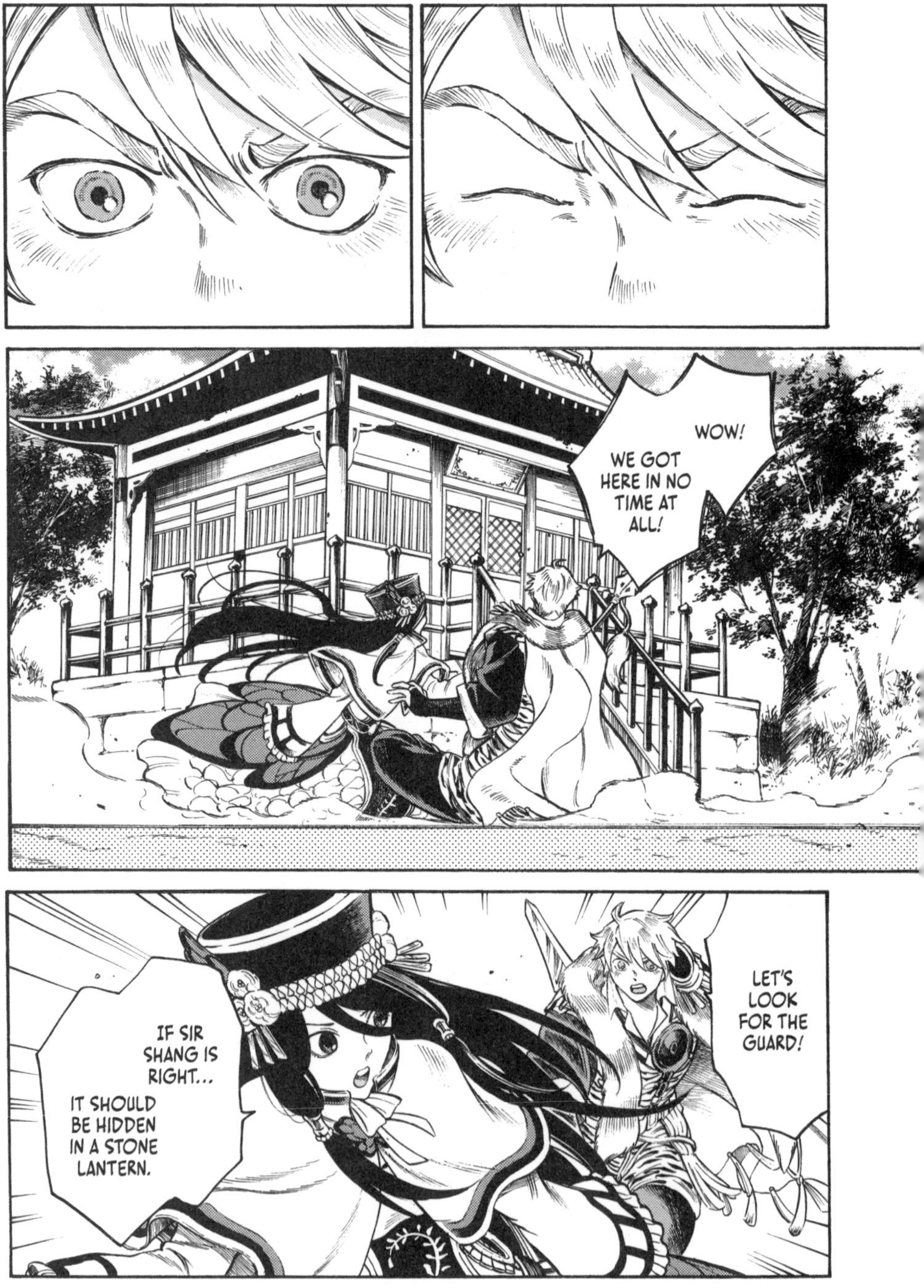
WOW!
WE GOT HERE IN NO TIME AT ALL!
LET'S LOOK FOR THE GUARD!
IF SIR SHANG IS RIGHT...
IT SHOULD BE HIDDEN IN A STONE LANTERN.

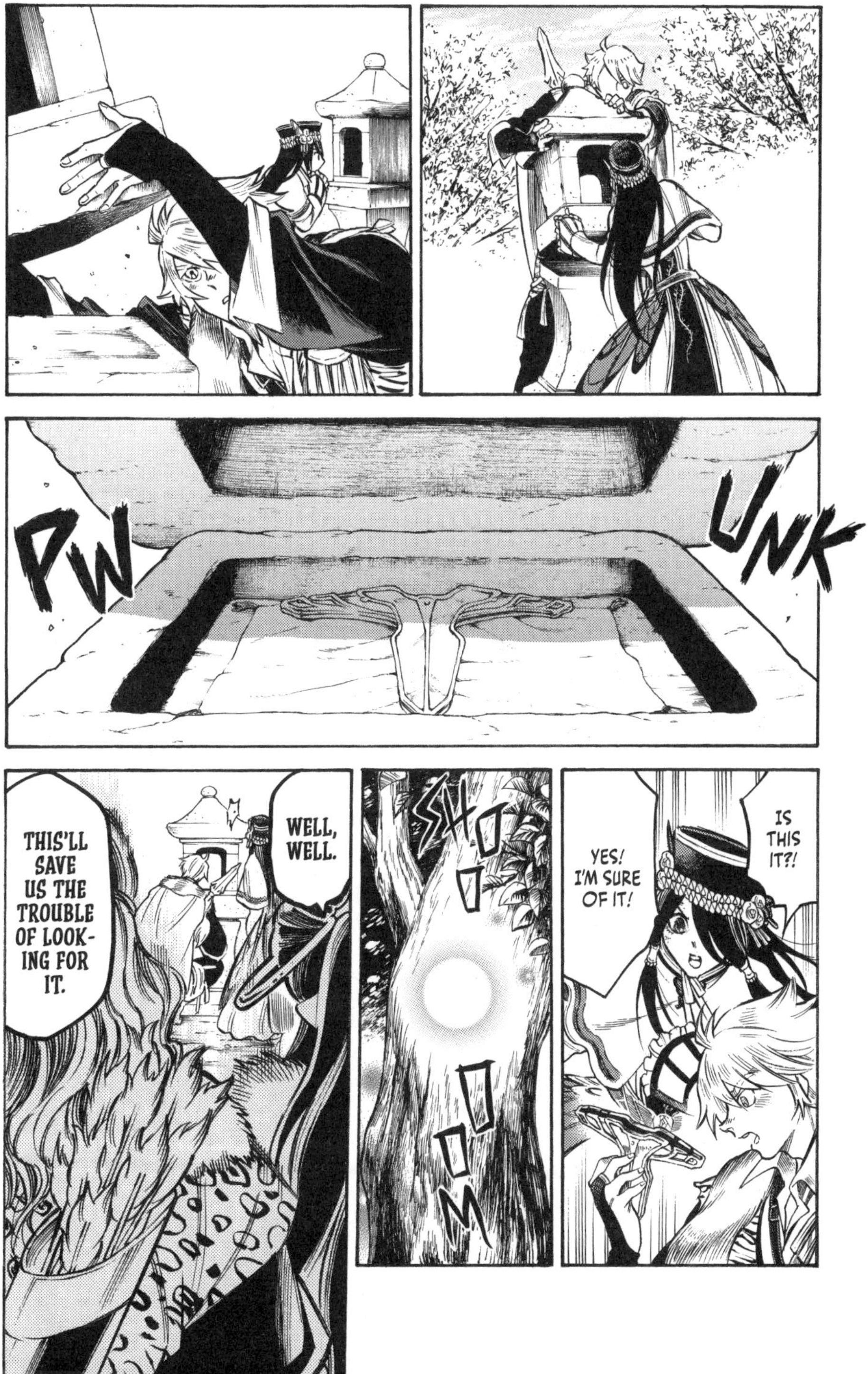
PWUNK
IS THIS IT?!
YES! I'M SURE OF IT!
SHOOOOOM
WELL, WELL.
THIS'LL SAVE US THE TROUBLE OF LOOK-ING FOR IT.

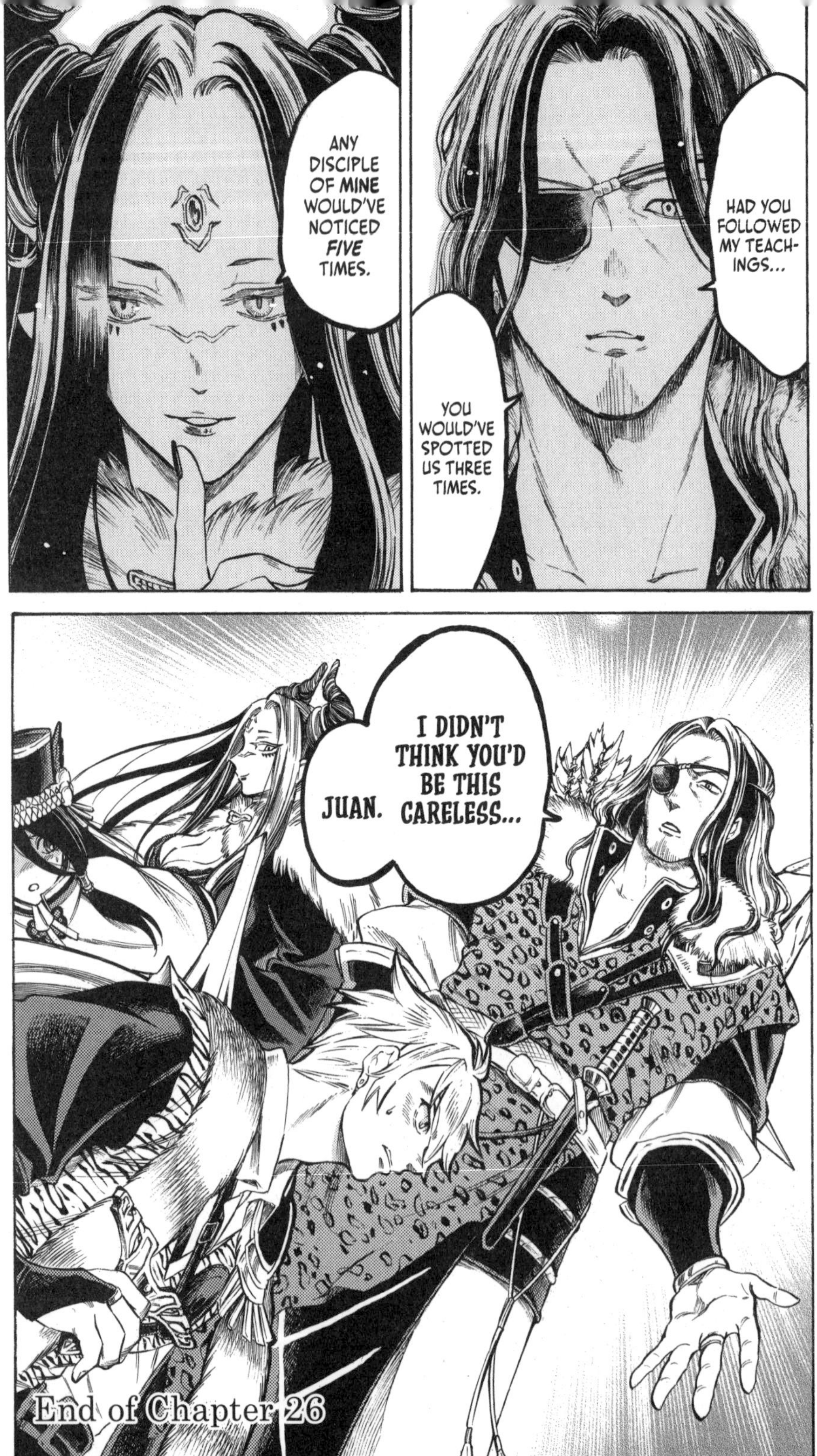
HAD YOU FOLLOWED MY TEACHINGS...
YOU WOULD'VE SPOTTED US THREE TIMES.
ANY DISCIPLE OF **MINE** WOULD'VE NOTICED ***FIVE*** TIMES.
I DIDN'T THINK YOU'D BE THIS CARELESS...
JUAN.
End of Chapter 26

◇◇ Chapter 27 ◇◇

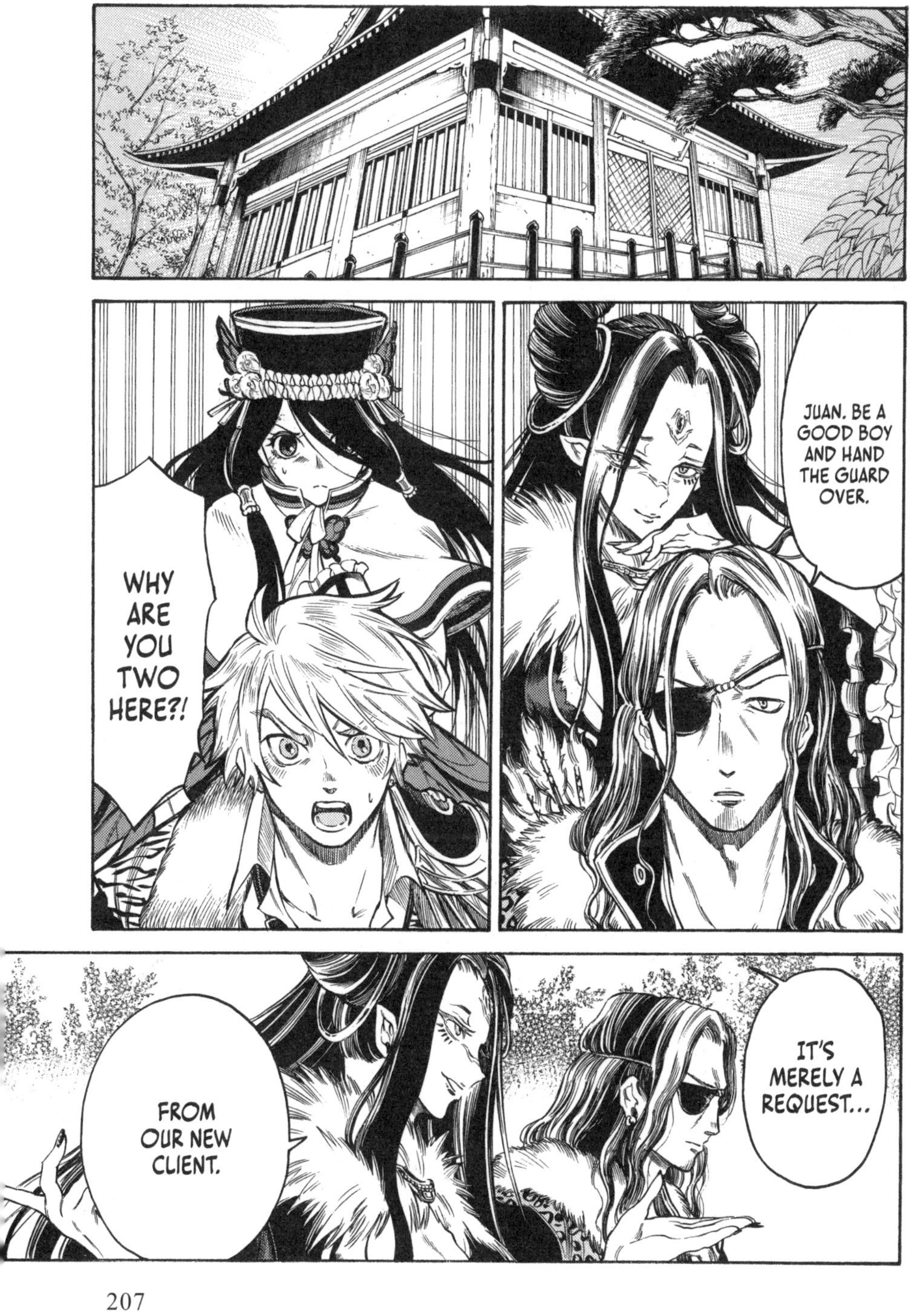
JUAN. BE A GOOD BOY AND HAND THE GUARD OVER.
WHY ARE YOU TWO HERE?!
IT'S MERELY A REQUEST...
FROM OUR NEW CLIENT.

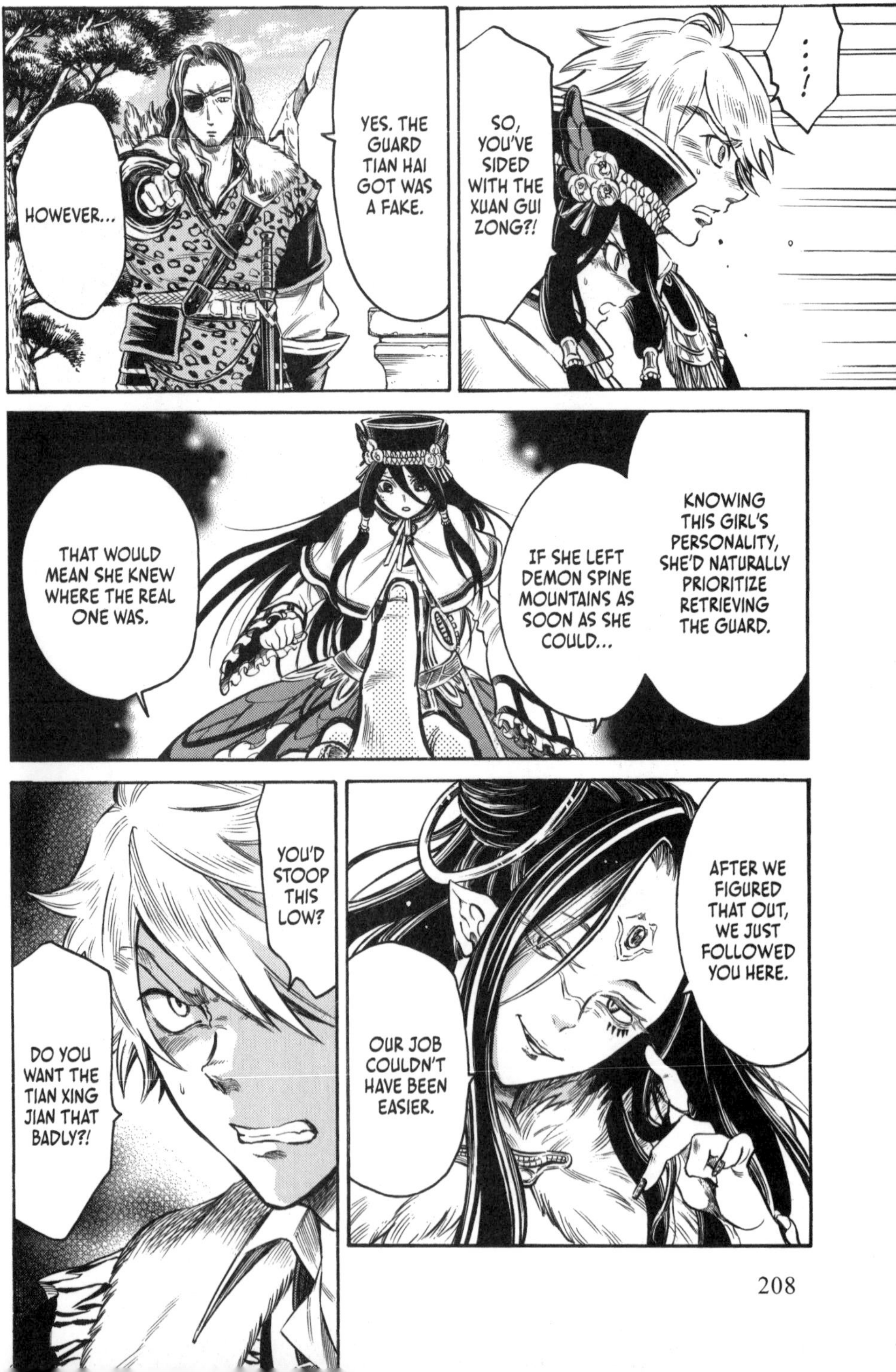
…!
SO, YOU'VE SIDED WITH THE XUAN GUI ZONG?!
YES. THE GUARD TIAN HAI GOT WAS A FAKE.
HOWEVER…
KNOWING THIS GIRL'S PERSONALITY, SHE'D NATURALLY PRIORITIZE RETRIEVING THE GUARD.
IF SHE LEFT DEMON SPINE MOUNTAINS AS SOON AS SHE COULD…
THAT WOULD MEAN SHE KNEW WHERE THE REAL ONE WAS.
AFTER WE FIGURED THAT OUT, WE JUST FOLLOWED YOU HERE.
OUR JOB COULDN'T HAVE BEEN EASIER.
YOU'D STOOP THIS LOW?
DO YOU WANT THE TIAN XING JIAN THAT BADLY?!

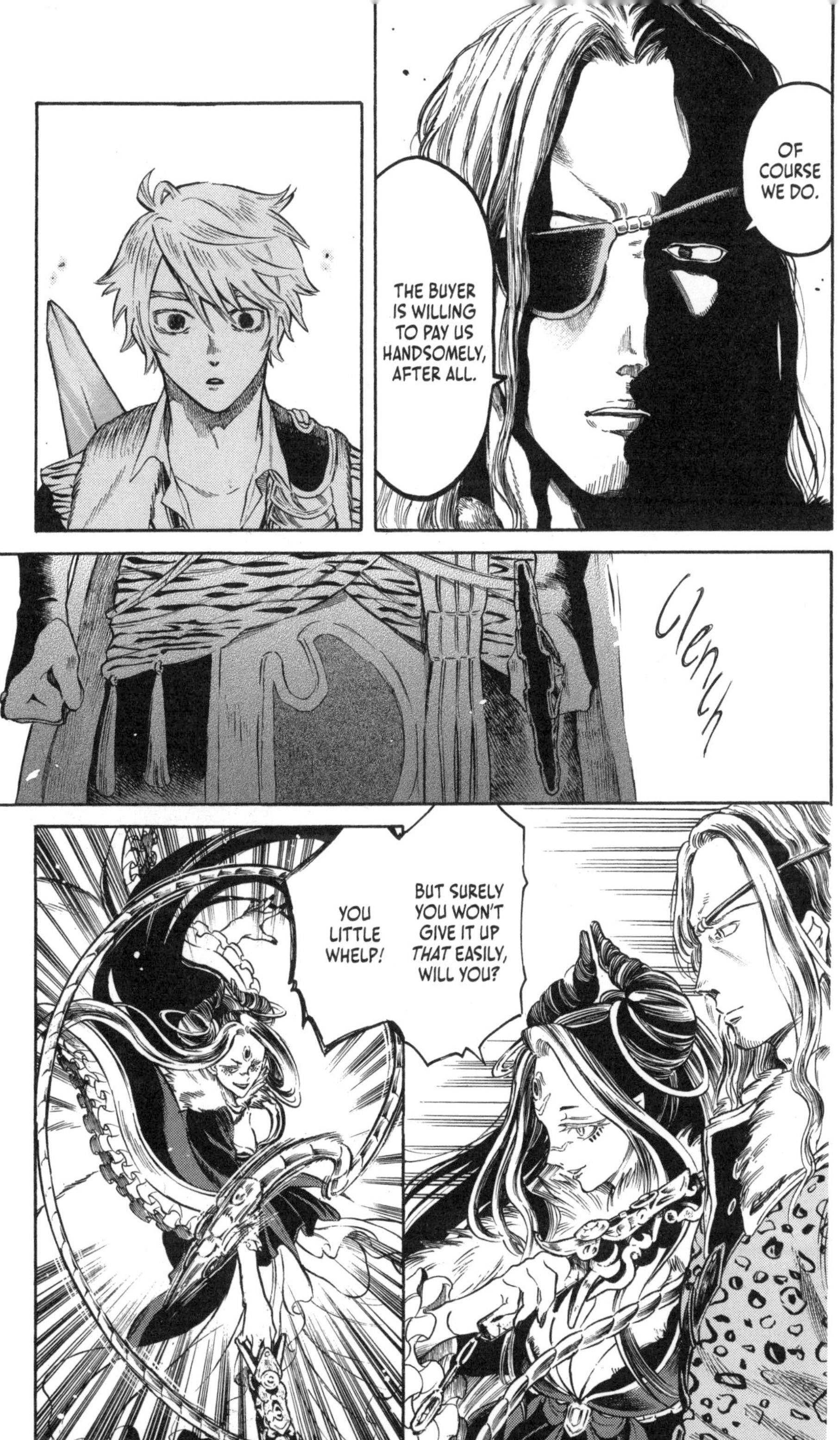
OF COURSE WE DO.
THE BUYER IS WILLING TO PAY US HANDSOMELY, AFTER ALL.
Clench
BUT SURELY YOU WON'T GIVE IT UP *THAT* EASILY, WILL YOU?
YOU LITTLE WHELP!

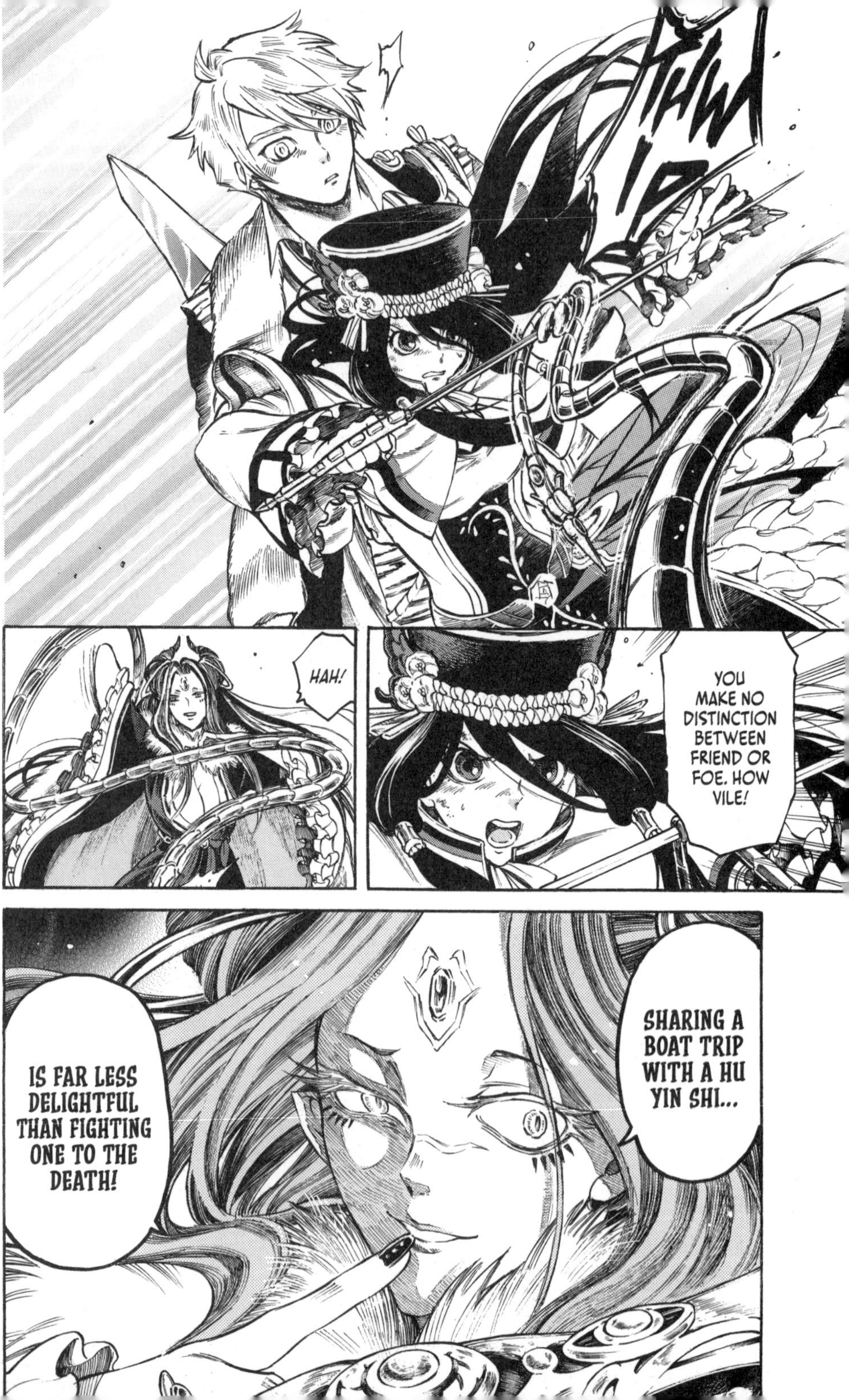
YOU MAKE NO DISTINCTION BETWEEN FRIEND OR FOE. HOW VILE!
HAH!
SHARING A BOAT TRIP WITH A HU YIN SHI...
IS FAR LESS DELIGHTFUL THAN FIGHTING ONE TO THE DEATH!

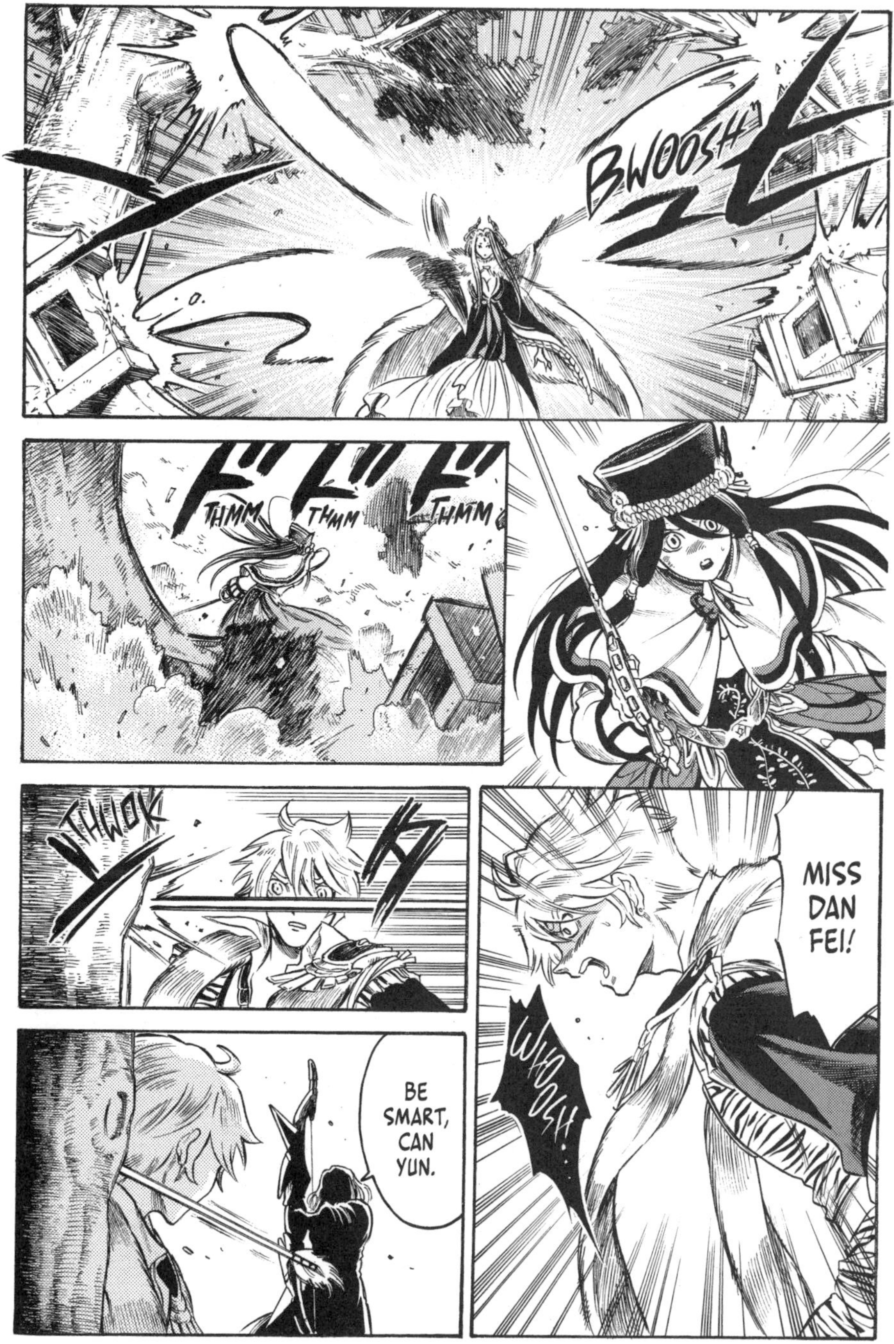
BWOOSH
THMM THMM THMM
MISS DAN FEI!
WHOOSH
THWOK
BE SMART, CAN YUN.

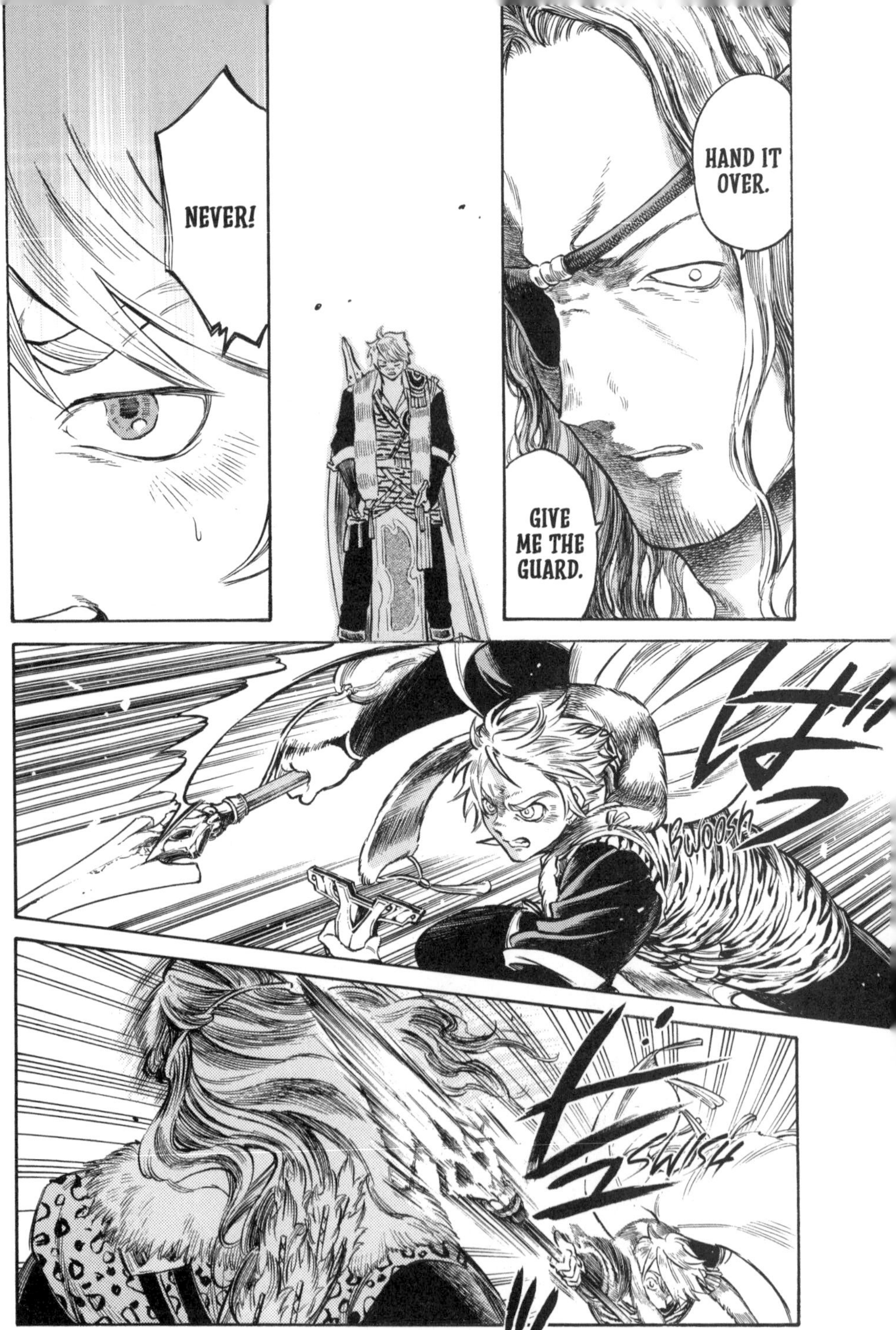
HAND IT OVER.
GIVE ME THE GUARD.
NEVER!
BWOOSH
SWISH

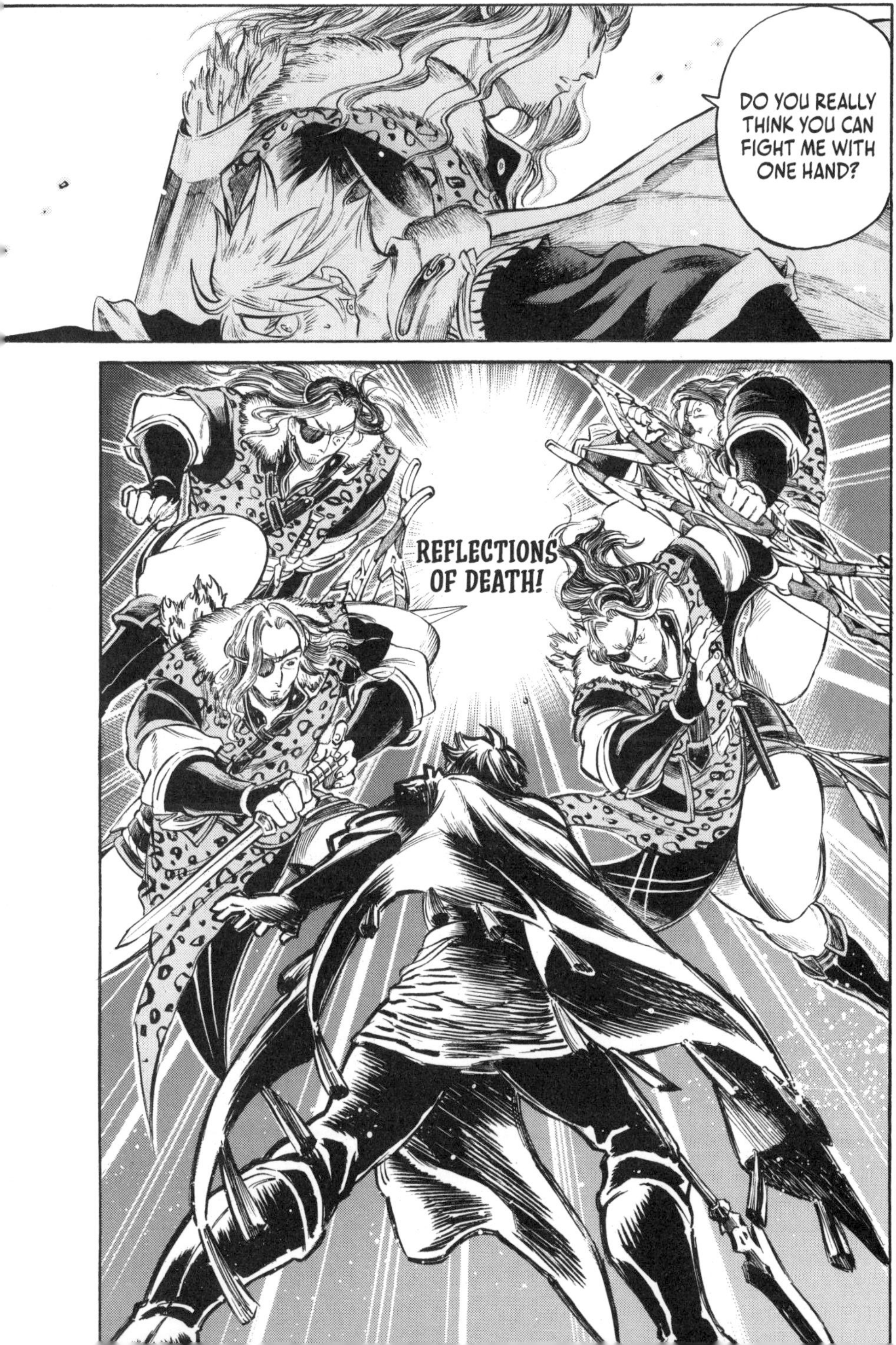
DO YOU REALLY THINK YOU CAN FIGHT ME WITH ONE HAND?
REFLECTIONS OF DEATH!

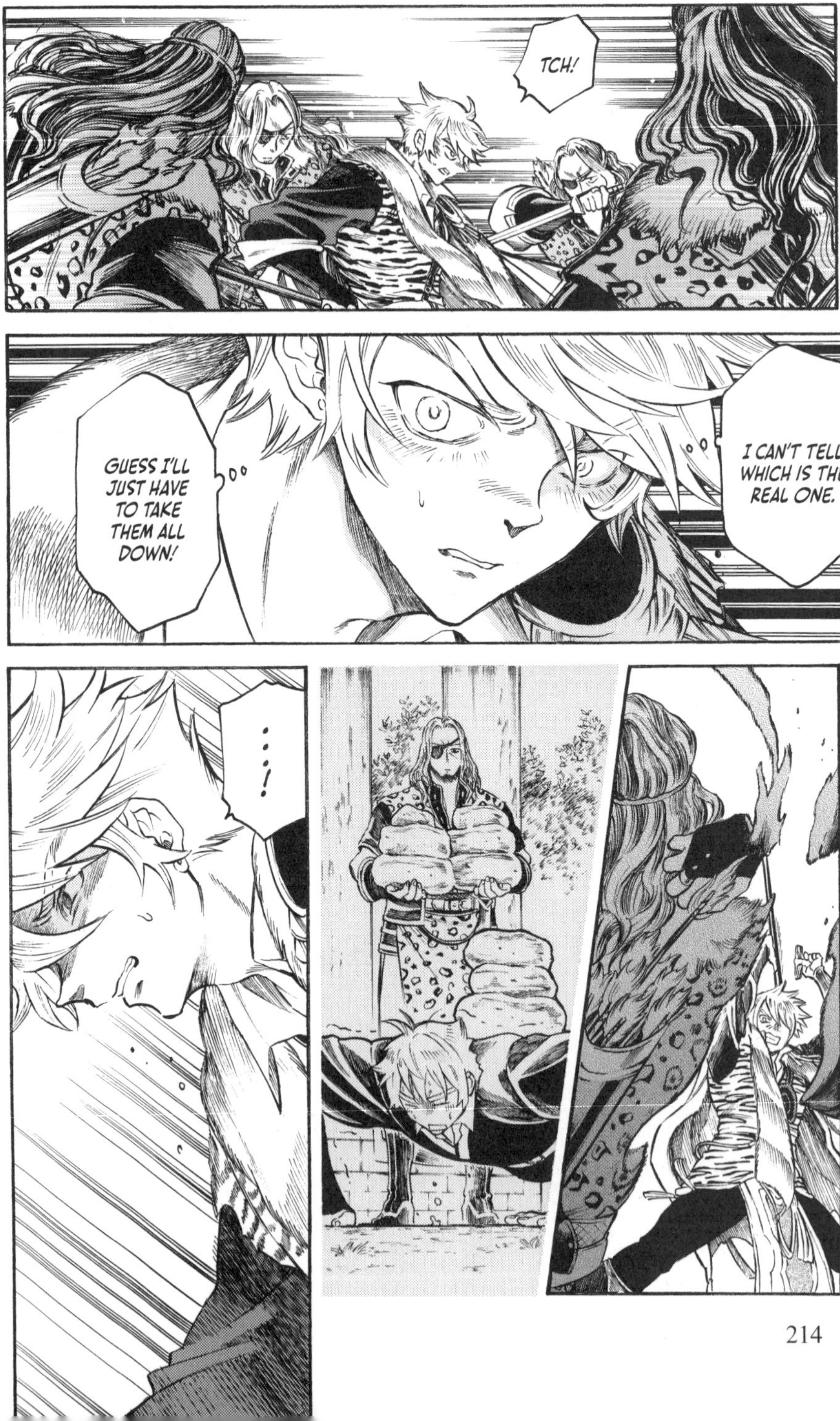
TCH!
I CAN'T TELL WHICH IS THE REAL ONE.
GUESS I'LL JUST HAVE TO TAKE THEM ALL DOWN!
...!

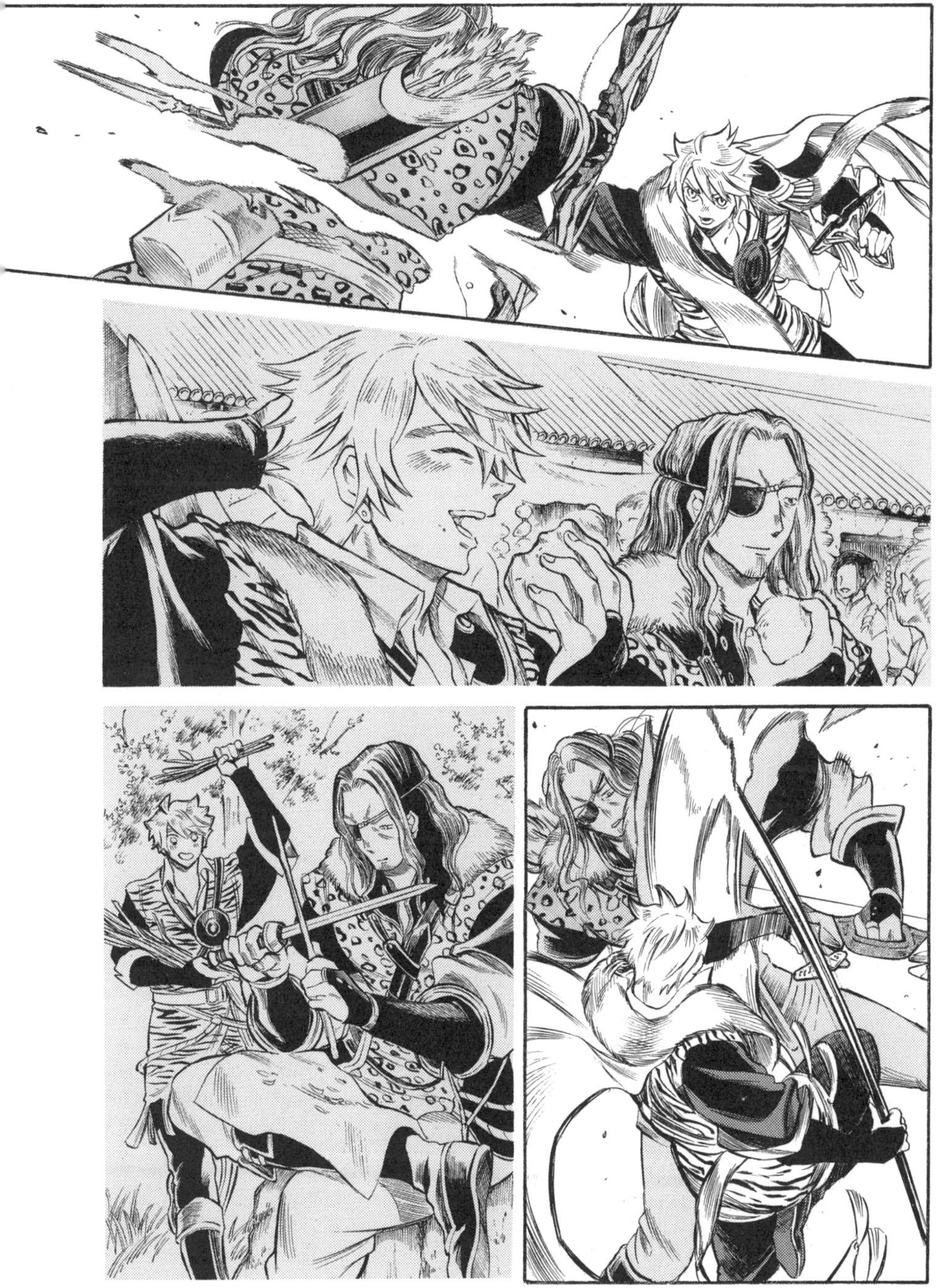

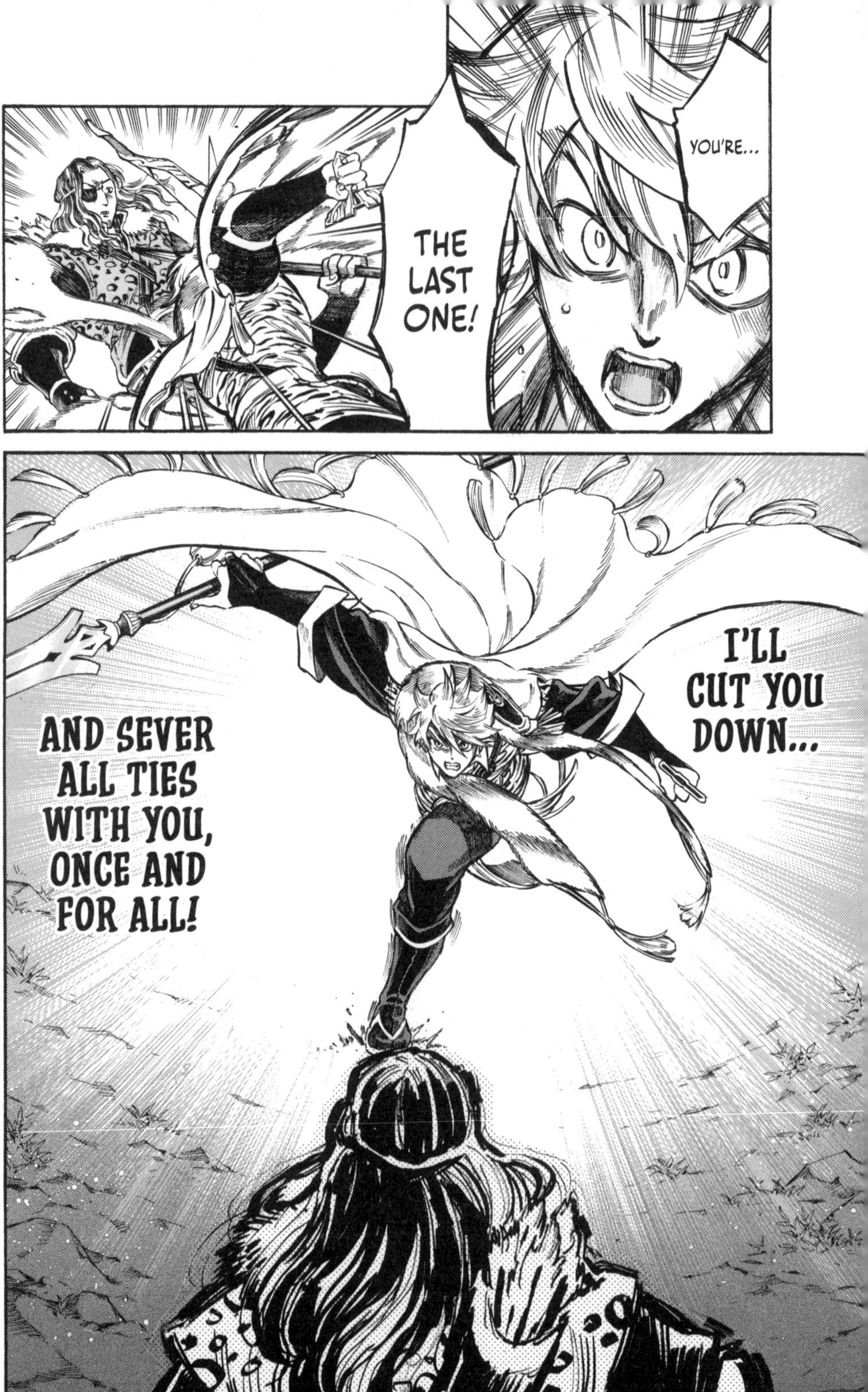
YOU'RE...
THE LAST ONE!
I'LL CUT YOU DOWN...
AND SEVER ALL TIES WITH YOU, ONCE AND FOR ALL!

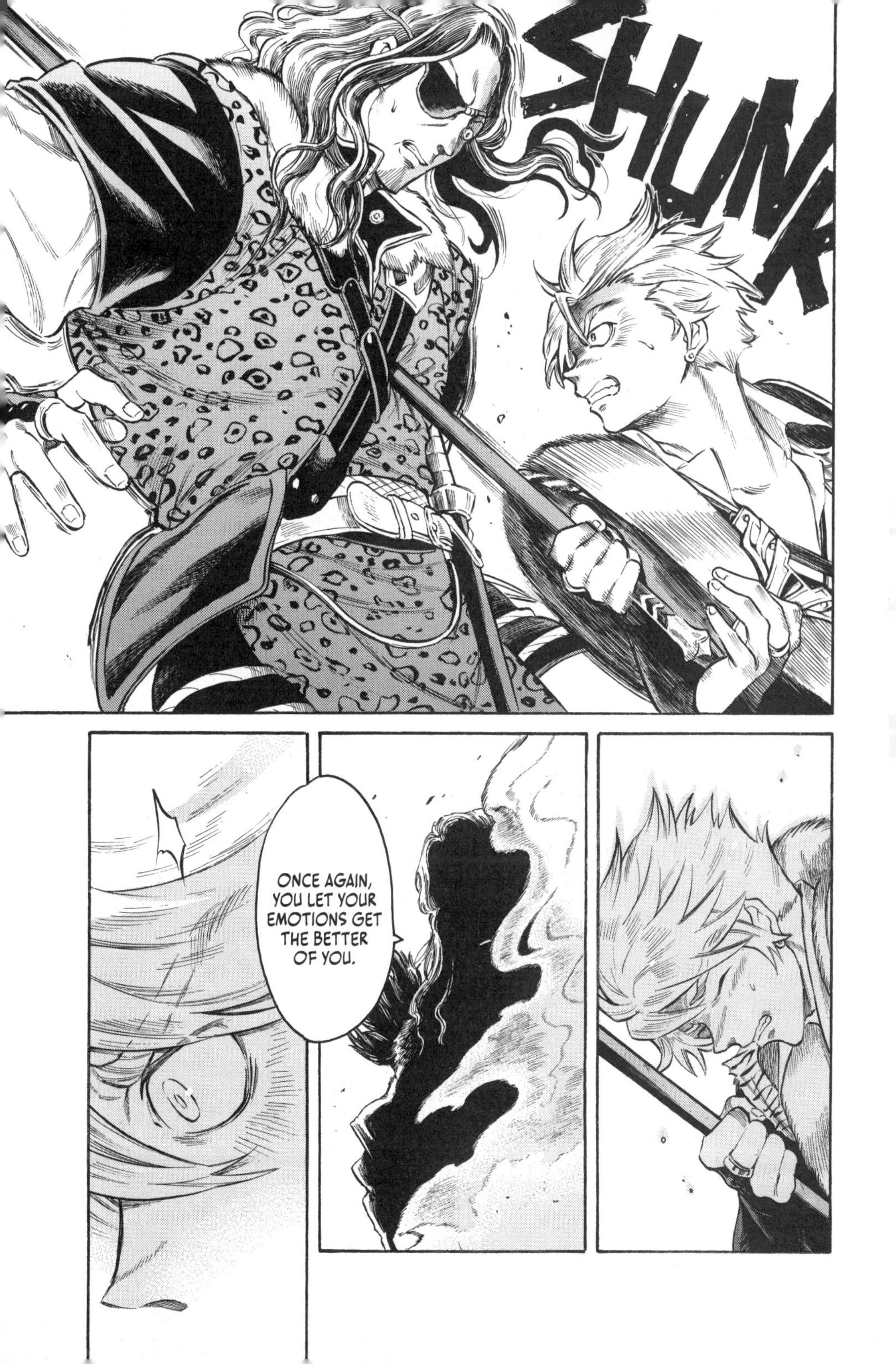
SHUNK
ONCE AGAIN, YOU LET YOUR EMOTIONS GET THE BETTER OF YOU.

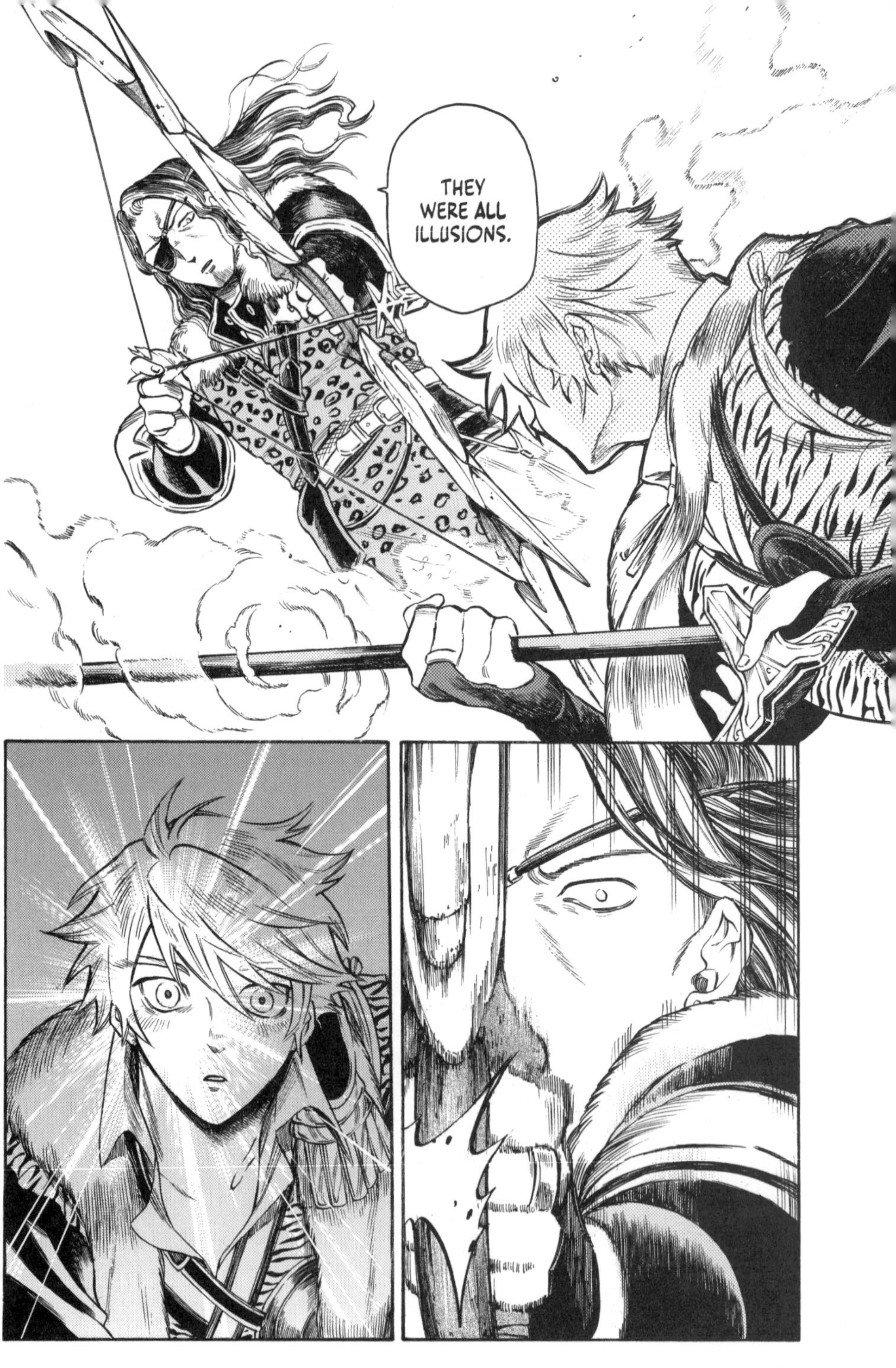
THEY WERE ALL ILLUSIONS.

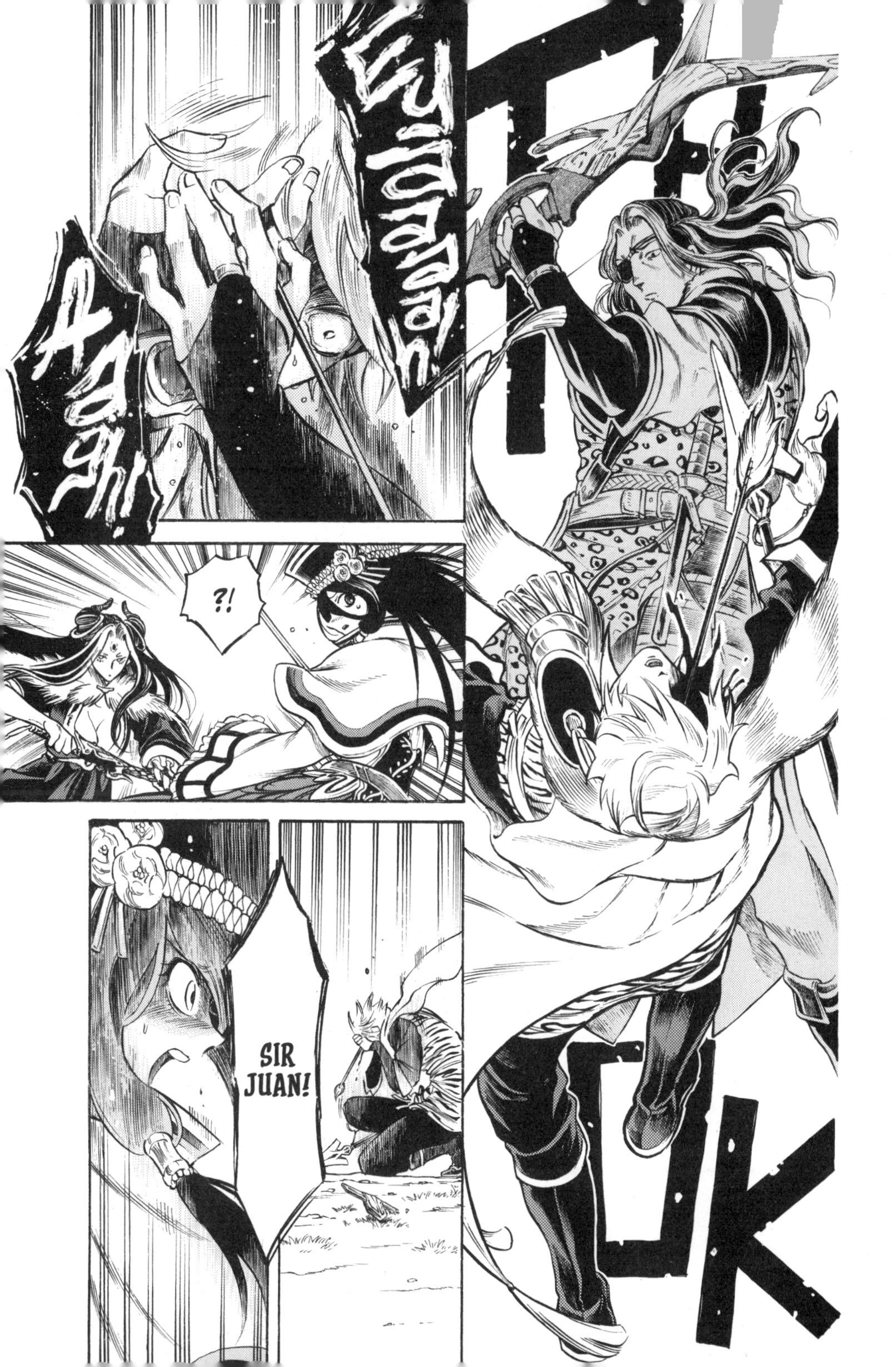
Agh!
?!
SIR JUAN!

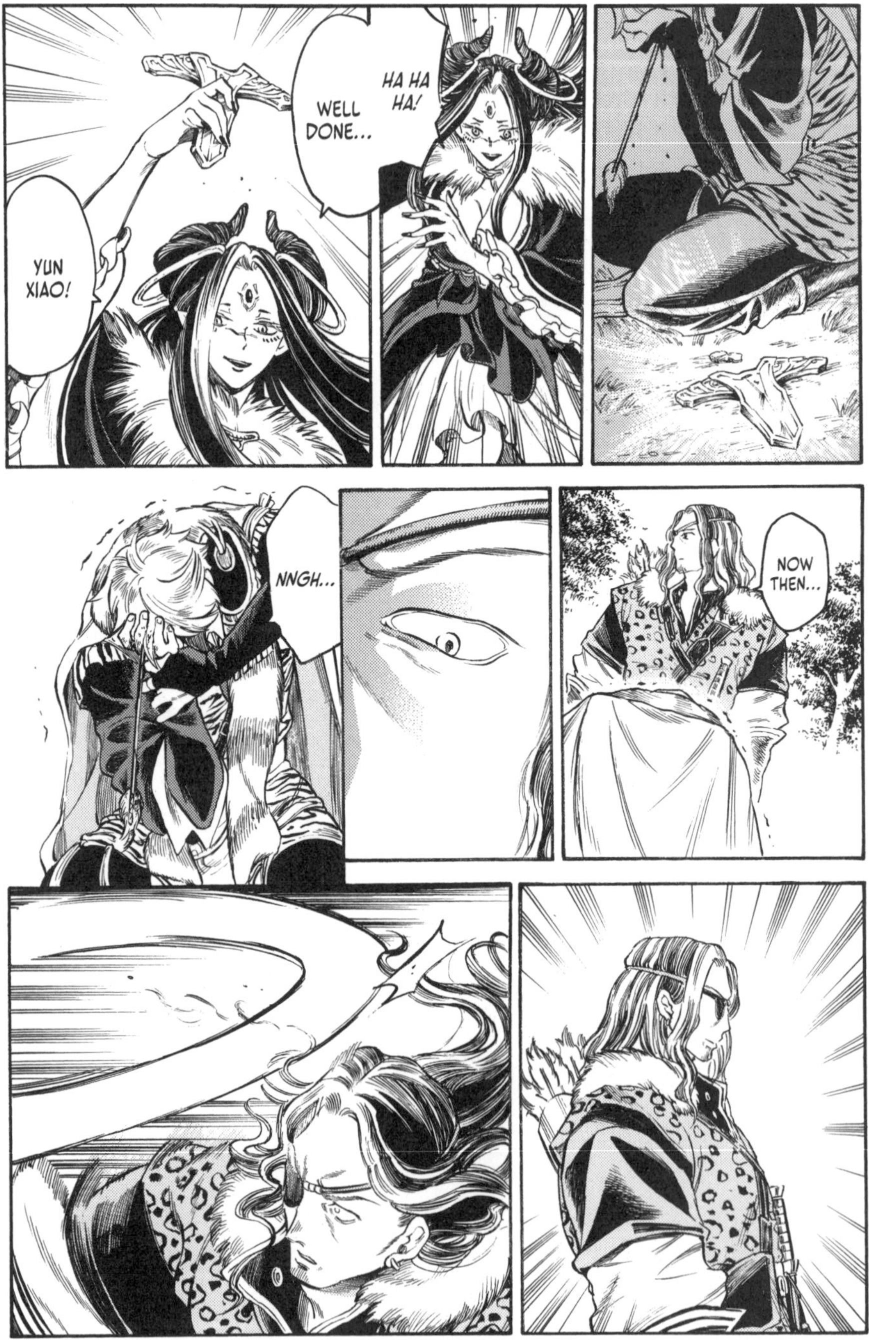
HA HA HA!
WELL DONE...
YUN XIAO!
NOW THEN...
NNGH...

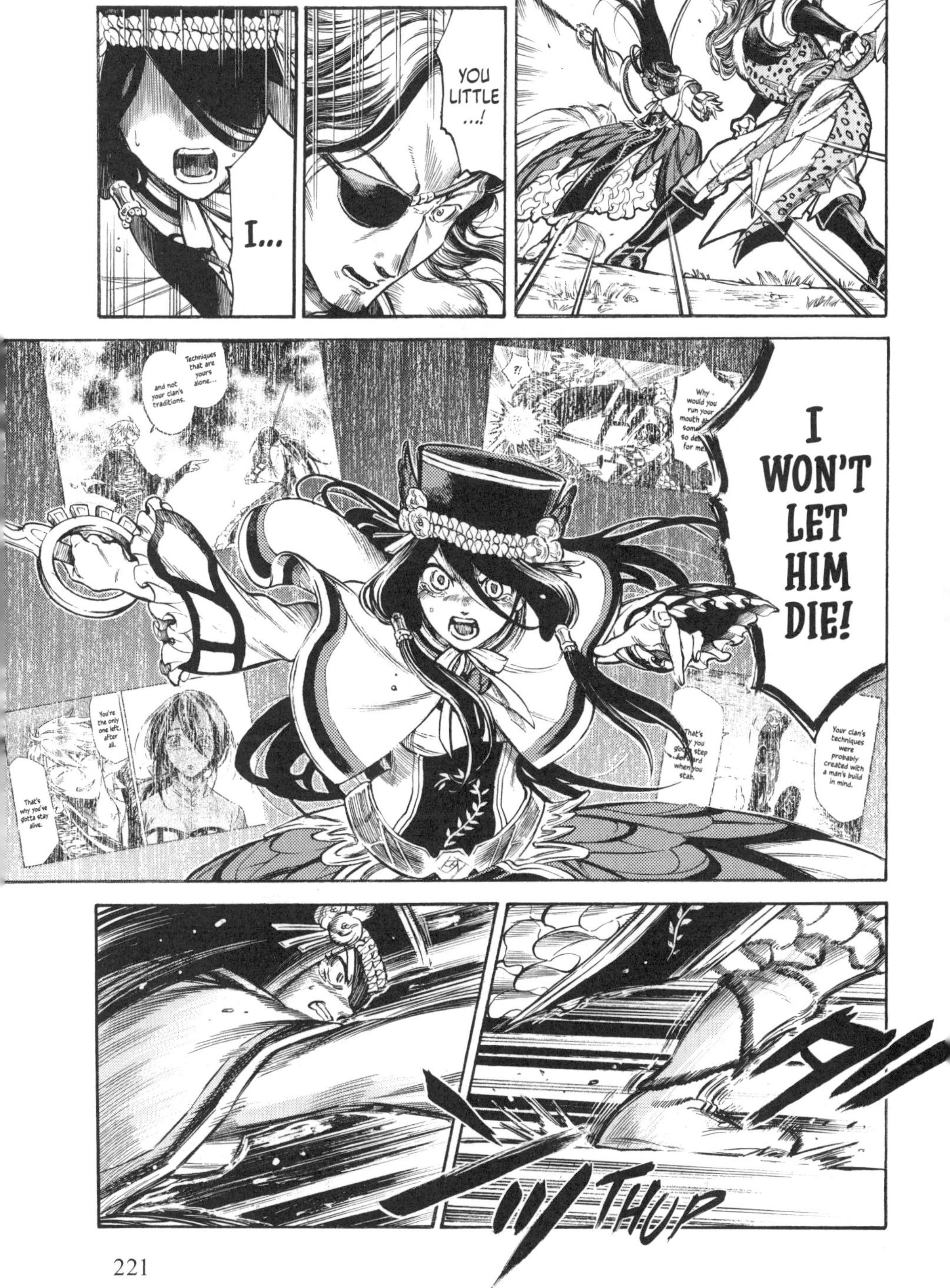
YOU LITTLE ...!
I...
Why would you run your mouth
I WON'T LET HIM DIE!
Your clan's techniques were probably created with a man's build in mind.
Techniques that are yours alone...
and not your clan's traditions.
You're the only one left, after all.
That's why you've gotta stay alive.
THUP

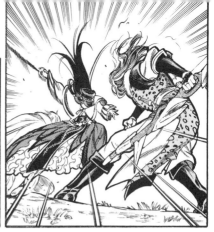

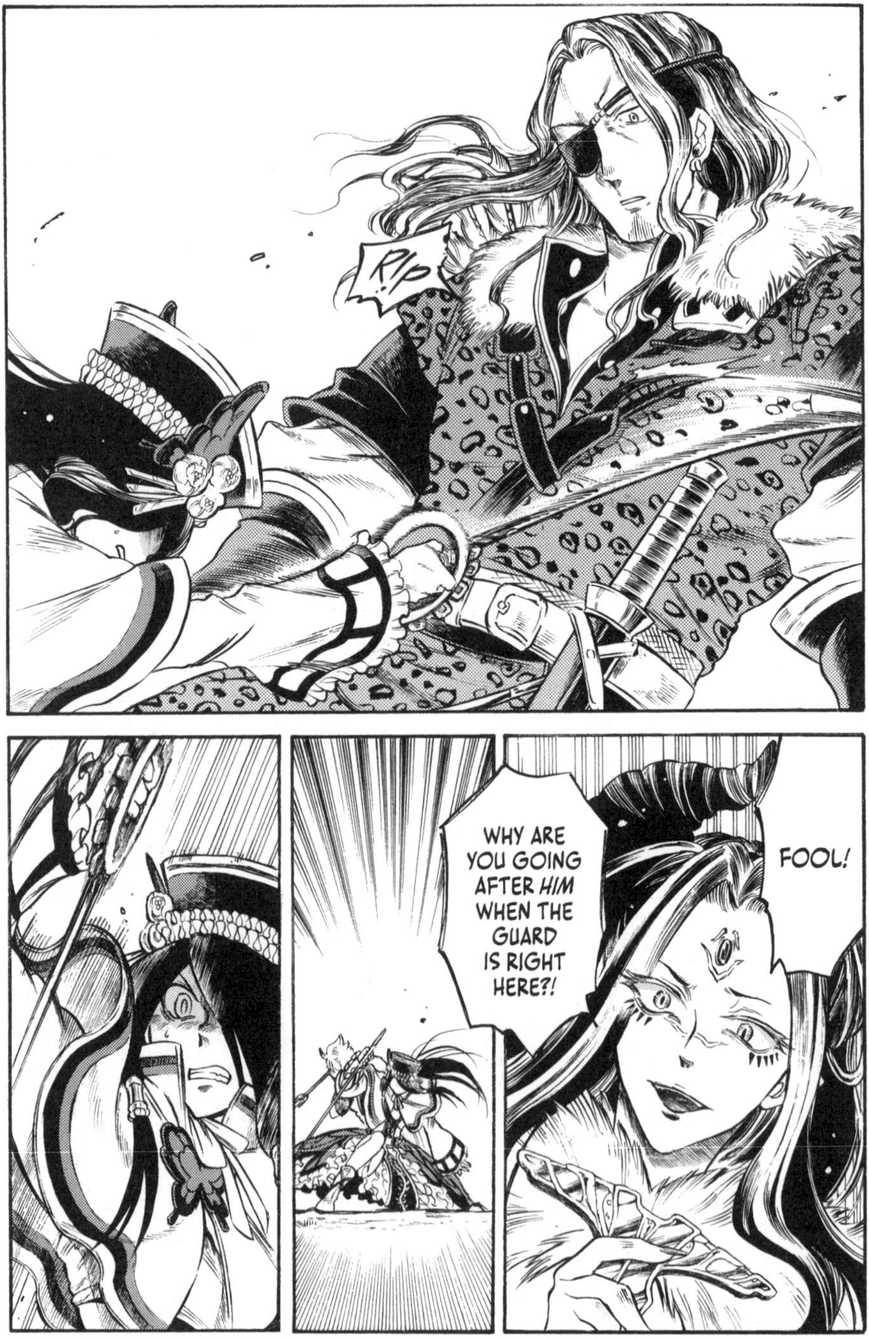
RIP
FOOL!
WHY ARE YOU GOING AFTER *HIM* WHEN THE GUARD IS RIGHT HERE?!

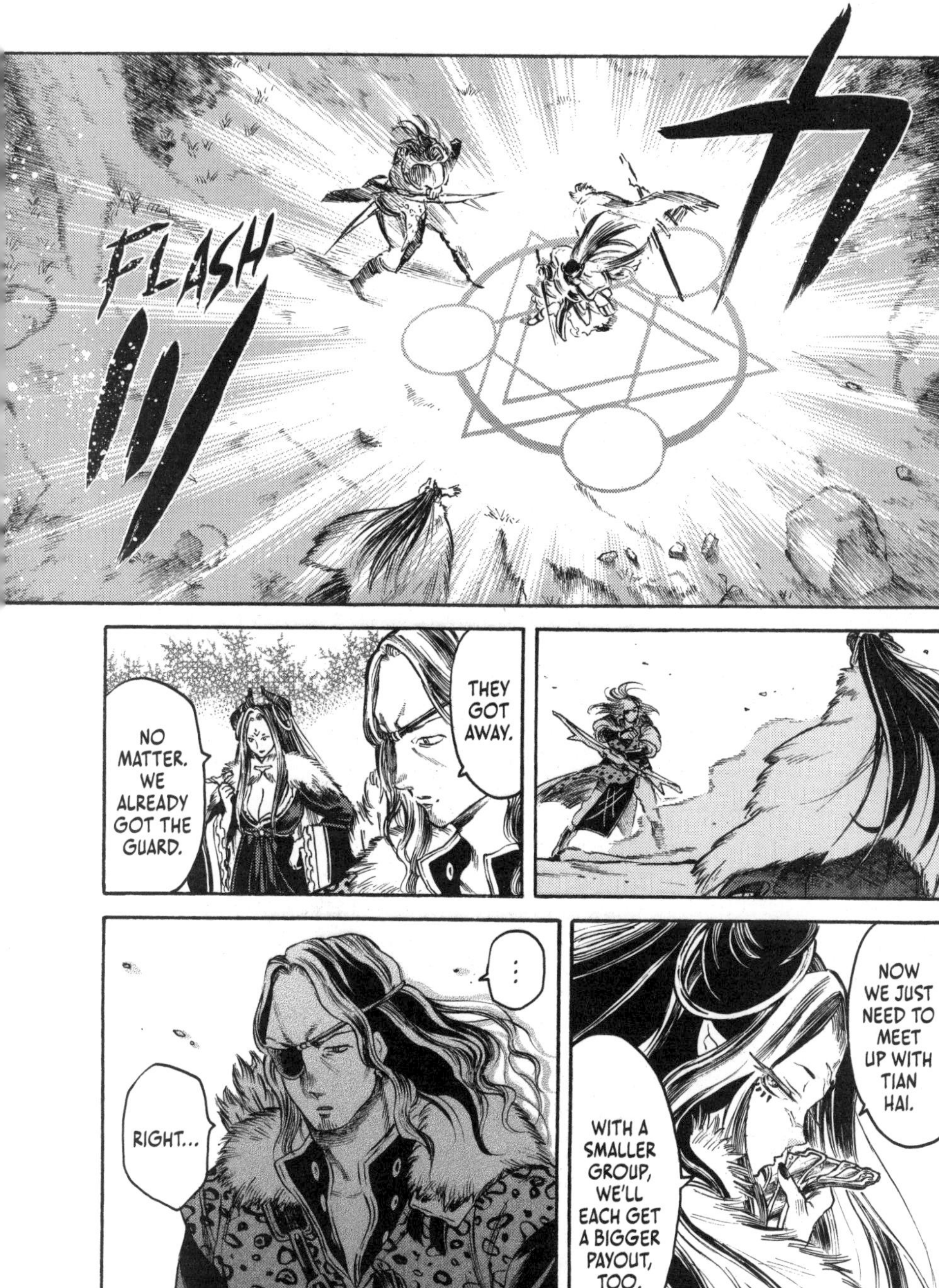
カ
FLASH
THEY GOT AWAY.
NO MATTER. WE ALREADY GOT THE GUARD.
NOW WE JUST NEED TO MEET UP WITH TIAN HAI.
WITH A SMALLER GROUP, WE'LL EACH GET A BIGGER PAYOUT, TOO.
...
RIGHT...

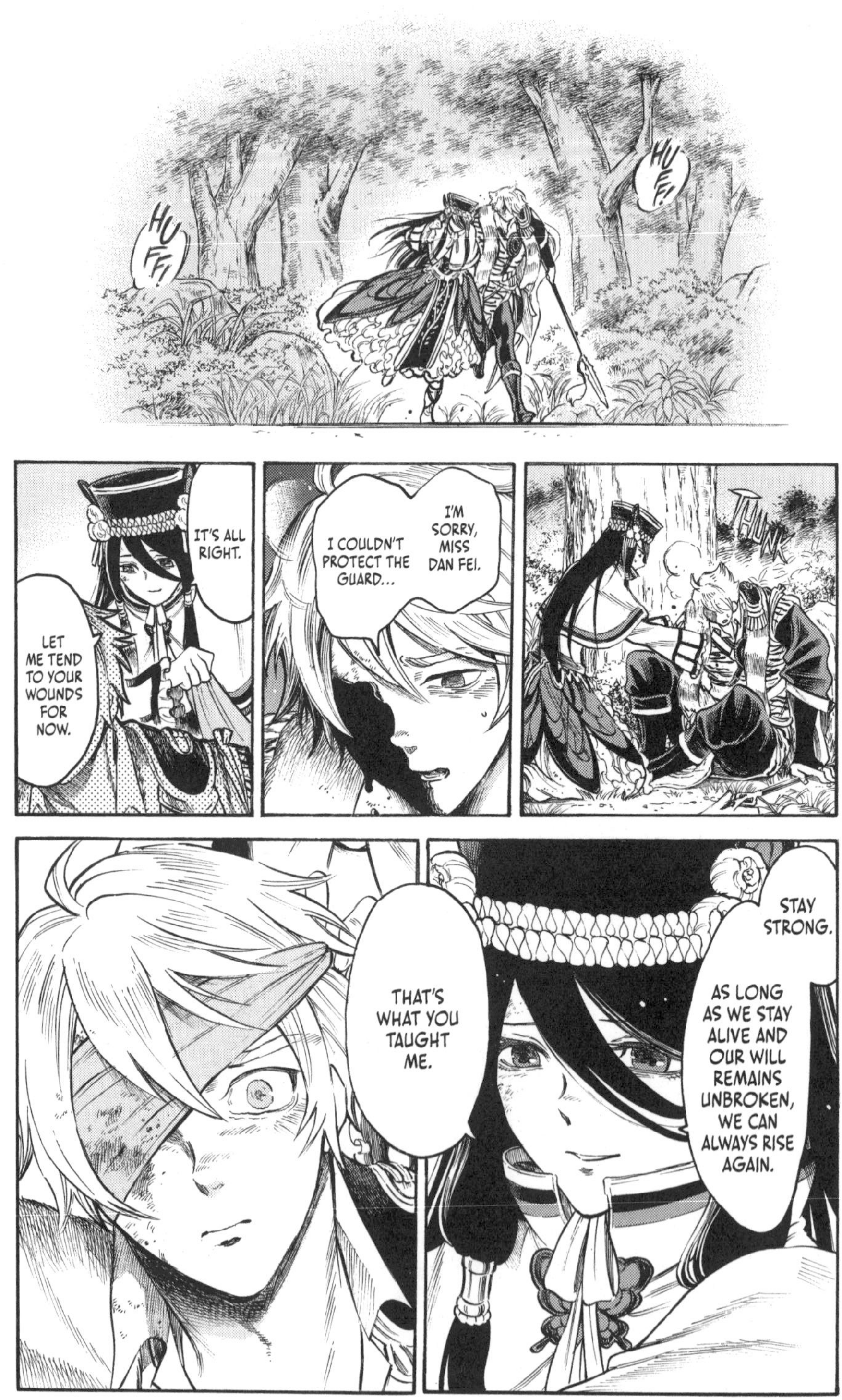
HUFF!
HUFF!
THUNK
I'M SORRY, MISS DAN FEI.
I COULDN'T PROTECT THE GUARD...
IT'S ALL RIGHT.
LET ME TEND TO YOUR WOUNDS FOR NOW.
STAY STRONG.
AS LONG AS WE STAY ALIVE AND OUR WILL REMAINS UNBROKEN, WE CAN ALWAYS RISE AGAIN.
THAT'S WHAT YOU TAUGHT ME.

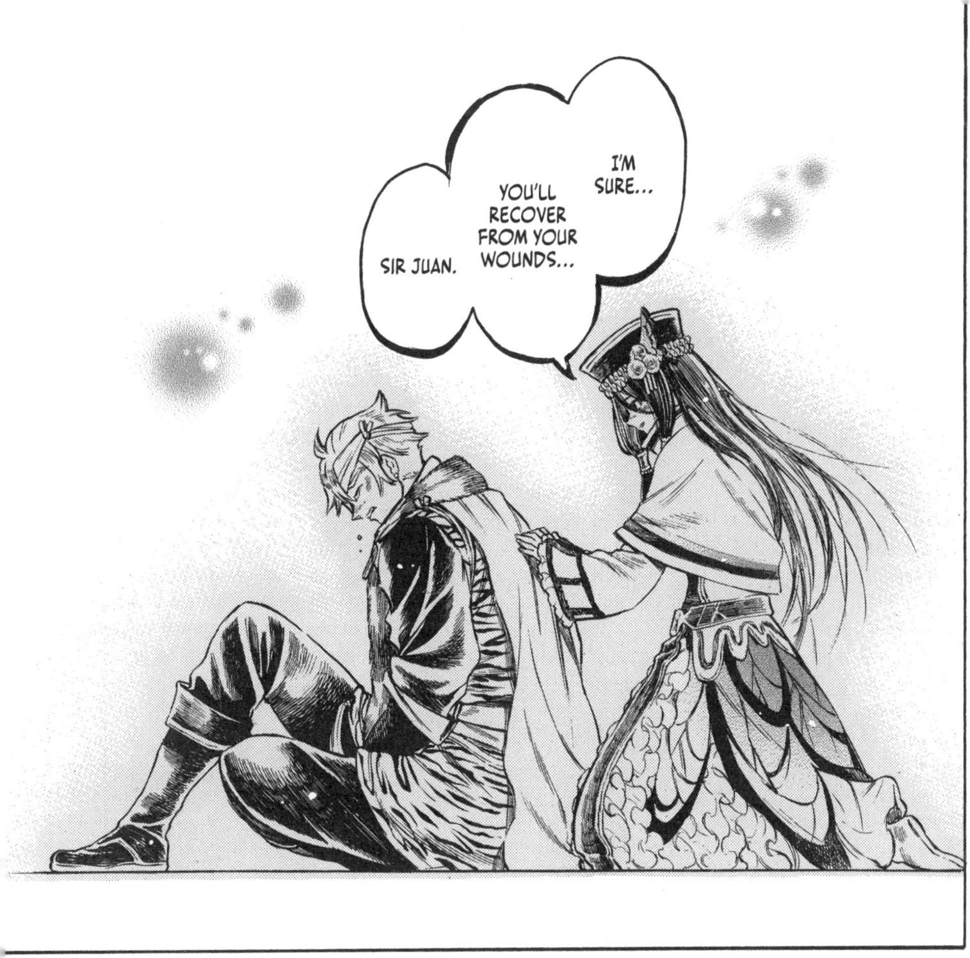
I'M SURE... YOU'LL RECOVER FROM YOUR WOUNDS... SIR JUAN.
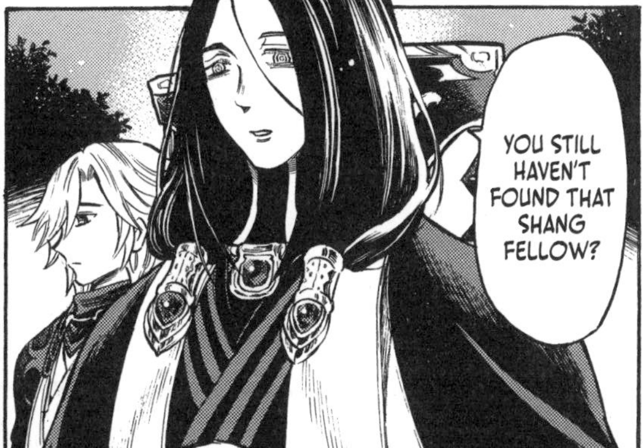
YOU STILL HAVEN'T FOUND THAT SHANG FELLOW?
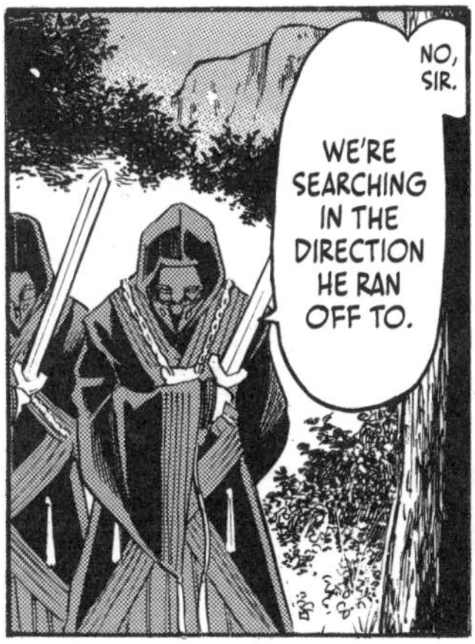
NO, SIR.
WE'RE SEARCHING IN THE DIRECTION HE RAN OFF TO.

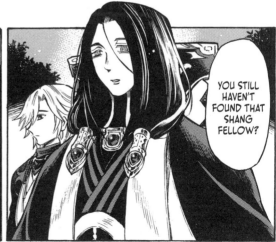

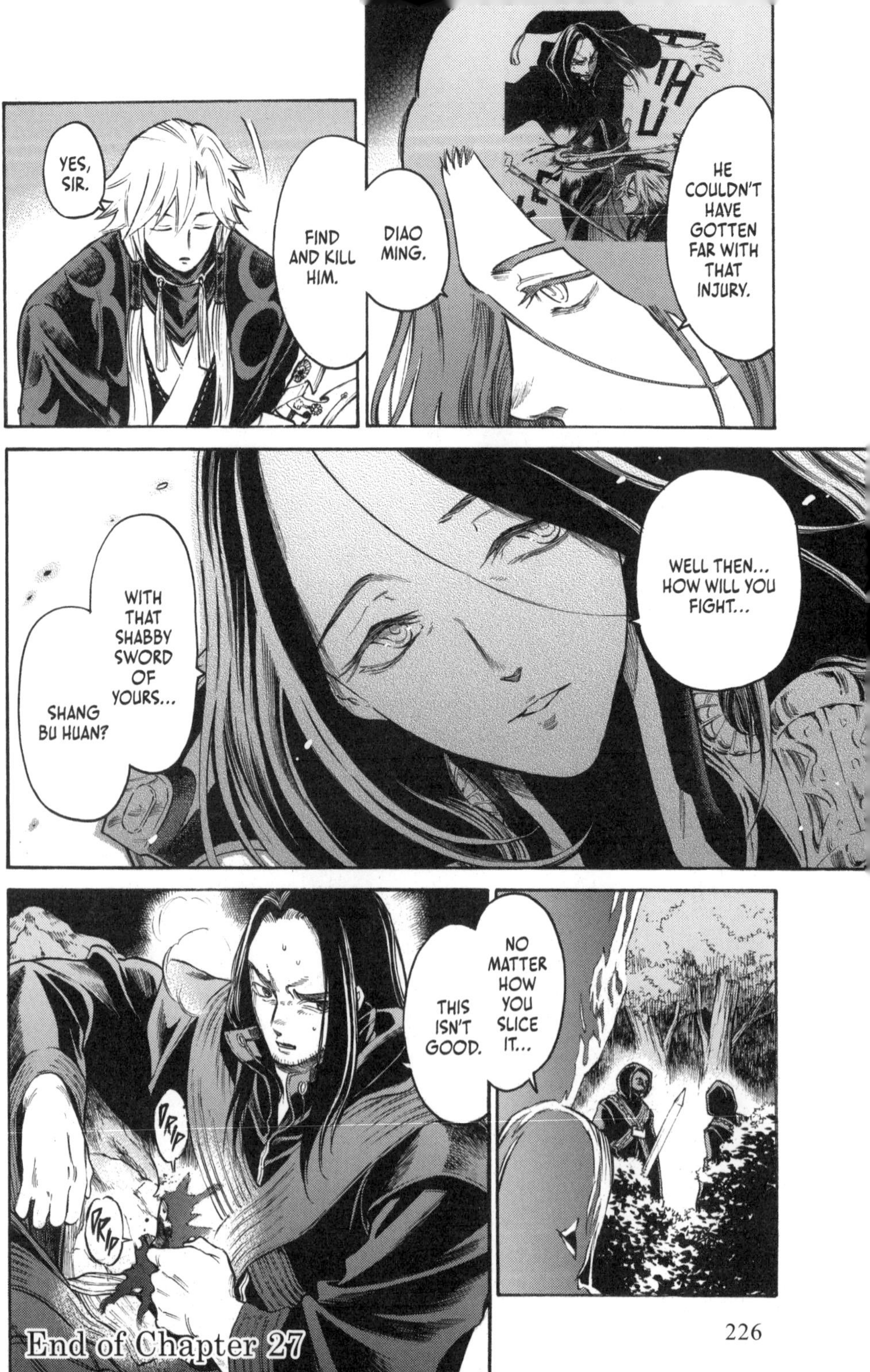
HE COULDN'T HAVE GOTTEN FAR WITH THAT INJURY.
DIAO MING.
FIND AND KILL HIM.
YES, SIR.
WELL THEN... HOW WILL YOU FIGHT...
WITH THAT SHABBY SWORD OF YOURS...
SHANG BU HUAN?
NO MATTER HOW YOU SLICE IT...
THIS ISN'T GOOD.
DRIP
DRIP
End of Chapter 27

◇◇ Chapter 28 ◇◇

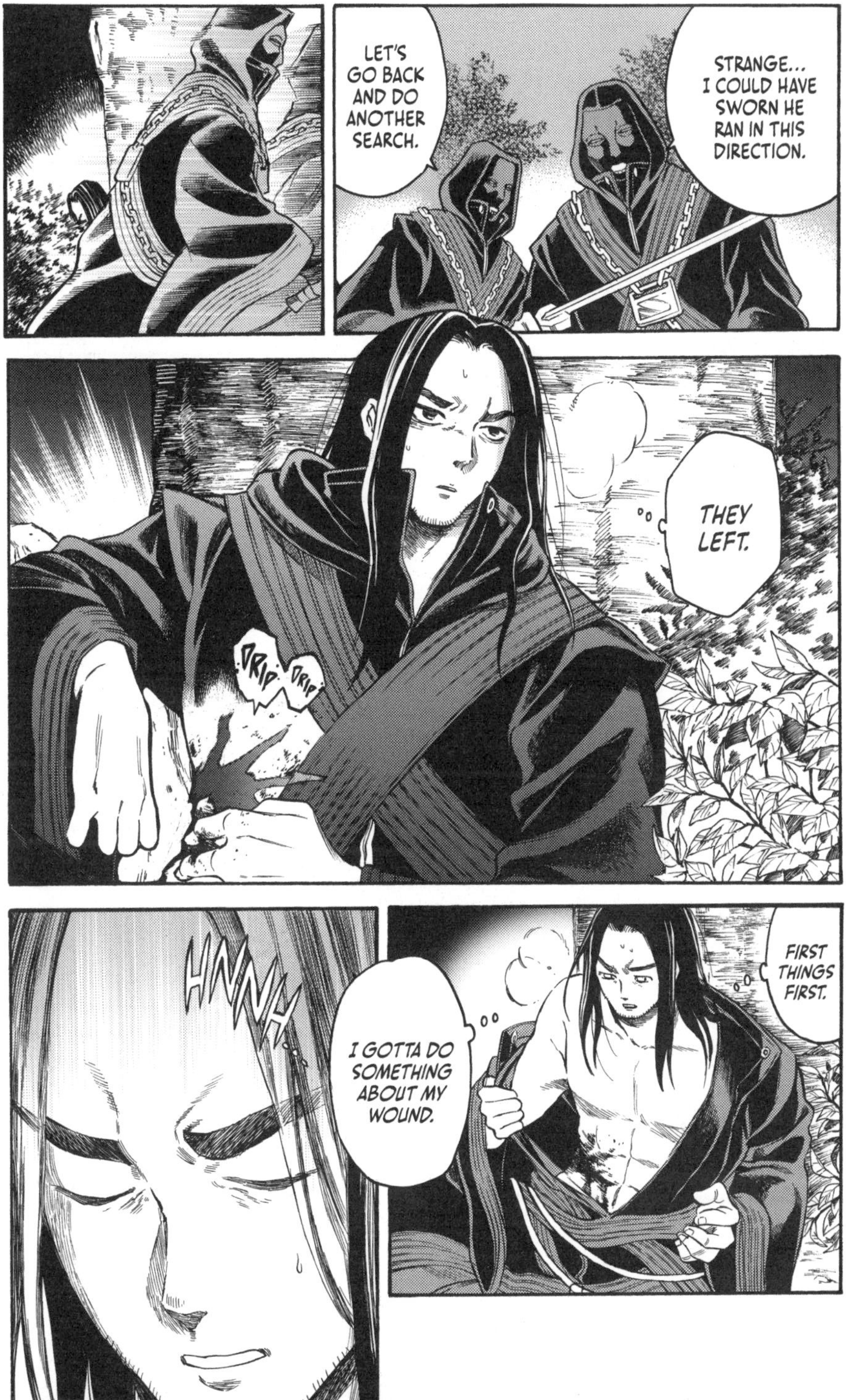
STRANGE... I COULD HAVE SWORN HE RAN IN THIS DIRECTION.
LET'S GO BACK AND DO ANOTHER SEARCH.
THEY LEFT.
DRIP DRIP
FIRST THINGS FIRST.
I GOTTA DO SOMETHING ABOUT MY WOUND.
HNNH

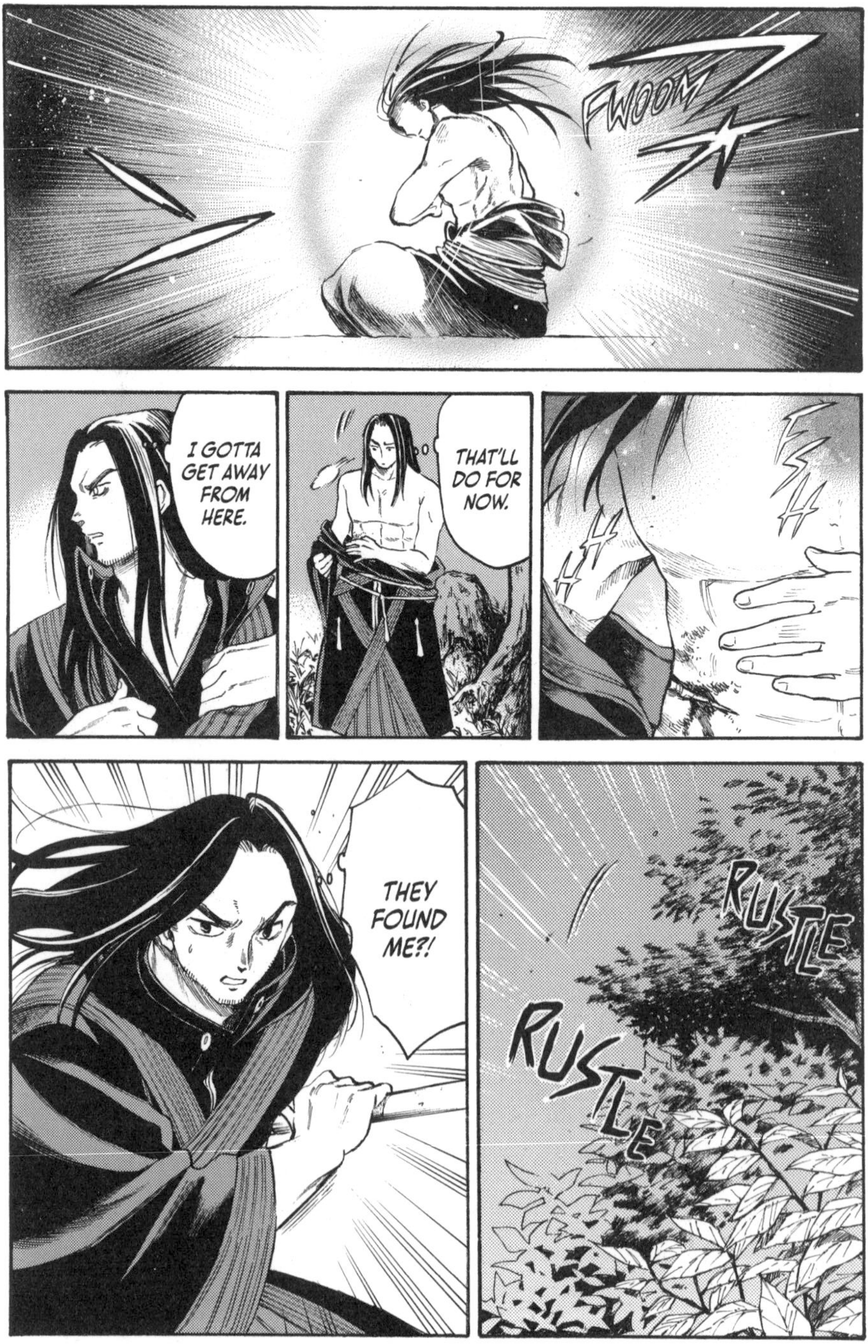
FWOOM
FSH
HH
THAT'LL DO FOR NOW.
I GOTTA GET AWAY FROM HERE.
RUSTLE
RUSTLE
THEY FOUND ME?!

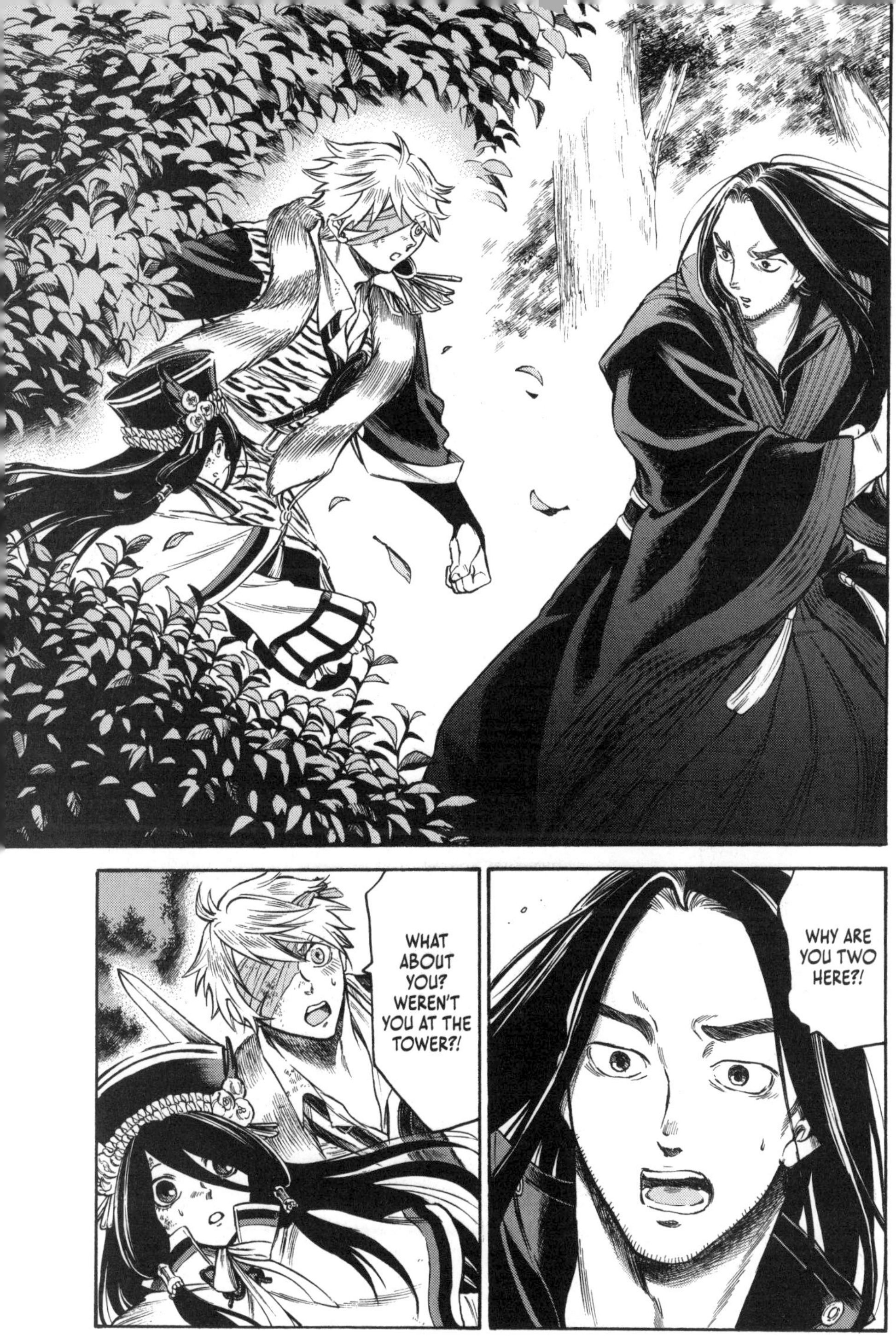
WHY ARE YOU TWO HERE?!
WHAT ABOUT YOU? WEREN'T YOU AT THE TOWER?!

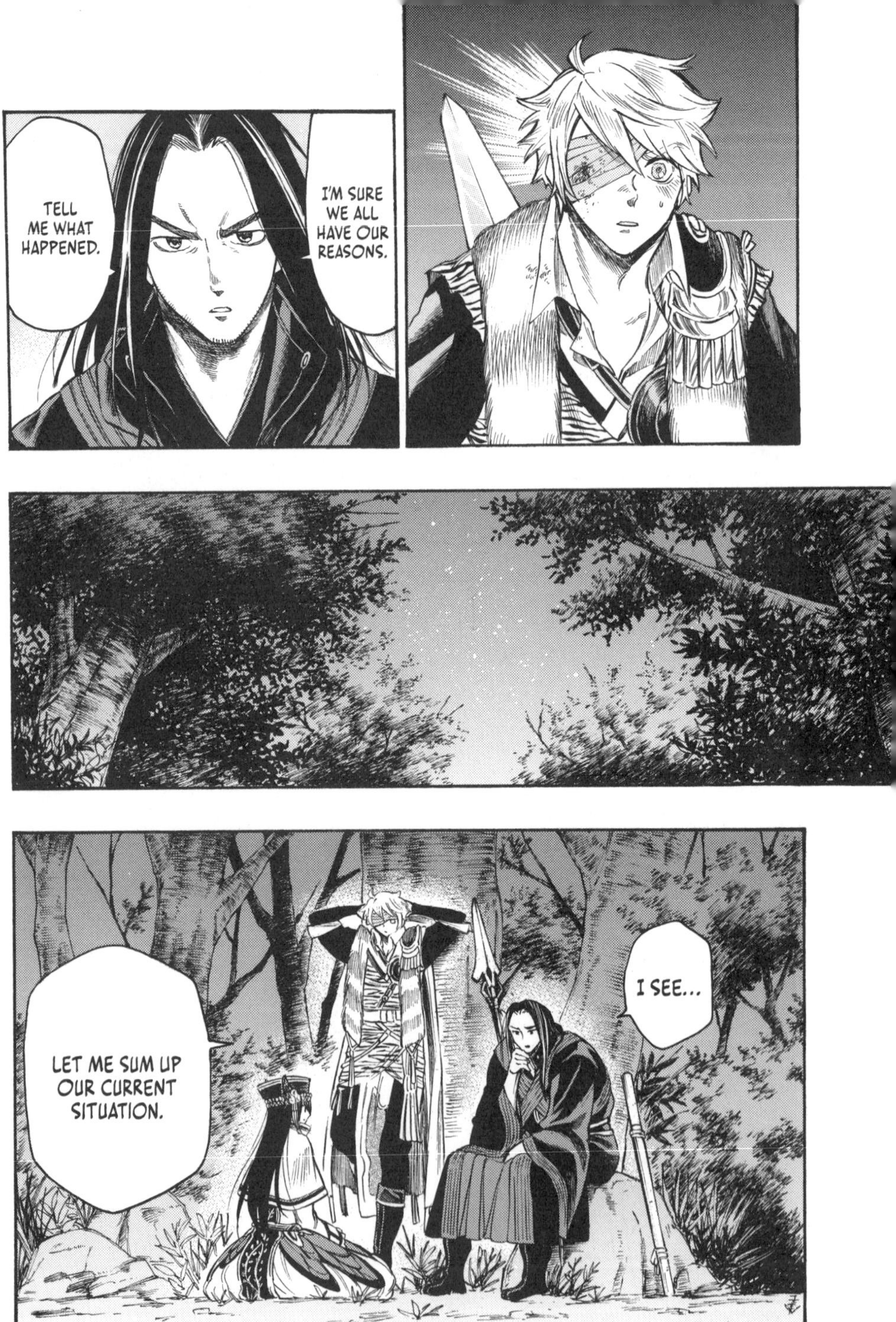
I'M SURE WE ALL HAVE OUR REASONS.
TELL ME WHAT HAPPENED.
I SEE...
LET ME SUM UP OUR CURRENT SITUATION.

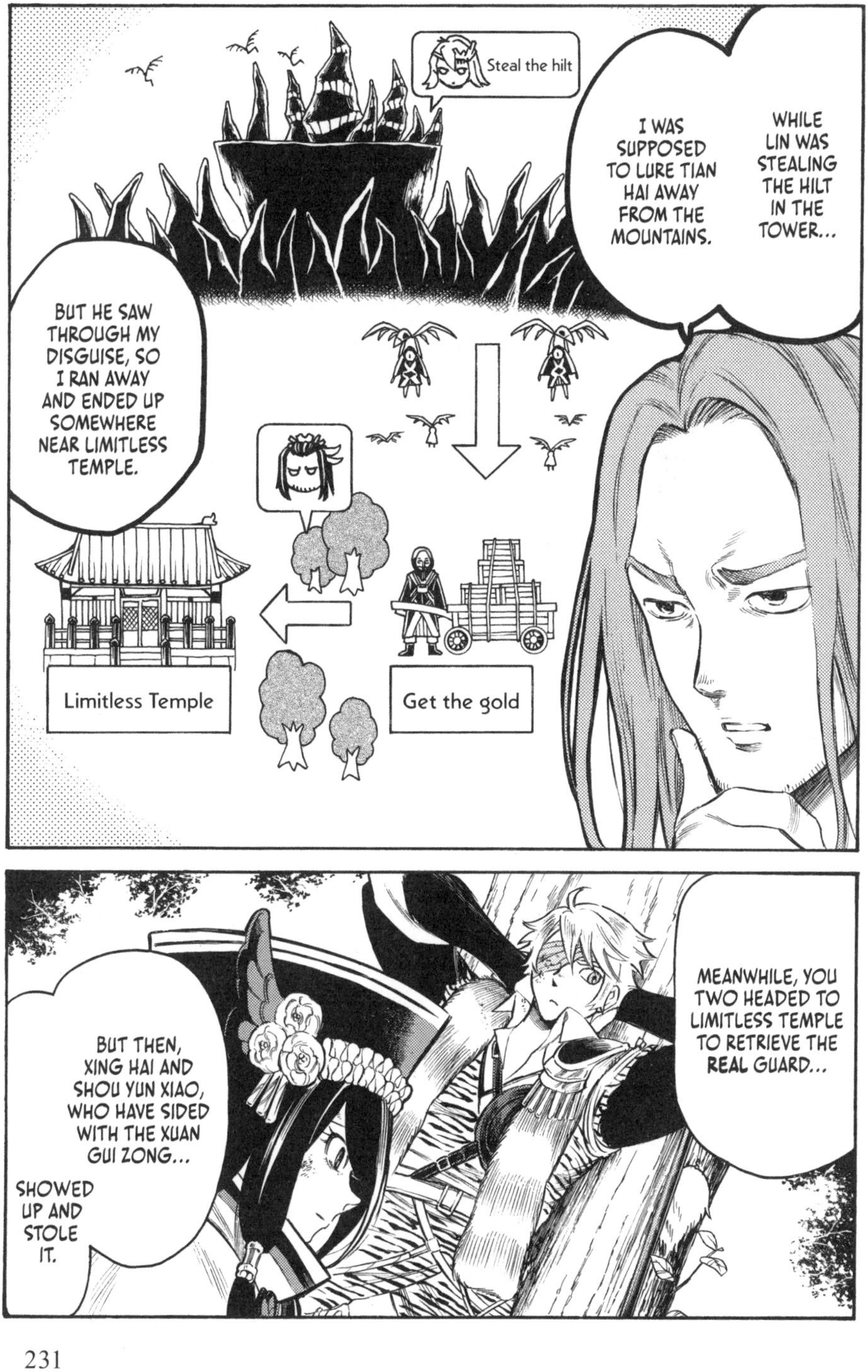
WHILE LIN WAS STEALING THE HILT IN THE TOWER...
I WAS SUPPOSED TO LURE TIAN HAI AWAY FROM THE MOUNTAINS.
Steal the hilt
BUT HE SAW THROUGH MY DISGUISE, SO I RAN AWAY AND ENDED UP SOMEWHERE NEAR LIMITLESS TEMPLE.
Get the gold
Limitless Temple
MEANWHILE, YOU TWO HEADED TO LIMITLESS TEMPLE TO RETRIEVE THE REAL GUARD...
BUT THEN, XING HAI AND SHOU YUN XIAO, WHO HAVE SIDED WITH THE XUAN GUI ZONG...
SHOWED UP AND STOLE IT.

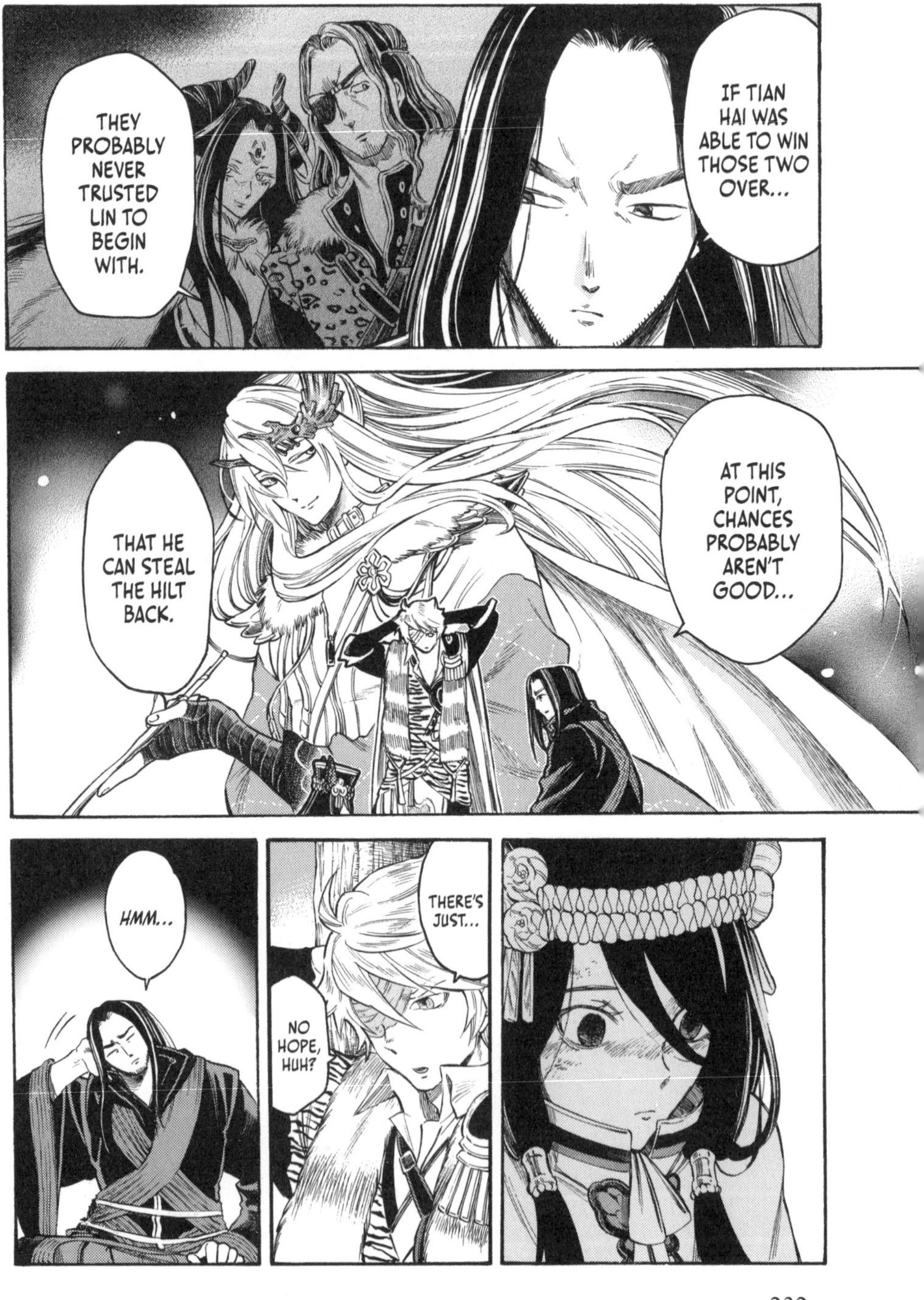
IF TIAN HAI WAS ABLE TO WIN THOSE TWO OVER...
THEY PROBABLY NEVER TRUSTED LIN TO BEGIN WITH.
AT THIS POINT, CHANCES PROBABLY AREN'T GOOD...
THAT HE CAN STEAL THE HILT BACK.
THERE'S JUST...
NO HOPE, HUH?
HMM...

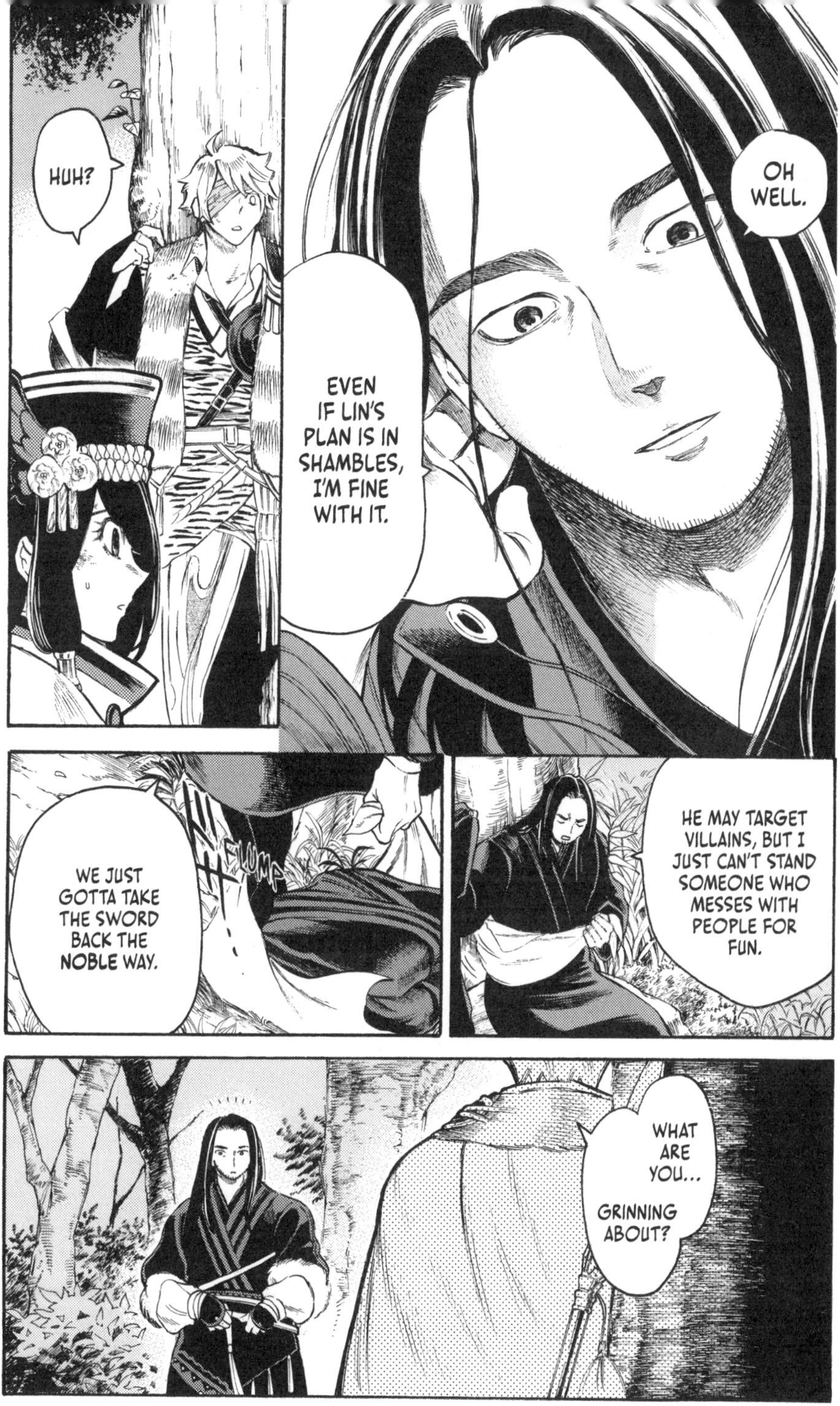
OH WELL.
EVEN IF LIN'S PLAN IS IN SHAMBLES, I'M FINE WITH IT.
HUH?
HE MAY TARGET VILLAINS, BUT I JUST CAN'T STAND SOMEONE WHO MESSES WITH PEOPLE FOR FUN.
FLUMP
WE JUST GOTTA TAKE THE SWORD BACK THE NOBLE WAY.
WHAT ARE YOU...
GRINNING ABOUT?

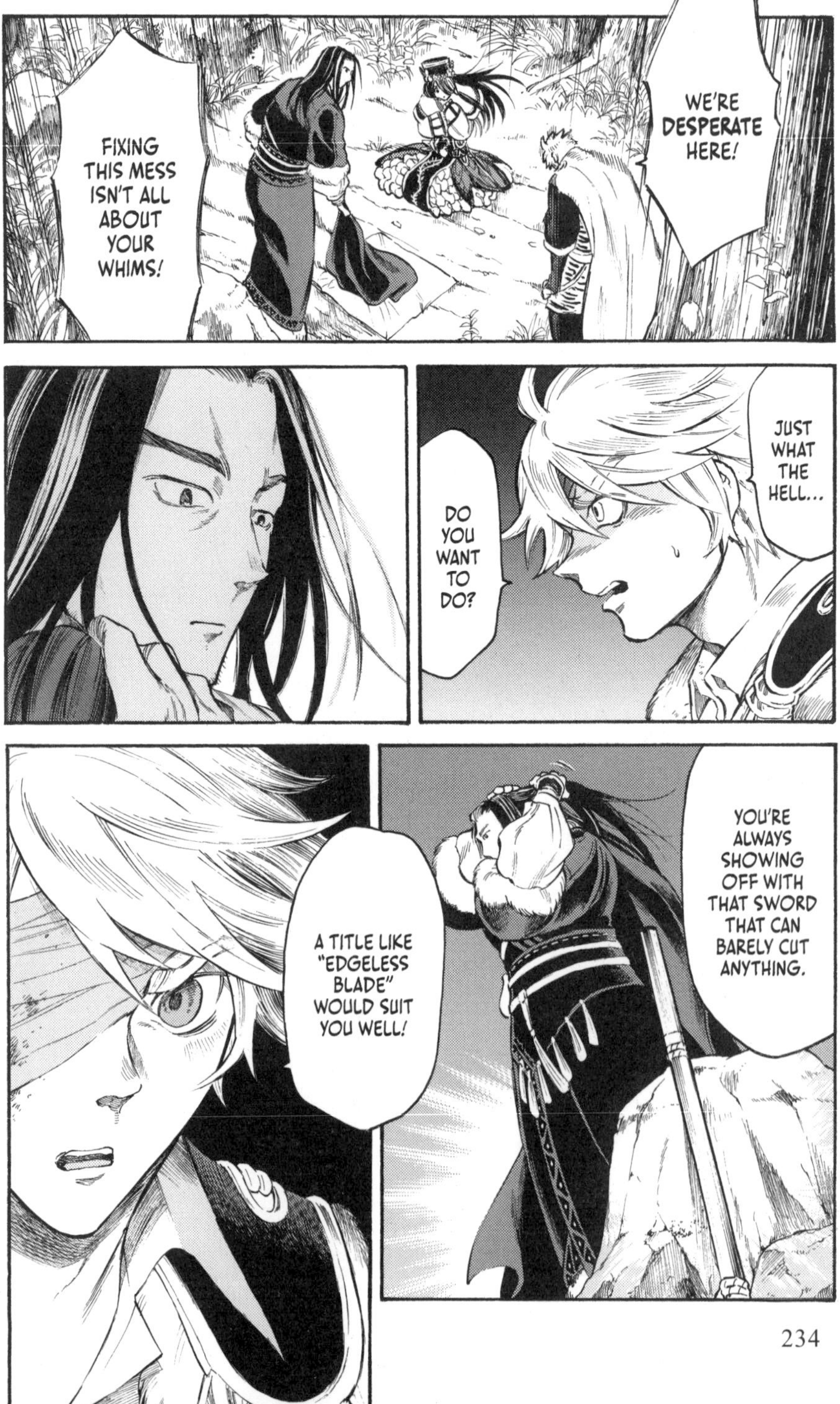
WE'RE DESPERATE HERE!
FIXING THIS MESS ISN'T ALL ABOUT YOUR WHIMS!
JUST WHAT THE HELL...
DO YOU WANT TO DO?
YOU'RE ALWAYS SHOWING OFF WITH THAT SWORD THAT CAN BARELY CUT ANYTHING.
A TITLE LIKE "EDGELESS BLADE" WOULD SUIT YOU WELL!

STOP IT, SIR JUAN...

"EDGELESS BLADE"...

A BLADE THAT DOESN'T CUT, HUH?

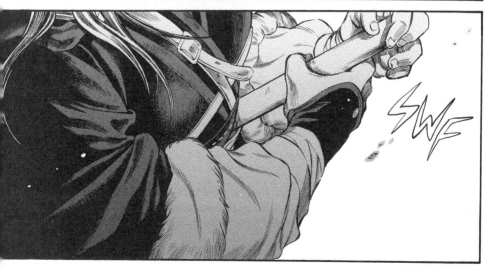

SWF

235

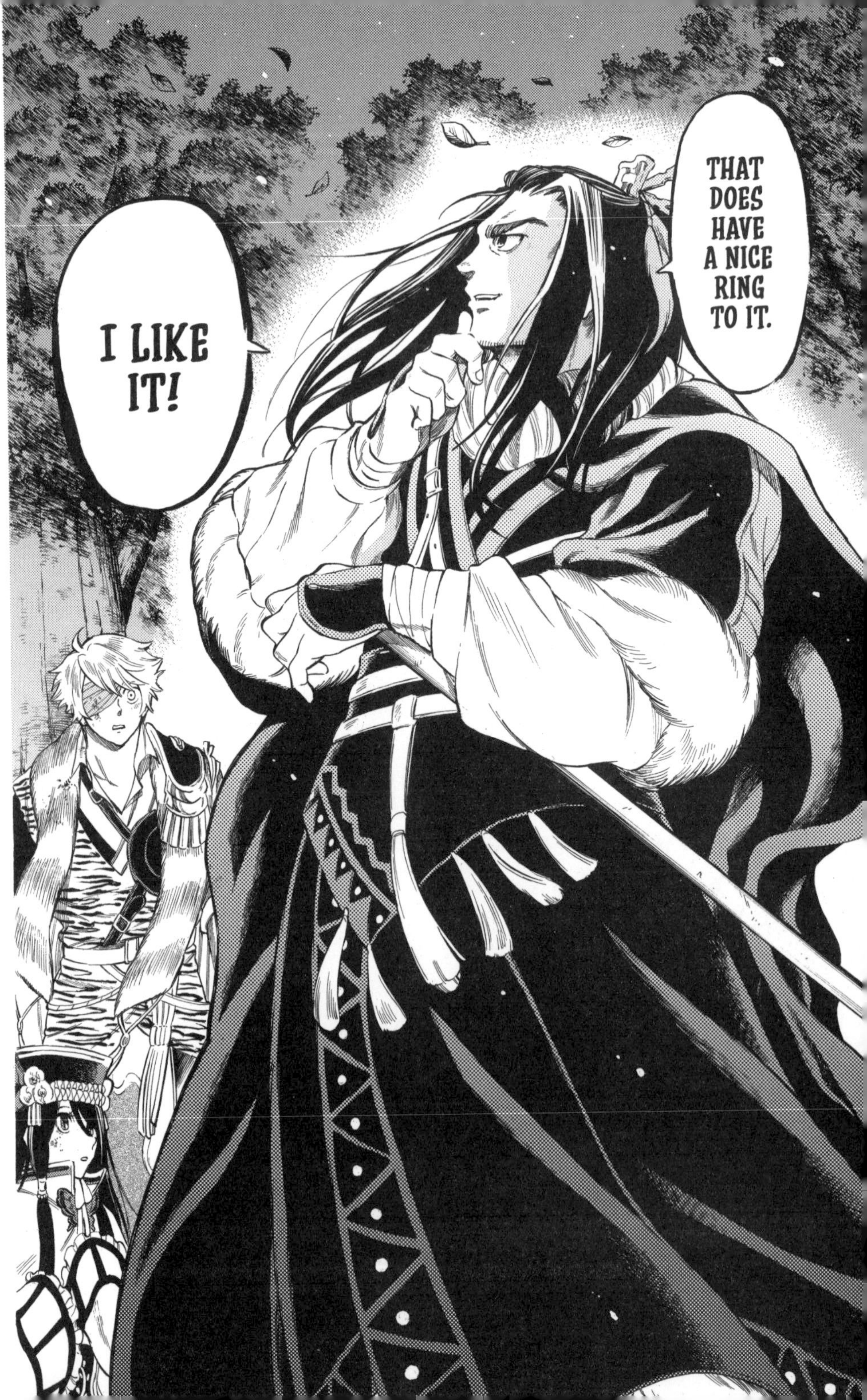
THAT DOES HAVE A NICE RING TO IT.
I LIKE IT!

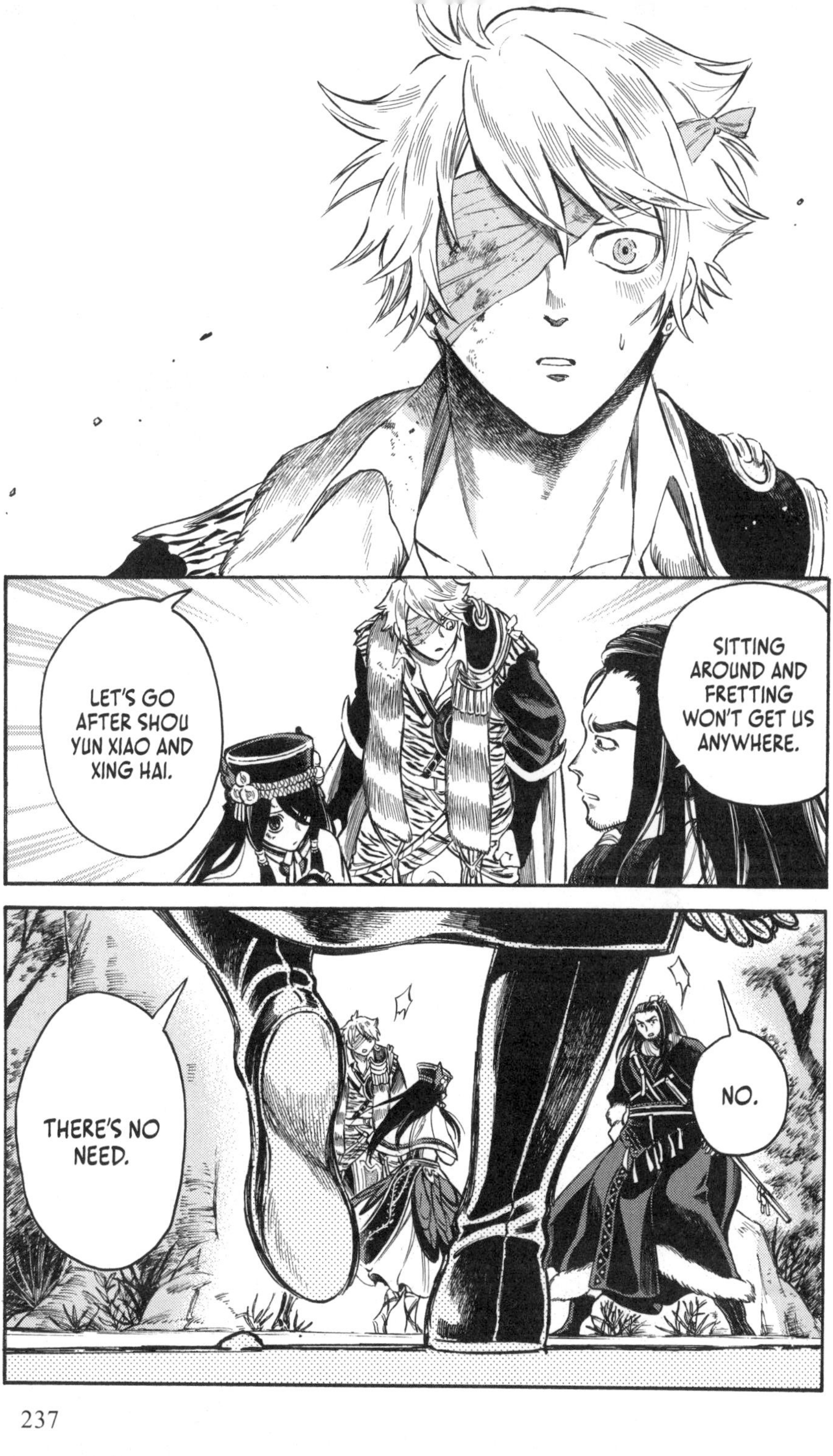
SITTING AROUND AND FRETTING WON'T GET US ANYWHERE.
LET'S GO AFTER SHOU YUN XIAO AND XING HAI.
NO.
THERE'S NO NEED.

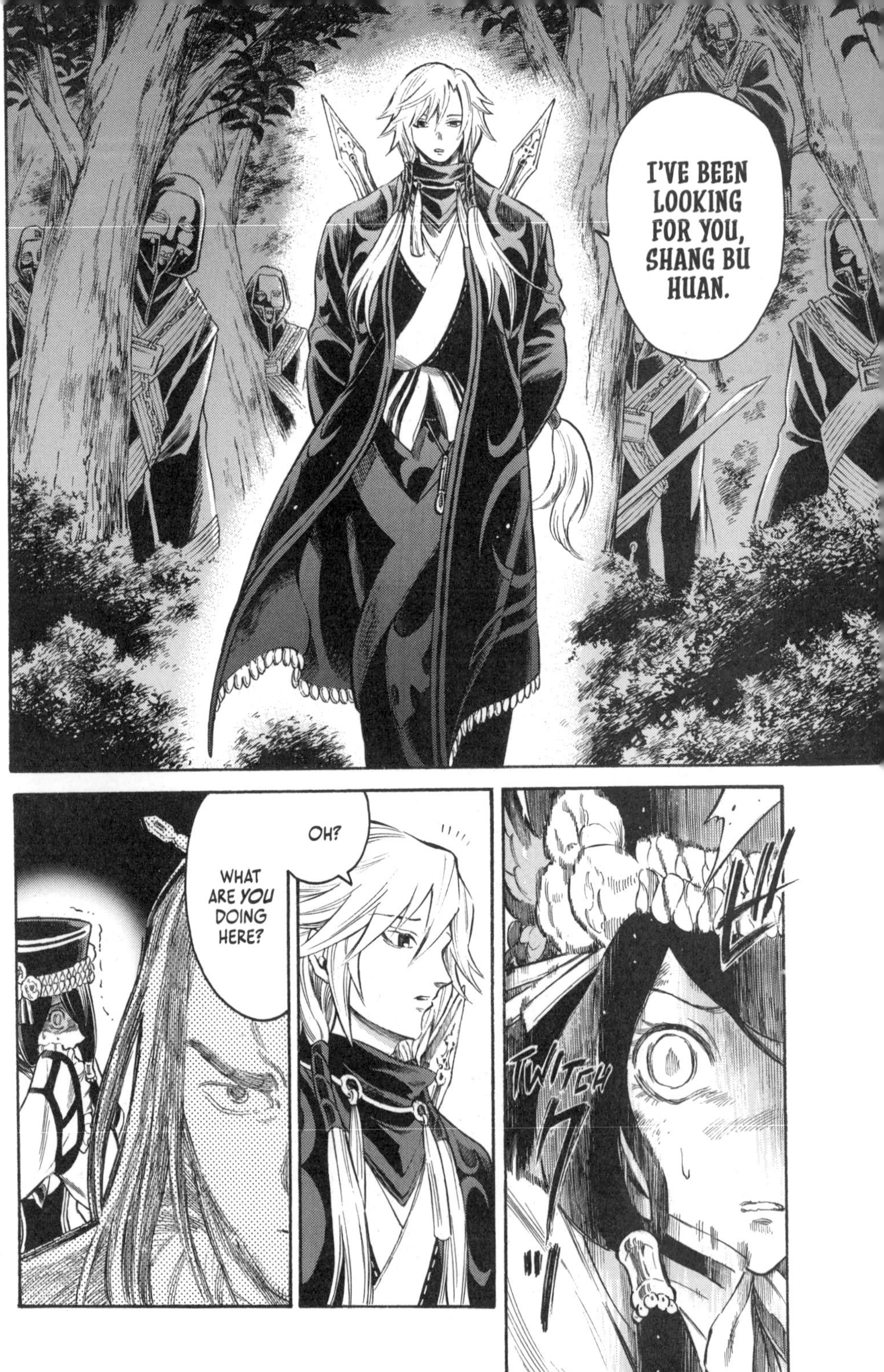
I'VE BEEN LOOKING FOR YOU, SHANG BU HUAN.
TWITCH
OH?
WHAT ARE YOU DOING HERE?

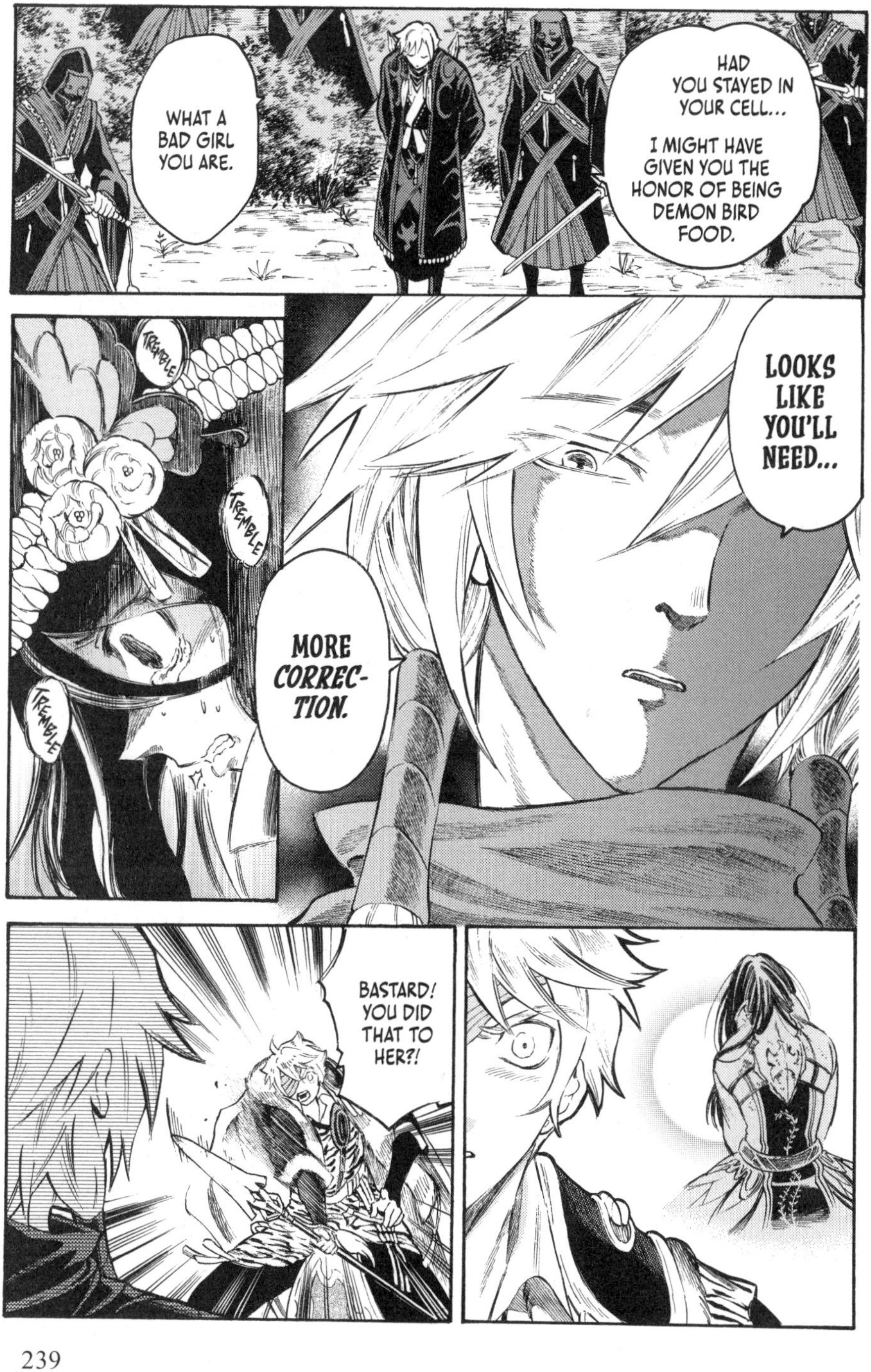
HAD YOU STAYED IN YOUR CELL...
I MIGHT HAVE GIVEN YOU THE HONOR OF BEING DEMON BIRD FOOD.
WHAT A BAD GIRL YOU ARE.
LOOKS LIKE YOU'LL NEED...
MORE CORREC-TION.
TREMBLE
TREMBLE
TREMBLE
BASTARD! YOU DID THAT TO HER?!

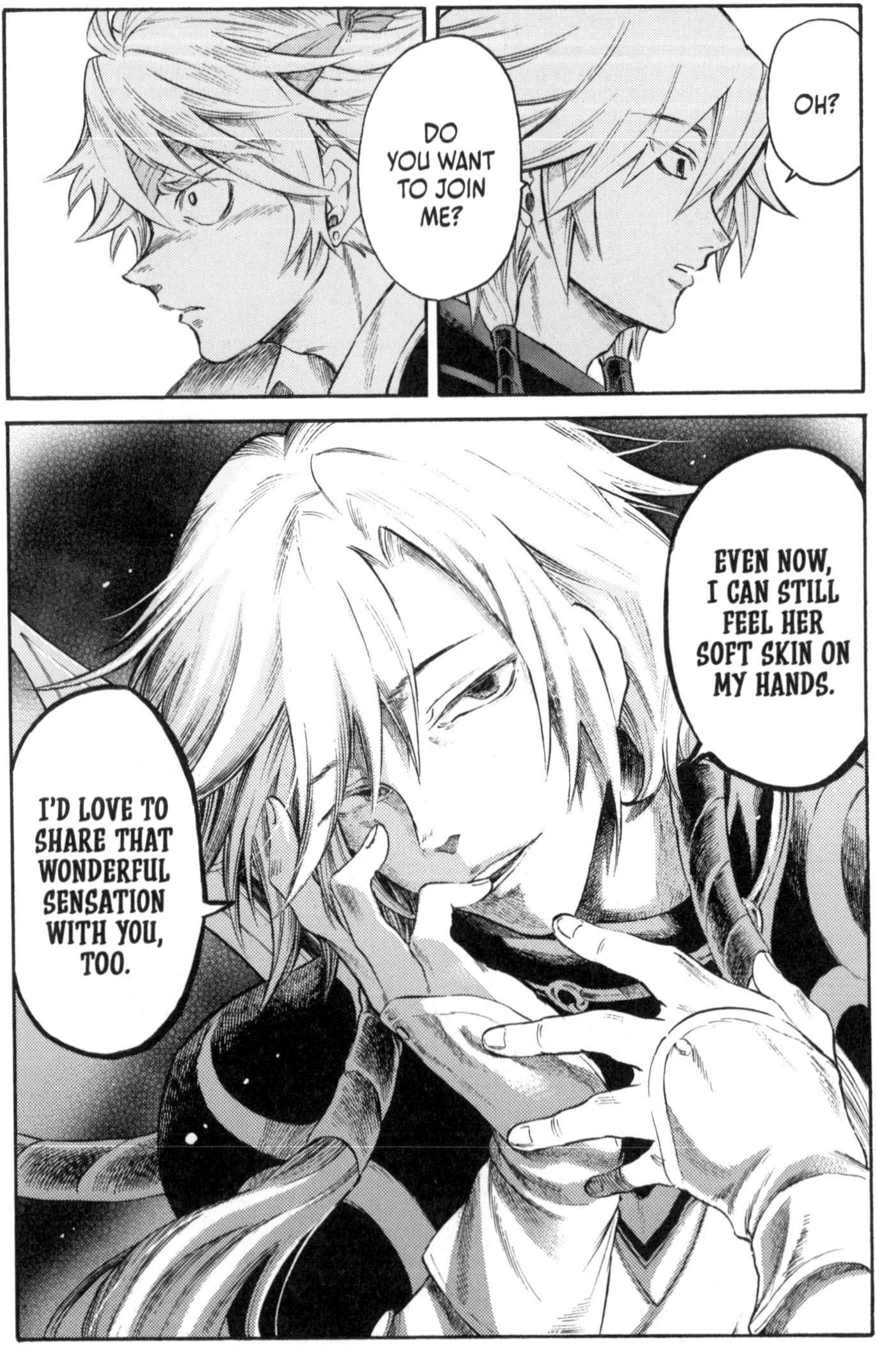
OH?
DO YOU WANT TO JOIN ME?
EVEN NOW, I CAN STILL FEEL HER SOFT SKIN ON MY HANDS.
I'D LOVE TO SHARE THAT WONDERFUL SENSATION WITH YOU, TOO.

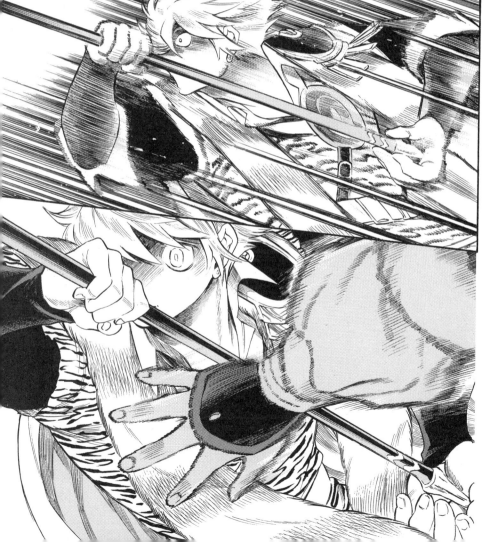

YOU PROTECT DAN FEI.

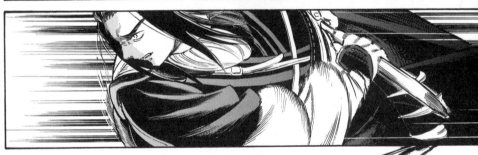

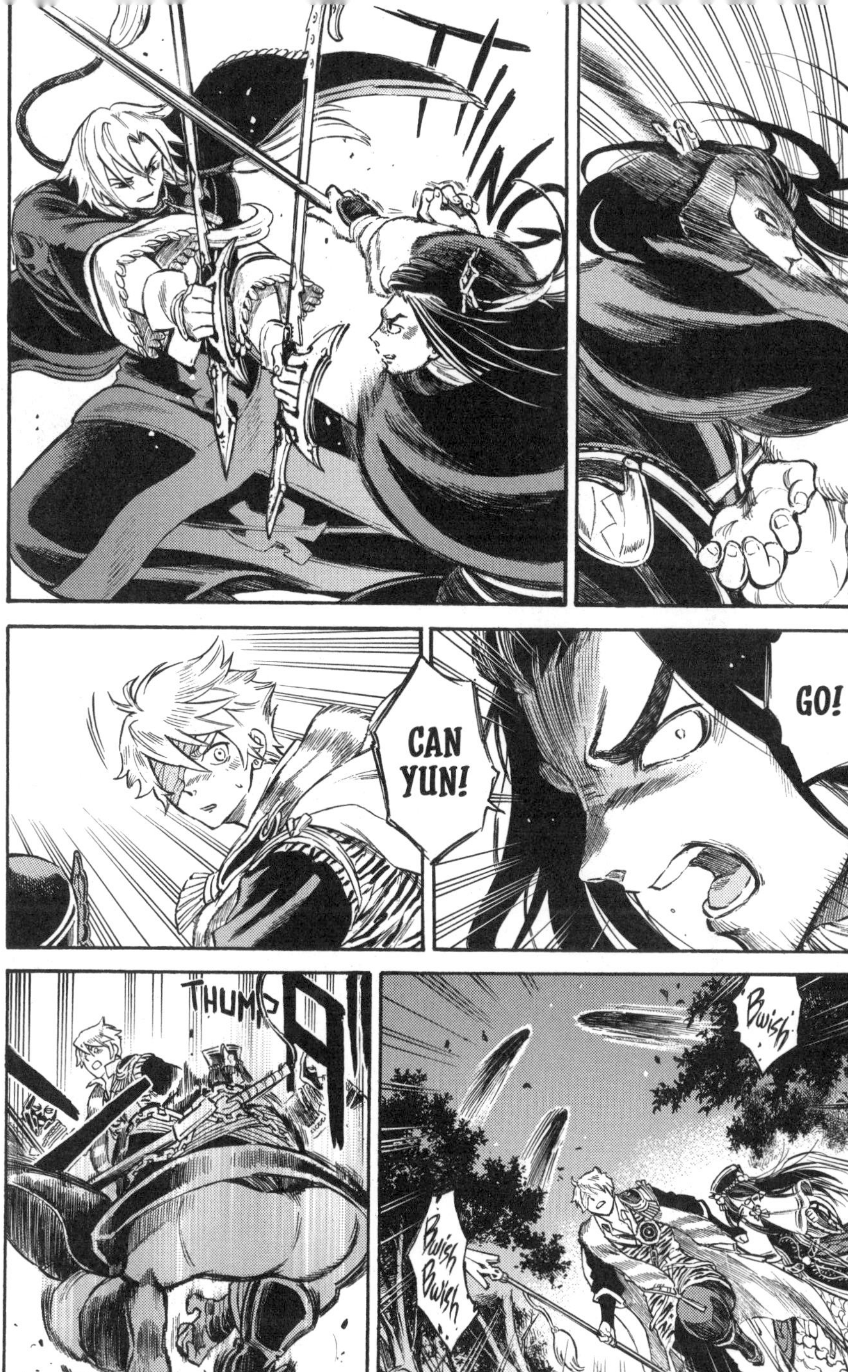
TIIING
GO!
CAN YUN!
'Bwish'
Bwish Bwish
THUMP

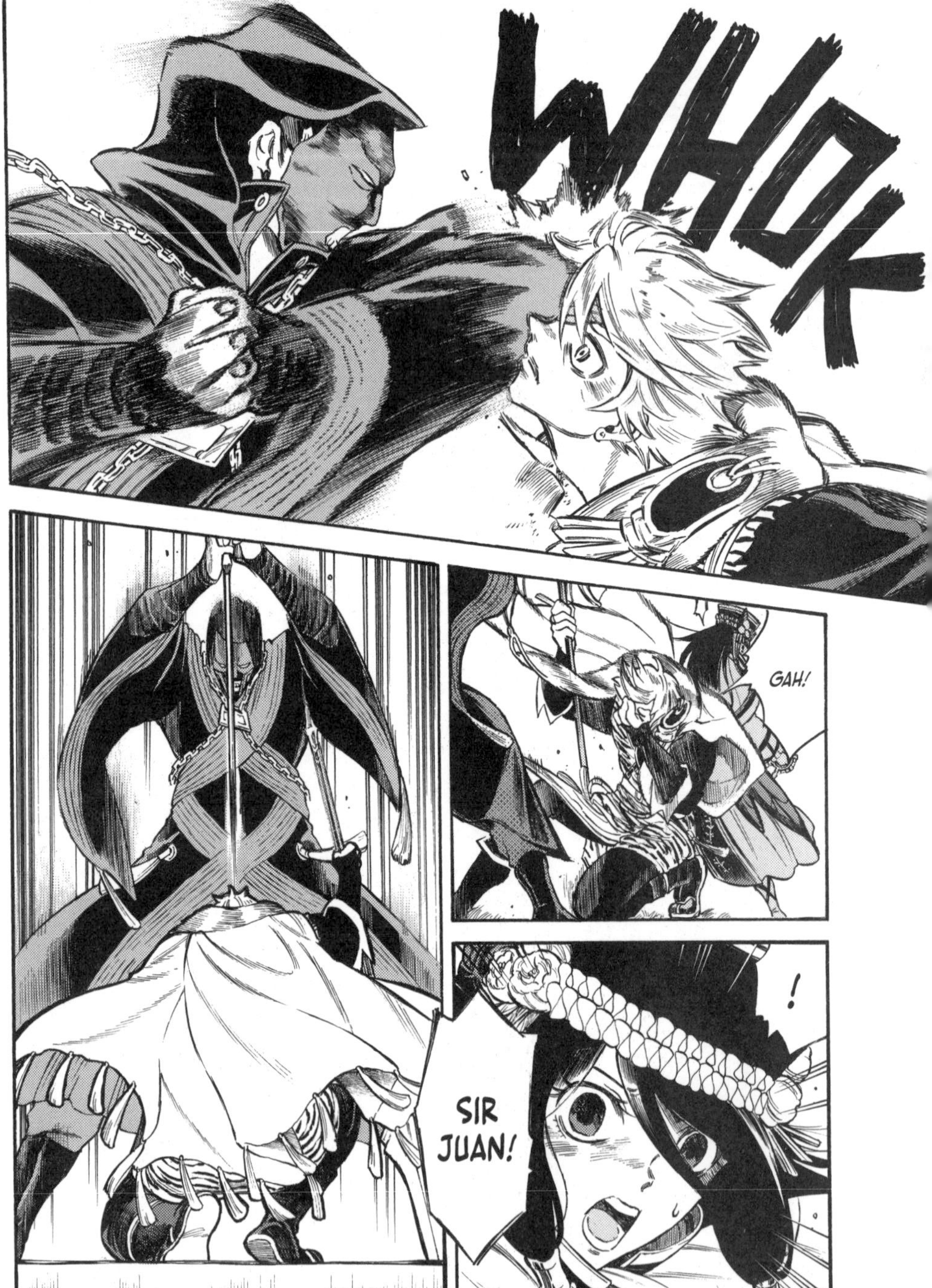
WHOK
GAH!
!
SIR JUAN!

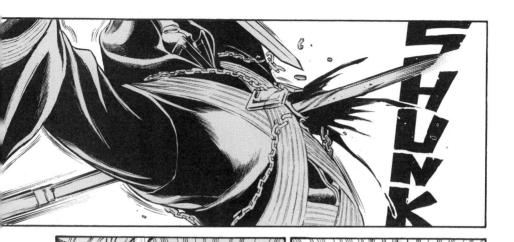

SHUNK

?!

PROTECT HER WITH ALL YOU'VE GOT!

YOU HEAR ME?!

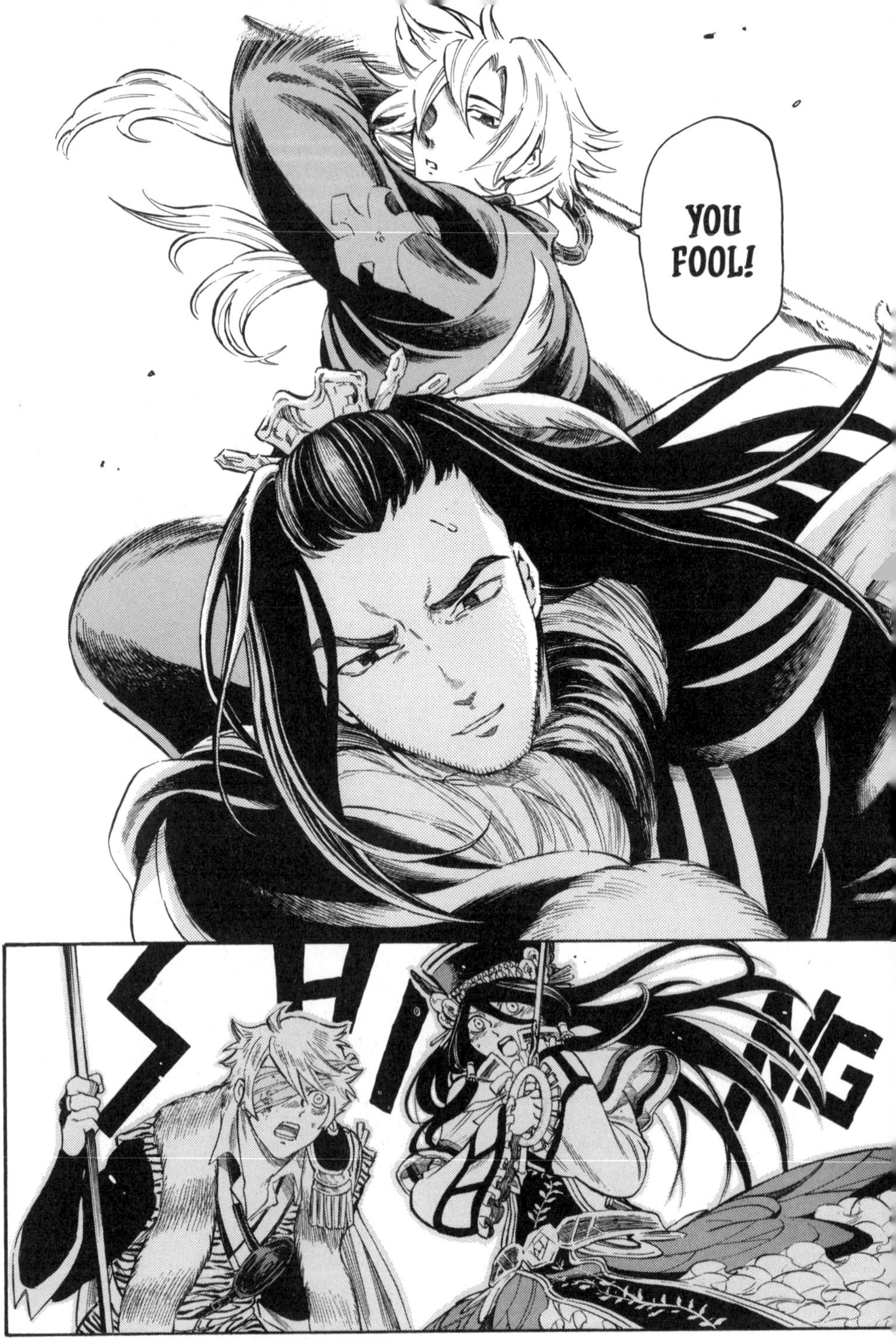
YOU FOOL!

End of Chapter 28

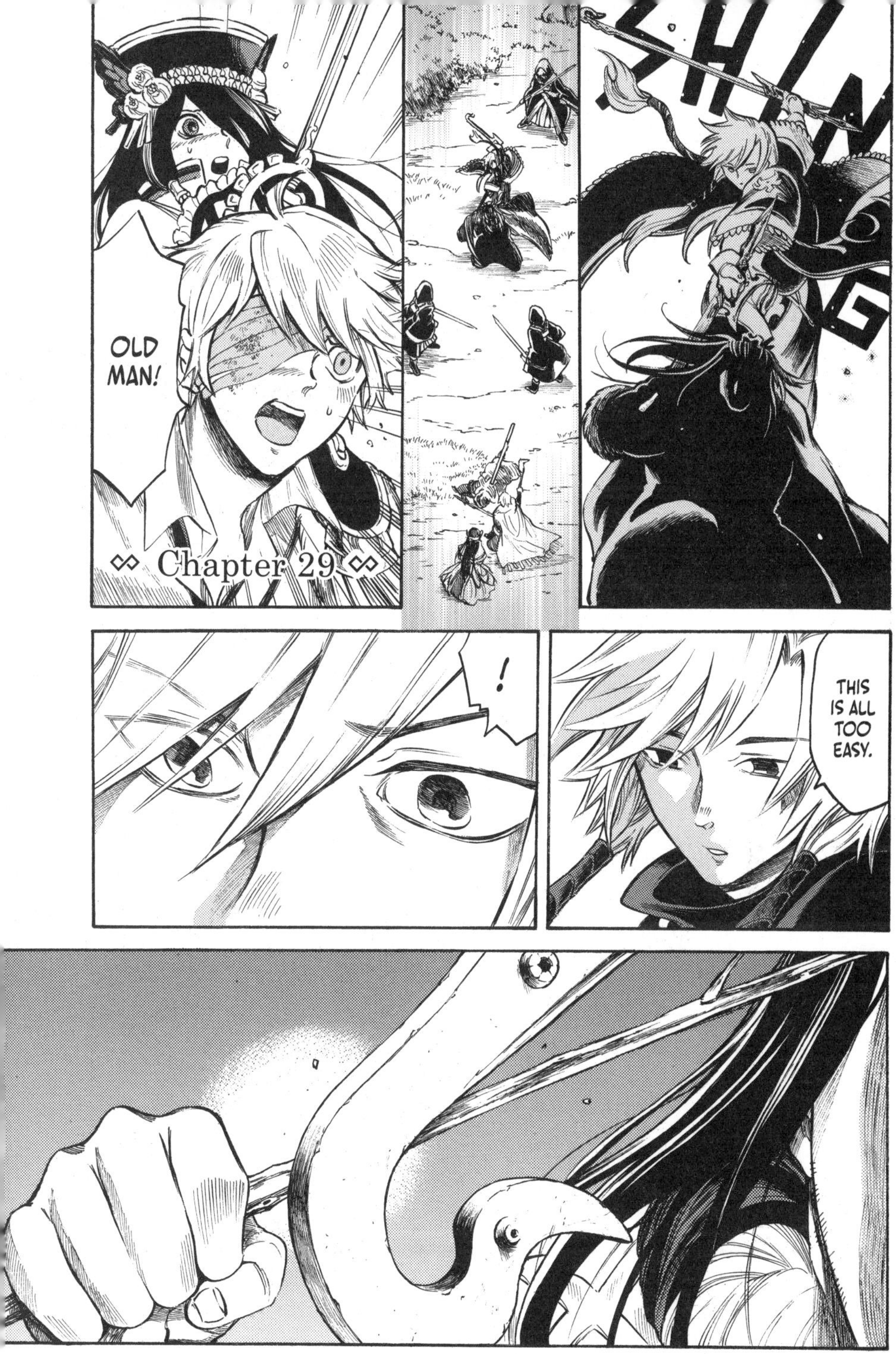
SHING
OLD MAN!
Chapter 29
THIS IS ALL TOO EASY.
!

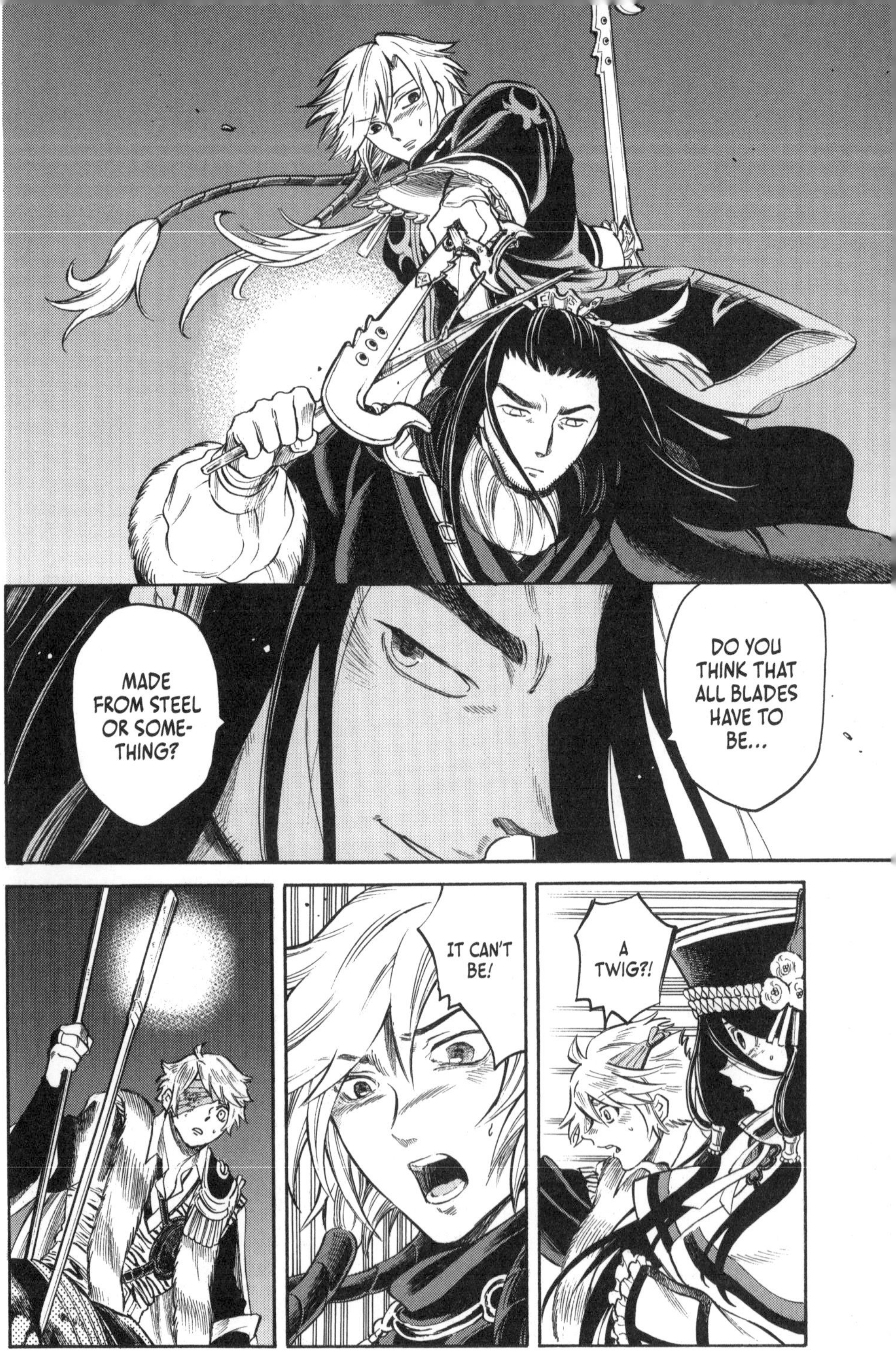
DO YOU THINK THAT ALL BLADES HAVE TO BE...
MADE FROM STEEL OR SOME-THING?
A TWIG?!
IT CAN'T BE!

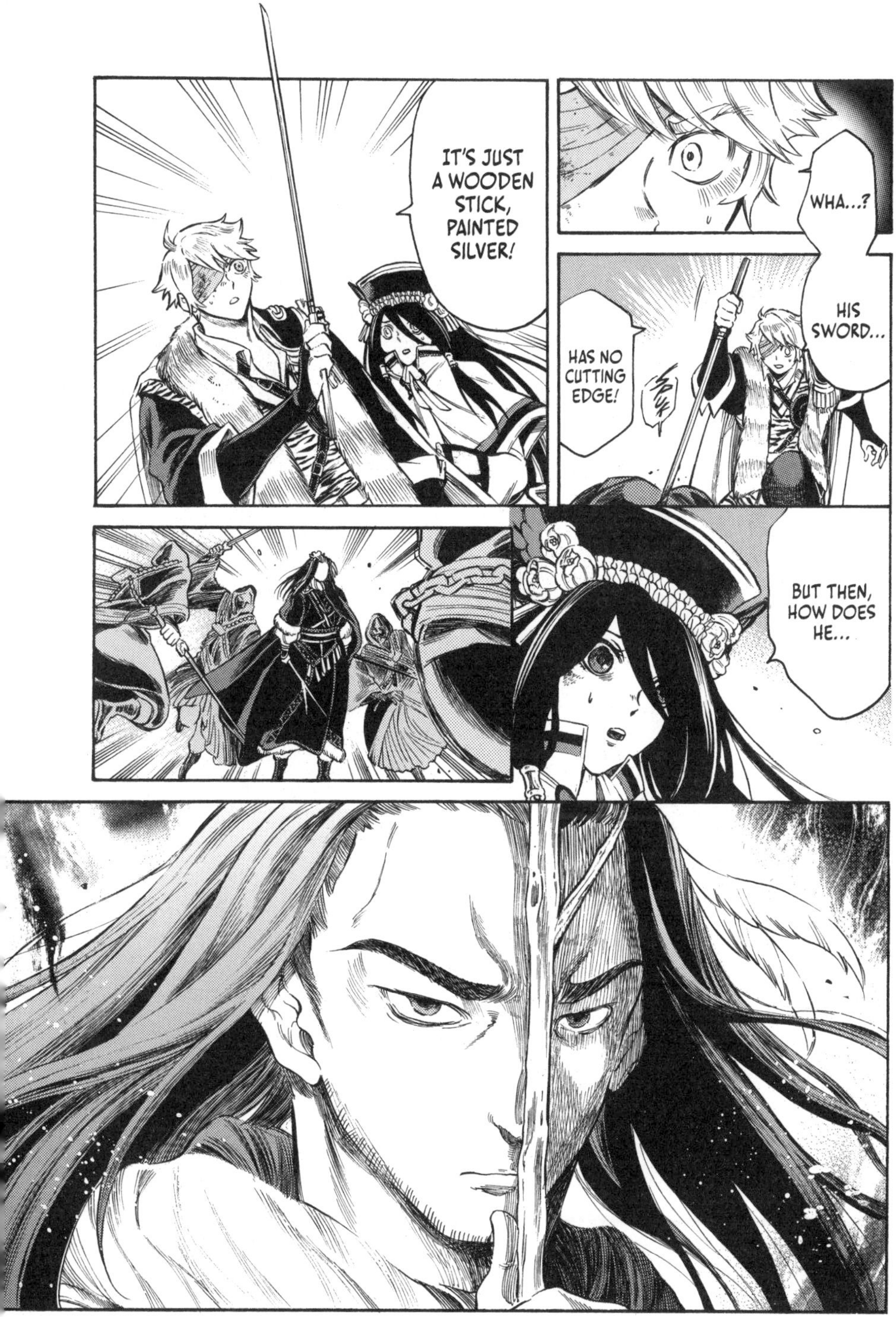
WHA...?
HIS SWORD...
HAS NO CUTTING EDGE!
IT'S JUST A WOODEN STICK, PAINTED SILVER!
BUT THEN, HOW DOES HE...

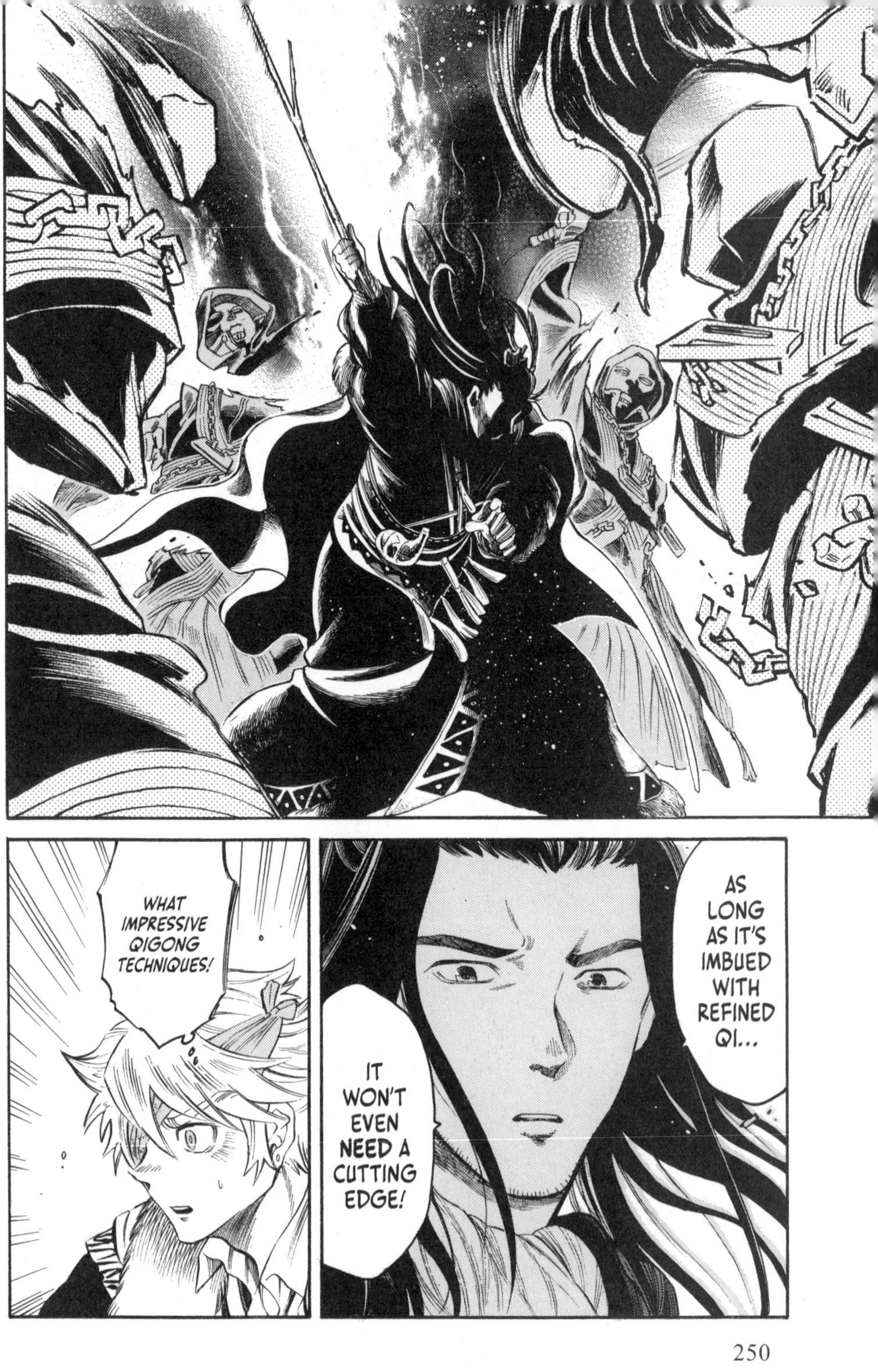
AS LONG AS IT'S IMBUED WITH REFINED QI...
IT WON'T EVEN NEED A CUTTING EDGE!
WHAT IMPRESSIVE QIGONG TECHNIQUES!

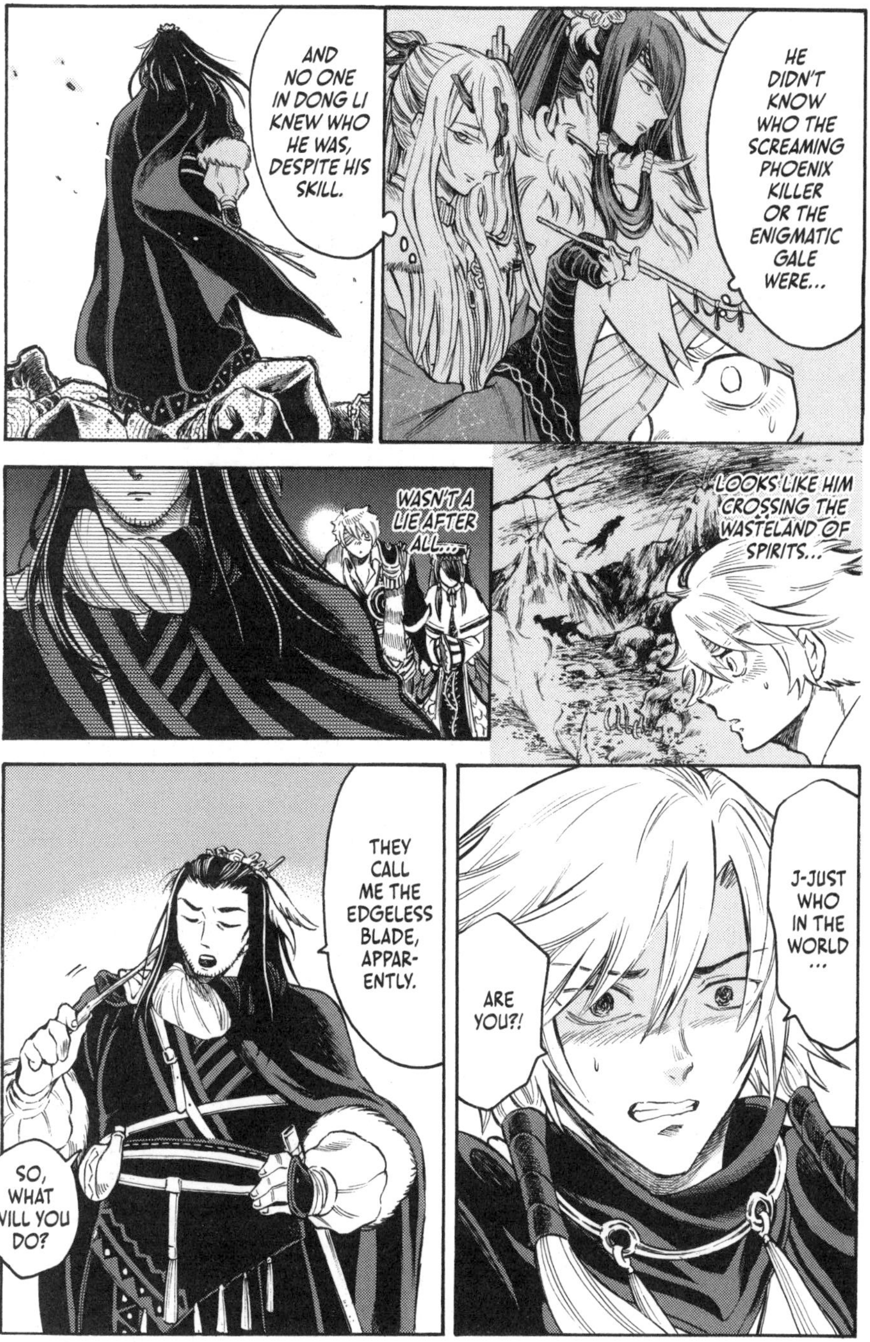
HE DIDN'T KNOW WHO THE SCREAMING PHOENIX KILLER OR THE ENIGMATIC GALE WERE...
AND NO ONE IN DONG LI KNEW WHO HE WAS, DESPITE HIS SKILL.
LOOKS LIKE HIM CROSSING THE WASTELAND OF SPIRITS...
WASN'T A LIE AFTER ALL...
J-JUST WHO IN THE WORLD ...
ARE YOU?!
THEY CALL ME THE EDGELESS BLADE, APPARENTLY.
SO, WHAT WILL YOU DO?

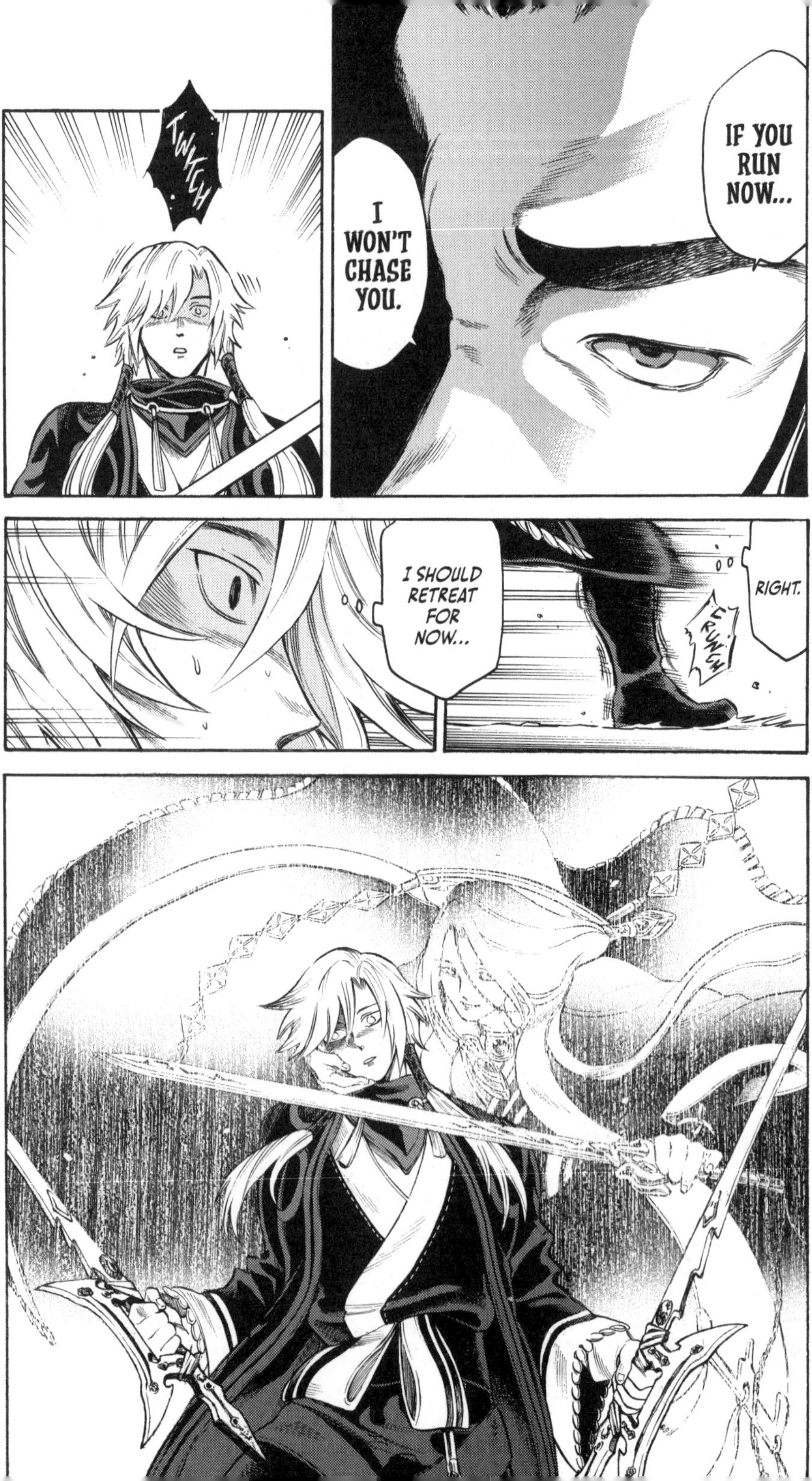
IF YOU RUN NOW...
I WON'T CHASE YOU.
TWITCH
RIGHT.
CRUNCH
I SHOULD RETREAT FOR NOW...

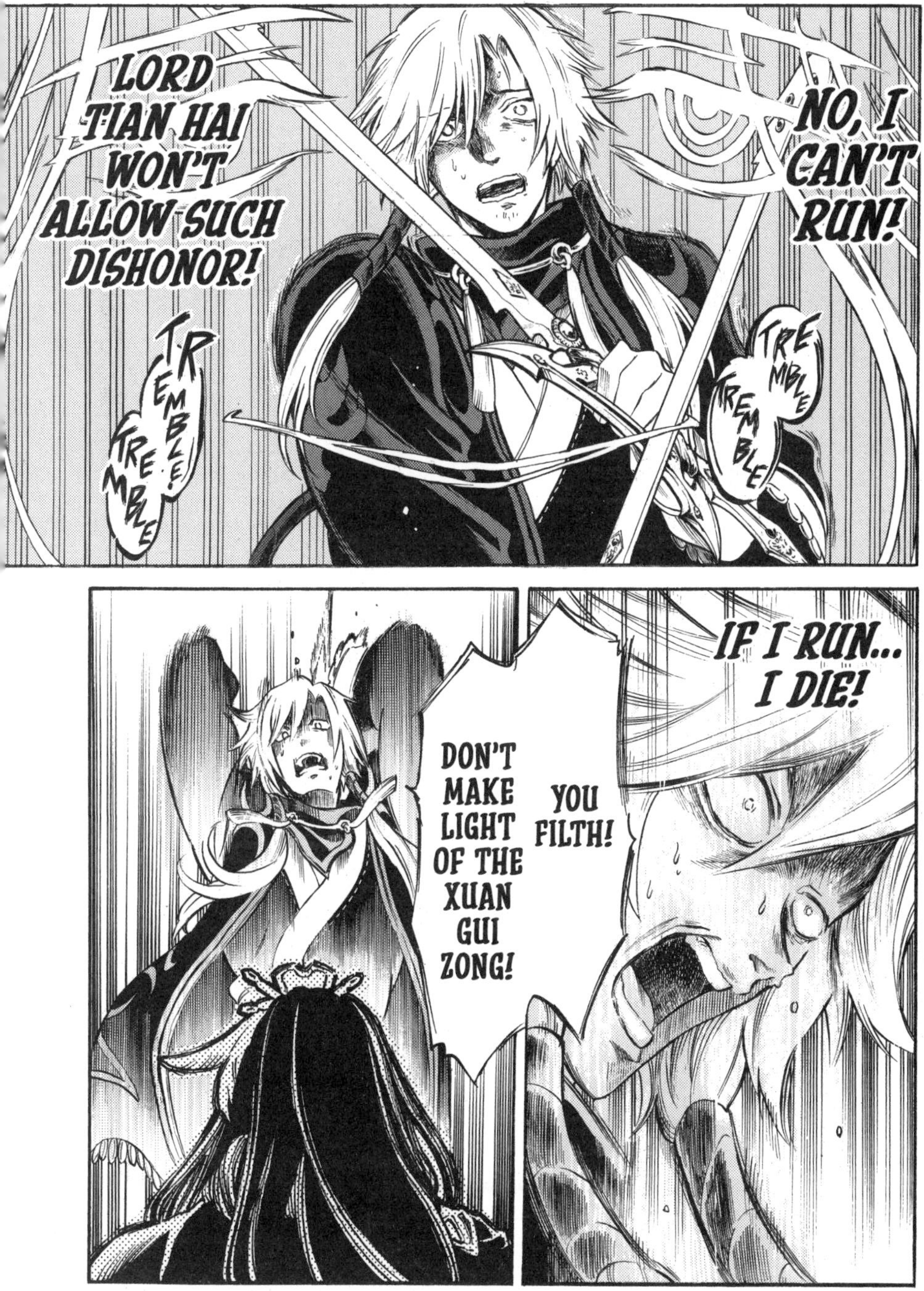
NO, I CAN'T RUN!
TREMBLE TREMBLE
LORD TIAN HAI WON'T ALLOW SUCH DISHONOR!
TREMBLE TREMBLE
IF I RUN... I DIE!
YOU FILTH!
DON'T MAKE LIGHT OF THE XUAN GUI ZONG!

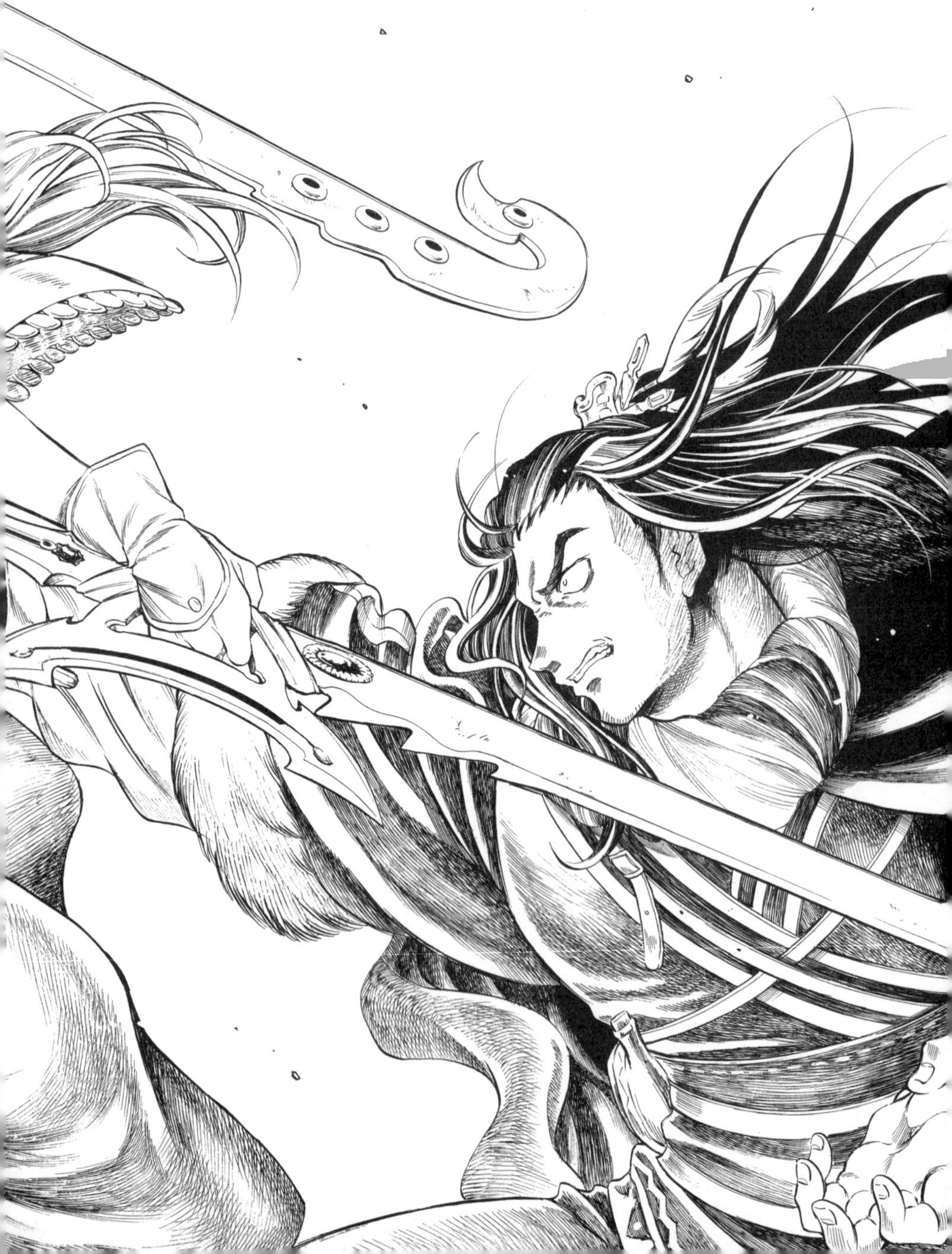

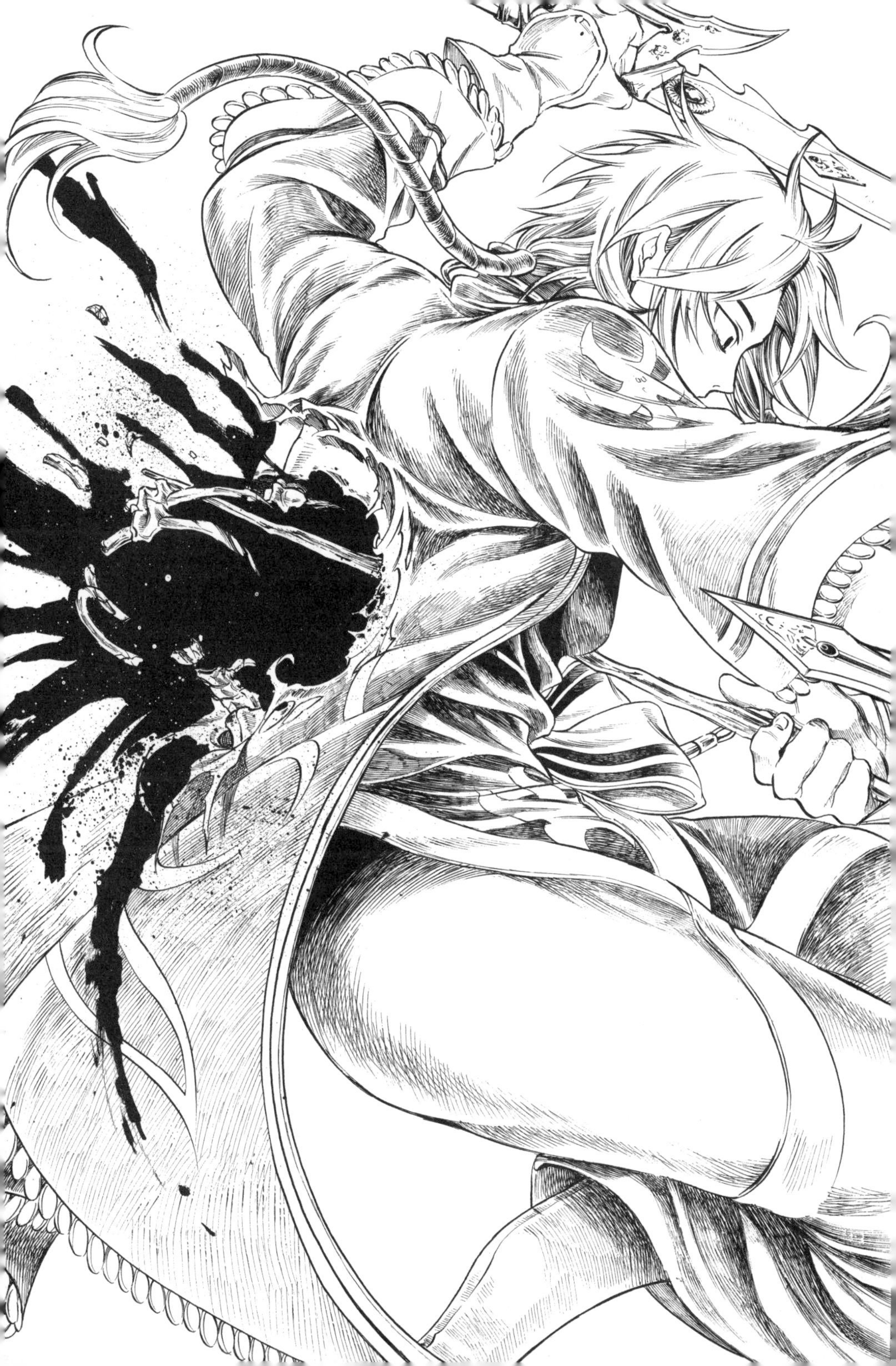

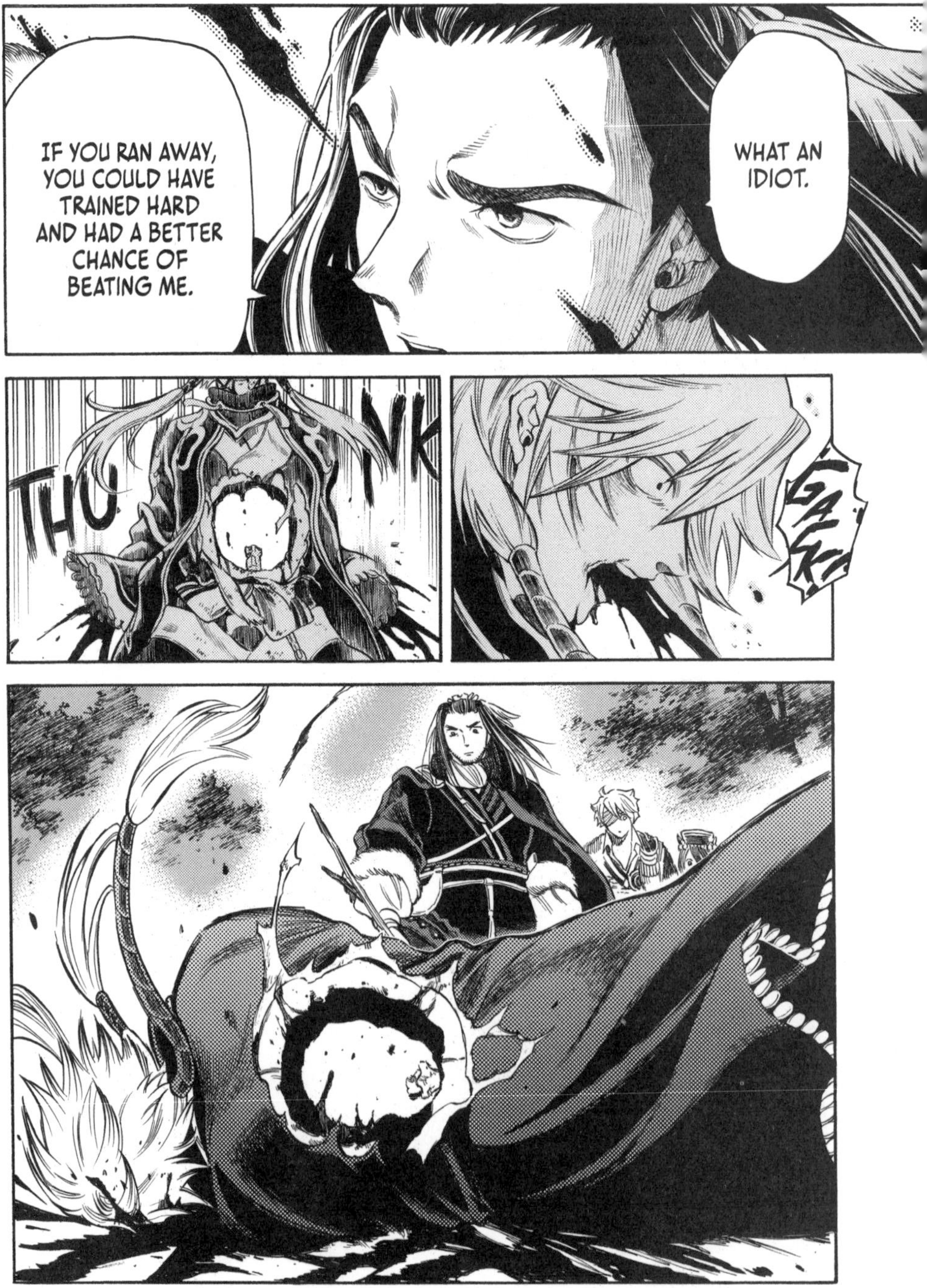
WHAT AN IDIOT.
IF YOU RAN AWAY, YOU COULD HAVE TRAINED HARD AND HAD A BETTER CHANCE OF BEATING ME.
GAK!
THUNK

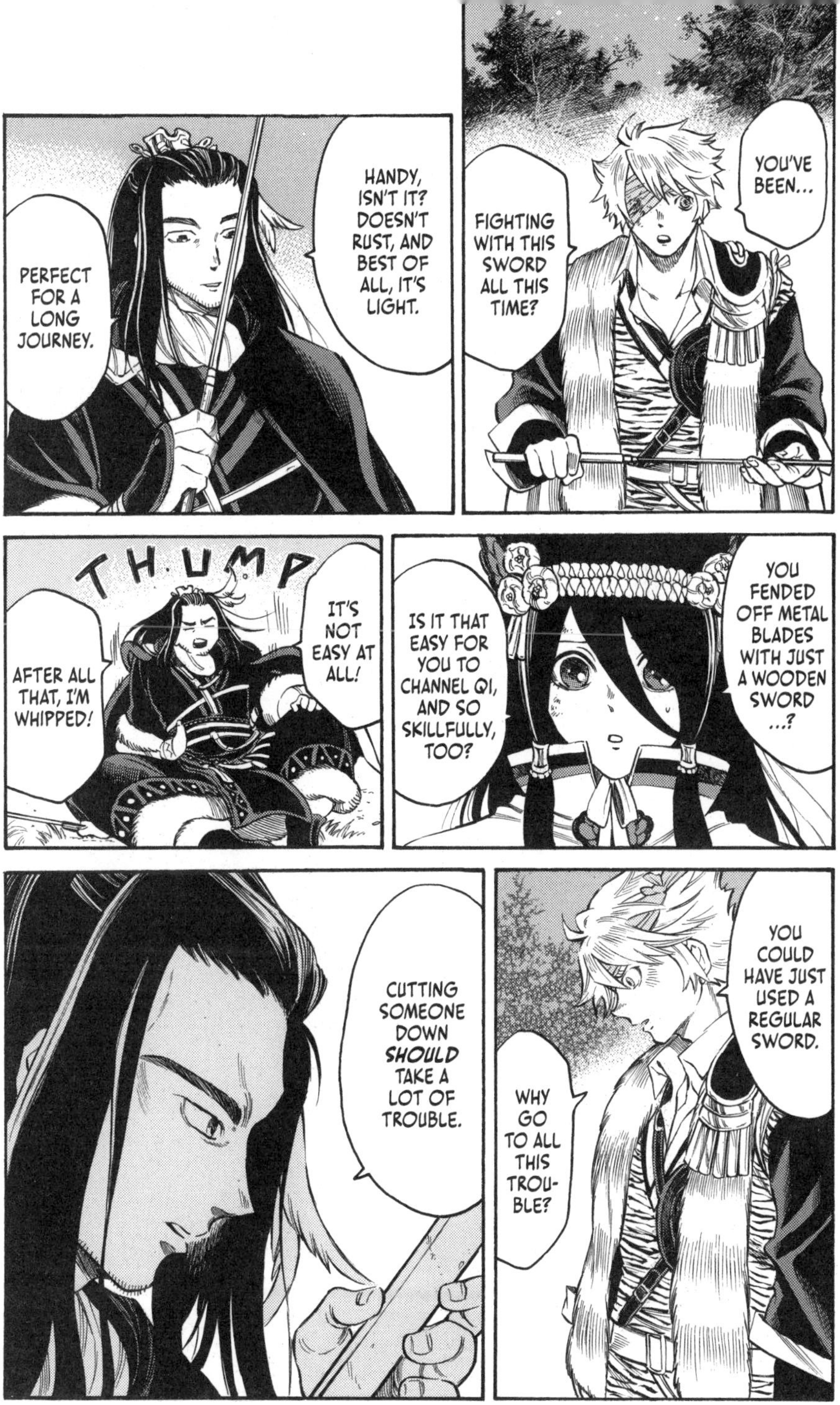
YOU'VE BEEN...
FIGHTING WITH THIS SWORD ALL THIS TIME?
HANDY, ISN'T IT? DOESN'T RUST, AND BEST OF ALL, IT'S LIGHT.
PERFECT FOR A LONG JOURNEY.
YOU FENDED OFF METAL BLADES WITH JUST A WOODEN SWORD ...?
IS IT THAT EASY FOR YOU TO CHANNEL QI, AND SO SKILLFULLY, TOO?
THUMP
IT'S NOT EASY AT ALL!
AFTER ALL THAT, I'M WHIPPED!
YOU COULD HAVE JUST USED A REGULAR SWORD.
WHY GO TO ALL THIS TROU-BLE?
CUTTING SOMEONE DOWN ***SHOULD*** TAKE A LOT OF TROUBLE.

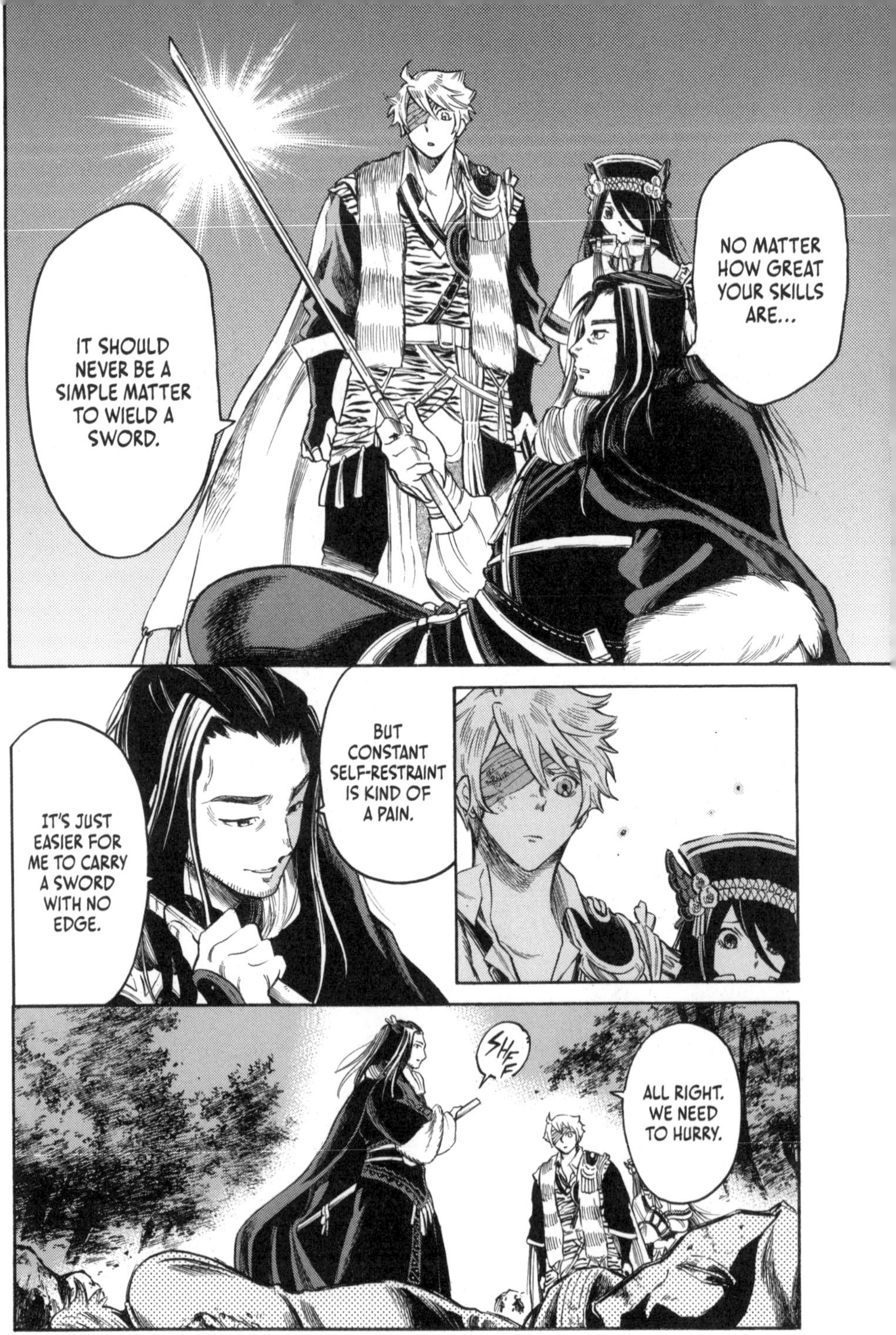
NO MATTER HOW GREAT YOUR SKILLS ARE...
IT SHOULD NEVER BE A SIMPLE MATTER TO WIELD A SWORD.
BUT CONSTANT SELF-RESTRAINT IS KIND OF A PAIN.
IT'S JUST EASIER FOR ME TO CARRY A SWORD WITH NO EDGE.
ALL RIGHT. WE NEED TO HURRY.
SHFF

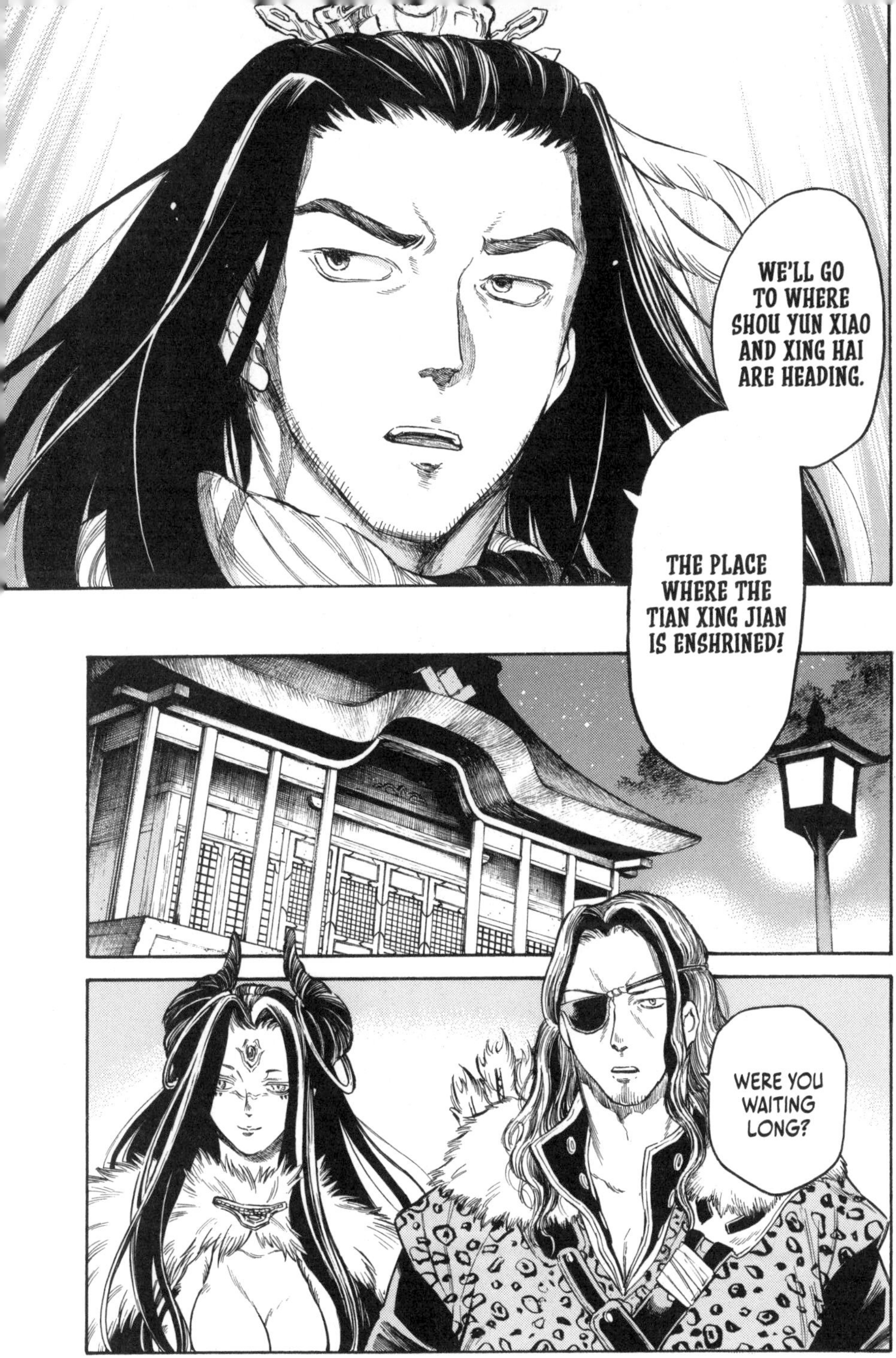
WE'LL GO TO WHERE SHOU YUN XIAO AND XING HAI ARE HEADING.
THE PLACE WHERE THE TIAN XING JIAN IS ENSHRINED!
WERE YOU WAITING LONG?

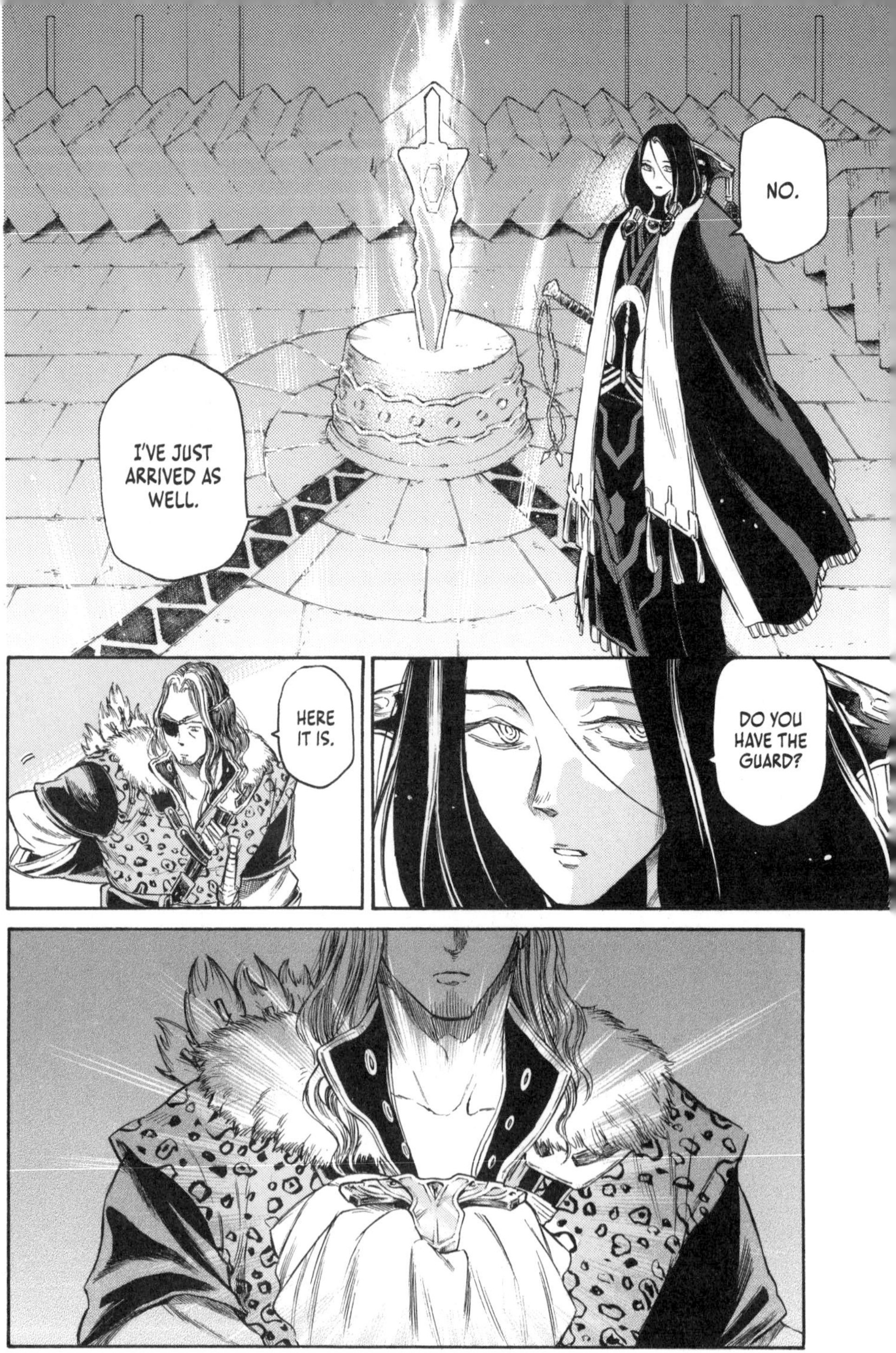
NO.
I'VE JUST ARRIVED AS WELL.
DO YOU HAVE THE GUARD?
HERE IT IS.

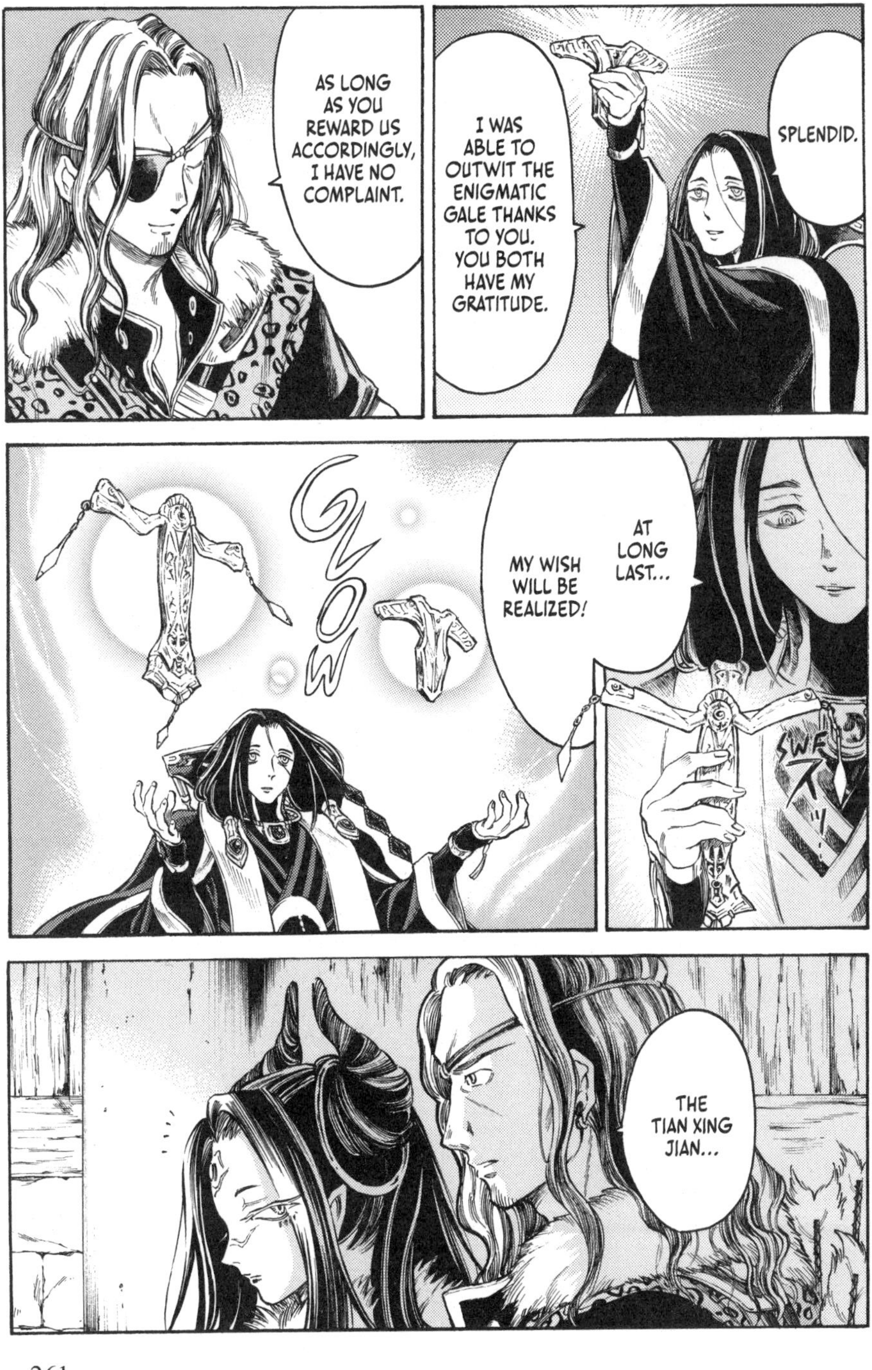
SPLENDID.
I WAS ABLE TO OUTWIT THE ENIGMATIC GALE THANKS TO YOU. YOU BOTH HAVE MY GRATITUDE.
AS LONG AS YOU REWARD US ACCORDINGLY, I HAVE NO COMPLAINT.
SWF
AT LONG LAST...
MY WISH WILL BE REALIZED!
GLOW
THE TIAN XING JIAN...

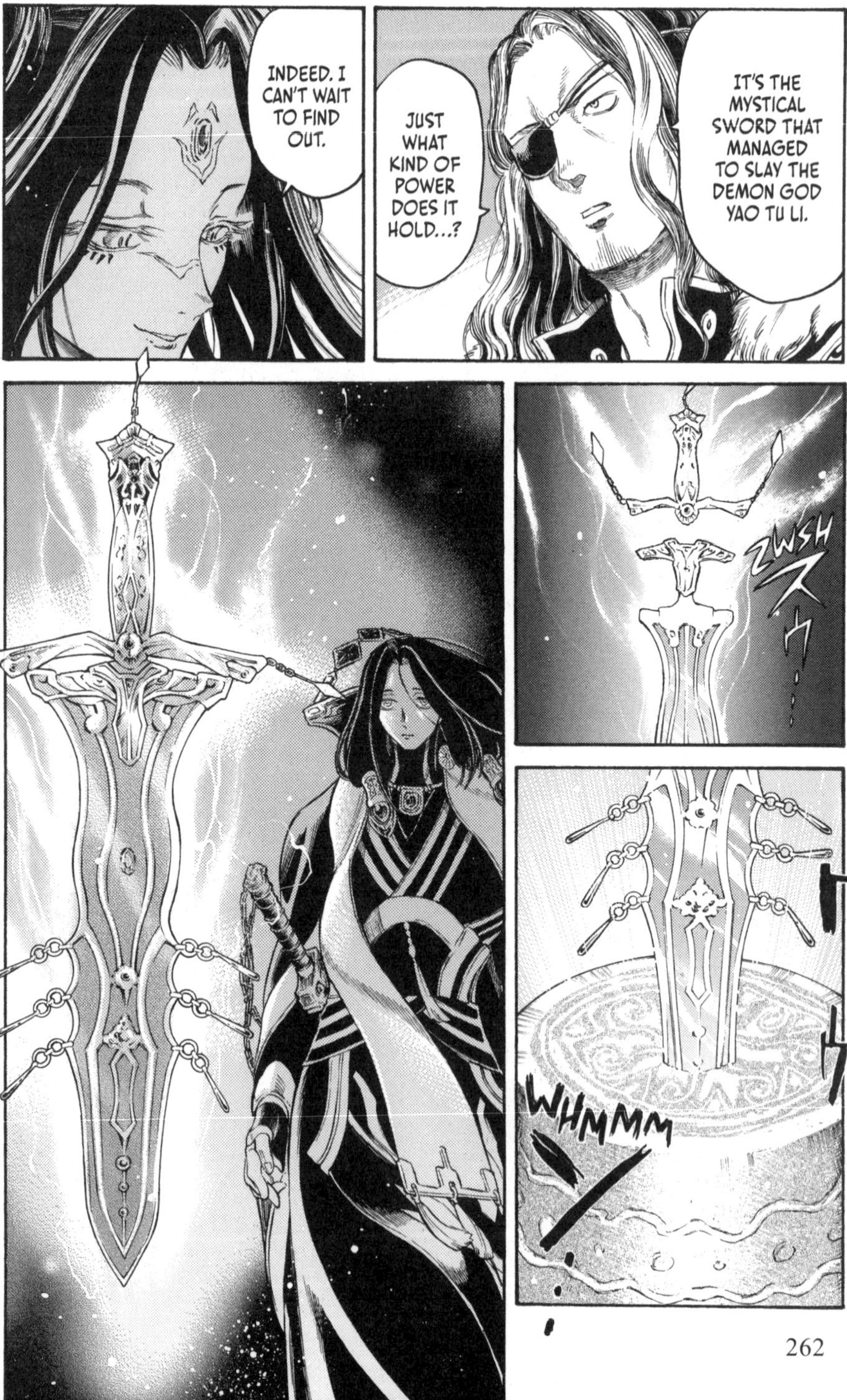
IT'S THE MYSTICAL SWORD THAT MANAGED TO SLAY THE DEMON GOD YAO TU LI.
JUST WHAT KIND OF POWER DOES IT HOLD...?
INDEED. I CAN'T WAIT TO FIND OUT.
ZWSH
WHMMM

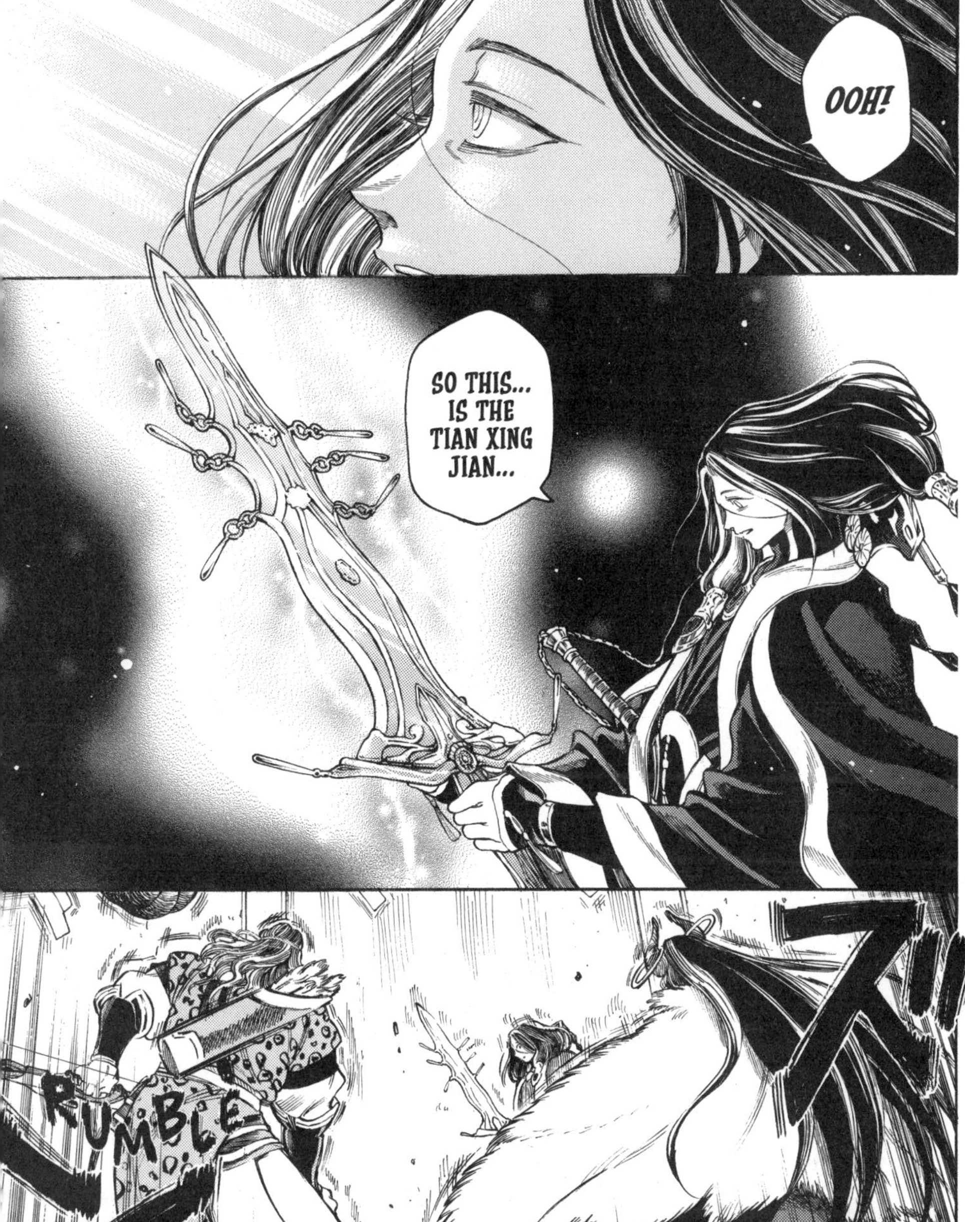
OOH!
SO THIS... IS THE TIAN XING JIAN...
RUMBLE

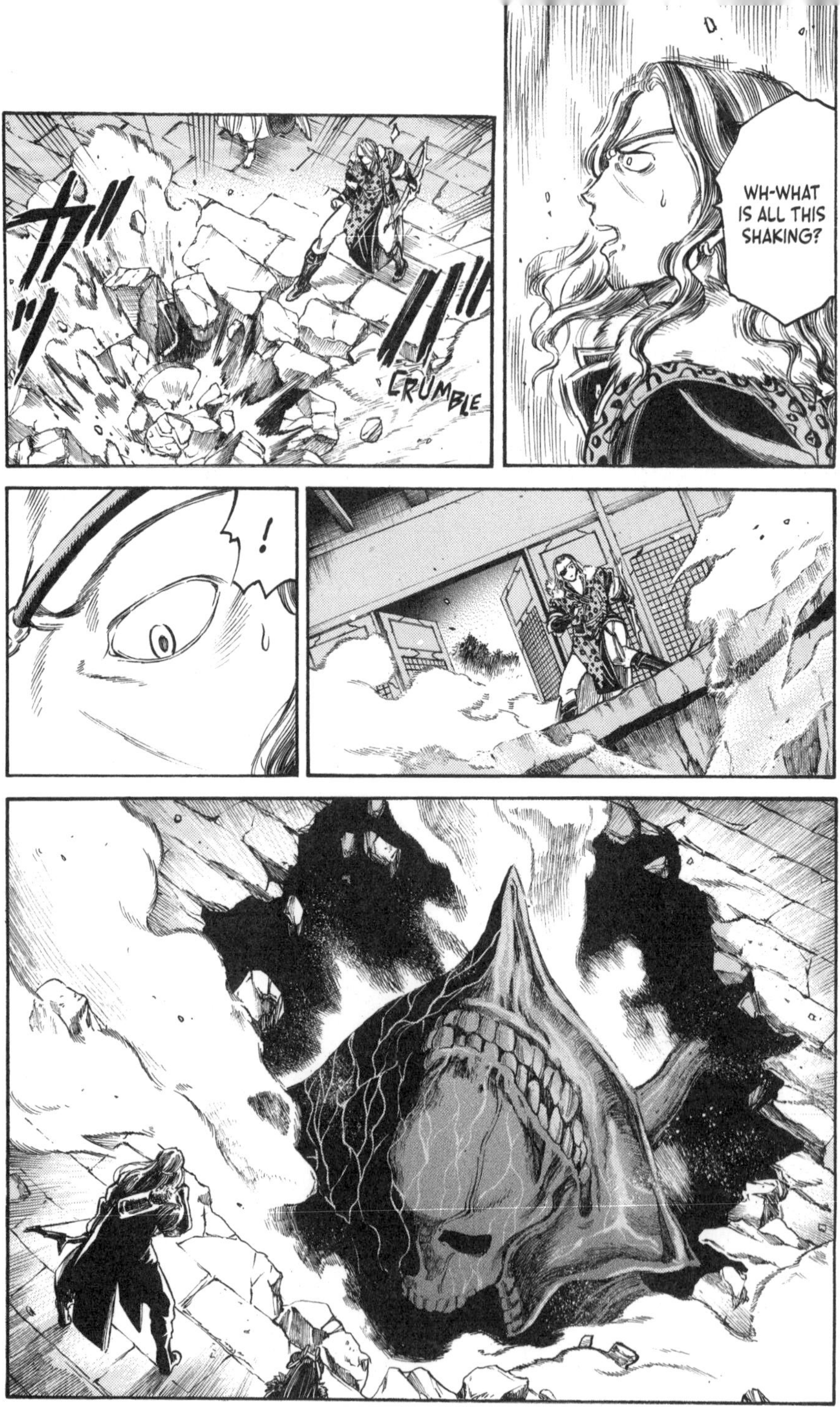
WH-WHAT IS ALL THIS SHAKING?
CRUMBLE
!

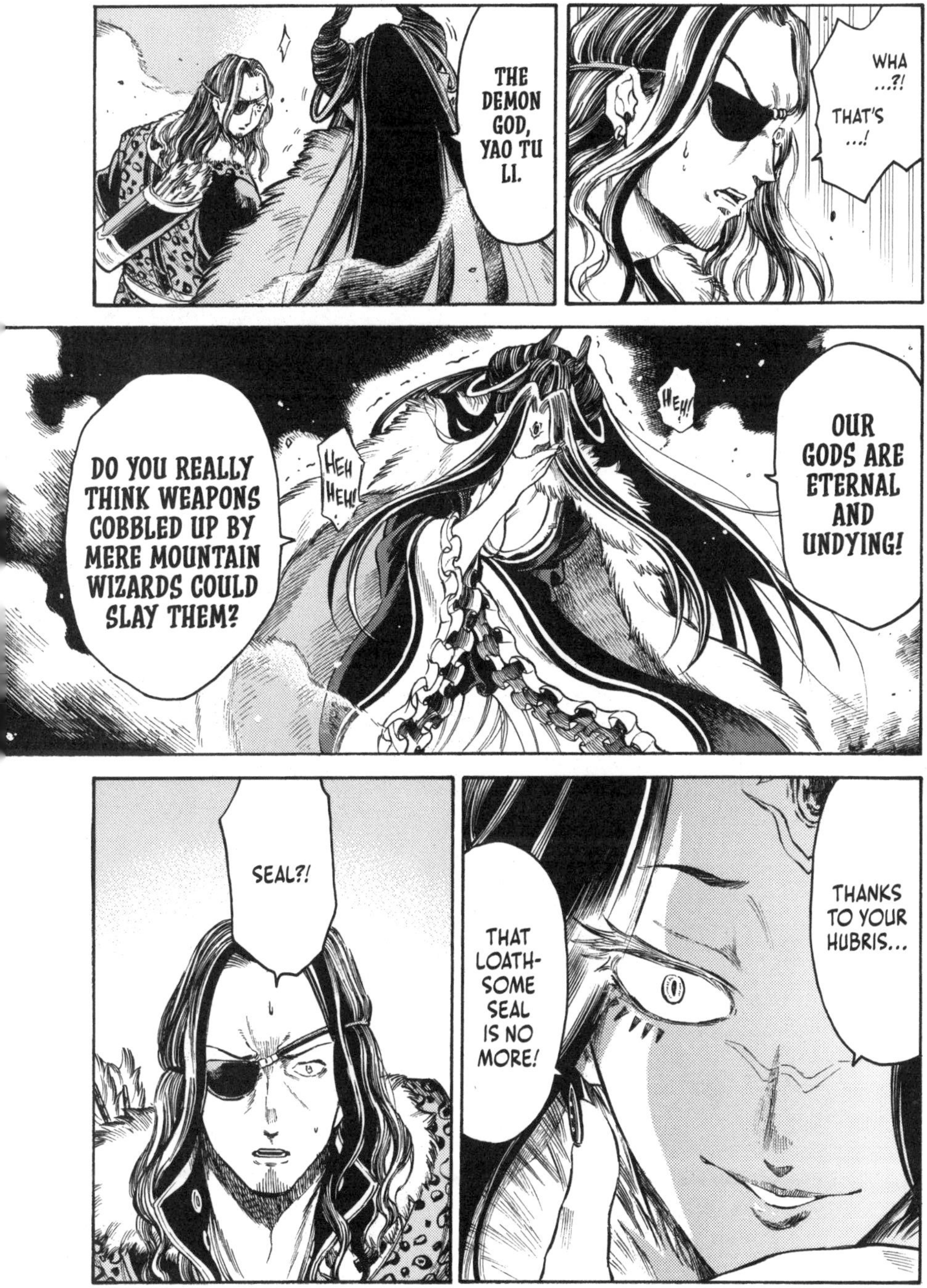
WHA ...?!
THAT'S ...!
THE DEMON GOD, YAO TU LI.
OUR GODS ARE ETERNAL AND UNDYING!
HEH!
HEH HEH!
DO YOU REALLY THINK WEAPONS COBBLED UP BY MERE MOUNTAIN WIZARDS COULD SLAY THEM?
THANKS TO YOUR HUBRIS...
THAT LOATH-SOME SEAL IS NO MORE!
SEAL?!

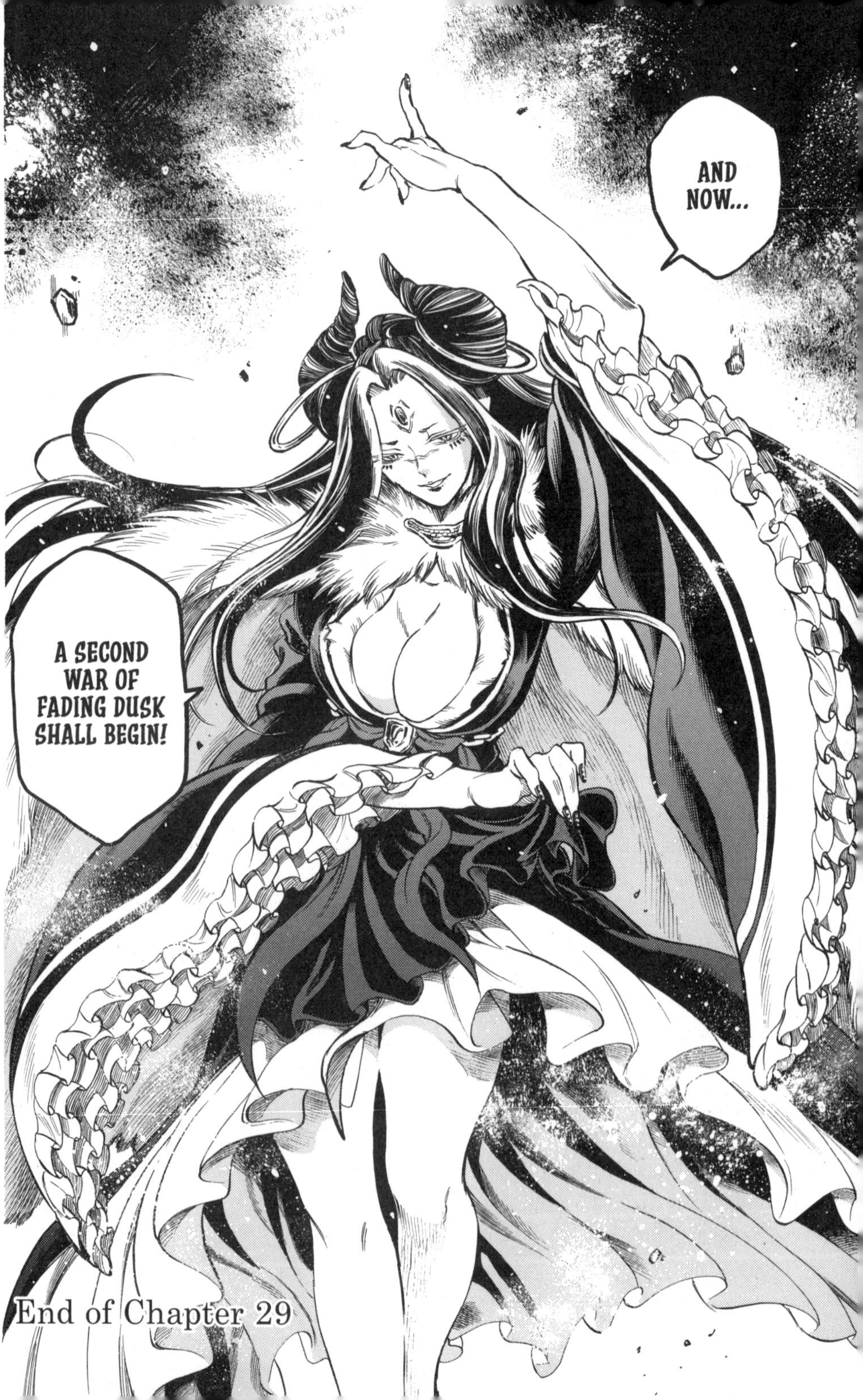
AND NOW...
A SECOND WAR OF FADING DUSK SHALL BEGIN!
End of Chapter 29

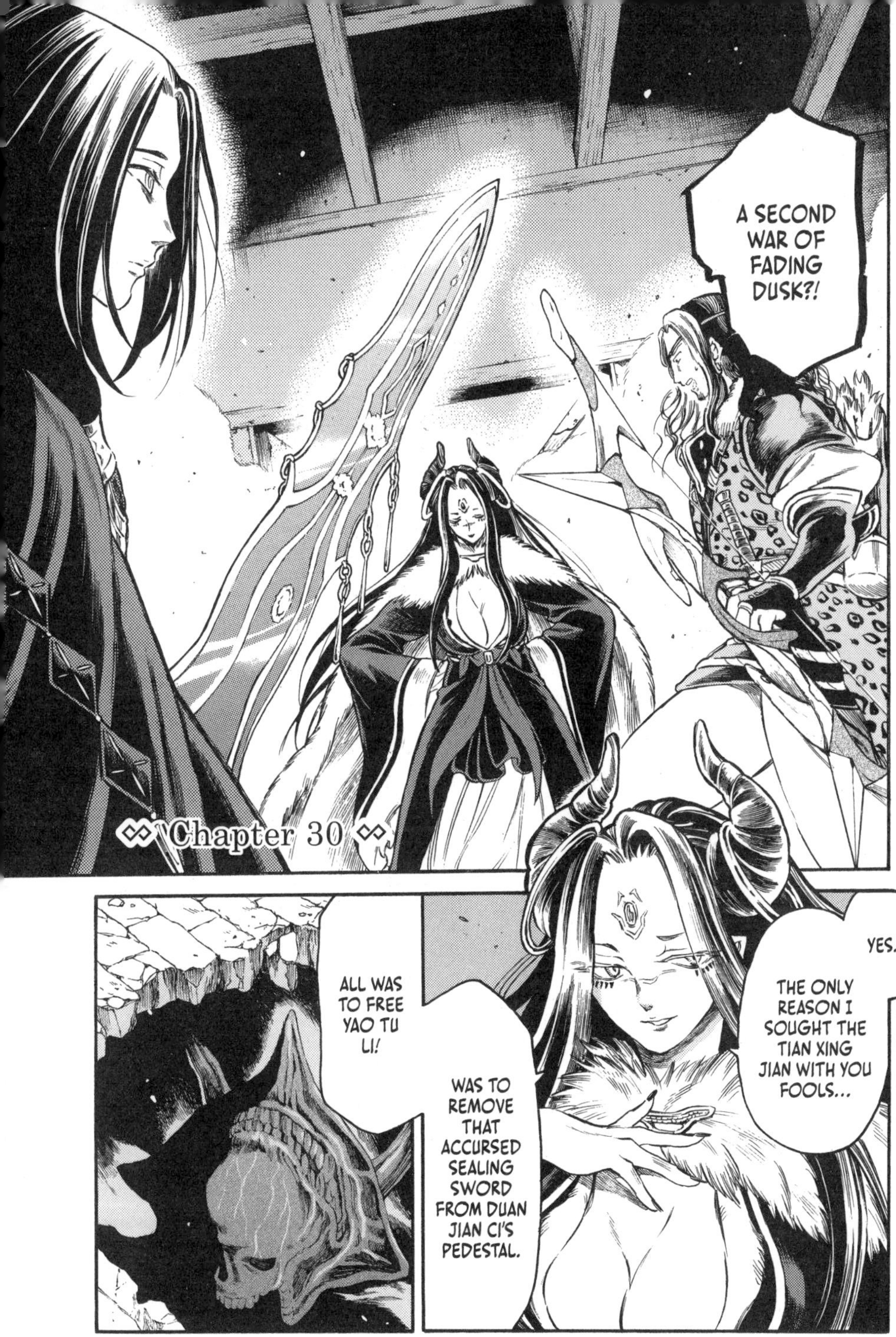
A SECOND WAR OF FADING DUSK?!
Chapter 30
YES.
THE ONLY REASON I SOUGHT THE TIAN XING JIAN WITH YOU FOOLS...
WAS TO REMOVE THAT ACCURSED SEALING SWORD FROM DUAN JIAN CI'S PEDESTAL.
ALL WAS TO FREE YAO TU LI!

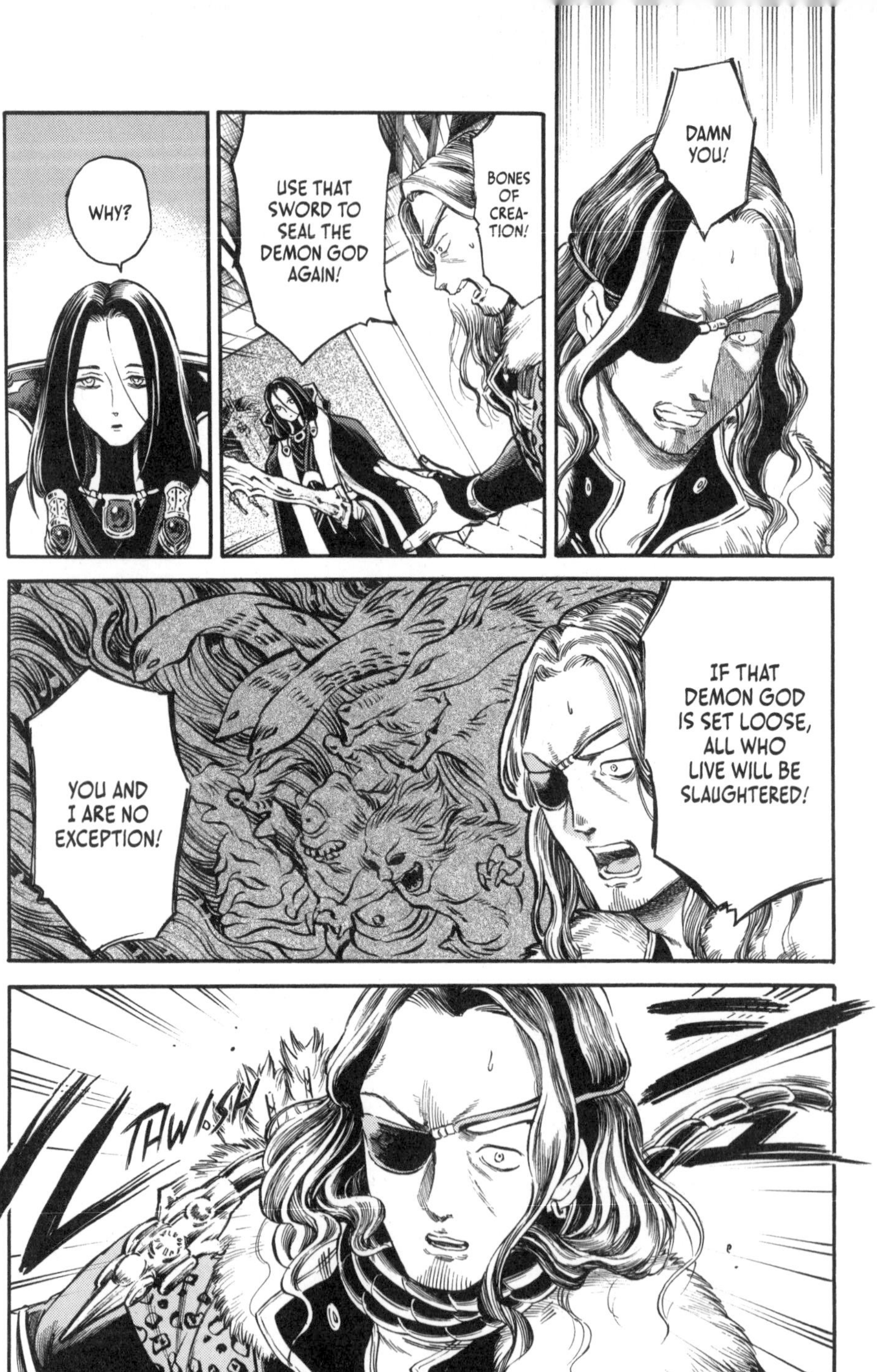
DAMN YOU!
BONES OF CREATION!
USE THAT SWORD TO SEAL THE DEMON GOD AGAIN!
WHY?
IF THAT DEMON GOD IS SET LOOSE, ALL WHO LIVE WILL BE SLAUGHTERED!
YOU AND I ARE NO EXCEPTION!
THWISH

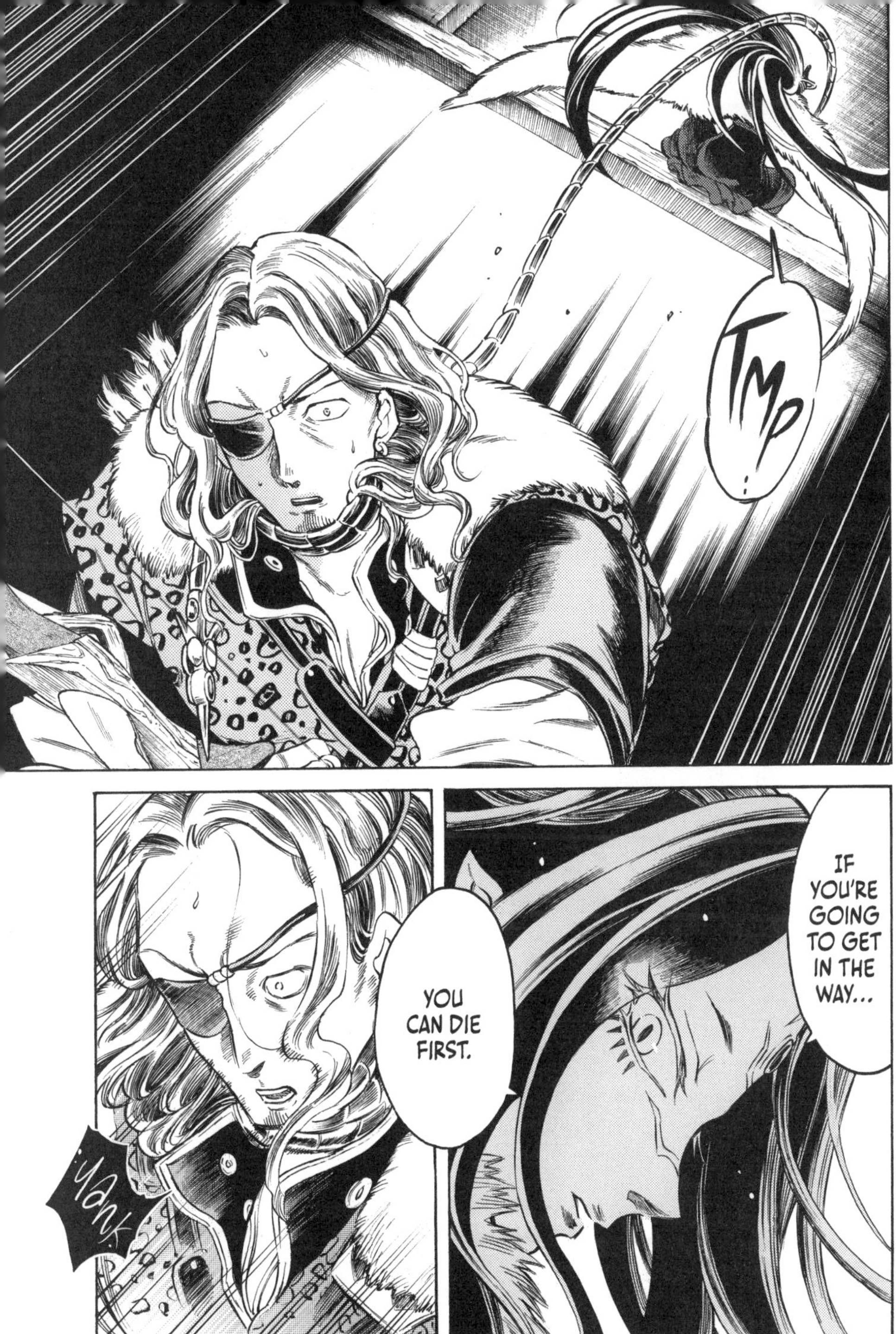
TMP!
IF YOU'RE GOING TO GET IN THE WAY...
YOU CAN DIE FIRST.
YANK!

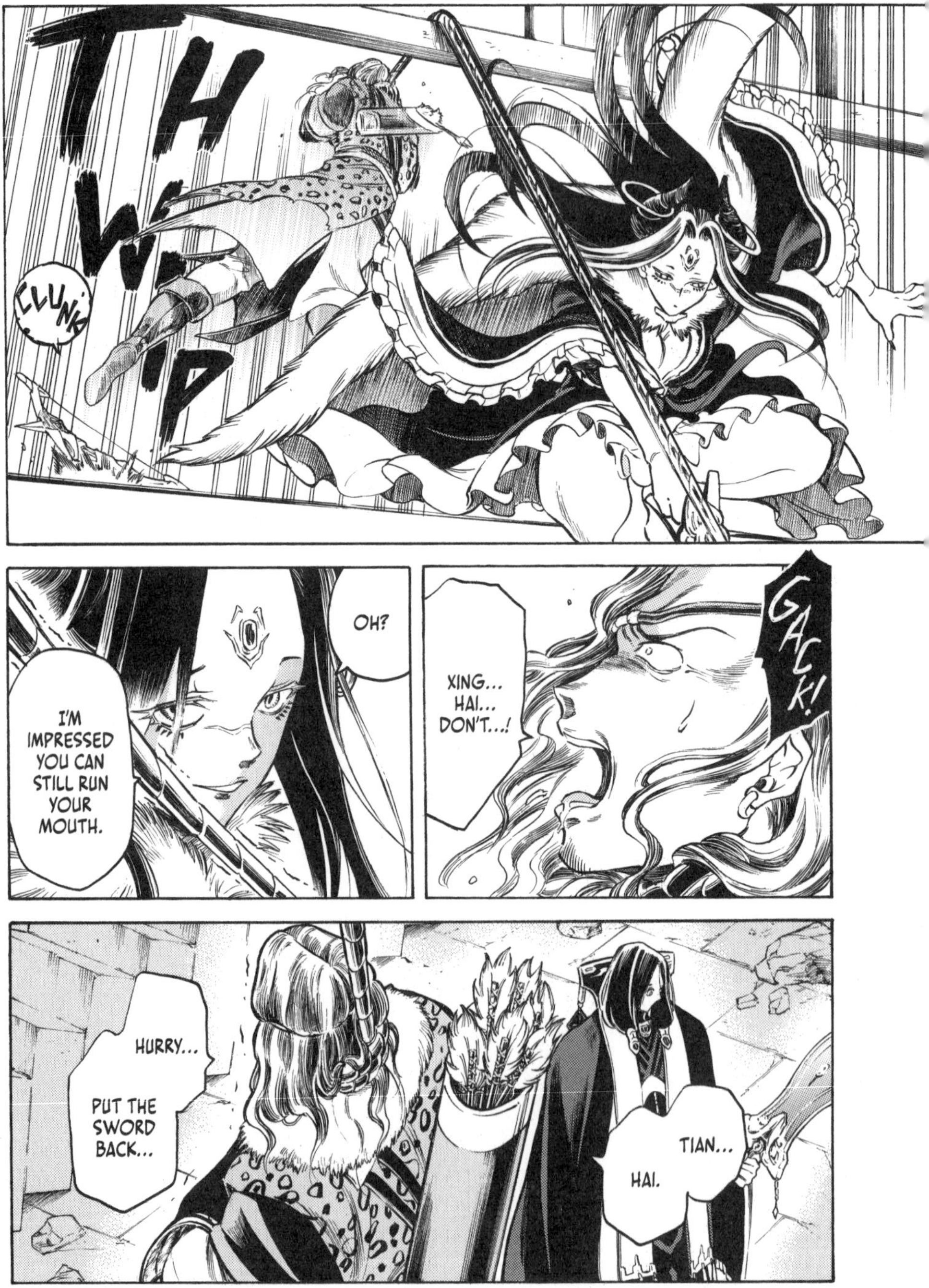
THWIP
CLUNK
GACK!
XING... HAI... DON'T...!
OH?
I'M IMPRESSED YOU CAN STILL RUN YOUR MOUTH.
TIAN...
HAI.
HURRY...
PUT THE SWORD BACK...

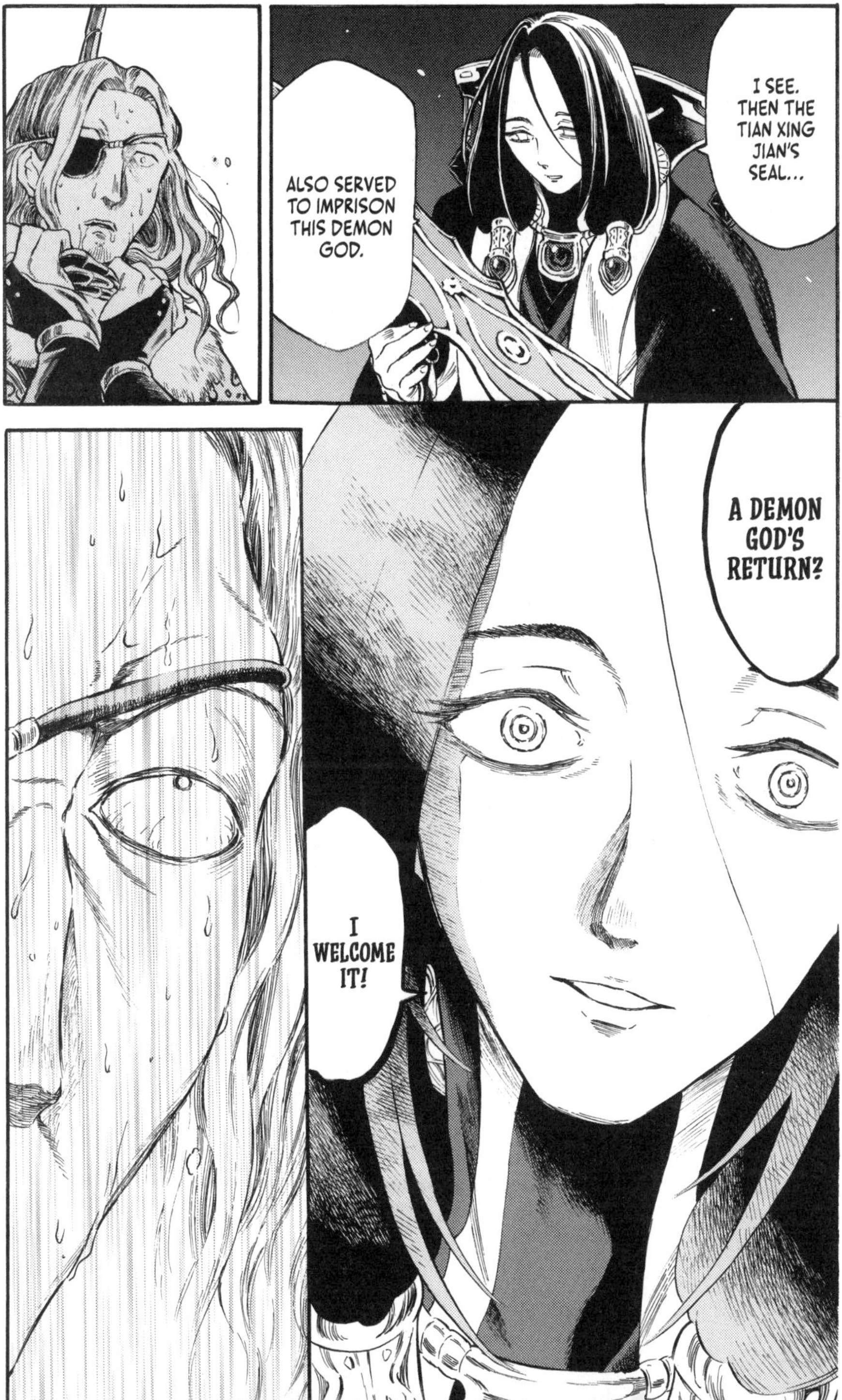
I SEE. THEN THE TIAN XING JIAN'S SEAL...
ALSO SERVED TO IMPRISON THIS DEMON GOD.
A DEMON GOD'S RETURN?
I WELCOME IT!

CREAK

Gah..

Gu..

GRIK

GRIK

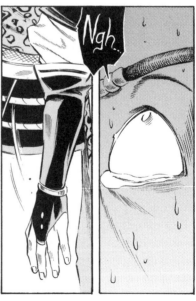

Ngh..

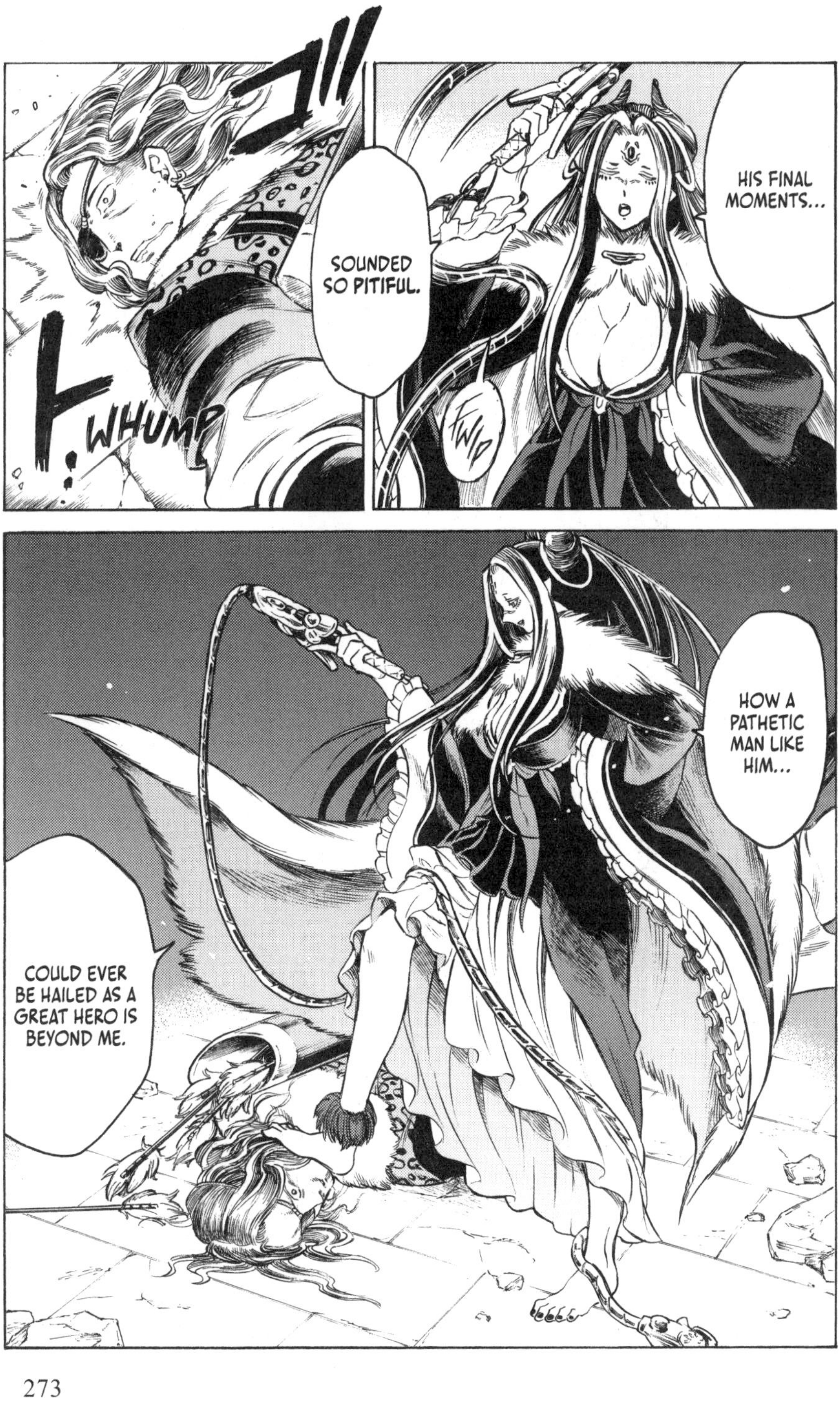
HIS FINAL MOMENTS...
SOUNDED SO PITIFUL.
FWIP
WHUMP
HOW A PATHETIC MAN LIKE HIM...
COULD EVER BE HAILED AS A GREAT HERO IS BEYOND ME.

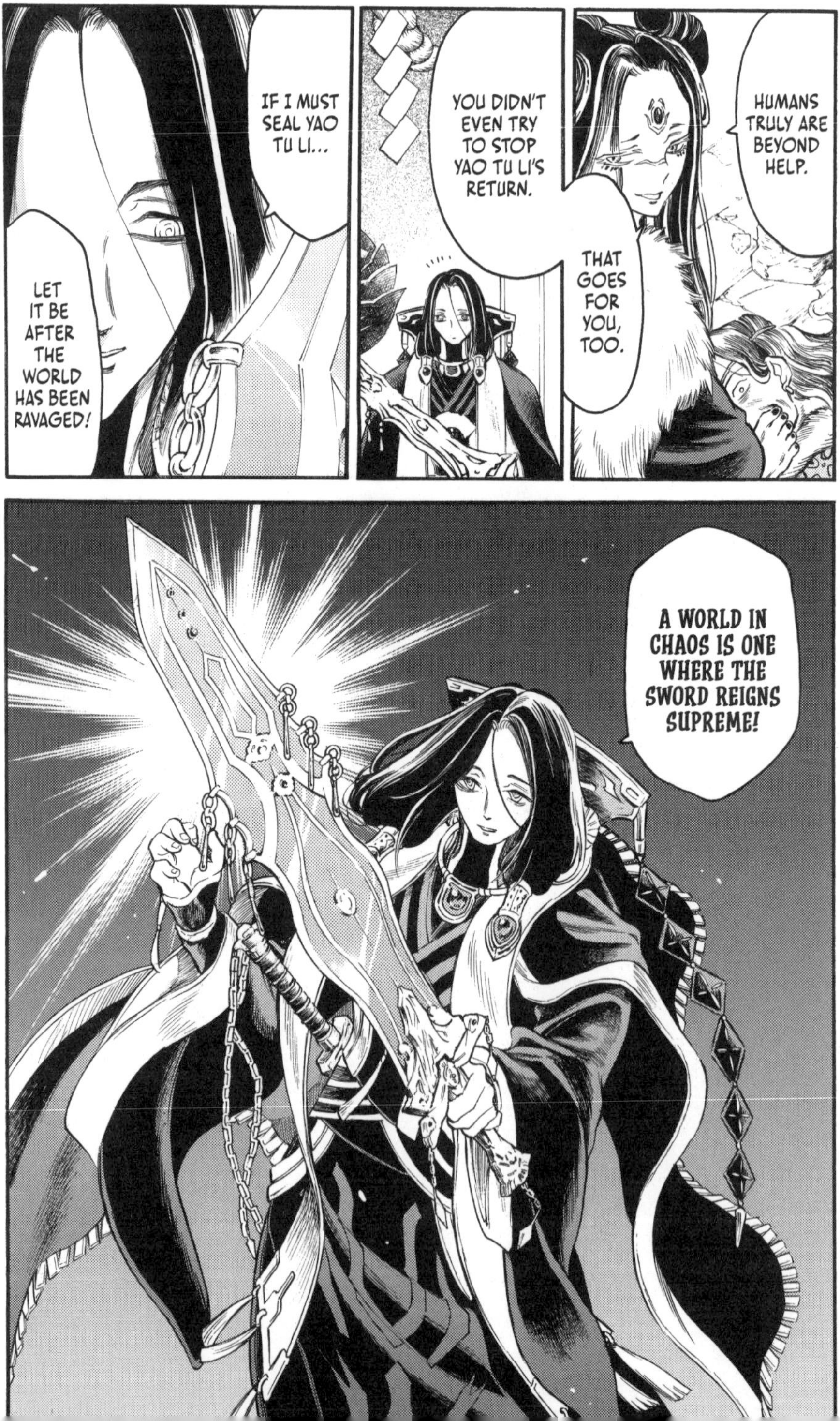
HUMANS TRULY ARE BEYOND HELP.
THAT GOES FOR YOU, TOO.
YOU DIDN'T EVEN TRY TO STOP YAO TU LI'S RETURN.
IF I MUST SEAL YAO TU LI...
LET IT BE AFTER THE WORLD HAS BEEN RAVAGED!
A WORLD IN CHAOS IS ONE WHERE THE SWORD REIGNS SUPREME!

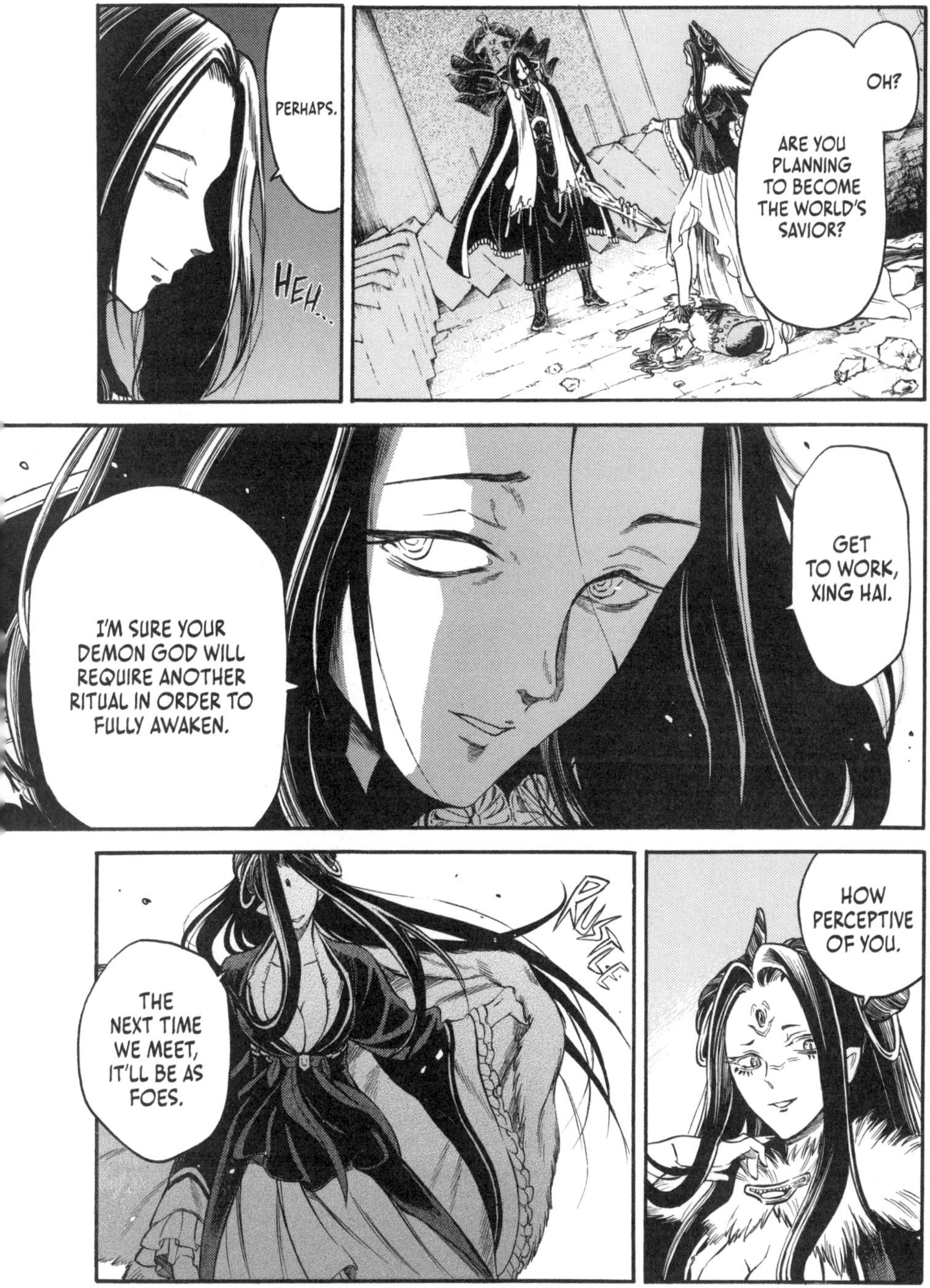
OH?
ARE YOU PLANNING TO BECOME THE WORLD'S SAVIOR?
PERHAPS.
HEH...
GET TO WORK, XING HAI.
I'M SURE YOUR DEMON GOD WILL REQUIRE ANOTHER RITUAL IN ORDER TO FULLY AWAKEN.
HOW PERCEPTIVE OF YOU.
RUSTLE
THE NEXT TIME WE MEET, IT'LL BE AS FOES.

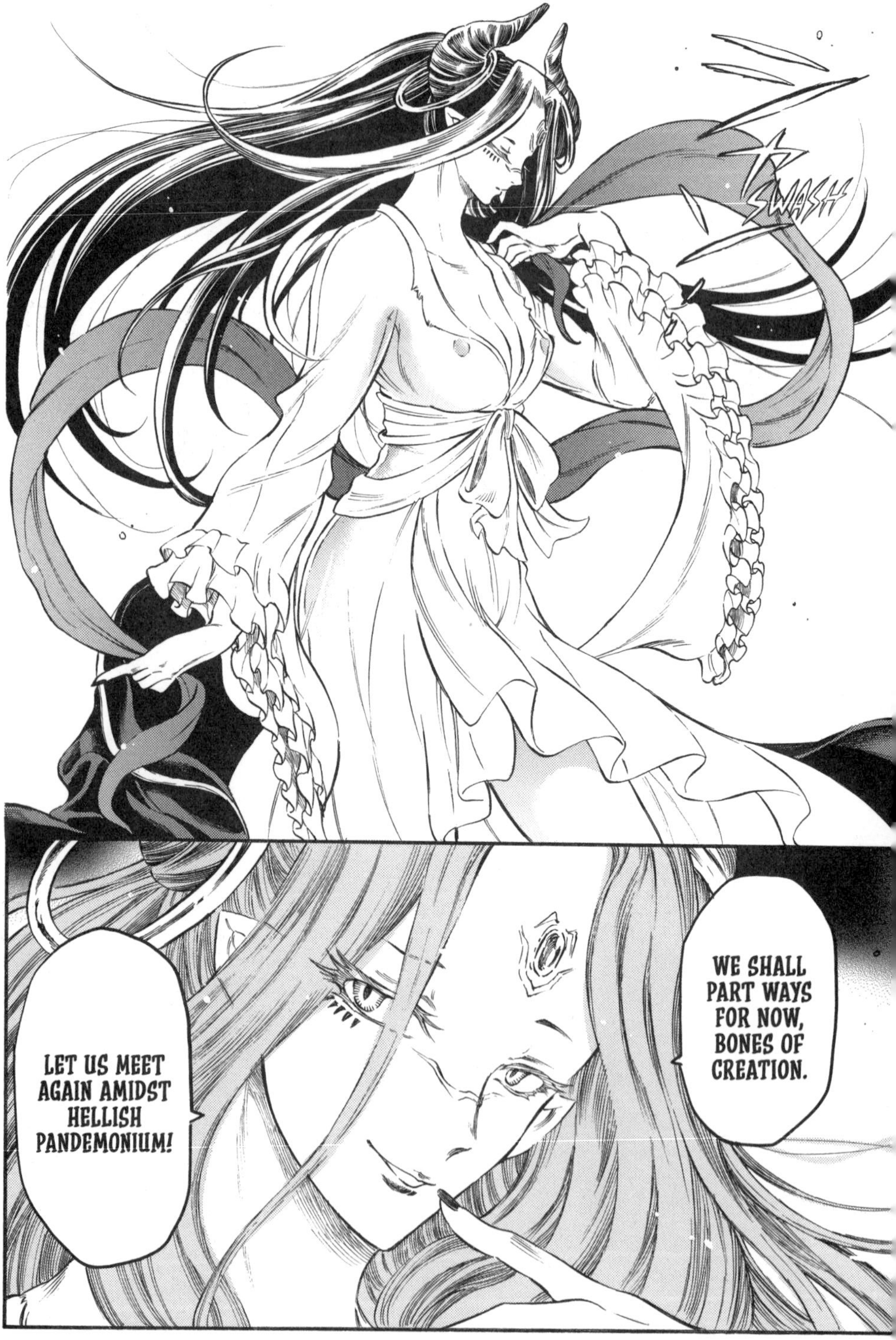
SWASH
WE SHALL PART WAYS FOR NOW, BONES OF CREATION.
LET US MEET AGAIN AMIDST HELLISH PANDEMONIUM!

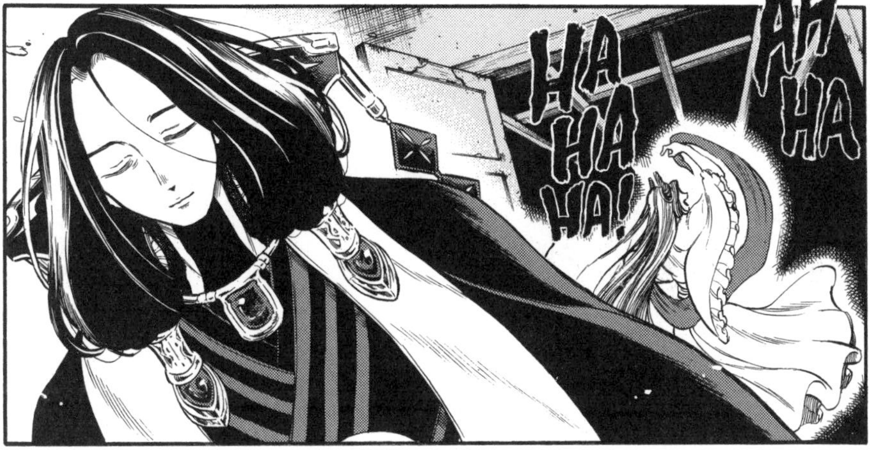
AH HA
HA HA HA HA!

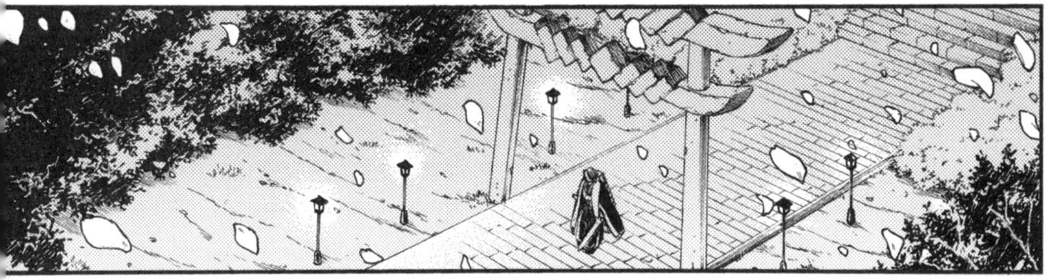

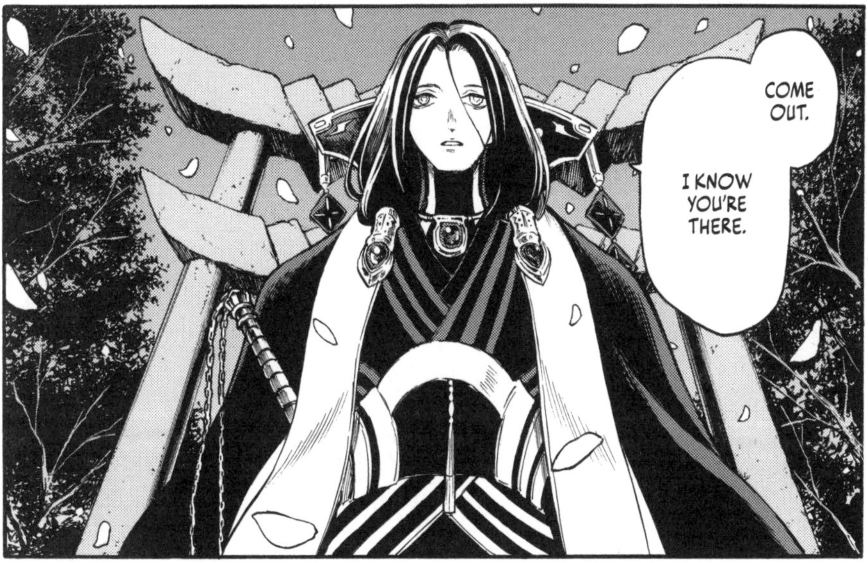
COME OUT.
I KNOW YOU'RE THERE.

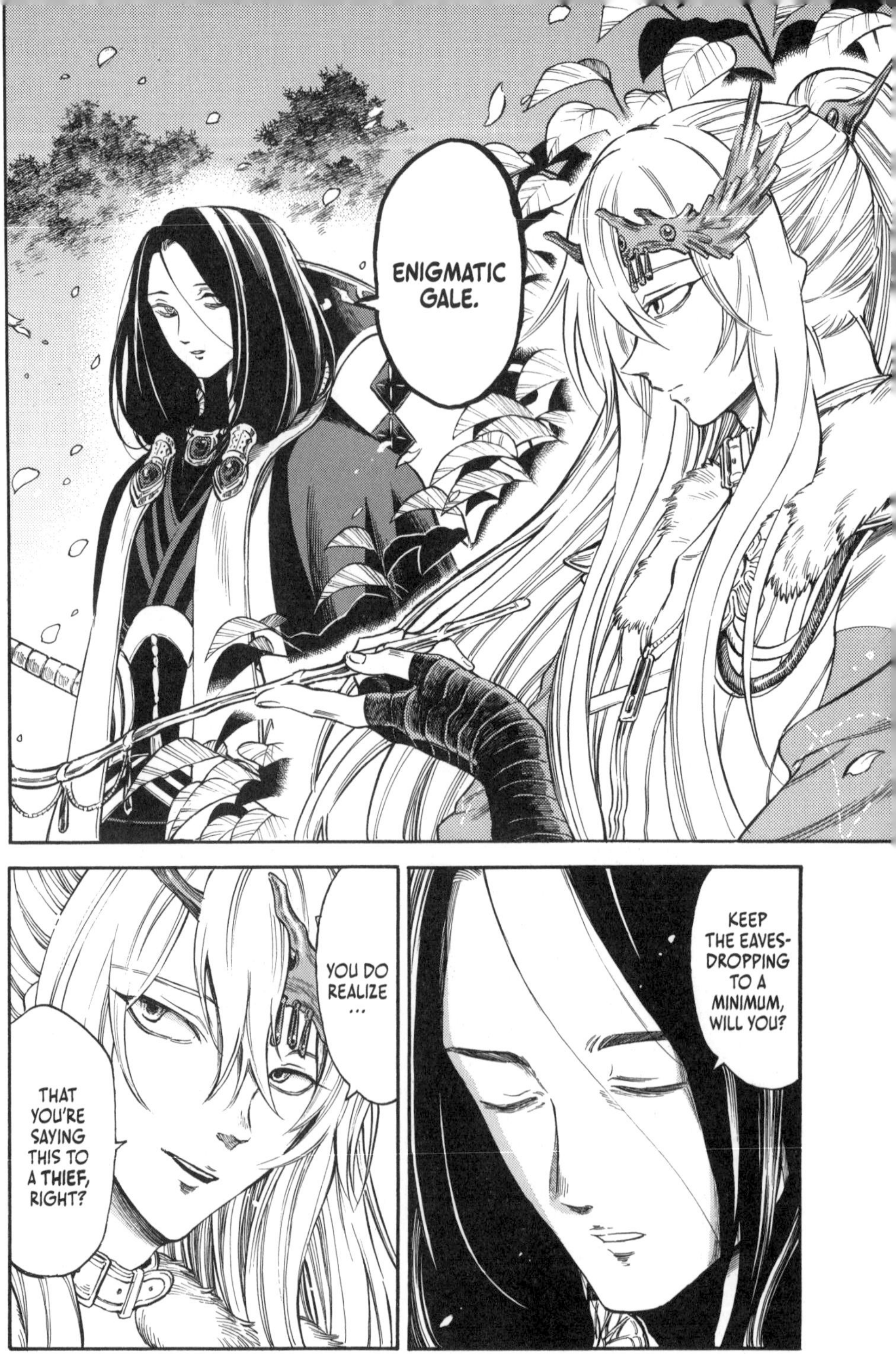
ENIGMATIC GALE.
KEEP THE EAVES-DROPPING TO A MINIMUM, WILL YOU?
YOU DO REALIZE ...
THAT YOU'RE SAYING THIS TO A THIEF, RIGHT?

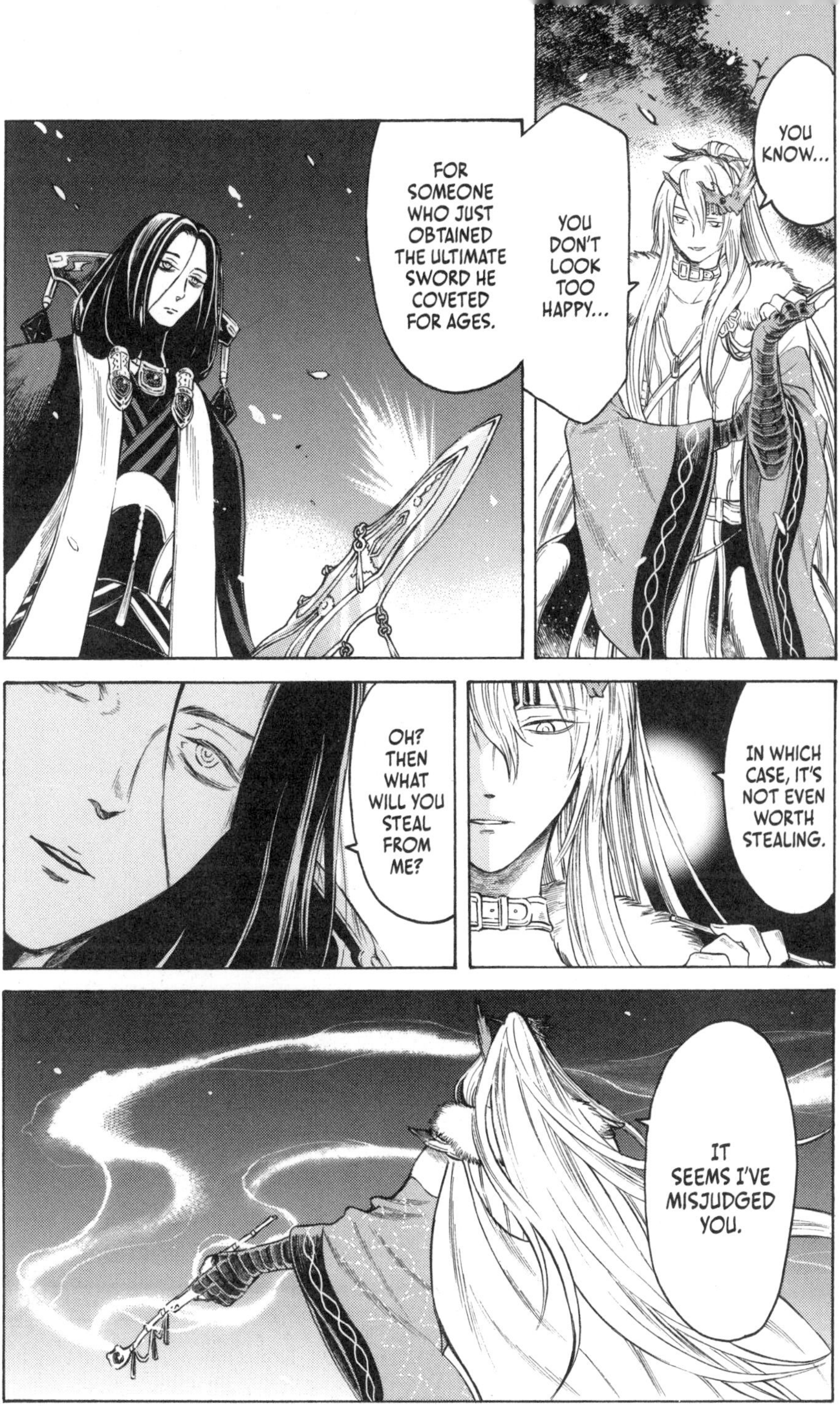
YOU KNOW...
YOU DON'T LOOK TOO HAPPY...
FOR SOMEONE WHO JUST OBTAINED THE ULTIMATE SWORD HE COVETED FOR AGES.
IN WHICH CASE, IT'S NOT EVEN WORTH STEALING.
OH? THEN WHAT WILL YOU STEAL FROM ME?
IT SEEMS I'VE MISJUDGED YOU.

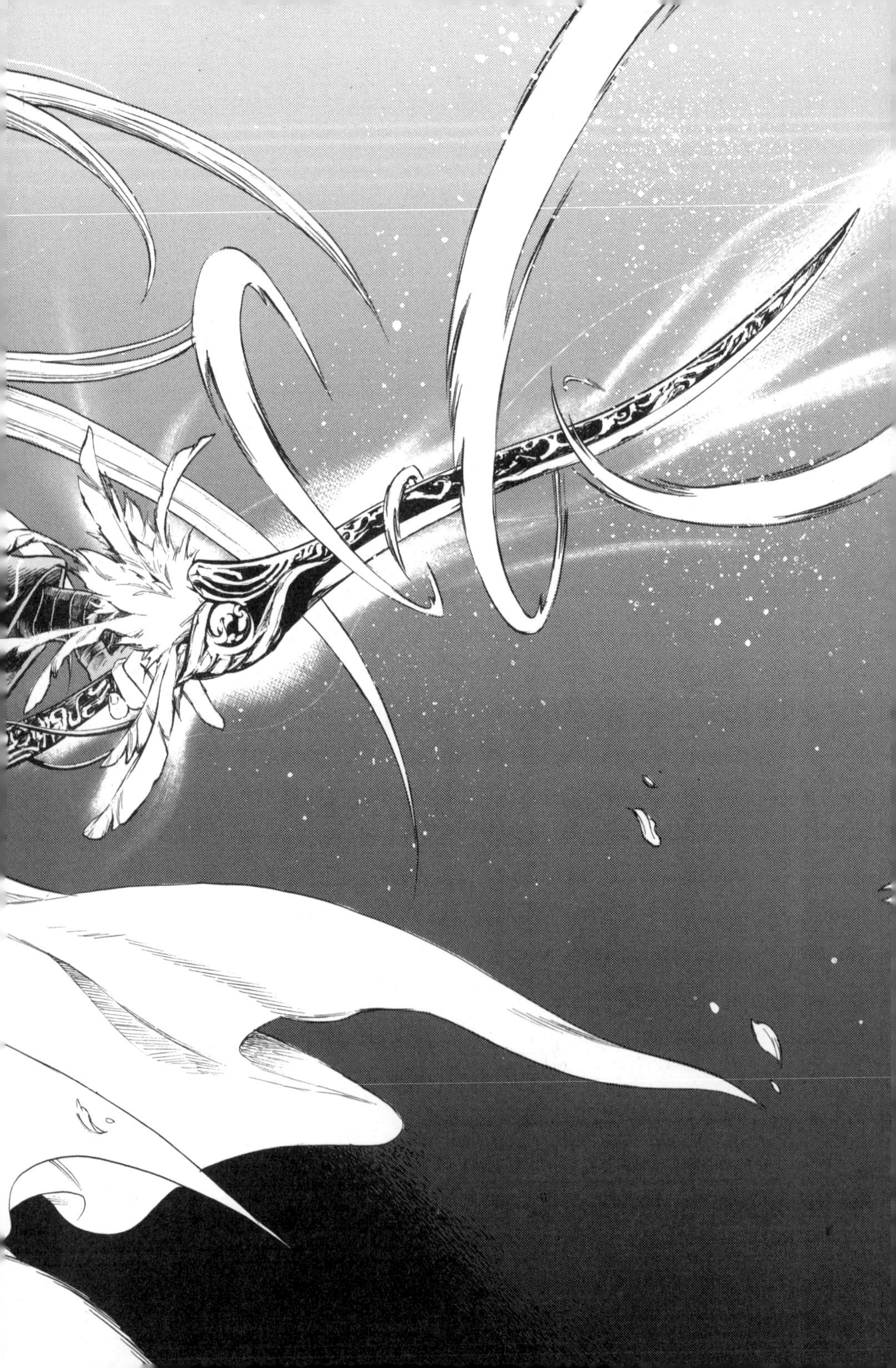

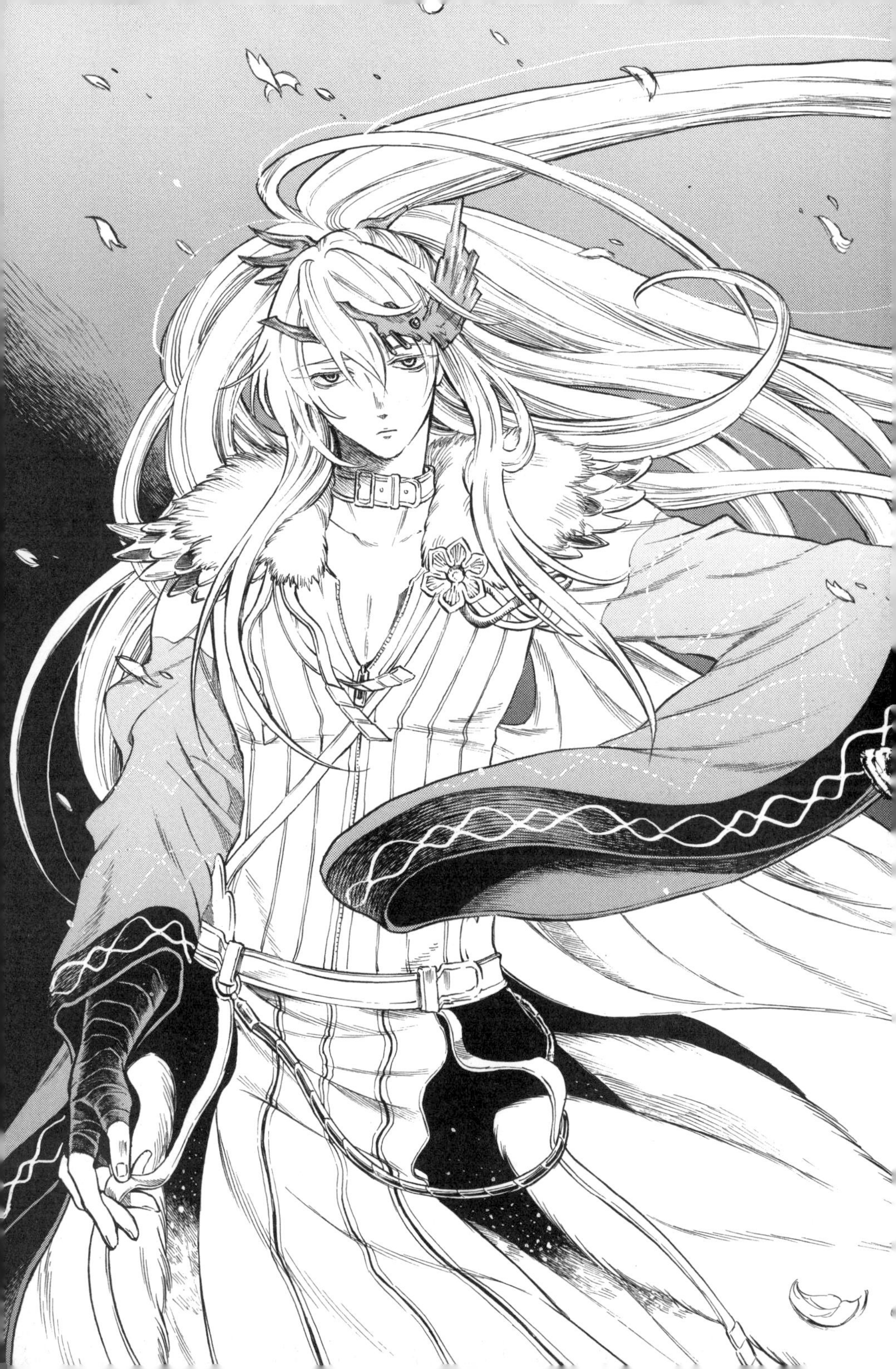

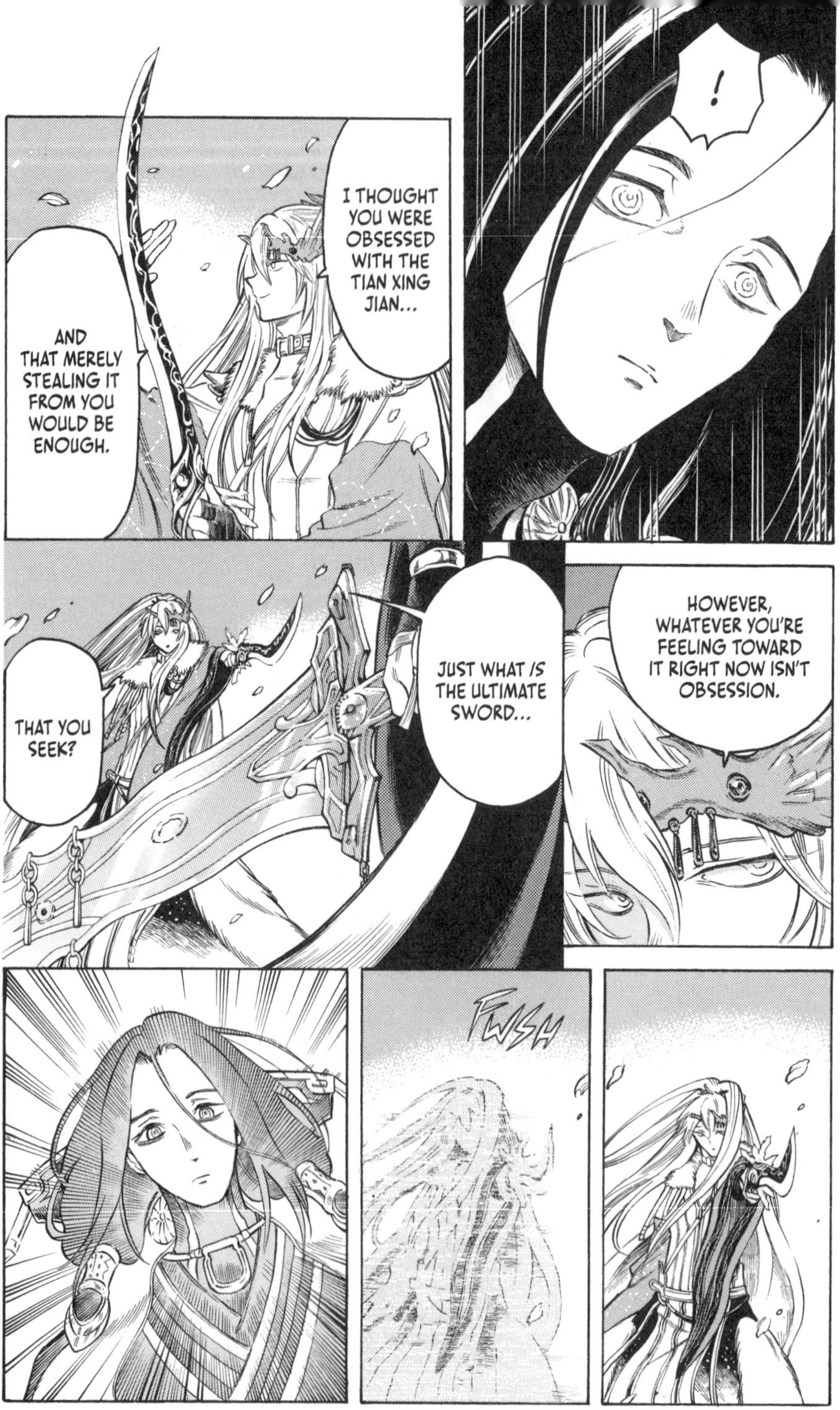
!
I THOUGHT YOU WERE OBSESSED WITH THE TIAN XING JIAN...
AND THAT MERELY STEALING IT FROM YOU WOULD BE ENOUGH.
HOWEVER, WHATEVER YOU'RE FEELING TOWARD IT RIGHT NOW ISN'T OBSESSION.
JUST WHAT *IS* THE ULTIMATE SWORD...
THAT YOU SEEK?
FWSH

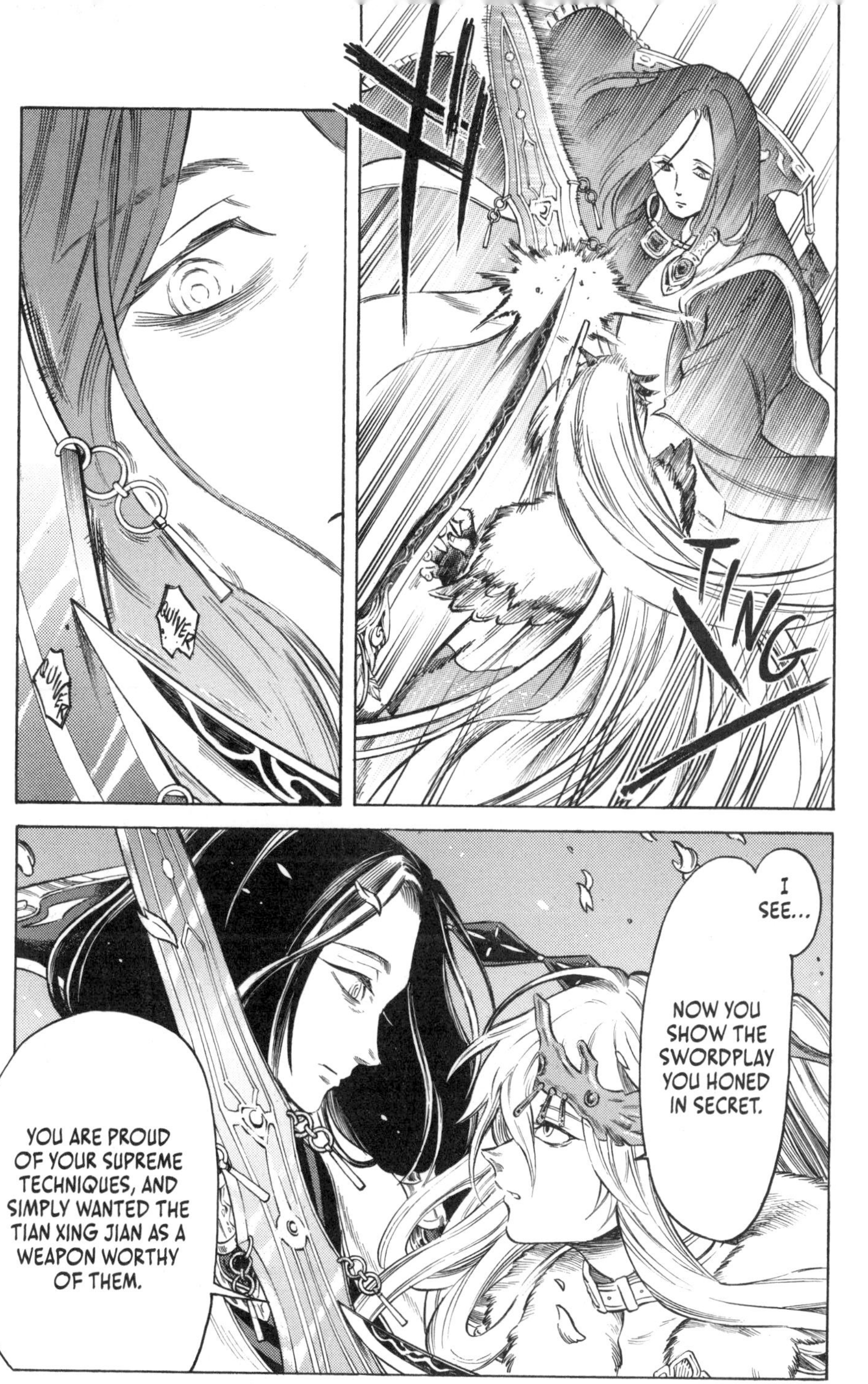
TING
QUIVER
QUIVER
I SEE...
NOW YOU SHOW THE SWORDPLAY YOU HONED IN SECRET.
YOU ARE PROUD OF YOUR SUPREME TECHNIQUES, AND SIMPLY WANTED THE TIAN XING JIAN AS A WEAPON WORTHY OF THEM.

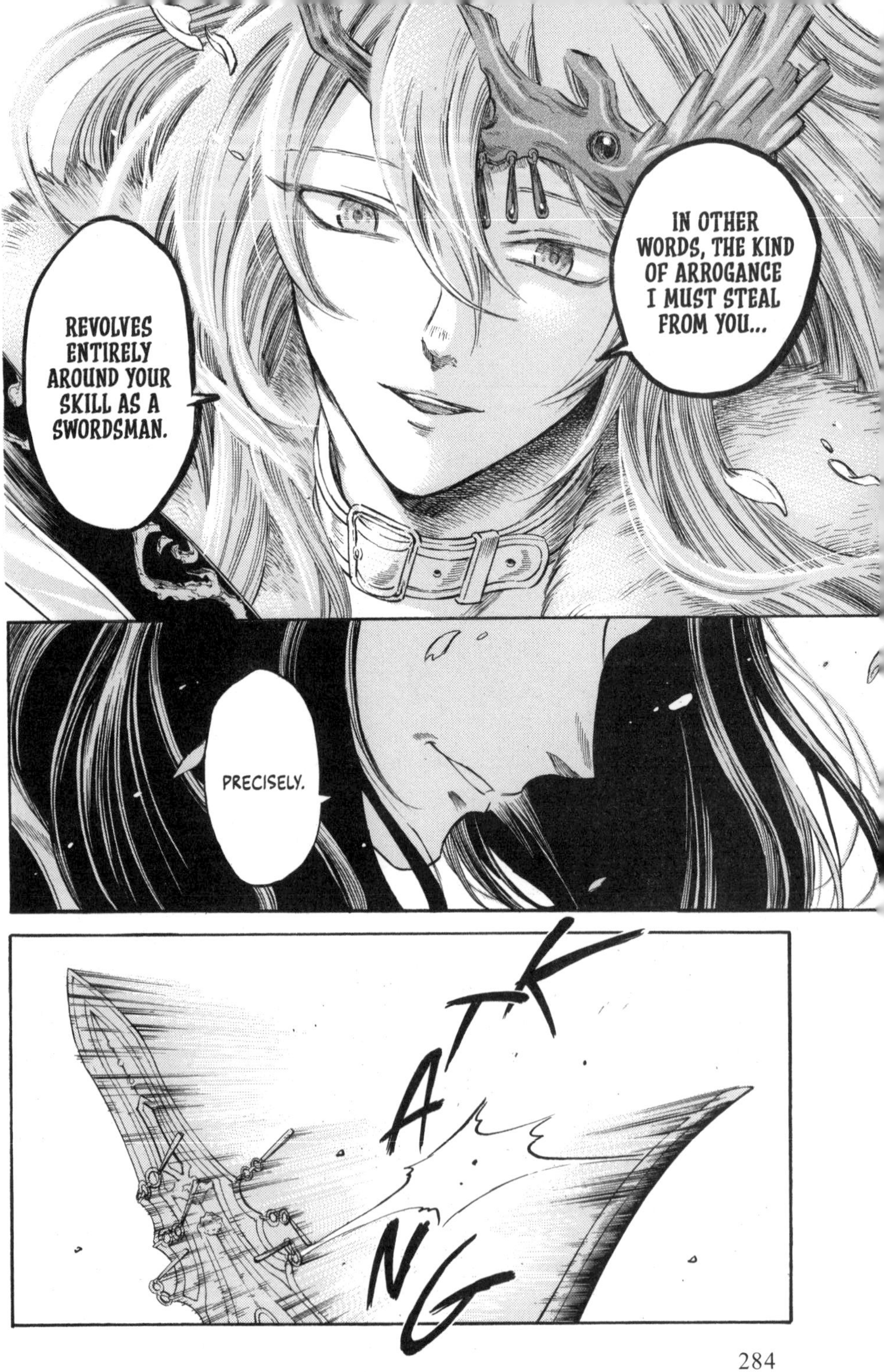
IN OTHER WORDS, THE KIND OF ARROGANCE I MUST STEAL FROM YOU...
REVOLVES ENTIRELY AROUND YOUR SKILL AS A SWORDSMAN.
PRECISELY.
TKANG

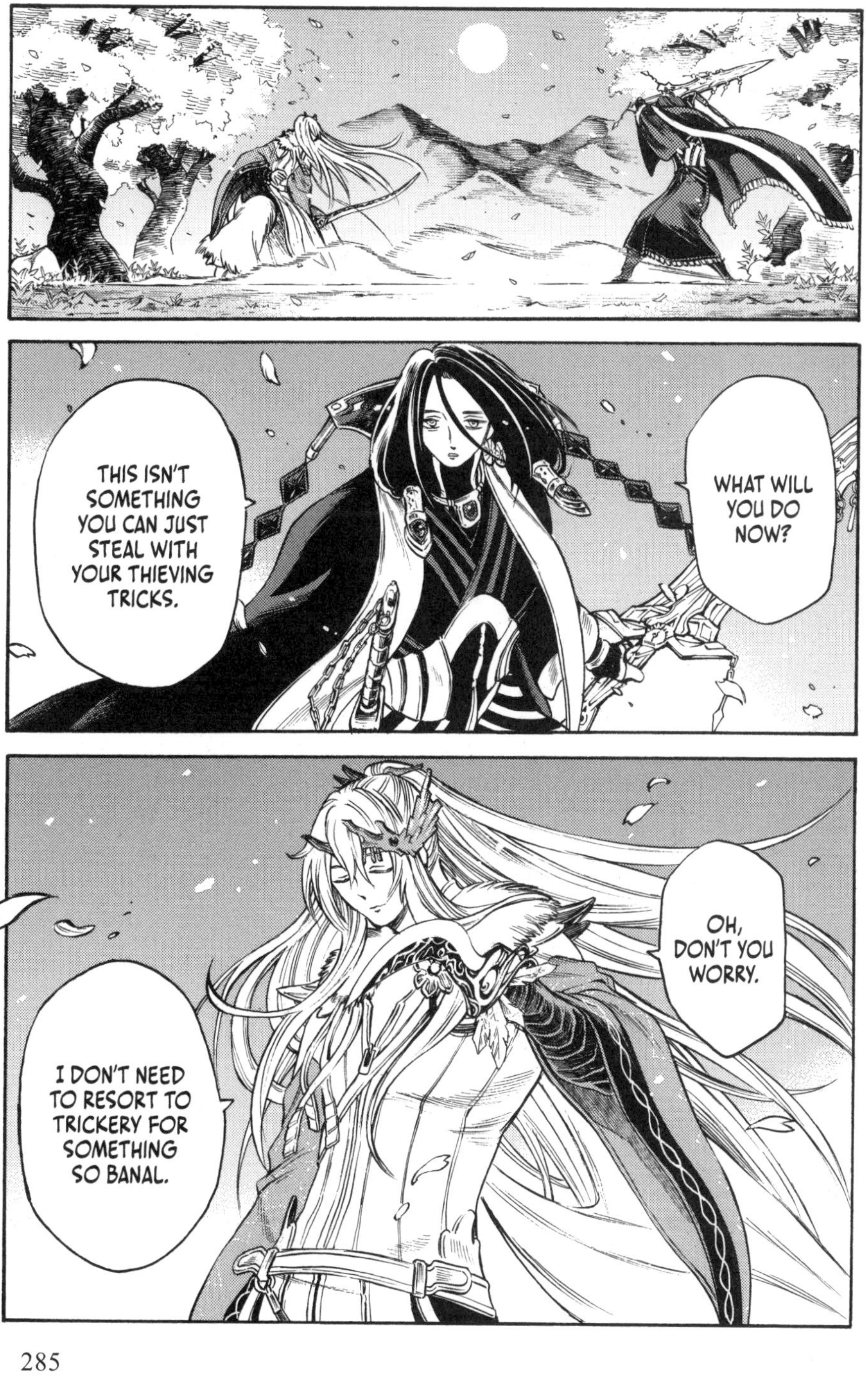
WHAT WILL YOU DO NOW?
THIS ISN'T SOMETHING YOU CAN JUST STEAL WITH YOUR THIEVING TRICKS.
OH, DON'T YOU WORRY.
I DON'T NEED TO RESORT TO TRICKERY FOR SOMETHING SO BANAL.

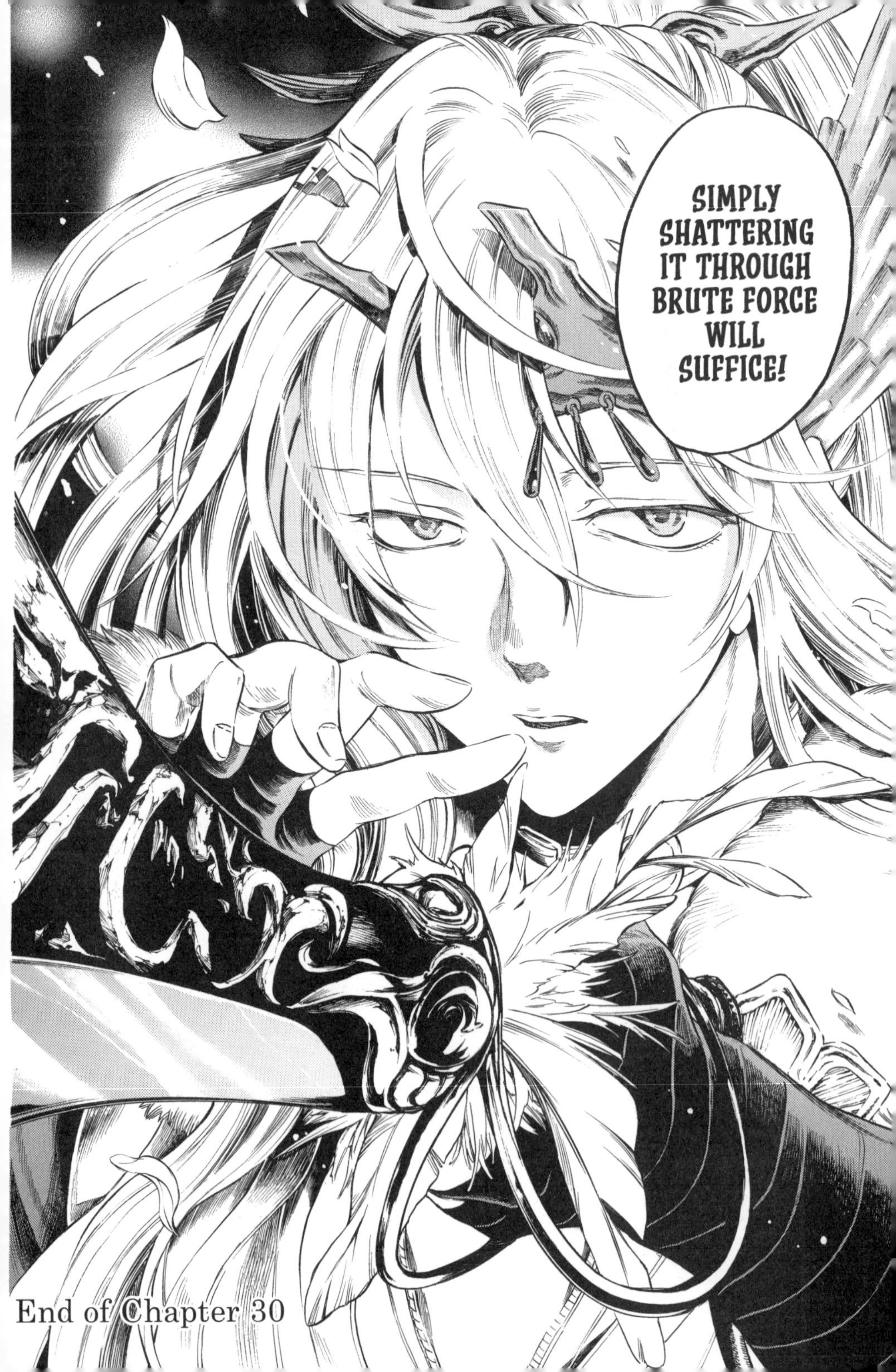
SIMPLY SHATTERING IT THROUGH BRUTE FORCE WILL SUFFICE!
End of Chapter 30

Character Designs

Here are a few character designs drawn by Yui Sakuma before the serialization of the manga began!

Shou Yun Xiao

Xing Hai

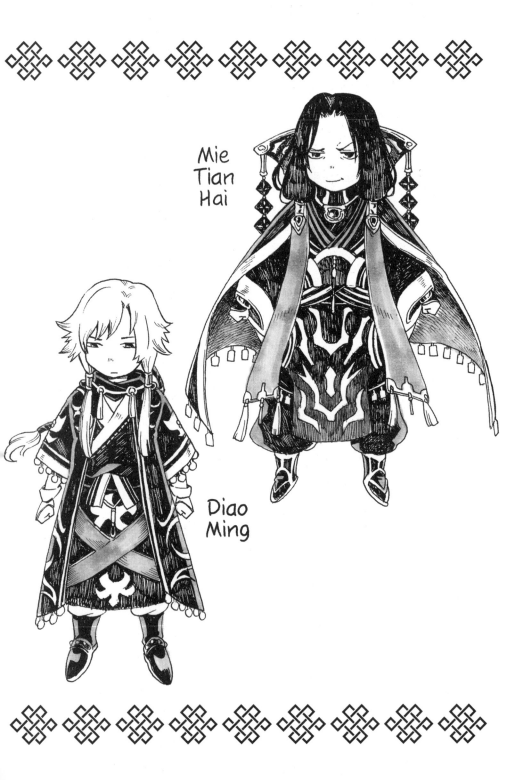

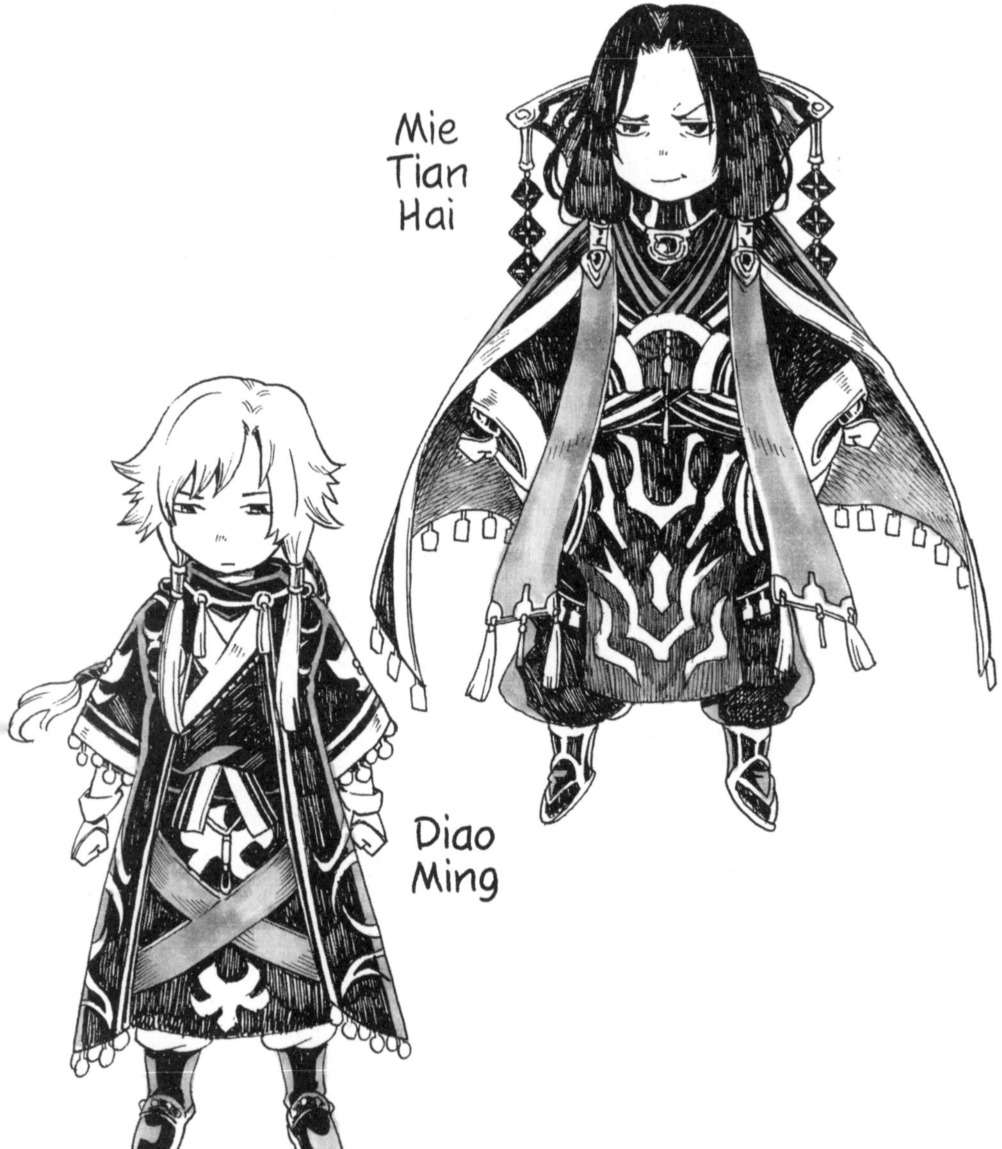
Mie Tian Hai
Diao Ming

Chapter 31

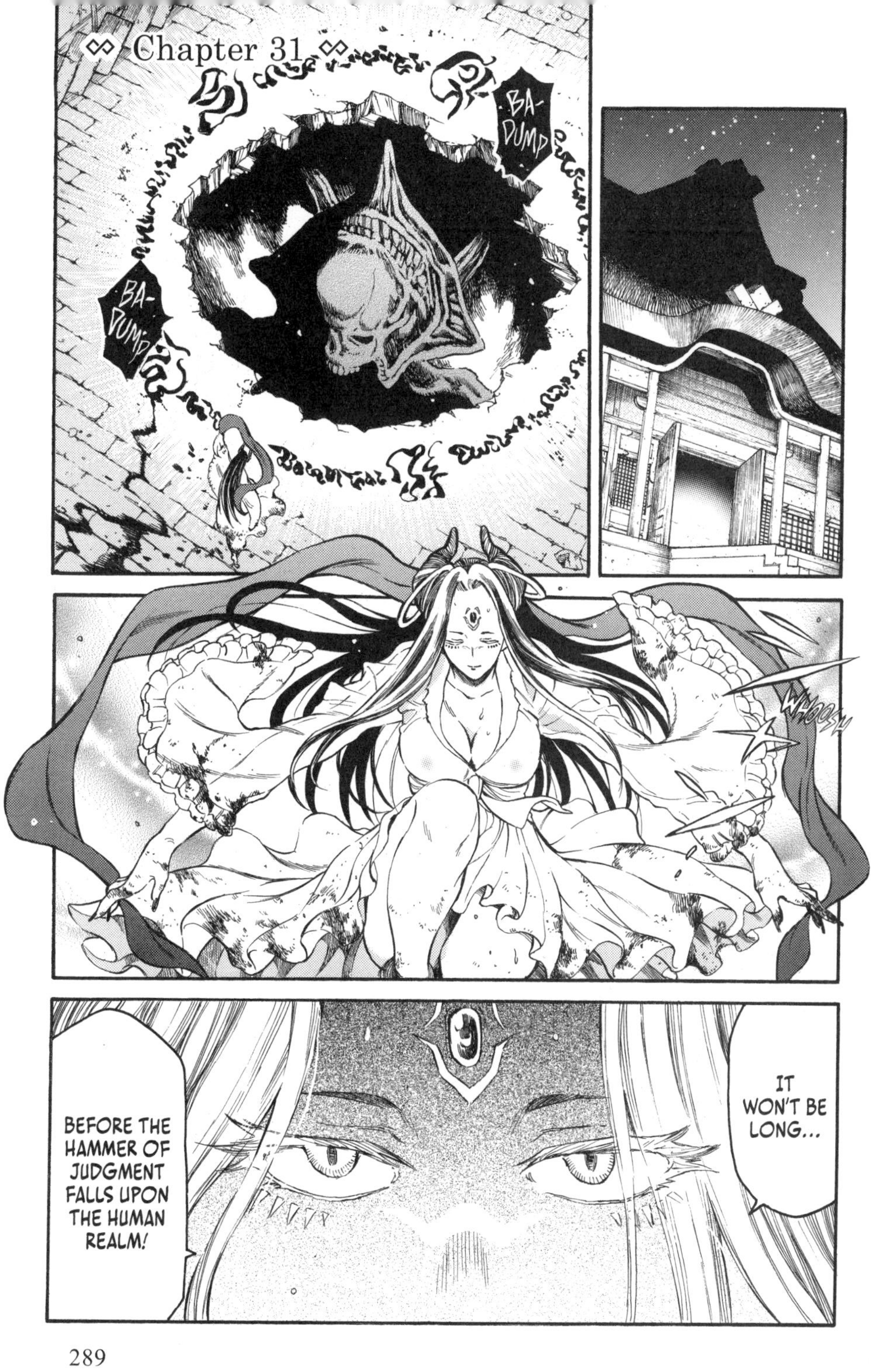
BA-DUMP
BA-DUMP
WHOOSH
IT WON'T BE LONG...
BEFORE THE HAMMER OF JUDGMENT FALLS UPON THE HUMAN REALM!

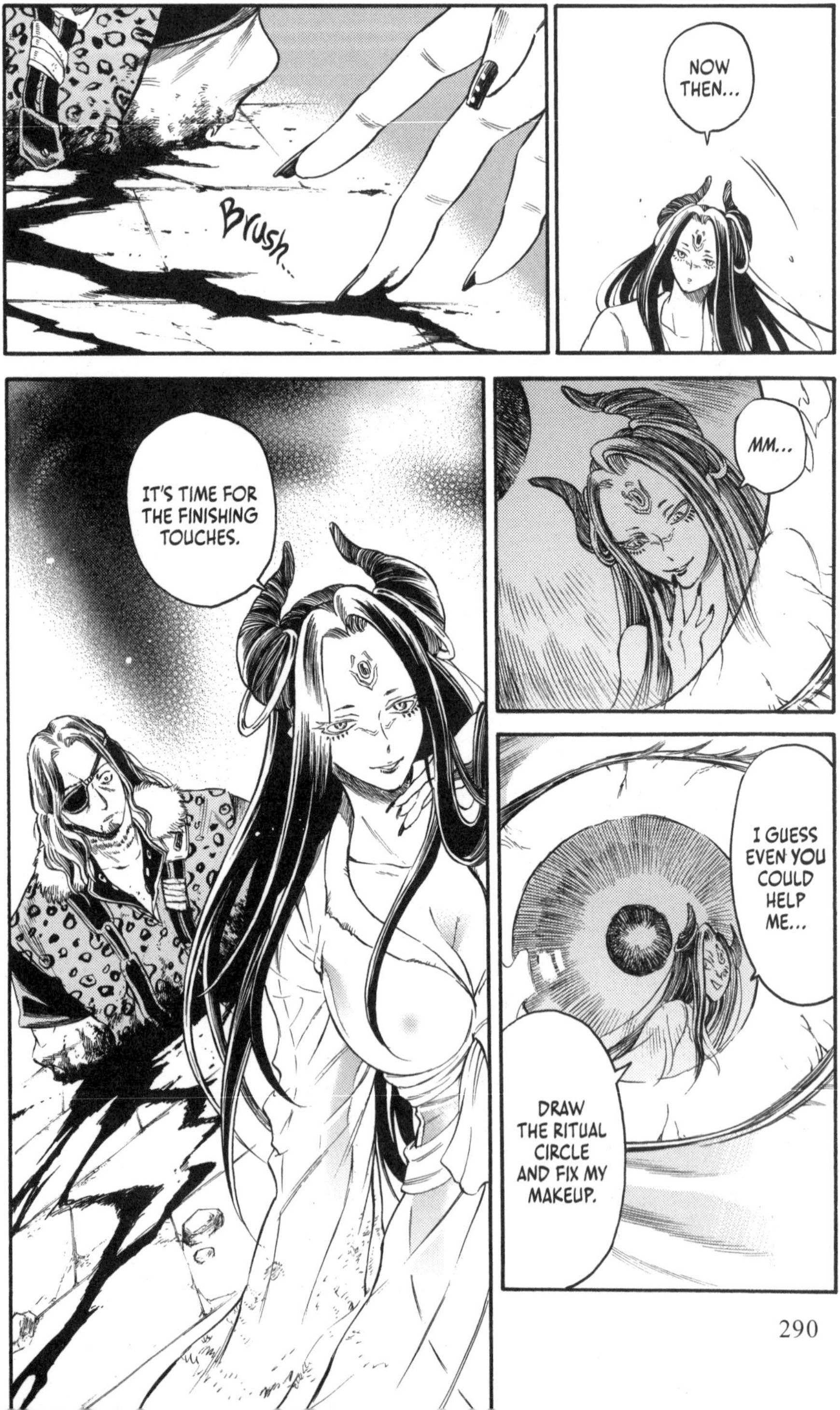
NOW THEN...
Brush...
MM...
I GUESS EVEN YOU COULD HELP ME...
DRAW THE RITUAL CIRCLE AND FIX MY MAKEUP.
IT'S TIME FOR THE FINISHING TOUCHES.

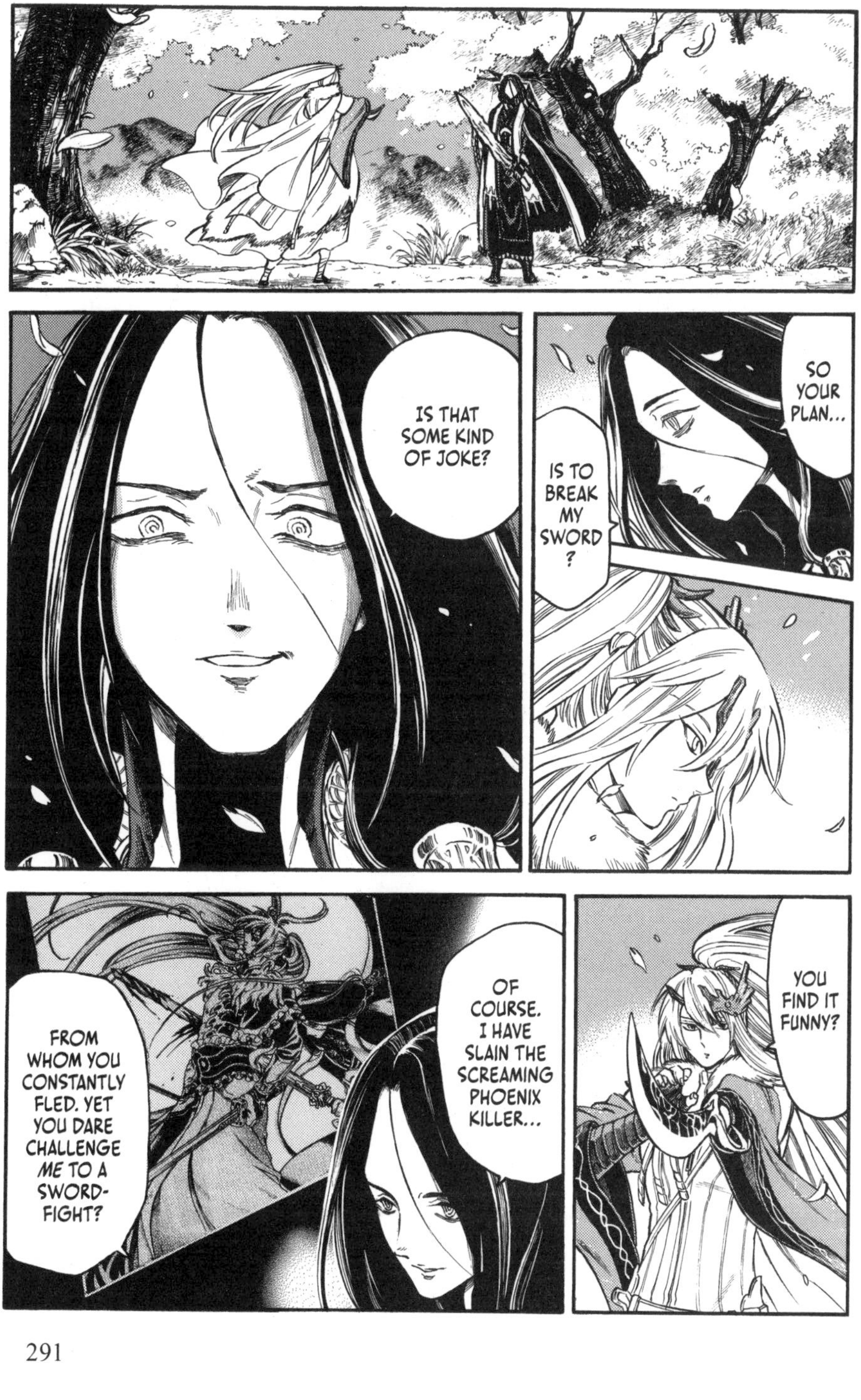
SO YOUR PLAN...
IS TO BREAK MY SWORD?
IS THAT SOME KIND OF JOKE?
YOU FIND IT FUNNY?
OF COURSE. I HAVE SLAIN THE SCREAMING PHOENIX KILLER...
FROM WHOM YOU CONSTANTLY FLED. YET YOU DARE CHALLENGE *ME* TO A SWORD-FIGHT?

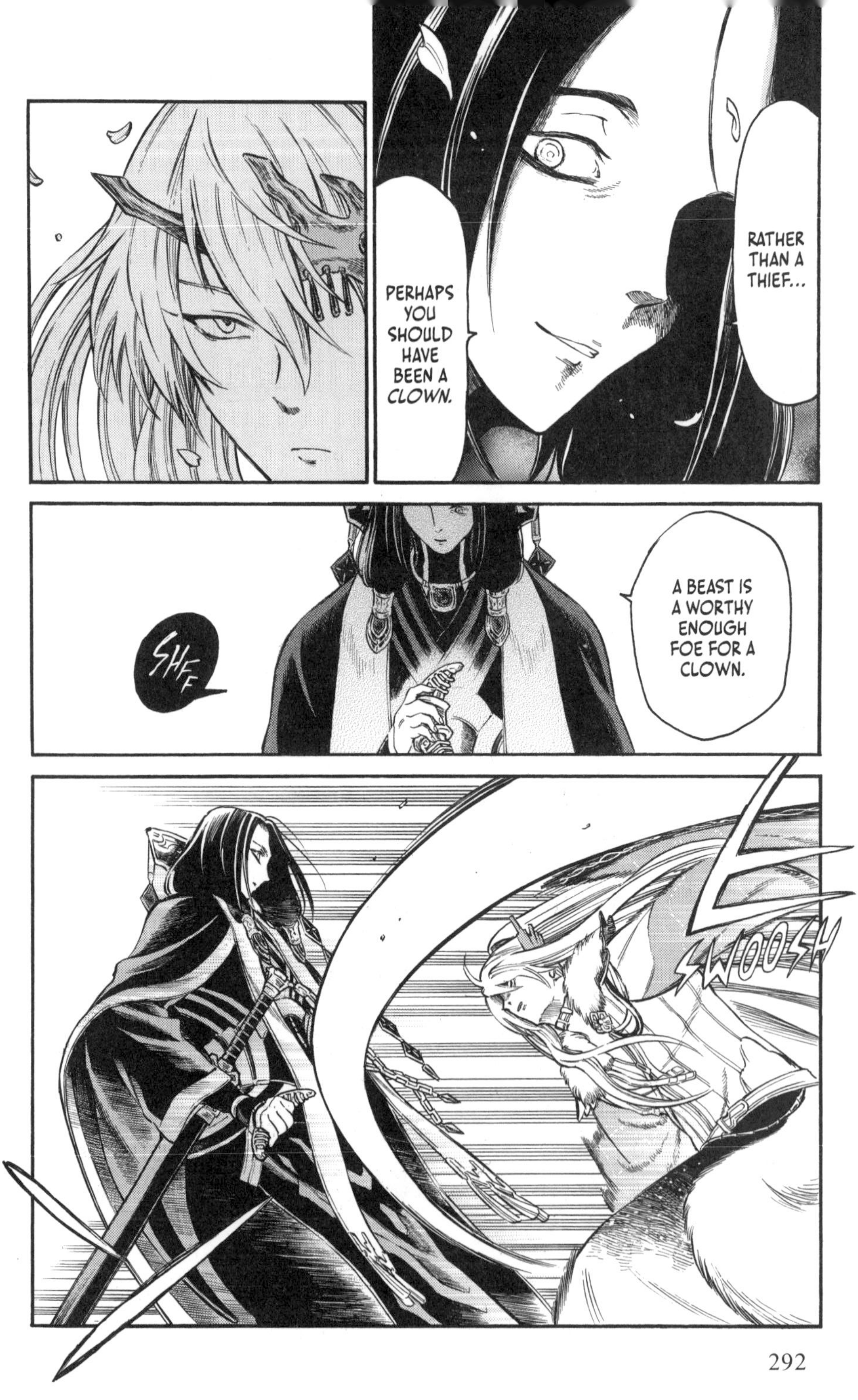
RATHER THAN A THIEF...
PERHAPS YOU SHOULD HAVE BEEN A *CLOWN.*
A BEAST IS A WORTHY ENOUGH FOE FOR A CLOWN.
SHFF
SWOOSH

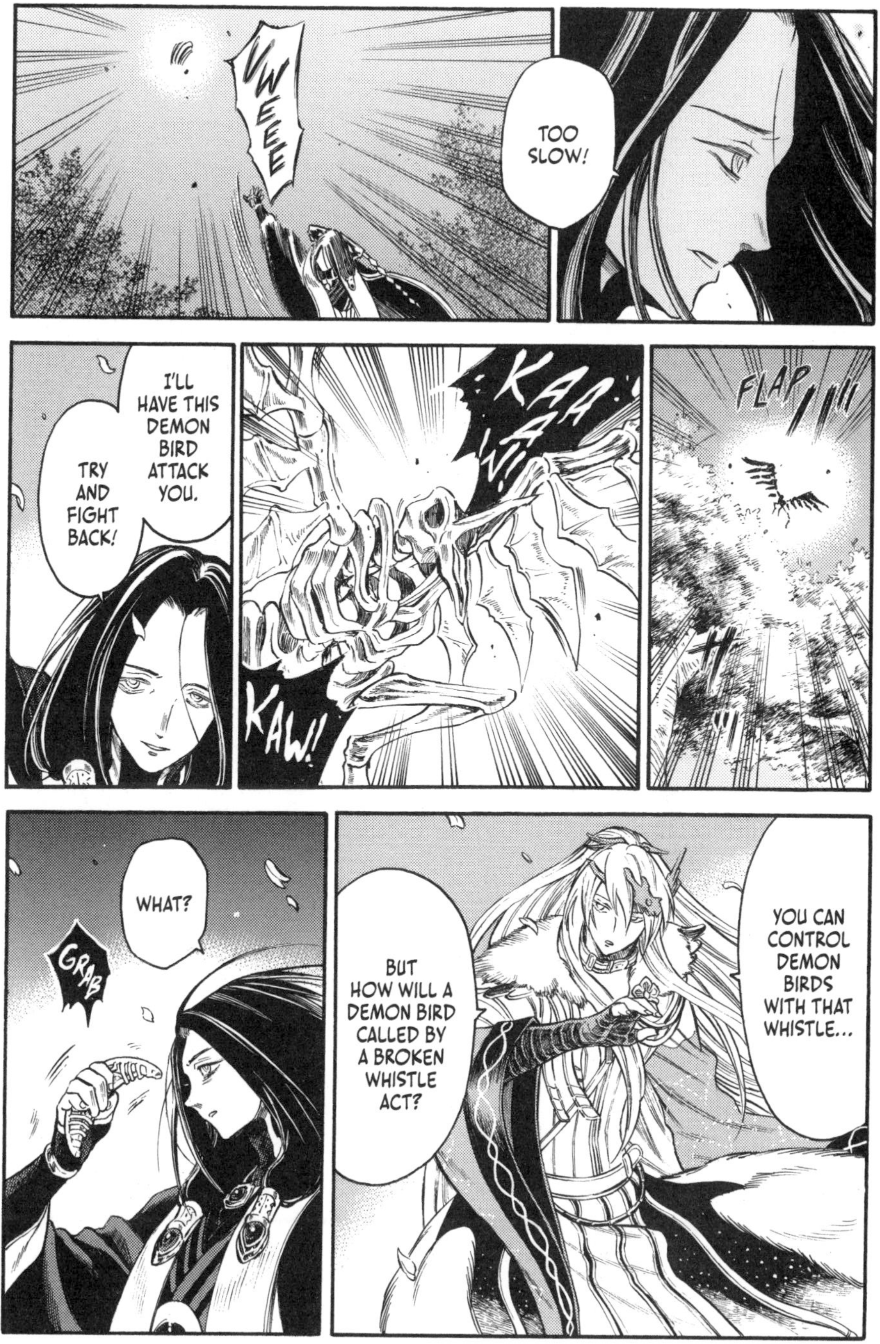
TOO SLOW!
UWEEE
FLAP
KAAAN!
KAW!
I'LL HAVE THIS DEMON BIRD ATTACK YOU.
TRY AND FIGHT BACK!
YOU CAN CONTROL DEMON BIRDS WITH THAT WHISTLE...
BUT HOW WILL A DEMON BIRD CALLED BY A BROKEN WHISTLE ACT?
WHAT?
GRAB

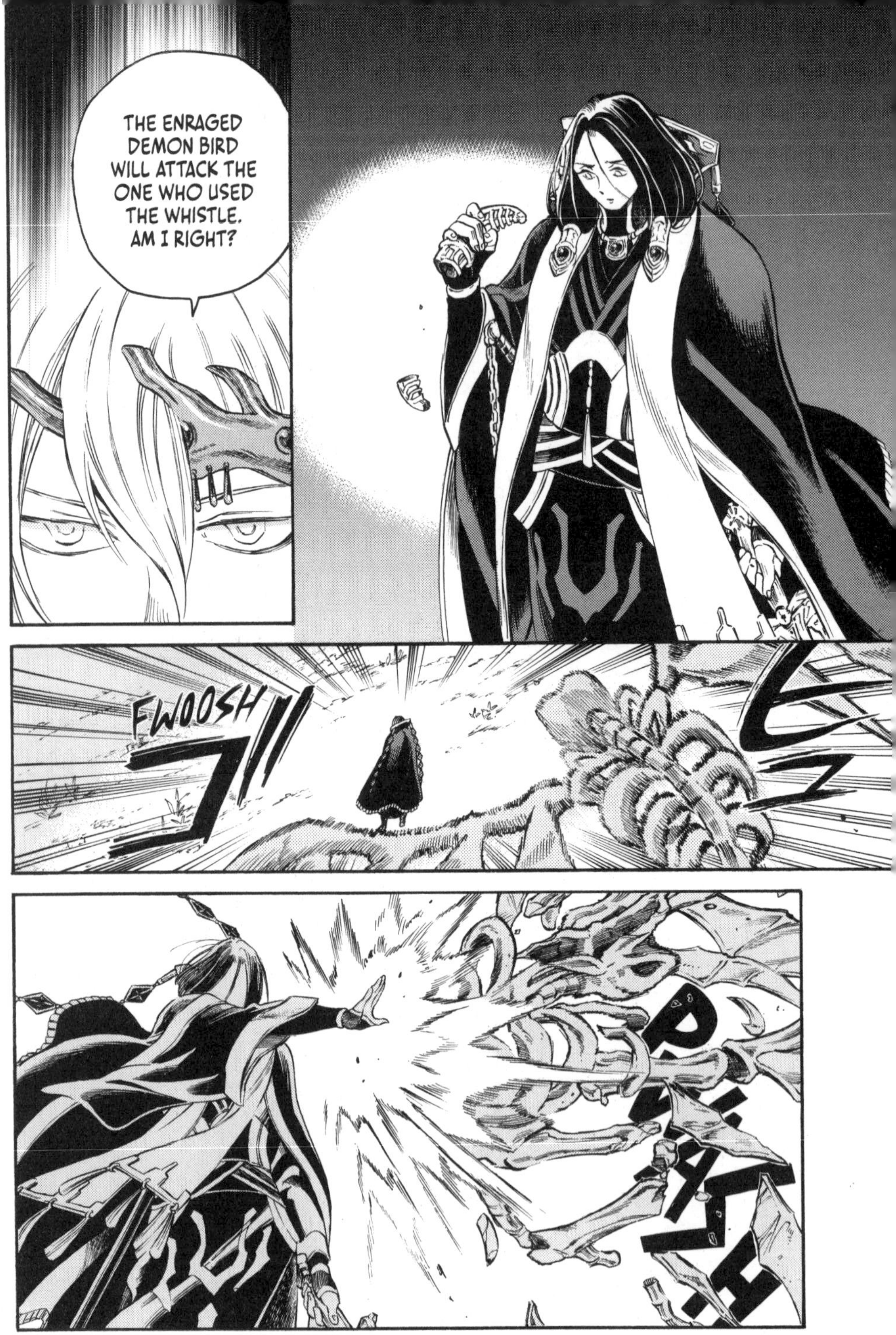
THE ENRAGED DEMON BIRD WILL ATTACK THE ONE WHO USED THE WHISTLE. AM I RIGHT?
FWOOSH

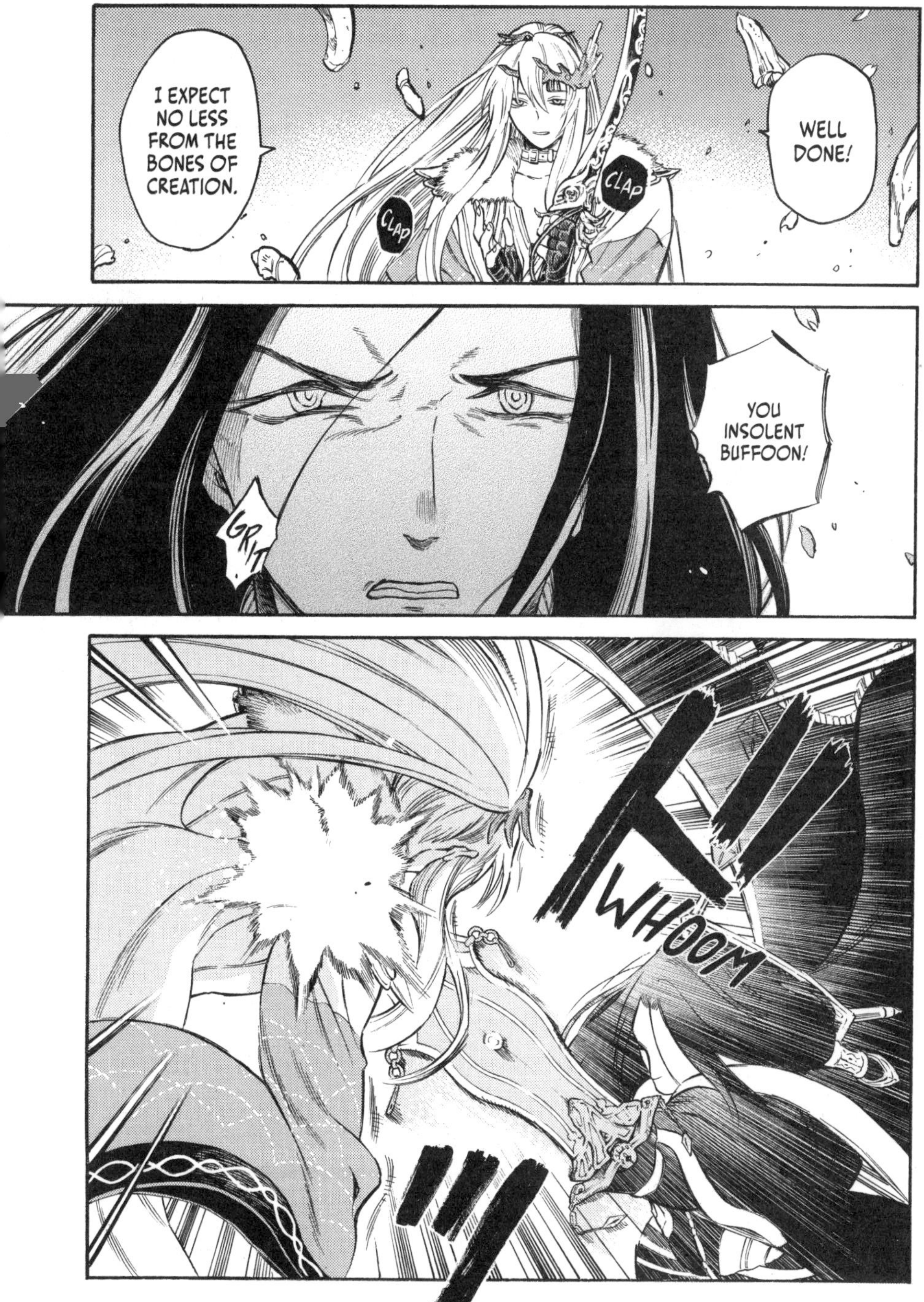
WELL DONE!
CLAP
CLAP
I EXPECT NO LESS FROM THE BONES OF CREATION.
YOU INSOLENT BUFFOON!
GRIT
WHOOM

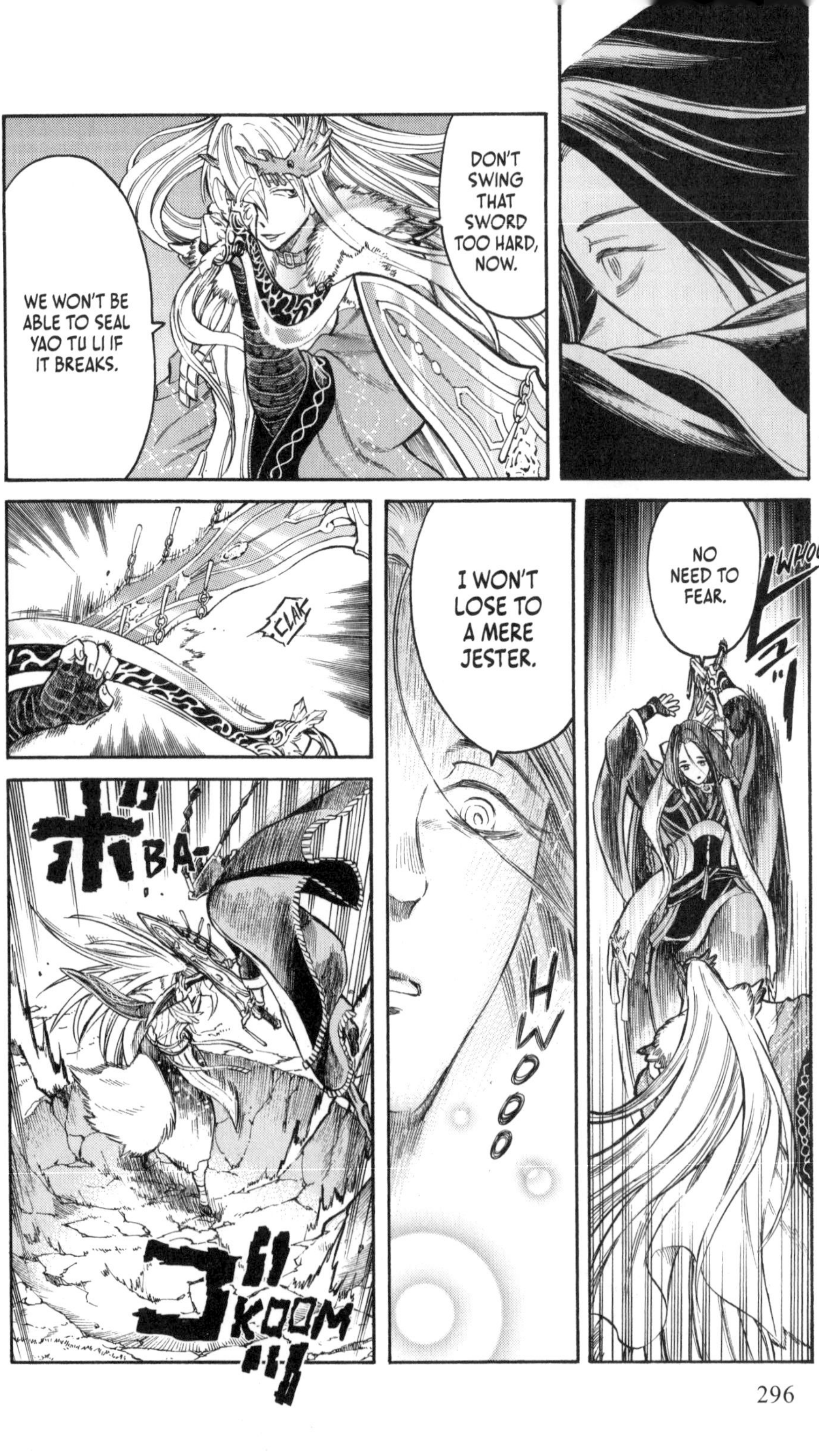
DON'T SWING THAT SWORD TOO HARD, NOW.
WE WON'T BE ABLE TO SEAL YAO TU LI IF IT BREAKS.
NO NEED TO FEAR.
WHOOSH
I WON'T LOSE TO A MERE JESTER.
HWOOOO
CLAK
BA-
KOOM

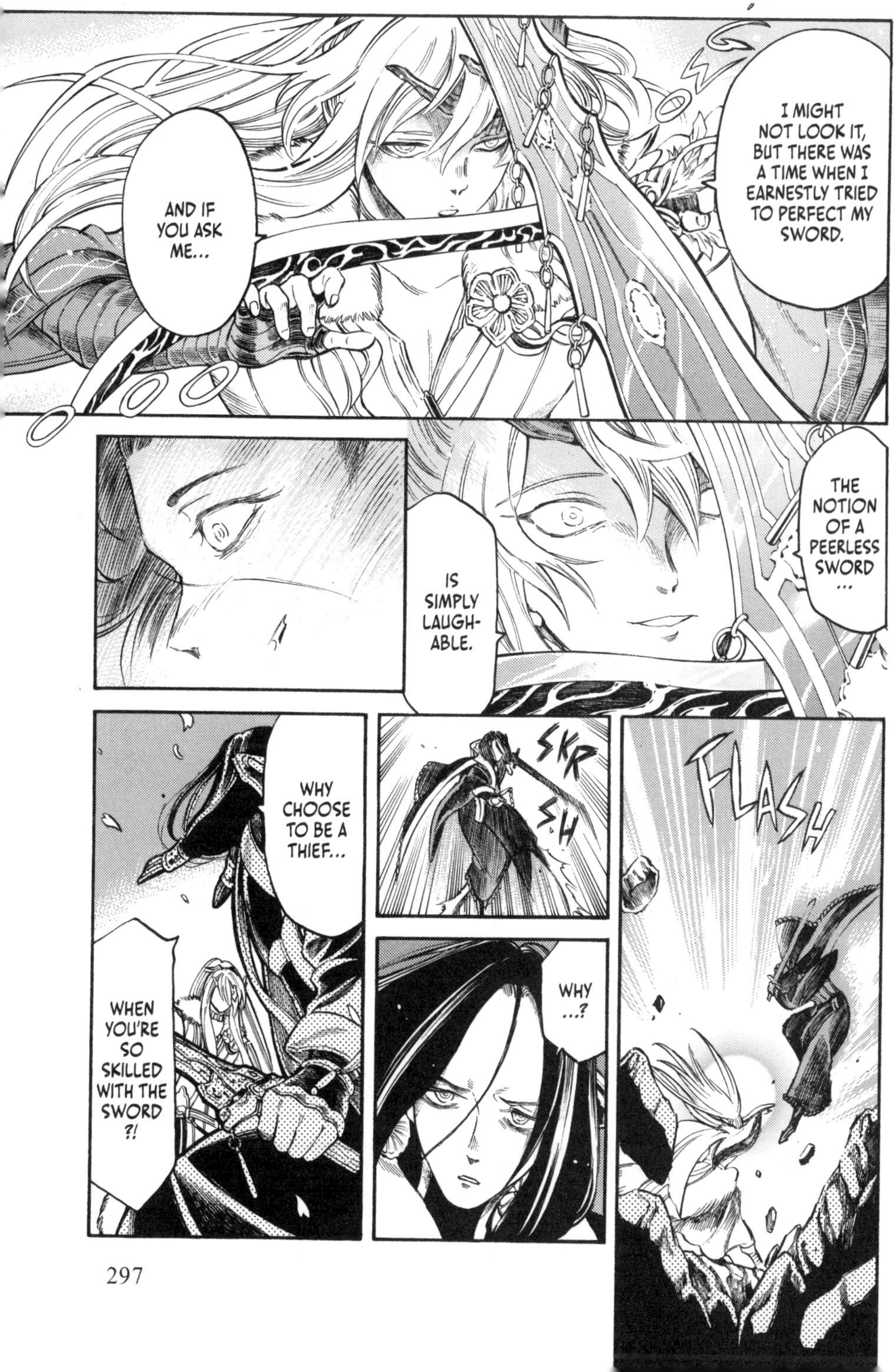
I MIGHT NOT LOOK IT, BUT THERE WAS A TIME WHEN I EARNESTLY TRIED TO PERFECT MY SWORD.
AND IF YOU ASK ME...
THE NOTION OF A PEERLESS SWORD...
IS SIMPLY LAUGHABLE.
FLASH
SKR SH
WHY ...?
WHY CHOOSE TO BE A THIEF...
WHEN YOU'RE SO SKILLED WITH THE SWORD?!

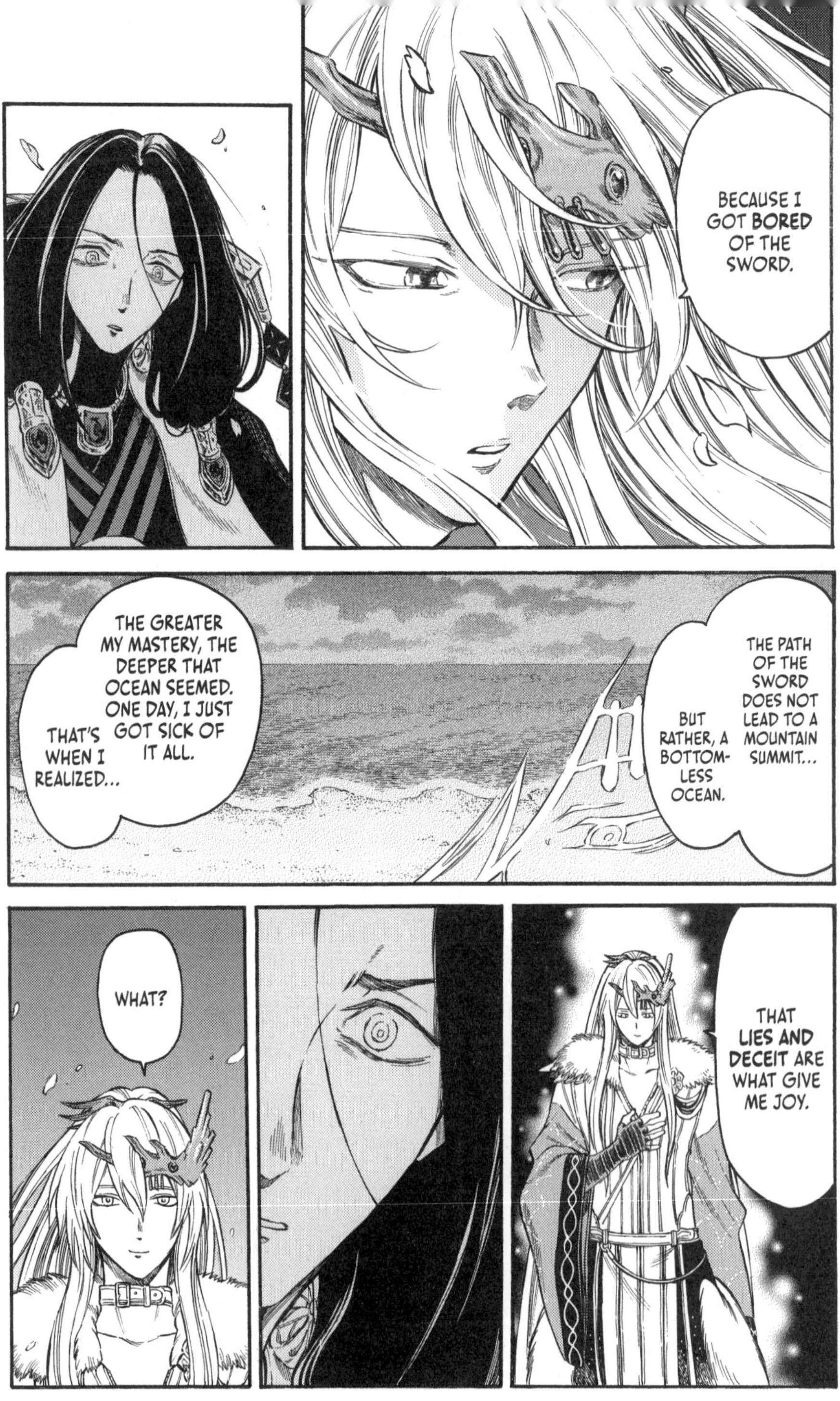
BECAUSE I GOT **BORED** OF THE SWORD.
THE PATH OF THE SWORD DOES NOT LEAD TO A MOUNTAIN SUMMIT...
BUT RATHER, A BOTTOMLESS OCEAN.
THE GREATER MY MASTERY, THE DEEPER THAT OCEAN SEEMED. ONE DAY, I JUST GOT SICK OF IT ALL.
THAT'S WHEN I REALIZED...
THAT **LIES AND DECEIT** ARE WHAT GIVE ME JOY.
WHAT?

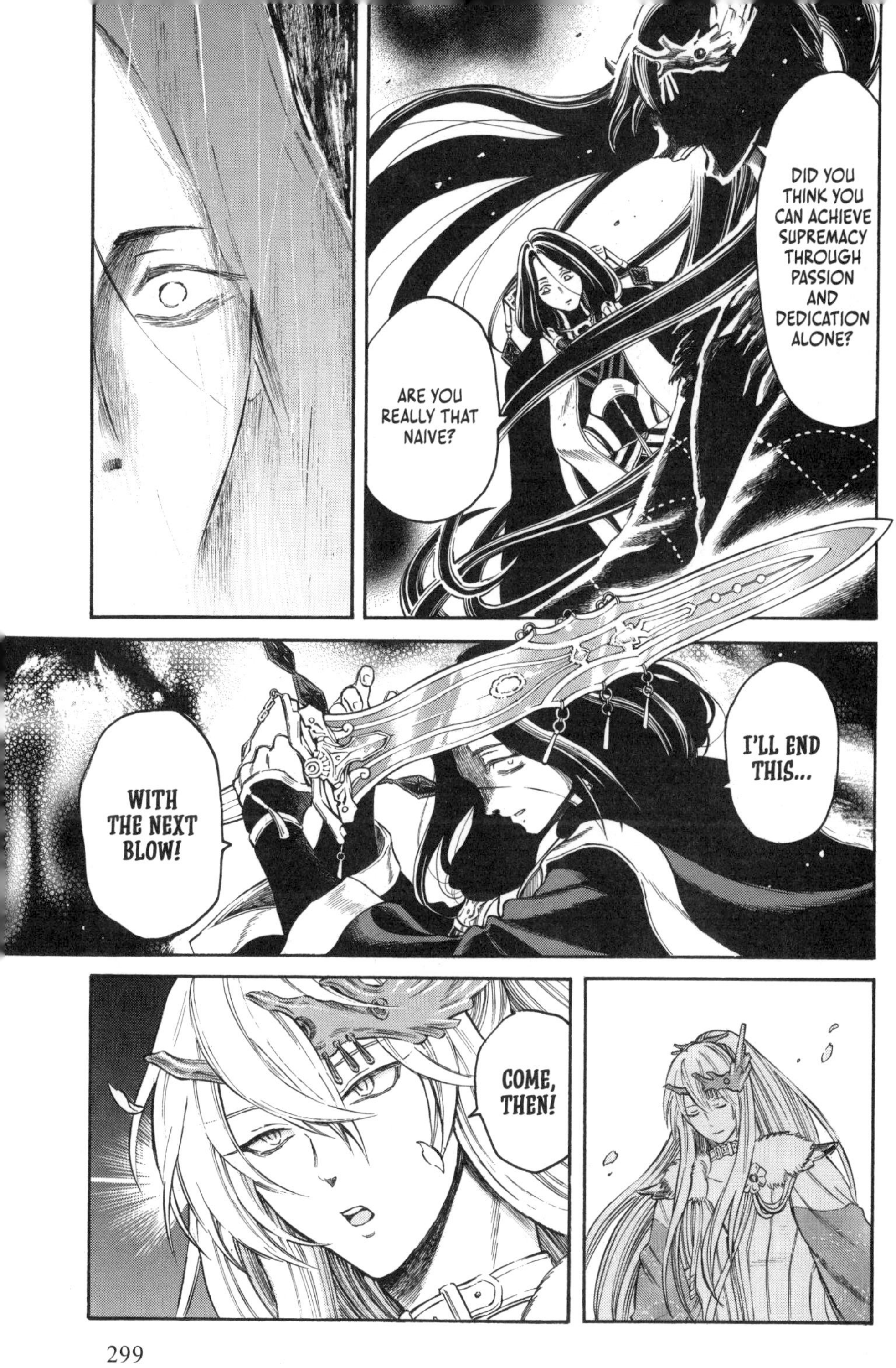
DID YOU THINK YOU CAN ACHIEVE SUPREMACY THROUGH PASSION AND DEDICATION ALONE?
ARE YOU REALLY THAT NAIVE?
I'LL END THIS...
WITH THE NEXT BLOW!
COME, THEN!

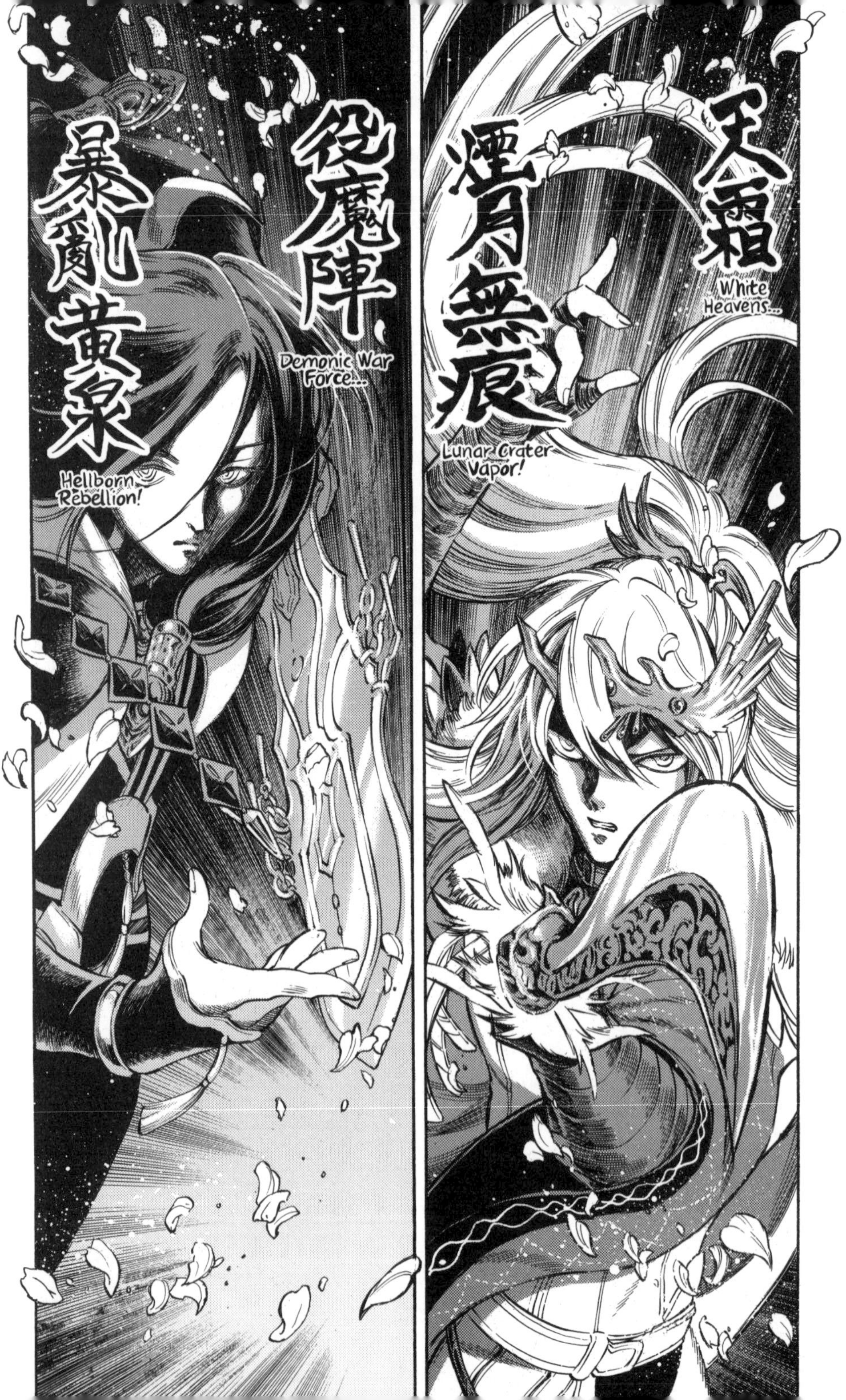
天霜
White Heavens...
湮月無痕
Lunar Crater Vapor!
殺魔陣
Demonic War Force...
暴亂黃泉
Hellborn Rebellion!

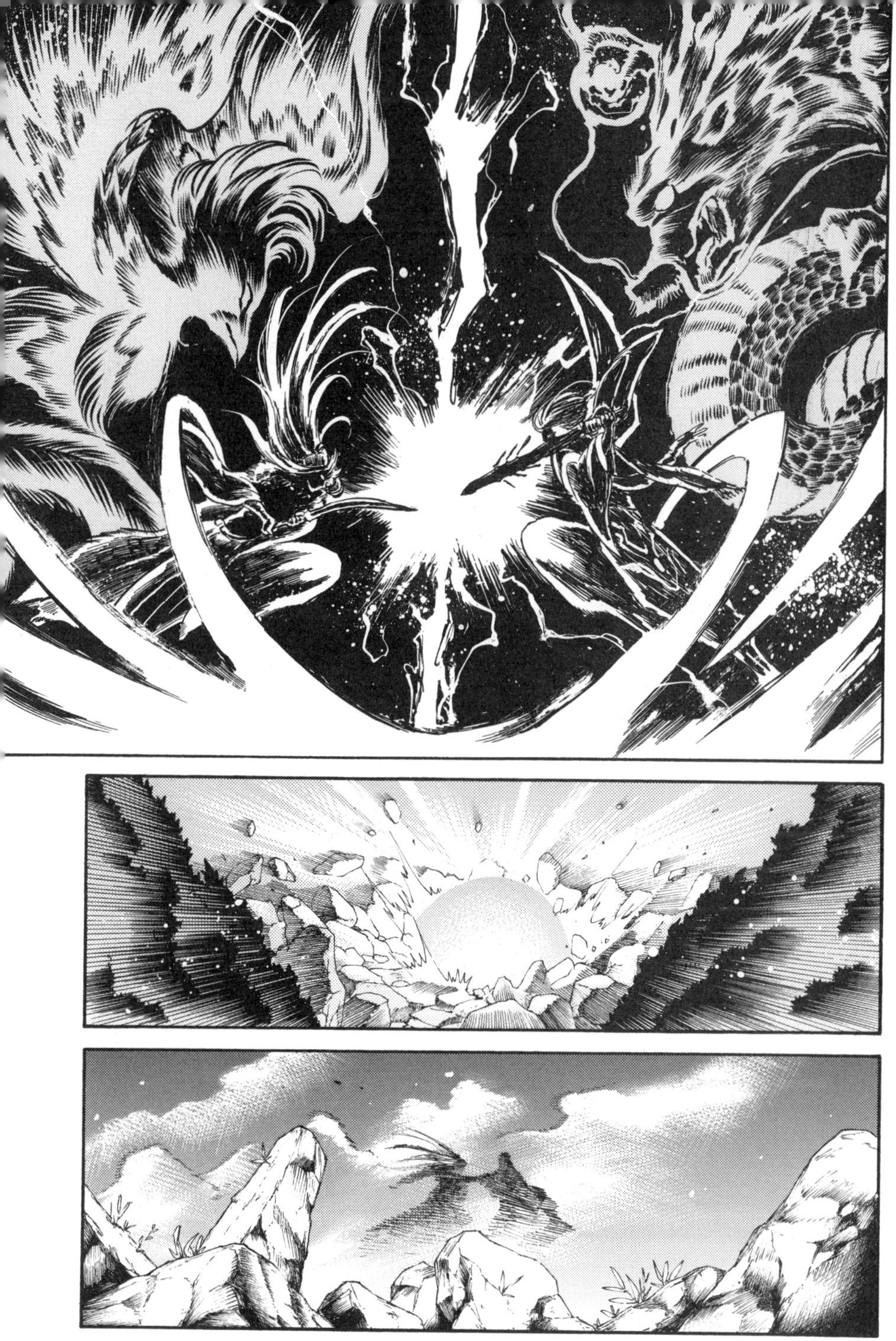

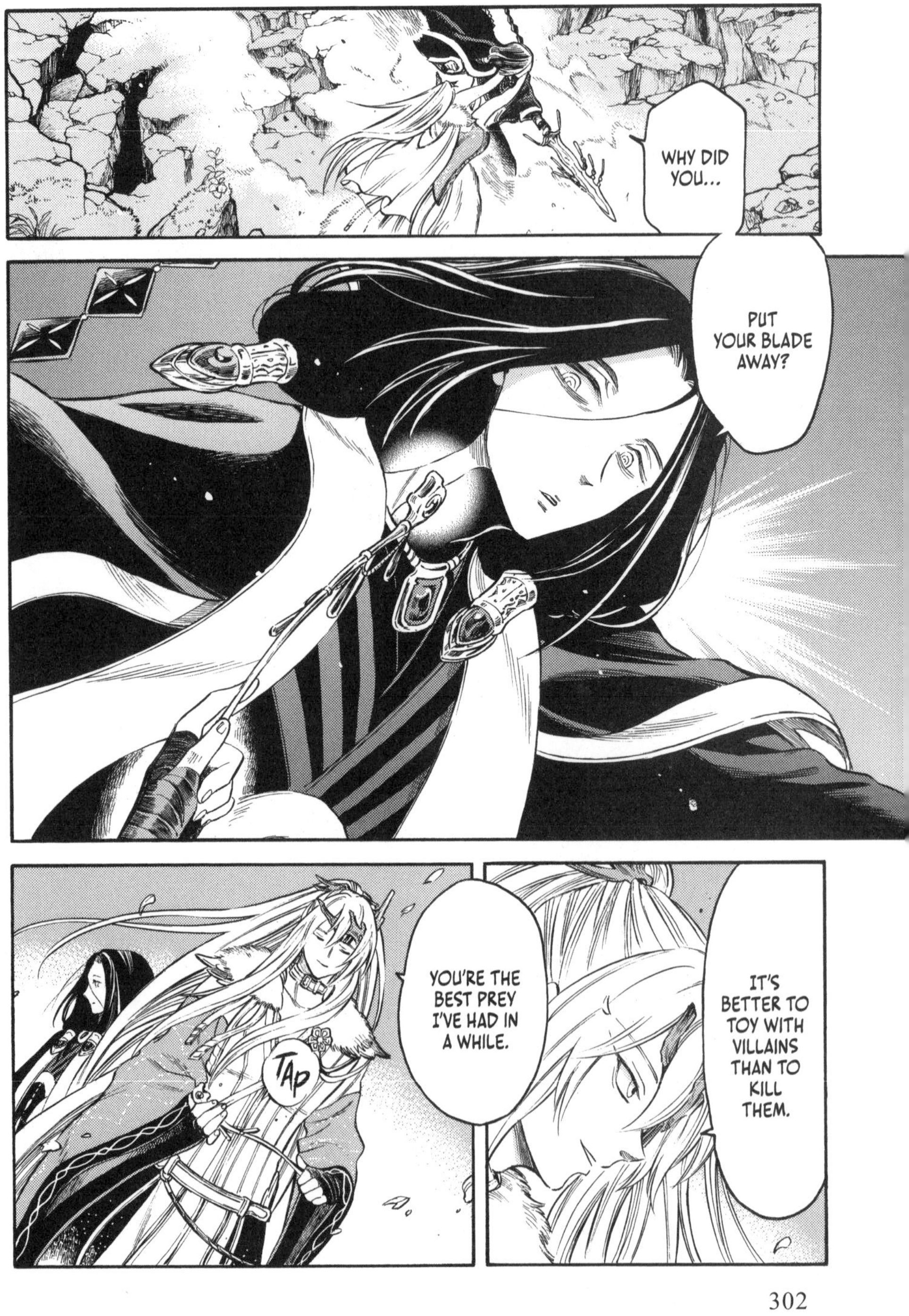
WHY DID YOU...
PUT YOUR BLADE AWAY?
IT'S BETTER TO TOY WITH VILLAINS THAN TO KILL THEM.
YOU'RE THE BEST PREY I'VE HAD IN A WHILE.
TAP

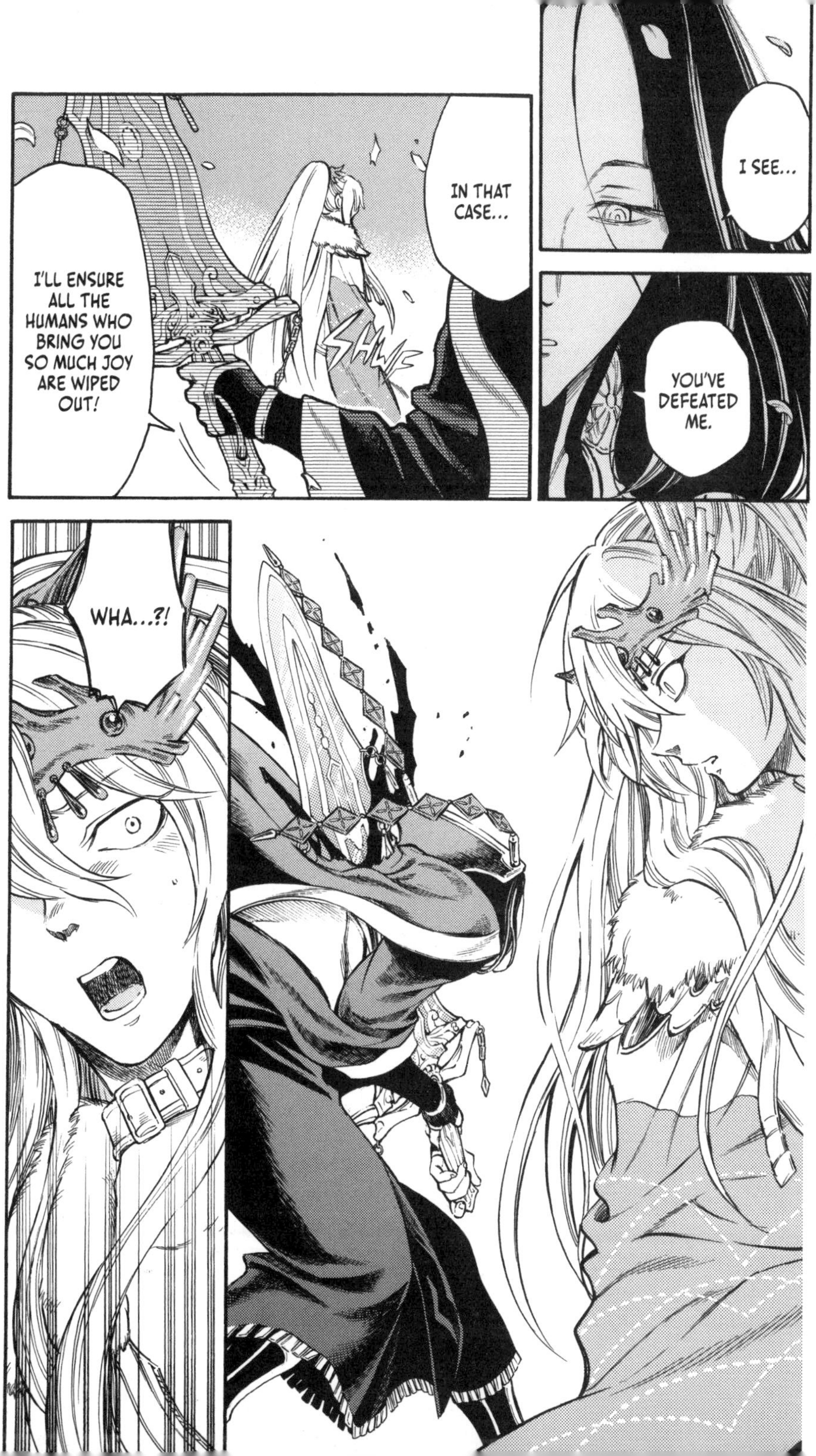
I SEE...
YOU'VE DEFEATED ME.
IN THAT CASE...
I'LL ENSURE ALL THE HUMANS WHO BRING YOU SO MUCH JOY ARE WIPED OUT!
WHA...?!

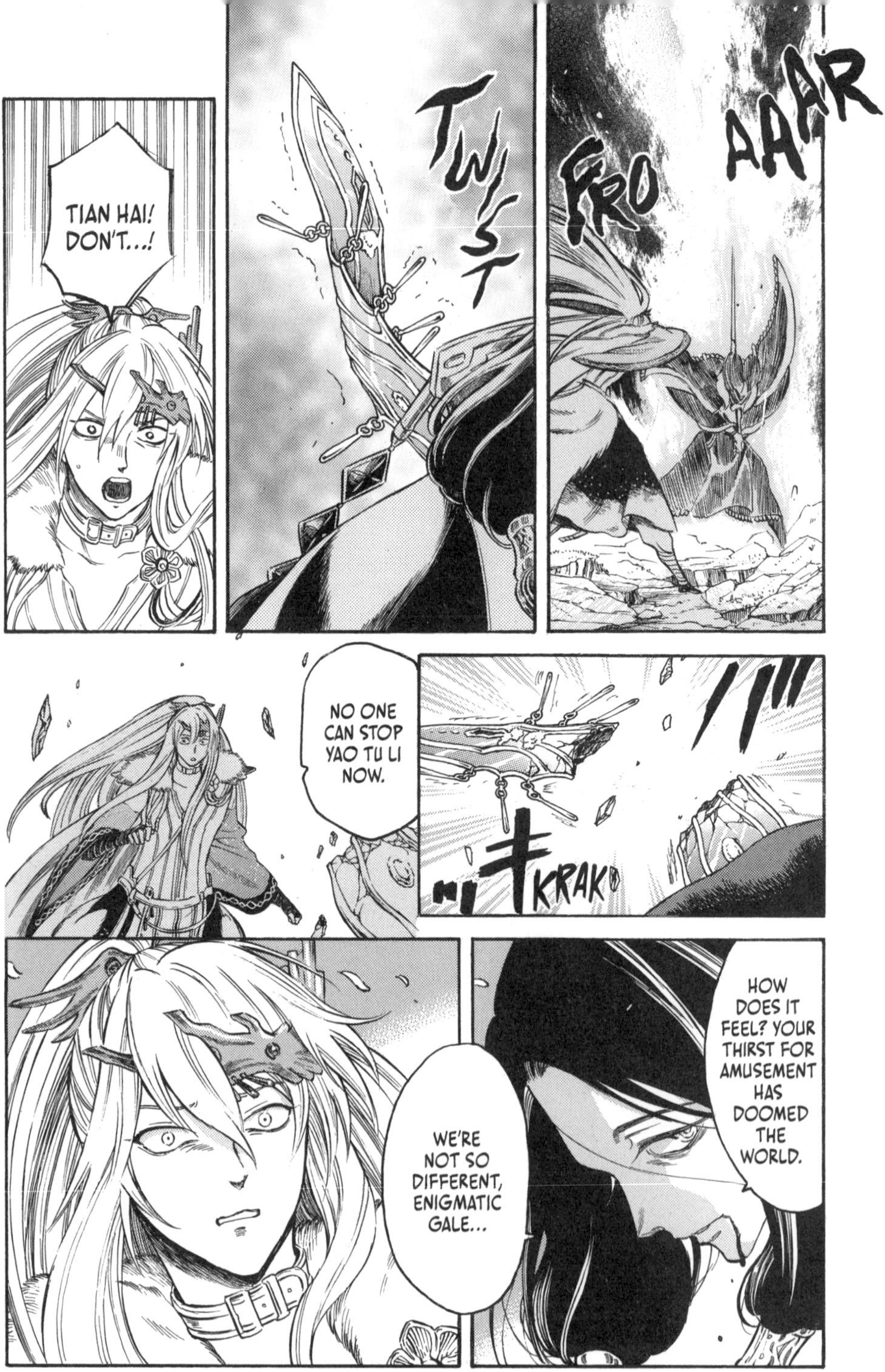
FRO AAAR
TWIST
TIAN HAI! DON'T...!
KRAK
NO ONE CAN STOP YAO TU LI NOW.
HOW DOES IT FEEL? YOUR THIRST FOR AMUSEMENT HAS DOOMED THE WORLD.
WE'RE NOT SO DIFFERENT, ENIGMATIC GALE...

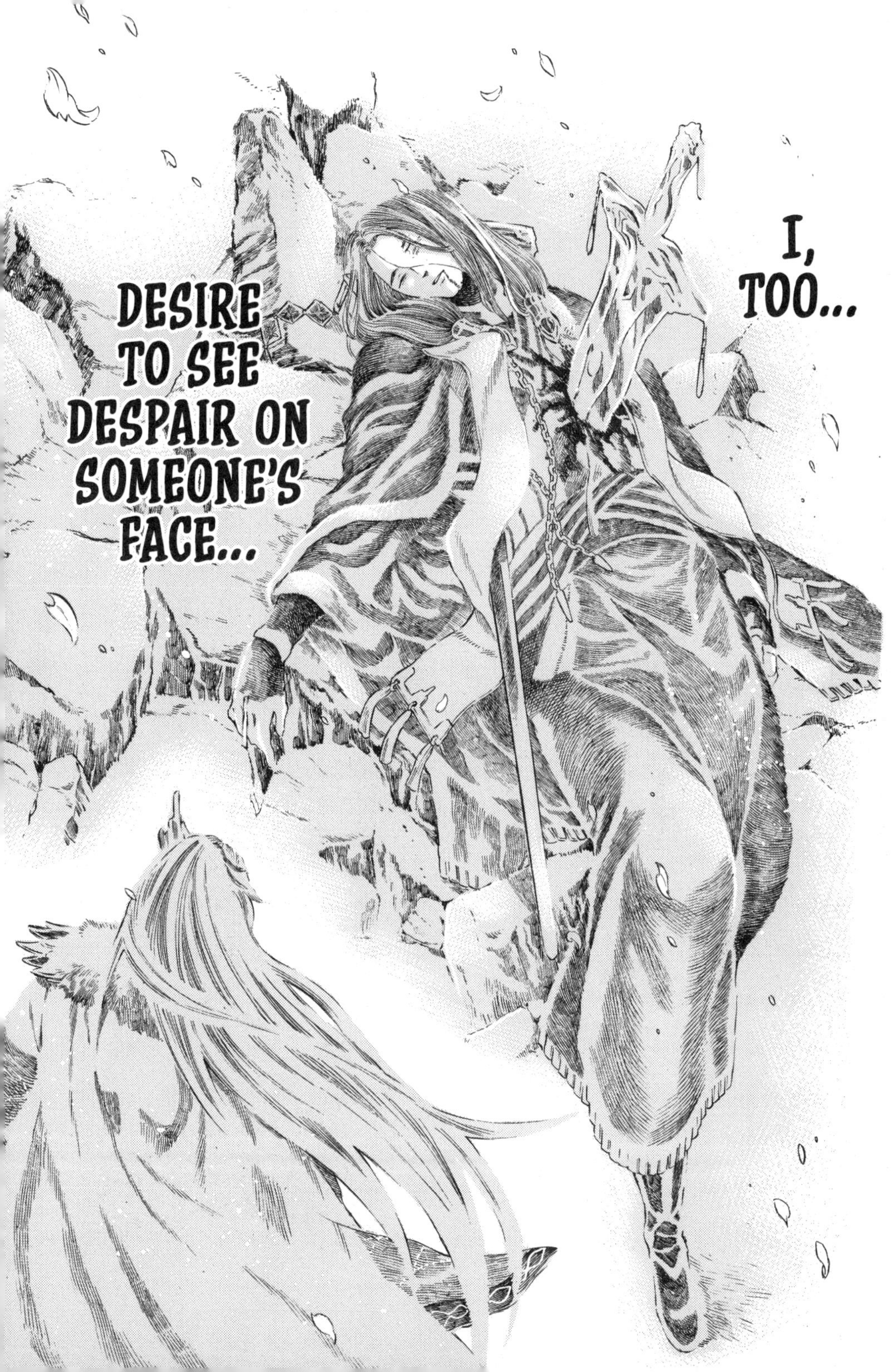
I, TOO...
DESIRE TO SEE DESPAIR ON SOMEONE'S FACE...

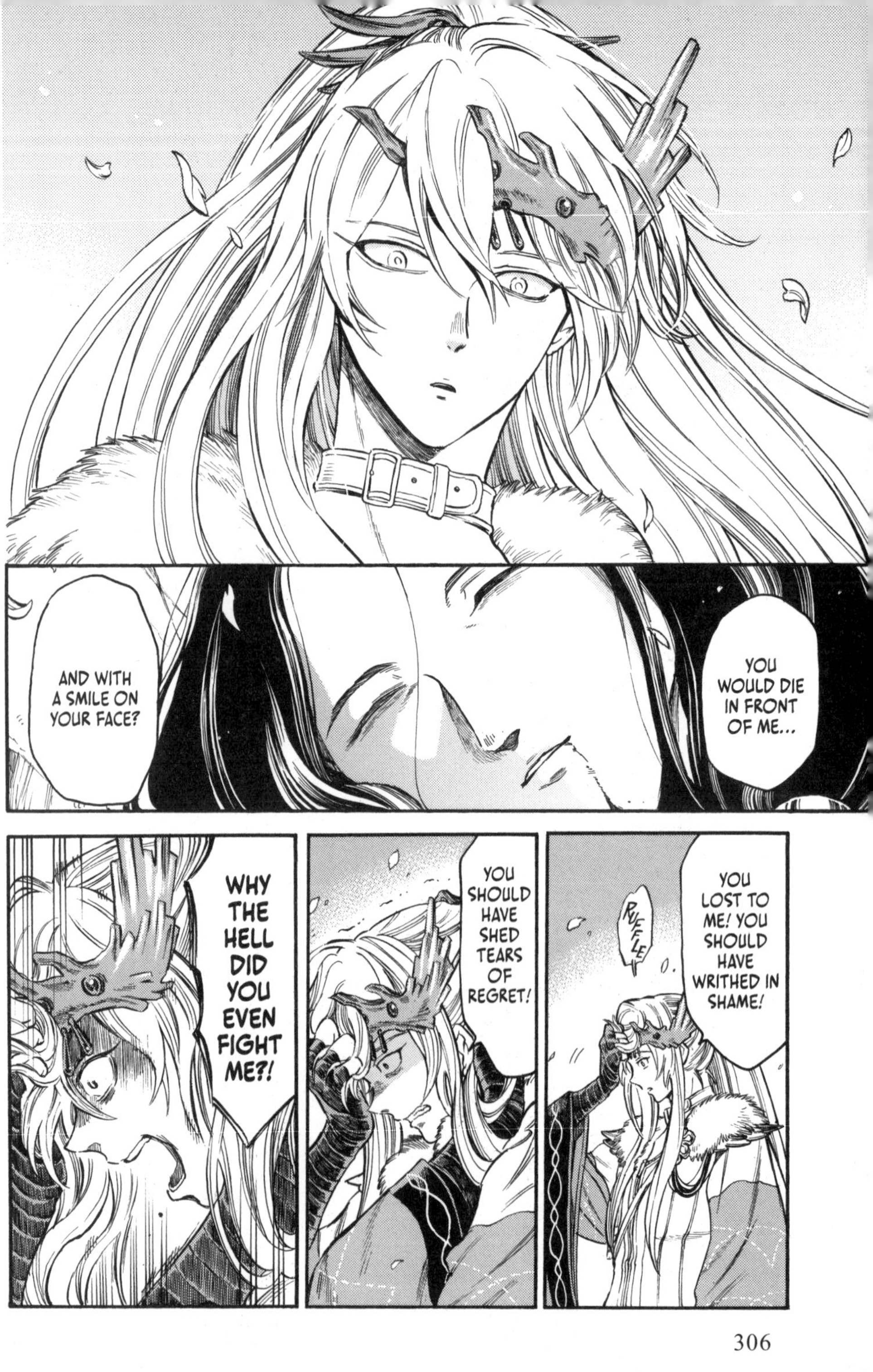
YOU WOULD DIE IN FRONT OF ME...
AND WITH A SMILE ON YOUR FACE?
YOU LOST TO ME! YOU SHOULD HAVE WRITHED IN SHAME!
RUFFLE
YOU SHOULD HAVE SHED TEARS OF REGRET!
WHY THE HELL DID YOU EVEN FIGHT ME?!

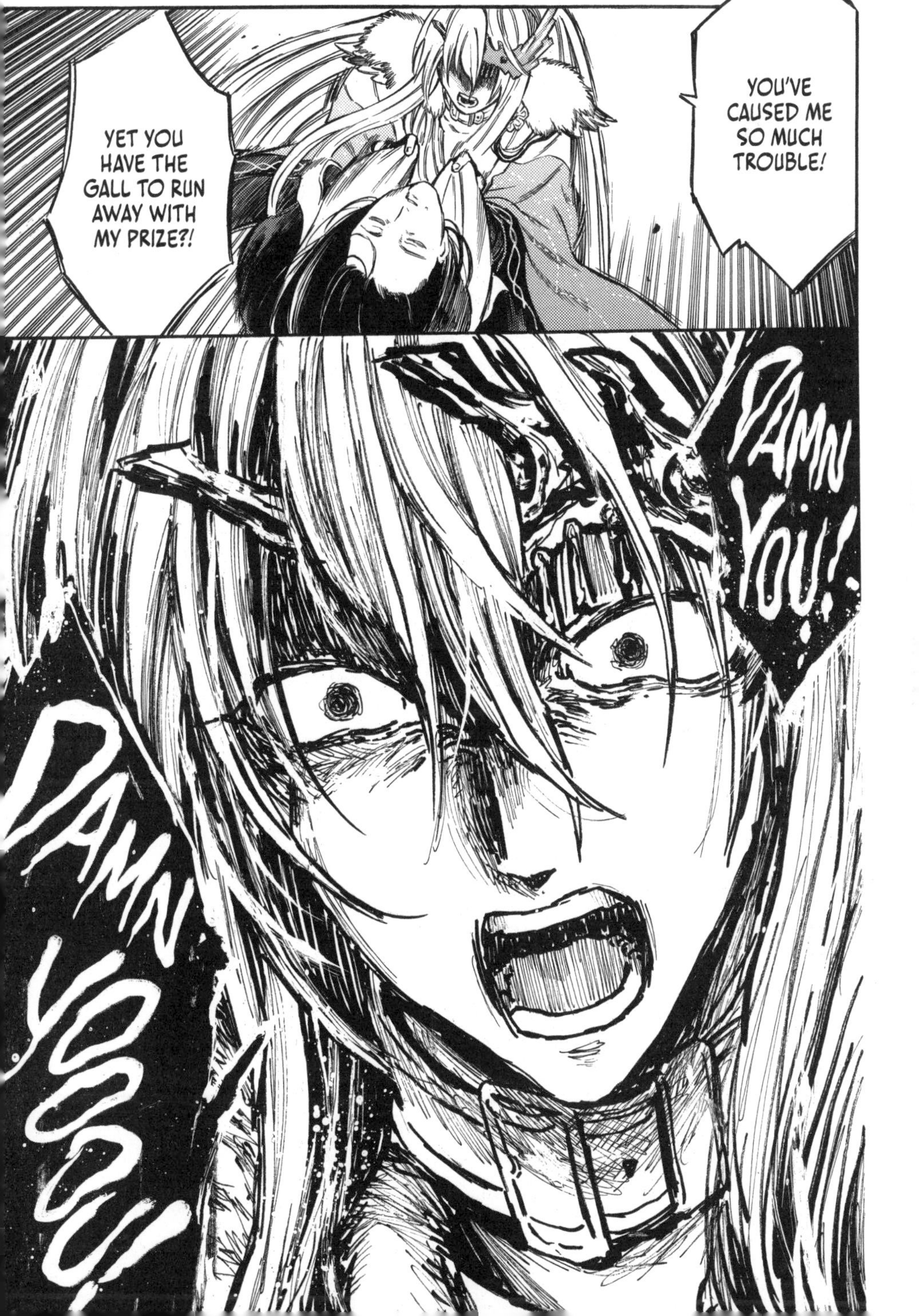
YOU'VE CAUSED ME SO MUCH TROUBLE!
YET YOU HAVE THE GALL TO RUN AWAY WITH MY PRIZE?!
DAMN YOU!
DAMN YOOOU!

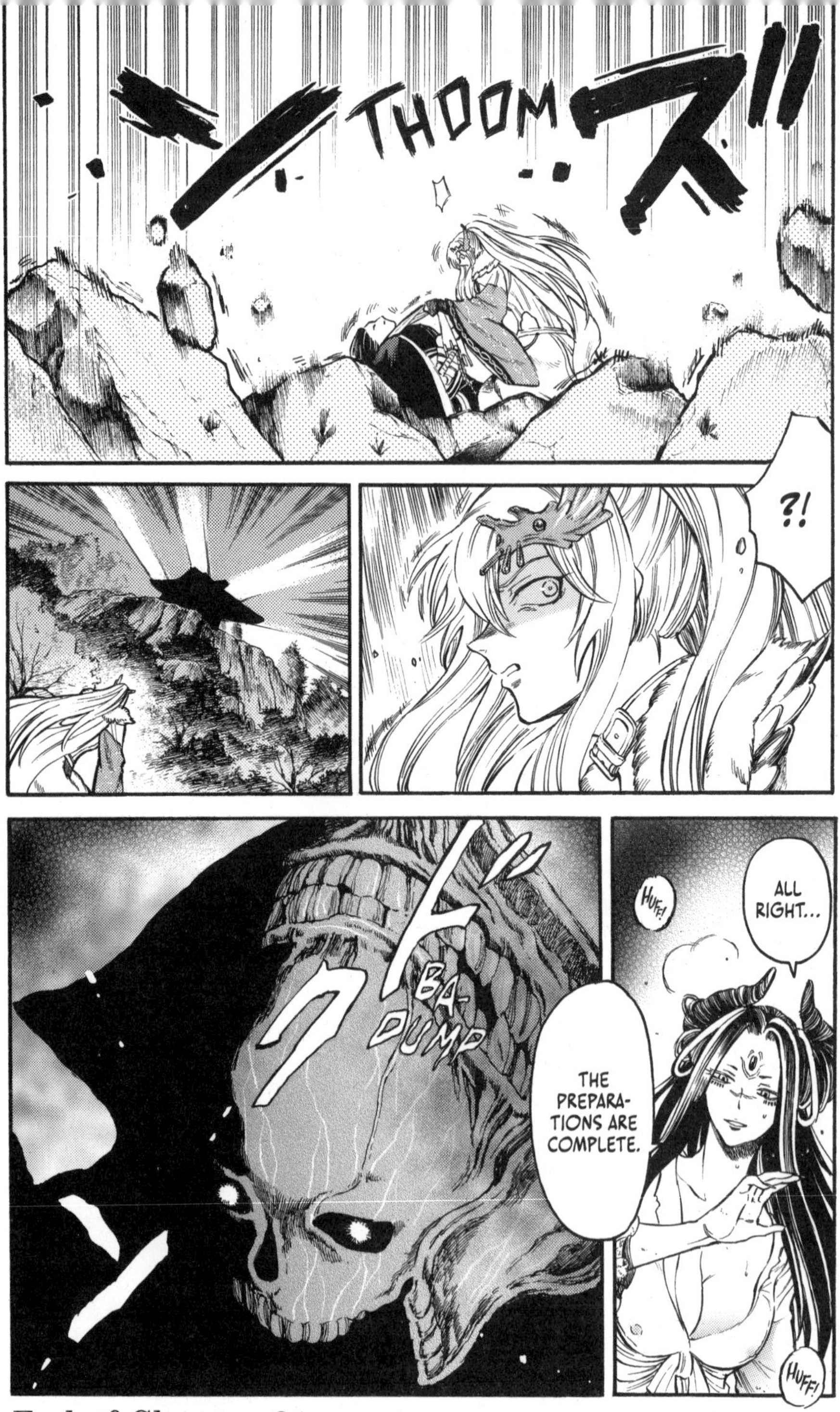
THOOM
?!
HUFF!
ALL RIGHT...
THE PREPARATIONS ARE COMPLETE.
HUFF!
BA-DUMP

End of Chapter 31

◇ Chapter 32 ◇

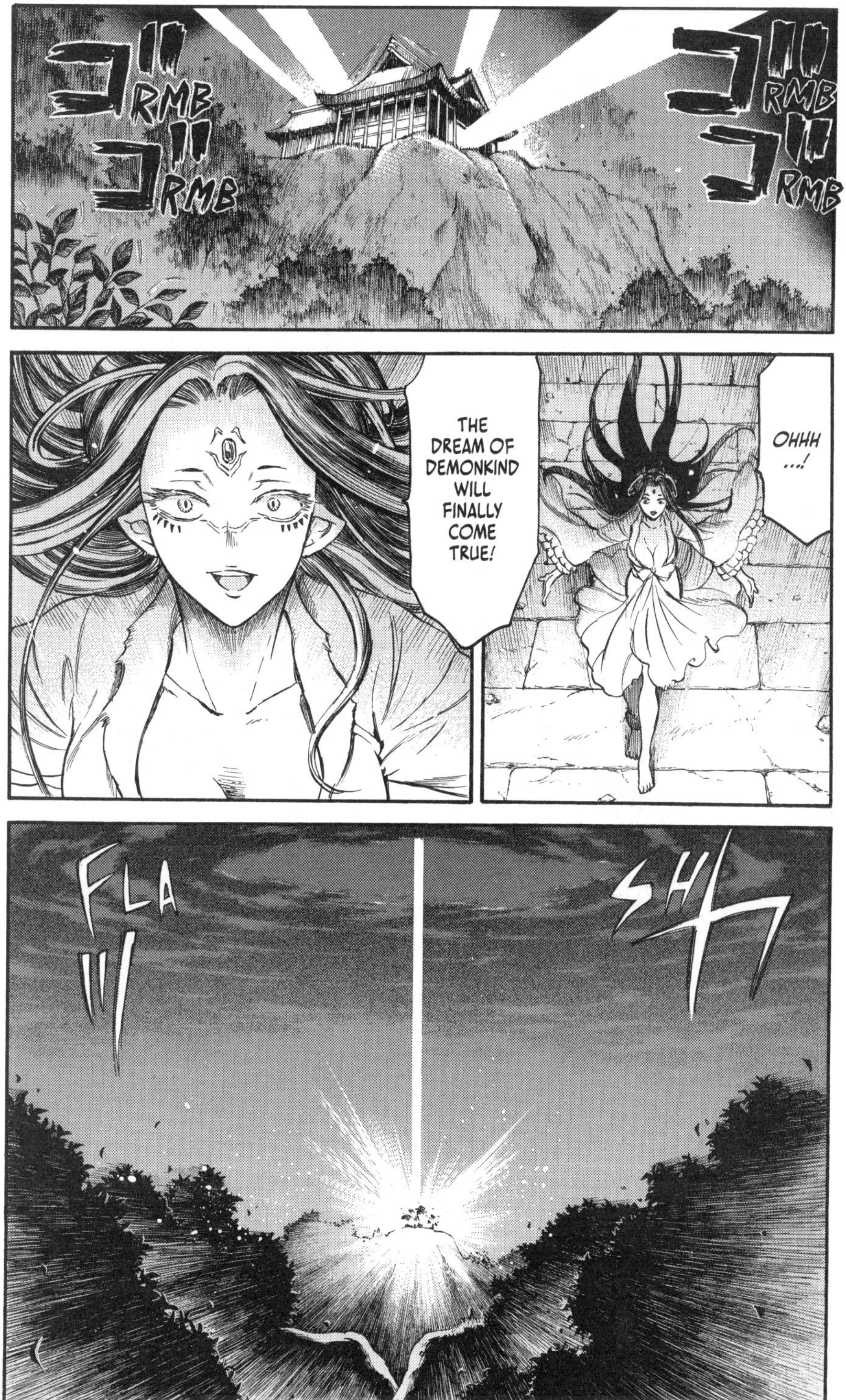
RMB
RMB
RMB
RMB
OHHH ...!
THE DREAM OF DEMONKIND WILL FINALLY COME TRUE!
FLASH

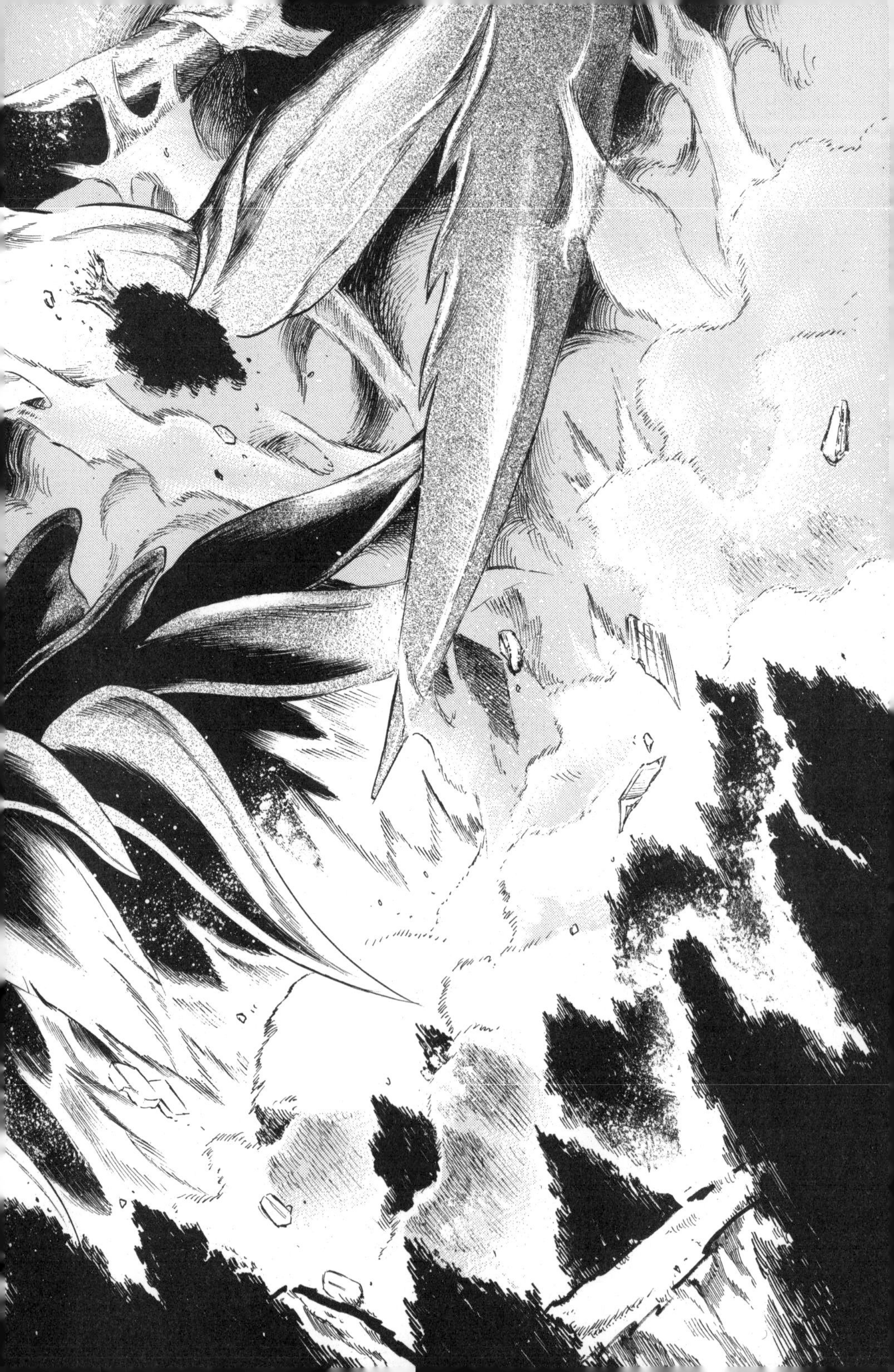

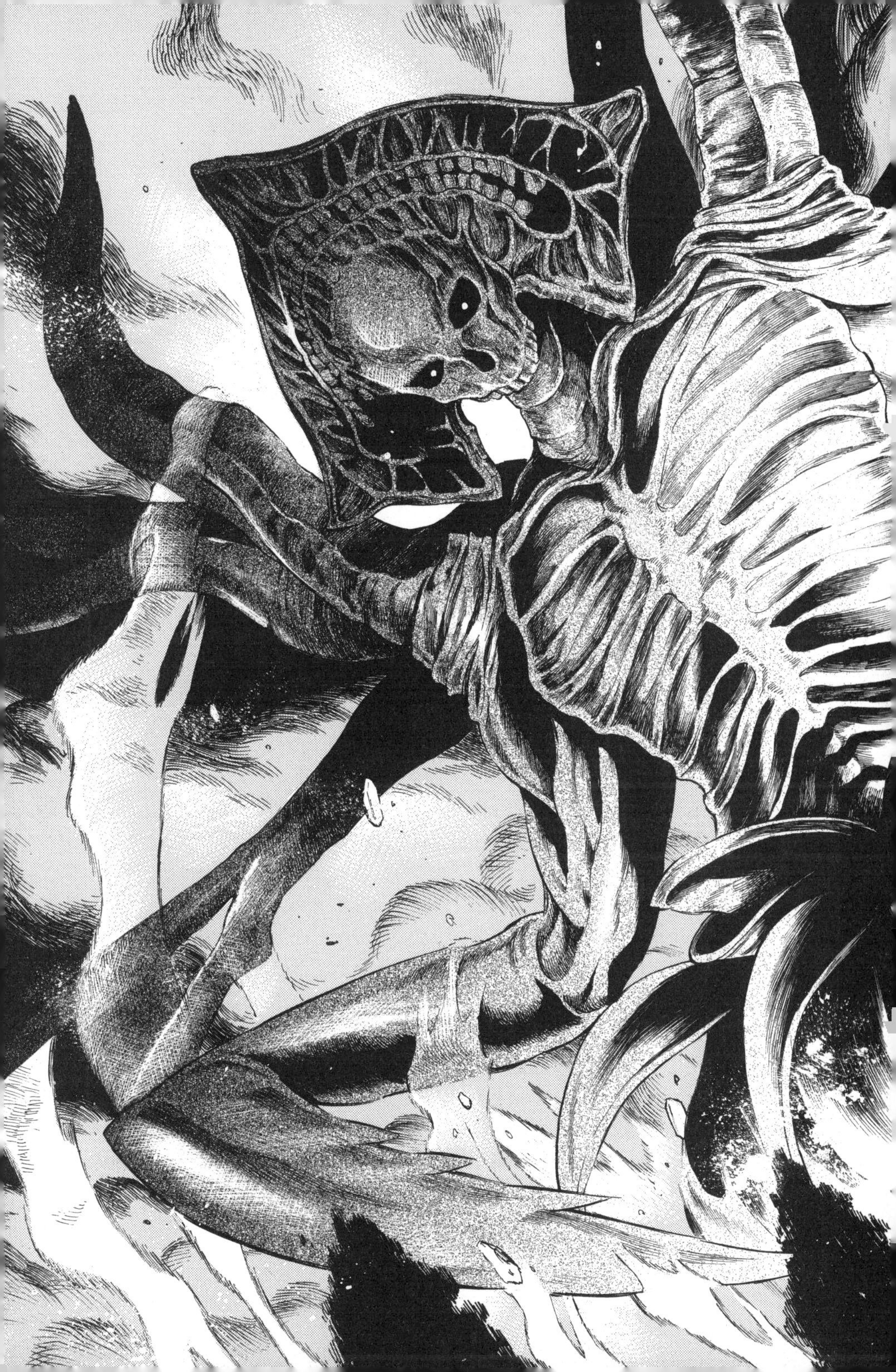

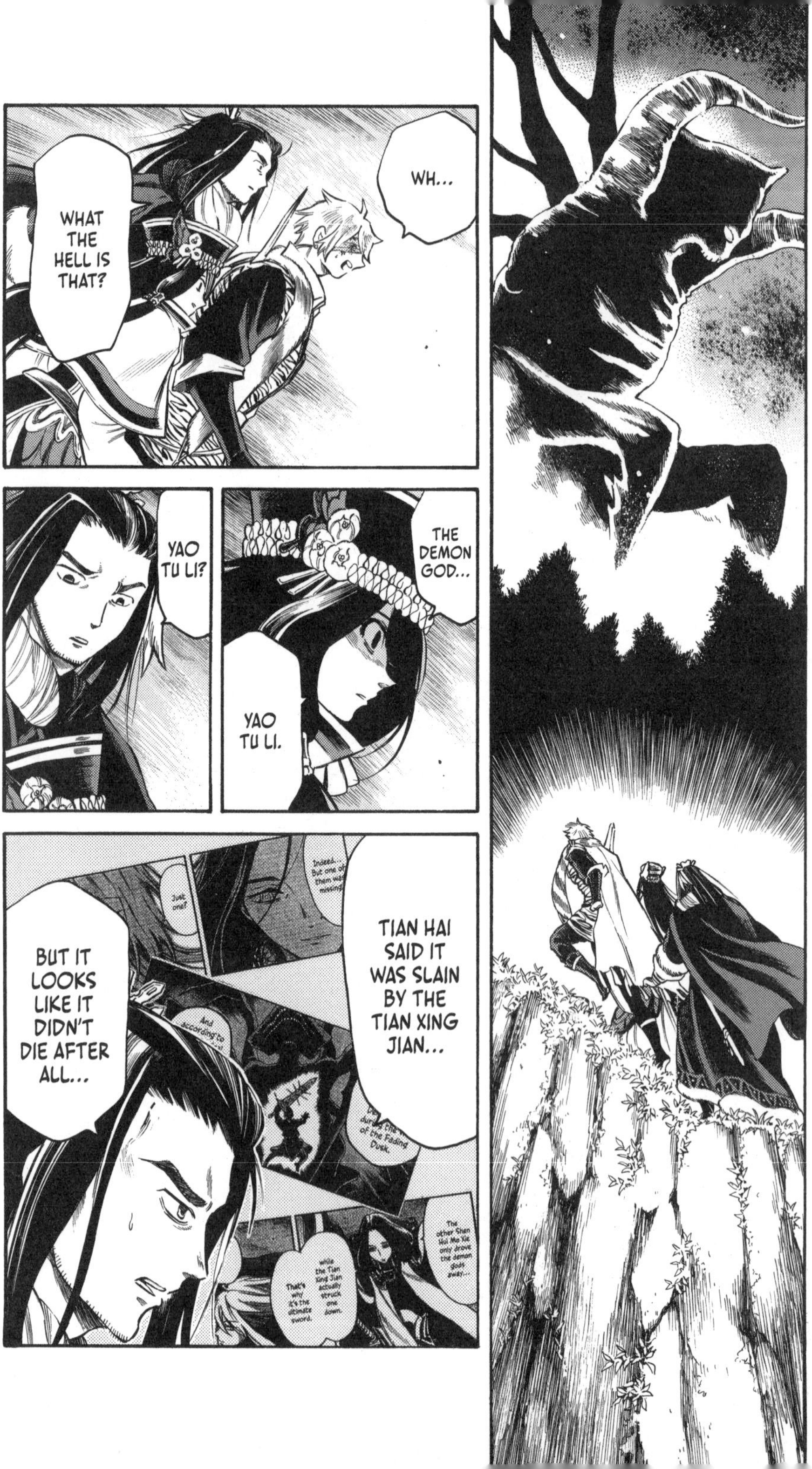
WH...
WHAT THE HELL IS THAT?
THE DEMON GOD...
YAO TU LI.
YAO TU LI?
TIAN HAI SAID IT WAS SLAIN BY THE TIAN XING JIAN...
Indeed... But one of them was missing.
Just one?
And according to
of the Fading Dusk.
The other Shen Hui Mo Xie only drove the demon gods away...
while the Tian Xing Jian actually struck one down.
That's why it's the ultimate sword.
BUT IT LOOKS LIKE IT DIDN'T DIE AFTER ALL...

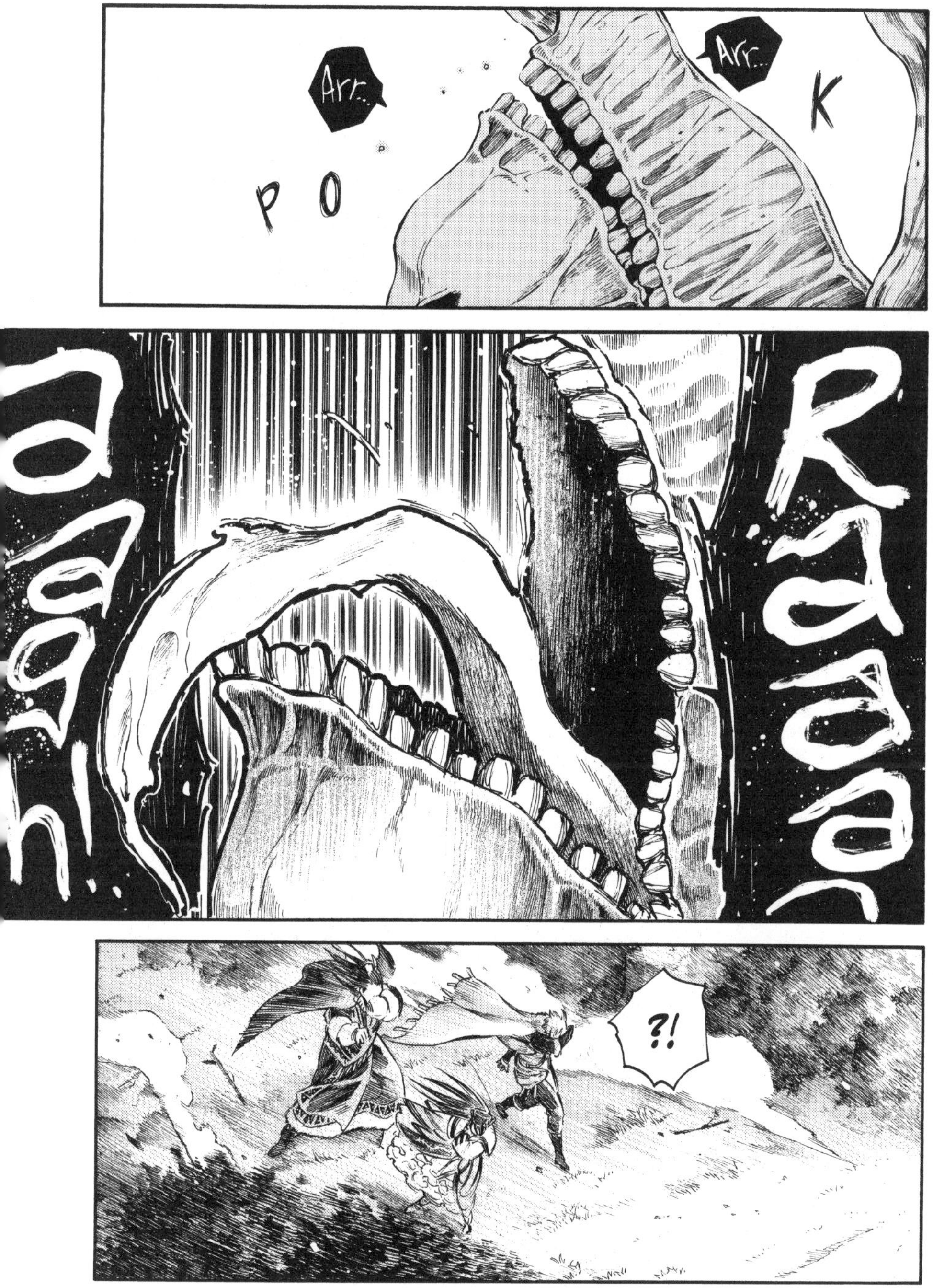
Arr...
K
Arr...
P O
Raaar
aaagh!!
?!

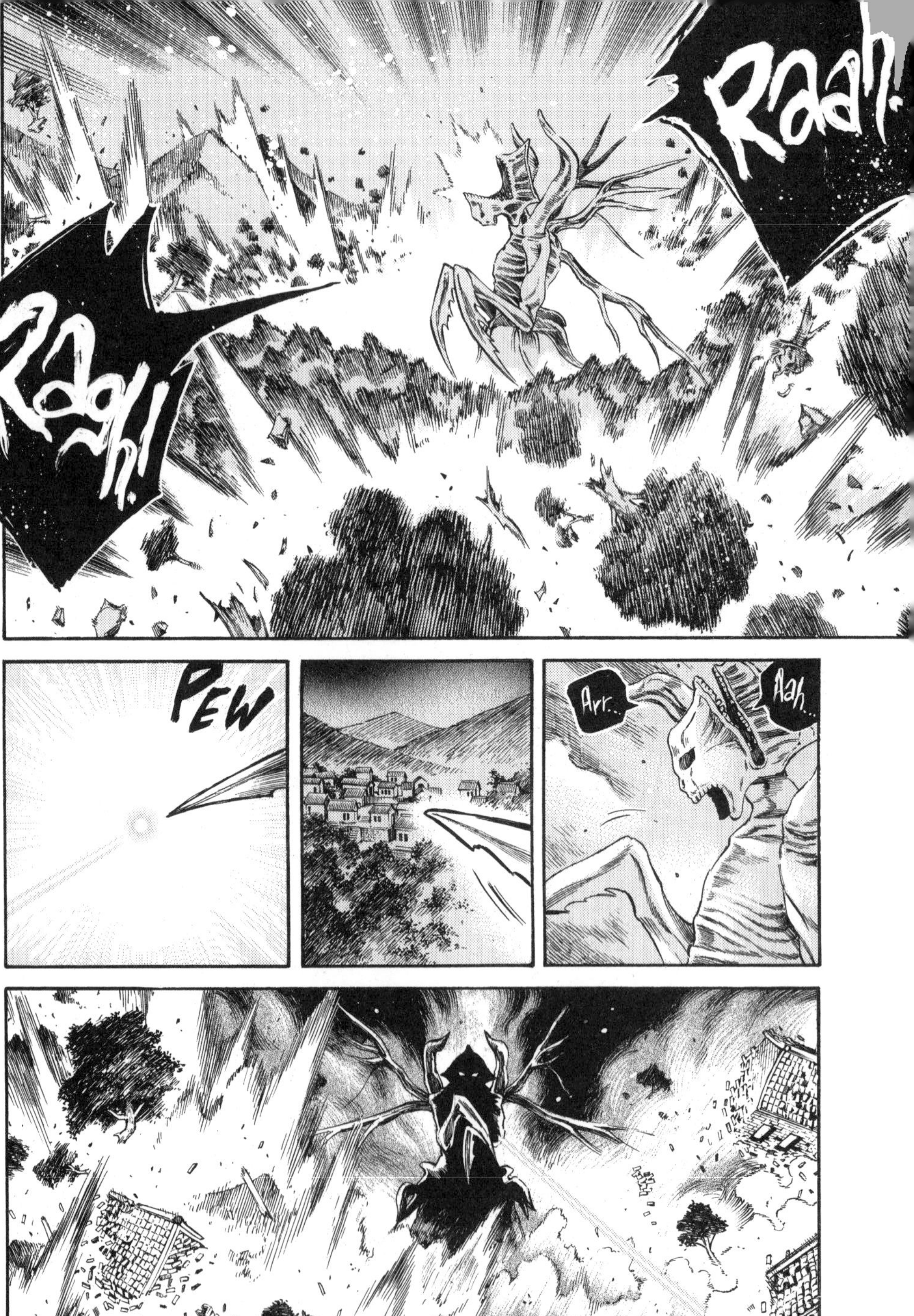
Raah!
Raagh!
Aah...
Arr...
PEW

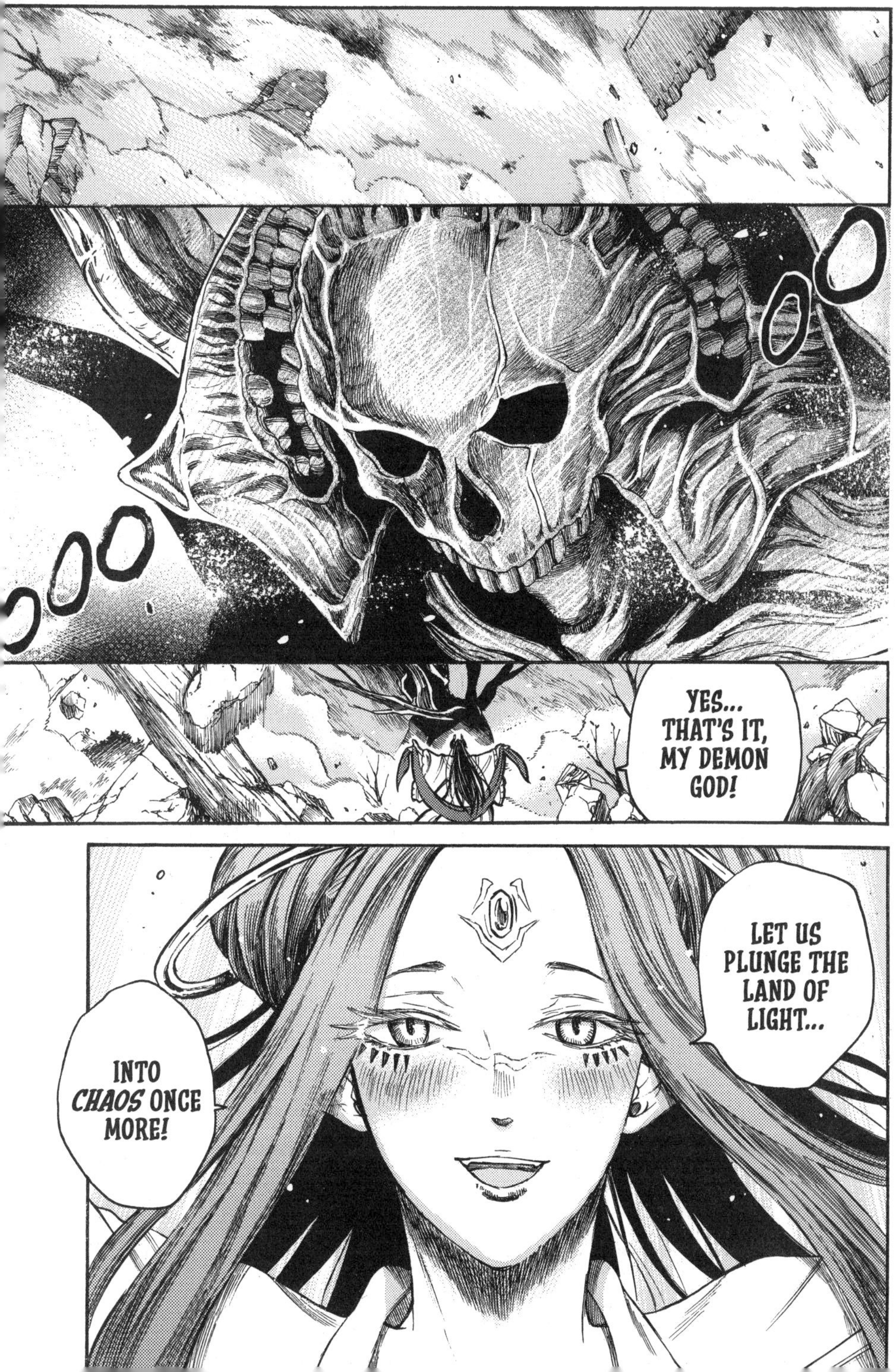
YES... THAT'S IT, MY DEMON GOD!
LET US PLUNGE THE LAND OF LIGHT...
INTO *CHAOS* ONCE MORE!

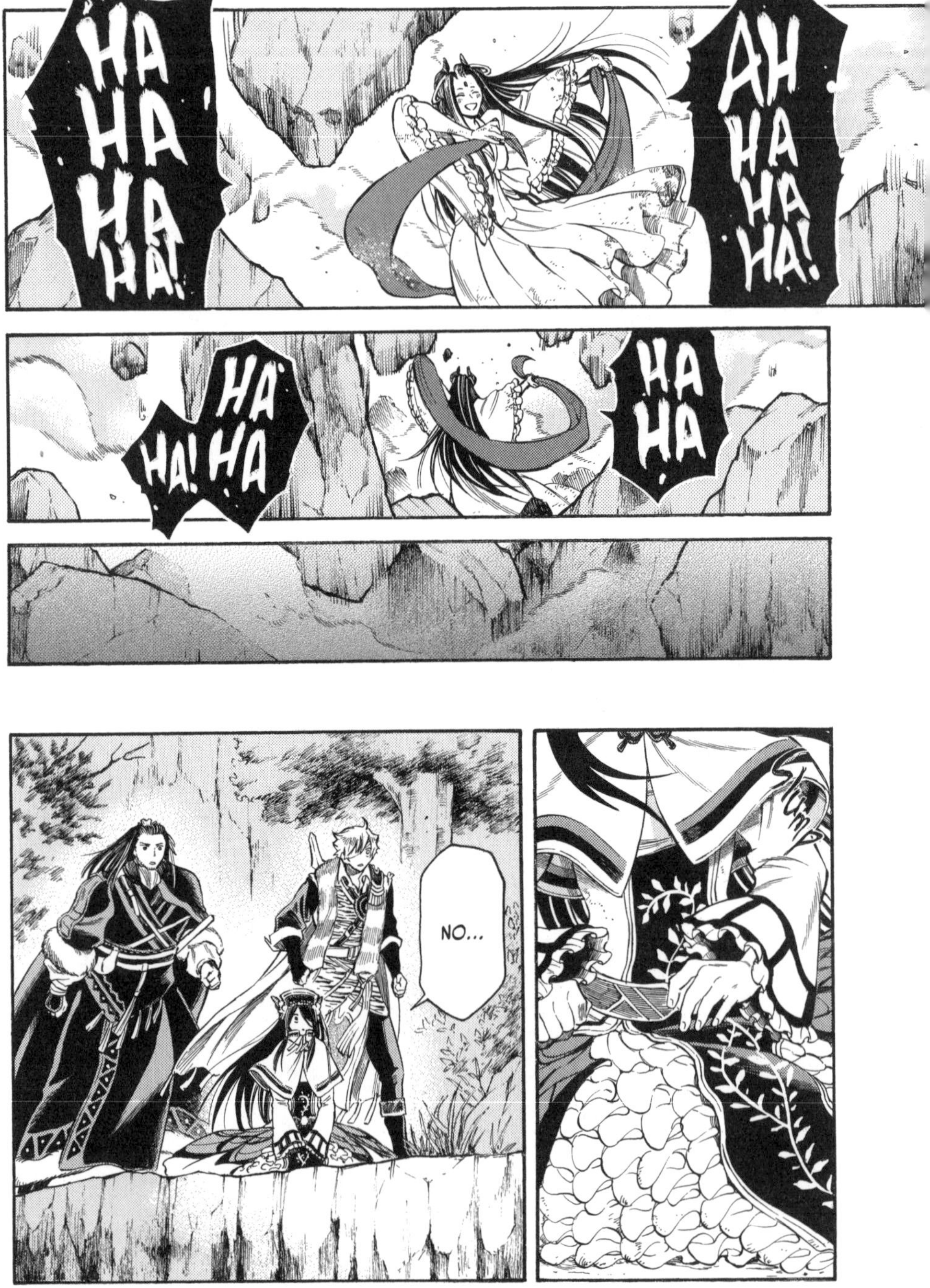
AH HA HA HA HA!
HA HA HA HA!
HA HA
HA HA HA!
NO...

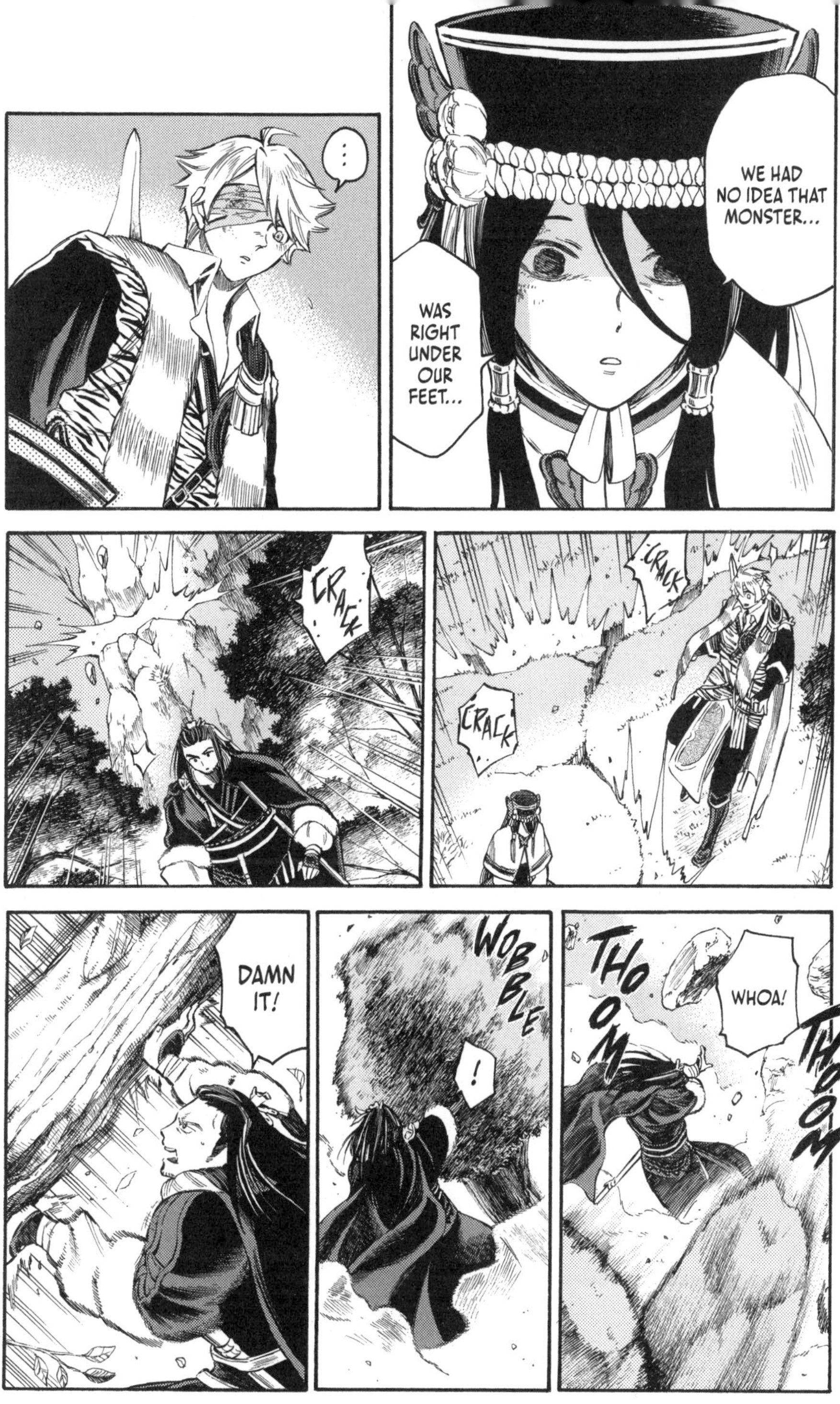
WE HAD NO IDEA THAT MONSTER…
WAS RIGHT UNDER OUR FEET…
…
CRACK
CRACK
CRACK
WHOA!
THOOM
THOOM
WOBBLE
!
DAMN IT!

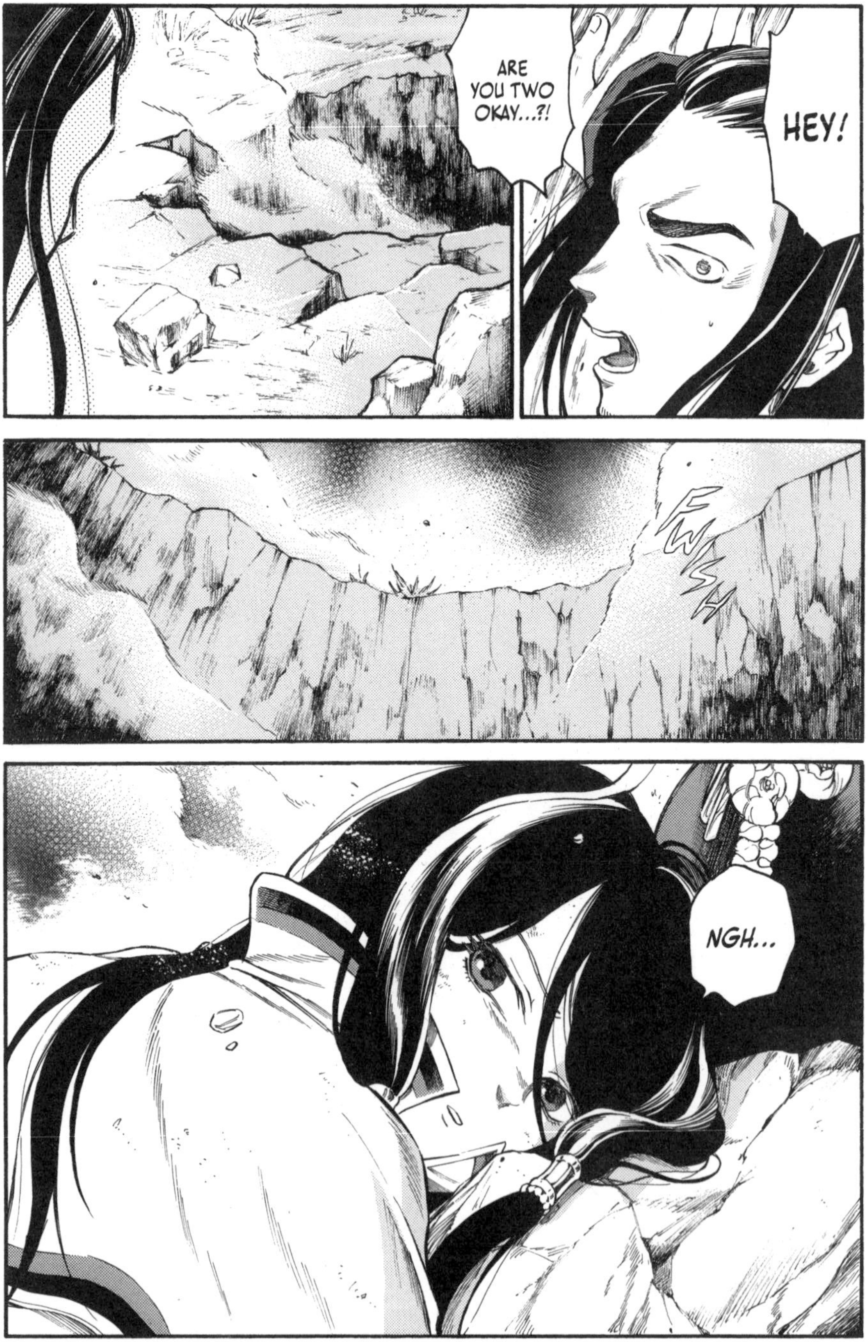
HEY!
ARE YOU TWO OKAY...?!
FWSH
NGH...

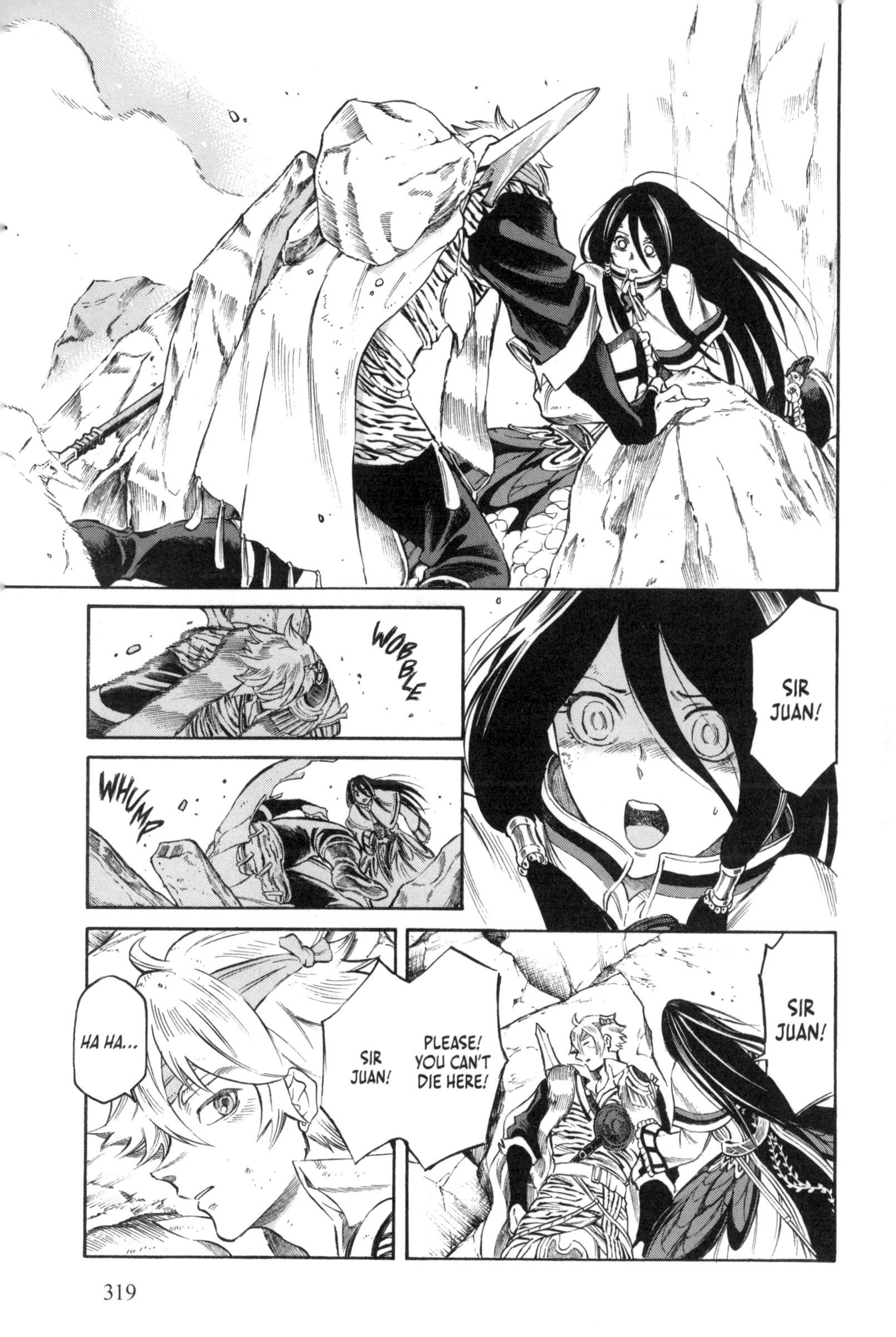
SIR JUAN!
WOBBLE
WHUMP
SIR JUAN!
PLEASE! YOU CAN'T DIE HERE!
SIR JUAN!
HA HA...

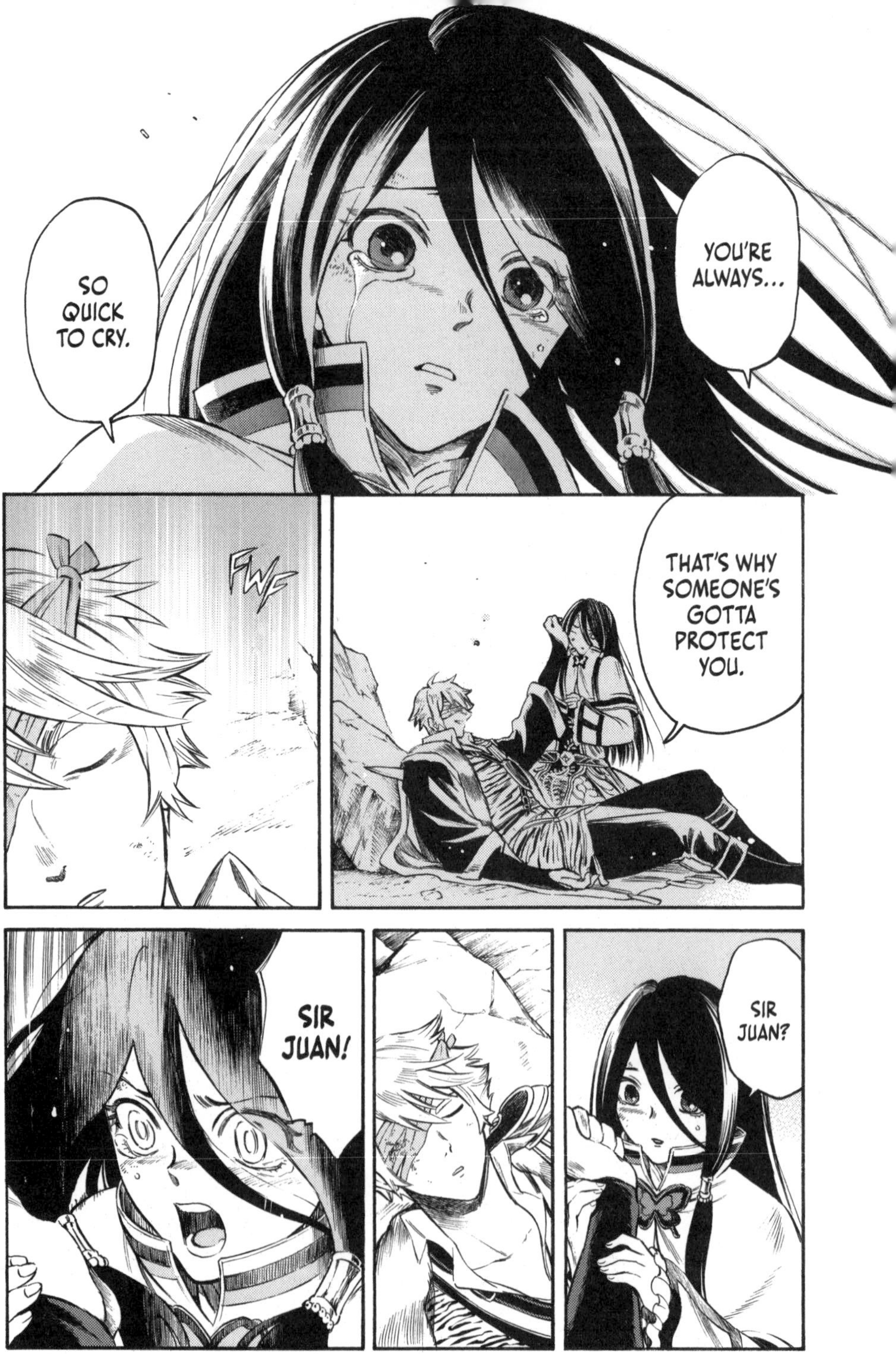
YOU'RE ALWAYS...
SO QUICK TO CRY.
THAT'S WHY SOMEONE'S GOTTA PROTECT YOU.
FWF
SIR JUAN?
SIR JUAN!

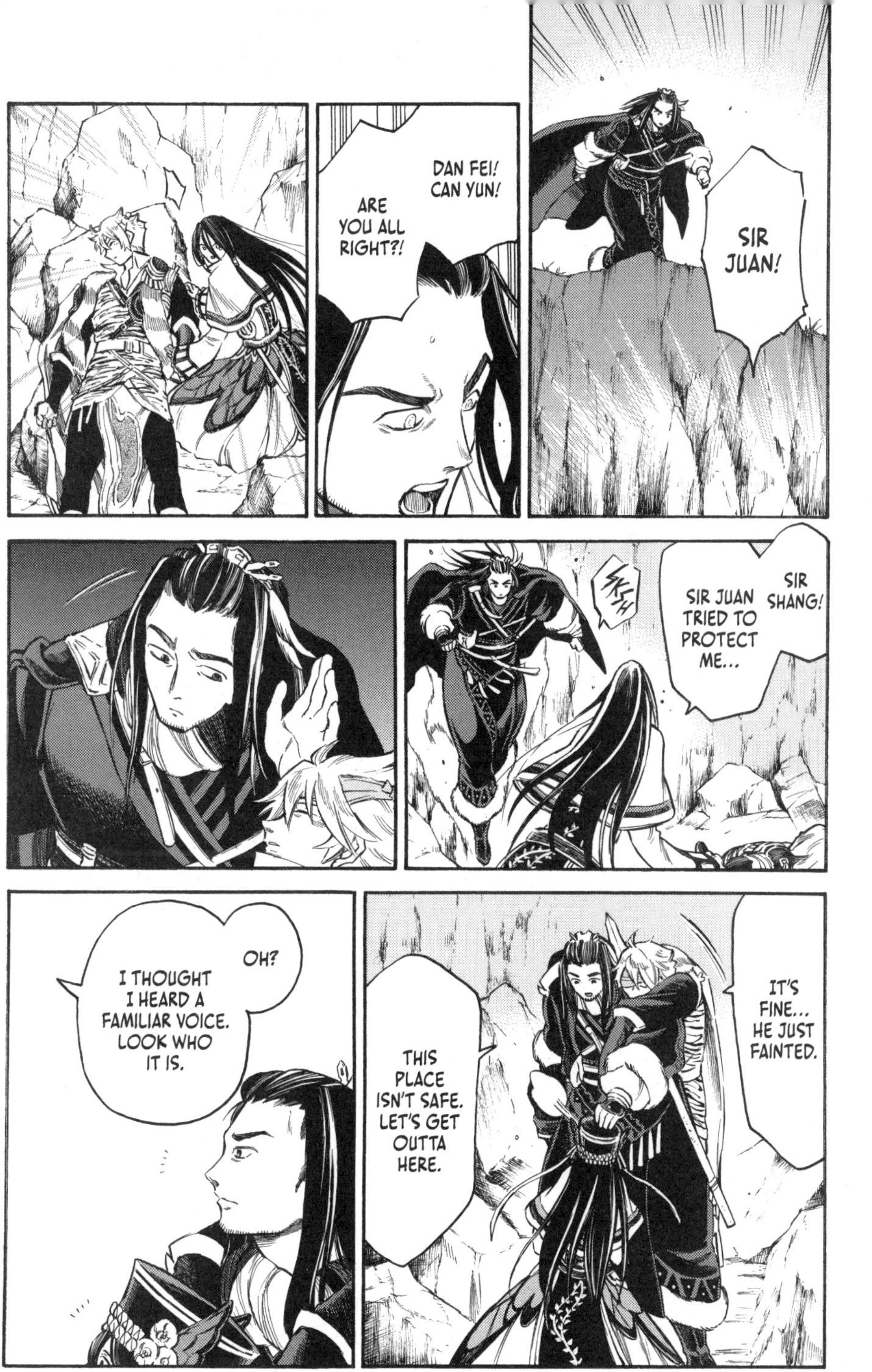
SIR JUAN!
DAN FEI! CAN YUN!
ARE YOU ALL RIGHT?!
SIR SHANG!
SIR JUAN TRIED TO PROTECT ME...
IT'S FINE... HE JUST FAINTED.
THIS PLACE ISN'T SAFE. LET'S GET OUTTA HERE.
OH?
I THOUGHT I HEARD A FAMILIAR VOICE. LOOK WHO IT IS.

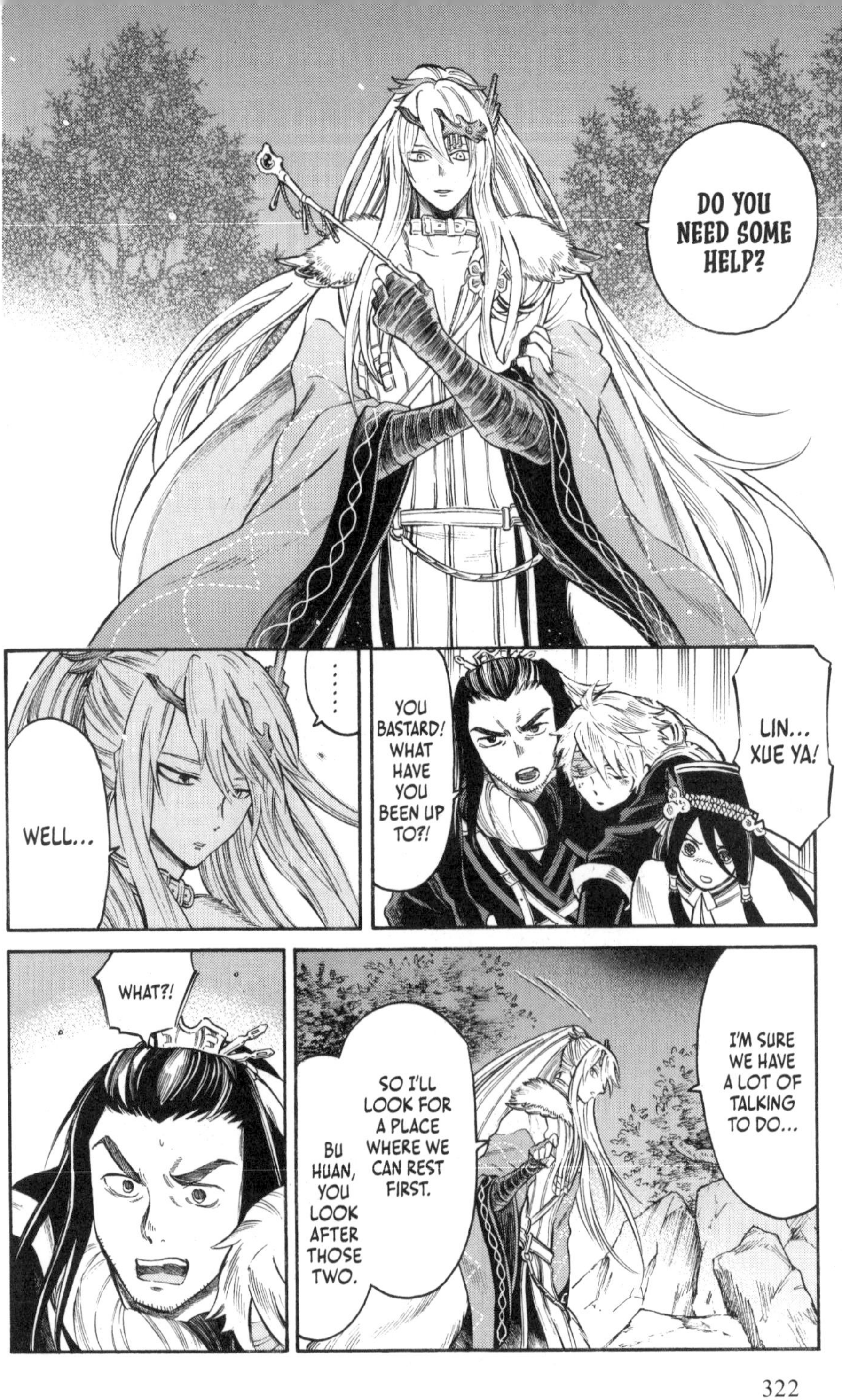
DO YOU NEED SOME HELP?
LIN... XUE YA!
YOU BASTARD! WHAT HAVE YOU BEEN UP TO?!
......
WELL...
I'M SURE WE HAVE A LOT OF TALKING TO DO...
SO I'LL LOOK FOR A PLACE WHERE WE CAN REST FIRST.
BU HUAN, YOU LOOK AFTER THOSE TWO.
WHAT?!

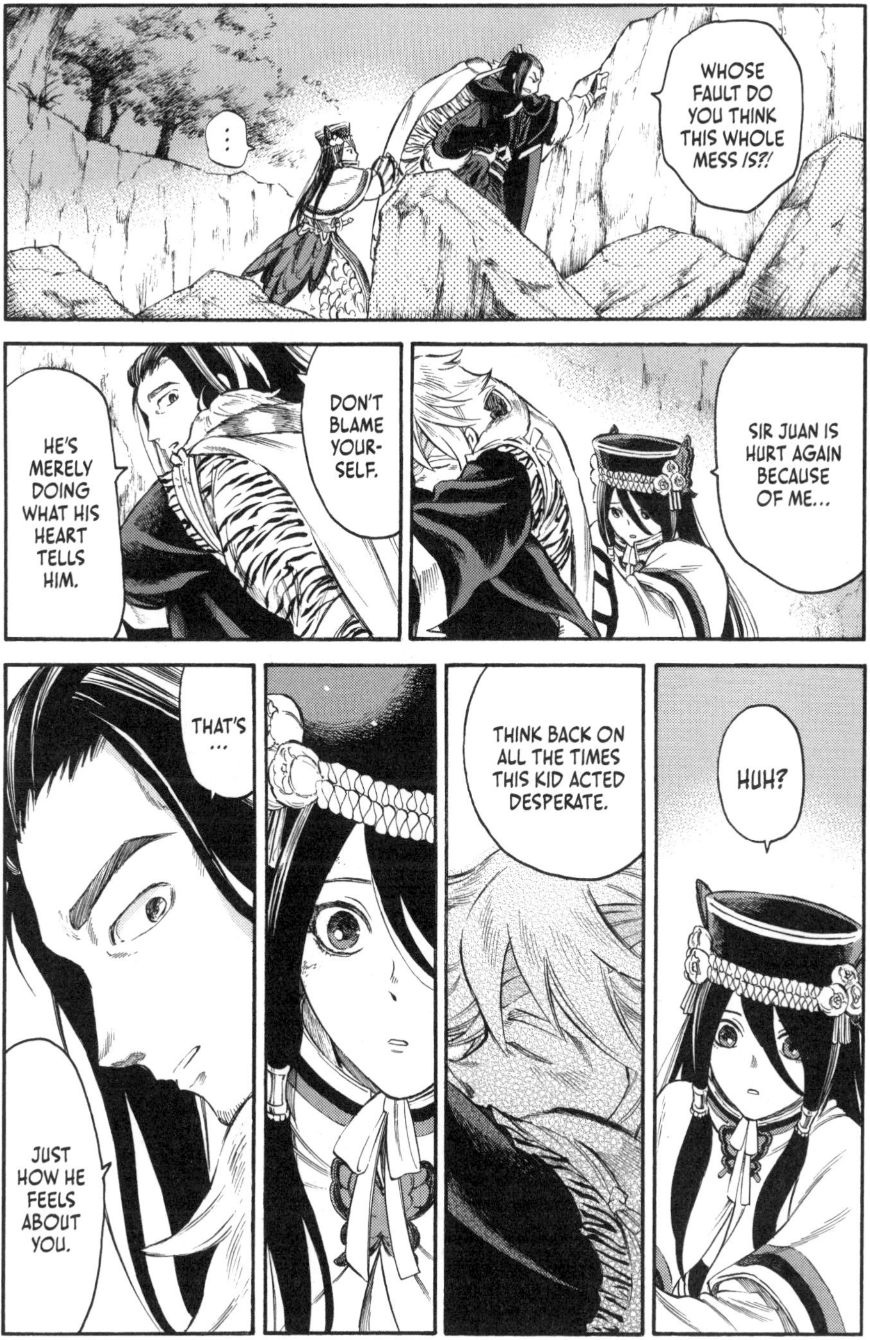
WHOSE FAULT DO YOU THINK THIS WHOLE MESS *IS?!*
...
SIR JUAN IS HURT AGAIN BECAUSE OF ME...
DON'T BLAME YOUR-SELF.
HE'S MERELY DOING WHAT HIS HEART TELLS HIM.
HUH?
THINK BACK ON ALL THE TIMES THIS KID ACTED DESPERATE.
THAT'S ...
JUST HOW HE FEELS ABOUT YOU.

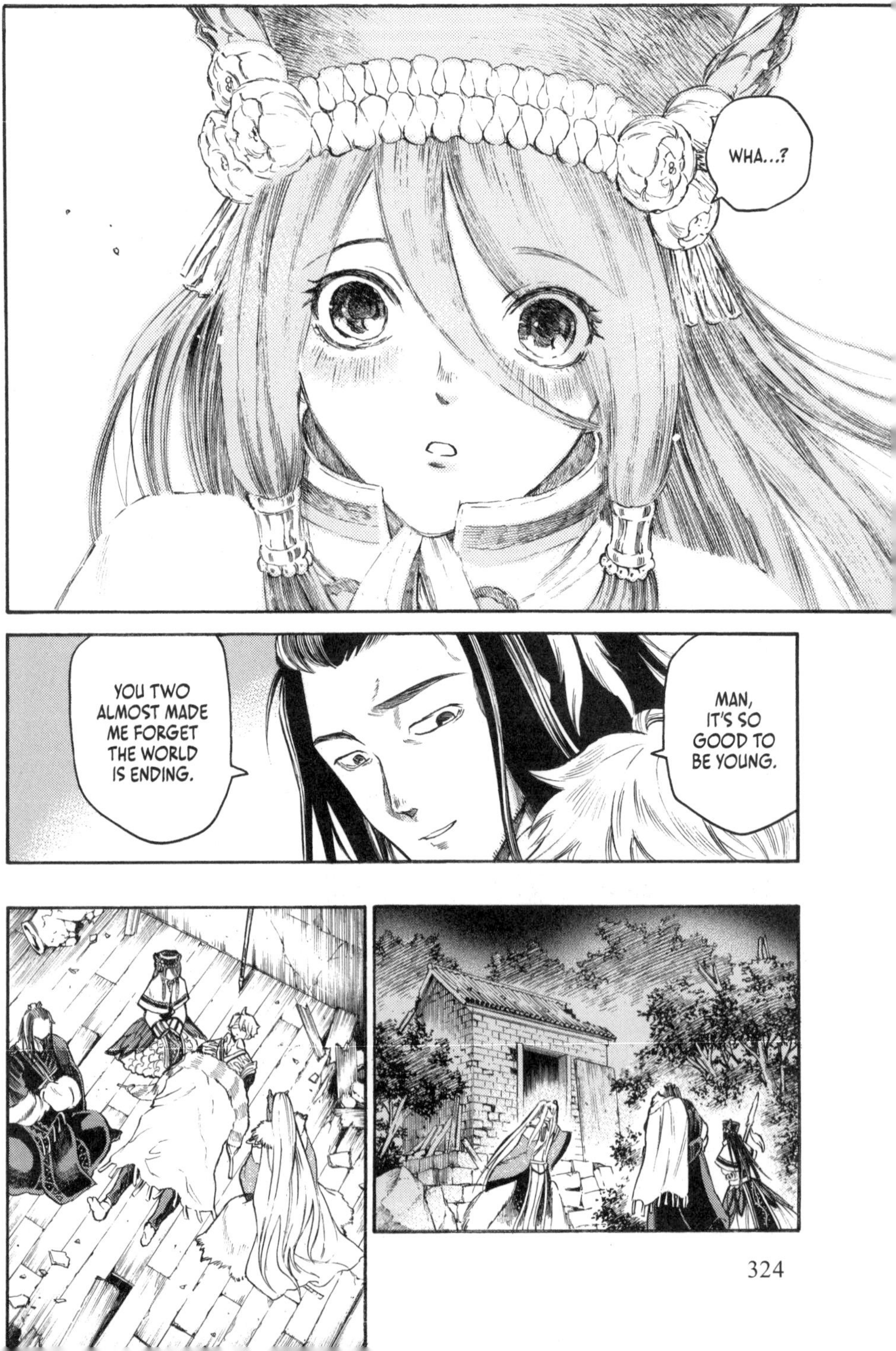
WHA...?
MAN, IT'S SO GOOD TO BE YOUNG.
YOU TWO ALMOST MADE ME FORGET THE WORLD IS ENDING.

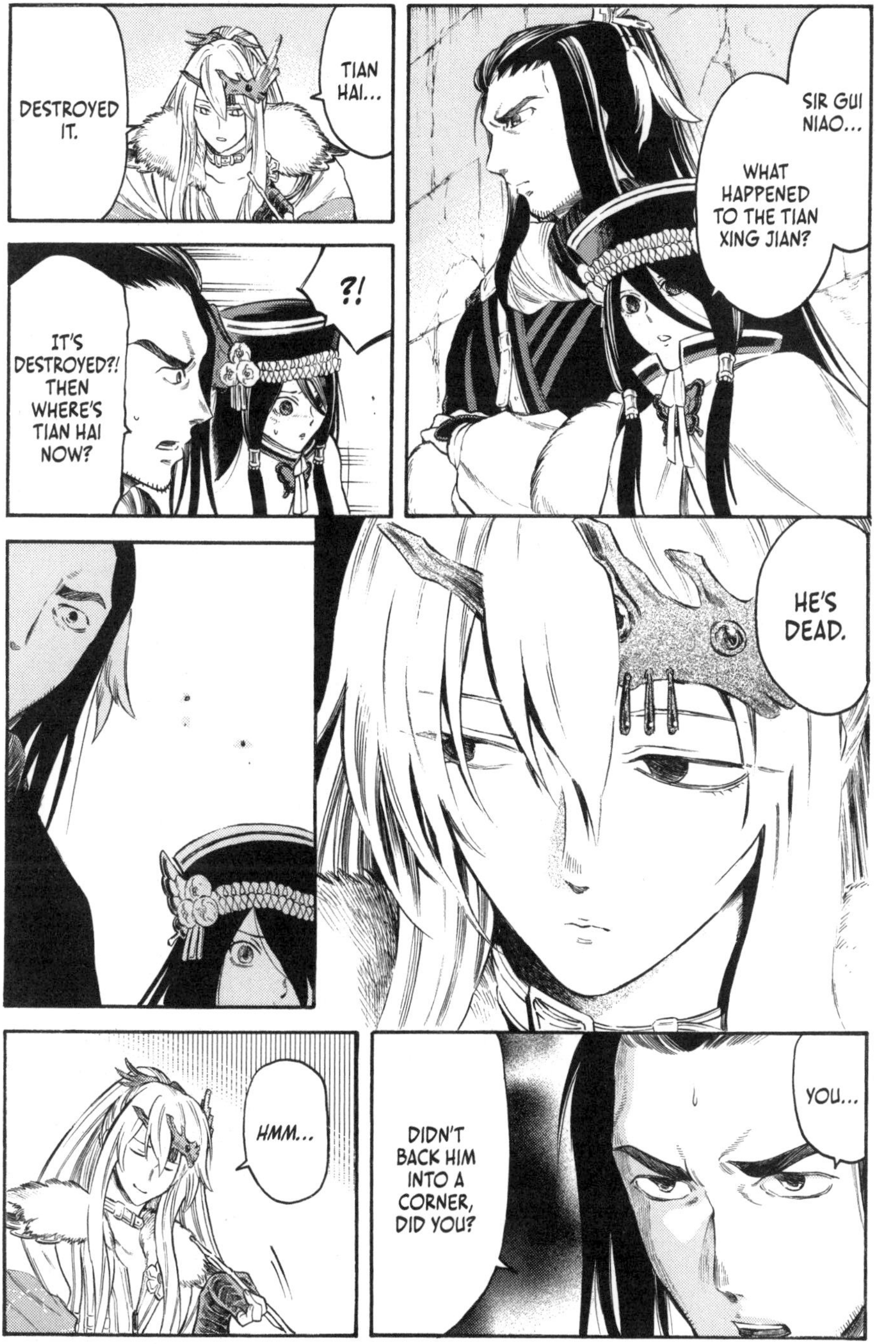

SIR GUI NIAO...
WHAT HAPPENED TO THE TIAN XING JIAN?
TIAN HAI...
DESTROYED IT.
?!
IT'S DESTROYED?! THEN WHERE'S TIAN HAI NOW?
HE'S DEAD.
YOU...
DIDN'T BACK HIM INTO A CORNER, DID YOU?
HMM...

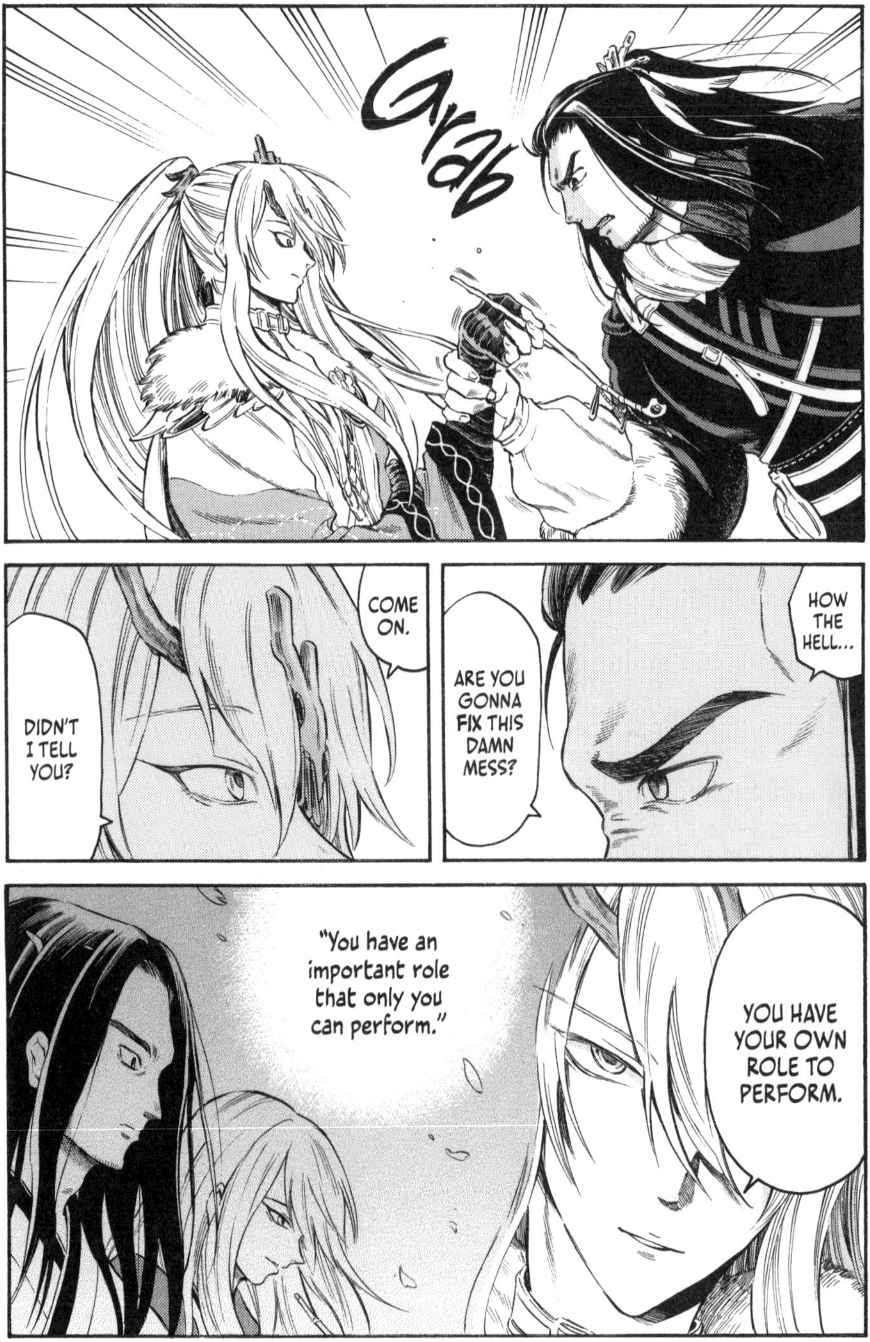
Grab
HOW THE HELL...
ARE YOU GONNA FIX THIS DAMN MESS?
COME ON.
DIDN'T I TELL YOU?
YOU HAVE YOUR OWN ROLE TO PERFORM.
"You have an important role that only you can perform."

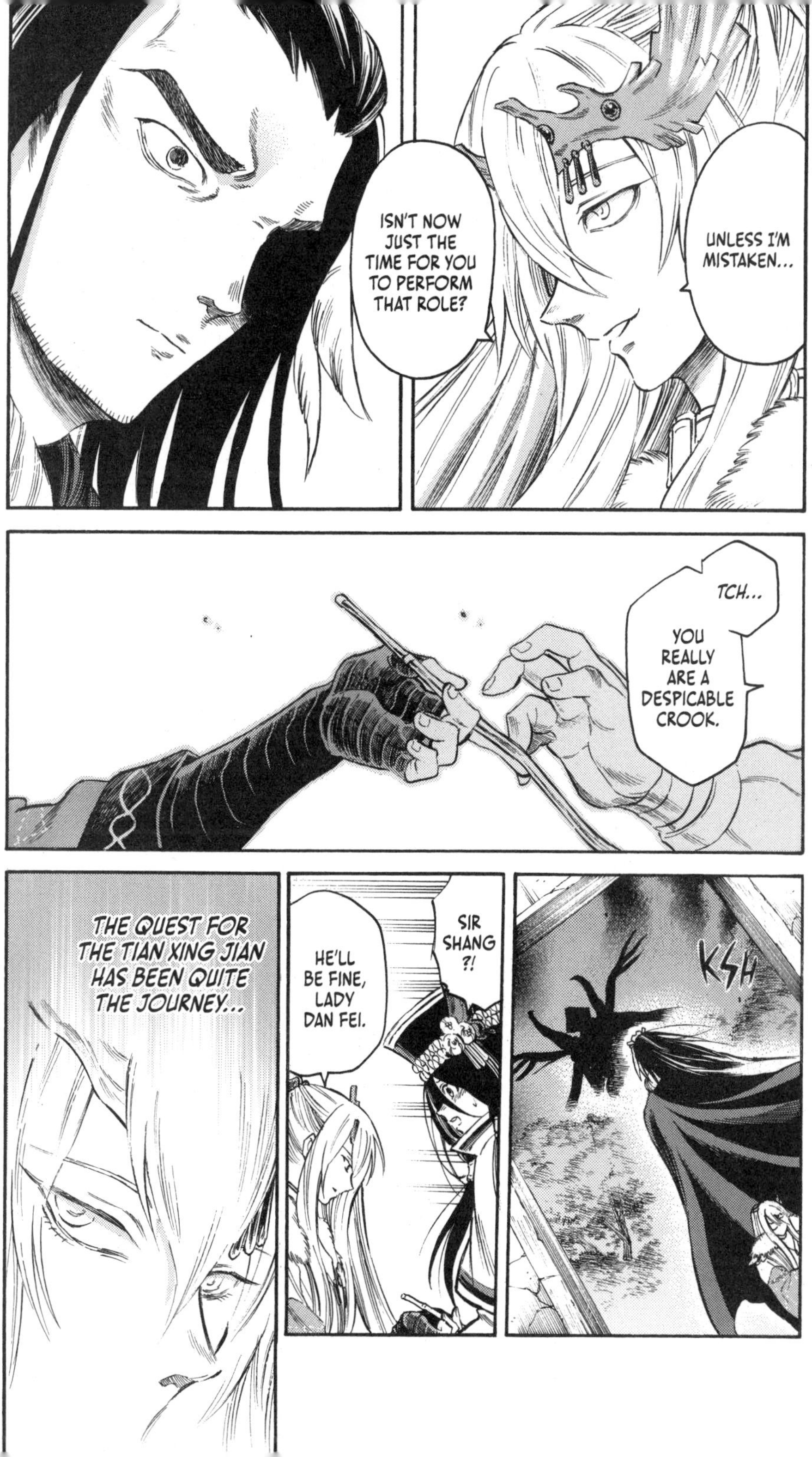
UNLESS I'M MISTAKEN...
ISN'T NOW JUST THE TIME FOR YOU TO PERFORM THAT ROLE?
TCH...
YOU REALLY ARE A DESPICABLE CROOK.
KSH
SIR SHANG?!
HE'LL BE FINE, LADY DAN FEI.
THE QUEST FOR THE TIAN XING JIAN HAS BEEN QUITE THE JOURNEY...

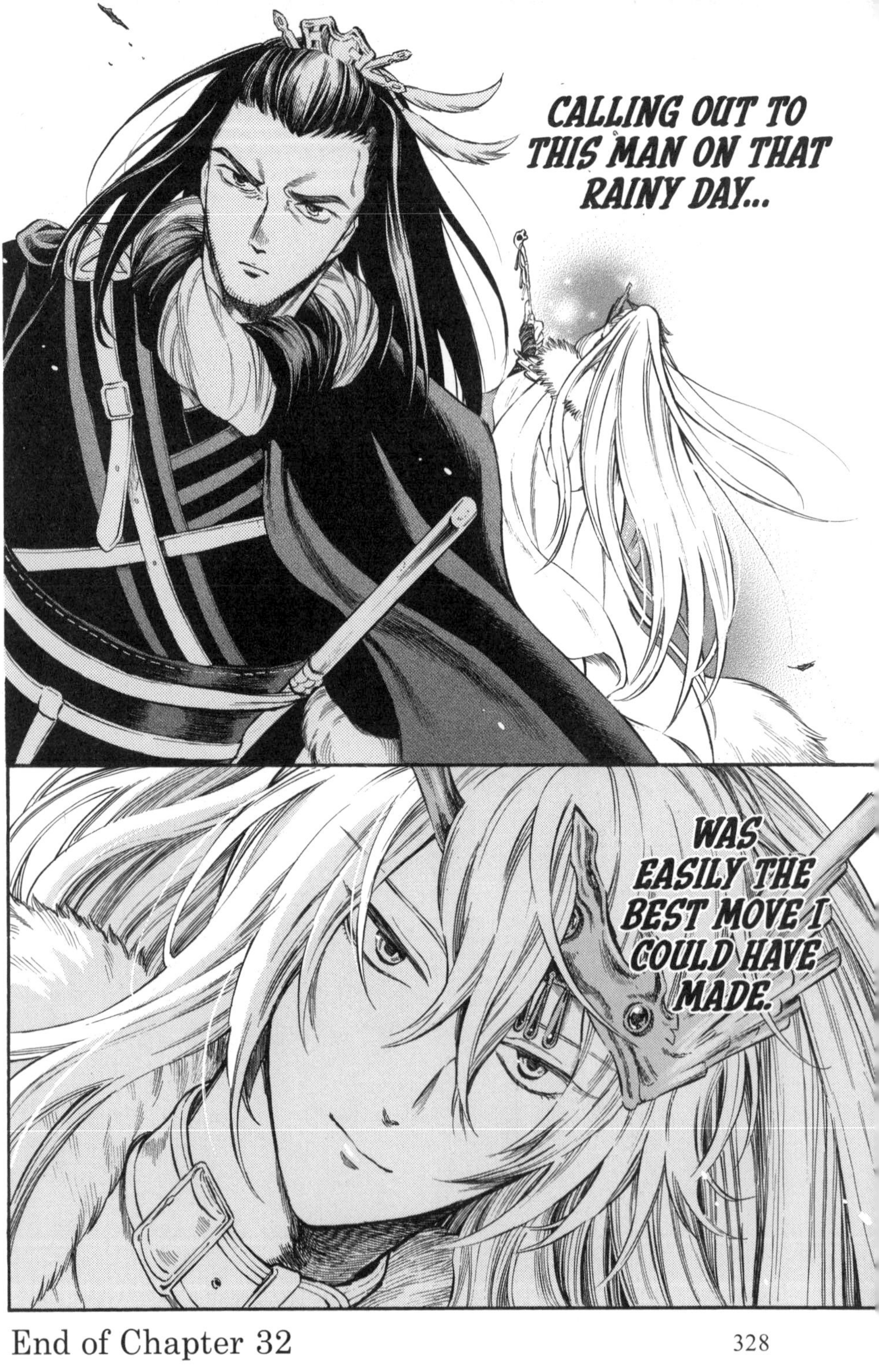
CALLING OUT TO THIS MAN ON THAT RAINY DAY...
WAS EASILY THE BEST MOVE I COULD HAVE MADE.

End of Chapter 32

∞ Chapter 33 ∞

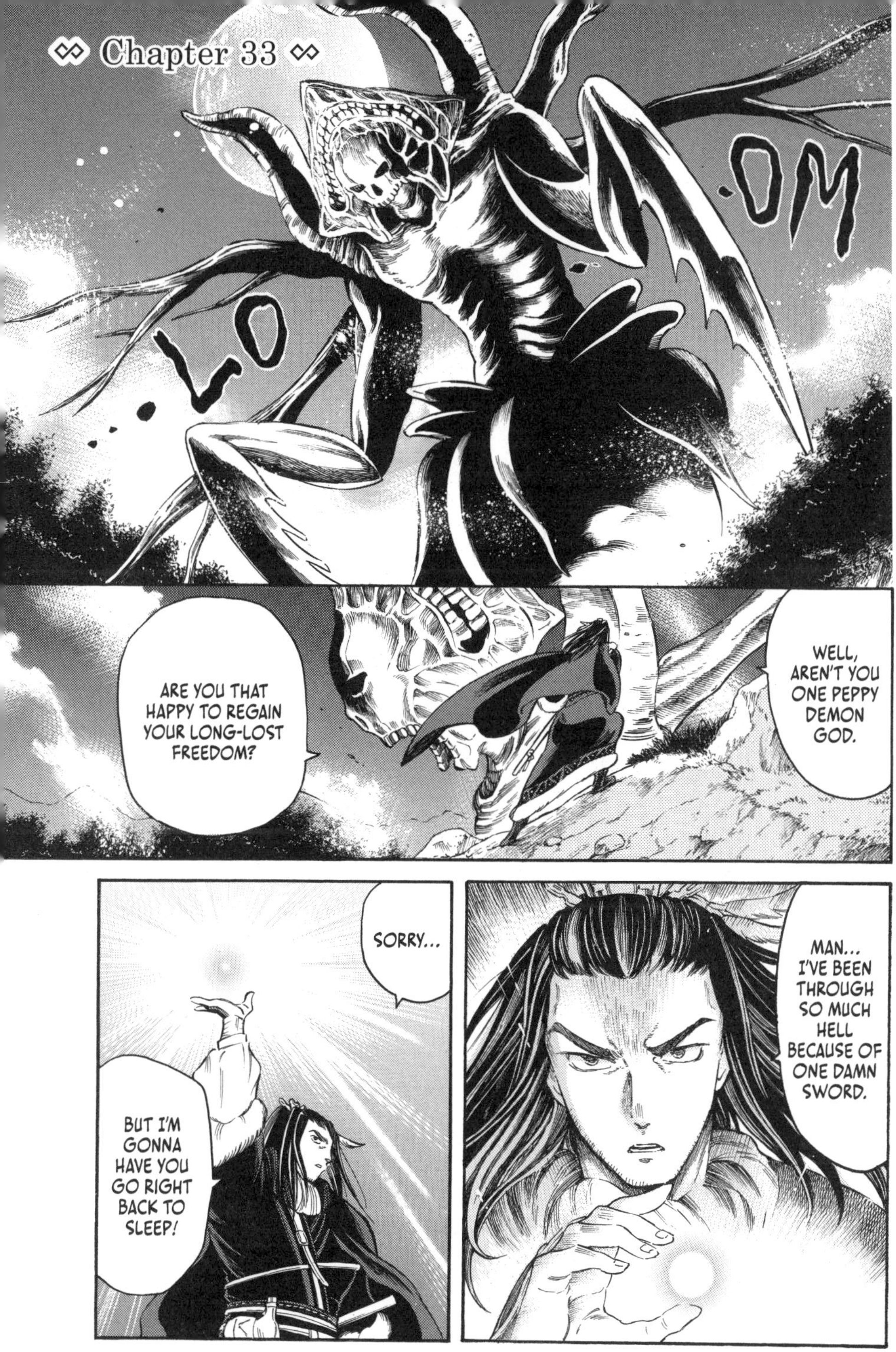

...LO·OM
WELL, AREN'T YOU ONE PEPPY DEMON GOD.
ARE YOU THAT HAPPY TO REGAIN YOUR LONG-LOST FREEDOM?
MAN... I'VE BEEN THROUGH SO MUCH HELL BECAUSE OF ONE DAMN SWORD.
SORRY...
BUT I'M GONNA HAVE YOU GO RIGHT BACK TO SLEEP!

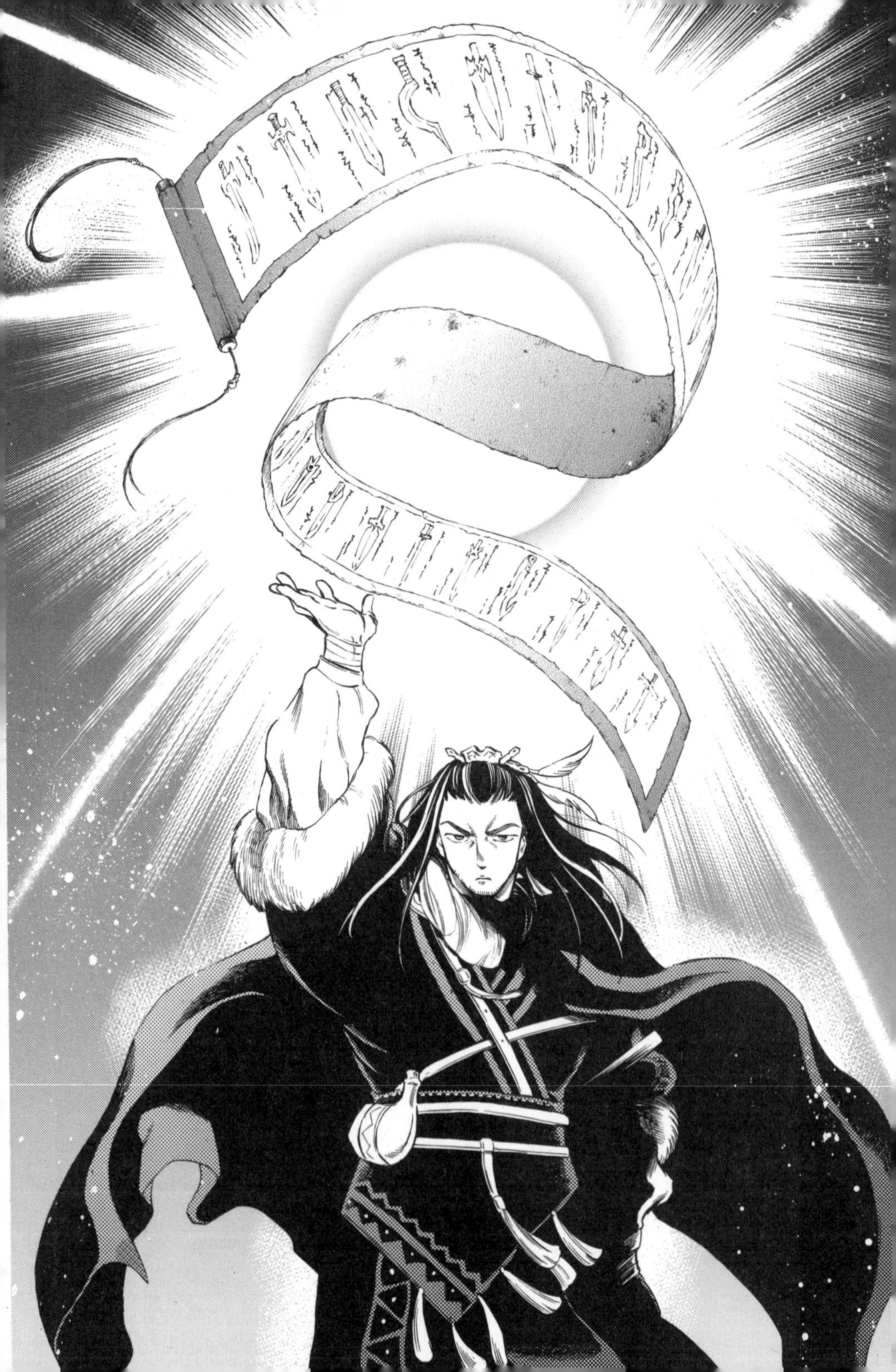

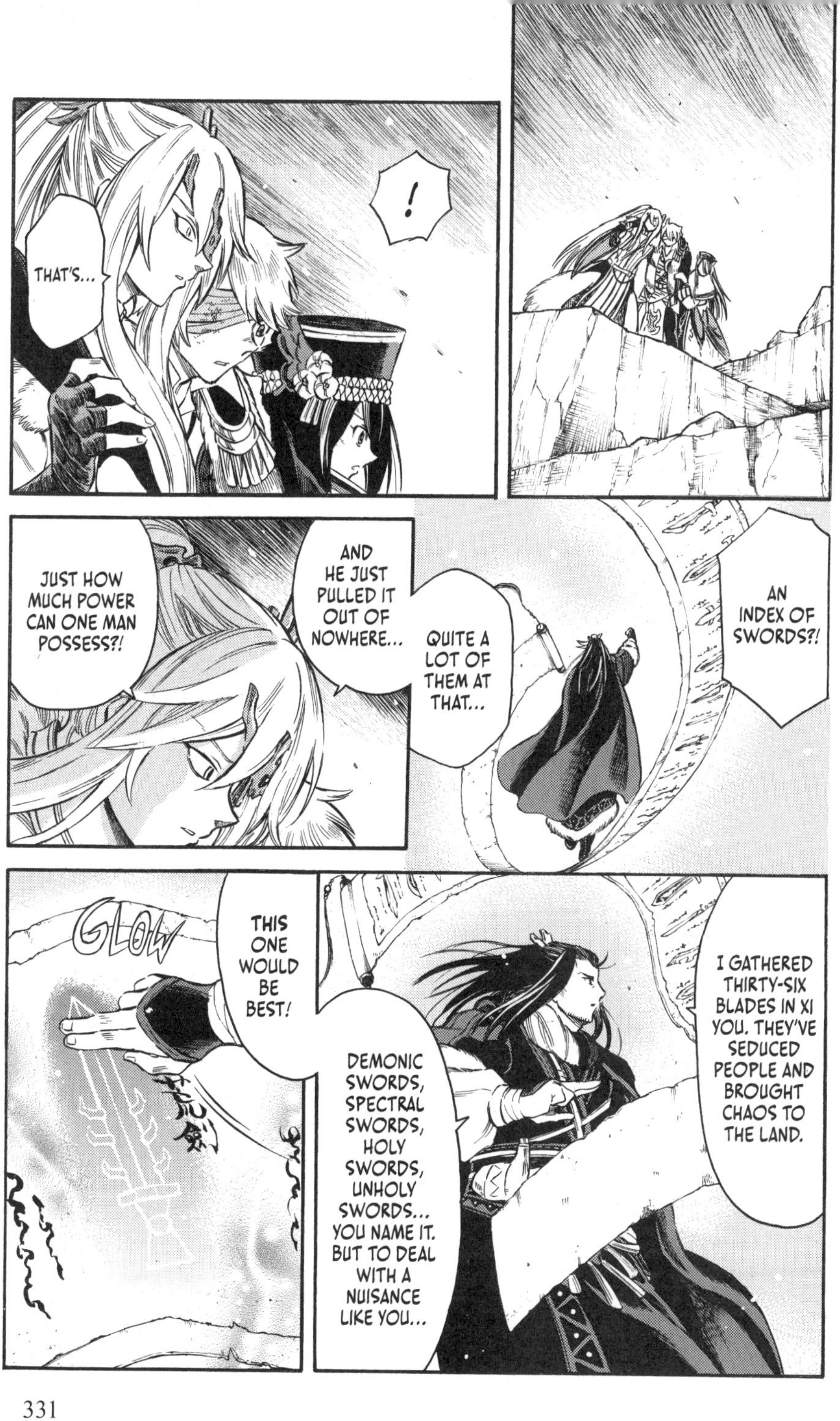
!
THAT'S...
AN INDEX OF SWORDS?!
QUITE A LOT OF THEM AT THAT...
AND HE JUST PULLED IT OUT OF NOWHERE...
JUST HOW MUCH POWER CAN ONE MAN POSSESS?!
I GATHERED THIRTY-SIX BLADES IN XI YOU. THEY'VE SEDUCED PEOPLE AND BROUGHT CHAOS TO THE LAND.
DEMONIC SWORDS, SPECTRAL SWORDS, HOLY SWORDS, UNHOLY SWORDS... YOU NAME IT. BUT TO DEAL WITH A NUISANCE LIKE YOU...
THIS ONE WOULD BE BEST!
GLOW

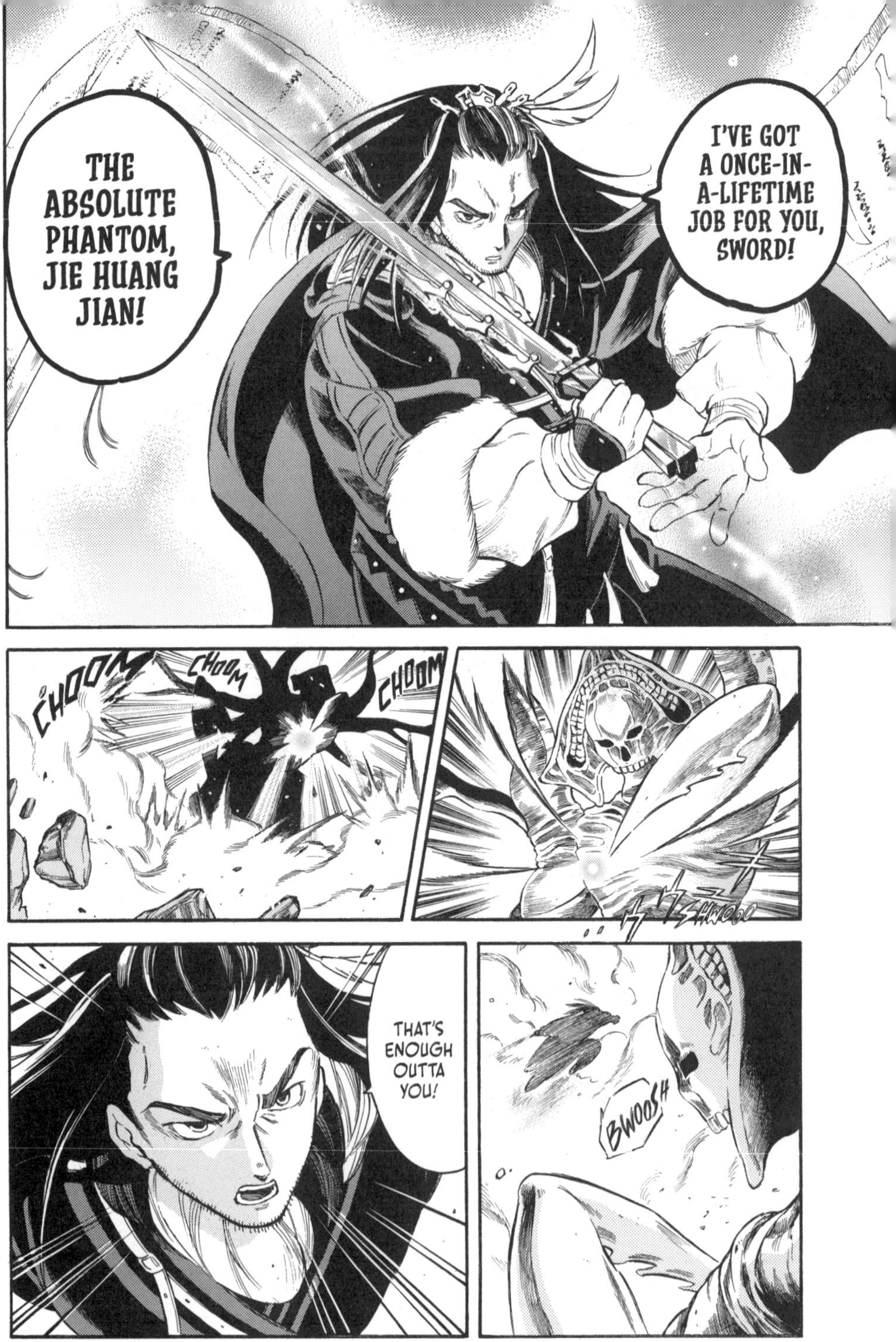
I'VE GOT A ONCE-IN-A-LIFETIME JOB FOR YOU, SWORD!
THE ABSOLUTE PHANTOM, JIE HUANG JIAN!
SHWOOO
CHOOM
CHOOM
CHOOM
BWOOSH
THAT'S ENOUGH OUTTA YOU!

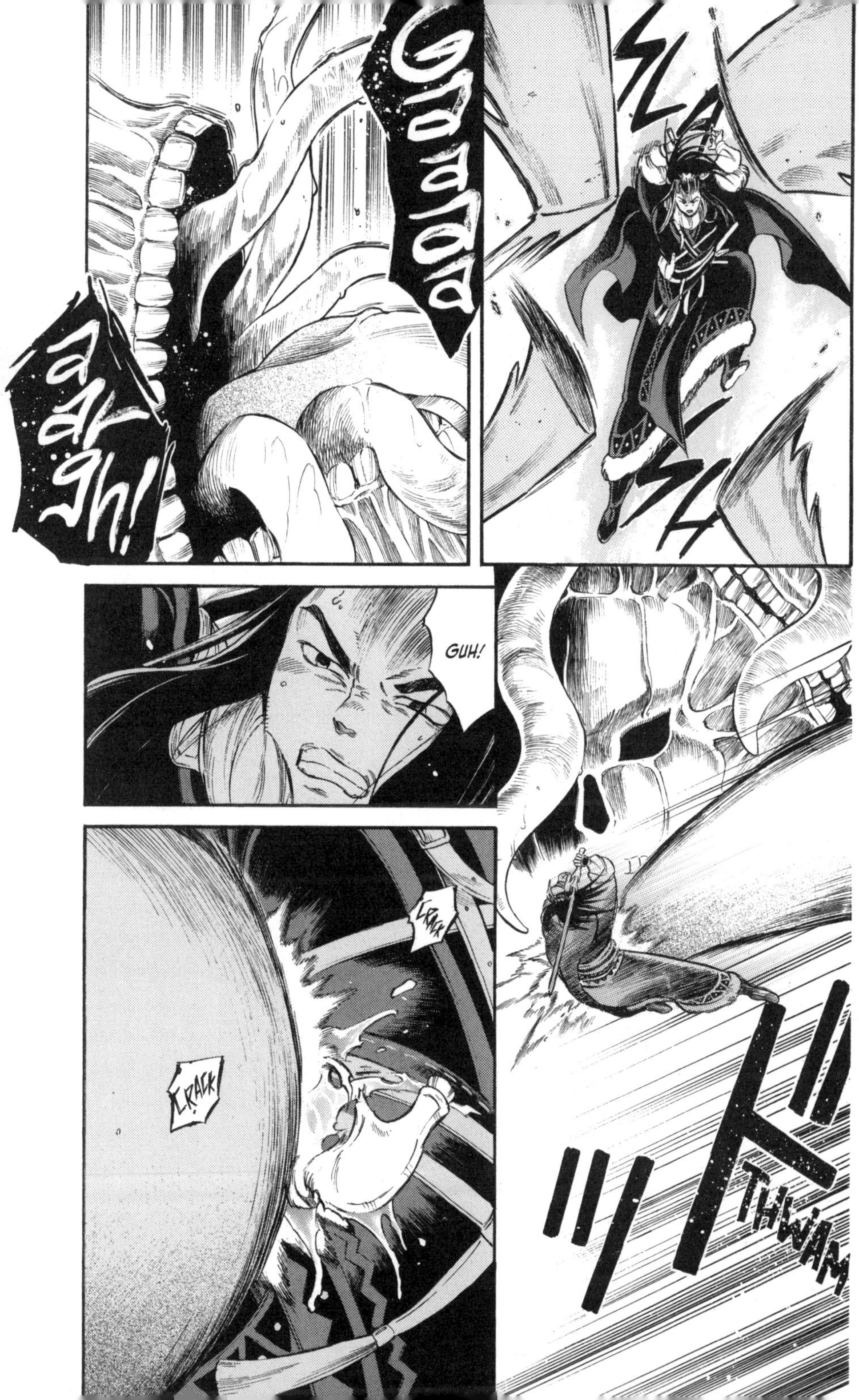
SLASH
GRAAAAA
AAARGH!
THWAM
GUH!
CRACK
CRACK

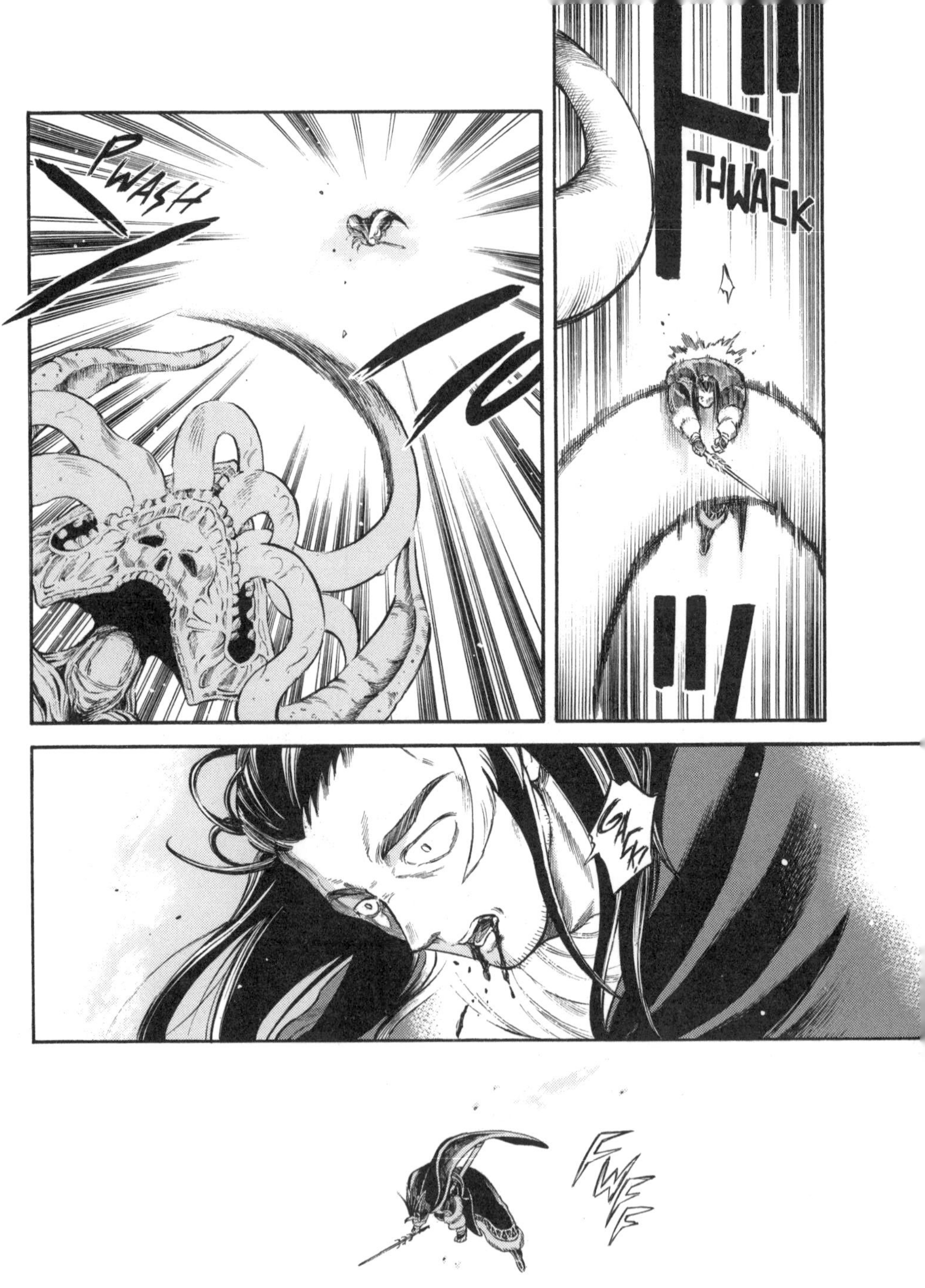
THWACK
PWASH
GACK!
FWEE

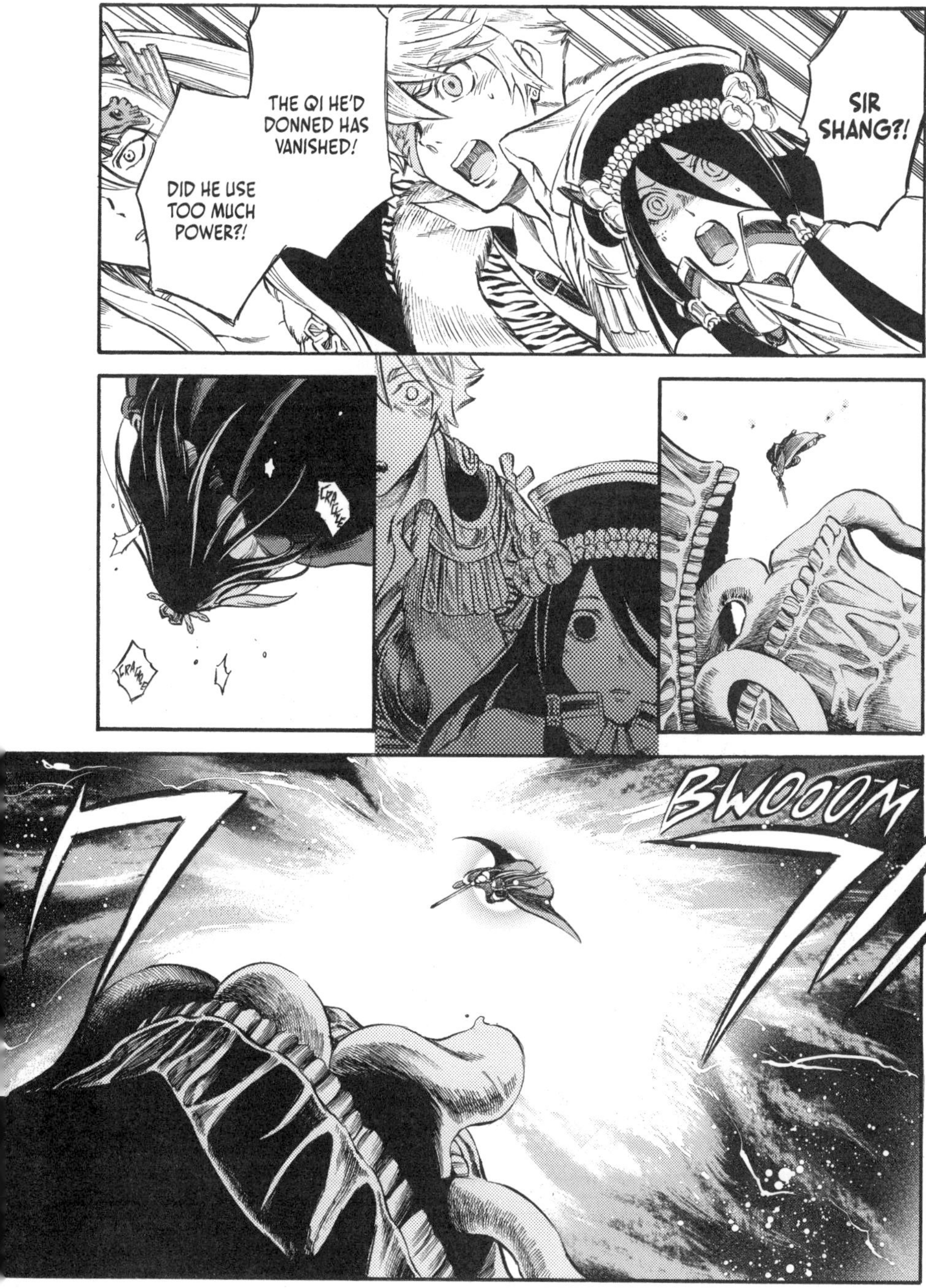
SIR SHANG?!
THE QI HE'D DONNED HAS VANISHED!
DID HE USE TOO MUCH POWER?!
BWOOOM

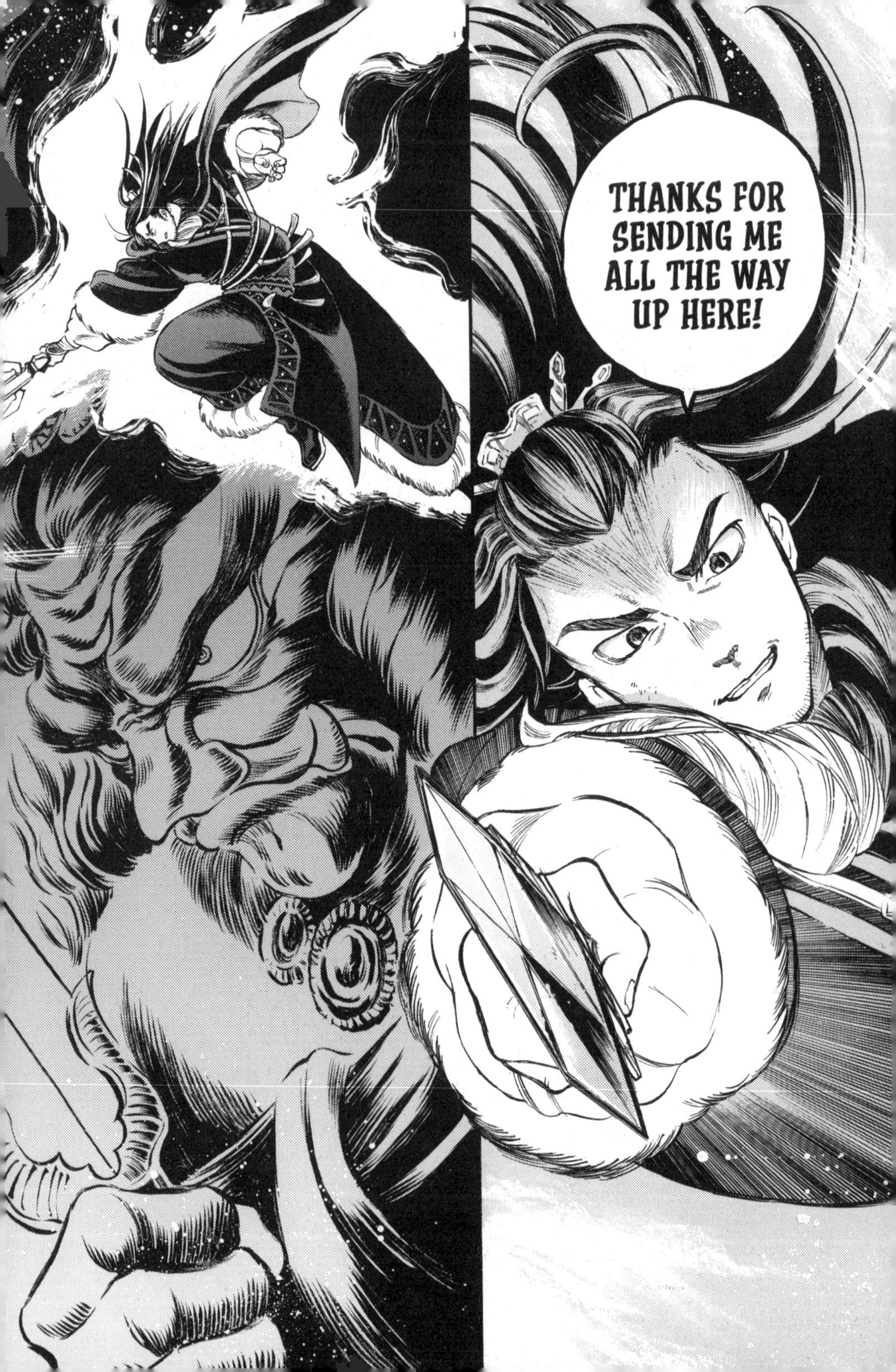
THANKS FOR SENDING ME ALL THE WAY UP HERE!

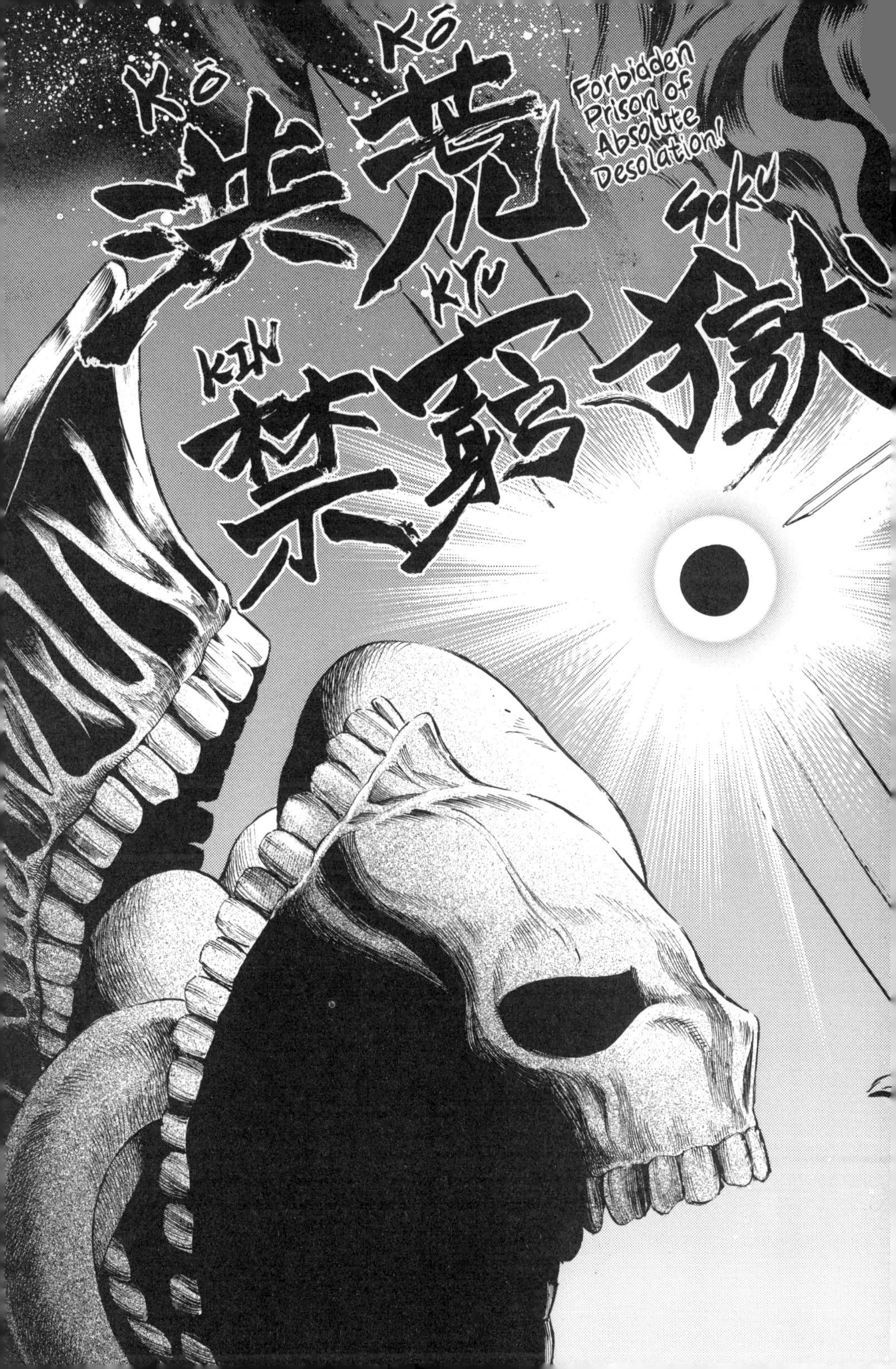

KŌ KŌ KIN KYU GOKU
Forbidden Prison of Absolute Desolation!

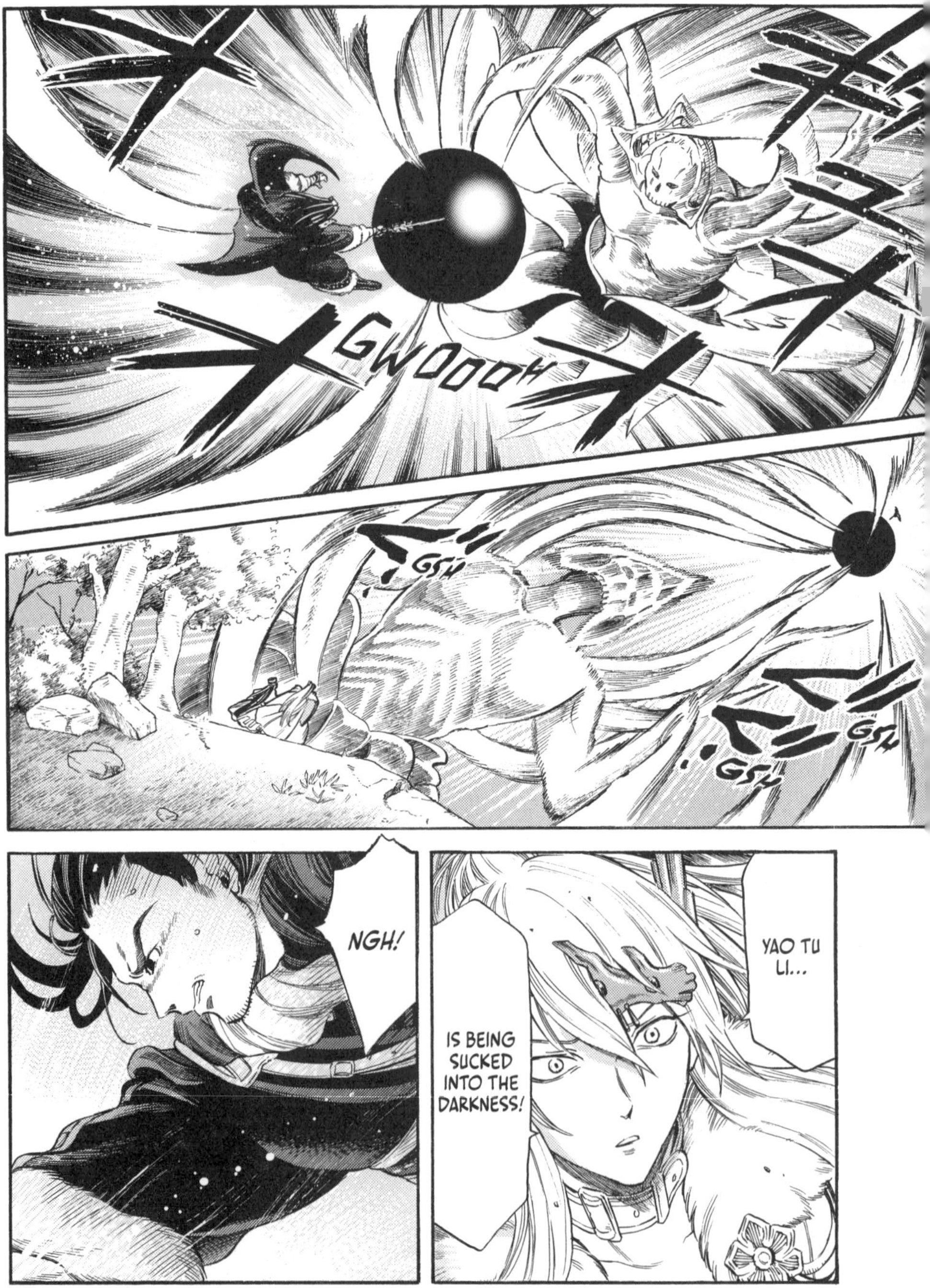
GWOOOH
GSH
GSH
GSH
YAO TU LI...
IS BEING SUCKED INTO THE DARKNESS!
NGH!

BWOOSH

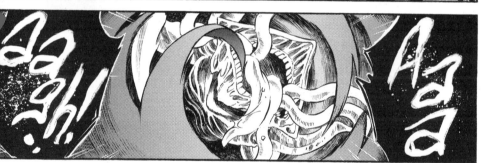

Aaah!

Aaa

SHOOM

HEH!

SO LONG!

339

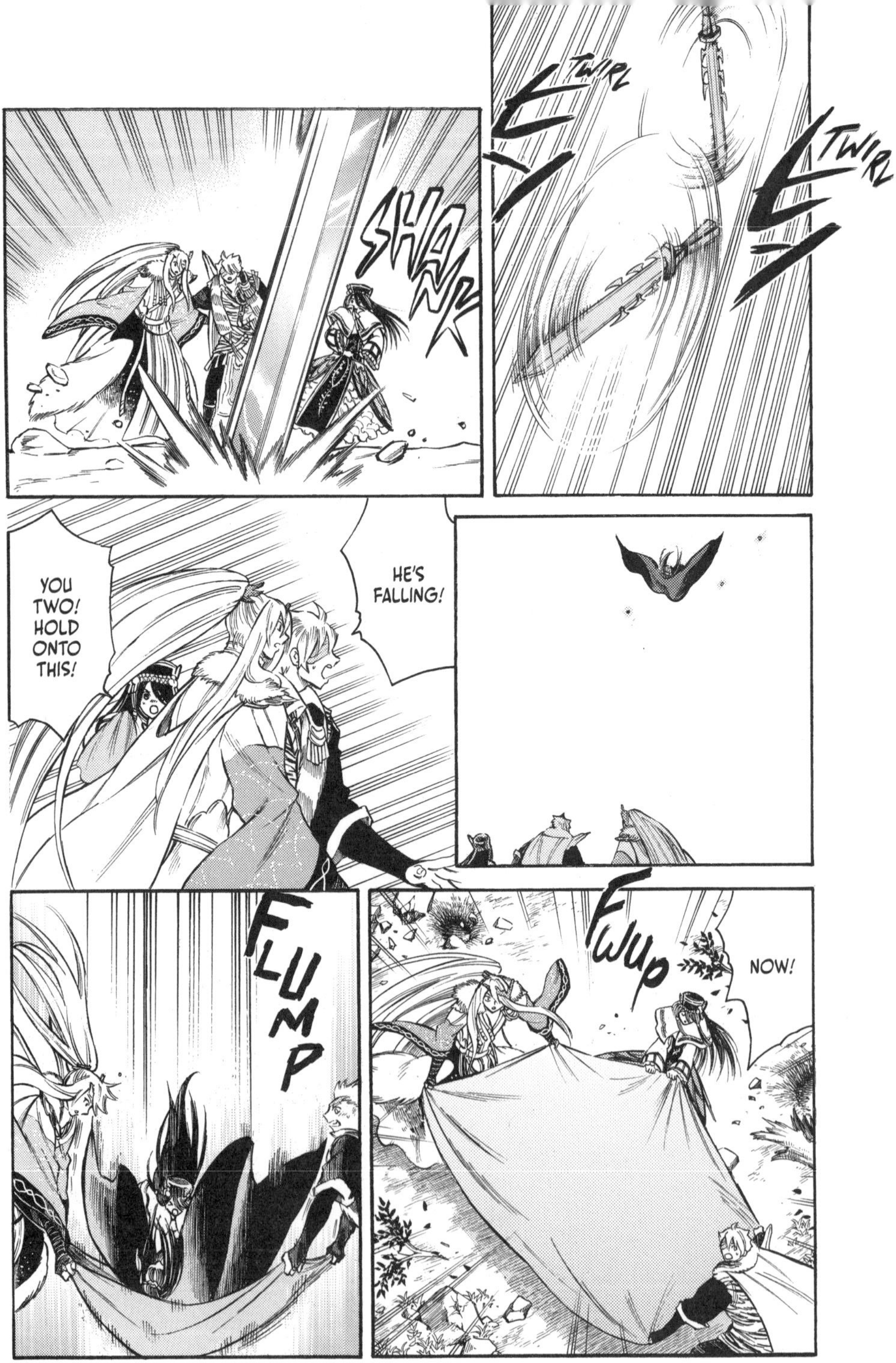
TWIRL
TWIRL
SHANK
HE'S FALLING!
YOU TWO! HOLD ONTO THIS!
FWUP
NOW!
FLUMP

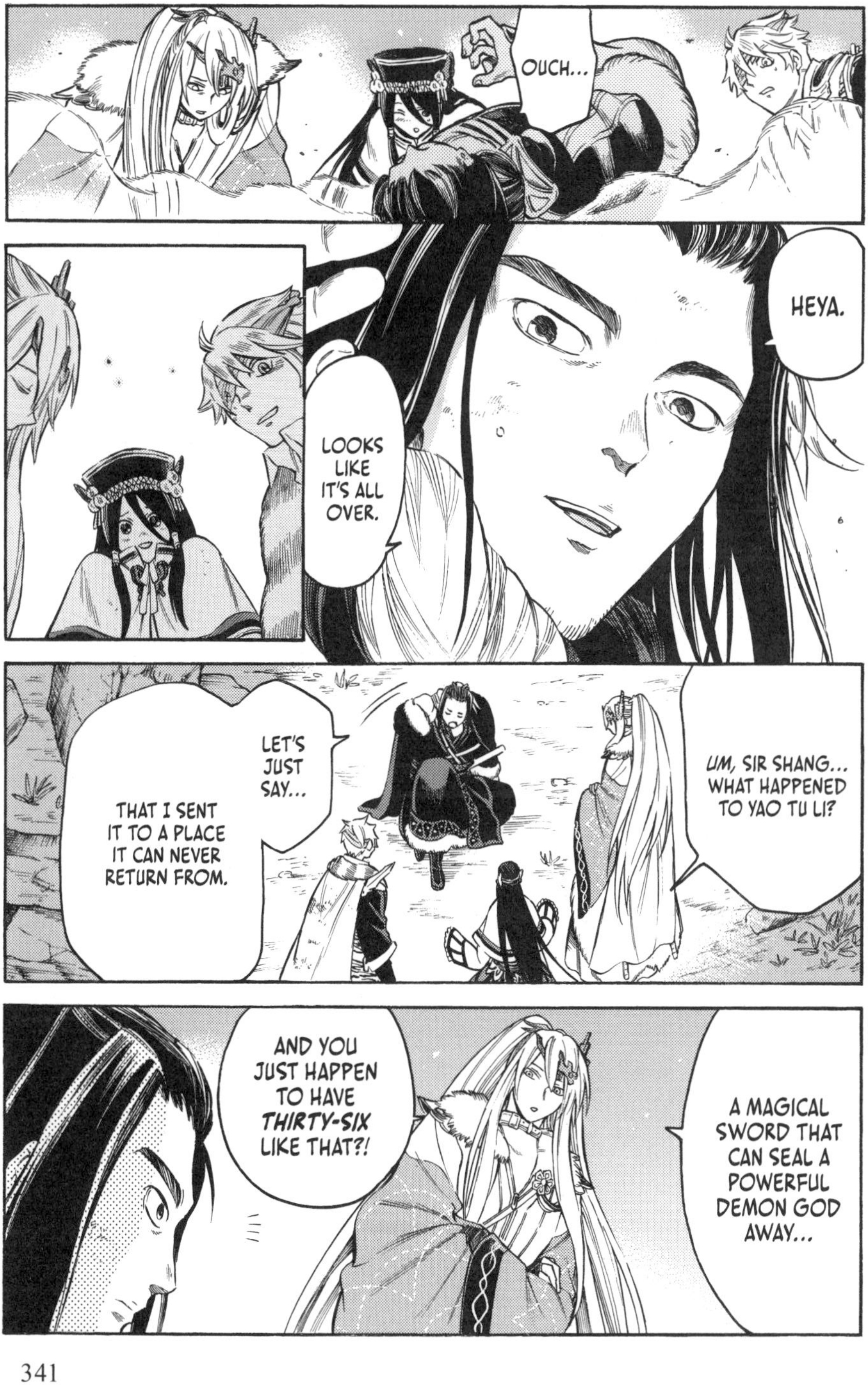
OUCH...
HEYA.
LOOKS LIKE IT'S ALL OVER.
UM, SIR SHANG... WHAT HAPPENED TO YAO TU LI?
LET'S JUST SAY...
THAT I SENT IT TO A PLACE IT CAN NEVER RETURN FROM.
A MAGICAL SWORD THAT CAN SEAL A POWERFUL DEMON GOD AWAY...
AND YOU JUST HAPPEN TO HAVE ***THIRTY-SIX*** LIKE THAT?!

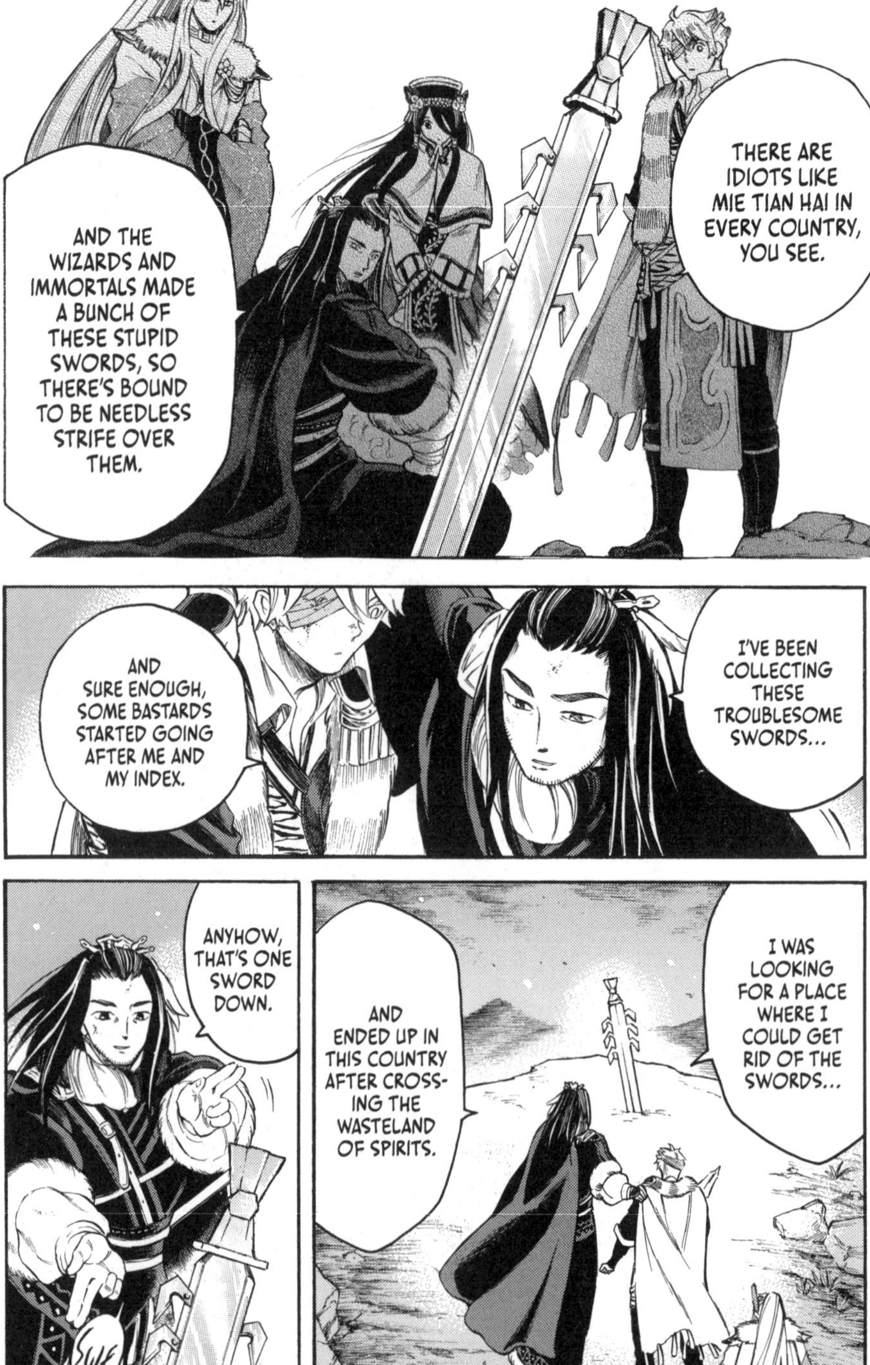
THERE ARE IDIOTS LIKE MIE TIAN HAI IN EVERY COUNTRY, YOU SEE.
AND THE WIZARDS AND IMMORTALS MADE A BUNCH OF THESE STUPID SWORDS, SO THERE'S BOUND TO BE NEEDLESS STRIFE OVER THEM.
I'VE BEEN COLLECTING THESE TROUBLESOME SWORDS...
AND SURE ENOUGH, SOME BASTARDS STARTED GOING AFTER ME AND MY INDEX.
I WAS LOOKING FOR A PLACE WHERE I COULD GET RID OF THE SWORDS...
AND ENDED UP IN THIS COUNTRY AFTER CROSSING THE WASTELAND OF SPIRITS.
ANYHOW, THAT'S ONE SWORD DOWN.
SWF

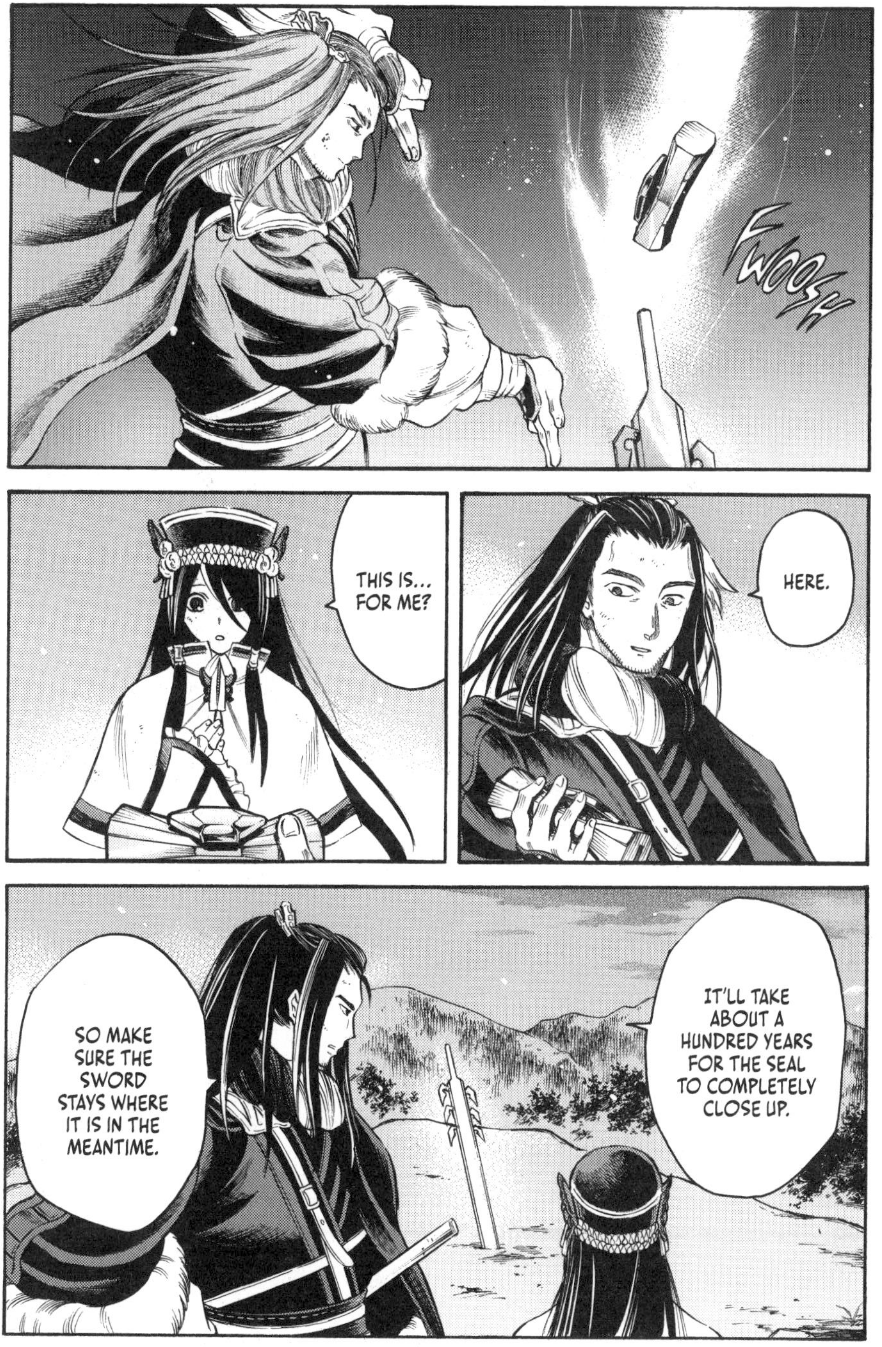
FWOOSH
HERE.
THIS IS... FOR ME?
IT'LL TAKE ABOUT A HUNDRED YEARS FOR THE SEAL TO COMPLETELY CLOSE UP.
SO MAKE SURE THE SWORD STAYS WHERE IT IS IN THE MEANTIME.

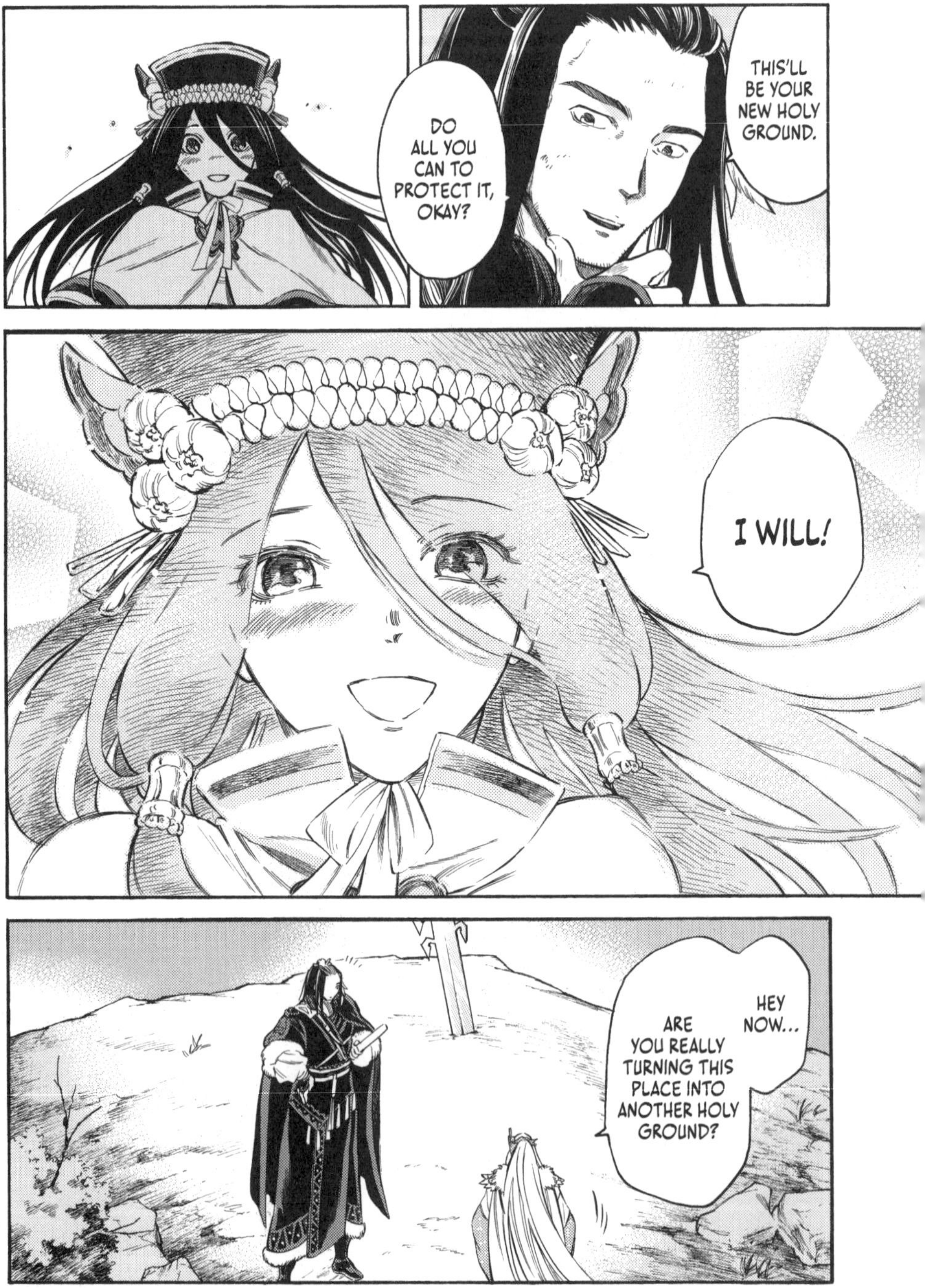
THIS'LL BE YOUR NEW HOLY GROUND.
DO ALL YOU CAN TO PROTECT IT, OKAY?
I WILL!
HEY NOW...
ARE YOU REALLY TURNING THIS PLACE INTO ANOTHER HOLY GROUND?

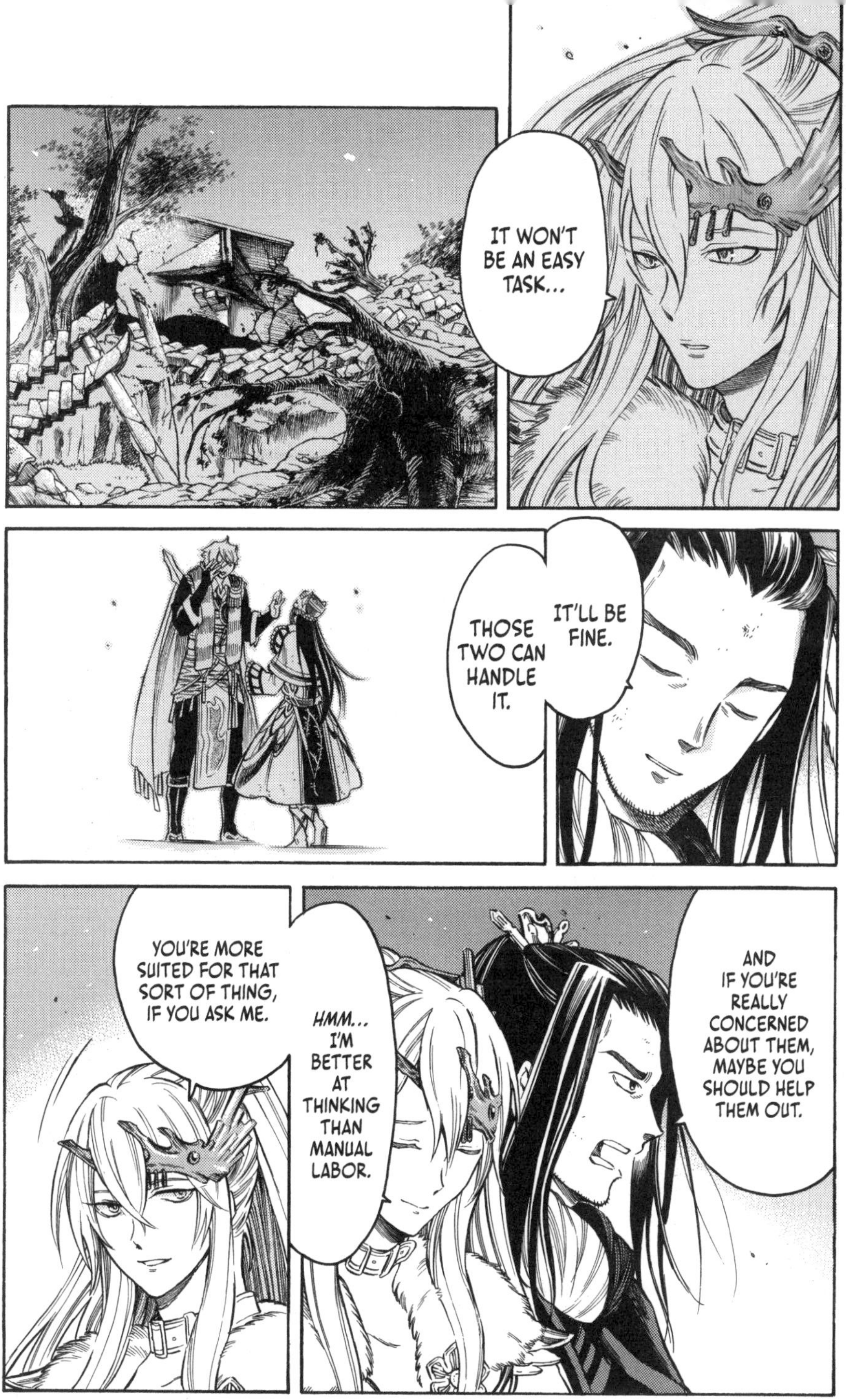
IT WON'T BE AN EASY TASK...
IT'LL BE FINE.
THOSE TWO CAN HANDLE IT.
AND IF YOU'RE REALLY CONCERNED ABOUT THEM, MAYBE YOU SHOULD HELP THEM OUT.
HMM... I'M BETTER AT THINKING THAN MANUAL LABOR.
YOU'RE MORE SUITED FOR THAT SORT OF THING, IF YOU ASK ME.

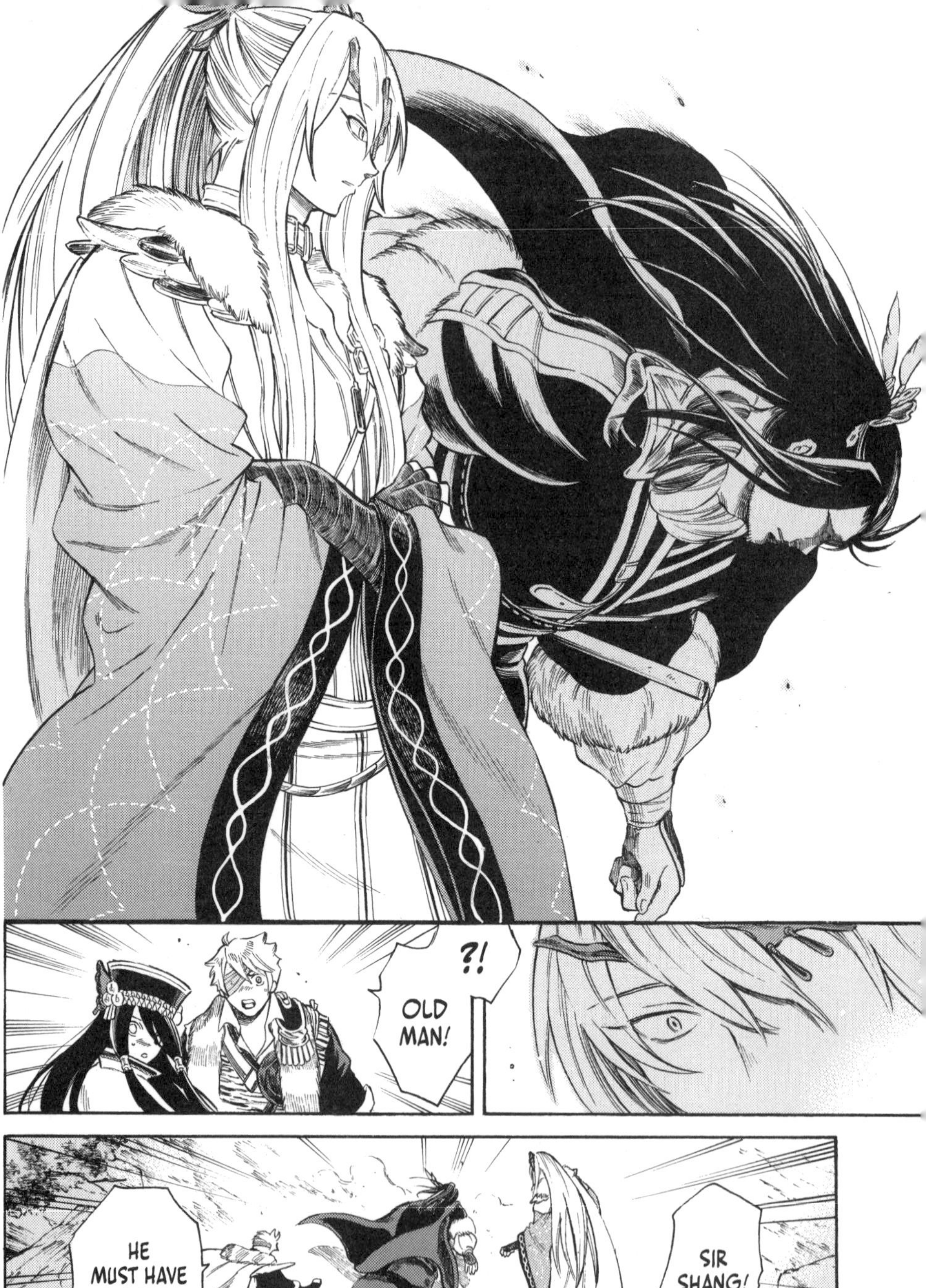
?!
OLD MAN!
SIR SHANG!
HE MUST HAVE GOTTEN A SERIOUS INJURY...!

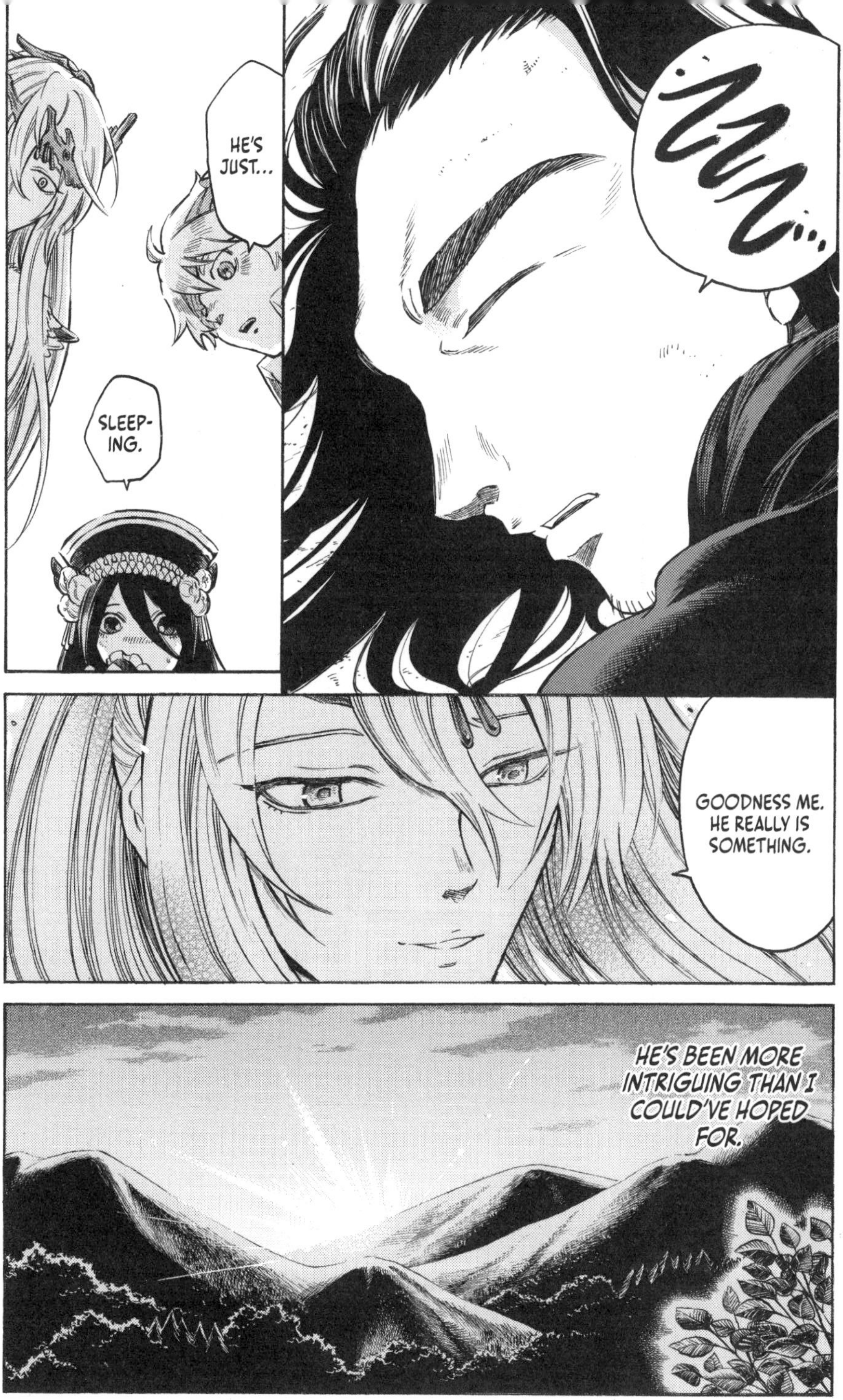
MM...
HE'S JUST...
SLEEP-ING.
GOODNESS ME. HE REALLY IS SOMETHING.
HE'S BEEN MORE INTRIGUING THAN I COULD'VE HOPED FOR.

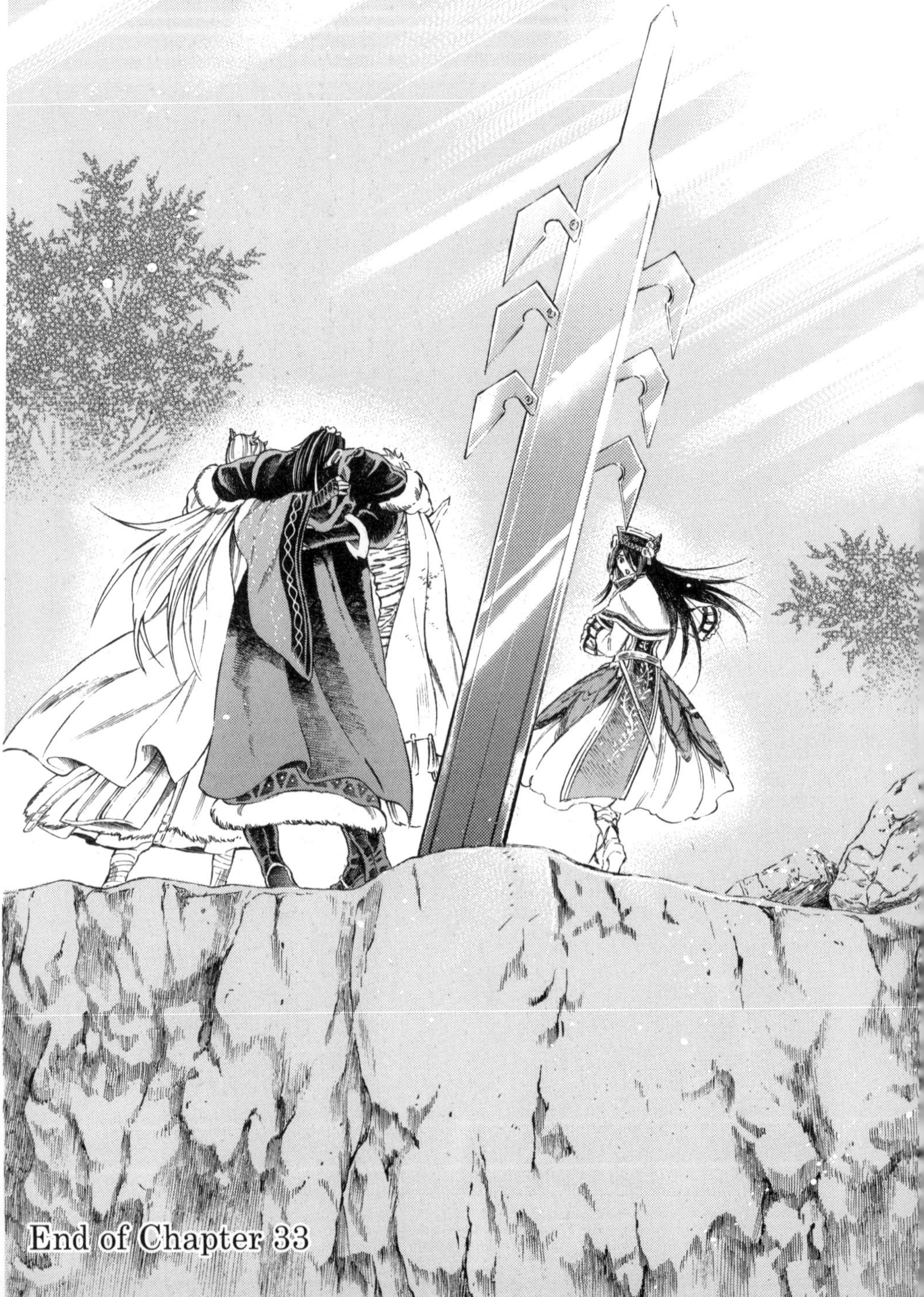
End of Chapter 33

Chapter 34

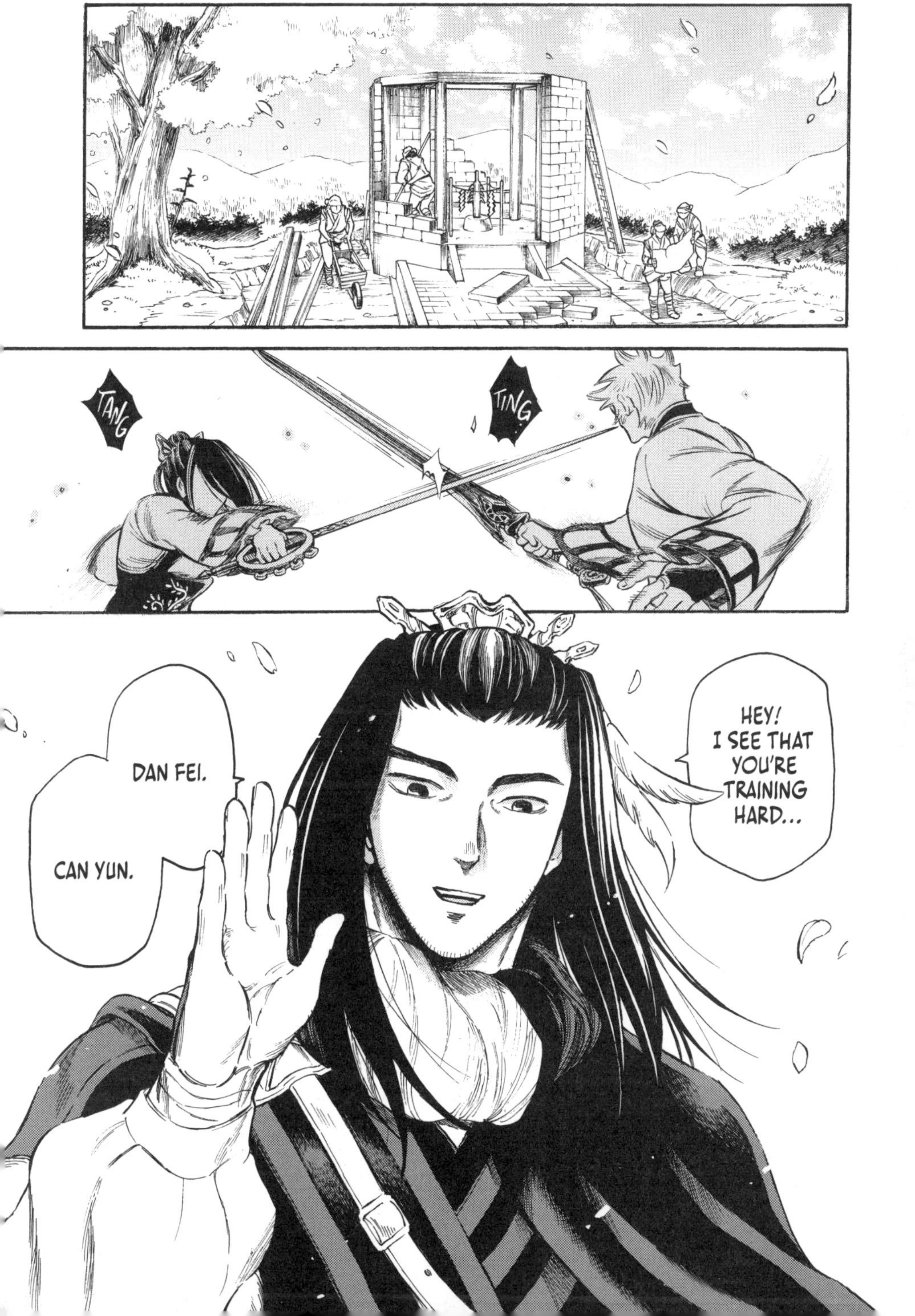
TING
TANG
HEY! I SEE THAT YOU'RE TRAINING HARD...
DAN FEI.
CAN YUN.

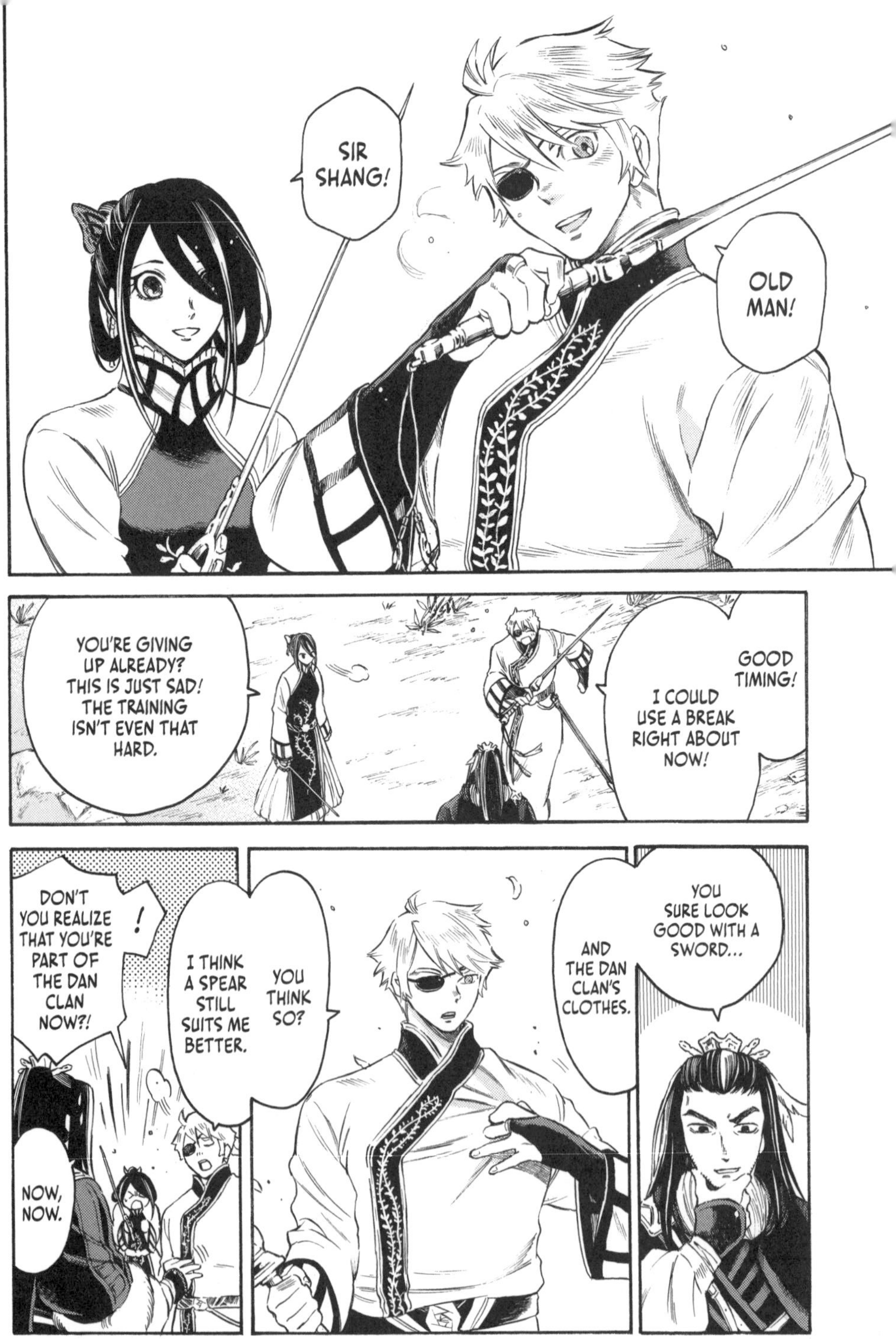
OLD MAN!
SIR SHANG!
GOOD TIMING! I COULD USE A BREAK RIGHT ABOUT NOW!
YOU'RE GIVING UP ALREADY? THIS IS JUST SAD! THE TRAINING ISN'T EVEN THAT HARD.
YOU SURE LOOK GOOD WITH A SWORD...
AND THE DAN CLAN'S CLOTHES.
YOU THINK SO?
I THINK A SPEAR STILL SUITS ME BETTER.
!
DON'T YOU REALIZE THAT YOU'RE PART OF THE DAN CLAN NOW?!
NOW, NOW.

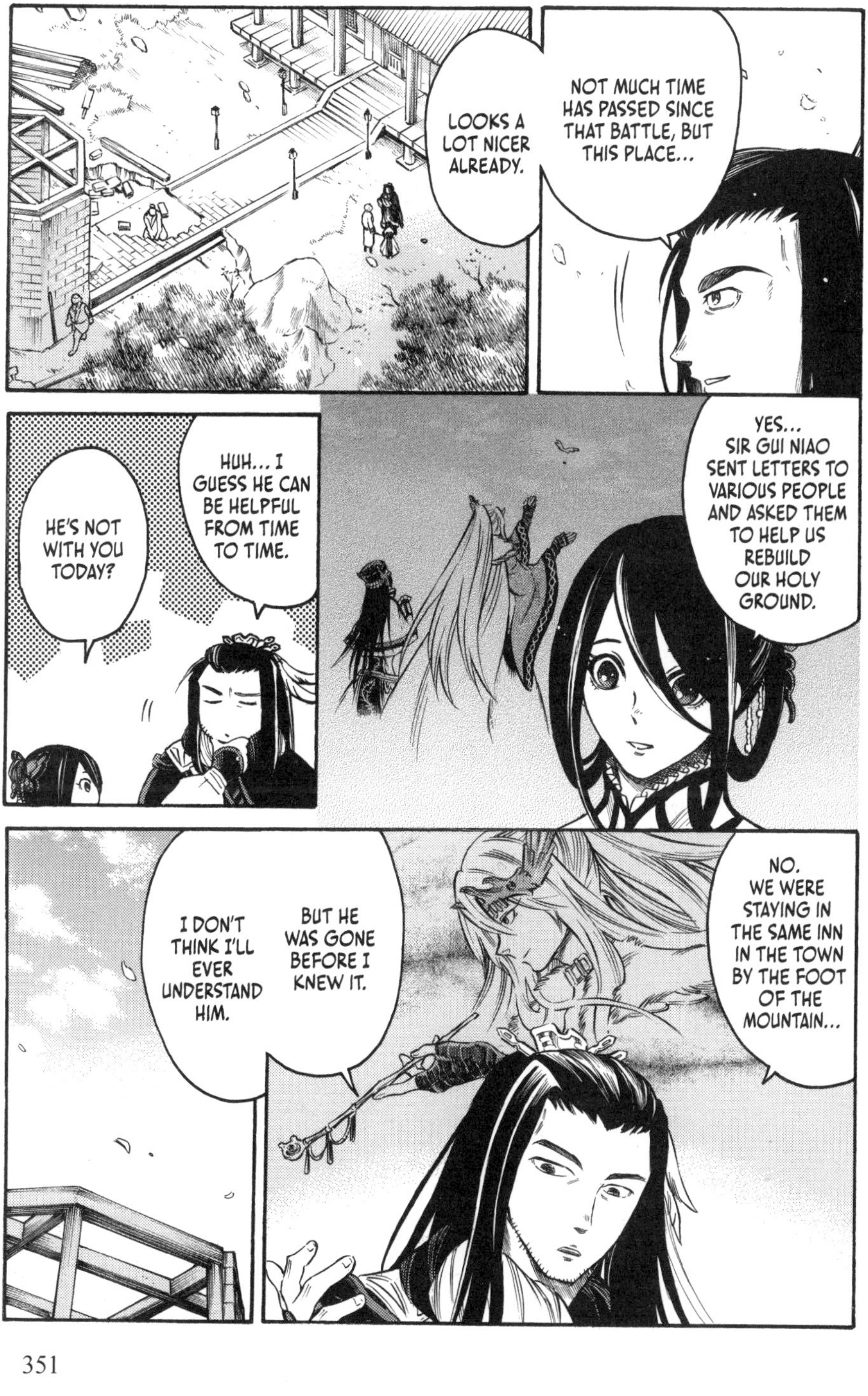
NOT MUCH TIME HAS PASSED SINCE THAT BATTLE, BUT THIS PLACE...
LOOKS A LOT NICER ALREADY.
YES... SIR GUI NIAO SENT LETTERS TO VARIOUS PEOPLE AND ASKED THEM TO HELP US REBUILD OUR HOLY GROUND.
HUH... I GUESS HE CAN BE HELPFUL FROM TIME TO TIME.
HE'S NOT WITH YOU TODAY?
NO. WE WERE STAYING IN THE SAME INN IN THE TOWN BY THE FOOT OF THE MOUNTAIN...
BUT HE WAS GONE BEFORE I KNEW IT.
I DON'T THINK I'LL EVER UNDERSTAND HIM.

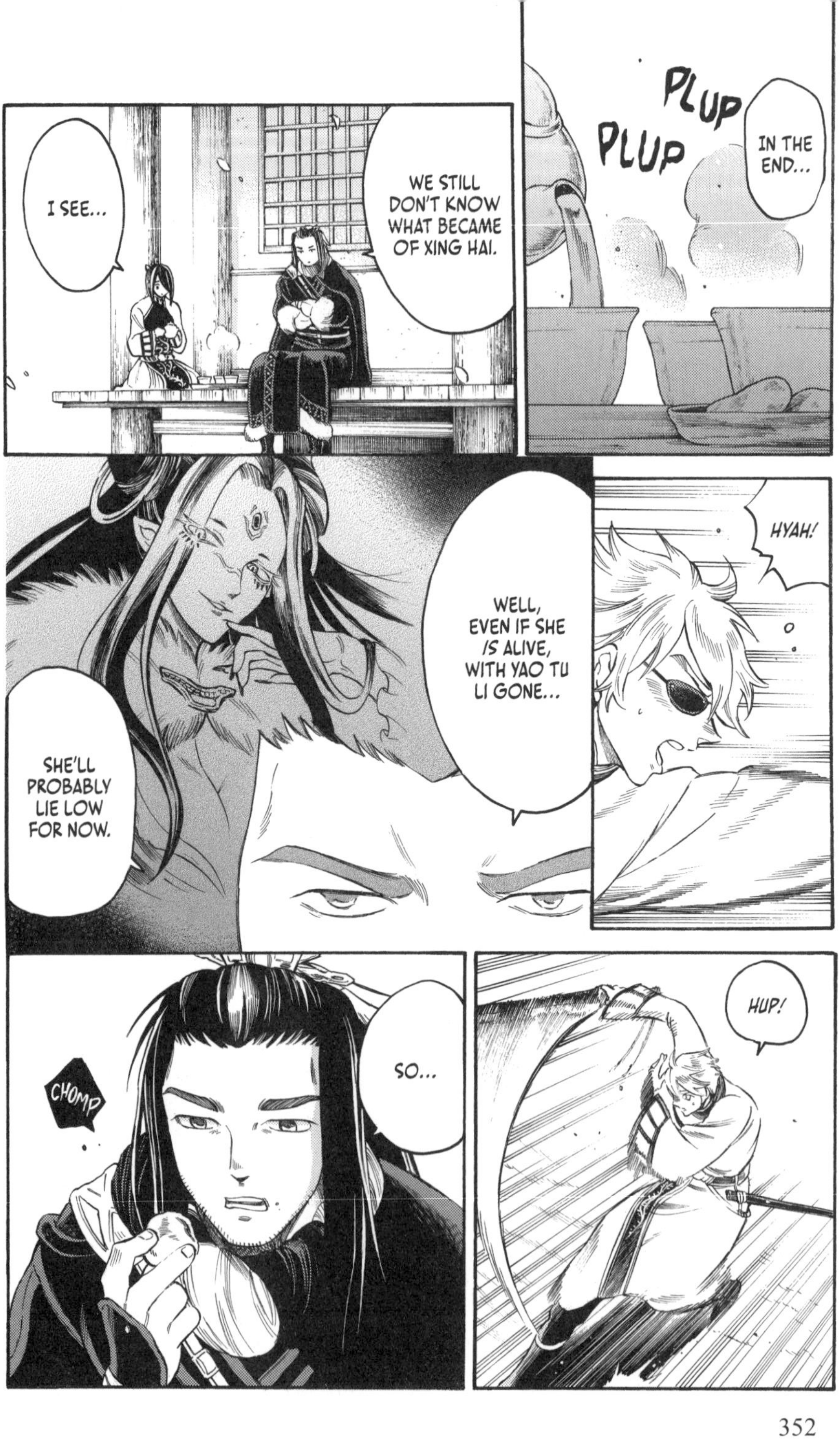
PLUP
PLUP
IN THE END...
WE STILL DON'T KNOW WHAT BECAME OF XING HAI.
I SEE...
HYAH!
WELL, EVEN IF SHE *IS* ALIVE, WITH YAO TU LI GONE...
SHE'LL PROBABLY LIE LOW FOR NOW.
HUP!
SO...
CHOMP

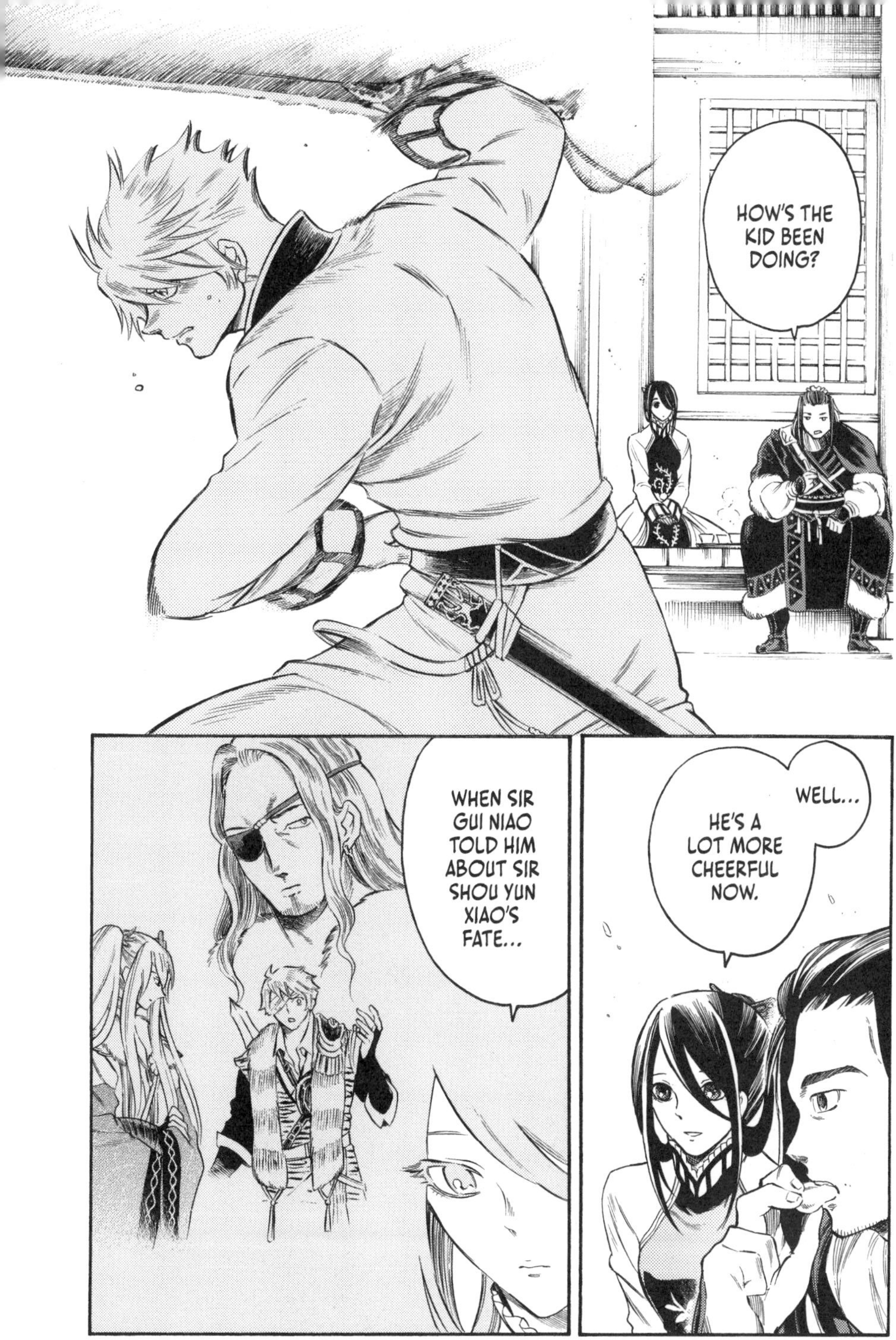
HOW'S THE KID BEEN DOING?
WELL...
HE'S A LOT MORE CHEERFUL NOW.
WHEN SIR GUI NIAO TOLD HIM ABOUT SIR SHOU YUN XIAO'S FATE...

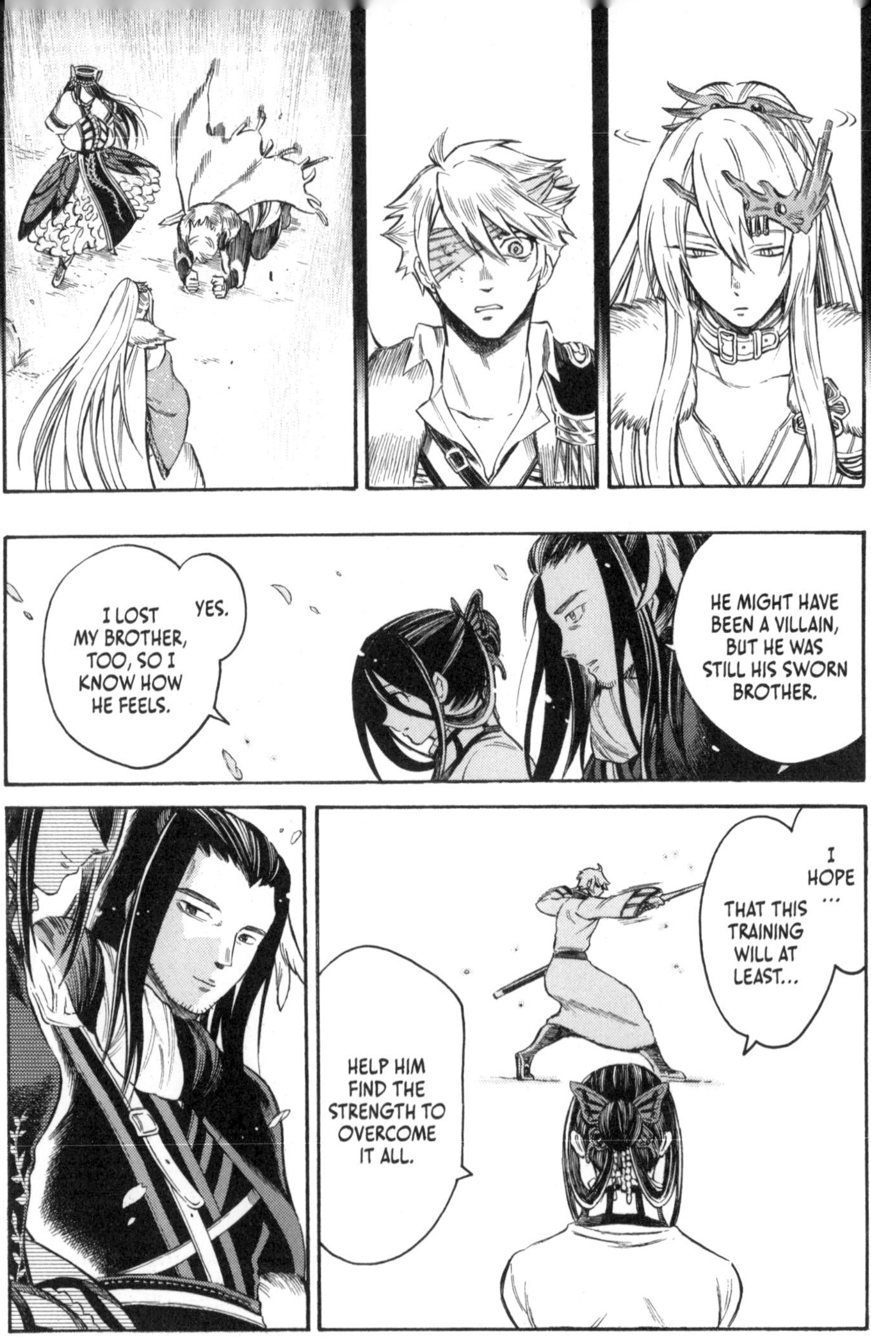
HE MIGHT HAVE BEEN A VILLAIN, BUT HE WAS STILL HIS SWORN BROTHER.
YES. I LOST MY BROTHER, TOO, SO I KNOW HOW HE FEELS.
I HOPE ... THAT THIS TRAINING WILL AT LEAST...
HELP HIM FIND THE STRENGTH TO OVERCOME IT ALL.

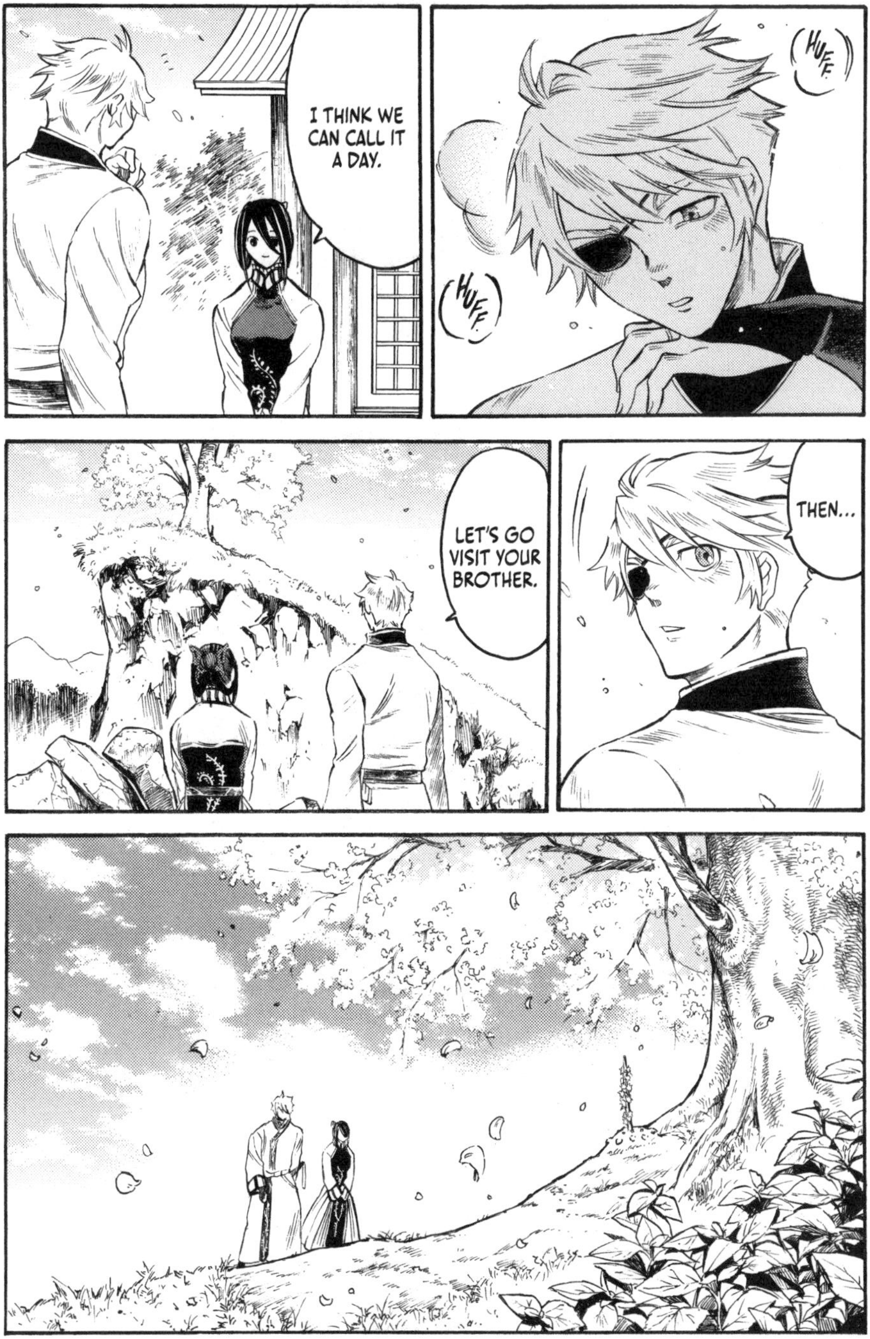
HUFF
HUFF
I THINK WE CAN CALL IT A DAY.
THEN...
LET'S GO VISIT YOUR BROTHER.

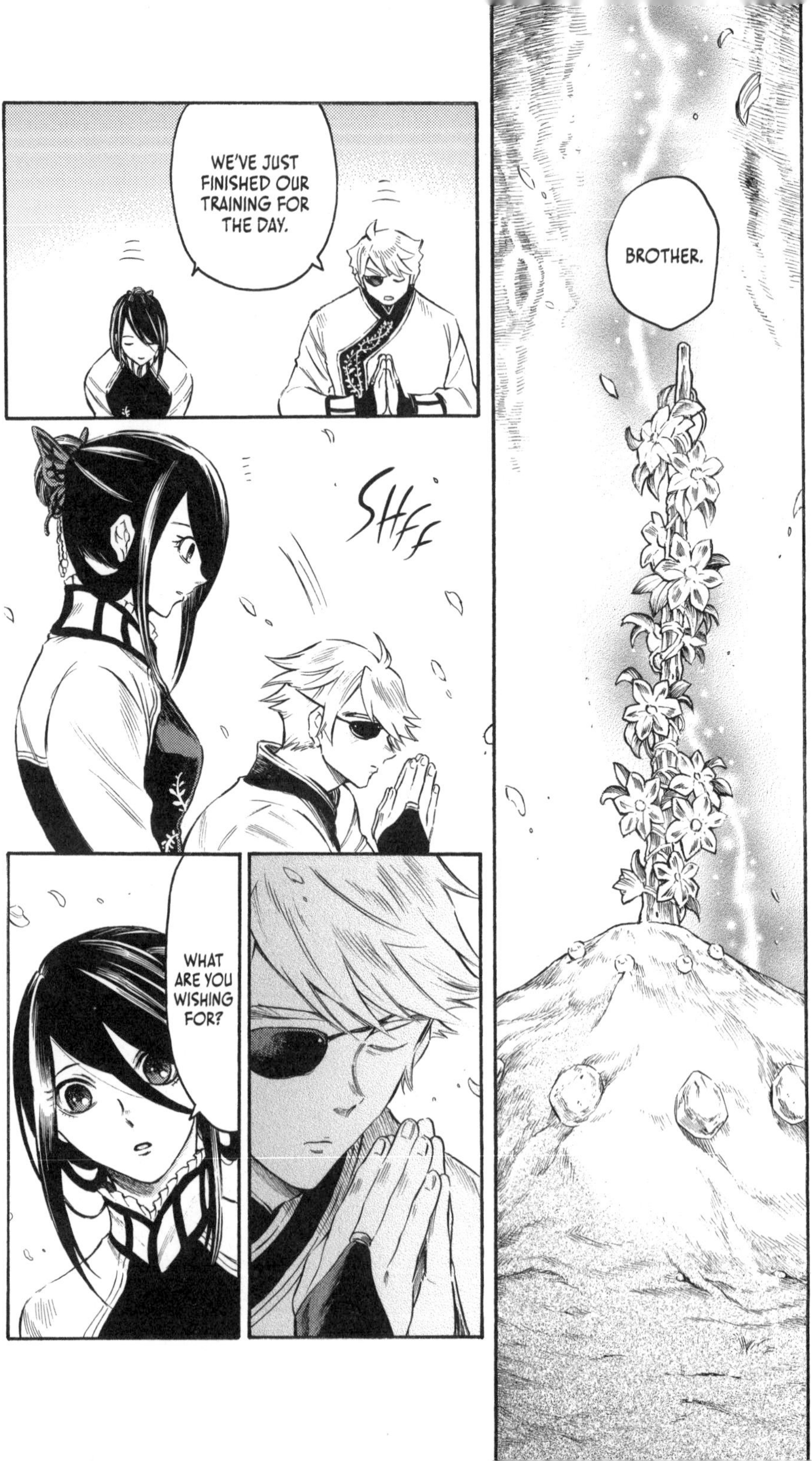
BROTHER.
WE'VE JUST FINISHED OUR TRAINING FOR THE DAY.
SHFF
WHAT ARE YOU WISHING FOR?

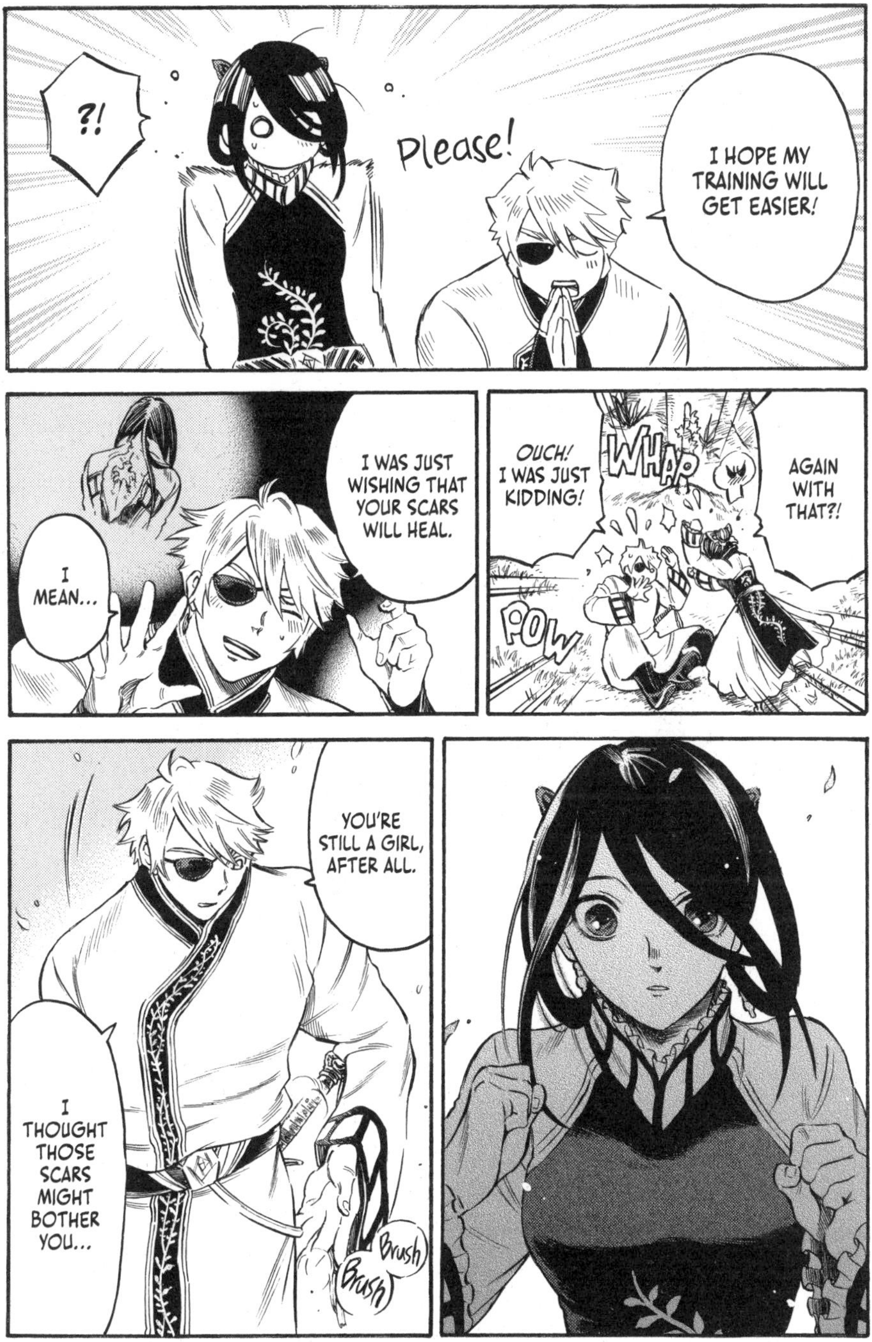
I HOPE MY TRAINING WILL GET EASIER!
Please!
?!
AGAIN WITH THAT?!
WHAP
OUCH! I WAS JUST KIDDING!
POW
I WAS JUST WISHING THAT YOUR SCARS WILL HEAL.
I MEAN...
YOU'RE STILL A GIRL, AFTER ALL.
I THOUGHT THOSE SCARS MIGHT BOTHER YOU...
Brush
Brush

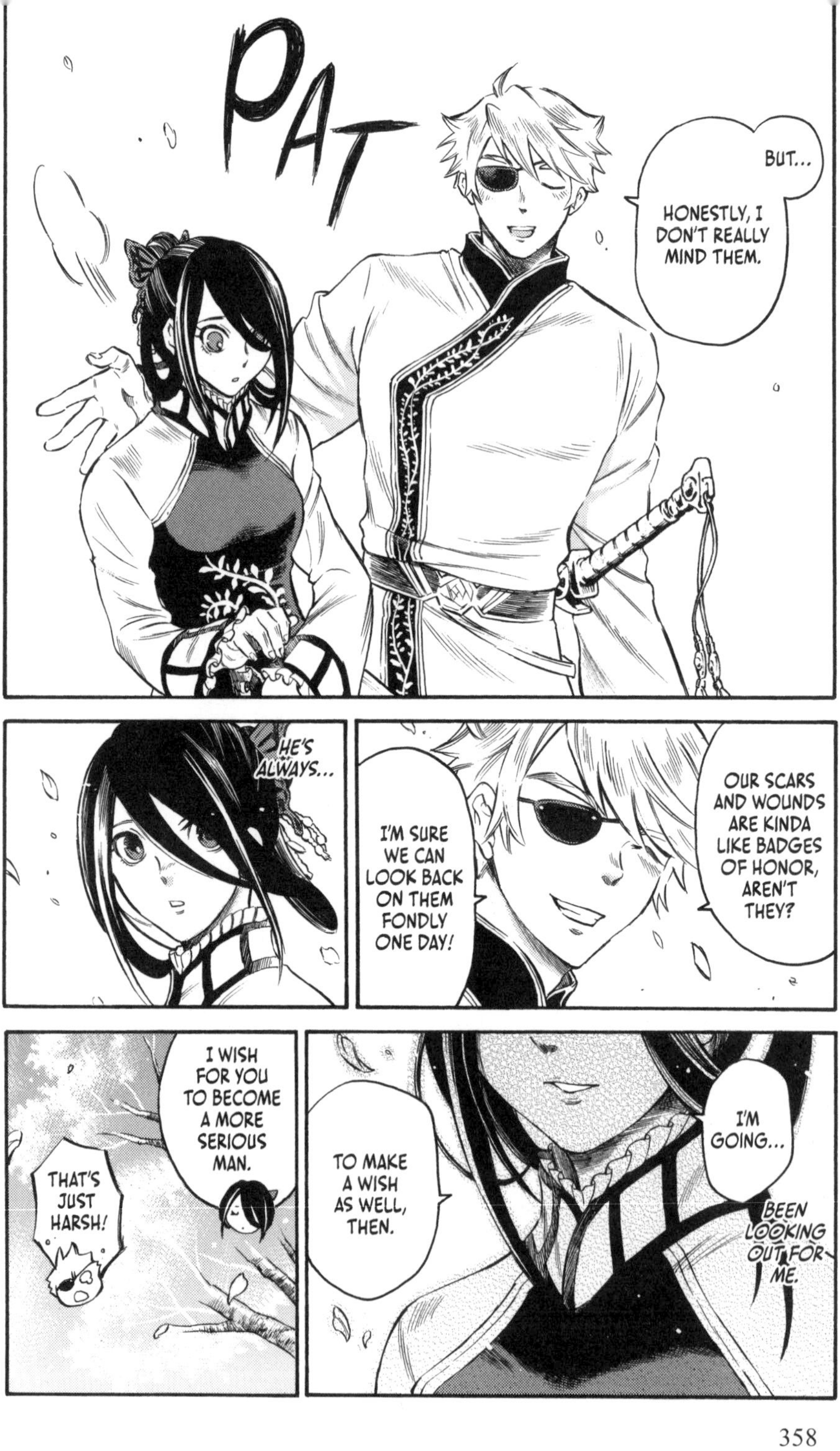
PAT
BUT...
HONESTLY, I DON'T REALLY MIND THEM.
OUR SCARS AND WOUNDS ARE KINDA LIKE BADGES OF HONOR, AREN'T THEY?
I'M SURE WE CAN LOOK BACK ON THEM FONDLY ONE DAY!
HE'S ALWAYS...
I'M GOING...
BEEN LOOKING OUT FOR ME.
TO MAKE A WISH AS WELL, THEN.
I WISH FOR YOU TO BECOME A MORE SERIOUS MAN.
THAT'S JUST HARSH!

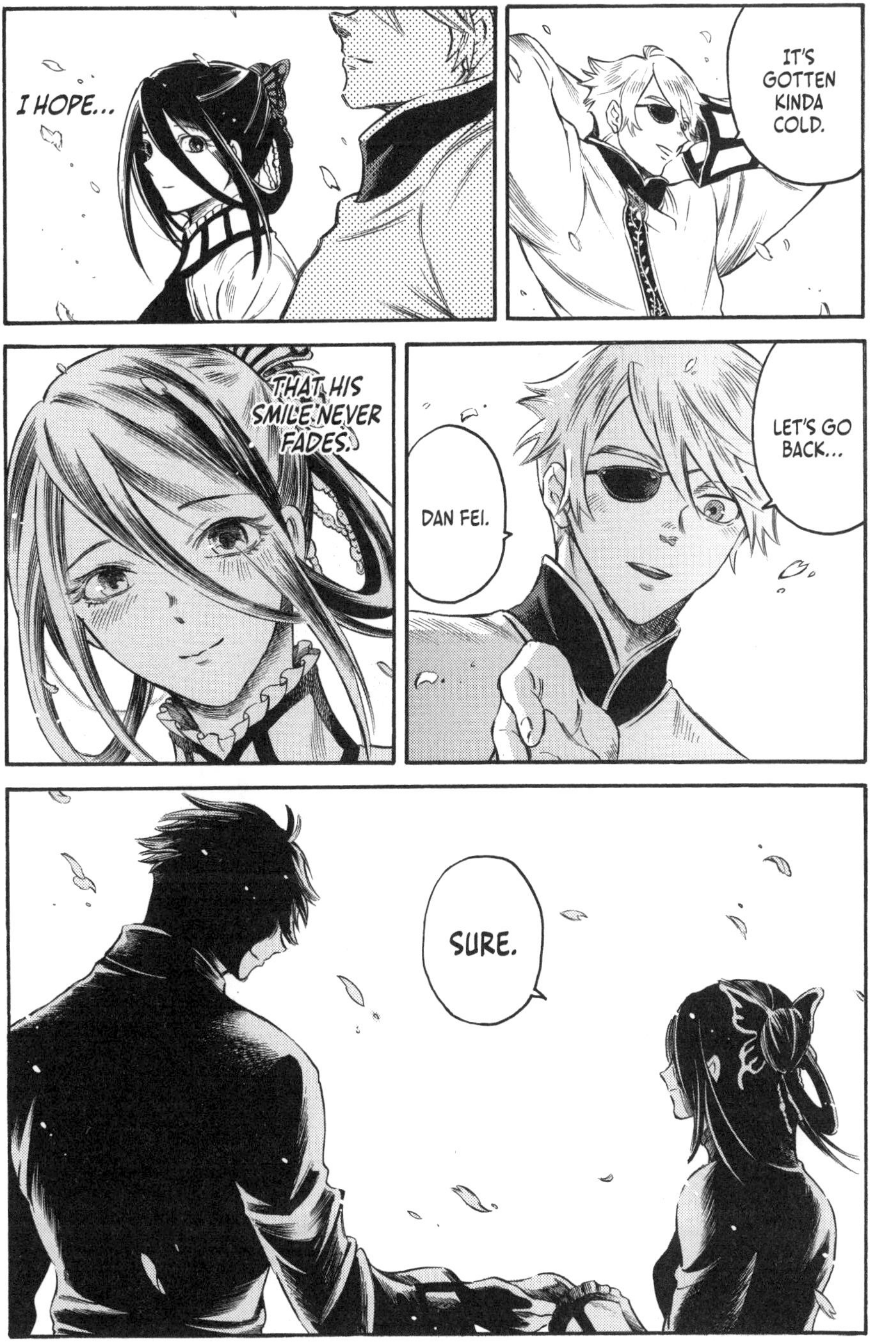
IT'S GOTTEN KINDA COLD.
I HOPE...
LET'S GO BACK...
DAN FEI.
THAT HIS SMILE NEVER FADES.
SURE.

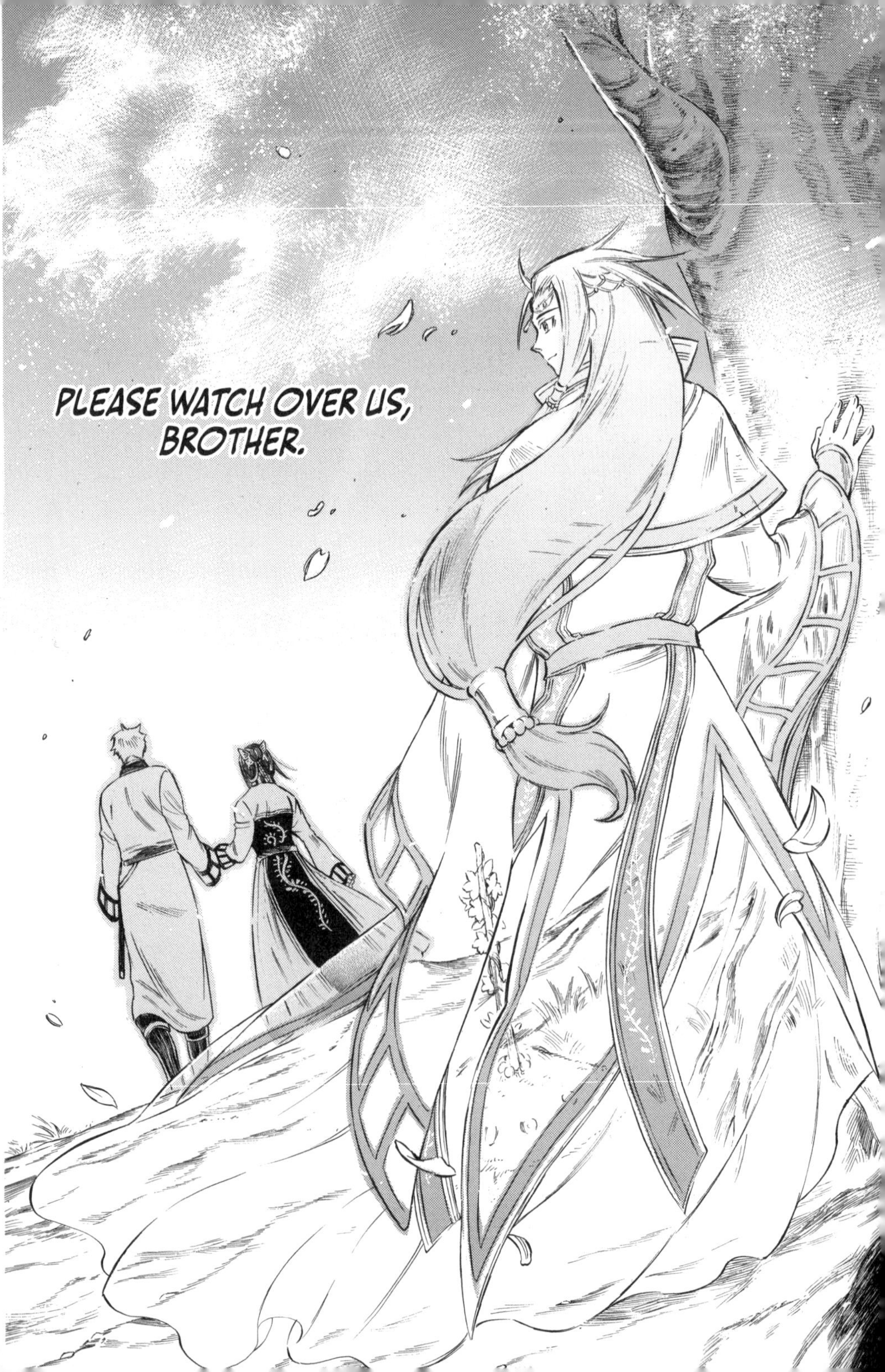
PLEASE WATCH OVER US, BROTHER.

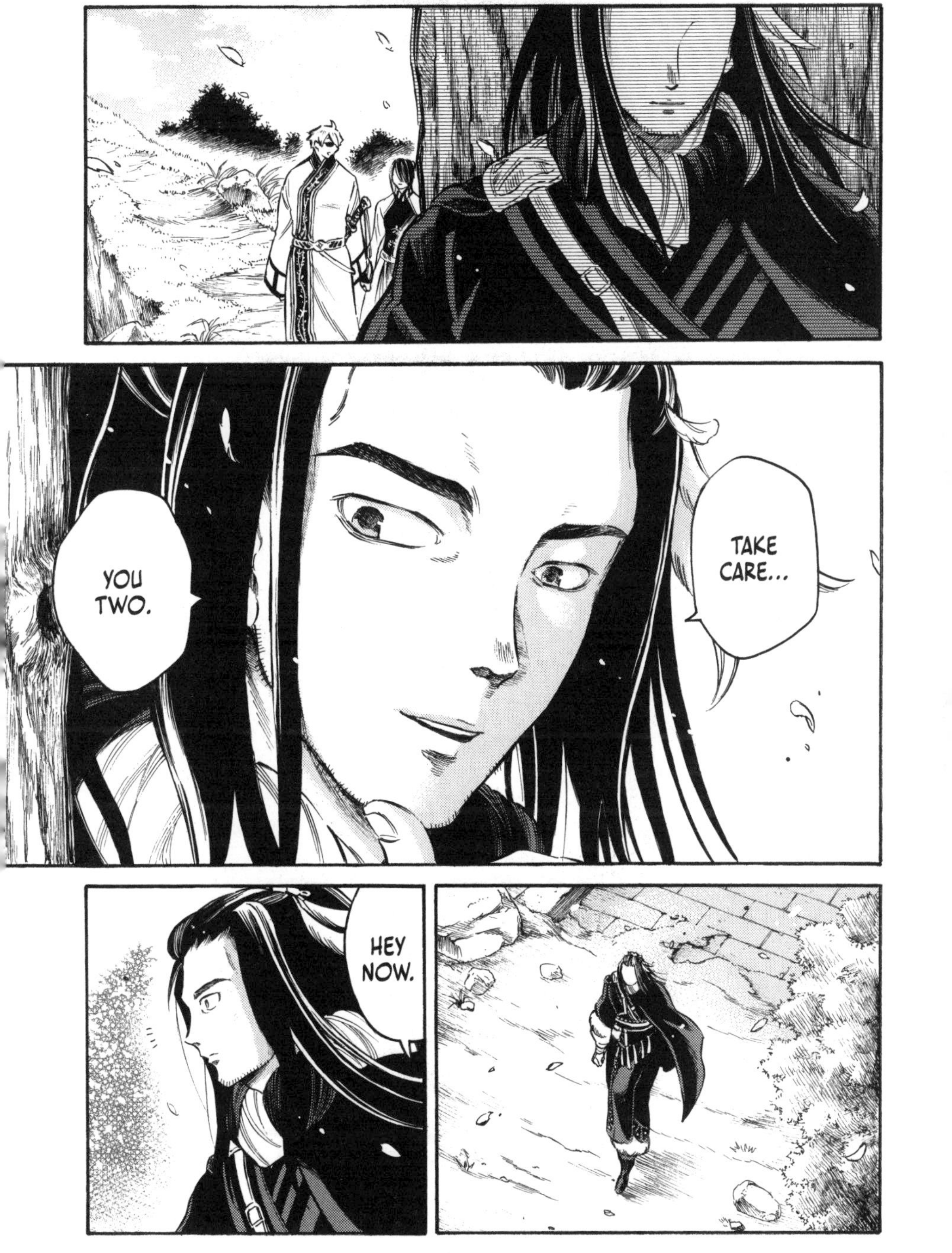
TAKE CARE...
YOU TWO.
HEY NOW.

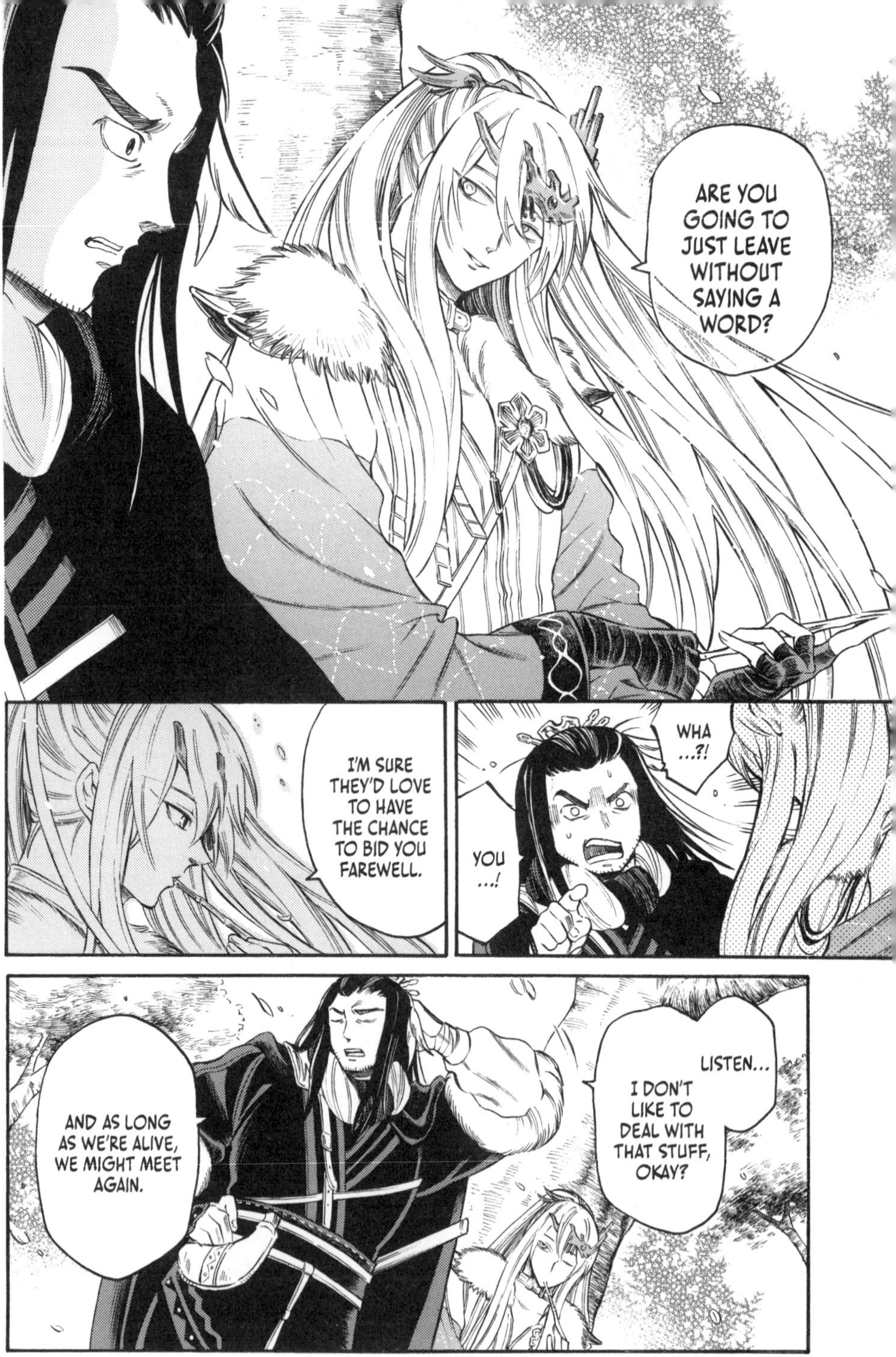
ARE YOU GOING TO JUST LEAVE WITHOUT SAYING A WORD?
WHA ...?!
YOU ...!
I'M SURE THEY'D LOVE TO HAVE THE CHANCE TO BID YOU FAREWELL.
LISTEN... I DON'T LIKE TO DEAL WITH THAT STUFF, OKAY?
AND AS LONG AS WE'RE ALIVE, WE MIGHT MEET AGAIN.

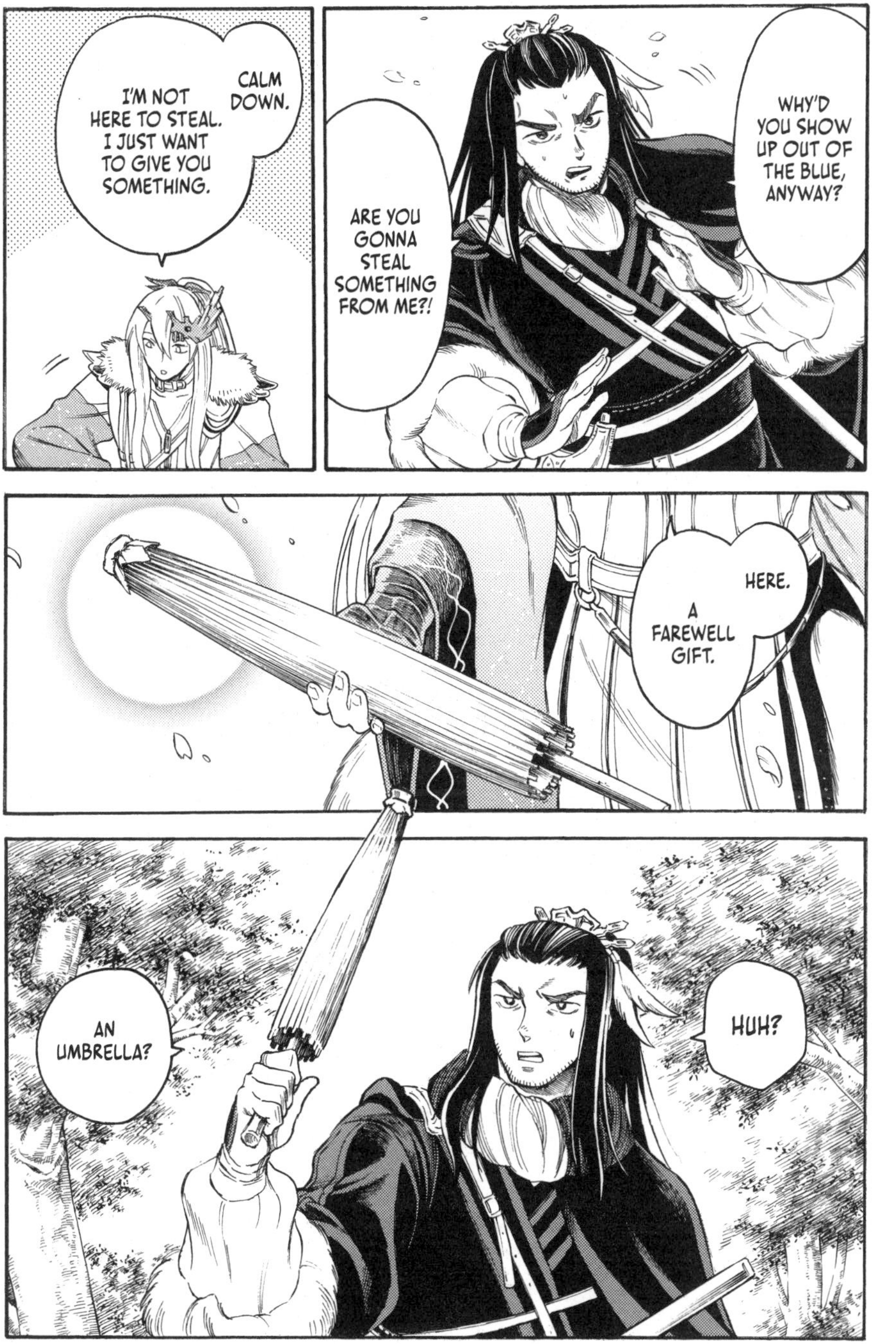
WHY'D YOU SHOW UP OUT OF THE BLUE, ANYWAY?
ARE YOU GONNA STEAL SOMETHING FROM ME?!
CALM DOWN.
I'M NOT HERE TO STEAL. I JUST WANT TO GIVE YOU SOMETHING.
HERE.
A FAREWELL GIFT.
HUH?
AN UMBRELLA?

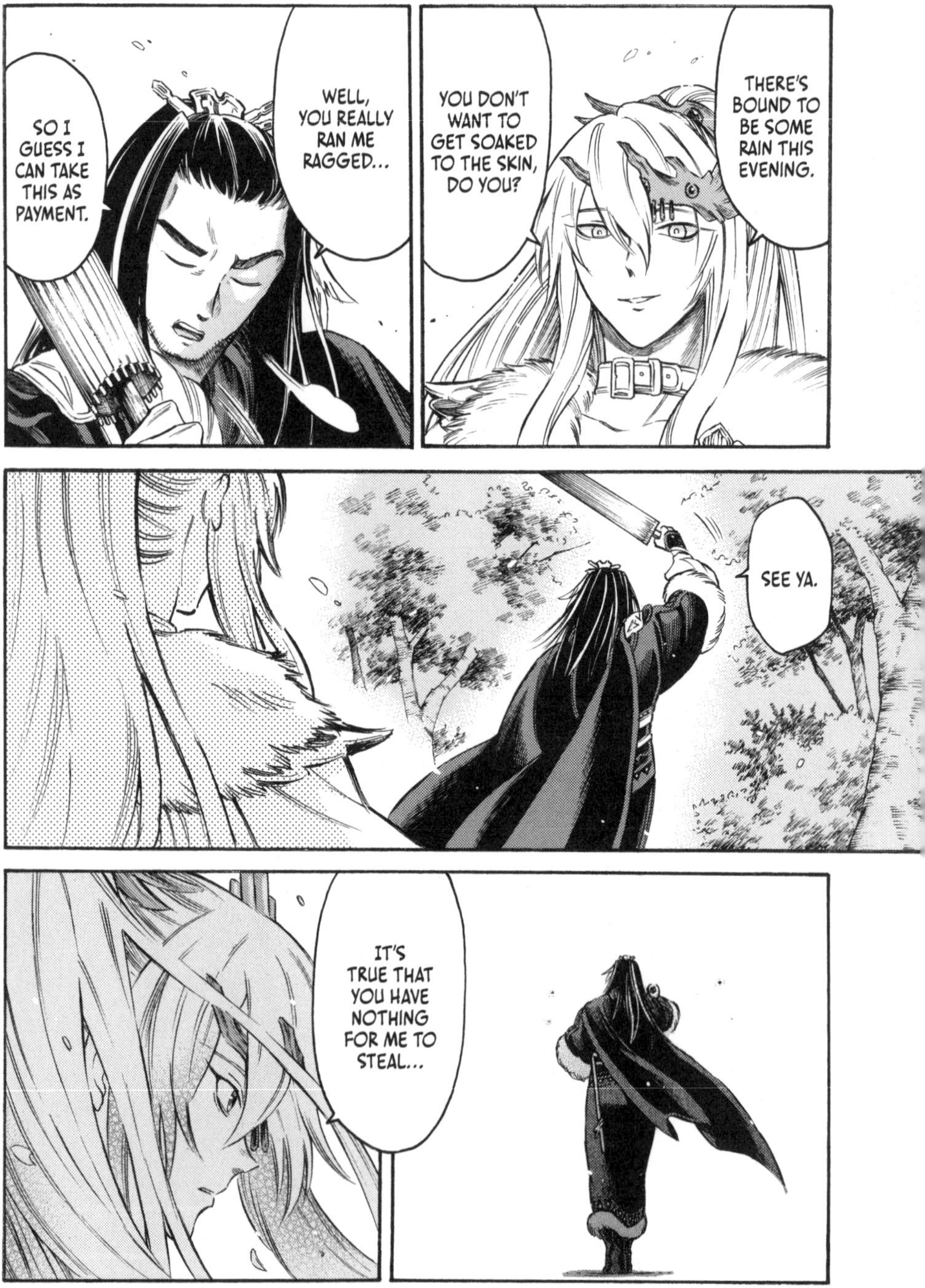
THERE'S BOUND TO BE SOME RAIN THIS EVENING.
YOU DON'T WANT TO GET SOAKED TO THE SKIN, DO YOU?
WELL, YOU REALLY RAN ME RAGGED...
SO I GUESS I CAN TAKE THIS AS PAYMENT.
SEE YA.
IT'S TRUE THAT YOU HAVE NOTHING FOR ME TO STEAL...

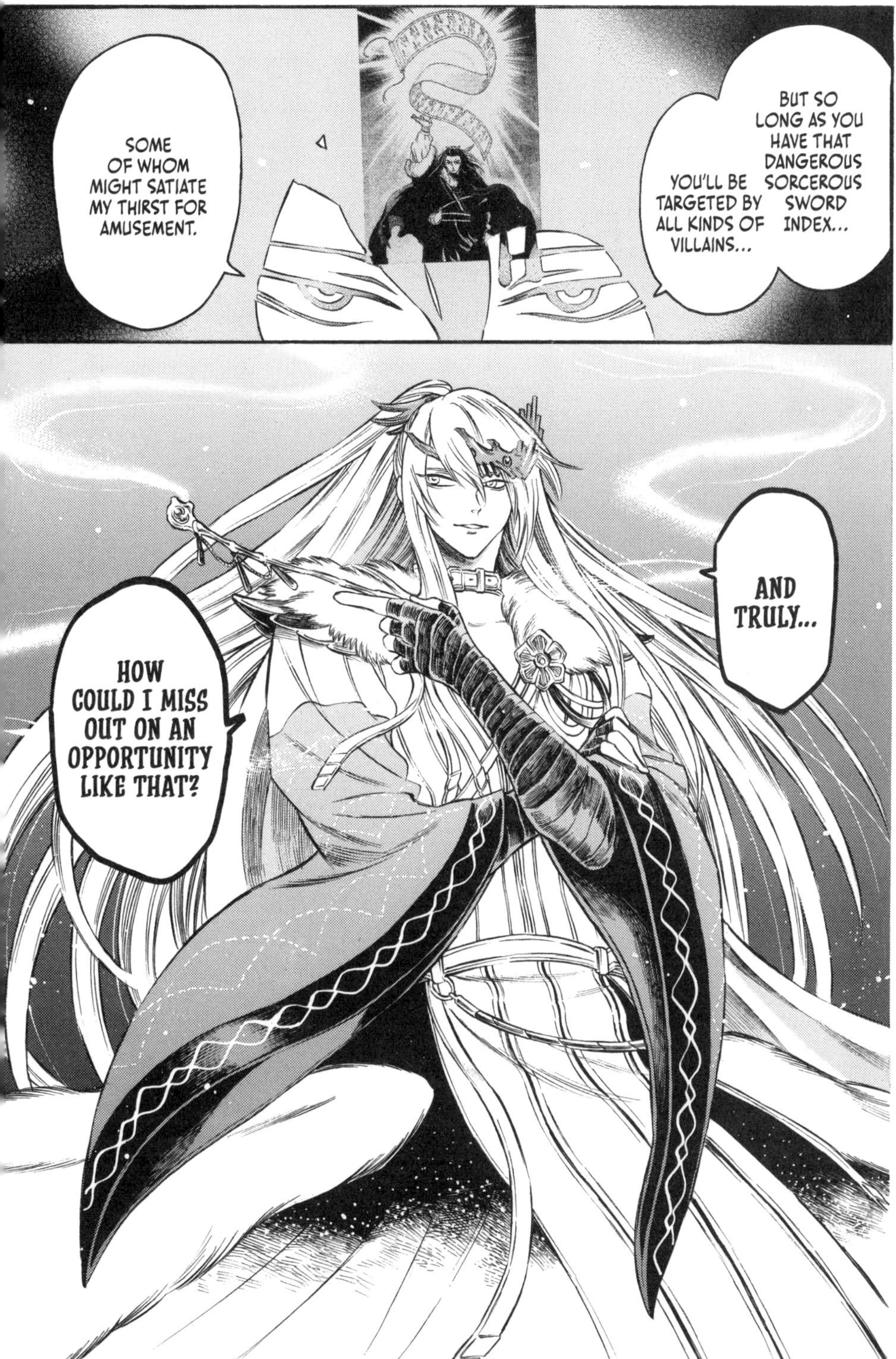
BUT SO LONG AS YOU HAVE THAT DANGEROUS SORCEROUS SWORD INDEX... YOU'LL BE TARGETED BY ALL KINDS OF VILLAINS...
SOME OF WHOM MIGHT SATIATE MY THIRST FOR AMUSEMENT.
AND TRULY...
HOW COULD I MISS OUT ON AN OPPORTUNITY LIKE THAT?

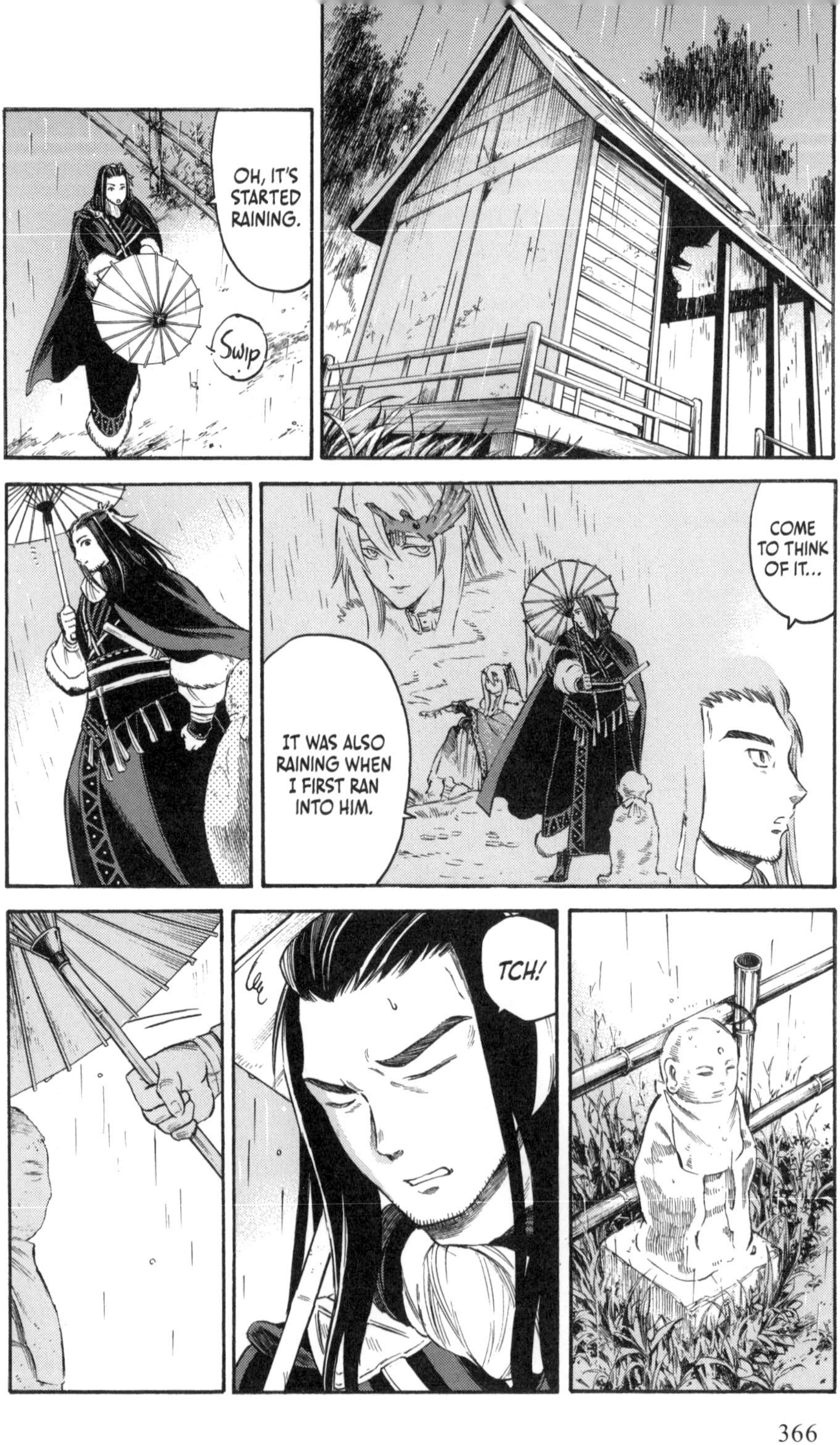
OH, IT'S STARTED RAINING.
Swip
COME TO THINK OF IT...
IT WAS ALSO RAINING WHEN I FIRST RAN INTO HIM.
TCH!

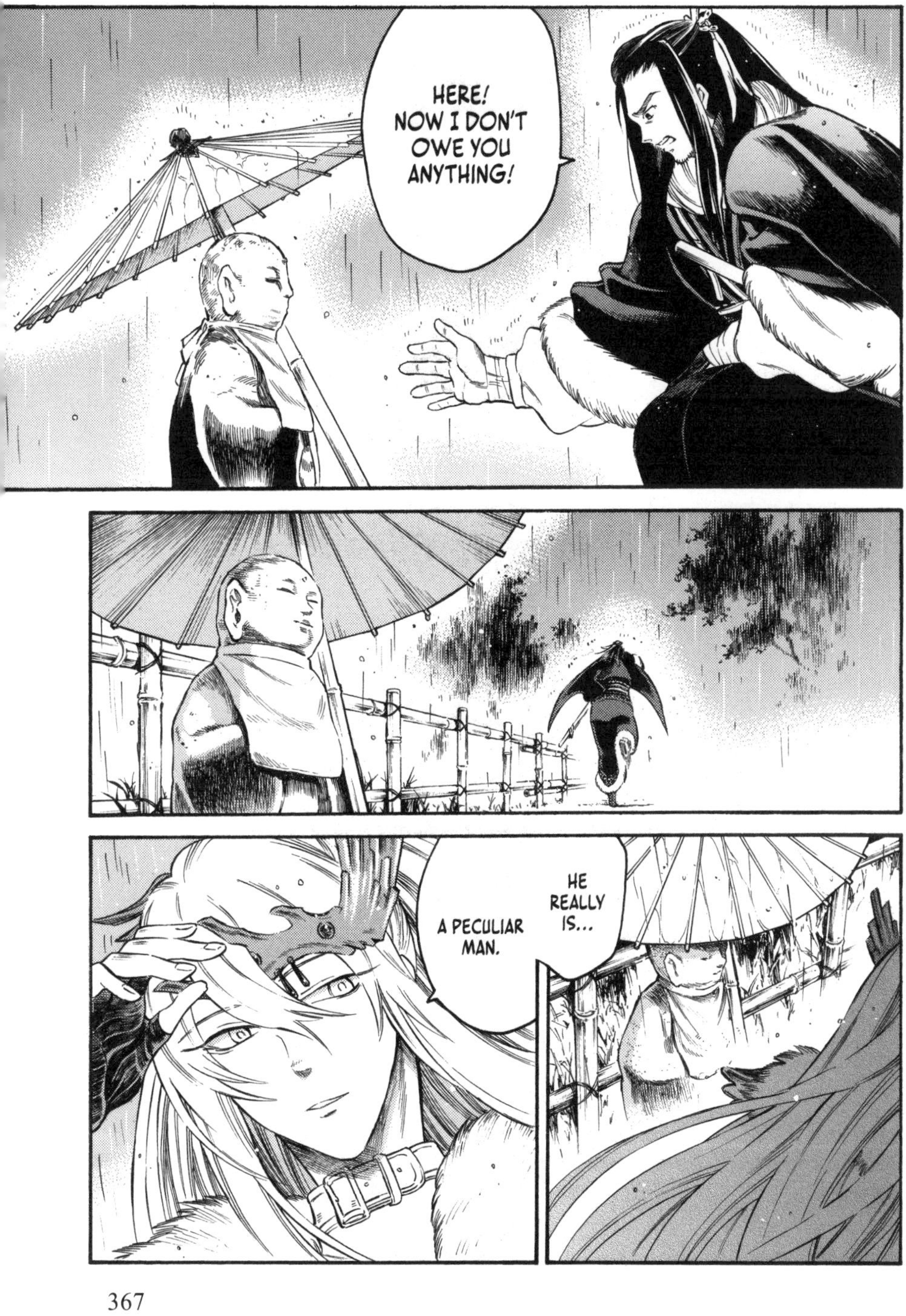
HERE! NOW I DON'T OWE YOU ANYTHING!
HE REALLY IS...
A PECULIAR MAN.

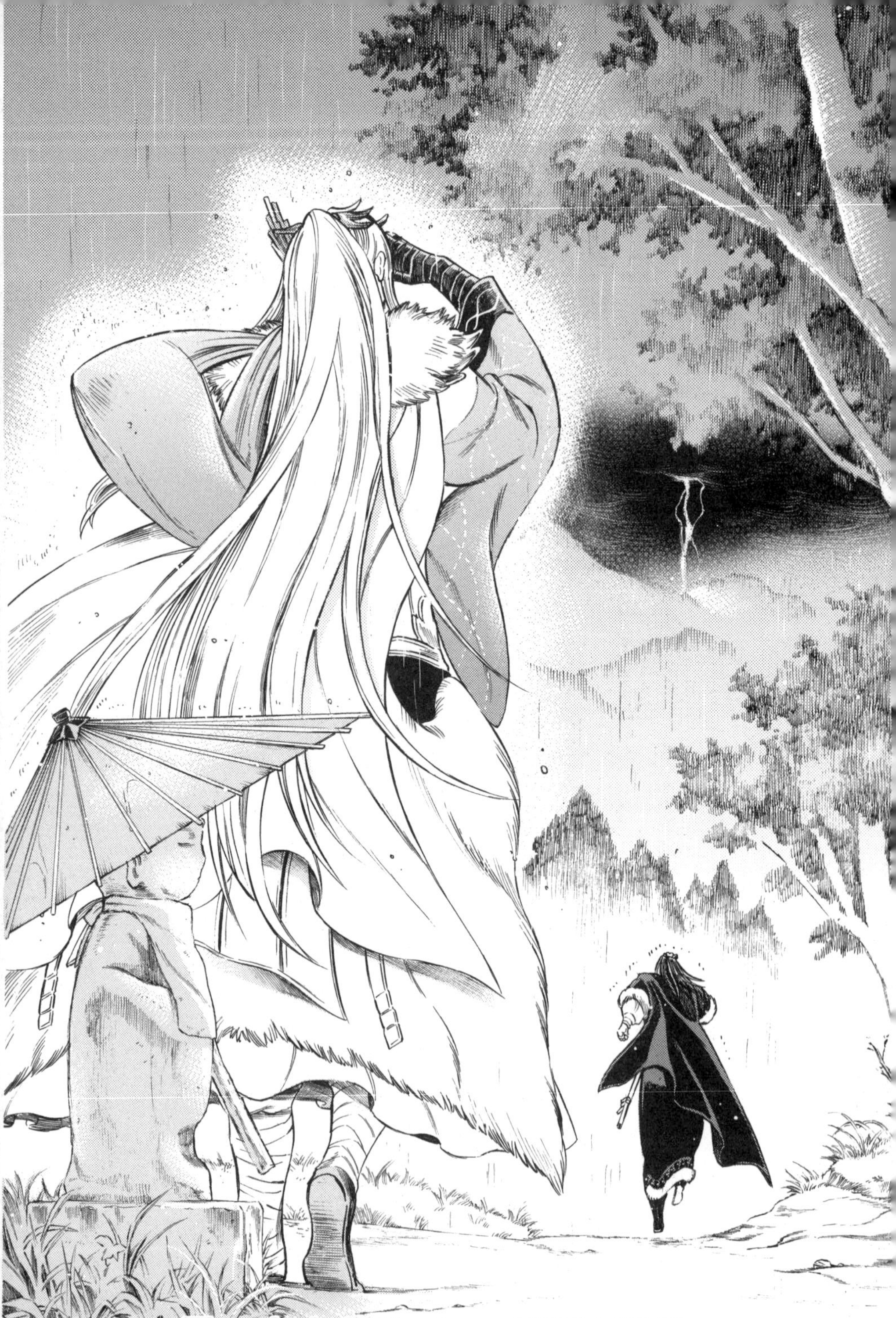

Thunderbolt Fantasy / THE END

Thunderbolt Fantasy
東離劍遊紀

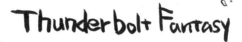

Thunderbolt Fantasy

REGULAR STAFF

Yoko

Ryo Haruta

EDITORS

Koji Terayama

Yoko Ueda

Natsumi Omichi

HELP STAFF

Hiroki Komatsu

Nagomu Haraguchi

Ranna Sato

Aena Miyasato

Yoshiki Miura

DESIGNER

Tadashi Hisamochi (hive)

COLLABORATION

Thunderbolt Fantasy Project

Before I knew it, we've already reached part three. Big thanks to everyone who purchased this book!

Yui Sakuma

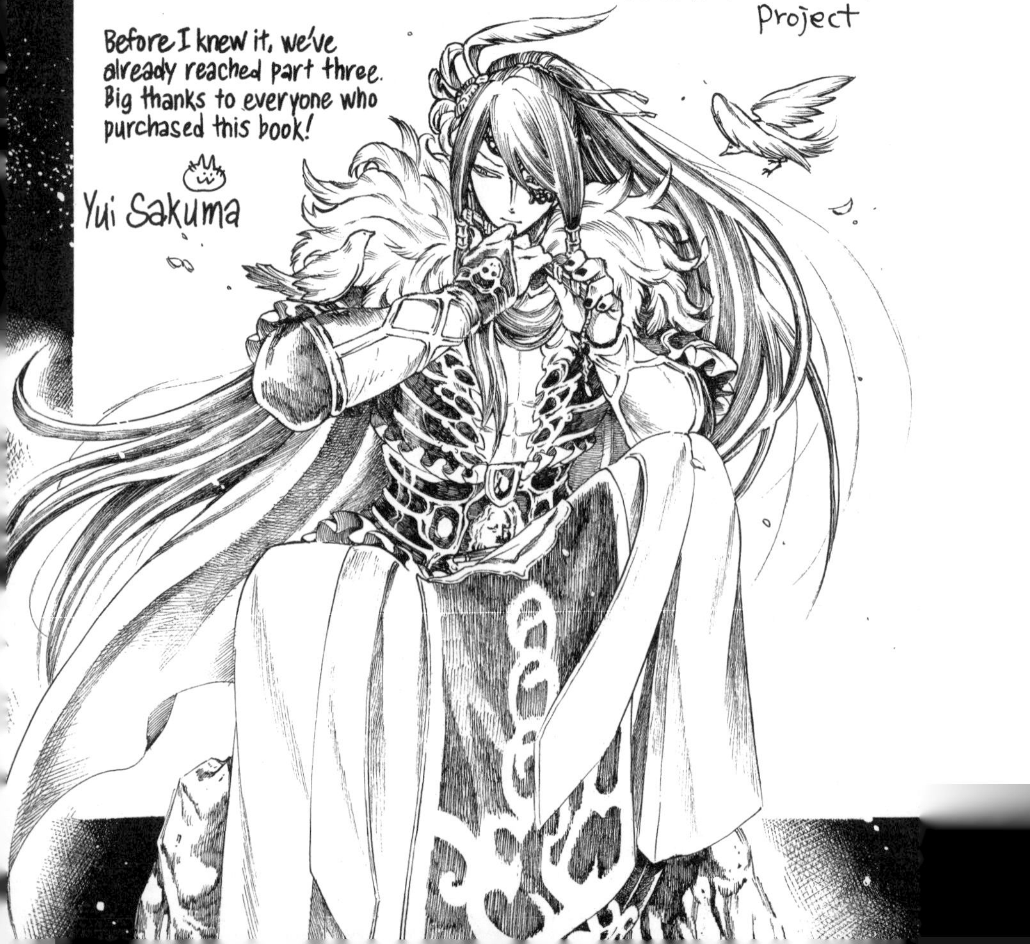

Thunderbolt Fantasy
Final Volume

Thank you so much for reading this manga all the way to the end!

The serialization lasted just barely over half a year, but it kinda felt like I was working on it for five years, lol. Every day I spent drawing it was just that fulfilling to me.

I hope we can meet again someday, somewhere.

Yui Sakuma

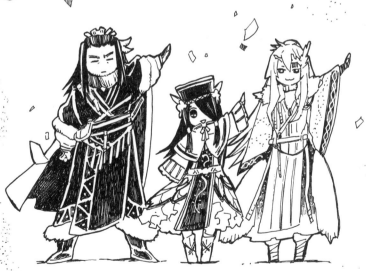

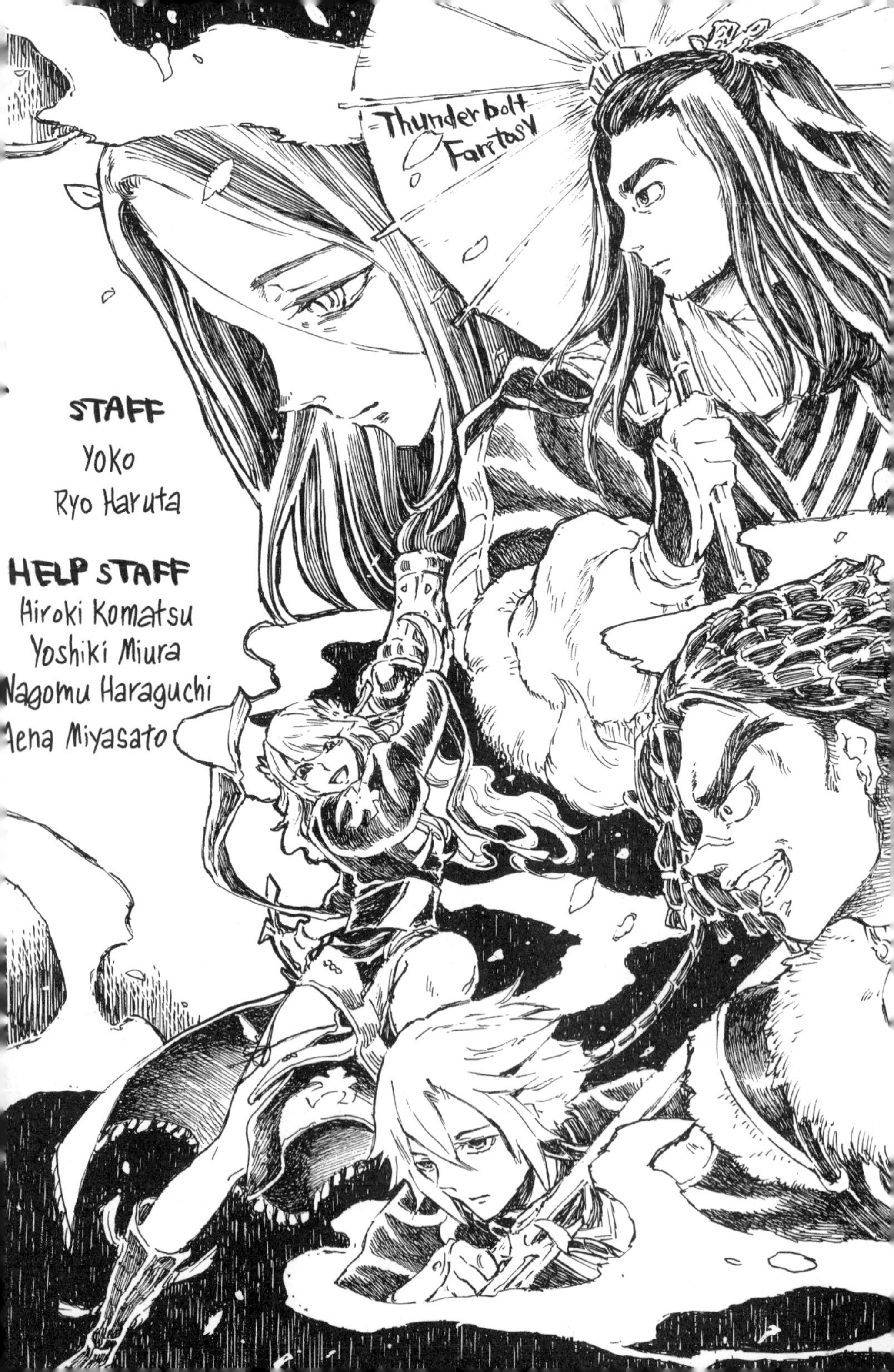
Thunderbolt Fantasy
STAFF
Yoko
Ryo Haruta
HELP STAFF
Hiroki Komatsu
Yoshiki Miura
Nagomu Haraguchi
Aena Miyasato

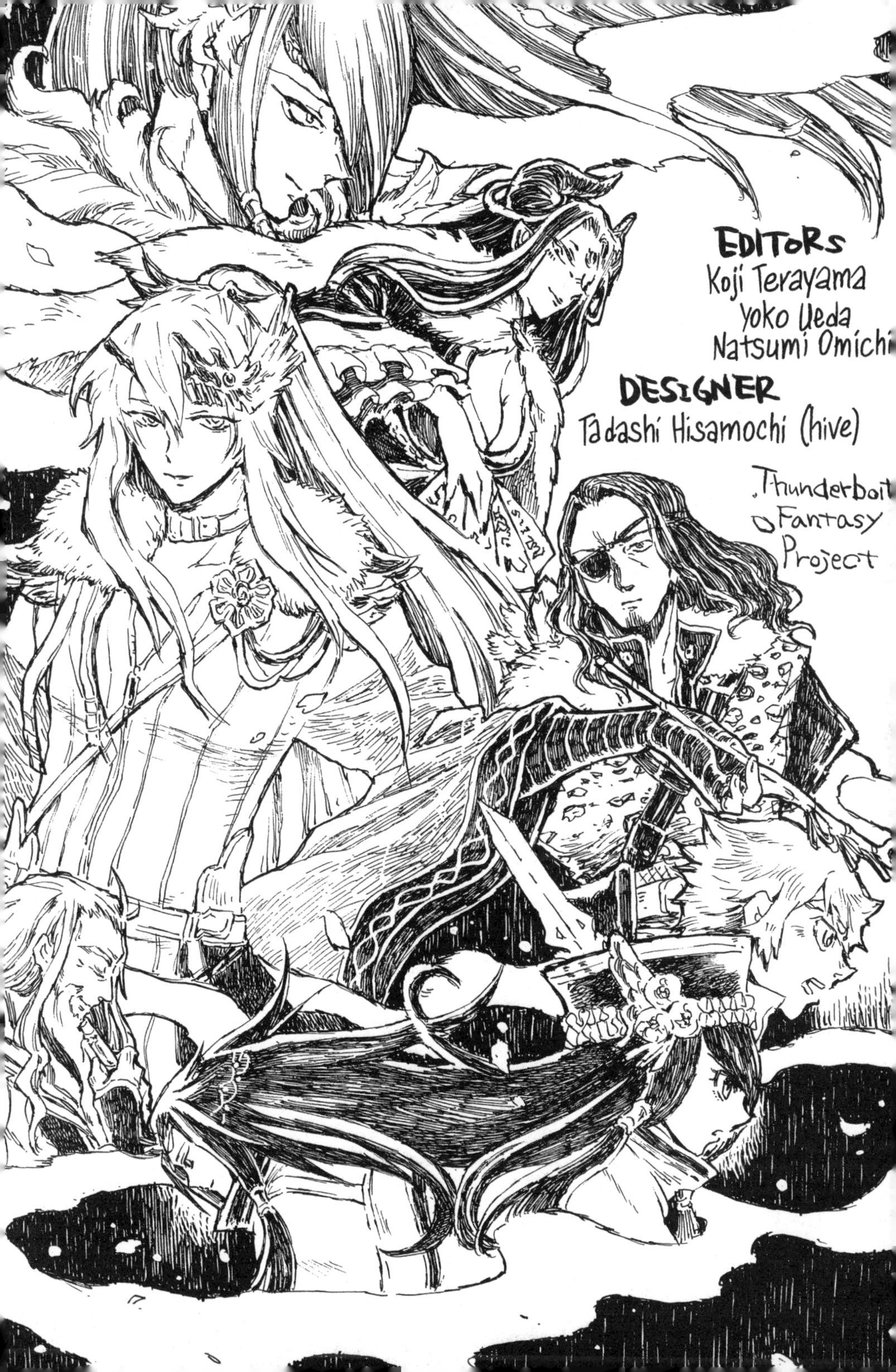
EDITORS
Koji Terayama
yoko Ueda
Natsumi Omichi
DESIGNER
Tadashi Hisamochi (hive)
Thunderbolt
Fantasy
Project

Thunderbolt Fantasy - ③

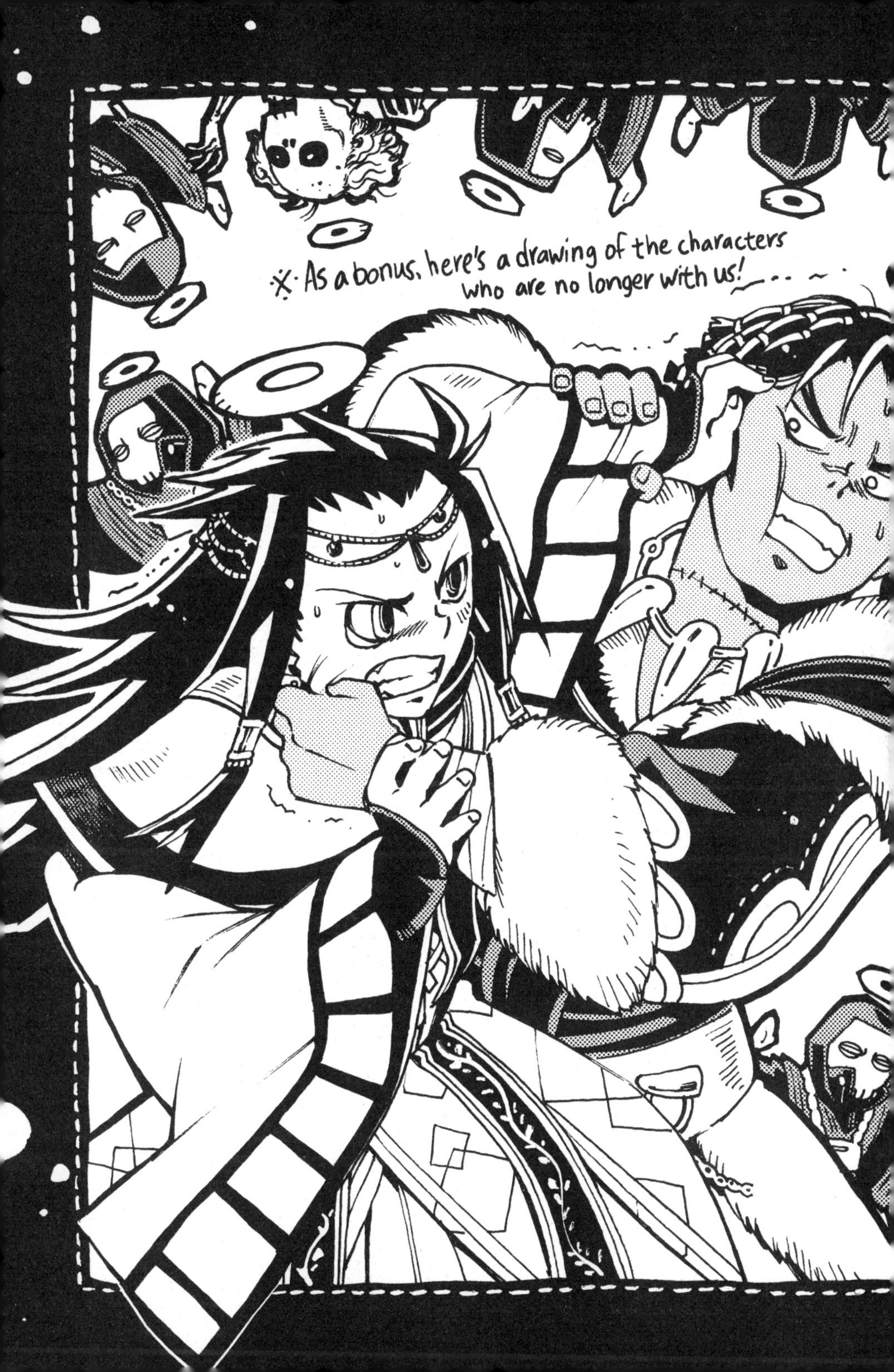
※ As a bonus, here's a drawing of the characters who are no longer with us!

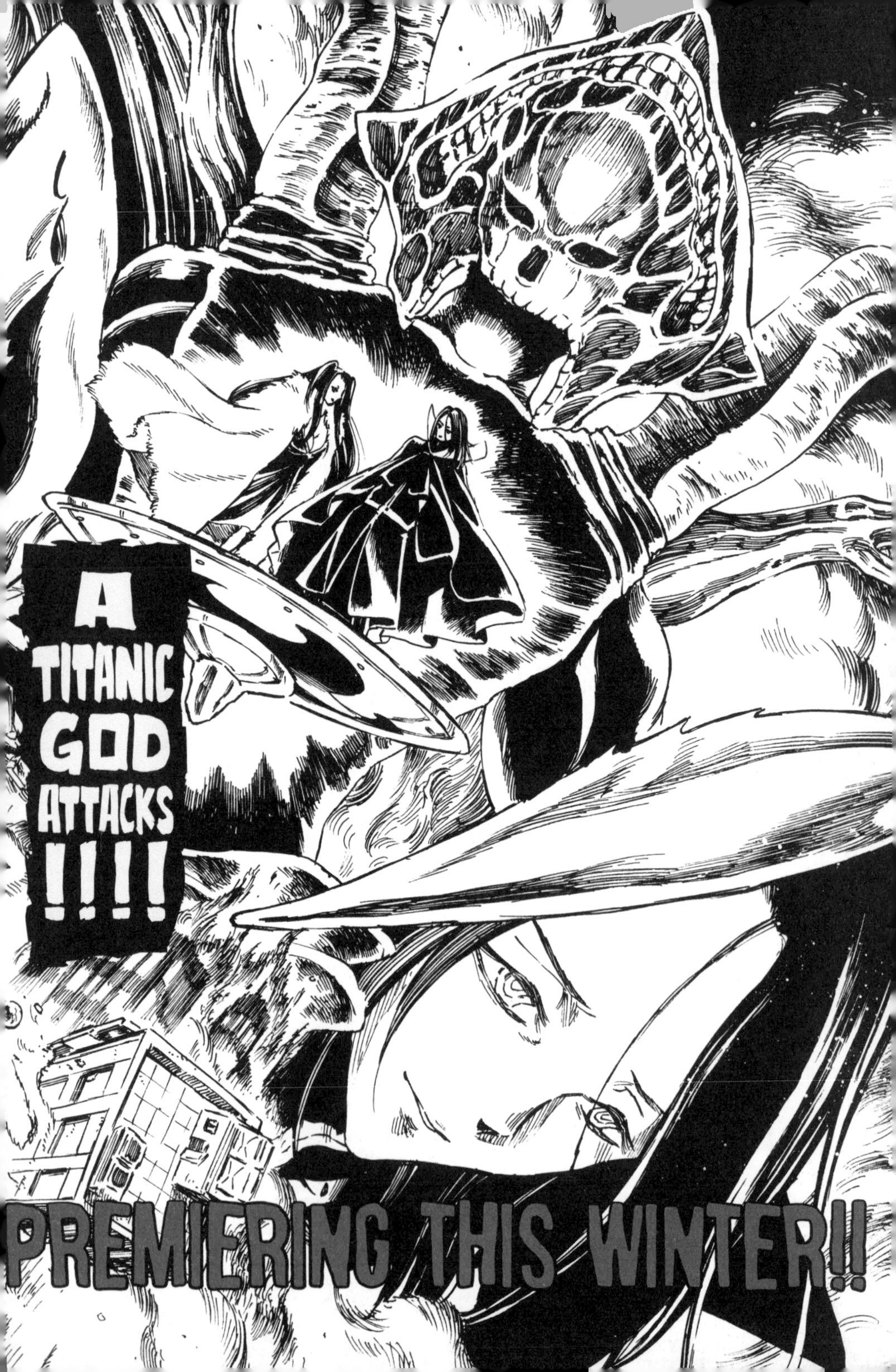
A TITANIC GOD ATTACKS!!!!
PREMIERING THIS WINTER!!

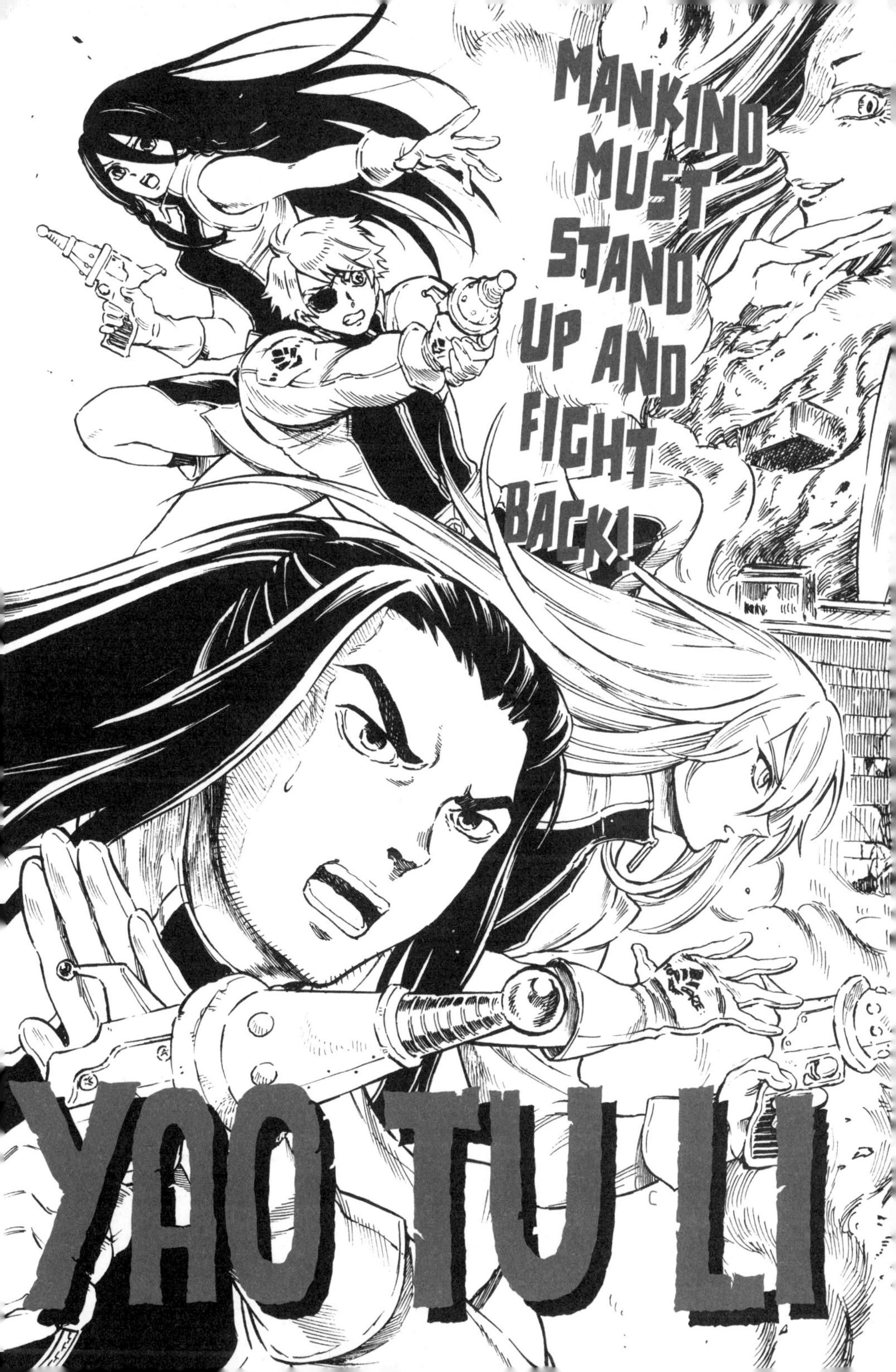
MANKIND MUST STAND UP AND FIGHT BACK!
YAO TU LI

SEVEN SEAS ENTERTAINMENT PRESENTS

Thunderbolt Fantasy VOL. 3-4

story by **GEN UROBUCHI** (Nitroplus) art by **YUI SAKUMA**

TRANSLATION
Anh Kiet Ngo

LETTERING
Aidan Clarke

COVER DESIGN
Nicky Lim

PROOFREADER
Krista Grandy

COPY EDITOR
B. Lillian Martin

SENIOR EDITOR
J.P. Sullivan

PRODUCTION DESIGNER
Christina McKenzie

PREPRESS TECHNICIAN
Melanie Ujimori
Jules Valera

PRODUCTION MANAGER
Lissa Pattillo

EDITOR-IN-CHIEF
Julie Davis

ASSOCIATE PUBLISHER
Adam Arnold

PUBLISHER
Jason DeAngelis

Seven Seas press and purchase enquiries can be sent to Marketing Manager Lianne Sentar at press@gomanga.com. Information regarding the distribution and purchase of digital editions is available from Digital Manager CK Russell at digital@gomanga.com.

ISBN: 978-1-68579-336-4
Printed in Canada
First Printing: January 2023
10 9 8 7 6 5 4 3 2 1

READING DIRECTIONS

This book reads from ***right to left***, Japanese style. If this is your first time reading manga, you start reading from the top right panel on each page and take it from there. If you get lost, just follow the numbered diagram here. It may seem backwards at first, but you'll get the hang of it! Have fun!!

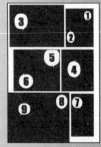

1
2
3
4
5
6
7
8
9